Swan Goose

Bean Goose

Pink-footed Goose

Greylag Goose

White-fronted Goose

Greenland White-fronted Goose

Lesser White-fronted Goose

Red-breasted Goose

WILD GEESE

by the same author:

THE WINTER BIRDS

DUCKS OF BRITAIN AND EUROPE

M. A. OGILVIE

Wild Geese

Illustrations by CAROL OGILVIE

BUTEO BOOKS
Vermillion, South Dakota

First published in 1978 by T. & A. D. Poyser Limited
281 High Street, Berkhamsted, Hertfordshire, England

Published in 1978 in U.S.A. by Buteo Books
PO Box 481, Vermillion, South Dakota 57069, U.S.A.

ISBN 0–931130–00–X

Library of Congress Catalog Card Number 77–94181

Text set in 10/11 pt VIP Bembo, printed by photolithography
and bound in Great Britain at The Pitman Press, Bath

To Hugh Boyd

Contents

Colour plates

List of tables

Preface and acknowledgments

In planning this book my original intention was to write a companion volume on geese to *Ducks of Britain and Europe*. However, even before I had completed the latter book I had come to the conclusion that the extra work involved in covering a wider field and producing a book dealing with the world's geese would be worthwhile. Because much of the research on geese carried out in Europe and in North America has been achieved in different circumstances and with differing objectives, bringing together information from the two continents produces more that is complementary rather than mere duplication. The North American goose biologists have one great advantage over their European counterparts, they can follow most of their geese throughout the year. In particular they can readily go to the arctic breeding grounds, and several fine long-term studies have been carried out there. Alas, for partly physical, partly financial, but mainly for political reasons, Europeans are much more restricted and far less work has been done on that crucial period of the goose's life cycle. In contrast, however, the winter studies in Europe are often more comprehensive than they are in North America. This arises because Europe is blessed with several well defined and comparatively small populations of geese which are amenable to regular and complete censusing, ringing, feeding studies, and refuge management. All of these tasks are carried out in North America, but nearly always on much larger population units with the result that the information gained is unavoidably less reliable, through no fault of the researchers concerned. I believe, therefore, that I have been able to produce a better all-round picture of wild geese by bringing together information from both continents than would have been the case had I restricted myself to Europe.

Little enough is known of the geese of Asia but I have included them for the sake of completeness. One goose that I have not included, however, is the Hawaiian Goose. It is confined to the Hawaiian Islands and is aberrant in a number of ways when compared to other geese. Although I could have pointed out all the exceptions as I came to them, it seemed simpler to exclude the Hawaiian Goose altogether, not least because it is the subject of a forthcoming exhaustive monograph to which the enquiring reader is directed.

The layout of this book follows *Ducks* in having some chapters in which each species, subspecies and, in this case, population, is dealt with in turn, and others of a more general character, such as that on breeding, where the complete cycle is followed through with references to the different species. I was criticised by a few reviewers of *Ducks* for constructing the book in this way and thus making it a little harder, but by no means impossibly so, for a reader to bring together all the facts relating to one particular species. I am completely unrepentant. I cannot conceive of anything more boring than a series of monographic chapters each dealing with a species or subspecies, which is what those reviewers seemed to be advocating. Gone would be the opportunity for comparison or contrast, for bringing out in one place the full and fascinating diversity of knowledge that there is about geese. Instead one would be forced into repetitious phrases, or even pages. One reviewer of this opinion was kind enough to add that there was a very full index to help the reader; I have tried to supply a similarly helpful one to this book.

I wish to thank a number of people for supplying me so readily with information about geese, both published and unpublished. Chief among these are my colleagues at the Wildfowl Trust, especially George Atkinson-Willes, Dr Janet Kear, Mike Lubbock and Dr Myrfyn Owen. My former colleague, Hugh Boyd, was especially helpful with details of numbers and distribution of some of the North American geese. J. Chattin, E. Ferguson, Dr Jack Grieb, O. J. Merne, H. Miller, Dr Austin Reed, C. Schroeder, M. Seago, J. van Impe, and James Voelzer have been very prompt in answering my written enquiries.

My publisher, Trevor Poyser, deserves grateful thanks for much hard work in unravelling my more tortuous sentences, and making sure that my meaning was clear to all and not, on occasion, to me alone.

Finally, I am once again very grateful to my wife for illustrating this book, as she did *Ducks*.

1 Introduction and classification

The geese form one of the three familiar divisions of the family of wildfowl, or Anatidae; the others are the swans and the ducks. They are quite readily, if superficially, identifiable by their long necks and long legs, and their habits are more terrestrial and less aquatic than their relatives. The swans are long necked but short in the leg, and the ducks nearly all lack stature in each respect.

The taxonomic category below the family is the tribe, of which there are ten in the Anatidae. It is at this level that the usual tripartite divisions of the wildfowl can be seen to be misleading, for it appears to give equal weight to each. However, the geese and the swans belong to the same tribe, the Anserini, while the remaining wildfowl, including the whistling ducks, sheldgeese, and all the great variety of ducks, are split between the other nine. This indicates that the swans and geese are more closely related to each other than they are to any other members of their family.

The classification below the tribe is the genus, of which the Anserini contains just four: *Coscoroba* and *Cygnus*—the swans; and *Anser* and *Branta*—the geese. In Britain we have the long-standing and widely used vernacular names of 'grey' geese for *Anser* and 'black' geese for *Branta*, but these names are neither strictly accurate, nor suitable for applying to North America, where there are also white Snow Geese and dark brown Canada Geese. The separation of the geese into two genera is based upon a number of physical characters which differ between the species in each genus. For example, *Anser* species tend to have uniform plumage colouring, in greys, browns and white, while their bills and legs are pink, orange or yellow. The *Branta* geese have more boldly patterned black or dark brown and white plumage, and their bills and legs are always black. The plumage patterns of the downy young differ too. *Anser* geese have quite prominent tooth-like serrations along the cutting edge of their upper mandible which are very small or absent in the *Branta* species.

Geese are, with the exception of introductions by man, confined to the northern hemisphere. Members of other tribes of wildfowl, including the sheldgeese and the perching ducks and geese, fill the available niche south of the equator for a large waterbird that feeds mainly by grazing on land or grubbing in marshes. Within the northern hemisphere the process of evolution, the effect of recent ice ages, the geography of suitable breeding and wintering areas, and the highly traditional nature of the use made of such areas by the geese, have combined to produce a considerable number of races

13

or subspecies, and discrete populations, within the relatively small number of whole species; just ten *Anser* and five *Branta*.

The fossil record of birds is very fragmentary, probably because of the fragile nature of their bones. Geese are no exception and although there are some remains from the Upper Eocene Period, between 50 and 40 million years ago, which are reported to be goose-like, it was not until the Miocene Period (25 to 12 million years ago) that recognisable geese attributable to both *Anser* and *Branta* occurred. In the Pliocene Period (12 to 1 million years ago) the number of species in each genus multiplied, and in the Pleistocene Period (1 million to 10,000 years ago) most of today's species have been found.

The Pleistocene Period ends with the last of the series of ice ages. These have clearly had an enormous influence on the evolution of the geese both into species and subspecies and into discrete populations. It can reasonably be assumed that the majority of the geese existing before and during the ice ages were, or became, adapted to breeding on open tundra habitat. When the ice began its long journey southwards the geese, successively, would have been pushed south before it and then allowed to spread back north in the various interglacial periods. There is also considerable evidence to show that some areas of the present arctic remained ice-free even during the maximum extent of the last glacial period, and that populations of birds including geese were able to survive within these refugia, as they are called, at least to breed, even if they had to migrate further south in winter. The combination of some populations of geese being forced to move south entirely, with others able to breed much further north, produced the necessary degree of isolation of populations which allowed evolution to take its course, leading to at first small, and then greater, differences, ending eventually in separate subspecies and finally species. Further separation of populations would have occurred as tongues of ice moved south, for example, down mountain chains, thus cutting off groups of geese from each other.

The principal refugia were in the region of the present Bering Sea where a land bridge joined North America with Asia, centred on Banks Island in the Canadian arctic, Peary Land in north-east Greenland, and parts of central arctic Siberia. Many smaller ice-free areas are thought to have existed but these may not have been able to support birds. When the ice retreated for the last time the geese in the refugia were able to spread east and west, while those forced to the south of the icesheets moved gradually north. Provided the separation had been for long enough, when birds from two different areas met, even though they had stemmed from the same original stock, they would have evolved sufficiently for them not to interbreed, and a new species would have been created.

We can now go through the list of goose species and subspecies, and comment on their possible evolution, current status in the vexed matter of subspecies, and lesser differences such as colour phases. Evolution is not a static thing but its rate of change is slow compared to our span of years on the earth. Thus, when we wish to examine the taxonomic categories of a group of birds such as the geese by deciding just how many species and subspecies there are, or to make judgements on their inter-relationships by placing them in a definite order, we are freezing, at a moment in time, a situation that is

entirely fluid and changing, albeit over a very long period. It is therefore not altogether surprising to find that people have differing views of the picture that is presented. The number of species and subspecies of geese that exists is a matter of opinion and has fluctuated widely over the years. The classification that I follow in this book divides the geese into 15 species and is a fairly widely followed practice. However, most authorities go on to list a further 22 subspecies, plus another that is extinct, and at this point I find myself differing from them.

I believe it to be far more meaningful to deal in terms of populations of geese rather than subspecies. Most geese require active management or conservation and this only makes sense if carried out on a population basis. However, some subspecies of geese are split between several identifiably discrete populations while some populations contain birds of two or more subspecies of the same goose. In fact, the exact subspecific status of a population is of little significance, particularly as many subspecies have been described on the basis of information that can now be seen to have been completely inadequate.

In the following species accounts I will point out where I differ from current taxonomic practice in the matter of subspecies and in Chapter 6 I will be discussing in depth the distribution and status of the various populations, of which over 60 have been identified, without concerning myself too much with which subspecies are involved. We start with *Anser* as it is considered the older more basic stock from which *Branta* probably evolved. It contains ten species, four of which are further subdivided into two or more subspecies.

Swan Goose *Anser cygnoides*

This is the most primitive of the geese and although it is wrong to regard it as a direct link between the swans and the geese it does demonstrate the close relationship between the two. From this species have descended very many of our domestic goose varieties, including the familiar Chinese and African Geese.

MAP 1. Breeding range of subspecies of Bean Goose *Anser fabalis*. ≋ *fabalis* and *rossicus*; ≡ *serrirostris*; |||| *middendorffi*.

Bean Goose *Anser fabalis* (Map 1)

The usual division of this species is into two groups each of three subspecies, the Forest and the Tundra Bean Geese, after their apparent breeding habitat preferences. The named Forest Bean Goose subspecies are the Western *A. f. fabalis*, Johansen's *A. f. johanseni*, and Middendorf's *A. f. middendorffi*, while the three Tundra Bean Geese are the Russian *A. f. rossicus*, the Thick-billed or Eastern *A. f. serrirostris*, and the Pink-footed Goose *A. f. brachyrhynchus*. In the classification that I am following, however, this last goose is given full species status, and will therefore be dealt with separately. Both groups of Bean Geese show a cline of increasing size from west to east.

Map 1 shows that the Bean Goose breeds right across northern Europe and Asia from Scandinavia to the Pacific coast, and it is assumed that before the last ice age there was a single species occupying this range. However, even then there was probably some differentiation into Tundra and Forest forms as, in the extremes these now take, the physiological differences would probably have required more time to evolve than the interval since the last glaciation. The main characters are bill length and body shape, with the shorter-billed, rounder-bodied geese breeding to the north of the longer-billed, longer-bodied ones. It is an advantage to the more northerly breeders to be smaller and to have small extremities as this reduces heat loss in cold conditions.

It can be supposed that when the Bean Geese were driven south by the advancing ice they were separated into a number of units, and that some of these evolved further differences. On moving north again as the ice retreated these would have come into contact once more and whilst habitat differences may have continued to separate some of them in the summer, there has clearly been much overlap and mixing in winter.

There is no complete agreement between authorities on the separation of Bean Geese into subspecies, and the Russians in particular have their own ideas. They consider it unrealistic to try to separate the Forest forms of *johanseni* and *middendorffi*, and instead lump them into a single subspecies *sibiricus*. The Russians also consider that in the west and centre of their country it is not practical to attempt to distinguish the Forest and Tundra Beans. Mixing between the two has taken place to such an extent that any differences that may once have existed have now virtually disappeared. This applies to *fabalis* and *rossicus* in western Russia, and to *johanseni* (or *sibiricus*) and *rossicus* in central northern Russia. In the east the Forest and Tundra forms apparently still remain more or less separate with *middendorffi* (or *sibiricus*) and *serrirostris* breeding as pure forms over quite large regions, although they too interbreed in the areas where they meet. There is an additional mixing factor in operation right across the U.S.S.R. Many immature non-breeding Forest Bean Geese migrate north in summer to special moulting areas on the arctic coast within the breeding range of the Tundra forms. It seems highly probable that at least some Tundra Bean Geese moult in the same localities and this could easily lead to them joining the Forest Bean Geese on their autumn migration. This would present strong opportunities for mixed pairings the following spring.

To sum up the Bean Geese, it is still practical to deal in terms of shorter-billed, rounder-bodied birds breeding to the north of longer-billed, longer-bodied ones. There is additionally a cline of increasing size from west to east, and of decreasing bill length and body length from south to north. Although at the extremes of the range it is possible to find individuals that fit the descriptions of the different subspecies, there are vast areas of overlap where intergrading between two or more forms completely nullifies any attempt to ascribe precise geographical ranges for each subspecies. The races have been named by museum workers using very small samples of skins. The more fieldwork that is done the more it becomes apparent that in any large flock of Bean Geese there are likely to be individuals close to one or more of these named subspecies, as well as every possible gradation between them. In such a situation it is clear that subspecific designations are not only not applicable but of no practical use.

Pink-footed Goose *Anser brachyrhynchus*

As already mentioned this goose is often treated as a subspecies of the Bean Goose, from which it differs only relatively slightly, being rather smaller and rounder in its body and, most obviously, having pink legs and pink on its bill instead of orange. For such differences to have come about from what is clearly its ancestor, the Bean Goose, separation must have occurred a very long time ago, almost certainly well before the last glaciation. The ranges of the Bean and the Pinkfoot are completely separate and this fact is one of the strongest arguments used by those who consider the Pinkfoot to be only a subspecies. One of the tests of a full species is that it can come into contact with its ancestral form and remain distinct, whereas two subspecies would readily interbreed. However, with the present distribution of the geese this is most unlikely to happen and one must use other criteria in coming to a conclusion. The Pinkfoot's breeding and wintering habitats, as well as size and coloration, differ from the Bean's sufficiently in some people's view, including mine, to warrant separation as a full species.

There are three breeding areas of the Pinkfoot: north-east Greenland, Iceland, and Svalbard (Spitsbergen). As will be shown in more detail in Chapter 6, the birds breeding in the first two countries form one population which is completely separated both in summer and winter from the Svalbard breeders. However, the separation can only be comparatively recent in evolutionary terms as no apparent morphological differences have yet arisen. It has been claimed that the Svalbard birds are a little larger than the others but insufficient measurements have been obtained to show this conclusively. However, a few hundred or thousand more years of separation might be enough to produce something more definite.

White-fronted Goose *Anser albifrons*

This species has an almost complete circumpolar distribution. The birds breeding in west Greenland have become the most differentiated and may well have been separated before the last ice age. They form a well-marked subspecies *A. a. flavirostris*, the Greenland Whitefront. Over the remainder of the range the usual practice until recently has been to name three races: the European *A. a. albifrons*, breeding from western arctic Russia east to about the Kolyma River at 160°E; the Pacific Whitefront *A. a. frontalis*, breeding in Siberia east of the Kolyma River to the Bering Strait, and in Alaska and arctic Canada; and the Tule Whitefront *A. a. gambelli*, a mysterious subspecies whose breeding grounds have never been found though it has been variously supposed that they must lie somewhere near the north coast of arctic Canada, or perhaps in interior Alaska.

The European and Pacific Whitefronts are very similar to each other but it has always been claimed that the Tule Whitefront is much larger and darker than the others. Very recently a further race, *A. a. elgasi* Elgas's Whitefront, has been described and named as being also large and dark but not so much as the Tule. With the evidence for the latter race already dubious there seems little justification for naming yet another race on the basis of a handful of skins that appear to have been selected for the differences that they show. The fact that they might be intergrades or even just showing natural variation from normal seems not to have been given serious attention by those naming the race.

Whitefronts are extremely variable in size and plumage colouring, as anyone who has spent any time looking at a flock of them will readily admit. This must be taken into account in any examination of possible subspecies. The very latest proposals acknowledge this and have simplified matters considerably by designating the Whitefronts of eastern Siberia and western Alaska (those from the latter area migrating down the west coast of North America) as the Pacific Whitefront *frontalis*, reserving *gambelli* for the birds breeding in eastern Alaska and arctic Canada. These latter average darker and larger than *frontalis* and almost certainly include within their number birds which in the past have been claimed as Tule Whitefronts. The vast majority of these birds migrate to winter on the Gulf Coast but a small offshoot crosses over to winter in California within the winter range of *frontalis*. Here, where the larger, darker birds exist in close proximity with the smaller, paler *frontalis*, is supposed to be the wintering area of the Tule Whitefront. But could it not be that the contrast between the two is what is striking to the observer, over-emphasising the difference which exists?

The new vernacular name of *gambelli* is the Interior Whitefront, reflecting its range and migration route. The mystery races, the Tule and Elgas's Whitefronts, with their unknown breeding grounds and supposedly very tiny and threatened populations, are dismissed as invalid. This seems to make very good sense to me, though it may take a little while before those still searching for the latter's breeding grounds are persuaded that they do not exist except as part of the range of the extremely numerous Interior Whitefront. There is a strong parallel here with the so-called Giant Canada Goose (see below) where selection of extreme individuals has been used to justify the naming of a race which, however, does not stand up to close scrutiny of large numbers of birds.

Returning to *frontalis*, it remains doubtful whether this is fully separable from *albifrons*. Certainly it is extremely improbable whether a Pacific Whitefront appearing in a flock of European Whitefronts, or vice versa, could be picked out, or even identified if it were shot. They intergrade where they meet in Siberia and individual variation in both races produces birds which could be mistaken for the wrong one. The bill of the Pacific Whitefront averages longer than that of the European race, but there is overlap and this seems slight evidence on which to base a subspecies. Additionally, there is evidence that as one goes from west to east across the range of the species in Russia, so the birds get slightly larger and slightly paler.

Lesser White-fronted Goose *Anser erythropus*

Undoubtedly this small goose sprang from the same stock as the Whitefront. The two overlap slightly in range but are separated by different habitat requirements. The Lesser Whitefront breeds, like the Whitefront, right across northern Europe and Asia, but always to the south in the scrub and forest zone and hardly at all in the tundra. The pair form a good example of Bergman's Rule which states that larger forms of the same species, or the larger of a pair of similar species, will live to the north of the smaller one. The explanation for this is that as body size increases the ratio of surface area to volume decreases, so that a larger bird has a smaller relative body surface through which to lose heat. Being more thermally efficient therefore than a smaller bird it is able to live more satisfactorily in colder climates.

It can be assumed that separation of the Lesser Whitefront from a common Whitefront-type stock took place a very long time ago and certainly well before the last glaciation. No apparent morphological differences have been found in birds from different parts of the range.

Greylag Goose *Anser anser*

There are two described races of the Greylag, the Western *A. a. anser* and the Eastern *A. a. rubrirostris*. As with the Bean Goose typical specimens of the two races look very different and are quite easily distinguished, but there is virtually complete gradation between them. It has been suggested that more races may be named in the future but it would seem much more satisfactory to treat the species as showing a clinal variation across its range and not try to lay down arbitrary divisions. Certainly there are separate populations with their own apparently discrete breeding and wintering ranges but they have not been separated for long enough to evolve into different races except for the two named. The differences between a typical Western and typical Eastern Greylag (with the former being smaller, darker and having an orange not pink bill) probably arose during separation at the time of the ice ages but the birds have rather spoilt things by coming together again, interbreeding and producing all shades of plumage and bill colour between the two races.

Bar-headed Goose *Anser indicus*

This localised species is classed as an aberrant grey goose or Snow Goose. It has obvious affinities with the latter but equally any common ancestor lies a long way back in time. The relatively restricted range has inhibited the formation of any possible subspecies.

Emperor Goose *Anser canagicus*

This species is much more similar, morphologically, to the Snow Goose than is the Barhead, and it too must have come from a common ancestor. Its range is restricted to eastern Siberia and western Alaska and, like many species of birds that now nest on both sides of the Bering Sea, this can be taken as evidence that they survived the last ice age in the Beringia refugium. This was an ice-free area that included a land bridge joining north-east Asia with north-west North America. The lack of spread from this area since the retreat of the ice may be due to competition with more successful species.

Snow Goose *Anser caerulescens*

The Snow Goose is well differentiated into two races: the Lesser *A. c. caerulescens* and the Greater *A. c. atlanticus*. These form a convincing demonstration of Bergman's Rule with the latter breeding to the north of the former. Subspeciation is apparently complete with virtually no range overlap and no interbreeding.

The Greater Snow Goose forms a single population with one wintering area and there is no suspicion of further evolution within it. The Lesser Snow Goose, by contrast, breeds in two well separated areas, the eastern Canadian arctic, and north-east Siberia. However, some mixing of populations takes place on the wintering grounds and there is no apparent difference between birds of the two regions.

The most fascinating aspect of Lesser Snow Goose evolution is the occurrence of the blue plumage phase, the birds having just a white head and neck, the rest of the body being blue–grey. These birds are usually called Blue Snow Geese, or just Blue Geese. For a great many years it was thought that they were the immature form of the Snow Goose and then, later, they were thought to be a separate species. Suspicions that they might be no more than colour phases of the same species were voiced many years ago but it was not until 1961 that it was convincingly demonstrated that this was indeed so. However, old beliefs took a long time to die and papers have been published quite recently trying to show that the two phases are different species. The evidence, though, is weak compared with the weight of data stacked against it.

The two colour phases of the Lesser Snow Goose are dependent upon the operation of a single pair of genes. It has been shown that the blue phase is dominant over the white, and also that there is no sex linkage. So, representing the two genes by the letters 'B' for the dominant blue, and 'b' for white, a male or female blue phase goose would have the genes 'BB' or 'Bb', while white phase birds would have 'bb'. If both birds of a pair are homozygotes, having the two genes the same, either 'BB' or 'bb', then all their offspring will be blue or white respectively. But if one of the parents is a heterozygote, having a mixed pair of genes, 'Bb', then on mating with a homozygote, some of the goslings will be blue and some white, in each case a majority of the former.

Although it is common to think solely in terms of the two colour phases, blue and white, there are in fact a number of intermediate forms. A total of seven have been described (numbered from 1 to 7 in increasing blueness). Numbers (1) and (2) are wholly white plumaged except for their black primaries, the only difference between them being that (2) has a certain amount of darkening on the alula or bastard wing, the small tuft of feathers on the outer edge of the wing near the bend. Both these forms are homozygotes with the genes 'bb'. Numbers (3), (4), (5) and (6) have dark wings, flanks and back, and decreasing amounts of white on the underparts, while in form (7) this is reduced to an occasional white feathering round the vent. Virtually all of forms (3) and (4) will be heterozygote 'BB', while forms (5), (6) and (7) will contain increasing proportions of the homozygote 'BB' as well as some 'Bb'. The great majority if not quite all of (7) will be 'BB'. The divisions are fairly arbitrary, and in some cases the plumage differences can only be seen in the hand, but essentially (1) and (2) can be described as white phase while all of (3) to (7) are blue.

The downy young Lesser Snow Geese also show polymorphism of a similar kind, but only five forms have been described of which three are genetically white, and two are blue. These, like the adult plumage, will be covered in more detail in the next chapter, on identification.

Another interesting aspect of the colour phases is that pairings of two white birds or two blue birds are commoner than one white with one blue. There is in fact a strong assortive mating so that like mates with like. This is true not only for the broad groupings of white and blue, but also shows up in each of the seven colour forms mentioned. However, as well as this assortive mating there is the preference of a bird to mate with a bird that looks like its parent. Offspring of a non-assorted pair may mate with either a blue or a white goose. It has been shown with captive geese that there is a definite attraction, probably based on the initial imprinting of the gosling on its parents, for the parents' colour. To add another dimension to the study some of the goslings and some of the adults were dyed pink! The preferences still held good.

One other feature is that the number of blue phase males mated with white phase females was found to be significantly greater than the other way round. It is assumed that the male goose plays the dominant role in the selection of a mate and therefore in order to have the difference mentioned one has to have more blue males with a white parent, than white males with a blue parent. And in the study in question the former were three times as common as the latter. However, this particular colony had a predominance of white phase geese. In a colony where blue phase geese were in the majority one would expect the ratios to be the other way round, with white goslings with a blue parent outnumbering blue goslings with a white parent. Thus, in mixed pairings those in which the male was white and the female blue would be more numerous.

These pairings dependent on parent colour phases raise the whole question of imprinting, namely the attachment of a newly hatched gosling, or other young bird or animal, for its parent; or in abnormal circumstances for the first, usually moving, object that it becomes aware of. It is not known in the case of these Snow Geese whether the young imprint on both parents or just the female, nor whether the colour of the other goslings in the brood has any significance in subsequent pairing preferences. Imprinting is certainly less than absolute as it can quite easily be changed within the first week of a gosling's life, and can still be broken at a later age.

It has been mentioned above that some colonies have more white than blue geese and vice versa. In fact there is a cline of increasing blueness as one moves from west to east across the Canadian arctic. Colonies in the eastern Siberian arctic have no blue phase geese at all nor do there appear to be any among the small number of Snow Geese breeding in northern Alaska. The westernmost colony in arctic Canada, at Kendall Island, has no blue geese, but the next ones east, a few hundred kilometres away at Anderson River, and on Banks Island, contain a handful of blue phase birds. Then at Perry River several hundred kilometres still further east there are about 9%, increasing in the colonies around Hudson Bay to about 25%. The colonies on Southampton Island have up to 35% blue phase birds while when one reaches Baffin Island the proportion shoots up to 41% at Koukdjuak, 61% at Cape Dominion, and 81% at Bowman Bay (see Table 1).

Not only is there this well-marked cline of increasing blue phase birds from west to east but it is in a state of change. In the 1950s and early 1960s the percentage of blue phase birds was increasing and spreading westwards at a rate of about 2% per annum. However, this trend has now stopped and even reversed in some areas as the Table shows.

The spread of the blue phase Snow Goose corresponds with a general warming of the Canadian arctic that has been taking place in the last few decades. It is of considerable interest that the apparent halt in the increase and spread has coincided with an apparent cooling of the arctic in the last five or ten years. The exact way in which the weather benefits one or other phase has been the subject of much detailed study. It appears that the blue and white phase birds are affected differently by the prevailing weather conditions on the breeding grounds, both on their arrival in spring and later in the incubation and rearing periods. Firstly, white phase geese have a marked tendency, presumably of genetic origin, to start to lay their clutches earlier than the blue phase geese in the same colony. Secondly, and in slight contradiction to this, the laying period of all the white phase geese in a colony is actually longer than that of the blue phase birds, starting earlier and carrying on later.

TABLE 1: *Percentages of blue phase Lesser Snow Geese in certain colonies, showing west—east cline of increasing blueness and changes during the last forty years*

Colony	Lat.	Long.	1930s	1940s	1950s	1960s	1970s
Wrangel Island	71 N	179 W	0			0	0
Kendall Island	69 N	135 W			0	0	0
Banks Island	72 N	125 W			<1	<1	<1
McConnell River	60 N	94 W		<1	8	24·5	24·2
La Perouse Bay	58 N	93 W			15	24	26·0
Boas River	63 N	85 W	5		25	33	23·1
East Bay	64 N	81 W			33		35·0
Cape Henrietta Maria	55 N	82 W			38		72·7
Bowman Bay	65 N	74 W	96		97	85	80·9
Cape Dominion	66 N	74 W	14		80	76	60·6
Koukdjuak Plain	66 N	73 W	10		45	57	41·4

Note 1: The last three colonies are virtually contiguous and the variation in the proportion of blue phase birds between them might be better expressed as segregation within one large colony.

Note 2: See Chapter 6 (Table 21 and Map 23) for details of the numbers of pairs of geese in each colony and their geographical position.

Cooch (1963), Kerbes (1975).

It has been found that the earliest clutches laid in a goose colony suffer a higher predation rate than later clutches, so that this predation would fall most heavily on white phase birds in any normally-timed season. A period of climatic amelioration, producing many more good summers than bad, would thus favour the blue phase goose over the white phase. In a bad season however, when cold weather delays the start of laying, the two phases will begin to lay at the same time. The white phase with its longer laying period, going on after the blue phase have stopped, will be at an advantage if, in that bad summer, there are spells of cold, wet weather capable of chilling eggs or killing off goslings. In these circumstances the worst effects tend to fall on eggs or goslings of much the same age. A larger proportion of the blue phase geese will be at the same stage of their breeding cycle than the white phase, and so will suffer more. This probably explains why the recent run of cooler, later seasons has stopped and reversed the spread of blue phase birds.

Another factor has been found which tends to favour blue phase geese regardless of the weather. In mixed clutches where some blue and some white phase goslings will be produced, the latter tend to be hatched from eggs laid towards the end of the clutch. This means that they hatch out very slightly later, perhaps only a few hours, and thus start life at a disadvantage. In a sample of mixed clutches in which the laying order of each egg was known, the first egg to hatch was always a blue phase, and the second egg was more likely to be blue phase than white. Normally a clutch of four or five eggs hatches within a period of about 24 hours and will be brooded on the nest until all the young are dry before the female leads them off to feed. In larger clutches, and Lesser Snow Geese will lay six or seven eggs, the last young will hatch significantly later than the first, and will therefore be weaker and less well rested. It is then more liable to straggle behind the family as they make their way to the feeding grounds, and be in danger of getting picked off by a predator. It is also more likely to be squeezed out to the edge when the parent is brooding the young, and thus benefit less from the protection against wet and cold that brooding gives. These last-hatched birds will nearly all be white phase.

A further disadvantage to white phase birds has been found on their autumn migration and is also linked to the weather. In normal seasons a higher proportion of white phase than blue phase geese interrupt their migration between the Canadian arctic and their wintering grounds in the Gulf of Mexico. More blue phase birds perform the journey in a single flight. The shooting pressure in the areas of central northern United States where the white phase birds stop off is higher than further south so relatively more white phase geese get shot, taking the winter as a whole. In very late seasons, however, the blue phase birds also stop en route, presumably because they have not been able to build up sufficient energy reserves to make their usual non-stop flight. In these years the kill of blue phase will equal or even exceed that of the white phase birds. Again the recent trend to poorer weather in the arctic will have favoured the latter.

There is one final factor which affects the two phases differently, but this time it is a human one. There is some evidence that shooters select white geese in preference to blue ones, though the reasons for this are not clear.

Ross's Goose *Anser rossii*

This, the smallest kind of Snow Goose, breeds in a fairly restricted area of arctic Canada and together with the Lesser Snow Goose is a good demonstration of Bergman's Rule as it nests to the south of the majority of the latter, as befits a smaller bird, less well adapted to the colder conditions further north.

Separation from the original Snow Goose stock probably occurred during a past glacial period when populations of Snow Geese became isolated geographically. This separation was sufficient to produce what can certainly be regarded as separate species, even though some hybridisation between Ross's Goose and Lesser Snow Goose does occur, and indeed appears to be increasing. The two species nest together in some areas and in large colonies competition for nest sites leads to eggs from both species appearing in one nest. The young hatched from these mixed clutches will all imprint on whichever species incubates and rears them, and also on each other. So Ross's goslings brought up with Snow Goose goslings by a Lesser Snow Goose, will naturally be attracted to the latter when they become old enough to pair. In this way hybrid pairs may well be formed. It has been estimated that as many as 1400 hybrids may be produced per year. While this is small compared with the present populations of about 30,000 Ross's Geese, the perhaps 2½ million Lesser Snow Geese are so much more numerous that, if all the hybrids are fertile, in the very long term the Ross's Goose could be overwhelmed genetically by the Lesser Snow Goose.

We have seen how the Lesser Snow Goose has two main colour phases which are detectable in the gosling. The Ross's Goose has just a white adult colour phase but interestingly the goslings show two distinct colour phases, with the downy plumage either predominantly grey or yellow. The former is the more common, outnumbering the yellow by about two to one. Broods in which all the young are grey are also much commoner than either pure yellow or mixed ones, showing that the grey carrying gene is the dominant one.

Canada Goose *Branta canadensis* (Map 2)

This is the first species of the second genus of geese, *Branta*. The most widely accepted classification divides it into the following 12 subspecies:

Atlantic *canadensis*	Western or Dusky *occidentalis*
Interior or Todd's *interior*	Vancouver *fulva*
Moffitt's or Great Basin *moffitti*	Aleutian *leucopareia*
Giant *maxima*	Bering *asiatica*
Lesser *parvipes*	Richardson's *hutchinsii*
Taverner's *taverneri*	Cackling *minima*

This list was compiled at a time when taxonomists relied very heavily on small numbers of museum specimens and when field observations backed up

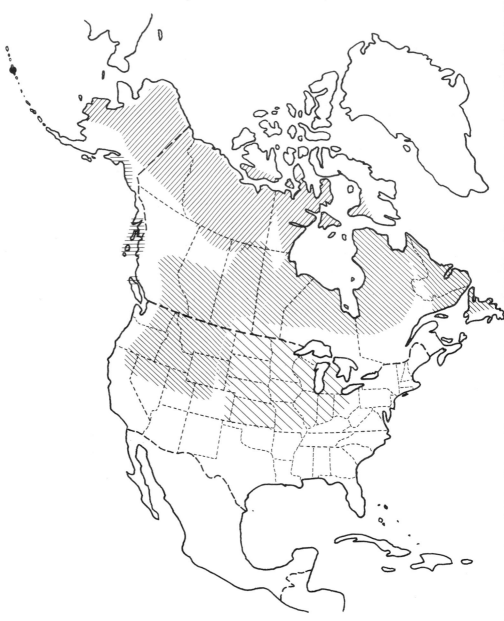

MAP 2. Breeding range of four 'groups' of Canada Geese *Branta canadensis*. ⧗Northern; ⧗ Southern;\\\\ additional range of sedentary 'Giant' Canada Geese; ≡Western; ● Aleutian.

by the now commonplace techniques of censusing and ringing were only just beginning on a country-wide scale. The accumulated evidence of recent years suggests that some of the original divisions into subspecies were too rigid and that there is much intergrading between several of them, both from east to west across the continent, and from north to south. Present-day interest in the Canada Goose in North America centres on their value as quarry birds, and it is the separation of the geese into populations, and the numbers and migrations of these, that is important. The precise name that should be given to a particular individual or group of Canada Geese is, in this context, of much less concern. In Chapter 6 we will explore the composition of the various populations, their allocation between the various flyways, as well as their current status and trends. The allocation of subspecific names to the birds making up these populations will be only a minor consideration.

The naming of subspecies is not something that can only be done by following rigidly laid down rules. It is largely a matter of personal opinion. It is quite usual to find intergrading in the area where two even quite well marked subspecies meet, while some species show a continuous cline of variation from one end of their range to the other. A few specimens taken arbitrarily out of this cline might well show sufficient different characteristics to warrant description and naming as subspecies. This is essentially what has happened in the case of the Canada Goose, though here one is dealing with a number of partially overlapping clines. Clearly evolution has been very active in this species, with geographical separation during glaciations producing some differences in size and colour, which have since become emphasised by the climatic variations between regions of the North American continent. Some of the differences have become quite marked but have become subsequently confused by meeting and mixing of previously discrete populations. We now have a situation where there is just one apparently isolated population, that on the Aleutian Islands, normally treated as a subspecies *leucopareia*, while every other named subspecies meets with and intergrades with at least one and often several others (see Map 2). Small numbers of specimens taken from a particular breeding or wintering area can often be found to be sufficiently like each other, and different from other Canada Geese, to be described as subspecies. But how far this should be taken remains an entirely subjective matter. Attempts have been made to lay down criteria by which subspecies should be judged, for example, that 50% or 75% of specimens should be identifiable, but no Canada Goose subspecies has really been put to this test.

Although my approach here will be to show that some of the current subspecific separations are probably not justified and should therefore be lumped together, it is only fair to draw attention to the other side of the coin, to the existence of 'splitters', those who believe in giving subspecific status and a separate name to every, even very slightly different, group of Canada Geese. Thus, one North American worker is reported to have named as many as thirty different races. He has not published the details and one can only surmise on his reasons for recognising so many. One must assume that he is basing his work on birds which have relatively discrete breeding or wintering areas, and have some morphological differences between them and other

Canada Geese, however slight. The existing races are, of course, separated on such criteria, including size, colour, shape of bill, etc. There is no doubt whatsoever that if one looks at small samples of Canada Geese critically enough one can detect many such differences. The essence of a splitter's approach is to believe that these are sufficient justification for giving such birds subspecific status. The major criticism that one can make of this is that it is frequently based on far too few specimens. As soon as one looks at large numbers of birds belonging to the same apparent group, the amount of individual variation present swamps the so-called subspecific criteria.

My own method of dealing with the Canada Goose is to divide it into four geographical groups (see Map 2). Three of these, which I have termed Southern, Northern and Pacific Coast, are large and contain birds of several of the currently named races. However, the intergradations that exist between the races are so great that it is simpler in my view to treat them as of a clinal nature within my grouping. The groups themselves are not discrete as there is also some intergrading between them, too. The fourth group consists of the single population on the Aleutian Islands, already mentioned.

The Southern Group of Canada Geese extends from the Atlantic seaboard west to the Rocky Mountain divide. This group contains the currently named subspecies Atlantic *canadensis*, Giant *maxima*, Interior *interior* and Moffitt's *moffitti*. All are large, rather pale Canada Geese. Looked at as a group it is apparent that *canadensis* and *interior* intergrade to a considerable extent, with overlap in both size and colouring, while *moffitti* and *maxima* are just not separable on any worthwhile characters and should clearly be treated as one (as they have been in a recent authoritative reference work). The usually stated criteria of size is certainly insufficient bearing in mind the extreme variability of these birds and the very high degree of overlap between their measurements. There has been a lot of publicity associated with the Giant Canada Goose and its rediscovery after supposed extinction, but too much emphasis has been placed on 'largest', to the exclusion of the true size range of the population. For example, hunters naturally boast of all very heavy birds they shoot and these have automatically been claimed as 'Giant'. Even the type specimen of *maxima* was described from the largest available bird. Other reported minor morphological differences do not bear close scrutiny of really large samples.

Intergrading between *canadensis* and *maxima/moffitti* occurs, as it does between the latter and *interior*. There is thus little justification for dealing even with three subspecies, let alone four, and as the populations increase as they have been doing in recent years, and as transplants of birds over the last two decades have resulted in considerable additional mixing of stocks, the tendency will be towards an increasingly amorphous whole. Distinct populations within the group may always be discernible, and the present ones will be discussed in Chapter 6, but any realistic separation into subspecies seems a particularly fruitless exercise.

The northern boundary of the Southern Group is not a fixed line on the map but peters out somewhere towards the latitude of 60°N. From here northwards lie the breeding grounds of the Northern Group, though many of them winter to the south of the Southern Group. The breeding range stretches across the arctic and subarctic from the north of Hudson Bay, across the Canadian mainland and into Alaska. The present named races involved here are, from east to west, Richardson's *hutchinsii*, Lesser *parvipes*, Taverner's *taverneri*, and Cackling *minima*. All the birds are small, though with a considerable size variation. *Hutchinsii* and *parvipes* are generally pale, while *taverneri* and *minima* are dark. The first two are being increasingly discussed in terms of the '*parvipes–hutchinsii* complex' by scientists working on them, which is surely just another way of saying that they are not fully separable. Where their supposed separate breeding grounds meet in the Canadian arctic, mixed pairs are commonplace and intergradation in size is complete. Only at the extremes of their ranges, and to a lesser extent in the wintering areas, is it possible to sort out the larger *parvipes* from the smaller *hutchinsii*, but even then one is faced with a complete size gradient in between. Clearly they should be considered as a single unit showing a cline in size.

One can treat *parvipes* and *taverneri* in a similar way. They show a complete gradation of colouring rather than size, from the pale *parvipes* in the east to the dark *taverneri* in the west. *Taverneri* has been regarded by many people as a very doubtful subspecies, and it certainly follows from the above that if two parts of a trio are both to be regarded as synonymous with the third part, that is *taverneri* with *parvipes* and *hutchinsii* with *parvipes,* then all three must be synonymous. *Hutchinsii* is the oldest name of the three and should survive if one wishes to use a subspecific name. We are left with a cline of increasing size from east towards the west, overlapping with another cline of increasing darkness in the same direction.

At the extreme west of the Northern Group breeding range is the named race of the Cackling Goose *minima*. It has some claim to be treated separately and it is often stated that it has completely separate breeding grounds, being confined to the coastal strip of western Alaska, while the geese of interior Alaska are all described as *taverneri*. This suggests firstly that there is a clear-cut dividing line between the breeding ranges of the two, which is not so, and secondly that it is easy to tell the two geese apart. Thus one is led by implication to believe that the coastal strip is known not to contain any *taverneri* In fact *minima* is one of the most variable of the Canada Geese both in size and in colouring, while we have already seen that *taverneri* is just part of a larger population showing clinal variation in both characteristics. As will be discussed in Chapter 6, the coastal breeding geese appear to have a more or less separate migration route southwards in autumn, but have extensively overlapping wintering grounds with the birds from the interior of Alaska. Thus while a different migration route could be put on the side of subspecific difference the opportunities for the formation of mixed pairs in winter, and the difficulty in telling the birds apart in summer, suggests on balance that it is best to treat *minima* as part of the Northern Group, though perhaps laying more claim to being treated as a separate entity than the other three described subspecies, which must certainly be considered as one.

There is a strong link between the Northern and Southern Groups in the form of intergrading between the largest and palest birds of the Northern Group, usually called *parvipes*, and *interior* of the Southern Group where their ranges meet close to the southern part of Hudson Bay, and also between *parvipes* and *moffitti* further west.

The third group, the Pacific Coast Group, consists of two named races, Western or Dusky *occidentalis* and Vancouver *fulva*. Both are large, dark-plumaged geese breeding on the south-east coast of Alaska and down the Pacific coast of British Columbia. The separation into two races appears to have been based on very slight size differences (there is in fact extensive overlap), and the fact that the breeding ranges are separated geographically with *occidentalis* lying to the north and separated by about 500 kilometres (300 miles) from the most northern outpost of *fulva*. Most of the former migrate to the south of the latter, which are largely sedentary, but there is some overlap and mixing during winter and on migration. There seems little justification for keeping them separate and it seems preferable to consider them as forming a cline, with a small decrease in size running from south to north.

There is a link between the Pacific Coast Group and the Northern Group through intergrading between the former and the dark birds of the latter under their subspecific name *taverneri*. Separation of their breeding grounds is, if anything, less than between *occidentalis* and *fulva*, while they certainly overlap on the wintering grounds and during migration, giving ample opportunity for the formation of mixed pairings. Birds from both groups are variable in size, and it is tempting to regard the birds of interior Alaska *taverneri* as the northern end of a cline running up the coast from *fulva* through *occidentalis*. There appears to be no link between the Pacific Coast Group and the Southern Group. The divide of the Rocky Mountains has been a sufficient barrier to prevent this.

The final group of Canada Geese is confined to just one named subspecies, the Aleutian Canada *leucopareia*, now apparently very rare and breeding only on the Aleutian Islands. The extinct, named subspecies Bering Canada *asiatica* could be thought to belong to this group but there is scant evidence to make one believe that *asiatica* was anything more than a very slightly paler form of *leucopareia* and certainly not justifying subspecific status. The race *leucopareia* is now restricted as a breeding species to a remote island in the Aleutian chain nearly 1500 kilometres (1000 miles) from the next nearest Canada Geese, *minima* on the west coast of Alaska. In former times it is thought to have been much commoner and to have migrated both westwards into Asia, and eastwards and southwards into the Pacific States of America. Whether any still perform the latter migration is uncertain. The remnant population, of under 1000 birds, would seem to have been isolated from other Canada Geese for a considerable period, for it to have developed the minor plumage differences which it has. Very recently, what seemed to be Aleutian Canadas have been identified among the large flocks of Cackling Canadas wintering in California, suggesting closer links with this race, and with the Northern Group, than hitherto supposed.

This then is my way of looking at the Canada Goose and the problem of how to subdivide it. Whilst it is easy to criticise what has been before it must be recognised that the approach of a taxonomist, used to working with museum specimens, is almost always directed towards finding differences rather than similarities. There is no doubt at all that the Canada Goose is still evolving, a process that man has speeded up by the massive transplanting and introduction schemes that have taken place, particularly with the larger birds belonging to the Southern Group. I happen to believe that not only are the present twelve named subspecies too many but that the category of subspecies is not particularly suitable when it comes to describing the various differently sized and coloured birds, hence my classifying them into Groups. Others think very differently and are prepared to believe in anything from eight to thirty subspecies. I am content to return to my initial theme, namely that when it comes to practicalities one must deal in terms of populations; the particular scientific name that one gives them is of slight importance.

Hawaiian Goose or Ne-Ne *Branta sandvicensis*

As mentioned in the Preface this species is not covered in detail in this book, being outside its scope and, more importantly, soon to be the subject of a detailed monograph. In evolutionary terms the Hawaiian Goose is a typical island form, a descendant of an ancestral stock that found its way accidentally to the remote Hawaiian islands, settled there and then gradually evolved in complete isolation from any congeners to its present highly adapted state. Among other adaptations is the partial loss of webbing from between the toes, an indication of the much more terrestrial way of life forced on it by the lack of major water bodies on the islands. Its ancestor must surely have been the same as that of the Canada Goose but beyond that it is unnecessary to probe.

Barnacle Goose *Branta leucopsis*

We return to a straightforward species with no described races or forms. The Barnacle Goose has some basic similarities with both the Canada Goose and the Brent Goose, and probably came from a common ancestral form. It is closer to the Canada, and its distribution suggests that it may once have spread east from some originally North American centre. As will be discussed in detail in Chapter 6, the Barnacle Goose presently has three discrete populations. However, not even the most ardent splitter has been able to find any grounds for considering that three separate races are involved, and one must assume that the separation into the three populations has been relatively recent, certainly since the last glaciation, and possibly much nearer in time than that. It is of course quite possible that if separation is maintained for a few more thousand years some morphological differences may evolve. The average weights of birds in the three populations are slightly different, which may be a first step.

Brent Goose *Branta bernicla*

The normally accepted taxonomic treatment of this species divides it into four subspecies: Dark-bellied *bernicla*; Light-bellied *hrota*; Lawrence's *nigricans*; and Black Brant *orientalis*. However I am adopting very recent thinking which omits Lawrence's Brent altogether as being without taxonomic validity, and transfers its subspecific name *nigricans* to the Pacific or Black Brant, while the latter's former name *orientalis* is dropped. Looked at in isolation *bernicla* and *hrota* are well defined and their breeding grounds geographically separated by a gap in the northern Russian arctic. However, going westwards across arctic North America and into eastern Siberia, one finds a clinal situation with intergrading between *hrota* and *nigricans* in eastern arctic Canada, apparently pure *nigricans* in western arctic Canada, Alaska and eastern Siberia, and then further intergrading between *nigricans* and *bernicla* in central arctic Siberia. It seems probable that *hrota* was entirely separated from the others for a considerable period as it is much better differentiated from either *bernicla* or *nigricans* than these two are from each other. Even so, through spread in the range of one or other of the races, *hrota* and *nigricans* have come into contact and, because their differentiation had only reached subspecific level not that of full species, they were capable of inter-breeding, which has been followed by the intergrading of plumage characters. The separation between *nigricans* and *bernicla* has probably never been so complete.

The position of Lawrence's Brent Goose must be regarded as highly suspect. It was described in 1846 when Brent Geese with dark underparts were sometimes found on the Atlantic seaboard of North America where, nevertheless, the Light-bellied race *hrota* was the common one. However, only three specimens were apparently available in museums at the time and one of these was in very poor condition. Some colour differences were found between these birds and typical Black Brant from the Pacific Coast and they were thereupon named as a new subspecies. To base a new subspecies on so few specimens was frequent practice in those days but it is somewhat surprising that it was not challenged until quite recently, and that it has found a place in the most recent full taxonomic revisions of all the wildfowl. The only qualification made is that it may now be extinct or that its breeding and wintering quarters are unknown. It is difficult to believe in fact that it ever existed and the latest view is that the specimens on which Lawrence based his subspecies were either Black Brant showing slight colour variation, or intergrades between Black Brant and Light-bellied birds, which are now known to occur quite widely.

Red-breasted Goose *Branta ruficollis*

The morphological differences between this goose and the other *Branta* species are so great that its evolution from some common stock must have taken place a long time ago, before either the Barnacle or the Brent Goose had stemmed from the same stock. There are no subspecies or plumage variations in existence, though it is of passing interest that the drawings, which are very clearly of this species, found on an Egyptian monument of about 3000 BC, do differ slightly in the colour pattern of the head and neck from the present-day bird. One is tempted to infer from this that a subspecies occurred there then.

This completes the survey of the present taxonomic status of each goose species and subspecies. It must be emphasised once again that evolution is a continuing process, and although the original classification that I have outlined and then discarded in places was without any doubt a most thorough and scholarly work there can be nothing sacred or immutable about it, any more than one believes that nothing has changed since the creation. In particular, I would hope that someone better qualified than I will come forward before too long with a rational classification of the Canada Goose, and perhaps also of the Bean Goose. It has been justifiably stated that the only good examples of many of the named races of these two species exist either in museums or zoos. Certainly few field observers would care to be categorical about which race or races might be present in a given flock of geese in the wild.

To conclude this chapter I am listing all the currently named species and subspecies of geese, many of which will be receiving their last mention in the book. I have tried to alleviate the dry list of English and Latin names by giving their derivations. These have been culled from a number of sources which will be found in the bibliography. My own opinion has been ventured on a number of occasions.

Swan Goose *Anser cygnoides*

The English and scientific names of this species allude to its obvious similarities with the swans on one hand and the geese on the other. However, this should not be taken as meaning that the species forms a link between the two, because this is not the case.

'Swan' has Anglo-Saxon origins, as does 'Goose', which in Anglo-Saxon was *gós*. In Icelandic, another ancient language, the word was *gás*. It has been hazarded that Swan comes from a root *svon* or *svan*, meaning 'to sound' or perhaps 'to sing', while both *gós* and *gás* may have stemmed from an old Aryan root *gha*, meaning 'to gape open'.

Anser poses rather more problems. It is obviously a Latin word, and was used in Classical Roman times for a goose. However, one authority considers that it is derived from *Anas* the generic name of all the dabbling ducks. The derivation of *Anas* itself is not too certain, though it is thought that it might come from a Latin root *no*, which has a form *na*, meaning 'to swim'. This seems a little far-fetched and I prefer another explanation which is that it is onomatopoeic, being a rendering of a goose's call. This is also claimed for the English word 'gander', a male goose, which comes from the Anglo-Saxon *ganra*, also very like the nasal honking of a goose.

Cygnoides is more straight-forward, being a form of *cygnus*, Latin for a swan, and could be roughly translated as 'swan-like'.

Western Bean Goose *Anser fabalis fabalis*

'Western' is an obvious geographic designation. 'Bean' is almost universally assumed to stem from the bird's supposed liking for beans, either at or after harvest time, or when new-sown in the ground. Apparently beans must have been grown in the past on a large enough scale for them to have attracted feeding geese. An old, now defunct, name for the species is 'Corn Goose' which perhaps more correctly describes one of its modern food preferences.

We have dealt with both 'Goose' and *Anser*. The specific and subspecific name *fabalis* comes from the Latin *faba*, a bean.

Johansen's Bean Goose *Anser fabalis johanseni*

This race was named in 1951 by Dr Jean Delacour in honour of Hans Christian Johansen, a Danish ornithologist who lived from 1897 to 1973. He travelled extensively in the U.S.S.R. between the wars and made many valuable contributions to that country's ornithology, including a notable series of papers on the birds of West Siberia. He was always very interested in, and wrote a number of papers on, the confused taxonomic situation of the Bean Goose.

Middendorf's Bean Goose *Anser fabalis middendorffi*

H. von Middendorf was a nineteenth-century Russian ornithologist who did extensive work in the far east of his country. This race of the Bean Goose was named after him by a fellow Russian, Severtzov. Middendorf had himself named this race *Anser grandis* but it was later found that this name had already been used for the domestic breed of the Swan Goose and so could not be used again. Severtzov's action could be said to be some compensation for this.

Russian Bean Goose *Anser fabalis rossicus*

Yet again we have both the English and scientific names meaning the same thing. The English name is an obvious, if poorly defined, geographical designation, while *rossicus* is a Latinised form of Russia.

Thick-billed Bean Goose *Anser fabalis serrirostris*

The thick bill of this race is one of its distinguishing characters. The scientific subspecific name, apart from being frequently mis-spelt, comes from the Latin *serra*, a saw, and *rostris*, a bill. This is presumably a reference to the saw-toothed appearance of the parallel lamellae along the sides of the bill. They are rather more conspicuous in these larger-billed birds than in others of its kind.

Pink-footed Goose *Anser brachyrhynchus*

The English name describes this species' feet.
Brachyrhynchus is derived from two Greek words, *brakhus*, short, and *rhunkos*, a bill. This refers to its comparatively small bill.

European White-fronted Goose *Anser albifrons albifrons*

European is something of a misnomer as the range extends over much of Asia too. It is sometimes called the Siberian Whitefront, which is perhaps more accurate. 'White-fronted' is descriptive of the white forehead patch of the adult birds.
Albifrons comes from the Latin *albus*, in fact its genitive *albi*, meaning of white, and *frons*, a forehead.

Pacific White-fronted Goose *Anser albifrons frontalis*

'Pacific' is a fairly good term because this race does occur on the Pacific coast of North America, and is absent from the Atlantic coast.
'Frontalis' is derived from the same Latin word *frons*, and in effect emphasises the fact that the forehead is the main distinguishing feature.

Greenland White-fronted Goose *Anser albifrons flavirostris*

This race is confined as a breeding species to Greenland.

The subspecific name comes from the Latin *flavus*, yellow, and *rostris*, bill, in recognition of one of the principal morphological differences separating this race from others in the species.

Tule Goose *Anser albifrons gambelli*

'Tule' is a colloquial North American name for bulrushes on which this supposed race was typically thought to feed in winter.

The race was named after William Gambel (1819–49). He was one of America's pioneer ornithologists, a protégé of Nuttall, possibly the greatest of his time. He crossed the continent to the Pacific coast in 1841, perhaps the first ornithologist to do so, and spent several years in California collecting and observing the bird life there, much of it very different from the east of the continent. He died of typhoid while attempting a mid–winter crossing of the Sierra range.

As mentioned, *gambelli* has recently been used for the Interior White-fronted Goose, whose vernacular name describes its range.

Lesser White-fronted Goose *Anser erythropus*

The word 'Lesser' reflects the smaller size of this species in comparison with the rather similar European White-fronted Goose, with whose range it just overlaps.

The scientific name *erythropus* is not very well chosen coming as it does from the Greek *eruthos*, red, and *pous*, foot, as its legs and feet are decidedly pink, not red.

Western Greylag Goose *Anser anser anser*

This race was designated 'Western' at the same time that the Eastern race was named, and will of course mean different things depending on your geographical standpoint. Perhaps it is just as well that there is no clear–cut boundary between the two described races. The origin of 'Greylag' is not at all clear. 'Grey' undoubtedly refers to the overall plumage colour, but 'lag' has two explanations. The most usual one is that when all the wintering geese in Britain have migrated away in spring, this species, being resident in some areas, 'lags' behind. I have never felt convinced by this reasoning, but it is certainly better than the alternative which is that 'lag' is a corruption of 'leg'. The leg colour is admittedly greyish in a very young bird but in all others is decidedly pink.

The scientific name calls for no comment except to say that it is a bit repetitive.

Eastern Greylag Goose *Anser anser rubrirostris*

'Eastern' has already been explained, above.
Rubrirostris comes from the Latin *ruber*, red, and *rostris*, bill.

Bar-headed Goose *Anser indicus*

This species is, indeed, barred on its head.
Indicus is a latinised form of India where the species winters.

Emperor Goose *Anser canagicus*

It is not certain where the name 'Emperor' originated, though most writers seem agreed that this is one of the handsomest of North American geese. It is perhaps relevant that its Russian names include 'Tzarski Goose', and when we remember that Alaska, the only part of North America where the species occurs, was Russian until 1867, it may be that 'Emperor' is merely a translation of its obviously earlier Russian name.

Canagicus is a latinised form of the name of one of the Aleutian islands, Kanaga. The local Eskimo name for the goose is *Kanagiamoot*, meaning 'people of the Kanag'.

Lesser Snow Goose and Blue Goose *Anser caerulescens caerulescens*

The term 'Lesser' is used to distinguish this race from the larger Greater Snow Goose. 'Snow' is an obvious reference to the white plumage. The Blue Goose, once thought to be a different species but now known to be just a colour-phase, was so called from the apparent blueness of its plumage, actually silvery-grey on dark brown.

Caerulescens comes from the Latin *caeruleus*, blue, and means blueish. In the days when *caerulescens* was reserved for the Blue Goose, the white Lesser Snow Geese had the specific name *hyperborea* which, literally translated from the Latin, means 'beyond the north wind', a delightful way of expressing the far northern parts where the bird breeds. Alas, the taxonomic rules of priority have meant that it has been supplanted.

Greater Snow Goose *Anser caerulescens atlanticus*

'Greater' separates this race from the 'Lesser'.
This race occurs on the Atlantic coast of North America where the Lesser Snow Goose is rather uncommon. The latinised form of Atlantic is, therefore, a satisfactory subspecific name.

Ross's Goose *Anser rossii*

The English and scientific names of this species refer to Bernard Rogan Ross, an Irishman born in Londonderry in 1827, who emigrated to Canada and became a Chief Factor of the famous Hudson Bay Company which virtually ran northern Canada in those days. Whilst working for the Company he travelled extensively and made observations of the birds and other wildlife that he saw. He corresponded regularly with the Smithsonian Institution in Washington, then as now a leading body in the study of the natural sciences. He died in Toronto in 1874. The species was named after him in 1861 by John Cassin.

Canada Geese

Perhaps, inevitably, the names of the twelve different described races of the Canada Goose are nearly as confused as the taxonomy. The races have received between them no less than 36 popular names in recent years, and they are only those published in reasonably authoritative works. Each also has vernacular names in different parts of its range, with a few names, such as 'Common', 'Western' and 'Lesser' being applied to different races in different parts of the country. There is no simple way of bringing order to such chaos, and in the following listing of the currently named twelve races I give the names most frequently met with, plus one or more additional appellations where they seem called for.

Atlantic (or Common) Canada Goose *Branta canadensis canadensis*

This described race of the Canada Goose is given a range which takes in the Atlantic seaboard of North America, hence its designation. It is also, for that heavily populated part of the continent, the 'Common' Canada Goose. Both 'Canada' and its latinised form *canadensis* refer of course to that country, from where the species was first described. The English ornithologist, Willughby, apparently first named the bird, from specimens in the King's collection in St James Park, London, in 1678, at a time when these and other wildfowl were being brought to England and released on park lakes.

It is not absolutely certain why Canada is so-called. One commentator points out that the name is very similar to the Iroquois name for a village or collection of huts, *kanata*. It is very tempting to infer from this that there was once a meeting between some early explorers and some of the natives, with the former trying to discover what the latter called their homeland. A simple misunderstanding as to what was being asked or conveyed would readily lead to the Indian indicating his village and saying '*kanata*', while the explorers took this to be the place name.

Branta will be dealt with below under Brent Goose, as the two names are so clearly related.

Interior (or Todd's) Canada Goose *Branta canadensis interior*

'Interior' refers to the stated range of this race (sometimes also called 'Central') which is largely confined to the interior provinces of Canada and the United States, though its range is also shown as including the southern part of the Atlantic coast.

This race was described and named by W. E. Clyde Todd (1874–1969), one of North America's leading museum ornithologists, who had equally sound field experience. He was for a great many years Curator of Birds at the Carnegie Museum, Pittsburgh, Pennsylvania. Among very many publications were the much-praised *Birds of Western Pennsylvania* and *Birds of the Labrador Peninsula*.

Moffitt's (or Great Basin) Canada Goose *Branta canadensis moffitti*

James Moffitt (1900–43) was originally a business man, but he deserted that life to become a full-time professional ornithologist, joining the California Department of Fish and Game in 1931. He was a pioneer in the regular censusing of goose populations, beginning with the Black Brant wintering on the Californian coast in the 1930s. He became Curator of the Department of Ornithology and Mammalogy in the California Academy of Sciences and among much other work began compiling material for a monograph on the Canada Goose. Alas he was to be killed on Active Service in the Aleutian Islands in 1943, leaving this and the promise of so much else uncompleted.

The Great Basin of North America is the bowl of land lying between the Rockies and the coastal range of the Pacific States.

Giant Canada Goose *Branta canadensis maxima*

Both 'Giant' and *maxima*, the latter from the Latin for largest, refer to the size of this race, supposedly larger than any other.

Lesser Canada Goose *Branta canadensis parvipes*

Size is again the rule in naming this race, *parvipes* being Latin for small.

Taverner's Canada Goose *Branta canadensis taverneri*

Percy Algernon Taverner (1875–1947) held a number of posts at the National Museum of Canada at Ottawa, joining their staff in 1911. He became successively Curator, Ornithologist, and Chief of the Division of Ornithology. He is best remembered for his classic *Birds of Canada* first published in 1934.

Western (or Dusky) Canada Goose *Branta canadensis occidentalis*

'Western' describes its continental position, while *occidentalis* is Latin for western. 'Dusky' refers to its rather dark plumage.

Vancouver Canada Goose *Branta canadensis fulva*

Vancouver Island is included in the range of this race. *Fulva* comes from the Latin word of the same spelling which means rufous or tawny, and is a fair description of the plumage of the darker forms of Canada Geese.

Aleutian Canada Goose *Branta canadensis leucopareia*

This race is confined to the Aleutian Islands as a breeding bird. *Leucopareia* is formed from two Latin words, *leucos*, white, and *pareia*, face.

Bering Canada Goose *Branta canadensis asiatica*

Another geographical term for the English name, with another in latinised form for the subspecific name.

Richardson's (or Hutchins') Canada Goose
Branta canadensis hutchinsii

We have already seen how a bird may be called after the person who described and named it, for example, Todd's Canada Goose, or after the person in whose honour it was named, for example Moffitt's Canada Goose. Here we have a case where both names are in current use, leading to a certain amount of confusion. However as both people concerned eminently deserve posterity in this fashion perhaps it is right that both alternatives are kept in being.

Sir John Richardson, who described and named the race, was the Scottish surgeon and naturalist on the first two of Sir John Franklin's expeditions to the Canadian arctic in search of the north-west passage, in 1819–22, and again in 1825–27. On the first of these he very nearly died of starvation. Fortunately for him he did not go on Franklin's third and ill-fated attempt on the passage from which there were no survivors. However, he did join in the extensive search for Franklin, leading a party that was in the field from 1847–50, looking in vain for traces of the lost expedition. Before that, though, he had published four volumes describing the zoological results of the first two expeditions, with the descriptions of 267 different kinds of birds, not to mention 114 mammals, 140 fish and over 1000 insects, many of them new to science. The birds included a small Canada Goose collected on the Melville

Peninsula north of Hudson Bay. He named this in honour of T. Hutchins of the Hudson Bay Company.

Hutchins (1730–90) was the English attaché to the Hudson Bay Company from the early 1850s to his death. He was one of the first people interested in birds to work in the interior regions of Canada, and spent some time on the south-west coast of Hudson Bay in the 1780s, describing the birds he found there.

Cackling (Canada) Goose *Branta canadensis minima*

'Cackling' is meant to be a description of the call.
Minima is Latin for smallest.

Barnacle Goose *Branta leucopsis*

We now come to the extremely confused situation surrounding the name 'Barnacle', its origins, derivations and usage. The favourite story, much quoted, and often garbled, is that the name comes from the belief that Barnacle Geese hatched from the sea barnacles, *Lepas anatifera*, shellfish that live on timber. They take the form of a bi-valve at the end of a short stalk, completely different from the limpet-like barnacle that lives on rocks and bottoms of ships. Some very early writers perpetrated this story, as early as about 1150. Although shown before 1350 to be a complete fabrication it was repeated and embellished by Gerard in his famous herbal of 1597. He included the drawing of a kind of tree on whose limbs were borne sea barnacles, from which were dropping tiny but perfectly formed Barnacle Geese. One justification for such an outlandish tale was that the true nesting places of the species were unknown, and were to remain so until the 1850s, and because the geese appeared each autumn, to spend the winter on sea coasts, and disappeared again in spring, they must in some way have come from a sea animal. It is said that the myth was kept in active being well into the last century by the folk of western Ireland who convinced their consciences, if nothing else, that Barnacle Geese, which occur on that coast, were fish not fowl, and as such could be eaten on Fridays, fast days, and in Lent. Whatever the ramifications of this fable there is now direct conflict as to which came first in nomenclature, the goose or the shellfish. There is also an alternative theory altogether for the origin of the name 'Barnacle'.

One school of thought, backed by the weight of the *Oxford English Dictionary*, says that the shellfish got its name first from the diminutive form *pernacula* of *perna*, Latin for a kind of shellfish. The goose was then named from the shellfish. However Dr J. A. H. Murray, who edited the *New English Dictionary*, completed in 1928, states that the bird was named first and the shellfish later. He traces the name to the Middle English word *bernekke*, or *bernekka*, which is supposed to refer to the 'burnt', i.e., black, appearance of the neck—'burnt-neck'. The word also has Celtic and Old French origins.

I doubt whether this controversy can ever be resolved, and it is with some relief that one can turn to *leucopsis* which is straightforward Greek *leukos*, white, and *opsis*, face or appearance. *Branta* will enmesh us under the next species.

Dark-bellied Brent Goose *Branta bernicla bernicla*

If Barnacle causes some difficulties, the situation with 'Brent' and *branta* is complete and utter confusion. There are about as many theories as writers on the subject. And just to start off on the right foot, the two species, Brent and Barnacle Geese, have for long been confused by observers and writers, hence the specific name for the Brent of *bernicla* which is merely the latinised form of 'Barnacle'. In different parts of the British Isles the Brent is called locally the Barnacle or Bernacle, as for example in Ireland; and the Barnacle is called the Brent, as in Cheshire. Perhaps this is not too surprising as both are strictly coastal species, with overlapping ranges.

Before investigating the origin of the word it is worth pointing out that it is by no means certain which came first, 'Brent' or *Branta*. The former was used by the Welshman Thomas Pennant in his *British Zoology,* published in 1778; and the Latin name *Branta* had been used by Scopoli in 1769. These dates are close enough together to make it uncertain which was coined first, and by whom. To avoid repeating both names hereafter I will only refer to Brent, but without meaning to imply that it has priority.

Just as Barnacle has been traced to a word with implications of being burnt, so Brent has been linked with a number of words meaning the same thing. The oldest of these are the Anglo-Saxon *brennan* or *bernan*, and *brand*, which come from the same root and mean 'burned' or 'charred'. It is perhaps relevant that the German name for the species is *Brandgans*. These words refer, as does *bernekke*, to the black colouring of the species, linking it in the mind with burnt or charred. The English word 'branded', meaning 'brindled' has also been invoked in this context. One school of thought has taken the origin of the name back several centuries to Aristotle, that earliest of ornithologists, who used the word *brenthos* to indicate an unknown bird. Quite how the link between this and the goose is meant to have come about is not explained.

A final suggested derivation, which, however, borders on the far-fetched, is that it comes from the Welsh word *brenig*, which means limpet. One cannot help feeling that its perpetrator was trying a little too hard to find a connection with the Barnacle Goose and had confused the two different kinds of marine barnacle. Probably the only safe conclusion is to say that we will never know.

Just in passing, 'Dark-bellied' is descriptive of the underparts of this race and separates it from the next to be dealt with, the Light-bellied Brent.

Light-bellied Brent Goose *Branta bernicla hrota*

'Light-bellied' is obvious, which just leaves us with *hrota*. This is an Icelandic name for the Brent Goose, and this is the race which occurs in that country, on passage.

Lawrence's Brent Goose *Branta bernicla nigricans*

George Newbold Lawrence (1806–95) who described and named this race, now considered invalid, was an American businessman turned ornithologist. His paper on the Brent Goose appeared in 1842 and was his first publication. He was an indefatigable worker and writer, particularly on the birds of Central America and the West Indies, and published his last paper only four years before his death.

He adapted the word *nigricans* from the Latin *niger*, black, as meaning blackish, because his birds were darker than the usual Light-bellied Brent Geese from which he was trying to differentiate them.

Black Brant *Branta bernicla orientalis*

Black Brant are no blacker than the Dark-bellied race but the term serves well enough to distinguish the darker of the two North American races. 'Brant' is merely an Americanised form of Brent.

Orientalis simply means eastern, from the Latin.

Red-breasted Goose *Branta ruficollis*

Both the English and scientific names refer to the colour of the bird's plumage, the breast in the case of the English name, while *ruficollis* comes from the Latin *rufus*, red, and *collis*, cheek.

2 Identification

It might be thought that the identification of a bird as a goose should not present too many problems but I have known individual geese firmly named as cormorant and diver (or loon); and flocks of geese, flying and on the ground, can be identified as Lapwings, Curlews and gulls, though admittedly the reverse identification is more likely, particularly when the observer is actively searching for flocks of geese. A goose by itself will, more often than not, be difficult to identify as a goose and to distinguish as to species.

A goose on the water floats high, has a longish neck (when not asleep) and a very characteristic straight back rising slightly towards the pointed tail, which projects beyond the waterline. Divers and cormorants sit much lower in the water and their tail remains flat on the surface. The Shelduck has a somewhat similar silhouette to a goose, but its neck is shorter and not so straight, and its head is smaller and differently shaped. In flight the long neck of the goose is again distinctive, and the combination of this with the long pointed wings and short tail should be a certain guide. Cormorants and shags have longer, thinner wings, and longer tails; and divers have much thinner necks, long, parallel-sided wings and long trailing legs, not to mention their very obvious hump-backed appearance in flight.

Flocks of geese should not be hard to identify as such if one is within hearing range of their calls, or can see their individual shapes. Beyond this range one must rely on such clues as the way they are flying, often in Vs or straight lines, without the rapid flock movements of the Lapwing or Curlew, and more purposefully than gulls.

Although identification of the bird or flock as geese is in most cases quite straightforward, there are several species of geese, particularly in Britain and Europe, which are quite similar in appearance. Furthermore, for the average goose watcher, observing conditions are often less than ideal, either because of poor weather and light, or the distance at which the identification has to be made. Much identification can be done by the process of elimination, by knowing what species are most likely to be seen in the particular area. But this only applies to large flocks, individuals of almost any species can appear virtually anywhere in the northern hemisphere, either wild or as escapes from captivity. The bulk of this chapter is therefore devoted to fairly detailed descriptions of each species which, when used in conjunction with the plates, should aid identification, particularly of single geese out of context. The beginner, too, should find them useful in the identification of the commoner species in their usual haunts.

Identification of a goose as to its correct species, or perhaps race, is usually enough to satisfy most bird-watchers, but some would also like to know the age and sex of the bird. These are both quite easy to determine when one has the goose in the hand, but much harder when the bird is walking or flying around. Shooters have long known how to age and sex the geese they have shot, and do so without going to the extremes of dissection. Biologists privileged to handle live geese caught for marking and release have adopted these techniques and evolved others so that it is possible to state whether a bird is male or female, in its first year or older; and, for many females, whether that bird has bred either recently or ever. In the field, one has to be content with being able to determine whether the goose is in its first winter or older, and even this is difficult if not impossible for some species, particularly late in the winter; and, though with rather less reliability, whether it is male or female.

Sexing geese in the hand is much easier to demonstrate than it is to describe; and easier to demonstrate than it is to teach. Briefly, the bird is held firmly in both hands, with its belly uppermost and tail pointing away from the handler. It is convenient either to sit down and rest the bird on one's knees, or to stand with the bird's head between one's legs. The hands should be grasping the bird round the lower half of the body, so that it is also possible to have the ends of the wings within the hands to prevent them from flapping. With the bird held thus, the middle or fourth fingers can bend the tail feathers back a little while the thumbs and first fingers locate the cloaca and then, with gentle pulling and stroking movements, gradually evert it. Some birds have very strong muscles keeping the cloaca closed, others less so, or perhaps they manage to relax more readily. With practice the cloaca can be made to gape open sufficiently for one to distinguish whether it is a male (in which case it will have a penis); or a female, when the clitoris and bursa fabricius will be visible (see Plate 16). Geese, swans and ducks are among the very few birds to have a fully formed male organ; most other birds mate by joining their cloacas together so that the male sperms are squirted into the female. Because waterfowl copulate in water, it has been necessary for them to evolve an intromittent organ to make more certain that the sperms will get into the female.

Whilst looking at the cloaca it is possible to age the geese with some reliability. In its first year a male has a comparatively small, whitish organ, perhaps a centimetre (less than half an inch) long in the larger species by the end of the winter—it is much smaller in the bird's first autumn. In the second year it grows considerably and becomes pinkish-purple. It twists into a spiral shape, and also develops slight corrugations. It may be possible with experience to tell second year birds from older ones but there is some doubt about this.

There is also dispute as to whether it is possible to age females from cloacal examination. Some workers consider that the depth of the bursa increases between the first and second year but others have found that this is unreliable. As both groups were dealing with Canada Geese there is need for further work on a wider range of species. In any case the depth of bursa is not a particularly easy measurement to take. What is more reliable is the presence of dark streaks in the ring of muscles surrounding the cloaca. When these are present in a female goose it indicates that the bird has laid eggs. The dark streaks are stretch marks. Another area which is stretched with the passage of the eggs is the gap between the bones of the pelvic girdle. This gap can be felt with the finger just in front of the cloaca and with experience one can decide whether it is still narrow, or has been forced open during egg laying. After the latter event it is not only wider but the bones feel looser. Once the bird has laid its first clutch the widened gap remains though it may partly close again during the winter. Females caught in the breeding season will have bare patches on their breast whilst they are actually incubating, where they have plucked the down with which to line the nest. The new feathers which grow in their place will show up against the unmoulted surrounding ones until the latter are shed later in the summer (see Plate 16). A bird showing this character will definitely have laid eggs that year.

With the bird in the hand there are a number of plumage characteristics that help in ageing birds. Some of these are also visible in the field, at least in good viewing conditions. In most goose species the adults have pale or whitish edgings to the feathers of the wing coverts and mantle. These edgings are even in width and, as the wing coverts lie in neat rows, they form parallel bars across the closed wing. In the first winter goose not only are the edgings less white, more brown in colour, but they are smaller and the wing coverts do not lie regularly. The barring effect is thus not so pronounced, if visible at all. An exception to this is the Brent Goose, in which the adult lacks any white edgings at all, and the young bird has brownish ones. Young Canada Geese show little difference from the adult in this respect.

The overall colouring of a young goose is always much duller, less clean looking than in the adult; the bill and legs as well as the plumage. These characters are quite visible in the field. One that is not, however, is the presence in a young goose of notched tips to its tail feathers. When the downy young gosling grows its first set of feathers, those in the tail are attached to the base of the down plumes that were growing there before. As the tail grows the down falls off or is abraded, leaving a slight notch in the tip of the feather (Plate 16). These feathers are retained for a variable length of time but usually well into the first winter, perhaps as late as March, so their presence can always be used to denote a first-year bird, but their absence is not a reliable guide to an older bird after about the New Year.

In the field, the first winter goose looks altogether more scraggy and gawky than an adult, with a more leggy appearance. Its plumage is less neat, lacks any regular barring on the wings and mantle, and has a tendency to be more mottled, less evenly coloured. There are, of course, a few obvious age differences in some species, as in the Whitefronts where the young bird lacks the white forehead and black belly bars, but for most species the characters are more subtle. Furthermore, the characters gradually disappear through the winter as the young bird undergoes at least a partial body moult, so that after the New Year it is often only the wing coverts which remain different, and even those may be less distinct. In the Canada Geese age differences are very slight indeed and it is considered almost impossible to age birds of some populations in the field.

Sexing in the field relies entirely on experience, and on having good views. The male goose tends to be larger than the female, to have a larger head and to be more often in the head-up alert position in a feeding flock. Judgements as to sex and age among geese may be helped by the presence of family parties, and of pairs without young, in goose flocks. Careful watching of a feeding flock will reveal small groups of geese moving as discrete units within it. They also usually take off and land together. These groups will be found to consist of two adults and from one to four or five, rarely more, young. Once a family party has been found it is comparatively easy to compare and contrast the differences between the adults and first winter birds. Closer scrutiny will also show which is the adult male and which the female, using the characters already mentioned. After these have been learned it should be possible to sex the birds of a pair without young, and even to have a go at lone birds, either within a flock of their own kind, or out of context among other geese or by themselves. Head size and shape is probably the best guide though, curiously, it is a distinction that is more apparent in the field than in the hand and more readily observed than detailed sets of measurements (which always show great overlap) would seem to suggest.

It may seem an unnecessary refinement to the average goose watcher to be able to sex and age the birds he is watching. But apart from the satisfaction this may give to some, it is of great importance to biologists as it enables them to assess with some accuracy the annual breeding success by studying autumn or winter flocks of geese. The only other method is to observe the geese on their breeding grounds, which is only possible with a few populations. By ascertaining the percentage of young in the flocks and the mean brood size, one gains information of real value in monitoring the well being of goose populations. This aspect will be thoroughly dealt with in Chapter 6.

Hybrid geese can present problems of identification. Almost every combination of hybrid is possible both within and between the two genera. Wild hybrids are comparatively rare but in captivity they are common and escapes are all too frequent. In many hybrids, characters from both parents will be obvious, as for example, in crosses between Canada Goose and Snow Goose, or Canada Goose and Greylag, when the head and neck are generally very dark with or without the white chinstrap, but the bill and legs are usually pink. Hybrids between closer relations than these will be harder to distinguish; for example, Lesser Snow Goose × Ross's Goose, and Bean Goose × Whitefront. There is no easy answer to their identification, only a continuing awareness that it is a possibility if a bird does not easily fit any single description.

Geese with aberrant plumage, usually darker or lighter than normal, can also confuse the goose watcher. Fortunately, they are not common and the types that are known to occur are mentioned under the appropriate species heading in this chapter.

Each species or subspecies description that follows is divided into a number of sections covering adult, first winter, downy young, voice and plumage variants. Not unexpectedly, first winter and downy young birds change as they grow older, the latter quite rapidly. It has been necessary to 'freeze' them at a particular age for the text descriptions and the colour plates. In the case of the first winter geese I have selected the first half of the winter, October to December. In all cases the differences between first winter and adult become less obvious as the winter progresses. The downy young are usually described and illustrated as day-olds, but in nearly all species the plumage colour changes quite noticeably, and quickly, in the first few days of life. In all the grey geese, snow geese, and some of the black geese, the downy young plumage has, first, an overall colour wash of yellow or green. This rapidly fades, perhaps by bleaching, and the gosling becomes duller and less well coloured. It retains this plumage until the first feathering appears at about three weeks old. The descriptions and plates, therefore, refer to this second stage of the downy plumage, as the longer lasting and therefore more likely stage to be encountered by an observer.

As well as plumage characteristics, size, shape and silhouette are also very important in identifying geese though by no means easy to convey in words. Size in particular is very difficult to grasp and actual measurements of length, wingspan or standing height have such large ranges, depending on age and sex, as to be of very little use. I have therefore restricted myself to three categories of size: small—geese up to about 60 cm (2 ft) in length from bill tip to tail tip, and with wingspan around 120 cm (4 ft); medium—approximately 60 to 75 cm (2 ft 0 in–2 ft 6 in) long and with wingspan between about 120 and 150 cm (4 ft 0 in–5 ft 0 in); and large—over 75 cm long, and up to 90 cm or more (2 ft 6 in–3 ft 0 in), and with wingspan more than 150 cm (5 ft). I should emphasise that these measurements are only meant to serve as a rough guide and that small or large individuals of a species may overlap into the adjacent category.

The way that flocks of geese behave on the ground and in the air can also be important in identifying the species, with differences in the density of feeding flocks and in the adoption of V-formations. These points are also covered.

Swan Goose (Plates 2, 3 and 15)

This is one of the largest geese, very long-necked and particularly long-billed. It is mainly brown with a dark cap and back of the neck, and is darker above than below. In flight it appears large and heavy, with a very long neck. Domestic forms of roughly the same pattern but usually different shape can be found widely, but the wild species is restricted to eastern Asia.

ADULT (Plates 2 and 3)

The large long head is buff-brown with a darker chestnut cap coming just below the eye, and running on down the back of the neck to the mantle. The sides and front of the neck are pale buff-brown like the face. The upperparts are brown to grey-brown with the coverts and mantle feathers edged with buff. This forms neat transverse barring across the closed wings and the back. The chest is buff-brown, darker than the front of the neck and usually with a fairly abrupt colour change. The belly is much the same colour but is barred on the flanks with dark brown. A thin white line runs down the flanks along the line of the closed wing. The upper and under tail-coverts and the lower

belly are white, while the tail feathers are brown tinged with white. There is a thin white line round the base of the bill in the majority of birds.

The bill is very large and long, forming a continuous line with the forehead. It looks too large for the bird, making the head nose-heavy and quite unlike any other species. The bill is black, the legs and feet are orange, and the eye is dark brown.

There should be no possibility of confusion with other species as both in size, shape and colouring the Swan Goose stands alone. It is only with domestic forms, perhaps strayed from a farm (and surprisingly some of them are good fliers), that there might be difficulty, but these are usually much rounder in the body, with a shorter, thicker neck and a more upright stance.

In flight the Swan Goose is a large slightly ponderous bird, with a very long neck, accentuated by the elongated head and bill. The wings are long and broad, and their action is slower and heavier than other geese. There is almost no pattern on the upperwing, but as in all grey geese the white upper tail-coverts form a band dividing the darker rump from the tail. At long range it could be confused with the Bean Goose, but closer to it is usually possible to see the contrast between the pale sides and front of the neck and the dark hind neck.

FIRST WINTER (Plate 2)
The only plumage distinction of the first winter Swan Goose is that the transverse barring on the wing-coverts and mantle of the adult are less obvious and regular, as the feather edging is neither so pronounced nor laid out in such regular rows. The bill is the same colour, the legs and feet orange-brown, and there is no white round the base of the bill.

DOWNY YOUNG (Plate 15)
The upperparts are yellowish-brown, the lower parts paler, tinged more

lemon yellow on the neck and undertail than on the belly. There is a faint brown or blackish band from the bill through and to behind the eye. The wings and sides of the tail have pale buff spots. The bill and feet are grey-black.

VOICE
The Swan Goose has the familiar strong trumpeting honk of the domestic Chinese Goose, its direct descendant.

VARIANTS
None recorded apart from domestic forms.

Bean Goose (Plates 1, 2, 3, 14 and 15)

The Bean Goose is essentially a large, long-legged and long-necked goose, with brown or dark brown plumage. The head and neck are noticeably darker than the body. The dark upperwings lack any contrasting pale patches. Most, though not all, have a fairly long narrow bill, giving the entire head an elongated appearance. Bean Geese are found throughout northern and central Europe and in Asia.

ADULT—ALL POPULATIONS (Plates 1, 2 and 3)
The head and neck are dark brown tending almost to black on the forehead in some individuals. The upperparts are an even dull brown, relieved only by the pale edgings to the wing-coverts which show on the closed wing as a series of narrow more or less parallel bars. The breast is a paler brown darkening towards the flanks. Both upper and under tail-coverts are pure white, while the tail itself is grey-brown with a narrow white tip. A thin white line runs down the flanks on either side, following the edge of the closed wing. A few birds have some white feathering round the base of the upper mandible, but this is rarely visible except at very close quarters.

The bill is a combination of black and orange, with the black at the base and tip, and the exact extent of the orange varying according to the race or population (see below). The shape of the bill, too, though generally rather long and heavy, varies considerably. The legs and feet are normally quite bright orange, but can be duller, or even yellow-orange. The eyes are brown.

Confusion is possible with the Pink-footed Goose at distances where the colours cannot be distinguished, but the latter has a much rounder dumpier shape, with a shorter neck and rounder head. Confusion with an immature Greenland Whitefront, particularly when it is a lone bird in a flock of another species, is quite frequent, but the Whitefront lacks the contrast between the head and neck and the rest of the body, and at close quarters has a white nail to the bill not a black tip.

In flight the Bean Goose reveals uniformly dark brown upperparts and upperwing, lacking any prominent lighter areas. Seen close to, the primary and secondary coverts are a little paler but this is a poor field character. The white upper tail-coverts form a white band at the base of the dark tail, as in most geese. In very bright light the primaries can sometimes be seen to be virtually black and so slightly darker than the rest of the wing. The contrast between the dark head and neck, and the paler chest, will show in good conditions. When seen just in silhouette or at a distance, the long thick neck and fairly long head should help to identify it. The Greenland Whitefront also looks evenly dark on top in flight, but has narrower wings than the Bean Goose and a shorter neck. All other grey geese, with the exception of the very differently shaped Swan Goose, have some kind of wing pattern.

Subspecies or population variation (Plate 1)

As related in Chapter 1, there are five named races of the Bean Goose whose differences are based mainly on overall shape, together with bill shape and size, and the extent of the orange on the bill. Although standard works illustrate typical specimens of each race, in practice it is not possible to assign many of the birds one sees in the field to a particular race, and is not really worth the attempt. Although some bird watchers are dissatisfied merely to record Bean Goose when they are aware that a number of named races exist, it would be more useful in the present state of knowledge, not to mention confusion, if drawings were made of the bill showing its shape and the extent of the orange and black. In this way it might be possible to assemble knowledge on the range of variation of Bean Geese in given areas, which would contribute to an understanding of the subspecies problem. Four typical bill shapes and colour patterns are shown in Plate 1.

In western Europe, including the British Isles, Bean Geese seem to fall into two main types, which hitherto have been referred to as the races Western Bean *fabalis*, and the Russian Bean *rossicus*. Essentially a Western Bean is described as the larger, longer-necked bird with an elongated bill on which the orange extends across the top and along the sides of the upper mandible. The Russian Bean is smaller, rounder-bodied and rounder-headed, with a shorter bill on which the orange is more or less confined to a narrow band over the top of the upper mandible, just behind the black tip. The combination of round head and shorter bill gives this named race a much more obvious and steeper forehead than the Western Bean. However, these remarks are only applicable to a minority of birds, as many that I have seen combine features of both races, with perhaps a rounded head and a long bill with or without plenty of orange. Bill shape is in fact highly variable, as is the amount of orange. The majority of the Bean Geese wintering in north-west Europe, at least, do not fit neatly into either of the two described races.

The other three races that have been named, Johansen's *johanseni*, Middendorf's *middendorfi* and Thick-billed *serrirostris*, have also been described on the basis of their size and bill shape. Differences in measurements exist but samples measured have been small and there is much overlap. Pinning down a race to a geographical area is virtually impossible and it is more satisfactory to treat Bean Geese in terms of clines as mentioned in Chapter 1. The most eastern birds in Asia are generally rather large and have long and heavy bills, with a considerable 'gape' between upper and lower mandibles. None of these, named as Thick-billed Bean Geese, have been reliably identified in north-west Europe.

FIRST WINTER—ALL SUBSPECIES OR POPULATIONS (Plates 2 and 4)

Like all first-year geese, the immature Bean is more scraggy than an adult bird, looking thinner, less well-groomed, and altogether more leggy. Its plumage is generally duller, and the regular transverse barring of the adult's wing-coverts is noticeably less well-defined, without the neat parallel rows of light feather edgings. The colour of bill and legs is duller than in the adult bird. These distinctions become less and less obvious from the New Year onwards.

In flight a first-year Bean Goose is virtually indistinguishable from an older bird. It can also be confused with an immature Whitefront, especially the darker Greenland race. It has a paler body, however, and so a more contrasting dark head and neck.

DOWNY YOUNG (Plate 15)

The upperparts are olive brown but initially with a yellowish tinge to the sides of the head, the neck and the mantle. A dark brown streak joins the bill and the eye. Indistinct spots below the wing, and a bar across it, are both pale yellow. The underparts are very pale yellow, with an olive brown wash on the sides and thighs. The yellow fades or bleaches as the bird gets older. The bill and feet are dark grey. There is no apparent variation between subspecies or populations, except perhaps in size.

VOICE

The Bean Goose is probably the least vocal of the grey geese, both in flight and on the ground. The principal flight note is a two-syllable 'wink-wink' or 'unk-unk', closely allied to the main call of the Pinkfoot but lower in pitch, more tenor to the Pinkfoot's alto or even treble. The sound of a flock in flight is deeper again than the Pinkfoot but a more musical sound than the equally deep or even deeper flock noise of Greylags. The sound made by a feeding flock consists of the repeated contact or conversation call, a deep 'ah-ah-ah', though louder calls can be made during aggressive encounters. A lone Bean Goose may utter a three- or four-syllable call, best rendered as 'ow-ow-ow-ow'. No variation in call has been reported from across the range of the species.

PLUMAGE VARIANTS

No melanistic Bean Geese have apparently been recorded but birds with pale, washed-out plumage, or with partial albinism, white feathering on the body or wings, have been seen very rarely. Another occasional variant has pink not orange on the bill but is otherwise similar to a Bean Goose.

Pink-footed Goose (Plates 1, 2, 3 and 15)

This is a medium to large goose with a rounded body, short neck and short black and pink bill, and pink legs. The overall plumage is a pinkish-brown, with noticeable darker head and neck. In flight there is a prominent grey forewing. The range is restricted in the breeding season to Greenland, Iceland

and Svalbard, and in winter to countries bordering the North Sea.

ADULT (Plates 1, 2 and 3)

The head and neck are dark brown, shading to paler brown in the lower part of the neck. Although the goose looks pinkish brown in the field, the upper body-feathers are in fact pinkish-grey close to. The wing-coverts on the closed wing show the usual series of regular transverse barrings formed from the light edgings to the feathers. The breast is pinkish-brown, merging with the darker neck above, and with the paler brown belly and flanks. There is an obvious white line down the edge of the flanks, following the line of the closed wing. The upper and under tail-coverts are white, and the tail is dark grey tipped with white. As in the Bean Goose a few birds have a very small amount of white feathering around the base of the bill.

The bill is short and black with a narrow band of pink over the upper mandible just behind the black tip. The pink occasionally extends along the side of the upper mandible. The legs and feet are pink. The eyes are brown.

Possible confusion with the Bean Goose at a distance has been dealt with under that species. In good light the essential 'pinkness' of the Pinkfoot is very obvious, though the apparent overall colour can vary tremendously depending on the background. Pinkfeet feeding on an autumn stubble field will look quite dark, while on ploughed land or a potato field, they appear much paler.

In flight the Pinkfoot shows a prominent area of pale grey on the primary and secondary coverts, which contrasts with the very dark brown of the flight feathers. Like the Bean and other grey geese there is a band of white across the base of the dark tail. The silhouette is of a short-necked bird. Flocks of Pinkfeet move easily, flying faster and with an easier wing action than other geese of similar or larger size. They very typically adopt the V-formation.

FIRST WINTER (Plate 2)

The young bird is a little darker than its parents, the pinkness being less obvious. The regular parallel barring of the wing-coverts is missing, because the feather edgings are browner, not so pale, and not arranged in neat rows. This gives a mottled appearance to the closed wing. The pink of the bill and legs is always duller, and the legs may not be much brighter than flesh colour. The differences become less as the winter progresses.

In flight the young bird is probably not separable.

DOWNY YOUNG (Plate 15)
This is essentially similar to the Bean Goose downy, though tending to be yellower all over at least at first. However, there is considerable individual variation and the yellow bleaches quite quickly.

VOICE
The most characteristic call of the Pinkfoot is a high-pitched 'wink-wink' or sometimes 'wink-wink-wink'. There is also a lower more nasal call 'ahng-ahng-ahng', similar to but higher-pitched than the Greylag call. A lone Pinkfoot has a very penetrating single-note call best rendered 'wing' or 'wang'. As a flock Pinkfoot give an impression of noisiness and urgency, but yet quite musical, lacking harsh notes such as Greylags have, but without the laughing quality of the Whitefront. A feeding flock produces a quiet buzzing sound derived from the conversational notes of the birds.

PLUMAGE VARIANTS
Pinkfeet with pale plumage turn up most years in the Iceland population. They lack much of, but not all, their pigment and so appear a creamy colour, though often still showing the slightly darker areas on the head, neck and wings. Total and partial albinos have been recorded but they are both very rare. Another rare variant has orange legs but retains the pink on the bill.

White-fronted Goose (Plates 1, 4, 5, 14 and 15)

Medium to large geese, the adults of all races have a relatively conspicuous steep white forehead, black bars on the belly, and relatively long narrow wings. The main colouring is grey-brown (darker and more olive-brown in the Greenland race) without any contrast between the head and the rest of the body, and with only a slight pattern on the upper wing. At a distance the birds look rather uniformly brown. Immatures lack the white forehead and black belly bars and lone birds can be confusing. Between them the races occur almost throughout Eurasia and North America though they are rare or absent in parts of eastern Canada and the United States. Whitefronts normally feed in more spread out flocks than other grey geese.

ADULT (Plates 1, 4 and 5)

European Whitefront
The head, neck and upperparts are grey-brown, the wing-coverts edged with very pale tips, combining to form a regular pattern of barring across them. White feathering surrounds the bill and extends up the forehead. This feature is variable and in a small number of birds reaches to above the eye. The underparts are paler than the upperparts, particularly on the chest, tending to darker brown on the flanks. The lower breast and belly is marked with a variable number of black blotches and bars, both thick and thin and of different lengths. Studies have shown that these are individually variable and probably stay constant once they have appeared after the immature bird's

moult of its belly feathers in its first spring. A very well-marked bird can appear almost black-bellied. There is the usual white flank line, and the upper and under tail-coverts are pure white. The tail feathers are dark brown, tipped white. The overall body plumage can vary through many shades of brown.

The bill is quite long but not deep, and is pink with a white nail. Some birds can appear to have an orangy bill though usually only near the tip and not as deep orange as the bill of the Greenland race. The legs and feet are orange. The eyes are dark brown. A proportion of birds, perhaps as many as one in five, has a pale yellow eye-ring but this is not usually very visible in the field. It can give rise to confusion with the Lesser Whitefront but the latter's eye-ring is much brighter and bigger and therefore more prominent. In any case identification of a Lesser Whitefront should never be on this character alone. In many Whitefronts the eye-ring is incomplete.

The European Whitefront in flight presents a fairly uniform grey-brown appearance. The upperwing shows a slight pattern with the forewing brown and the flight feathers grey-black, but this is only visible in good light. The white forehead and black belly bars can be seen even at some distance in good conditions. This race is much paler overall than the Bean Goose and has a shorter, thicker neck but distant views may be impossible to resolve. Fortunately, though, the Whitefront is very vocal in flight, which the Bean Goose is not, and the calls are quite different (see Voice).

Pacific Whitefront

This race is only separable from the European Whitefront on bill length, with an average of about 52 mm compared with 47 mm for the latter. However, the published ranges of bill length are respectively 47–57 mm and 43–56 mm which is an indication of how variable both races are. Body plumage, too, is very variable and Pacific Whitefronts have been described as both paler and darker than European Whitefronts, even by the same author. It is doubtful in the extreme whether one could identify either race in the 'wrong' area.

Interior Whitefront

The larger Whitefront of North America, the Interior race is a bigger, heavier version of the Pacific or European Whitefront, more massive in every dimension. It is also generally darker in plumage though not as dark as the Greenland race. It has a pink bill. Separation in the field is only possible with experience, and even then identification is probably safer when encountered in areas where the race is known to occur. Its flight is said to be less buoyant and free than the other races, and it is also reputed to fly lower, but these indications should be taken merely as a sign that the geese are worth a closer look when they land and not as conclusive characters in their own right.

Greenland Whitefront

In most conditions the Greenland Whitefront adult is clearly distinguishable from the other races. The overall body colour is much darker, more olive brown in most lights. The white face patch is normally less extensive and is generally surrounded by a narrow border of very dark brown feathers, darker than the rest of the head. The black belly bars are also usually more extensive than in the other races, and this adds to the overall darkness of the bird.

The bill of the Greenland Whitefront is orange or orange-yellow in colour, very different from the pink of the other races. The nail is white. In addition, the bill is longer and heavier than either the European or Pacific Whitefront's. The legs and feet are orange.

In flight Greenland Whitefront are evenly dark. Confusion is most likely with the Bean Goose but the Whitefront has much narrower wings, narrower even than in the other Whitefronts and forming a good separation character.

FIRST WINTER—ALL RACES (Plates 4 and 14)

The immature Whitefront of all races lacks the white face patch and black belly bars of the adult. The white patch will begin to appear in January, rarely in December. It is sometimes preceded by new black feathers on the forehead. By March or April the white patch can be quite extensive, but the belly bars do not appear until after the first complete moult during the late spring or early summer. Thus, in late winter the absence of belly bars is a certain indication of age, while the forehead patch gradually ceases to be of use. Young birds also lack the neat pale barring on the wing-coverts of the adults, having instead uneven pale feather tips producing a faintly mottled appearance. The mottling also shows on the breast and belly. The bill, legs and feet are similar in colour to the adults of the particular race, but always duller.

An immature Whitefront seen away from others of its kind is one of the more confusing grey geese. A pink-billed bird can be confused with a Greylag, which, however, has a much more massive bill, and is a much stouter, heavier-built goose with a shorter neck. When it flies it shows conspicuous pale patches on the forewing. An orange-billed first winter

Greenland Whitefront is darker than other immatures and is most likely to be muddled with a Bean Goose. However, the latter has black at the base and tip of its bill and also has a darker head and neck contrasting with the paler body, while the Whitefront is more uniformly brown.

Confusion is quite possible with the first winter blue phase Lesser Snow Goose, but the latter has dark grey legs changing to pink as it matures, not yellow-orange, and a large pink bill with a prominent gape or 'grinning patch' along the sides.

In flight the immature Whitefront will be very difficult to identify with certainty unless the bird comes very close, though with experience the narrower wings are a good guide while the voice (see below) can be conclusive. Blue phase Snow Geese in flight have grey not white upper tail-coverts so do not show the typical white tail band of the Whitefront as they fly away.

DOWNY YOUNG—ALL RACES (Plate 15)

The upperparts, including the crown and hindneck, are olive brown and the underparts are yellowish. There is a yellowish tinge to the cheeks, and stronger yellow on the chin, and a bar across the wing. There is a dark line from the bill through the eye. The legs and bill are dark grey. The only racial difference reported is that the Pacific race is rather greyer in tone, less brown.

VOICE—ALL RACES

The call of the Whitefront is a high-pitched, musical sound, almost laughing in character, best rendered in words as 'kow-lyow', or sometimes 'lyo-lyok'. It can sound more metallic and harsher but this is usually when the birds are alarmed. The normal flight call has a contralto pitch. A feeding flock produces a curious buzzing sound, audible over considerable distances. Much of this arises from the calls produced by the birds when families meet in aggressive encounters. Whitefronts are quite noisy geese and this can be very useful when identification is in doubt in poor light or at a distance.

The immature Whitefront seems to have a more distinctive voice than most other young geese, sounding squeaky, as if its voice had not yet 'broken'.

There seem to be no racial differences in the calls.

PLUMAGE VARIANTS

Melanistic and leucistic Whitefronts are recorded from time to time, particularly among the well-watched European race in north-west Europe. The melanistic birds are very dark brown, to black, all over though still with a white forehead, and showing pure black barring on the wings. Leucistic geese lack most though not all of their pigment and have a rather creamy-brown appearance. Partial albino Whitefronts have also been reported. One type which has been seen a number of times in the Greenland race has the whole of the head white, when it resembles the blue phase Snow Goose at a distance, or most of the front half of the head white. The forehead patch is quite variable in the European race and may extend to above the eyes or run back on either side to form white eyebrows.

Lesser White-fronted Goose (Plates 4, 5 and 15)

A small dainty goose, the Lesser Whitefront is superficially a smaller version of the European Whitefront. Separation is possible, however, on a number of good features provided a really good view is obtained. It is further a rounder-bodied goose with a smaller more rounded head, and very short bill. It breeds across most of northern Europe and Asia, wintering to the south.

ADULT (Plates 4 and 5)
The general colouring is similar to that of the European Whitefront. The white forehead patch is more extensive, however, extending to most of the fore crown, reaching back to above the eye, an amount only rarely found in the European race. The patterning on the wing and the white flank line are as in the other races. The closed wings usually, though not invariably, extend beyond the tip of the tail, whereas those of the other Whitefronts rarely if ever do so. The extent of the black belly barring, often said to be less than in other races, is not a reliable feature.

The bill of the Lesser Whitefront is short and the upper mandible meets the lower at the tip at a considerable angle. This combines with the steep forehead to emphasise the small, round-headed appearance. The bill is pink with a white nail. The legs and feet are orange. The dark brown eye has a conspicuous eye-ring of yellow. This is visible even at some distance and is brighter and more prominent than the pale eye-ring shown by a proportion of European Whitefronts.

When grazing the Lesser Whitefront walks more quickly and pecks at a faster rate than larger geese. One of the best ways of spotting a single Lesser Whitefront in a flock of another species is to look for a bird moving more rapidly than its neighbours.

In flight the Lesser Whitefront moves quickly and daintily, its small size, coupled with the short neck, giving a slight resemblance to a large duck.

FIRST WINTER (Plate 4)
The white forehead and black belly bars of the adult are lacking but the eye-ring is present and equally distinctive. The white forehead begins to appear during the second half of the winter. The transverse barring on the upperparts is also lacking, as in the European Whitefront. The wings projecting beyond the tail, plus the small bill and round head, and the more rapid walking and feeding movements, will all help to pick out an immature Lesser Whitefront from a flock of another species, just as they do for the adult.

DOWNY YOUNG (Plate 15)
The overall effect is very similar to the European Whitefront though with a tendency to be darker brown above and less yellow below. However, there seems to be some individual variation, and in any case the bird becomes darker after the first few days.

VOICE

The flight calls of the Lesser Whitefront are higher pitched than those of the European Whitefront and form a trisyllabic version of the laughing call, rendered 'lyee-lyee-lyeek', or 'yow-yow-yow'. An experienced ear can pick out a flying bird from among a flock of European Whitefronts. A flock of Lesser Whitefronts has a treble pitch, in comparison with the contralto of the Whitefront.

PLUMAGE VARIANTS

None have apparently been recorded, apart from slight variation in the extent of the white forehead.

Greylag Goose (Plates 1, 2, 3 and 15)

This is a large, grey, goose, with a prominently large head, noticeable on the ground and in flight, set on a thicker neck than other species. In flight a conspicuous pale grey forewing can be seen. Greylags occur throughout Europe and much of Asia. A cline of colour exists with pale birds to the east.

ADULT (Plates 1, 2 and 3)

Western Greylag

This description applies to birds breeding in Britain and Iceland and wintering in the British Isles, and to those breeding through most of Scandinavia and around the Baltic and wintering in western and central Europe. Intermediates between this form and typical Eastern Greylags occur widely, especially in eastern Europe, and may occasionally be seen in Britain, for example southern England.

The head and neck are fairly pale grey, the neck being marked with dark

diagonal lines formed by indentations of the feathers. The upperparts are grey-brown, with the usual parallel barring formed by the pale feather edgings to the wing-coverts. The underparts are paler, more grey than grey-brown. The belly usually has a small number of black blotches or spots, only very rarely forming bars or showing as much as on even a lightly marked Whitefront. There is a sloping white flank line, as in other grey geese. The upper and under tail-coverts are pure white, contrasting with the dark grey tail feathers which are finely tipped with white. The rear flank feathers have blackish centres to them, producing a finely barred effect on many but not all birds.

The bill of the Greylag is deep and heavy, virtually triangular in outline, and is coloured pale orange with some indication of pink just behind the white nail. The legs and feet are pink. The eye is brown and has an orange ring round it.

In flight the Greylag shows by far the most contrasting wing of any grey goose with a very pale almost blue-grey patch on the upper wing-coverts showing most conspicuously against the deep grey or grey-black of the flight feathers. There is a similar striking contrast on the underwing. The flight silhouette is of a large goose with a relatively thick neck, though still quite a long one, on the end of which is a noticeably large head which can be spotted at considerable distances. Whilst all grey geese fly with equal facility in given conditions, the flight of the Greylag is perhaps a little more laboured than that of other species. In making short flights they seem a little less prone to adopt V-formation, preferring straggling lines.

Eastern Greylag

Although basically similar to the Western Greylag in shape, the typical Eastern bird is a little larger on average and considerably paler in plumage, with much of the brown of the Western race replaced by white or very pale grey. The overall effect is of a much greyer, less grey-brown bird. The bill is longer and is completely pink apart from the white nail. The legs and feet are pink. In flight the pale forewing is if anything even paler than in the Western race.

True Eastern Greylags are not normally found west of the Black Sea but intermediates are very frequent in eastern and central Europe and have been introduced further west. They take in the complete colour range of plumage, and bill colour varies from completely orange to completely pink.

FIRST WINTER (Plate 2)

Western Greylag

The immature bird in its first winter lacks the even barring on the wing-coverts of the adult, with the regular pale tips replaced by very irregular edging, often looking quite brown. The bill and legs are duller than the adults and sometimes appear tinged with grey. There are no black belly or flank markings.

Eastern Greylag

Differentiation of the young from the adult is similar to that for the

Western race. The young Eastern Greylag can be told from the young Western by its larger size, longer pinkish bill, and much paler plumage.

DOWNY YOUNG—BOTH RACES (Plate 15)

The upperparts are olive brown, the forehead, throat and rest of the underparts are yellowish though it is variable and in any case soon fades. A dark brown line runs through the eye. There is a pale yellow bar across the wing. The legs and feet are dark grey-brown. The overall colouring tends to get paler and yellower going from west to east.

VOICE

The Greylag has the most raucous call of any grey goose and it closely resembles the cackle of the Emden and other farmyard geese descended from the Greylag. The call is two or three syllabled, 'aahng-aahng-aahng' often of different pitches within the same call, rising or falling. The sound made by a flock is, overall, deeper and more bass than other geese but within it there is probably also a greater range of calls, both in pitch and tone. Part of this comes from a conversational contact call, 'uhng-uhng' particularly heard on the ground. Like most geese, Greylags have an alarm call consisting of a single note similar to those of their flight call but sharper and more penetrating.

PLUMAGE VARIANTS

Melanistic and leucistic plumage forms occur but neither at all commonly. Total and partial albinos have also been seen.

Bar-headed Goose (Plates 8, 9 and 15)

This is a light grey bird of medium size, very pale grey on the back, with black and white markings on head and neck. It has a characteristic, head-forward, standing position. In flight it presents an overall pale appearance with a dark trailing edge to the wing. The range is restricted to eastern Asia, though escapes from captivity are common in western Europe.

ADULT (Plates 8 and 9)

The head and top of the neck are white with two broad black bars round the back of the head. A white stripe continues down each side of the neck to the shoulder separating the black back of the neck from the brown or russet-brown front. The upper- and underparts are pale grey with transverse pale barring on the wing-coverts, and a little dark barring on the flanks and underparts. The upper flanks are tinged with russet-brown, and there is a diagonal white flank stripe following the closed wing edge. The upper and under tail-coverts are white, the tail pale grey, tipped with white.

The bill is yellow with a black nail and the legs and feet are orange.

In flight the Barhead shows a predominantly very pale grey wing, with a dark tip and trailing edge formed from the secondaries and the outer half of the primary feathers, which are dark grey or black, so that at a distance the wing pattern is not dissimilar to that of a Snow Goose, though the black is more extensive. Apart from possible confusion with this species, the Barhead ought not to be an identification problem.

FIRST WINTER (Plate 9)

The young bird lacks the white barring on the wing-coverts, having instead irregular brownish feather edgings, which make the whole upper surface look less evenly pale. The bill and legs are both duller.

DOWNY YOUNG (Plate 15)

The upperparts are a pale grey-brown, with yellowish patches on the wings, under them, and on the flanks. The head and neck are yellowish with a grey patch on top of the head. The underparts are pale yellow. The legs and feet are blue-grey.

VOICE

The call of the Barhead is a low sonorous 'honk'.

PLUMAGE VARIANTS

None have been described.

Emperor Goose (Plates 8, 9 and 15)

A medium-sized goose with a round almost dumpy body, the Emperor has been well likened to a tea-cosy! The neck is short and thick, and it has a rounded head. The head and hind neck are white, while the overall body colour is grey, including the wings and the tail-coverts. At a distance it gives the impression only of a dark body and white head. It occurs on the coasts and islands of the Bering Sea and straggles south as far as California.

ADULT (Plates 8 and 9)

The head, cheeks and hind neck are white, though very often heavily stained orange from ferrous salts in the water. The chin and front of the neck are dark grey or black shading to bluish-grey plumage on the body. The

upperparts look lighter than the underparts because of white edgings to the wing-coverts, forming neat transverse bars across the back of the standing bird. The coverts have a subterminal band of black then a wide white tip, though the black is not very visible in the field. The white feather edgings extend to the flanks and the bird shows no appreciable diagonal flank line unlike all the other geese dealt with so far. The underparts are darker than the upperparts and have smaller pale edgings. Unique among the geese the Emperor lacks any white on the upper or under tail-coverts, which are dark grey; instead the whole of the tail feathers are white or off-white. Thus, a bird flying away gives a totally different appearance to any other goose, all other dark geese having a white band at the base of a dark tail.

The Emperor Goose has a very small bill, pink above and blackish below, with a white nail and, usually, a little black at the base of the upper mandible. The legs and feet are yellowish-orange.

In flight the wings and back are uniformly dark contrasting strongly with the white head and upper neck, and the white tail. The silhouette of the Emperor in flight is of a heavy rounded goose with a short thick neck and relatively short wings. The flight is laboured, somewhat slow, though with rapidly beating wings, and usually low over the water or land.

Confusion is really only possible between this species and the blue phase of the Lesser Snow Goose. However, the ranges of the two are well separated. The white undertail, the much larger deeper bill of the Snow Goose and the white of the head extending under the chin and well down the front of the upper neck are points to look for. In flight the blue phase Snow Goose has contrasting pale grey wing-coverts and black flight feathers, as well as a very different shape with a longer thinner neck and longer wings.

FIRST WINTER (Plate 9)

The immature Emperor Goose is little different from older birds at a distance, though at closer range the white edgings to the wing coverts will be seen to be tinged brownish, and not in regular parallel lines. Its bill and legs are duller in colour. The bird has a completely dark head and neck at first but white feathering begins to appear almost at once and by about October the extent of the white is about the same as in the adult, though it is still flecked with dark feathers. The latter will all have gone by the New Year.

continued page 65 after colour section

COLOUR PLATES

The colour plates are designed as an aid to the identification of the different geese and should be used in conjunction with the text descriptions in Chapter 2. The postures of the flying geese are deliberately stereotyped and it is not pretended that geese ever raise or lower their wings into a vertical position, except perhaps when turning sharply or when taking off in alarm. Normally the wings rarely go more than about 45° above or below the horizontal. The purpose of these plates has been to present the full plumage details of the upper and under wing, together with its size and shape relative to the rest of the goose. The latter aspect, together with head shape and neck length in proportion to the body, is important in identifying distant birds where colour or pattern may not be visible.

Six pairs of plates each show a group of species standing and flying. The standing geese are all drawn to one scale and include adult and first winter birds, with the exception of the dark Canada Geese where the latter are indistinguishable. The flying geese are all drawn to a second scale, slightly smaller than the standing birds. They are all of adults. An additional plate illustrates three often-confused immatures. Another plate shows the heads of a number of potentially confusing species and races, or illustrates the range of variation, as in the Bean Goose. The plate of downy young portrays them at about a week to ten days old rather than the more usual one day old. In nearly all species there is a loss of colour overtones during the first few days of life, probably due to bleaching, and unless an observer finds a newly-hatched brood the goslings are unlikely to appear as bright or well-coloured as described in most reference books. The colouring as painted is usually seen in goslings for about two weeks, before the first feathering begins to appear. The final plate is devoted to a series of paintings of the cloacas and tail feathers of geese to illustrate ageing and sexing characters of the goose in the hand.

Pink-footed Goose
Anser brachyrhynchus
adult

Bean Goose
Anser fabalis

four varieties of bill
and head size and
shape

adults

adult

**Lesser
White-fronted Goose**
Anser erythropus
adult

**European
White-fronted Goose**
*Anser albifrons
albifrons*

adult

**Greenland
White-fronted Goose**
Anser albifrons flavirostris

1st winter

1st winter

1st winter

Lesser Snow Goose
*Anser caerulescens
caerulescens*

adult

Pacific White-fronted Goose
Anser albifrons frontalis

adult

Ross's Goose
Anser rossii

adult

adult

adult

adult

Western Greylag Goose
Anser anser anser

**Eastern
Greylag Goose**
*Anser anser
rubrirostris*

Greater Snow Goose
*Anser caerulescens
atlanticus*
C. Ogilvie

2: GREY GEESE

Swan Goose
Anser cygnoides

adult

1st winter

adult

Bean Goose
Anser fabalis

1st winter

Pink-footed
Goose
*Anser
brachyrhynchus*

adult

1st winter

adult

Western Greylag Goose
Anser anser anser

1st winter

C. Ogilvie

**European
White-fronted Goose**
Anser albifrons albifrons

**Greenland
White-fronted Goose**
Anser albifrons flavirostris

**Interior
White-fronted Goose**
Anser albifrons gambelli

Lesser White-fronted Goose
Anser erythropus

C. Ogilvie

6: SNOW GEESE

Lesser Snow Goose
white phase
*Anser caerulescens
caerulescens*

adult

Lesser Snow Goose
blue phase
Anser caerulescens caerulescens

adult

1st winter

1st autumn

Greater Snow Goose
*Anser caerulescens
atlanticus*

adult

Ross's Goose
Anser rossii

adult

1st winter

1st winter

C Ogilvie

Lesser Snow Goose
white phase
*Anser caerulescens
caerulescens*

Lesser Snow Goose
blue phase
*Anser caerulescens
caerulescens*

Greater Snow Goose
*Anser caerulescens
atlanticus*

Ross's Goose
Anser rossii

C. Ogilvie

Bar-headed Goose
Anser indicus

adult

1st winter

Emperor Goose
Anser canagicus

adult

1st winter

adult

Red-breasted Goose
Branta ruficollis

1st winter

C Ogilvie

Bar-headed Goose
Anser indicus

Emperor Goose
Anser canagicus

Red-breasted Goose
Branta ruficollis

C. Ogilvie

10: CANADA GEESE

1st winter

large pale adult

large dark adult

Canada Goose
Branta canadensis

medium pale adult

medium-sized dark adult

small pale adult

small dark adult

Aleutian Canada Goose

C. Ogilvie

medium-sized dark

small pale

large pale

Canada Goose
Branta canadensis

C. Ogilvie

Barnacle Goose
Branta leucopsis

adult

1st winter

Light-bellied Brent Goose
Branta bernicla hrota

adult

1st winter

Dark-bellied Brent Goose
Branta bernicla bernicla

adult

1st winter

Black Brant
Branta bernicla nigricans

adult

1st winter

C Ogilvie

Barnacle Goose
Branta leucopsis

Light-bellied Brent Goose
Branta bernicla hrota

Dark-bellied Brent Goose
Branta bernicla bernicla

Black Brant
Branta bernicla nigricans

C. Ogilvie

White-fronted Goose
Anser albifrons

Bean Goose
Anser fabalis

Lesser Snow Goose
Anser caerulescens
blue phase

C. Ogilvie

15: DOWNY YOUNG

Swan Goose
Anser cygnoides

Bean Goose
Anser fabalis

Pink-footed Goose
Anser brachyrhynchus

White-
fronted
Goose
*Anser
albifrons*

Canada
Goose
large
Branta canadensis

Greylag Goose
Anser anser

Lesser
White-
fronted
Goose
*Anser
erythropus*

Greater
Snow
Goose

*Anser
caerulescens
atlanticus*

Canada Goose
small
Branta canadensis

Lesser
Snow
Goose

*Anser
caerulescens
caerulescens*

yellow phase

grey phase

Ross's
Goose
Anser rossii

Emperor Goose
Anser canagicus

Bar-headed Goose
Anser indicus

Barnacle Goose
Branta leucopsis

Brent Goose
Branta bernicla

Red-breasted Goose
Branta ruficollis

C. Ogilvie

tail feathers — 1st winter bird

tail feathers — adult

female—immature

female—adult

cloacas

male—adult

male—immature

adult female showing
refeathered brood patch

C. Ogilvie

DOWNY YOUNG (Plate 15)

The plumage is a pearly-grey, darker above, nearly white below, with a narrow pale ring round the eye and whitish around the base of the bill. The head, neck and back vary considerably in their relative darkness compared with the rest of the body, even within the same brood. The bill and feet are olive green.

VOICE

The Emperor Goose is not particularly vocal but when it does call its voice is both loud and distinctive. The principal call is a repeated 'kla-gha, kla-gha'. There is also a high-pitched alarm note 'ullee'.

PLUMAGE VARIANTS

None have been recorded.

Lesser Snow Goose (Plates 1, 6, 7, 14 and 15)

A medium-sized goose, the Lesser Snow has a relatively large bill showing a prominent gape between the mandibles set on a largish head. The neck is quite thin. Body colour is either pure white or blue-grey, with variable white on the head, neck and chest. Black quills are noticeable in flight, particularly on white phase birds. The species occurs throughout North America, in eastern Siberia and as a vagrant and escape in Europe.

ADULT WHITE PHASE (Plates 1, 6 and 7)

There should be nothing easier than the identification of an adult Snow Goose, pure white all over except for black primaries. However, easy as this is, it still leaves us a choice between Lesser, Greater and Ross's Goose. Separation of all three is much more difficult. Just to complete the description, the bill of the white phase Lesser Snow Goose is quite long and deep and coloured pink, even rose-pink, with a pale pink or whitish nail. It additionally has a very distinctive black edge to the mandibles, which gape towards the rear forming the well-named 'grinning patch' characteristic of the Lesser and Greater Snow Geese but absent in the Ross's Goose. The legs are dark pink, sometimes looking purplish. The eye is brown. Orange ferrous staining on the head and upper neck is frequent.

In flight the bird is long-necked and long-winged, with black primaries, sometimes as few as seven, sometimes all eleven plus three or four adjacent secondaries, and pale-grey primary coverts. The remainder of the bird is white. The flight action is powerful and fluid, with birds in flocks forming irregular lines rather than neat V-formations. They also tend to float up and down as they fly so that the lines undulate.

It is virtually impossible to tell the Greater and Lesser Snow Geese apart in the field at a distance, whether on the ground or in flight, unless the two are together for comparison, or unless the observer is very familiar with both. Really good, close views are needed for positive identification. In North

America there is fairly complete geographical separation of the two subspecies, enhanced by the fact that the nearest population of Lesser Snow Geese to the range of the Greater Snow Goose has a very high proportion of blue phase birds in it. So, in general terms, one can identify a flock of geese by the locality (see Chapter 6 for maps and distributional details), or if in a possible overlap area by the presence or absence of blue phase birds.

At a sufficiently close range, or if both subspecies are present together for comparison, the much larger, heavier bill of the Greater Snow Goose should be apparent. It averages nearly 12% longer and is correspondingly deeper at the base too. A lone Snow Goose in a flock of another species, such as occurs both in North America and quite usually in Europe, enables one to compare the bird's size with whatever species it is associating with. A Lesser Snow Goose is about the same size as a Pinkfoot, or all the Whitefronts except for the largest Interior. It is not as long in the neck as the Whitefronts. The Greater Snow Goose has a greater body bulk than all Whitefronts except some Interior, closer to the size of a Greylag. A combination of body size, plus size and shape of bill should always be used for identification.

Separation of the white phase Lesser Snow Goose from the Ross's Goose is easier than from the Greater Snow Goose. Ross's is much smaller (averaging 40%) and has a quite small, almost triangular bill with a bluish base. In the hand the base of the bill can be seen to be comprised of warty protuberances. The black 'grinning patch' is completely absent.

ADULT BLUE PHASE (Plates 1, 6 and 7)

The typical blue phase Lesser Snow Goose has its head and foreneck white, with dark grey extending up the rear of the neck for a variable distance. The upperparts are all dark grey with black barring and show a distinct blueish tinge on the mantle, wing coverts and scapulars, though tending to paler grey towards the rump. The underparts are grey, with a brownish tinge and with some buff feather edgings. The upper and under tail-coverts and the belly to the rear of the legs vary from grey to white, contrasting with the dark grey, though white-tipped, tail. The scapulars show as prominent white-edged drooping feathers on the side of the closed wing, a feature not found in any other goose.

The bill, legs and feet of adult blue phase Lesser Snow Geese are similar to those of the white phase. The head and neck are frequently stained orange.

In flight the blue phase Snow has a two-coloured wing, with black primaries as in the white phase, whereas the wing-coverts are a pale blue-grey. The underwing, too, shows some contrast with the white axillary feathers dividing the grey of the wing from the grey flank. The flight silhouette and general shape of the blue phase is the same as the white phase. In common with many white-headed birds seen at a distance and against a pale sky, the white head can apparently disappear leaving an impression of a very short-necked bird or one with its head and neck tucked back into its shoulders, but this is only in certain circumstances.

Although the typical and most usual blue phase plumage is as described above, the existence of a number of intermediates between it and the white phase was mentioned in Chapter 1. The full range has been numbered from one to seven. The first type (1) is the pure white phase Snow Goose with a minimum of seven black primaries, and little or no grey on the coverts. The second (2) is a minor variant of this in which all eleven primaries are black, plus up to four secondaries, while the primary coverts and the tiny alula feathers, or bastard wing, a group of feathers on the leading edge of the wing near the base of the outer primary, show a varying amount of greyness. The third type (3) is much closer to the blue phase in that the wings are mainly dark as are the back and flanks. However, the underparts remain white, apart from some dark feathering around the neck, usually up the back of it a short way. This is perhaps the commonest intermediate form. The next three types show progressive darkening of the underparts starting at the neck, where it joins the body to give a dark breast (4), then dark back to the sternum (5), then dark to the legs (6). The final type (7) is the pure blue phase in which all the underparts are grey, though with occasional small amounts of white around the vent, and mostly pale or even white between the legs and the tail.

Possible confusion with the Emperor Goose is dealt with under that species.

FIRST WINTER WHITE PHASE (Plate 6)
The young bird starts off with its first complete plumage an overall greyish-white, darker on the top of the head, the back of the neck, and the upperparts. The underparts are mostly white, though tinged greyish-brown. The larger wing-coverts and the scapulars have dark centres, while the primaries are dark brown or black. The bird steadily whitens through the winter until by about March the general body plumage is largely white, though grey is still to be seen on the closed wings, head and back. The bill and legs are grey-brown at first and will have a distinct pinkish tinge before the autumn is through. The black primaries contrast well with the grey-white of the rest of the wing. Separation from Greater Snow and Ross's Geese must be on size, and size and shape of bill as in the adult.

FIRST WINTER BLUE PHASE (Plates 6 and 14)
The young blue phase is generally dark without any white on the head or neck, except for a small amount under the chin of most birds. The body colour is a dark slaty-grey with only slight relief from pale feather edgings. It tends to be browner than the adult, and a little paler below. The under tail-coverts are white, the upper are grey, and the tail is grey tipped with white. The bird changes little through its first winter though some white feathers may appear on the head and neck. The bill, legs and feet are dark grey, becoming pinkish during the autumn, and usually pink by November.

In flight the immature blue phase is very dark, except for its white under tail-coverts. The upper wing-coverts are not as pale as in the adult and so some of the contrast between them and the primaries is lacking.

Possible confusion between this bird and the immature Whitefront was dealt with under that species.

DOWNY YOUNG (Plate 15)
There are five types of downy young plumage. The first (1), often called golden, is generally greenish yellow with a wash of grey on the back and

wings. There are brown patches on the crown, the nape and as a line through the eye. Yellow patches, rather blurred in outline, occur on the back and wings. There is a brown band from the thigh to the flanks. The bill and legs are grey. Type (2) is darker than (1), especially on the brown areas, and the line through the eye is almost black. The third type (3) is more olive green than yellow and tending to black on the head and upperparts. There is a yellow chin patch and a yellow line from the bill to the eye. The bill and feet are black. In the fourth variety (4) there is almost no yellow present but the plumage bleaches as the bird gets older, to look patchily pale. The darkest type of all (5) is a dark brown to black all over, slightly paler underneath, with a whitish patch under the chin. There is no trace of yellow.

VOICE

Snow Geese are probably the noisiest of wildfowl and a flock of them keeps up a constant clamouring, audible over considerable distances. The main notes are a single or double syllabled 'kowk' or 'kow-luk', which has a resemblance to the shrill barking of a small dog when heard separately, but seems much more musical coming from a flock. The complete range of notes is very varied with high and low pitched calls emanating from a feeding flock. The alarm call is a penetrating 'kaah-ahh'.

PLUMAGE VARIANTS

Perhaps not surprisingly there are a few exceptional birds which do not belong within the usual seven forms. Pure white birds have been seen rarely though it is uncertain whether these are albinos as such or merely completely white in plumage but with normally coloured bill and legs. Another variant seen a few times is one in which the body is completely white but the wings are of the sort found on a blue phase bird. Leucistic Lesser Snow Geese have also been recorded.

Greater Snow Goose (Plates 1, 6, 7 and 15)

ADULT

The identification of this race has already been covered under Lesser Snow Goose white phase. A close view is necessary if separation is to be certain, or better still a direct comparison.

FIRST WINTER (Plate 6)

This is essentially similar to the white phase Lesser Snow, and it too can only be distinguished on size, and bill size and shape when on its own.

DOWNY YOUNG (Plate 15)

Similar to the type (1) of the Lesser Snow Goose.

VOICE

The calls of the Greater Snow Goose are apparently not distinguishable from those of the Lesser Snow Goose.

Ross's Goose (Plates 1, 6, 7 and 15)

This species is a small pure white goose with black wing tips. Relative to the Lesser Snow Goose it has a smaller head and bill and a shorter neck. It breeds in the central Canadian arctic and winters principally in California.

ADULT (Plates 1, 6 and 7)

The body plumage is pure white, while the primaries are black, tending to grey at the base. There is grey on the primary coverts. As in the Lesser Snow Goose the extent of the black is variable, from seven or eight primaries to all the primaries plus three or four secondaries.

The short bill is pink but greenish or bluish at the base and a paler pink or whitish nail. It completely lacks any 'grinning patch'. The green or blue areas have a number of warty protuberances which are not present in young birds nor in a proportion of adult females.

The Ross's Goose is a much smaller (40%) version of the Lesser Snow Goose and has a smaller, rounder head emphasised by the steeply sloping, almost triangular bill. On the ground its movements are quick, with rapid walking and pecking and these features can serve to pick a lone bird out of a flock of Lesser Snow Geese as they do with a Lesser Whitefront among European Whitefronts.

In flight this species flies with very rapid wing beats, much faster than the Lesser, while the shorter neck makes for a different silhouette. There is no grey on the primary coverts.

FIRST WINTER (Plate 6)

The young Ross's Goose is grey or grey-brown in its first winter, like the white phase Lesser Snow Goose. However, it is much paler than the latter and is particularly more whitish on the upperparts which on the Lesser Snow tend to be the darkest area. The bill, legs and feet are grey, turning pink by about November.

DOWNY YOUNG (Plate 15)

Although there is no plumage dimorphism in the adult Ross's Goose, it is present at the downy young stage as already mentioned in Chapter 1. There are two described forms, the yellow and the grey. Birds of the first form are a yellowish grey, darker above than below, with a light yellow head and a dusky patch in front of the eye. In the grey form the yellow colour is absent and the overall effect is whitish grey. The bill of both forms is grey and the legs olive green. The down of the Ross's gosling is unusually long and soft.

VOICE

The principal call is much higher pitched than that of the Lesser Snow Goose and more squeaky, less musical in tone. It is best rendered as 'luk-luk'. The flock sound is definitely soprano in pitch.

Canada Goose (Plates 10, 11 and 15)

Size, shape, relative body proportions and overall colour tone are all variable in this species, yet the essential identification characters of a black head and neck, white 'chinstrap' and brown body remain common to every one of the possible types. The largest are larger than any other goose, the smallest no bigger than the Redbreast, Brent or Ross's goose.

As already explained in Chapter 1, the normal classification into eleven extant subspecies is not being followed here, instead I have divided the Canada Geese of North America into four groups and the descriptions which follow are based on these.

ADULT (Plates 10 and 11)
Southern Group
This group includes the largest Canada Geese, grading down to about middle-sized, and has a plumage colour range from the palest to moderately dark. The colour follows an approximate cline from east to west. The range lies to the south of about 60°N and extends from the Rockies to the Atlantic.

The most typical Canada Goose plumage in this group has dark brown upperparts with a tinge of grey, with narrow buff edgings on the wing coverts forming rather faint parallel barring. The underparts are pale buff. There is a sharp contrast between the pale chest and the black of the neck. The head, too, is black but there is a creamy white throat and cheek patch, or 'chinstrap'. In some of the larger birds this has a decidedly backward pointing hook to it at the top of the cheek. This feature has been claimed as a characteristic of the Giant race, *maxima*, but birds from outside the given range of this race also show it, for example on the Atlantic coast.

In the darker birds the underparts become nearly as dark as the upperparts, and the contrast between the chest and the base of the neck is less obvious. The flanks of all birds tend to be darker than the breast or belly. The rump is always blackish, but the upper and under tail-coverts are white, as is the lower belly from the legs rearwards. In dark birds this contrasts with the rest of the belly. The tail feathers are black.

The bill, legs and feet are black in all races. The size and shape of the bill is variable, but is mostly quite large and long, though not particularly deep at the base.

The combination of black head and neck is unlike any other goose. The Barnacle is superficially similar but the black on the neck extends right down to the chest. Its cheek patch is much more extensive so that almost the whole face looks white, including the chin and forehead. The shape of all the Canadas in this group is of very long-necked birds, and in most the neck also appears noticeably thin.

In flight the Canada Goose presents a dark appearance with no contrast on its wings, either above or below. The dark head and neck stand out on the pale-breasted birds, less so on the dark ones. In all this group the long, thin neck is an excellent flight characteristic. The wings, too, are long, though quite broad as well. The face patch is not always easy to see in flight, and at long range confusion might be possible with Whitefronts, whose wings, however, are much narrower. The largest birds typically have slow, precise wingbeats, relatively shallow in arc. Canada Geese frequently form into Vs or diagonal lines when flying.

Northern Group

The breeding range of this group lies in the subarctic and arctic to the north of about 60°N. They winter in the southern half of the United States.

In size the birds of this group go from middle-sized down to small, and from very dark to pale throughout the size range. The smaller birds have proportionately shorter necks and so do not have the distinctive long, thin neck of the larger kinds. They also have a much more rapid wingbeat and deeper wing movement. Confusion with other species should not occur in North America, except perhaps with Brent, though the latter have much shorter necks and are black not brown on the body. In Europe a lone small Canada among Barnacle Geese can be surprisingly hard to pick out even when known to be present in a flock. Presumably the reverse would also be true. A white neck ring is sometimes present (see Aleutian Canada Goose).

Western Group

The birds of this group inhabit the Pacific coast of Alaska and British Columbia. They are overall very dark, some of them almost rufous brown. Their size ranges from medium to large and they possess proportionately long necks.

Aleutian Canada

This is a fairly well marked and relatively isolated race, though formerly close to and perhaps intergrading with the now extinct Bering Canada Goose. The Aleutian Canada is a small, fairly pale bird. Its most obvious feature is a distinct white ring separating the black neck from the pale chest. It is found in most if not all Aleutians, and although it is also sometimes found in other small Canada Geese, it is then rarely if ever so broad.

FIRST WINTER—ALL GROUPS (Plate 10)

The immature Canada Goose is especially difficult to separate from the adult in the field, far harder than for any other goose species. The transverse barring on the coverts of the adult, so useful in ageing other species, is rather less obvious whereas the barring on the juvenile is more pronounced and regular. The difference between adult and juvenile is therefore very slight, even non-existent.

It has been found for some populations, of both large and small birds, that the black neck of the immature merges quite gradually into the paler chest, whereas in the adult there is a sharp cut-off. In some small Canada Geese there is a slight white collar at the base of the neck and it has been suggested that only adults show this, but confirmation is required. Adults additionally have an irregular pattern of light and dark brown barring on the breast, but the first winter bird lacks the barring and therefore looks paler with a diffuse appearance to the plumage. This arises because the breast feathers of the first winter bird are only half as wide as those of the adult and lack a pale terminal bar. These characteristics are just visible in the field in good conditions but as the first-year bird moults its body plumage through the winter they will gradually disappear; although found in both small and large Canada Geese, they have only been described for the pale plumaged birds and it seems probable that even if they existed in the dark birds they would be impossible to see in the field. It has been claimed that immature Canada Geese have black speckling on their white cheeks but this would hardly be visible in the field, and other studies have found the speckling to be variable without regard to age.

The bill, legs and feet of the immature are black as in the adult. Breeding males, in particular, develop a hard bony protuberance on the carpal joint, a kind of spur, which may become unfeathered through abrasion. In young birds this spur is small and feathered. Its existence in females appears to be variable.

DOWNY YOUNG—ALL GROUPS (Plate 15)

There is some variation in the plumage of downy young Canada Geese from the different ranges of size and colouring, but less than might be expected. The typical downy young of a pale Canada Goose has olive green upperparts, together with the hindneck, the crown of the head and an area around the eye. The remainder of the neck, head and underparts, plus patches on the trailing edge of the wings, and on the body below the wings, are bright yellow, though fading as the gosling grows. The bill and legs are blue-grey. The gosling of a dark Canada Goose is much browner above and whiter below, having less olive green and less yellow. The pattern is the same, though.

VOICE

The popular name of the Canada Goose in North America is the 'honker', derived from its most familiar call, a double-note 'ka-ronk', or 'ah-onk'. There is a rising inflexion on the second part. The call varies from deep, long and slow, and very sonorous, in the largest birds, to the much higher-pitched, short, quick notes of the smallest. In addition there are various other more conversational notes used in feeding flocks, or between birds of a pair.

PLUMAGE VARIANTS

Pale, washed-out Canada Geese have occurred in both large and small populations, the black neck appearing as medium brown or light tan, while the brown body plumage comes out as pale brown, or just a pinky-white. Varying amounts of white occur with some degree of regularity in Canada Geese, particularly spotting and flecking on the head and neck, and less often on the wings and body. Among small Canada Geese as many as 10–20% have some white feathers on the forehead, and a few have white feathers on the under wing-coverts.

Barnacle Goose (Plates 12, 13 and 15)

This is a small, black, grey and white goose, with a rounded body, fairly short neck and round head. The black on the neck extends down on to the chest, while the white on the face is more extensive than on the Canada Goose. The species is confined as a breeding species to East Greenland, Svalbard, and NW arctic Russia, and winters in Britain and Ireland, the Netherlands and West Germany.

ADULT (Plates 12 and 13)

Superficially the Barnacle Goose is like the Canada Goose with a black head and neck, and a white face patch, but there is no real excuse for confusing the two. The Barnacle has a white, or rather creamy-white face and forehead, and the white extends under the throat and up to the bill, much more extensive than the Canada's chinstrap patch. A narrow and sometimes indistinct line of black joins the bill and eye. The top of the head is black, as is the nape, joining the black neck and chest. There is a sharp demarcation between the black chest and white, or silvery white, lower breast and belly. The upperparts are bluish grey, while the wing-coverts have a subterminal band of black and then white tips. These latter are missing in some birds, however, giving them a much darker appearance on the back. The white tips, when present, form a regular transverse barring, as on nearly all other geese. The flanks are grey barred lightly with brown-grey. The upper and under tail coverts are white, as is the lower belly. The tail is black.

The short bill is steep, emphasising the steep forehead and rounded head, and is black, as are the feet and legs.

In flight the Barnacle shows a dark upper surface and a dark and light under one. The wings are dark above, silvery grey beneath. When the birds twist and turn in flight as they quite often do as a flock, this produces a repeated flashing of dark–light–dark, much as occurs from a flock of Lapwings. The wings are quite pointed and beat rapidly. Flocks of Barnacles are usually well packed, occasionally in straggling lines, and rarely in V-formation. A prominent feature of the flock of Barnacle Geese on the Solway Firth in Britain is their wader-like flying. They adopt this if threatened by an aerial predator such as a Peregrine, or by an aircraft, but will also do it at other times. The whole flock of a few thousand birds will turn and twist in unison. This behaviour is rare or absent in the other populations of Barnacle Geese and among other species has only been recorded regularly in the Brent Goose. Confusion with the Brent is possible in flight at a distance but the Brent has a much shorter neck and narrower wings.

FIRST WINTER (Plate 12)

The difference from the adult is the same as in most other species, namely the regular transverse barring on the wings and mantle is replaced by irregular, buffish tips producing a more mottled appearance. The face patch tends to have some dark fleckings in it but this is not invariable and only observable from very close quarters. The black of the neck and chest also tends to be less pure, often showing duller, and containing a few brown feathers. The grey-brown barring on the flanks of the adult is absent in the young bird at least in the early part of the autumn. The bill and legs are black.

DOWNY YOUNG (Plate 15)

The centre of the crown, breast and upperparts is grey-brown. There is also a dark grey line from the bill to the eye. The rest of the head starts pale yellow quickly fading to whitish, similar to the underparts. There are whitish spots on the wings and rump. The legs and bill are dark grey.

VOICE

Barnacle Geese are very vocal birds. The main call is a single syllable harsh note, 'gnuk', sometimes strung together and rapidly repeated. The sound of a flock is not unlike that of a lot of yelping dogs, at least to some ears. There is quite an amount of pitch variation and a flock of Barnacles, either feeding or flying, gives off a considerable range of sound. Conversational notes include 'hoog' and 'wrack'. The alarm call is an intense 'arrk'.

PLUMAGE VARIANTS

Birds with reduced pigment have been recorded in the Greenland and Svalbard populations, varying from coffee-coloured to pure white.

Brent Goose (Plates 12, 13 and 15)

The features common to all Brent Geese are their small size, short necks, small heads without much forehead, and typical head-pointing-forward attitude on land and water. Mainly black above, and with a black neck and chest, the underparts vary from very dark grey to silvery white. They occur on coasts on both sides of the Atlantic and Pacific, though rarely in the Asian Pacific.

ADULT (Plates 12 and 13)
Dark-bellied Brent Goose
The head, neck, chest and upper back are sooty black, the wings and remainder of the upperparts, very dark grey-brown, except for the upper tail-coverts which are white. There is a small whitish patch on either side of the neck, variable in width and height, not normally joining in the front, though it does so in a small number of birds. The wing-coverts lack any obvious edgings and so the wings present a smooth, even, dark grey surface. The lower chest and belly are slate grey, rather variable in tone, but most often little if any lighter than the upperparts, and grade into the black of the chest. The rear belly, well behind the legs, and the under tail-coverts are pure white, with a sharp demarcation line between them and the rest of the belly. The tail is black but rather short so that it shows as a black bar at the end of an otherwise white stern. There is normally a white flank bar following the line of the closed wing but this is variable from nil to very broad.

The bill, legs and feet are black. The bill is rather short but not steep and follows the line of the head so that the bird has little apparent forehead.

Brent Geese normally feed on mudflats, either in a close flock or more spread out. On fields inland of the seawall they are usually very close packed, walking very fast as a tight flock. On the water they float high with a cocked-up tail.

In flight Brent Geese are fast manoeuvrable fliers, with a short rapid wingbeat action of their narrow wings. Indeed they can readily be confused when single or in small numbers with large ducks such as Mallard. However, the neck is shorter and the wings narrower than a duck's. Both the upper and under wing surfaces are dark and the only relieving whiteness is the rear end, where it is very conspicuous. Brent often fly in tight packs and may perform simultaneous aerial twists and turns. At other times they fly low over the water which only the Emperor Goose also does regularly.

Light-bellied Brent Goose
The colouring of the upperparts is as the Dark-bellied race. The underparts are pale silvery grey with some barring on the flanks from darker tips. The effect in flight is of a dark–light–dark pattern as the birds turn, not dissimilar to the Barnacle Goose, but the silhouette is very different with a much shorter neck and narrower wings. Intergrades between this race and the Black Brant are quite common and all shades of underpart colouring can occur, some of which will produce the effect of a flank stripe which is not normally visible in

this race. The white neck mark is similar to that of the Dark–bellied race, and
the bill, legs and feet are also black.

Black Brant

The basic colouring is as in the Dark–bellied race, but the white neck mark
and flank bar are each generally more extensive and therefore conspicuous.
The neck bar extends to join in the front of the neck and on average is rather
deeper than in the Dark–bellied Brent. The flank bar is always very broad.
However, a Dark–bellied Brent can show a very broad flank bar and this
cannot be used for racial identification on its own. Even a neck mark,
complete in front, has been found in otherwise typical Dark–bellied birds.

FIRST WINTER—ALL RACES (Plate 12)

Contrary to the situation in other geese it is the first year Brent Goose
which shows noticeable pale edgings to its wing-coverts and mantle, whereas
in the adult they are completely absent. The pale edgings may combine to
form more or less regular barring, but at other times they are scattered more
diffusely. Another distinctive feature of Brent in early winter is the lack of a
white neck mark. It begins to appear in the New Year.

DOWNY YOUNG—ALL RACES (Plate 13)

The gosling is grey-brown, darker above than below, especially on the
crown and around the eyes. The underparts are pale grey though there is a
brownish grey band across the chest. There are whitish spots on the wings
and flanks. Racial variation is restricted to the Black Brant being darker than
either of the other two, with the crown being almost black. The bill, legs and
feet of all races are dark slate.

VOICE

The Brent Goose is a vocal bird but not particularly noisy. The main call is a
two–note 'rott-rott', rather hard and brief. A softer 'rronk' is also common. A

flock calling together produces a low babble of sound. The alarm call is a nasal 'wauk'.

PLUMAGE VARIANTS
Very occasional partial albinos have been noticed. The plumage of the first winter bird is prone to fading or bleaching and individuals with a brown, not black, overall appearance may be seen in late winter.

Red-breasted Goose (Plates 8, 9 and 15)

This small goose has an unmistakable pattern of black, white and red. Its head is rounded with a tiny bill, the neck short and the body round. The breeding range is restricted to central arctic Siberia and the wintering range to areas around the Black and Caspian Seas, and south into Iraq and Iran.

ADULT (Plates 8 and 9)
The head is patterned in black, white and red. The black covers the crown, nape and front of the face, with a white spot behind the bill and a large chestnut red patch on the cheeks, outlined in white. The front of the neck and the chest are also a rich chestnut-red separated from the black rear neck and black underparts by a thin white line. The upperparts are black except for two narrow white lines or bars across the wing-coverts. There is a broad white flank bar, and the upper and under tail-coverts and the lower belly are also white. The tail is black. The white on the belly extends a variable amount forward of the legs, but does not extend up to the flanks.
The very small bill, the legs and the feet are black.
Identification should pose no problems though a single bird is surprisingly hard to pick out of a feeding flock of another species, when at a distance. The broad white flank bar is then a good character to look for.
In flight Red-breasted Geese have even, black wings above and dark grey beneath. Two narrow white bars on the upper wing are only visible in good light. The flank bar is conspicuous and the white-edged face and chest show up well. The flight action is fast with rapid wingbeats.

FIRST WINTER (Plate 8)
Although the appearance is similar to that of the adult, all the colours are duller and less well defined. In particular the black areas look much browner and may be spotted with white, while the reddish areas may have both white and black flecking. The wing-coverts show several irregular lines of pale buff edgings and lack the two white bars of the adult. There is a narrow white tip to the tail. These distinctions become less easy to see as the winter progresses.

DOWNY YOUNG (Plate 15)
The overall colour is greenish brown, darker above, toning to greenish yellow underneath. The forehead is lighter, and there are paler spots on the wings and sides. There is a dark ring round the eye. The bill, legs and feet are grey-black.

VOICE

The Red-breasted Goose has a high-pitched double call 'kik-wik', or sometimes 'kee-kaa', and a flock keeps up a constant calling in somewhat shrill tones.

PLUMAGE VARIANTS

Variants are almost unknown, though one partial albino with white feathers in one wing has been recorded.

3 Ecology, food and feeding

Geese live much more terrestrial lives than their aquatic relatives, the ducks and swans. Water is an essential requirement for drinking, bathing, and copulation, and provides a safety barrier to protect roosting or nesting birds, but most geese obtain the greater part of their food on land, and spend most of their waking hours walking, not swimming. They use estuarine mudflats, fresh and salt marshes, natural grassland, and especially farmland, both pasture and arable. The great majority of geese feed on farmland from autumn until spring, and many also do so at migration stopping places. Only in the breeding season are geese found largely in natural habitats, uninfluenced by man. A few populations breed in temperate lands, in marshes, on lakes, or beside rivers. Here they still find farmland on which to feed, though many will be living on the lush natural vegetation surrounding such wetlands. Most geese, however, breed in the arctic or in the scrub and forested zones lying immediately to the south, where their foods will be entirely natural.

Some geese are relatively restricted in the habitat they occupy and the foods that they eat, but most, although they may once have been comparatively specialised feeders, have proved very adaptable when it comes to exploiting farmland. And whether remaining entirely dependent on natural food, or now relying to a great extent on farmland, geese vary their diet in such a way as to obtain the maximum food value at different times of the year.

Farmland feeding geese, in particular, have taken full advantage of the considerable range of foods available to them, such as waste grain, waste potatoes, grass and sprouting cereals. These have their counterparts in the natural state, but the cultivated varieties are all richer in carbohydrates and/or proteins, and the geese are able to exploit each in turn as it reaches its peak of abundance. The varying nutritional value of the different foods is taken account of at the different stages of the annual cycle. Thus, in the spring, prior to migration and breeding, both of which require large energy reserves, the geese are feeding mainly on young growing vegetation which contains maximum levels of protein at this time. Similarly, the growth peak of vegetation in the arctic, where most geese breed, occurs at a time when the eggs are hatching, and so it is available to provide the necessary nourishment for the growing goslings. Towards the end of the summer many geese change their diet and seek the ripe berries of the creeping arctic shrubs. These have a high sugar content and are therefore an extremely potent source of energy. The geese continue on a carbohydrate-rich diet on their arrival on the wintering grounds when they are still requiring to build up their weight before the start of the cold weather.

Winter goose-feeding areas can be broadly divided into natural, semi-natural and farmland. Before man so completely changed the face of the landscape, becoming a herder of flocks and a cultivator of the land, geese would have been restricted to wholly natural winter habitat—mudflats, coastal marshes, sand-dunes, and areas grazed by wild animals. For many species the presence of short vegetation for grazing is an essential requirement and it is difficult to see where in Britain, for example, such areas existed, of adequate size, before man began clearing forests and keeping herds of domestic sheep and cattle. The wild forebears of these herds were apparently never very numerous. On the continent of Europe, however, and in North America, there were sufficient grasslands kept short by roaming herds of buffalo and horses, to provide feeding places for geese.

Relatively few geese now feed exclusively on natural habitat, if only because this is fast disappearing. The Brent Goose, its relative the Black Brant, and the Emperor Goose, still feed largely on estuarine mudflats and sheltered sea coasts, where their principal food is eel-grass *Zostera*, of which there are a number of different species. In most places the geese walk over the mud, exposed as the tide goes down, feeding on the long thin ribbon-like leaves and the short juicy rhizomes. Although a good eel-grass bed will give an appearance of continuous green when viewed from a distance, on walking out to it one finds the plants quite scattered, with plenty of mud visible in between. As a result, a flock of feeding Brent Geese will soon spread over a wide area and not remain as a compact group. In a few areas, most notably at Izembek Bay, Alaska, eel-grass grows in thick mats in shallow water, and here the geese graze, up-end, or just dip their heads below the surface to pull off the long strands. Up-ending, which also occurs elsewhere, is dependent on water depth and therefore on the state of the tide.

Once the eel-grass in a locality has been eaten out, which can happen quite quickly after a poor growing season, the geese turn to one or more algae also growing on the mudflats. Emperor Geese in Alaska also eat algae that grow on tidal rocks. The main species is *Enteromorpha* and another important one is *Ulva*. Both have wider shorter leaves than eel-grass. Depending on the numbers of geese and the weather conditions, this diet will probably last through to the spring. At that time both Brent Geese and Emperor Geese change their feeding area and move on to the salt marshes fringing the estuaries. Here they take succulents such as glasswort *Salicornia*, and grasses such as poa *Puccinelia* and fescue *Festuca*.

There is a distinct advantage to the geese in eating the plants in this sequence as the timing more or less coincides with the most active growth periods for the respective plants, and at these times there will be the maximum amounts of protein and nitrogen in the growing tips. However, the selection of foods is also governed by preference and if the stocks of eel-grass remain high, or start growing again in spring after a mild winter, the geese will choose them instead of feeding on the saltings.

In the 1930s a strange disease attacked the eel-grass on both sides of the Atlantic, and to a much lesser extent on the Pacific coasts. It was associated

with a mycetozoan called *Labyrinthula* and caused whole beds of eel-grass to be completely wiped out within a few years. The effect on the Brent Geese was apparently an immediate and serious decline in their numbers. However, counts made in those days were nothing like so complete as nowadays and there has recently been some suggestion that in North America, at any rate, the direct cause and effect relationship is not as clear cut as was once thought. Be that as it may, the Brent Geese clearly had to find alternative foods and it is thought that they turned not only to the algae, in a bigger way than before, but also began feeding on saltmarshes and, occasionally, on fields over the seawall. Eel-grass has made a steady comeback since the 1930s, though it is still absent or greatly reduced in some areas where it was once abundant, and often it is a smaller-leaved species that has returned while the larger-leaved kind, which in theory should provide more food, has remained scarce. However, the conditions of mud consistency, depth of water at high tide, and purity of the water that eel-grass requires for growth may not now be available so widely as before.

In recent years there has been a striking increase in the numbers of Dark-bellied Brent Geese visiting north west Europe, and this has been accompanied by a marked change in their feeding habits. Hitherto it had been widely assumed that this was an unadaptable goose, unable to alter its feeding habits sufficiently in changed circumstances, hence the apparent decrease after the disappearance of the eel-grass. Saltmarsh and field feeding were uncommon in the 1930s but this may have been as much the risk of being shot as an inability to use these areas, that kept the geese away. However, in recent years the Brent Goose has shown that it is perfectly well able to feed on grass and winter wheat on fields close to the seawall. The habit is still a relatively new one and it remains to be seen whether it will become a permanent feature.

When the Brent Geese feed on fields they show an interesting behavioural difference to their feeding on the mudflats. Instead of spreading out to feed, as they do when grazing eel-grass, or as other grazing geese tend to, they stay in an extremely tight pack, moving quite fast over the field, and pecking at a very high rate. Their feeding also remains linked to the tides. When feeding on the mudflat they can do so only when it is uncovered or under shallow water. At high tide they sit in a flock just off shore or sometimes stand on the tide edge, preening and bathing. They will feed twice each day if both of the low tide periods fall in daylight, or at night too if there is sufficient light from the moon or stars to see by. So far, they have been slow to learn that they can feed all day on the fields. Many flocks stay on the mudflats until they are pushed off by the rising tide, and only then fly to the fields to feed. This is in part a reflection that field feeding has a lower priority to mudflat feeding. They still prefer the latter foods if they are available.

This recent development of field feeding by Brent Geese has two sides to it. Firstly, by opening up a new and very large food resource, the population has broken away from its previous dependence on eel-grass and algae, which are relatively restricted in distribution and quantity. With the amount of food now available to them in winter they should have much better prospects for the future. If the killer disease returned, the effects on the geese would be less disastrous, and in very hard winters, when the eel-grass quickly dies off, the geese will be less hard hit. On the other side of the coin however, farmers whose fields border the river estuaries and coasts where field feeding has become common are not at all happy about the amount of grass and winter wheat that the geese might eat. The question of conflict between wild geese and agriculture will be dealt with in Chapter 8.

Both Brent Geese and Emperor Geese take a certain amount of animal matter, the Brent probably largely by accident, the Emperor perhaps deliberately. Eel-grass and other marine plants are often hosts to fish eggs, small crustaceans and worms, either directly attached to the leaves, or living in the densest parts of the vegetation. Under these circumstances it is not surprising that small quantities should get eaten inadvertently by a goose grazing on the plants. However, the amounts found in the Emperor Goose, up to 10% at times, seem to indicate some selection. This is a long way, though, from earlier statements that the species was wholly or largely dependent on animal food.

Still dealing with natural habitat, we can turn from estuarine mudflats to coastal and inland marshes. The main goose food plants that grow in marshes include bulrushes *Scirpus*, cat-tails *Typha*, spike-rush *Eleocharis*, cordgrass *Spartina*, and horse-tails *Equisetum*. The geese that feed in marshes are Greater and Lesser Snow Geese, the larger Whitefronts and Canadas, the Greylag and the Swan Goose. All these geese have relatively long and powerful bills. They eat not only the leaves of the plants but dig down and eat the roots and underground storage organs, and also take the seeds. This is not food that a short-billed primarily grazing species could exploit. The vegetation is generally rather tall and coarse, and provides shelter and cover for the geese in addition to food.

Marshes of all kinds are threatened habitat. Inland freshwater marshes have largely disappeared from Britain, for example, having been drained and turned into agricultural land. Others, both in Europe and North America, have been saved by conservation agencies, but can still deteriorate unless there is adequate control over water levels and the flow of rivers. Coastal marshes can be embanked and reclaimed, or polluted by industrial effluent. It

is perhaps all to the good that almost every population of geese currently wintering in marshland has also proved itself able to spread on to adjacent farmland and sustain itself there.

The Greater Snow Geese winter on the Atlantic coast of the United States, on the salt and brackish marshes bordering the great estuaries and sea bays of North Carolina and Virginia. They roost at night on the water and move to feed in the daytime by swimming to the nearest marsh, or by flying short distances. The geese eat several species of bulrush, as well as cordgrass, taking the leaves, the seeds, and digging for the roots. An area that has been heavily used by them is recognisable by the uprooted plants, and broken off leaves and stems, left behind by the feeding birds. In some places the feeding is even more intensive and the geese do not leave what was once a lush marsh of tall plants until it is nothing more than a waste of mud, pock-marked by the holes left by their probing bills. Such areas may take three or four years to recover fully and the birds consequently require a far larger area for wintering in than they will use in any one season. The population of Greater Snow Geese has been steadily increasing in recent years and perhaps under pressure of the larger numbers, feeding on agricultural land adjacent to the marshes has been getting more common. Here they eat grass, growing cereals, and take waste grain from stubble fields.

Greater Snow Geese have also moved on to farmland at their traditional migration stopping place at Cap Tourmente, on the St Lawrence River near Quebec. The geese have stopped here regularly in spring and autumn for as long as records have been kept. Until recently they were only to be found on the wide belt of saltmarsh fringing the river, eating mainly bulrushes, only occasionally going on to farmland, and usually in spring when they ate a certain amount of grass. In the last few years, however, the greatly increased numbers have fed more and more on farmland, stubbles in the autumn and grass in spring. Once again conflict has arisen with the local farmers.

Whitefronts wintering in the Central Valley of California feed in swampy fresh marshes. Their diet consists of the various species of bulrush and cat-tails, both the leaves and stems but particularly the underground rhizomes, which are rich in starch. Some of the larger Canada Geese formerly had a very similar diet but their use of marshes has declined in most parts of North America in the last few decades.

The main European marshland goose is the Greylag, but it only lives in this habitat in relatively few areas now, having become adapted to farmland over most of its range. Other European geese, too, such as the Bean and the Greenland Whitefront have largely deserted marshes and upland bogs, often forced to do so by the disappearance of the habitat, but also because they have found better feeding elsewhere. When feeding on marshy areas Greylags take particularly bulrushes and sedges *Carex*. Greenland Whitefronts still live on acid bogs in a few places in Ireland and Scotland and one of their main foods is the beaked sedge-grass *Rhynchospora*. They take large numbers of bulbils, underground storage organs, which they find by probing and digging in the wet surface layer.

The only remaining habitat used by geese which is not entirely man created, although nowadays certainly man-influenced, is short grassland. In its natural state it will be composed of a mixture of grass species and short herbs. Grass as a climax vegetation occurs only where there is grazing pressure to prevent the invasion of scrub and then trees, or in maritime situations where salt spray and to some extent salt in the soil, kills off all but the shortest vegetation. Additionally, in a few places of very poor soil, only certain grasses will grow.

Wintering geese seeking grassland areas on which to feed, require that the grass is not too long, as it becomes much less palatable when long and also unmanageable for the short-billed birds. The growing tips of grass are the parts containing the most protein and nitrogen, both of which decrease rapidly with age. So, short regularly cut or grazed grassland is both more nutritious and easier for the geese to graze. Unless the grass has been kept short during the summer it will not be in a suitable state for the geese on their arrival in autumn. The steppelands of central Europe and Asia, and the prairies of North America were the traditional wintering and passage areas for grazing geese as they also supported large herds of grazing animals. They are still used by the geese today but the grazing is done by domestic stock, in those areas which have not gone under the plough.

High saltmarsh, sand-dunes and machair, and offshore islands, can all hold flocks of short-billed grazing geese, such as Barnacles, Whitefronts, Pinkfeet and small Canadas. Nowadays most areas like these are grazed in summer by sheep and cattle, but even if they were not it is likely that strong winds laden with salt spray would serve to keep the vegetation sufficiently short. Several species of grass, for example fescue, rye-grass *Lolium*, and meadow grass *Poa*, as well as clover *Trifolium*, will be found here and most of these will be eaten by the geese. The grasses have fine leaves and are clearly palatable. Clover forms an important part of the diet of Barnacle Geese feeding on high saltmarsh. They take some clover leaves but feed principally on the stolons, starch-rich storage organs lying just below the surface. The average stolon is perhaps 15 millimetres long (a little over half an inch) and a few millimetres wide. The Barnacle Goose does not have a heavy, powerful bill suitable for digging deep into the soil for roots, but manages very well, probing into the mat of grass stems for the clover stolons lying just beneath.

Seeds form a common food for geese on grassland and in marshes. Depending on the size of the seed the goose may pick them individually off the ground or out of the water or in the case of the Swan Goose may filter them out of the water, rather like a swan. Most geese are also capable of stripping seeds from the standing heads, by pulling the stem through their closed bills. Various grasses, sedges, bulrushes, and wild cereals are treated in this way by, for example, Canada Geese, Barnacles, Greylags and Bean Geese.

The main winter habitat for geese nowadays is undoubtedly agricultural land. In broad terms the birds make use of each stage of the farming cycle between the months of August or September and April to May. The relatively small number of resident flocks of geese may feed on farmland through the year. Migrant geese on arrival at an autumn staging post or wintering grounds make for the cereal fields. An early arrival will find these still unharvested, in which case the larger geese, particularly the Canadas, will go straight in and start stripping the grains out of the heads. If it has been harvested, then the spilt grains among the stubble prove a great attraction to almost all species of geese, even those which still spend most of their time on marshes or grassland. Corn (or maize), wheat, barley, oats, millet and soybeans, are all taken in this way, and spilt grain must have been the first product of farming to become a regular food of geese.

Soybeans can be a dangerous food for geese, because if the birds eat them after they have become hard and dried, they will swell inside the bird's gut as soon as it has a drink of water, often with fatal results. In 1966, as many as 3000 Canada Geese died in this way in Illinois out of a population in the area of about 50,000. Scaring techniques have been adopted to prevent a recurrence, though fortunately it only happens in unusually dry years in which the geese arrive early, before other foods are available.

Another important autumn food is also a waste product of farming, namely potatoes. After harvesting, a potato field is littered with fragments sliced by the harvester and with tiny tubers that escaped the riddle. In clearing these up the geese are performing a service to the farmer who would otherwise be faced with potato rogues in his crop the following season. In Britain potato-eating by geese is fairly recent in origin and has been fully documented.

Potatoes themselves have been grown in Britain for nearly four hundred years but only widely for the last two centuries. From being a food grown in small patches by crofters and smallholders, potatoes became an important crop which was planted in large acreages. This in turn brought about the development of mechanical harvesters which inevitably leave bits and pieces of potato, and small whole ones, on the field. In some areas pigs were then turned on to the fields to glean but otherwise the remains were just left to rot. Although Mallard have been reported for 150 years or more as feeding on harvested potato fields, and on complete crops attacked by blight and therefore left unharvested, the first record of geese doing so was of Pinkfeet in Lancashire in the last quarter of the 19th century. It is not known exactly how they first discovered that potatoes were a good food. It may be that the geese were attracted to a potato field by the sight of many Mallard feeding there, or alternatively they may have found pieces of potato left on a field of newly sprouting winter wheat, a crop which often followed potatoes in rotation.

The habit did not spread very quickly from Lancashire. Indeed it was not until the 1920s that it became widespread, which may have had more to do with the distribution both of the geese and of potato growing, than a genuine slowness to adapt to potato-eating. In the 1920s potato-eating by Pinkfeet was reported from eastern Scotland, Yorkshire and Lincolnshire. It now occurs wherever the distribution of potatoes and Pinkfeet overlaps.

The other common farmland goose of Britain, the Greylag, took to potatoes later than the Pinkfoot and it did not become a widespread habit for this species until the late 1940s. This is slightly surprising as the two species can often be found feeding in mixed flocks.

Geese commonly graze the young sprouts of autumn sown cereals. Winter wheat is grown widely in parts of Europe, and Greylags, Pinkfeet, Whitefronts and Bean Geese all move on to such fields as soon as the growing shoots are a few centimetres high. After a few days a once green field can quickly revert to brown. However, the apparent destruction of the crop is not in fact taking place. The cropped shoots will sprout again, and indeed do so more strongly and more thickly than if the geese had not been there. In areas where there are no geese the farmers either turn their sheep on to the field for a few days to eat the shoots, or flatten the blades of wheat with a heavy roller. These processes produce the same effect as the geese, breaking the seed's first shoot, or biting it off altogether, and ensuring that three or more shoots come up in its place. One name for it in England is tillering.

Unfortunately the geese do not necessarily confine their attentions to the growing wheat at this stage of its development only. If grazing takes place later, when the wheat is getting taller, the crop can be set back permanently, though this is not very common as the geese are less attracted to the much taller growth.

Once the geese have finished gleaning from stubble and potato fields, and have tillered the winter wheat if present, they switch to grass. Sown leys, as opposed to natural pastures, have been normal farming practice since the early 1790s. Mixtures of rye grass and clover have been found to produce good pasture for stock, or to make hay. The geese were probably not slow to discover the better feeding that was available for them, too. Nowadays, rough pasture is a rarity in many areas, and all leys are reseeded periodically. Feeding on these fields by the geese in the winter months causes little or no loss to the farmer. The grass is hardly growing, if at all, and only in mild areas will the stock be wintered out, and even then will be provided with supplementary feed. In temperate latitudes the grass does not start growing again until March or even later, and in many areas not until after the geese have departed northwards.

It is now common farming practice to top-dress one or more fields on a

farm each winter in order to encourage earlier growth for the stock, the 'spring bite'. These fertilised fields can be told by their brighter green appearance, and not surprisingly the geese can also detect the difference. There is then direct conflict between the farmer and the geese with the grass, deliberately brought on for the stock, being eaten by the geese.

When feeding on a grass field the geese will be selecting both for length and succulence and for species. Most sown leys have several species in them, and some are clearly more palatable than others, while at different times through the winter there will be variation in height and in the amount of dead material present, each of which will affect the feeding geese. In snow and frost the tall grasses will get eaten, being more readily available to the birds, while at other times the shorter species will be preferred. It seems likely that the geese choose a height range which allows for optimum grazing efficiency. They certainly prefer areas with the minimum of dead material. The length of grass will dictate to some extent the species of geese that will use a particular field, with the short-billed geese, such as Barnacle, Redbreast, small Canadas, Brent and Ross's Goose on the very shortest grass, and larger-billed birds, the Pinkfoot, Greylag, Whitefront, large Canadas, Barhead, Bean and Lesser Snow, able to utilise taller growth.

Another food item obtained from farmland is the swede turnip. Geese have from time to time been recorded as taking the green tops of turnip and kale, but usually only in hard weather when snow had covered their normal feeding grounds, and they were attracted to the green tops because they stuck up above the snow. From this it is but a short step to attacking the tuber of the turnip itself. This was first noticed in Scotland, where the swede turnip is quite widely grown as a foodstuff for sheep, in the very severe winter of 1946–7. In subsequent winters the geese returned to the turnips, occasionally going into the unharvested fields, but usually finding them when the sheep were put out on to the crop. The green tops were therefore already off, exposing the tubers more fully. With their powerful bills the Greylags are able to make considerable inroads into a turnip in direct competition with the sheep and therefore the farmer. Fortunately, perhaps, it is only in the relatively mild west of Scotland that the turnips are left in the ground and the sheep put in the fields. In frost-prone areas the turnips are lifted and clamped, and then fed to the sheep by scattering them in a grass field. In this way many fewer are available at a time and the geese able to eat much less.

A similar food to the turnip is sugar beet, eaten in parts of North America by Canada Geese. This is normally taken in years when other more usual foods are unavailable, as for instance in drought conditions when grass is short, or when the harvest is delayed and stubbles are not present.

The problem of the conflict between geese and agriculture, which has now been mentioned a number of times, will be discussed more fully in Chapter 8.

The preceding paragraphs have emphasised the dependence of the majority of geese on farmland, but no geese can feed there at all unless it is within daily flying distance of a body of water on which they can roost at night. River estuaries, sheltered arms of the sea, lakes, broad rivers, and reservoirs, will all serve. The amount of farmland within reach of geese has been greatly increased by the construction of reservoirs in previously dry regions. Thus, in the Lothians area of Scotland the geese formerly used one or more shallow bays on the Forth estuary as their roosts, flighting inland to feed. As the nearby city of Edinburgh expanded, several drinking water reservoirs were built in the hills behind and these have been gradually adopted by the geese as their roosts. Not only were the reservoirs often closer to suitable farmland feeding areas than the coastal roosts, but the latter were heavily shot whereas shooting on the reservoirs was usually prohibited.

The great plain of the Hortobágy in Hungary was once a vast marsh frequented by tens of thousands of geese. In the second half of the 19th century it was drained and further flooding prevented, and it became a huge and waterless area. The geese left, because although there was plenty of food on what was now farmland, there was nowhere for them to roost. Then in the first part of this century numerous large ponds were constructed for the rearing of fish. These were soon adopted by the geese as roosts, and large flocks once more feed on the Hortobágy.

On the prairies of North America, the goose population has increased and spread greatly as man has built irrigation dams. Not only are there more wintering geese, but many Canada Geese now breed on the dams and rivers where formerly they were completely absent.

The traditional pattern for goose feeding on farmland is for night-time roosting and day-time feeding. Geese will feed at night under a full moon but

even then they will use the roost for part of the night. If the moon rises before sunset they remain on the fields, flighting to roost later in the night. If the moon rises after dark, the geese which will have already returned to the roost at sunset, fly out again when there is sufficient light.

When roosting on estuaries with varying tidal water levels, the geese stand on exposed mudbanks when they can, but take to the water as the tide rises. Depending on circumstances, they may swim or even fly short distances to avoid being drifted too far on the tide. On bodies of fresh water the geese most often stay on the water all night, seeking the shelter of an island or the lee of a shore, and avoiding exposed and choppy conditions. Only where they feel really safe from humans, foxes or other predators, will they stand on the shore. The area of the water body is highly variable. It can be as small as one hectare (about 2½ acres) and a water this size can readily support 5000 geese. But this is perhaps exceptional and only possible when the lake or pond, and an area around, is strictly protected. More usually, goose roosts are larger than this but many carrying thousands of birds are not more than 5–10 hectares (12–15 acres). On the really large lakes and estuaries the precise position of the roosting geese may vary from night to night depending on wind strength and direction, and on the tide.

The geese leave the roost at first light. A large flock may take an hour or more to completely vacate the water, but the start of the flight is related to the amount of light rather than to time. Thus on cloudy days it will be later than on sunny ones. There is also some correlation with temperature, with the geese leaving later, the colder it is. Similarly the return flight in the evening is controlled by the amount of light. However, there is an over-riding time element involved, so that in mid-winter when the days are at their shortest the geese will flight earlier relative to sunrise and later in relation to sunset than they do in the autumn or spring. This gives them the maximum possible feeding time on the fields. Studies of marked individuals and families of geese, using radio transmitters attached to them, have shown that there is great variability in their flight times even though the flock of which they are a part may be exhibiting great regularity in its timing.

Geese vary greatly, both between species and for the same species in different areas, in the distances they will fly from roost to feeding area. Some species rarely move more than a few kilometres while others may fly regularly up to 15 kilometres and occasionally up to 30. The Pink-footed Goose in Britain has the tradition of the longest flights, but looking at the feeding ranges from all roosts one finds that the average is not so very far, perhaps 5–10 km, and only a very few flocks go further. Such long flights can only be worth making if the food supply at the end of it is a good one. The expenditure of energy in making a long daily flight has to be offset by improved feeding, and such flights also reduce the amount of daytime available for feeding.

From a large roost the geese may flight out in a number of directions, which will depend to a great extent on where the birds were feeding the previous evening, though this is not invariable. Strong winds will also tend to influence the direction in which the birds fly, as they are reluctant to head far into a gale even though there may be a good feeding area in that direction. The first flocks to leave the roost are usually quite small, and sometimes just a lone bird is first away. This has given rise to the widespread belief that this is a scout, checking to see whether it is safe for the rest of the flock to flight. There is, however, no good evidence that there is any deliberate, socially beneficial behaviour of this kind by geese. It could just as plausibly be a bird that got separated from its mate or parents the previous day, perhaps because of shooting, and is still looking for them. Certainly these lone geese often call a great deal, which one would not expect a scout to do. On reaching the selected feeding field, the flock may circle a number of times, gradually getting lower before the first birds settle. Thereafter, each succeeding flock will pitch straight in, reassured by the sight of geese already on the ground, and feeding peacefully.

During the longer autumn and spring days the geese will spend more time not actually feeding, a feature also of periods when they have been able to feed at night under the moon. Then the flock may remain on the fields, but the birds sit down and sleep. Alternatively, they may move to a special resting area, usually a wide open site with good all-round visibility, such as a stretch of moorland, or large unfenced fields near a river. The latter, which may sometimes be flooded, can also be used as a night-time roost.

The return flight to the roost is, like the dawn flight, a fragmented affair, particularly in some species where small numbers may start flighting back in the early afternoon. In others, however, virtually the whole flock lifts off the field together and flies back to roost. As with the first arrivals on the feeding

field, there may be a certain amount of hesitation before the geese touch down on the water, but once some have landed the remainder come straight in. In places where there is shooting on the water's edge the geese quickly learn to come in high until well over the water, and then to drop steeply. They manage this by a technique known widely as 'whiffling', which is accomplished by side-slipping first one way then the other. A skein of geese suddenly breaking up into a vertical column of tumbling, twisting bodies is a thrilling sight. There is also an accompanying tearing noise as the air spills between their widespread pinions. This behaviour is not confined to flocks dropping into a roost. A flock flying between feeding areas may suddenly begin to whiffle for no apparent reason, except perhaps that they enjoy it. When twisting like this a goose may turn completely over on to its back, though photographs have shown that it keeps its head the right way up by twisting the neck.

During the day the birds may change their feeding field, and even feeding areas, depending on the amount of food available to them at any one site, and on the disturbance they suffer from farming or other activities. There is usually a general lessening of feeding activity around the middle of the day, and where the flock is quite close to the roost, some or all of the birds may return there for a drink and a bathe. This is quite regular behaviour in Greylags and other species which tend not to fly far from their roost, but much less common in the longer distance flyers. The latter content themselves with drinking from any pool of floodwater on or near their feeding fields, or they may go without water until their evening return to the roost.

Observations on individually marked geese, and on birds carrying radio transmitters, have shown that families of geese tend to use the same roost and feeding areas for extended periods, while lone geese are more variable. There are a number of reasons why this makes good sense. Firstly, it means that if one member of the family gets separated from the rest it has two familiar places to make for, at each of which it stands a chance of finding them again. Secondly, it means that the food resources round a roost will be used more efficiently than if the birds were behaving in a random fashion. It may also be a reflection of the general wariness of the geese in that they prefer to use known places, and although they may suffer losses from shooting there, they are still better off than if they were constantly seeking new sites, and facing the problems of the unknown.

The summer habitats of geese are much less varied than in winter. This reflects their overall breeding distribution, with the great majority of the geese in the arctic, smaller numbers in the subarctic and boreal zones lying to the south, and only comparatively few in the temperate zone. The suitable habitats and food available particularly in the arctic, are strictly limited.

Those geese that breed in the temperate latitudes do so nowadays in places where they are at least to some extent under man's protection. Formerly they bred much more widely but persecution and destruction of the habitat drove them out. The Greylag Goose has probably always been the most widespread temperate breeding goose in Europe and western Asia. Areas where it still breeds include the north-west of Scotland and the outer islands, where there are numerous lakes (or lochs) surrounded by thick heather moor. Many of the lakes have islands which the geese prefer as nesting sites, being safe from predators. Grassy and boggy patches round the lakes provide grazing areas for them. In other parts of Europe the Greylag are found in thick marshy vegetation surrounding large water bodies, such as Lake Neusiedl in eastern Austria. Here there is an abundance of cover for nests and food for the geese.

In North America the Canada Goose is the most southerly breeding species. Large pale forms nest in most of the central and western States. Here they seek lakes, reservoirs and large rivers. The preferred nest site is on an island or in thick vegetation on the banks. Many of these birds are able to continue feeding on farmland through the summer, usually seeking grass, but occasionally other forage crops.

In Asia both the Bar-headed Goose and the Swan Goose breed quite far south in latitude but because their breeding areas are at quite high altitudes, on the mountain plateaus of Tibet and northwards, their habitat is much closer to subarctic than to either temperate or boreal.

The forest zone lying between the arctic and the temperate is inhabited by a number of kinds of geese including Canada Geese in North America, and Bean Geese and Lesser Whitefronts in Europe and Asia. The geese seek swampy clearings in the forest and become more common as one goes north and the high trees peter out into scrub. Nests are always close to water, with open patches of marsh or bog where the geese can feed. Grasses and sedges are

TABLE 2: *Summary of principal winter habitats and foods of the different geese.* † = common, * = secondary

	HABITATS					FOODS										
	Arable farmland	Pastureland	Fresh marsh	Salt marsh	Mudflats	Cereal grains	Rice grains	Other seeds	Growing cereals	Grass	Roots, tubers	Marsh plants	Salt marsh plants	Marine grass	Algae	Invertebrates
Swan Goose		*	†							†		†				
Bean	†	†	*			†				*	†	†				
Pinkfoot	†	†		*		†				*	†	†	*			
Whitefront																
European race	*	†	*	*						*	†		*	*		
N. American races	†	†	*			†			*	†	*	†				
Greenland race	†	†	†			*					†	†	†			
Lesser Whitefront		†	*			†				*	†					
Greylag	†	†	†	*		†	†			†	†	†	†	*		
Barhead	*	†	†					*			†	†				
Emperor			*		*								†		*	
Lesser Snow	†	†	†	†		†	†	†	*	†	†	†	†			
Greater Snow	*	*		†		*					†	†				
Ross's	†	†	†			†					†		*			
Canada																
Small	†	†	†			†				*	†		*			
Medium	†	†	†	†		†		*	†	†	†	†				*
Large	†	†	†	†		†	†	*	†	†	†	†	†	*	*	*
Barnacle		†		†					*		†	*	*			
Brent	*	*			†					*	*			†	†	†
Redbreast	†	†	†			†				*	†					

the principal foods in spring and summer, but in autumn, before the geese migrate, they may eat large quantities of berries, which being rich in sugar, provide a very suitable diet for building up weight after the breeding season and annual moult. There are several species of berry-bearing bushes in the low arctic and northern boreal scrub, with various local names, including blueberry, bearberry, snowberry, and so on, nearly all belonging to the heath family.

Arctic tundra, where the majority of geese find their summer habitat, consists of low vegetation, with scrub up to a metre or two in sheltered areas of the low arctic but nothing over half a metre, if that, in the high arctic. The geese nest in a wide variety of situations here, depending whether they are solitary or colonial, desirous of protection from foxes, or able to look after themselves. Islands offshore or in lakes or rivers, cliff ledges, rock pinnacles, steep slopes, and flat bare ground are all used. The requirement for feeding is wet marshy ground, which occurs in abundance in much of the arctic, where precipitation is usually small but drainage bad or non-existent because of the under-lying permafrost. The vegetation includes several species of grass, creeping willow, of which the geese eat the leaves, and mosses, which they probably eat to a small extent. In the better vegetated areas there are also berried plants for food in the autumn before migration. Probably the principal arctic food plants for all geese are cotton-grass *Eriophorum*, sedges *Carex*, horsetail *Equisetum*, and various grasses. Arctic plants may be small in stature but they have to grow fast in the short summer and are consequently high in nutritional value. In areas of high goose numbers the birds will have a very noticeable effect on the tundra vegetation, leaving it very heavily grazed by the end of the summer.

The breeding season foods of geese are much less well differentiated than at other times of the year. The over-riding requirement of a safe breeding site dictates, to some extent, what vegetation will be available to eat. The choice of the arctic for breeding by the majority of the geese means that many different species, with widely varying bill structures well adapted for specialised feeding in winter, will nevertheless have broadly similar diets during the short summer period.

This survey of the habitat and foods eaten by geese is summarised in Table 2. It will have revealed that geese are primarily grazing birds, although also capable of picking up small items such as seeds. Some of the larger species have additionally evolved more powerful bill structures, adapted to dig and probe in soft ground for roots and other vegetative organs, whilst still remaining suitable for grazing. A few species have shown remarkable adaptability in their feeding, discovering techniques for removing pieces from turnips and potatoes, or stripping seeds from the heads of plants.

The principal grazing technique uses the side of the bill. The head is held slightly on one side and the part-opened bill is poked into the vegetation. The bill is then closed, trapping pieces of plant such as grass leaves and stems between the interlocking transverse ridges (lamellae) which run along the edge of each mandible. The head is then jerked back, firmly, plucking off the vegetation. This is then pushed down the bird's oesophagus by the action of the tongue, and by pressure of more food which follows.

This main grazing method is only suitable if the vegetation is relatively long and coarse. Where the food consists of very fine grasses, or when it is already quite short, the nail at the end of the bill is used, with the head held more vertically. The sharp edges of the nail clip off some of the grass and hold other bits which are broken off when the head is retracted. Some species, for example the Barnacle Goose, feed mainly on very short grassland and therefore rely more on this method, while the larger-billed geese prefer longer vegetation where possible, using the sideways grasping and pulling technique.

When gouging pieces of turnip or potato, the geese use the nail of their bill to make the first incision, then scoop out thin slivers, helped by the tongue and the lamellae. Turnip and sugar beet eating is restricted to geese with large, powerful bills, such as Greylags and large Canadas, but geese with much

smaller bills, like the Pinkfoot, can manage potatoes quite easily. It used to be thought that even a Greylag could not make the first incision into a turnip, but could only eat from one that had already been damaged or bitten into by a sheep, but this is now known not to be so. Equally, a Pinkfoot can eat from a whole potato without difficulty. A similar difference of opinion arose over carrot-eating by Pinkfeet, an unusual and restricted food for them. The geese were found to be eating them while still in the ground and thus damaging a potentially valuable crop. At first it was thought that the geese could only manage to eat from a whole carrot that had first been frosted and so softened, and incidentally rendered unfit for human consumption. But later evidence showed that the geese could tackle a whole, unfrosted carrot without too much difficulty.

Digging for roots and stolons of plants is done mainly by those geese with rather elongated bills, but the small-billed geese can find clover stolons which lie only just below the surface. Greenland Whitefronts dig and probe five centimetres (two inches) or more into boggy ground, and find bulbils of plants such as beak-sedge *Rhynchospora*. Greylags, Greater Snow Geese and Whitefronts in North America, all of which feed on the roots and underground tubers of bulrush, often feed in 15–30 cm (6–12 in) of water. Here they can be seen trampling with their feet in order, presumably, to loosen and clear the mud away. Sometimes they also shake roots in the water in order to clean them before swallowing.

The other main feeding technique practised by nearly all species is picking up small items in the tip of the bill and swallowing them whole. These items are mainly grain of one kind or another, wheat, maize or corn, barley, and so on. Geese do not have teeth with which they chew food before swallowing, although there are in fact tooth-like serrations on the roof of their mouths, and food items can be gripped between them and the tongue, both when grasping and when swallowing. The tongue itself has backward pointing hair-like projections which must also assist this process.

Seed-stripping by geese has not been closely observed in many species but they appear to do it the following way. The stem is grasped below the seed head and then by pulling backwards the bill travels up the stem peeling off the seeds, which are caught against the sides of the mandibles.

The digestive system of a goose is peculiarly inefficient when it is remembered that grass and other vegetation form a major part of the diet of all species. Unlike a cow or other ruminant animal eating similar food, a goose completely lacks the ability to digest the cellulose which forms a major part of a plant leaf or stem. Not only would this cellulose be a valuable source of food, but by dissolving the walls of the plant cells this would release the cell juices, which are rich in sugars and proteins, and readily digestible. However, a goose is quite unable to do this. A cow digests cellulose with the aid of bacteria, a high concentration of them living in a special part of the digestive tract called the rumen. In addition the cow can regurgitate food from this organ and masticate it again 'chewing the cud'. In all, the food will spend about twelve hours in the rumen after which time it has been thoroughly broken down. Many other animals have a similar system. Rabbits manage another way. They have a bacterially aided digestion but cannot regurgitate their food. Instead they pass the partially digested grass as pellets, which they then eat and chew a second time.

The goose, then, is at a serious disadvantage. The most that it can do is to break down as many of the cell walls as possible before the plant material reaches the stomach where the digestive juices can get to work. These by themselves cannot digest the cellulose, only bacteria can do that. At the lower end of the oesophagus, the goose, and many other birds, have their gizzard, an extremely thick-walled part of the gut, the walls being virtually solid muscle. In a medium-sized goose the gizzard will be about 10 cm long by about 4 cm thick ($4 \times 1\frac{1}{2}$ in). In the gizzard is a certain amount of fine grit and sand, perhaps up to 15 grams ($\frac{1}{2}$ oz) in weight. Whilst the food is in the gizzard it is ground to and fro by the action of the walls and, as this goes on, the grit and sand particles rupture the cell walls quite effectively, so releasing some of the cell contents. The gizzard then empties and the food passes into the stomach, thence along the intestine and out through the rectum. Most of the grit stays in the gizzard and is replenished at intervals by the goose picking up the correct sized particles.

The passage of food through a goose is remarkably fast, taking only about one and a half to two hours on average. Clearly in this short time comparatively little digestion can have taken place. One consequence of getting relatively little goodness out of each mouthful of grass is that the goose has to eat a comparatively large quantity in order to get sufficient nourishment to supply its energy requirements. This is the reason why, if one watches a flock of geese that spends a whole day on grass, they will use up to 90% or more of that day feeding, particularly in the middle of winter when daylight is restricted. As long-distance migrants geese would, in fact, find a more elaborate digestive system with storage organs, either a crop or a bacteria-filled rumen, something of a disadvantage as they would be carrying the unwanted extra weight of the organs and the food they contained.

Some detailed work has been carried out to discover just how much geese eat in a day and the rate at which they take it in. For example, the European White-fronted Goose has been found to peck at a rate of about 80–100 pecks per minute at the beginning of the day's feeding, gradually increasing through the day to a mean maximum of about 130 pecks per minute. There is also a tendency for the mean pecking rate to increase during the winter as the grass becomes shorter and the birds are needing to put on weight prior to migration. Thus, the bird compensates for a reduced food supply by a faster rate of intake.

There is some selection of grasses by the feeding bird, as it chooses green growing leaves in preference to the numerous brown and shrivelled ones present in a winter sward. There is also some selection for species of grass, but this is mainly done by the bird choosing a promising field or area within a field, rather than blade by blade selection as it pecks. A high intake is more important than the choice of just the nicest or juiciest bits of grass. However, when the geese find a better area of vegetation as they walk across a field, it is noticeable how their speed of walking decreases so that they can make the most of it. Thus they can help to increase their food intake, and therefore their protein intake, by fairly minor behavioural changes. It is not certain how the geese detect 'better' vegetation, as they have rather poorly developed taste buds. However, they are probably able to recognise vegetation with a high water content by its apparent 'succulence', and it is known that a high water content in grass and other plants also means a high protein content.

Juvenile geese feed at a rate about 10% faster than adults, walking more quickly and pecking more quickly. They are apparently less selective than adults but as they also spend less time looking around with their head up they are able to take in more food during a day, which helps them to grow and put on weight, as they must in their first winter. They actually eat about 6–7% more per unit time than adults.

White-fronted Geese were found to eat between 650 and 800 grams of fresh food per day (about $1\frac{1}{2}$–$1\frac{3}{4}$ lb), or rather more than 25% of their body weight. This represented about 130–160 grams of dry weight (the usual way of measuring food intake and equal to 4–6 oz). Similar work on the Barnacle Goose found that although the birds pecked at a slightly higher rate, up to 150 pecks per minute, they probably took in less per peck because of their smaller bill and tendency to feed on shorter grass. Their daily intake was very much the same, at 135–158 gm dry weight. This was estimated to represent about 6–700 kilocalories. Their feeding efficiency, or the proportion of their food intake that they actually absorb, is reckoned to be only about 33%, or between 205–240 kcal.

Because grazing geese digest none of the cellulose in a plant leaf it passes through the gut almost unchanged. A goose dropping, from a bird feeding on vegetation, is a dark green cylinder about a centimetre in diameter and up to four centimetres long ($\frac{1}{3} \times 1\frac{1}{2}$ in). These measurements are for a medium-sized goose, for example, a Whitefront. A large Canada Goose will produce a considerably bigger dropping; that from small geese like the Brent will be correspondingly smaller. The droppings are slightly moist when they first appear, and usually have some whitish substance at one end. These are crystals of uric acid; the kidney excretion of the goose. If one takes a dropping and breaks it up in a dish of water, then examines a small portion of it under a low-power microscope, completely recognisable fragments of grass or other plant leaves and stems will be visible. At a higher magnification it is possible to see clearly the structure of the leaf fragments. Each is very thin and the epidermal cells show up well. It is possible to tell from the dropping what the goose has been eating because these epidermal cells are different for each species of grass or other plant. Small samples from each dropping are analysed to show not only what species the goose has been eating but in what relative quantities. In this way detailed studies have been made of the diets of grazing geese in different habitats and at different times of year, and all without disturbing a single goose.

Before the discovery of the technique of analysing droppings the only certain method of finding out what a goose had been eating was to shoot it and examine the contents of the gizzard and stomach. Wildfowlers who were interested in more than just the sport of shooting provided virtually all the early data on what geese ate, but nowadays we can find out much more by just looking at the droppings. And this can be done on the breeding grounds as well, where previously it would have been necessary to shoot the birds.

Droppings of geese feeding on items other than grass or similar vegetation will also contain fragments of that food, whether grain, potatoes or turnips. The amount of these foods that the goose can digest is greater, including all the starch and sugars contained in them. Only the cell structure will be left and in these cases it forms a much smaller part of the original intake. The droppings are of similar size to those composed of grass fragments, but pale brown or whitish in colour.

Droppings analysis not only reveals what the geese are eating but enables the researcher to rank the plant species into some order of preference. The logical follow-up to this is to provide the preferred plants in greater quantity, by ploughing and reseeding old grassland with more palatable mixtures, or by selective fertilising, so that the habitat will support more geese by providing them with more food. This has been done on a number of goose refuges and it not only provides better feeding for the geese but by concentrating them on the refuge for longer periods may prevent or alleviate possible conflict with farming interests in the neighbourhood.

Geese produce droppings at regular intervals through the day after a pause of about one hour while their gut fills up after the night-time period when there has been no feeding. For both Whitefront and Barnacle the defecation rate is about one dropping every three and a half minutes. This means that in an eight-hour day the birds are going to produce about 120 droppings. Knowing this fact, sample counts of the number of droppings on a field can be made and from their density it is possible to estimate how many goose hours or goose days have been spent in that field. Thus, without ever seeing a goose, but merely by collecting or counting the droppings, it can be discovered what the birds have been eating and how many have been using a particular field. Where a goose feeding area is large and perhaps not easily visible without disturbing the birds, counts of droppings make it possible to provide assessments of the usage of different fields, and therefore, once again, the birds' preferences. Only this time it is not necessarily the food preference that is measured but the preference for particular fields, chosen perhaps on their freedom from disturbance, or distance and direction from the roost. Here again this is information of great value to those trying to manage land for geese by enabling them to provide optimum conditions.

The importance of goose droppings, therefore, can hardly be over-estimated, but there is another side to it, however. Many farmers believe that sheep and cattle will avoid fields which have a large number of droppings on them. However, tests have been carried out which have shown that there is only a slight avoidance of droppings when they are fresh, but within a day, or even hours, the unpleasantness, probably the uric acid, evaporates and the animals become indifferent to them. The droppings gradually break down in rain and disappear over periods of days or weeks. In a few areas stock are actually known to eat droppings, probably because they contain trace elements, such as potassium or calcium, ingested at the goose roost, perhaps, of which the animals are deficient. This is probably the place to state that I know from personal experience that a fresh goose dropping from a bird feeding on grass has little or no taste, except perhaps that of chewed grass.

4 Breeding

The smaller kinds of geese become mature and capable of breeding when they are two years old, but most of the larger species do not breed until they are three. Exceptions occur in both directions with the very occasional precocious bird breeding at one year old, though nearly always with an older mate, while many birds do not breed in their first mature year but delay at least one more year. There is not a great deal of detailed information on the subject and what there is tends to be contradictory. The situation may well change from year to year in the same population depending on the weather and the food supply. In one population of large Canada Geese in North America 10% of males bred in their first year, but no females did; 70% of females bred in their second year compared with 90% of males. But in another study, also of large Canada Geese, no birds bred in their first year, around 30% did so when two years old, and all did so at three.

The pairing of young geese begins as they enter their first summer, but most will not form permanent pairs until well on into their second winter, or even later. Geese pair for life and so have little need for the elaborate displays and plumages favoured by the ducks, which have to renew their pair bonds each year. Male and female geese have the same plumage and although it is the male which takes the initiative he has no display peculiar to his sex, the female responding to him with the same actions that he makes.

The single most important display involved in pair formation is the Triumph Ceremony. It also serves to cement the bond throughout the life of the pair, and has a part to play, too, in the maintenance of the family bond when young are present. The Triumph Ceremony gets its name because it is used when the male has just driven off another goose which has encroached on his preserves, either the nesting territory or the area he chooses to defend around his mate and family. On successfully driving away the other bird he runs back to his mate with his head and neck stretched out towards her, calling loudly. She adopts the same attitude and calls as well. Without anthropomorphising too much it is clear that he is saying: 'How clever I have been to defend you against that intruder', and she is replying: 'Yes, you have been clever', and both are saying that they acknowledge each other as their mate. The 'triumphant' aspect of the display, particularly on the part of the male, is very obvious to the onlooker. If goslings are present they frequently join in, stretching their necks forward and adding their thin and piping voices to their parents' deeper calls.

The exact posture adopted by the pair differs slightly, depending on the species, and some examples are illustrated. Essentially the head and neck are held forward and parallel to the ground, but the bill may be pointed upwards, as in the Bar-headed Goose, while both the Canada and the Barnacle Goose move their head and neck to and fro. In the majority of the *Anser* geese, the pairs hold their heads still and close together, almost calling in each other's ear.

The first steps towards the formation of a pair are difficult to note, but the male seems to take the initiative, following the female of his choice and then displaying to her by showing off his white under tail-coverts. This he does by swimming in front of her, cocking his tail in the air. Such displays are infrequent and are not often seen, even in a captive flock. Another occurrence that appears to be involved in pair formation is the flight together of three, or occasionally four, birds. This has been observed in a number of species and although it has been assumed that the birds are probably two or three males pursuing one female, as happens in many duck species during courtship, the lack of obvious sexual differences in the geese make this difficult to know for certain.

Courtship between geese may be prolonged over several weeks, or even months, but is not carried out in the same demonstrative way it is in the ducks. It seems slightly surprising that a pair bond which is going to last the life of the birds is formed with comparatively little fuss, whereas the bond between a pair of ducks, involving elaborate plumages and displays, lasts for little longer than the time spent in forming it. Pairing between two geese can be said to have taken place when they perform a mutual Triumph Ceremony, though the male may have done it without a response from the female on a number of earlier occasions.

Once the pair bond has been formed it will normally last until the death of

one of the birds. Although there are cases of captive birds not taking another mate after the death of the first, this is probably rare in the wild, unless the surviving bird is very old. Immature geese probably take days, or rather weeks, to form their pair bond, but older birds can form one in a matter of hours. A female Canada Goose whose mate was killed in a fight with a Black-throated Diver (Arctic Loon) flew away from her nesting lake but was back within a matter of hours complete with a new mate. She had already begun laying her clutch, and completed it after finding a new partner. This might be an exception but clearly in those circumstances it is an advantage to be able to form a new pair very quickly.

Sufficient studies of individually marked geese have not yet been carried out to establish whether pairs ever break up and the birds take new mates. Divorce and re-pairing of this kind has been found in the Mute Swan in Britain but not, so far, in the related Bewick's Swan. The latter are migratory, like most geese, and a stronger pair bond is of greater value to them than to sedentary birds like the Mute Swan. If divorce is ever found in geese then it would be most likely to occur in non-migratory populations. However, studies of captive and therefore sedentary goose flocks have not yet revealed it. Nor apparently do immature pairs begin to form and then separate but this may be because the initial stages of pairing are so difficult to observe.

The Triumph Ceremony is performed between a pair after the male has successfully defended his territory, mate or family. He has a number of aggressive displays, too, which can also be made by the female if necessary. They vary slightly from species to species but essentially there are three principal postures, called Erect, Diagonal Neck, and Forward. The names are given to them by behaviourists and are largely self-explanatory. In the Erect posture the bird stands very upright with its neck stretched upwards and bill pointing skywards. This emphasises the furrowed neck pattern which is present in virtually all the geese, though far more obvious in the *Anser* than the *Branta* species. At the same time the neck feathers are vibrated rapidly, further exaggerating their pattern. When adopting this posture the bird is frequently sideways on to its opponent, which will give the latter a better view of the neck. The wings are sometimes raised slightly or even flicked up and down alternately. The Bar-headed Goose is apparently alone in actually spreading its wings wide whilst in the Erect posture.

The second main threat posture is the Diagonal Neck. Here the neck is held at an upwards angle to the ground or water, with the head pointing at the opponent. The angle of the neck in relation to the ground, and of the head in relation to the neck, may vary according to the intensity of the threat. The neck feathers are also frequently vibrated. This posture is common to the *Anser* geese and to some of the *Branta*, but both the Canada and Barnacle Geese perform the Bent Neck posture instead, in which the neck begins horizontally but then takes a sharp bend downwards about half way along. The head follows the line of the upper neck so that the bill is pointing at the ground just in front of the bird. The kink in the neck stretches the furrows in the feathers and makes them more conspicuous. Normally they are rather indistinct in the black necks of these species.

The third and most aggressive threat is the Forward posture, and it most

often precedes actual attack, though it may be enough in itself to drive off the intruder. The head and neck are held low to the ground and parallel to it. As the aggressive intensity increases the bird may open its bill, raise its tongue, and hiss quite loudly. In this most extreme threat the bird faces directly at its rival, whereas in the other two it may stay sideways on. If all this is not sufficient to cause its opponent to retreat the bird launches itself into the attack, running fast over the ground still in the Forward posture, or if on the water, raising itself on to the surface and half-flying, half-splashing with its feet, projecting itself forward.

There are some obvious similarities between the threat postures and the Triumph Ceremony, and the threats are clearly derived from the latter. Threat postures are often the result of conflicting urges to attack and to flee, which explains why the threatening bird is often sideways on to its opponent in the milder forms of threat. Apart from neck vibrating, geese do not emphasise their actions much by pattern of plumage as the ducks do. The Bar-headed Goose has slightly more elaborate displays than the other geese, which perhaps makes up for its somewhat limited vocal repertoire. It has Rotary and Lateral Head Shakes (which explain themselves) and when threatening an opponent it alternates the Forward and Diagonal Neck postures. All these actions emphasise the prominent head stripes. The Emperor Goose when in Forward Threat shows a strong contrast of its white head against its dark body, which may also serve to enhance the threat. The Canada Goose and the Barnacle Goose both have Lateral and Rotary Head Shakes, which show off their white cheeks.

Actual fights are rare among wild geese, the attack following on the Forward threat is usually sufficient to see off the most persistent intruder. In captivity, however, when the opponent cannot retreat so far, particularly if pinioned, the aggressor will try to catch hold of it with his bill and then to hit with his wings. The Canada Goose has quite pronounced spurs on the carpal joints, especially the adult males. Little damage is done in these encounters, the loss of a few feathers perhaps. And at the conclusion of each aggressive threat or fight, the successful bird will return to its mate and go immediately into the Triumph Ceremony, cementing the pair bond a little further.

Copulation between a pair of geese virtually always takes place on the water, though they are capable of performing it on land. Only the highly terrestrial Hawaiian Goose, living where water is scarce, regularly copulates on land. Geese, like other waterfowl, have developed a male organ, the penis, which is inserted into the female as their cloacas are brought together, instead of, as in most other birds, the semen being squirted into her without the assistance of penetration. This is no doubt necessary because of the added problem of having to float on water while the male mounts on top of the female and twists his tail sideways to meet hers twisting in the opposite direction.

The copulation sequence is usually initiated by the male. He swims up to his mate, riding high in the water with his tail cocked well up and head raised. Then he begins to make regular head-dipping movements, plunging his head and neck into the water and raising them again almost vertically. There is little of the body-plunging as when bathing, yet the action is clearly similar, though carried out more deliberately. This behaviour on the part of the male usually, though not always, stimulates the female to copy him. Sometimes she takes no notice and the male then gradually stops. On other occasions both birds head-dip for a few moments and then cease, perhaps disturbed by something or unable to work up to a sufficient intensity. The female's movements are less exaggerated than the male's, but more or less synchronised with them. The two birds usually stay side by side until the male swims behind the female and mounts her. He does not usually wait for her to assume a prone posture on the water but begins to scramble on to her back forcing her down. He grasps the nape of her neck in his bill and often pushes her head under water whilst copulating. Union lasts for about five to ten seconds.

Just as copulation is preceded by a special display, so it is followed by one. As the pair are about to part the male opens his wings slightly, or in the case of the Bar-headed Goose, opens them wide, then slips off the female and takes up station alongside her again. Then both birds rear up in the water, stretching their heads up, cocking their tails high in the air, and raising their wings. The latter remain folded but are lifted off the back. Both birds paddle vigorously with their feet and also call loudly during this display. Then they subside on the water, the male may flap his wings a couple of times, and both start to bathe and preen, and may go on doing so for several minutes.

These descriptions of pre- and post-copulatory display fit all species of geese though there are minor species differences. For example, the Brent Goose head-dips very vigorously before copulation, almost upending at times, while the post-copulatory display is more subdued, with little if any raising of the wings. The Red-breasted Goose performs very exaggerated movements both before and after mating.

The significance of the pre-copulatory display is to bring both birds to the point of readiness to copulate. The post-copulatory behaviour is equally important in that such mutual displays further the strengthening of the bond between the pair, just as does the Triumph Ceremony. Pairs will begin to copulate sometimes many weeks before the laying period starts and will do so for many more times than is necessary merely to fertilise the eggs. Copulation, like the Triumph Ceremony, serves an important function in welding the pair together. It is essential that the pair bond should be strong because both birds are involved in rearing the family.

The next stage in the breeding cycle, following the establishment of a pair, is their arrival on the breeding grounds, the taking up of a nesting territory, and the selection of a nest site. A significant proportion of all geese nest in the arctic or in conditions where the climate exerts a considerable influence on events. It therefore seems appropriate to insert here a brief description of the main factors which affect these birds in comparison with those breeding further south. It will make more clear some of the features of the breeding cycle to be covered later in this chapter.

The arctic has a number of important advantages to geese as a place to breed. It also has several disadvantages, and to overcome these the birds have had to adapt in various ways. Firstly, much of the arctic provides excellent habitat for wetland birds which feed on vegetation. The ground only thaws to a limited extent in the summer, remaining permanently frozen just below the surface, at 15–20 centimetres (6–8 in) in the far north, the high arctic, to as much as a metre (3 ft) further south. This impermeable barrier prevents drainage down through the ground. Thus, although precipitation is comparatively small over most of the arctic, such water as there is from summer rain or the melting winter snows remains on or close to the surface where it acts as a reservoir available to plants. On flat ground it creates vast areas of marsh, with intricate networks of small streams and innumerable pools. Although arctic vegetation grows slowly and is not very diverse, there is sufficient, particularly in the marshes, to provide nourishment for geese, some areas supporting dense colonies.

Two important additional factors benefit grazing geese in the arctic. The first is the absence of much competition for the food. Grazing animals such as caribou (or reindeer) and muskox do occur in some areas but the fact that they must either migrate overland for the winter, or stay and survive on much more limited food supplies, greatly restricts their numbers and therefore the pressure that they can exert on any one area. The further south one goes from the arctic the more prolific becomes the vegetation, but so the competition for it from other animals increases. The second advantage to the geese is the continuous daylight which enables them to feed for more hours each day, perhaps as many as 20, with the minimum set aside for rest and bathing.

An area of marshland with lakes and pools will naturally provide suitable nesting sites for ground nesting birds such as geese which generally desire to be close to water. It is also likely to offer some protection from ground predators. Where they can, geese prefer to nest on islands and this holds true for the arctic as well as for further south in temperate latitudes. Foxes, badgers, racoons, coyotes, wolves and rats will all take goose eggs given the chance, and though most of these can swim if they have to, not all will do so in order to rob nests. In the arctic the land predators are reduced to two, the wolf, which is nowhere common, and in any case much reduced or even exterminated in several areas, and the arctic fox. The latter, despite much trapping, is still widespread and relatively common. In some areas, indeed, it has made something of a comeback since regular trapping declined with the establishment of fox farming for furs before the last war.

Some of the larger geese can probably stand up to an arctic fox and successfully drive it off, but the smaller species would be more vulnerable. One defence against predators is to nest in large colonies, and this is the course adopted by, for example, the Snow Geese. The small geese for whom even this might not be sufficient protection nest on islands in lakes and rivers or, where these are not available, on offshore islands or on cliff ledges and other precipitous places where foxes cannot easily get. It is, of course, fortunate that the arctic fox cannot migrate like the geese but must survive the winter and its food shortages in the arctic. The rigours of winter regulate its numbers however abundant food may be in the summer at a seabird or goose colony.

Geese cannot escape from avian predators by nesting in the arctic but even so there are fewer species and smaller numbers of them capable of taking an egg or gosling in the far north than there are elsewhere. The principal arctic species are the Glaucous Gull and the Raven, with a smaller threat coming from the larger skuas, or jaegers. Further south one would have to add Crows, usually far more numerous than Ravens, other large gulls such as the Black-backed and Herring Gulls, and possibly Magpies and Jays.

The worst predator that geese have is man. Breeding geese were formerly found widely throughout the temperate latitudes but were gradually driven out until by the time man became interested in conservation only small pockets held out in remote or inaccessible places, or where some form of protection had been given. It cannot be said that these geese were forced northwards but it is true that the further north one goes so the density of human beings drops until one reaches the arctic where only a few areas are inhabited. Either the geese deliberately colonised these areas where they were safe from man, or else they colonised all suitable habitat and have only been able to flourish where man did not go.

Some exploitation of arctic nesting geese has been traditional among the indigenous tribes, such as the Eskimos and Samoyeds, for hundreds if not thousands of years. Only comparatively recently has large-scale egg-collecting and rounding-up of flightless adults ceased, but these practices were probably always confined to relatively small areas and there is no evidence that large populations were ever exterminated by this harvesting.

So the arctic provides large areas of wetlands with food and safe nesting sites, restricted numbers of predators, and particularly, remoteness from man. These near-ideal conditions have to be paid for by others that are less favourable. The very fact of the arctic's remoteness means that birds which breed there have to be capable of long migratory flights, often over the sea or over equally inhospitable land. All the geese are powerful fliers, and certainly a flight of several hundred miles non-stop will take many fewer hours for them than for some of the other breeding birds of the arctic, such as the Wheatear or the Lapland Bunting (or Longspur). On the other hand the smaller the bird the more extra energy reserves it can carry in the form of body fat. A Wheatear may add nearly its own weight in fat before undertaking a long migration and still be able to fly efficiently, whereas a goose probably cannot put on more than 20–25% extra weight without seriously threatening its flying ability. It may seem paradoxical that the smaller bird can carry the greater load in proportion to its own weight but this has to do with the relative wing-loading of different sizes and shapes of birds. The larger you are the less extra weight you can carry although this is compensated for by the greater speed of travel. To continue our comparison, a goose can fly at around 65 kilometres per hour (40 mph) and so do a journey of 1300 kilometres (800 miles), the distance from Greenland to Britain, in about 20 hours. A Wheatear can only average about 25 kph (15 mph), and so will take more than twice as long. It must therefore be able to carry extra fuel for survival.

The principal disadvantage of the arctic as a breeding place, however, is the climate. The arctic is generally defined as the area in which the mean temperature of the warmest month of the year, usually July, does not rise above 10°C (50°F). It is often divided into the high arctic and low arctic, with

the former having a mean July temperature of no more than 5°C (41°F). The arctic is therefore a comparatively cool place even in summer, but more important for the geese than just the maximum temperature is the sheer brevity of the season. The spring thaw of the winter's ice and snow in the high arctic does not come until June, sometimes not until the middle of the month. There is then a bare two and a half months before winter sets in with freezing temperatures and snowfall towards the end of August. It is a slight exaggeration to say that there are only two seasons in the arctic, winter and summer, but spring and autumn are so brief as to be almost unnoticed. Even further south in the low arctic, or the subarctic region that borders it, where low trees and scrub can grow, the period between spring thaw and the return of winter is not a great deal longer.

Into this short summer period the goose has to cram its breeding season. The difficulty will be apparent when one adds together the number of days required for each stage of the nesting cycle. Taking as our example the Brent Goose, which has about the shortest incubation and fledging periods of any of the geese, one must allow an absolute minimum of two days for the selection of the nest site and the small amount of nest-building that geese do; five or six days for the laying of the clutch of four or five eggs, as one day is usually missed in the normal one egg per day sequence; 24–26 days incubation; and about 40 days for the young to fledge. They will then require a few more days gaining strength and ability on the wing before being ready to migrate. This comes to a total of 71 days, and more probably 75 to 80. In the high arctic where Brent Geese breed the snow-free period is about two and a half months, or roughly 75 days. As the figures for the nesting cycle are the shortest possible it is clear that to have any sort of safety margin the geese must either start earlier, before the snow melts, or run the risk of prolonging their season at the end of the summer. They adopt the first alternative.

Not only the Brent Goose but most other geese nesting in the arctic, actually start nesting before the onset of the main spring thaw. They do this by arriving on the breeding grounds when snow is still lying, selecting snow-free patches of ground for their nests, and commencing egg-laying and incubation straight away. Precipitation in the arctic is mostly very small, and even where substantial falls of snow occur, the ever-present wind soon blows it about so that bare ground is nearly always visible when the geese arrive. Their traditional nesting localities, and indeed nest sites, will in any case be in those places where this normally happens. In years when there is no snow-free ground the geese will not be able to breed.

Non-breeding by arctic birds has received a lot of attention from biologists, though some misunderstandings have confused the issue. It was not always realised by those who first observed that in some years a high proportion of some species of arctic birds were not breeding, that delayed maturity meant that there might be large numbers of one and two year olds in the population which were not ready to breed, whatever the weather. It was also not recognised so clearly as it is now that most arctic bird populations are perfectly well able to withstand periodic breeding failures, even as often as every other year. This aspect and how it affects goose populations will be left to the next chapters. Here it is relevant to discover what stops geese breeding and how they react to these conditions.

As already mentioned, the geese arriving on their arctic breeding grounds must have at least some snow-free ground on which to make their nest and lay their eggs. If this is not available they can only afford to wait a limited time before it becomes too late to breed for that year. Birds with a shorter breeding cycle can delay the start of their nesting for two or three weeks in these circumstances, but the geese cannot afford to do so without a considerable

risk of not getting their young on the wing before the region becomes uninhabitable again. Consequently, they wait at most a fortnight before abandoning any attempt at nesting that season. And even if the melt comes within that time, the geese are likely to lay smaller clutches. This is because the female, if she cannot lay her clutch at the right time, or within a few days of it, begins to resorb the egg follicles; follicular atresia as it is called. The longer the wait the more of the uncompleted eggs she resorbs, until they all go. This has two effects. Firstly the resorbed follicles provide the female with nourishment which she is likely to need anyway if the ground is snow-covered, and secondly it effectively prevents laying too late, which would not only jeopardise the young but also the adults themselves, which would be moulting later than normal and in danger of being caught by the autumn freeze-up.

It would theoretically be possible for the geese to move elsewhere if their normal breeding sites were unsuitable. There is some evidence that this may actually happen in the case of the Brent Geese breeding in arctic Canada, but not only are late springs, which are mainly responsible for snow-covered nesting grounds at laying-time, usually very widespread in their effects but the chances of the geese finding another area which was entirely suitable seem both improbable and very risky. It is no use locating an area where there is snow-free ground for nesting if there is not also an adequate food supply in the neighbourhood, and it is difficult to see how the birds could acquire this knowledge. The only well-documented case of nest sites in late seasons being shifted concerns Greater Snow Geese which moved to the opposite side of a valley because their preferred sites were snow-covered. But this was a comparatively minor change which left them in reach of familiar feeding areas to which to take their goslings.

Very late springs which completely prevent breeding are comparatively uncommon but, even in a normal year, when the geese arrive to find sites for their nests they are still faced with other problems. The main one is that there is very little food available for them at this time and there will not be an increased supply until after the thaw and the start of vegetation growth. Fortunately, the latter follows quickly on the former, within a few days, but even so the geese have to survive a period during which there will be very little to eat, and this may be as long as two or three weeks. At this time they will have to live on energy reserves built up during the winter and spring, some of which they will already have expended on their migration north. The female has the additional strain of having to find the energy to produce a clutch of four to five eggs, and to incubate them with only short intervals available for feeding during three to four weeks. Thus, the amount of fat and muscle tissue that the female in particular is able to lay down during the winter and spring is of very great importance and may well control the overall breeding success rate of arctic breeding populations.

In order to arrive at the nesting grounds in peak condition the geese need to have fed on a plentiful supply of nourishing food during the late winter and spring. As plants start to grow again after their dormant period their growing tips are indeed rich in nitrogen which the geese can make excellent use of. But if spring comes late one year, or frosts destroy the young growth, the geese

may not be able to find sufficient food to lay down large enough reserves of energy. In those years their full breeding potential would not be realised, however kind the weather on the breeding grounds. There is increasing evidence, among the low arctic breeding geese at least, that the body condition of the females is as important as any other factor. In the case of high arctic breeders, however, it would seem that the weather at the time of arrival on the nesting grounds, and during egg-laying, is paramount. Conditions are certainly more extreme than those only a little further south, and it is not uncommon for the thaw to come too late for successful laying. For example, the Dark-bellied Brent Geese nesting in Siberia have complete breeding failures about one year in two or three. Nevertheless, in good years they almost always have a very high success rate, but if body condition was a major factor one would expect only moderate success from time to time.

Once the egg-laying is under way, the arctic weather can still have a drastic effect on the success of the breeding season. Because time is so short the great majority of geese over a wide area, and certainly within a large colony, will start laying and then incubating almost simultaneously. It is not uncommon for less than a week to separate the timing of many thousands of nests. A consequence of this is that if a spell of really bad weather occurs at a critical time it will affect a majority of the geese. Cold and precipitation are the two worst components, as they can cause chilling and death of eggs, particularly if the females have to leave the nests to feed, as they have to if spring conditions generally have been poor, but more especially in the hatching period when the downy young are at their smallest and most vulnerable. The weather need not be extreme for large numbers of goslings to die from cold and wet. Freak snowstorms in summer, which can occur, will of course have an even greater effect and have been known to bury nests and eggs. If the young can survive their first two or three weeks of life then weather by itself will rarely cause great mortality.

The dangers brought about by synchrony of nesting are avoided by geese breeding further south. A comparison of large numbers of Canada Geese nesting in the arctic with those nesting in California, showed that the former began their nests within a period of no more than 10 days, while the latter spread the start of their egg-laying over at least 50 days. Clearly only a small proportion of these would be at exactly the same stage and therefore vulnerable to the same adverse conditions.

With such a short breeding period in the arctic there is a tendency for most species of geese that nest there to be small in size, though there are exceptions. A smaller bird lays fewer and smaller eggs, requiring a shorter laying and incubation period, and raises young which take less time to grow to flying stage. These adaptations enable them to breed more safely in the far north. Large geese will manage all right in good seasons and so are likely to move northwards during periods of climatic amelioration.

The size of birds in relation to latitude has been formulated as a biological rule by a Swedish biologist, Bergman, who stated that, in the northern hemisphere, larger birds tended to live further north than smaller ones. The principal reason for this is that in conditions when loss of body heat might be critical to the continued survival of the birds, the larger the bird the smaller will be the heat loss relative to its size. This stems from the physical characteristic of any solid object that the larger its volume, the smaller the body surface relative to that volume. Thus, a small bird has a larger proportionate body surface through which to lose heat than a larger bird, and is therefore less fitted for surviving in cold weather.

Bergman's Rule is widely taken to apply solely to breeding birds and there are indeed many examples where the more northerly breeding population, subspecies, or species, is the larger of a pair, or sometimes the largest of a cline. This is true of the Wheatear, the Ringed Plover and the Eider Duck, for example. And among the geese there are the Whitefront and the Lesser Whitefront, and the Greater and Lesser Snow Geese, with the first named breeding to the north of the second. However, also among the geese the reverse is true, with the smaller Canada Geese, for example, breeding to the north of the larger ones. This apparent contradiction of Bergman's Rule is, however, explained by the wintering distribution. The small Canadas perform a 'leapfrog migration' from the arctic, where they are better adapted for breeding successfully within the short summer than their larger relatives, to more southerly wintering areas, leaving the larger birds further north in the cold winter conditions. These latter birds probably have a longer, cooler winter period than the small birds' summer, so they are rightly adapted to it by their larger size.

With some species following Bergman's Rule and others contradicting it in the summer, it is clear that the geese are at a critical size when it comes to balancing the advantages of being larger, and therefore reducing heat loss, with being small enough to complete the breeding cycle in the shortest possible time. Below the size of a goose, virtually all arctic breeding species showing size variation follow Bergman's Rule. The only birds larger than geese to breed in the arctic, namely the swans, show the reverse, with the smaller Whistling and Bewick's Swans breeding to the north of the larger Trumpeter and Whooper Swans. The various goose species have split

TABLE 3: *Latitude range of breeding distribution, and normal period of egg-laying for the different geese*

	Lat. range °N	Normal egg-laying period—¼ months
Swan Goose	35–55	IV April–II May
Bean—tundra races	65–75	I June –II June
—forest races	50–65	II May –I June
Pinkfoot—Svalbard	76–80	III May –I June
—Iceland	64–66	II May –IV May
—Greenland	70–77	IV May–I June
European Whitefront	67–76	IV May–II June
Pacific Whitefront	60–66	III May –I June
Interior Whitefront	64–72	IV May–II June
Greenland Whitefront	63–71	III May –IV May
Lesser Whitefront	65–74	IV May –I June
Greylag—Iceland	63–66	II May –IV May
—Scotland	57–59	I April –I May
—Eurasian continent	39–68	I April –II May
Barhead	38–50	IV April–IV May
Emperor	59–67	III May –II June
Lesser Snow	58–71	IV May –II June
Greater Snow	72–82	II June –III June
Ross's	66–70	IV May–I June
Canada—large	40–48	IV Feb –IV April
—small	60–70	IV May –II June
—Alaska	59–65	III May –II June
Barnacle—U.S.S.R.	70–75	I June –II June
—Svalbard	76–80	IV May–I June
—Greenland	70–75	IV May–I June
Dark-bellied Brent	71–79	II June –III June
Light-bellied Brent	63–82	II June –IV June
Black Brant	60–76	III May –II June
Redbreast	66–73	III May –II June

between the two possibilities, apparently with more or less equal success.

That, in summary, is sufficient about the arctic and its effect on the geese breeding there to enable the rest of the breeding season information in this chapter to be placed in context without further elaborate explanations. Other peculiarities and adaptations forced on the geese by the arctic will be mentioned as they fit into the relevant part of the cycle.

We can now return to the moment of arrival of the pair or pairs of geese on the breeding grounds. They may or may not have had to make a long migration to reach their chosen place. If they have, then the mechanics of that migration and the various routes will be dealt with in Chapters 6 and 7. Here, it is enough to say that their migration is timed to bring them to the breeding grounds, if in the arctic, at the earliest practical moment for starting to nest.

Their arrival date remains remarkably constant from year to year but in late years it too may be delayed, presumably because the geese have sensed, or been held up by, adverse conditions when further south. In more southerly latitudes the geese will begin to breed earlier, though not too early, because there has to be a good growth of vegetation, not just for the adults, but more particularly for the young when they hatch. Many birds, not only geese, time their breeding season so that the hatch takes place to coincide with the maximum availability of food for the young.

Geese which have not had to migrate to reach their nesting place, or which have only to make a short journey or none at all, may begin to show interest in the nesting area well before egg laying starts. Birds belonging to sedentary populations will begin to show territorial behaviour, staking out a claim to a nest site and possibly defending an area around it, as much as a month before they will actually lay. The overall controlling factor bringing birds into breeding condition is the stimulation provided by the steadily increasing day length as the spring progresses. In theory, this should produce a regular starting date for breeding each year, but in practice the date can be advanced by warm weather and retarded by cold. Thus, these first signs of interest in a nest site may be an on–off affair, initially, as the weather changes. Staking out their territory like this over a longish period is presumably of some advantage to those birds able to do so, but can of course be dispensed with altogether in arctic breeding populations.

Geese in temperate latitudes, such as Greylags and Canadas in England, and Greylags in other parts of Europe across to Austria, will lay in April, at the beginning of the month or even in late March in an early spring, though some birds in the same localities may not lay until May. Similarly, the large races of Canada Geese in the United States, breeding from the midwest States through to California and Oregon, will lay from mid-March onwards in favourable seasons. Some at least of the later breeders in any area are likely to be younger birds, breeding for the first time. Moving north in spring, so the beginning of the breeding season becomes steadily later. The latest to start are probably the Brent Geese in Canada and Siberia whose first eggs are generally laid about the first ten days of June. Some average dates for the timing of the season are set out in Table 3.

The various species of geese vary greatly in the density in which they will breed. All species defend territories around the nest but of very different sizes depending on the species; the individual, the terrain, and whether or not the birds are nesting colonially or on their own. Several of the goose species are normally colonial nesters, including the Greater and Lesser Snow Geese and Ross's Goose, the Greylag and the Pinkfoot, and the Barnacle and the Redbreast. Some Canadas are colonial, mostly the larger southerly breeding populations, while others nest in scattered associations which are not really colonies. This is also true of the Brent Goose, the Whitefronts, the Bean Goose and the Emperor Goose. Some of the arctic nesting Canada Geese are completely solitary breeders and lone pairs of most species can be found in some areas.

The Lesser Snow Goose nests in the largest colonies, up to 120,000 nests in one colony, while some colonies of Barnacle Geese or Red-breasted Geese

have perhaps only half a dozen nests. But whatever the size the reason is the same, safety in numbers. There will be more pairs of eyes on the look-out for danger, and although the largest colonies will undoubtedly attract predators to this rich potential source of food, the damage they can do in relation to the size of the colony will be small; although the individual may suffer, the colony as a whole will not be seriously harmed. The alternative to this is solitary nesting, where defence against predators is attained by being inconspicuous. Clearly there is a place for both types and it is difficult to say that one is more successful than the other.

Once a pair of geese has been formed, the male will defend his mate against the attention of other geese, especially other males. In this way he is forming a small territory around the female which he regards as sacrosanct. The territory naturally moves around as the female moves around, and has no fixed boundaries, nor is the attack distance the same all the time. In crowded conditions where the birds may be feeding or drinking close together, the territory will shrink almost to nothing. As the breeding season draws nearer the area is liable to expand. A great deal depends upon the aggressive tendencies of the individual male. Studies of captive flocks have shown that there are dominant males who will defend a much larger area around their female than will subdominant males. The dominance is usually, though not always, related to age, and sometimes to size.

Once a nest site has been chosen, the male begins to defend an area around it, as well as around his female if the pair move away from the site. The boundaries will still be fluid and will vary according to the nearness of neighbouring birds, perhaps also establishing themselves at nest sites. But as time goes on, the boundaries begin to be less flexible, until about a week from egg-laying they become fixed into the position which will remain until the young hatch. Thus, the male's territorial defence of his female as she moves around before choosing a nest site, becomes fixed as she settles down in a single spot.

The above account presupposes a pair of geese arriving on the breeding grounds with plenty of time before they need lay their eggs. In the arctic, the same process is gone through but is much speeded up, so that the site is chosen and the territory boundaries become fixed within a few days.

The earliest birds to select their territory are almost invariably the older pairs which bred in the same place the previous season. Young birds breeding for the first time will be forced to the fringes of a colony, into perhaps less suitable territories. They may also be smaller than those of older birds, as the males will be subdominant and less able to defend a large area. Better territories will become available to them in future years on the death of the older birds.

The prime purpose of a nest territory is to prevent harassment of the female by other geese. She is at a critical time, having expended much energy in producing the clutch of eggs, and she is too intent on incubating them to be able fully to defend herself. In very crowded colonies of highly territorial geese, such as Canadas, the nest success can drop significantly because of desertions and nest destruction caused by incessant fights and bickerings between neighbours. The situation probably arises because a shortage of nesting sites forces the birds to crowd closer together than normal. If the only suitable nesting place is perhaps one small island, then every pair will want to nest there, and nowhere else. The result is a self-regulating mechanism, usually termed 'density dependent', whereby, because the birds have become too numerous, their breeding success drops and further increase in growth is restricted. The same would happen if the less aggressive birds gave up trying to nest on the one island and moved out to fringe sites on mainland banks. There they would be subject to greater predator pressure and so breed less successfully.

A recent hypothesis suggests that, normally, the territory in some arctic breeding species, notably Ross's Goose, is also the place where the male can feed during the incubation period. In this way he is able to be present throughout the incubation period, whereas if he has to leave the territory to feed this leaves the female vulnerable to interference from neighbouring birds. The hypothesis goes on to relate territory size to the requirements of the male in this respect so that it is large enough to provide food but is small enough to be readily defended. The final size may be affected by the reserves of fat that the male has retained on arrival on the breeding grounds, which would affect in turn how much further food he would need. This theory is not supported, however, by a study of colonially breeding Pinkfeet where there was little or no attacking of the female by other geese and the males commonly fed out of the territory. It is suggested instead that the territory provides food for the female in the important period when she is laying the clutch. The Pinkfeet nest in the low arctic and there is a certain amount of vegetable food available, including last years seeds.

The exact size and shape of a breeding territory will depend not only on how naturally aggressive the birds are, or how much food they require from it, but also on the configuration of the ground. In hummocky ground or in scrub, pairs of geese will nest much closer to each other than in open ground where they can more easily see each other. Exceptionally, nests may be only a few metres apart, but because of an intervening hummock or dense bush this is still tolerable. In these situations the pairs may still have sizeable territories stretching out in other directions. I have seen this state of affairs in Canada Geese and in Pinkfeet, and it doubtless occurs in others.

Colonially nesting geese generally have quite small territories, thus for Ross's Geese they averaged about 16·5 square metres (175 square feet) on nesting islands in one area studied. The mean distance between closest nests was about 5 metres (16 feet). This is similar to that found in the Greater and Lesser Snow Geese. The large colonies of the latter average about 390 nests to the square kilometre (1000 to the square mile). Not that the density will be uniform right through the colony; local topography will see to that. In an aerial survey of the Pinkfeet colony in central Iceland it was found that the average density, over the whole colony of about 10,700 nests, was about 131 nests per square kilometre (340 per square mile); but it ranged from as low as 36 per sq km (93 per sq mile) to as high as 544 per sq km (1400 per sq mile), with distinct zones of high density where the ground was well ridged, providing a maximum of usable nest sites. The low density areas were in marshy places where dry sites for nests were few and far between.

Small colonies of Canada Geese and Greylags, numbering perhaps 20 or 30 pairs, may nest quite densely on available islands but the density expressed in terms of the total island and water area available is of course much lower. Both species sometimes nest only a matter of a metre or two apart, though this is usually when they are out of sight. The Greylag is much more tolerant in this respect than the Canada.

Many Canadas are not colonial at all. In the arctic around Hudson Bay the small races breed at an average density of no more than seven nests per square kilometre (18 per sq mile), and often much less, down to about two per sq km (5·2 per sq mile). Here the alternative strategy to colonial nesting is carried out to perfection. No predator is going to be able to make a living searching for such widely scattered nests. The only nest to be found will be by chance. It is relevant to point out that the Canada Goose is quite well camouflaged on the tundra, whereas the Snow Goose, after the spring thaw, is not, and so colonial nesting is its best defence. Whether blue phase Snow Geese can breed just as successfully out of colonies as within them, or whether they have ever tried, is not known.

In areas where there are ample nest sites, the larger Canadas too will not be particularly colonial. Nest densities of 10 per hectare (4 per acre), between 25 and 75 per hectare (10–30 per acre), and up to 100 per sq km (260 per sq mile), have all been reported. The precise figures depend on the definition of the area involved, but all show a degree of spreading out.

Some species seem not to mind whether they nest close together or well scattered. Colonies and well spaced nests exist within the same nesting area of, for example, Emperor, Brent, Barnacle, Whitefront, Bean, Swan Goose and Barhead. The only species which appears always to be a solitary breeder is the Lesser Whitefront. Table 4 (p. 125) summarises nest sites and dimensions.

The choice of the actual nest site is dictated by a number of considerations, though it is not always easy to see which is of prime importance and which is only secondary. The great majority of arctic breeding geese nest on comparatively flat open tundra, where, there is a strong tendency to select any slight hummock or ridge projecting only a little above the general ground surface. If available, the geese may also nest on rocky outcrops or other larger eminences. A degree of protection is sometimes also sought beside a rock, or by a tussock of vegetation. Three principal reasons are commonly advanced for the choice of an elevated site; a good all round view for the sitting bird and her mate as a defence against arctic foxes and man; to be above the level of floodwaters produced by the spring thaw; and because raised spots will be the first to become free of snow.

The relative importance of these three reasons is not easy to judge though it is tempting to link each with the period of the nesting season at which observations may have been made. Thus, until fairly recently, the majority of people visiting goose nesting grounds only did so towards the end of the incubation period, or found nest sites after the hatch, when any snow or meltwater had long since gone, and a defence against predators would present itself as the most obvious advantage of the site. Those who have seen nests during the spring melt will naturally notice that the nests are safe above the flood water. But only those comparatively few who have arrived on the breeding grounds at the same time as the geese, or who have realised what conditions must be like at that time, will have alighted on what must be the prime reason, the requirement that the site is free of snow at the time of laying. The other benefits of being above floods and giving a good view will naturally accrue from this but it is probably wrong to give them too much importance in site selection.

A reinforcement of the belief that freedom from snow is the most important consideration is found in those species nesting on small islands, where snow melt is unlikely to produce floods, and where arctic foxes do not normally occur. Hence, indeed, the choice of the island in the first place. Here, too, nests are generally placed on some slight hummock.

This use of small islands, whether offshore, or in a river or lake, is very common in the smaller species of geese, such as Ross's Goose, Barnacle, Brent and small Canadas. These are the species which are probably unable to stand up to or drive off an arctic fox, even in the protection of a colony. A surrounding barrier of water is therefore almost essential. There have been a number of recorded cases where a bridge of ice remained, or reformed, connecting an island with the mainland, whereupon an arctic fox crossed to the colony and wiped it out. The species which do not make a habit of island nesting may, nevertheless, nest in wet, marshy areas, through which any fox would have to make its way to reach the nests. There is clearly some protection to be gained here. Even the larger geese, capable of defending their nest and eggs against a fox, especially when acting as a pair, still nest in such defensive sites if they are available. These include Greylags, Bean Geese and Pinkfeet. In western Alaska, where Whitefront, Emperor Geese, small Canadas and Brent all nest, the latter two choose small islets as first preference, while the first two species, much larger geese, will nest on any dry spot whether island or not.

If there are no islands on which to nest then some of the smaller species, and occasionally the larger ones too, will make use of the other kind of barrier, a vertical drop. The Barnacle Goose is the species most usually found nesting on cliffs, though it will nest on flat ground on islands, too. The cliffs it chooses are usually inland ones, though occasionally seacliffs are used. The steep-sided U-shaped glacial valleys of East Greenland, for example, provide Barnacle Geese with nest sites some hundreds of metres above the valley floor. The hills or mountains forming the sides of the valleys have steep scree slopes at their feet, running back up for perhaps two hundred metres. There are often some bands of harder rock forming vertical cliffs, 20–30 metres (60–100 ft) high, usually much broken and providing many suitable ledges. A typical nesting site would be on a ledge between one and two metres wide and up to 75 cm from front to back (3–6 ft by 2½ ft). The nest ledge is often made quite visible from a distance by a patch of bright orange lichen, fertilised no doubt by the goose's droppings. An alternative type of site, but just as inaccessible, is on the top of a rock pinnacle, found sometimes in river gorges or standing free from the mass of a cliff. Barnacles in Greenland and Svalbard, and Pinkfeet in Iceland, have been recorded in such situations. Bar-headed Geese, too, nest in rocky and precipitous places, while Canada Geese will also nest on cliff ledges, though usually not in the arctic, but further south. The arctic breeding Canadas seem content with islands or marshy ground.

As one moves south so the geese take more advantage of vegetation for protection and concealment. The Bean and Lesser White-fronted Geese nesting in the scrub zone of Eurasia, and the Canada Geese in the equivalent areas of North America, will place their nests under thick bushes, while further south again one finds Greylags and large Canada Geese siting their nests at the foot of large trees, which will give them some shelter from the weather and render them less conspicuous. These latter two species, but especially the Greylag, also nest in dense stands of reed and bulrush, starting on a foundation of old dead stems from the previous year, or sometimes choosing a mat of floating vegetation. The great majority of nests will be protected by water in some way, either deep in a marsh, or, more usually, being placed on an island in a lake or river. In Britain the great increase in gravel workings in the last 20 years has provided excellent Canada Goose habitat as the flooded pits very often have islands of spoil left in them when digging has finished.

A more unexpected site for geese to nest is the crown of a pollarded willow. This is not uncommonly used by Greylags in central Europe, as many as 20% of a large sample in Czechoslovakia. Bar-headed Geese nest in the tops of broken tree stumps, as do Canada Geese in North America, and the latter will also choose the tops of leaning or fallen branches, indeed any part of a tree broad enough and sufficiently stable to take their nest. They have extended this type of site to include the old nests of other birds, particularly herons and Ospreys, both of which make large, relatively long-lasting structures. Heights above ground of as much as 30 metres (100 feet) have been recorded. In one remarkable case a pair of Canada Geese hatched seven young in an Osprey's nest in mid-April. The day after the young had left an Osprey was seen at the nest apparently eating the eggshells or perhaps the membranes. Two weeks later a pair of Ospreys were occupying the nest; and they laid eggs and reared two young.

This tree-nesting preference of the larger Canada Geese has been taken advantage of by people seeking to increase both the number of nest sites available to the geese in a given area and the safety of those nests. Platforms of wood, placed in trees up to 20 metres (60 ft) above the ground, or fastened to the tops of poles up to about three metres tall (9–10 ft), where there were no suitable trees, have been quickly adopted by the geese. In one area where about 70 pairs of Canadas were nesting, over half the pairs had adopted aerial platforms by the fourth breeding season after their erection. A particularly cheap and simple form of artificial nesting site for Canadas is the sawn-off end of a wooden barrel, or the old-fashioned wash-tub, about 60 centimetres (24 in) across and up to 30 cm (12 in) deep. These can be placed in trees, or on poles, with the latter sited in water for additional safety. The advantages include not only the increase in the number of available sites, and therefore of

pairs that can breed, but also a significant increase in the breeding success of the tub-nesting birds. Nest predation and losses to floods were all greatly reduced, while desertion was down and hatching rate up. Of course these birds nesting in the temperate areas of North America have not only foxes to contend with but raccoons, rats and even bears, so sites have to be out of the reach of all of these to be safe, and tubs on poles set in the water achieve this.

Another type of artificial nest site is the floating raft. This has been used with success in America and Europe for encouraging Canada Geese, while other waterbirds such as grebes and coots will also use them. The floating part of the raft is often constructed from railway sleepers, though metal girders supported on oil drums have been used. The raft must have soil placed on it, and be planted with clumps of rushes for cover. The whole must be anchored to the bottom and must not rock too much if there is a danger of large waves building up. Rafts can be used where the water is too deep for tubs on poles.

Geese, particularly Canadas, will use a wide variety of other sites given the opportunity. Often a shortage of conventional sites has a part to play in the selection of the less usual ones. Muskrats are common in many marshy areas of North America and they build houses of branches, twigs and reeds, projecting out of the water. The tops of these form tiny dry islands in an otherwise wet environment. It is, therefore, perhaps not surprising that

Canada Geese readily adopt these as the bases for their nests. In some places, indeed, such muskrat islands make an important contribution to the number of available sites. There have also been records of the tops of beaver lodges being used in the same way. Hay and straw stacks also find favour with Canada Geese, and what is probably the record nest density for the species was no less than eleven on one haystack in Oregon. Sometimes, instead of using the shelter of the base of a tree, the geese will site their nest at the foot of a board fence or even the wall of a hut. In such places it is clear that they have little fear of man and may indeed have been under his protection for generations.

These temperate zone nesting geese, then, are quite catholic in their choice of nest site. Availability seems to be the over-riding consideration, for which the birds require a certain amount of protection from predators, most often provided by water, and a degree of visibility so that either the sitting female or her mate nearby can see, if not all round, at least partly. This latter factor is not an invariable one, however, and both it and the type of cover used are secondary.

There is one last type of nest site which is involved in one of the more extraordinary relationships known in the bird world. The breeding grounds of the Red-breasted Goose in Siberia have only been visited relatively few times by ornithologists, but the great majority of nests that have been found have been close to the nest of a Peregrine, or more rarely some other bird of prey. The geese nest in small colonies of from three to twenty pairs and each colony is placed round the nest of the Peregrine. In the area of Siberia where the Redbreasts breed, the Taymyr Peninsula, the only eminences in an otherwise flat and featureless tundra, are low hills thirty to fifty metres high, beside some of the rivers. Occasionally they are cut into by the river to produce a steep gully or low cliff, but in their absence the Peregrine nests on the top of the hill. The Redbreasts place their nests there too. Each species seeks slight depressions, protected perhaps by a boulder or clump of vegetation. The distance between the falcon's nest and the goose's is usually between ten and thirty metres (30–90 ft), occasionally as much as 100 metres (300 ft), once only 1·5 metres (4½ ft). To emphasise the dependence of the Redbreasts on the falcons, of 22 nests of the latter which were located, no less than 19 had Red-breasted Geese nesting close by. The Peregrines were nesting between 7 and 10 kilometres apart (4–6 miles), which appeared to represent a reasonable density based on the available food supply. The only other places where Redbreasts were found nesting were alongside the nests of Rough-legged Buzzard, and a couple of times among Herring and Glaucous Gulls.

It has to be concluded from this remarkable evidence that the Red-breasted Goose depends upon the Peregrine for protection against the arctic fox. There are hardly any islands in the region, whether in the rivers or lakes, and those there are appear to be subject to spring flooding. There are no rocky cliffs and the geese have therefore to nest on the ground. There are some reports of them choosing steep slopes but these are in short supply. They have thus, in some extraordinary way, evolved the habit of nesting in the one place where they can receive the protection they seek. There are many other instances of one species of bird choosing to nest alongside another better able to defend itself, and therefore by proxy its neighbours, from predators, including well-known examples of waders and ducks nesting in tern colonies. The selection of a bird of prey capable of striking down the species seeking protection is a different matter. There are many unsolved problems concerning this interesting relationship but alas the breeding grounds are closed to western biologists and hardly ever visited by the Russians either. Maybe we will never have detailed observations on the behaviour of the one species to the other, of their interactions both during nest site selection and incubation, and after the hatch. For example, do the adult geese refrain from flying to and from their nest, and so avoid presenting a target to the Peregrine, or does the latter in any case refrain from making a kill close to his eyrie in the same way that rabbits are thought to be able to live in safety in a fox's earth?

Unfortunately for the Red-breasted Geese the Peregrines on which they rely so heavily are in decline. Pesticides taken in, probably on their wintering grounds in southern Eurasia, have led to a reduction in numbers. The Redbreasts too have been decreasing and it is almost certain that the two declines are linked. One of the few records of another species of goose nesting close to a Peregrine's nest concerned Barnacle Geese on Novaya Zemlya, and when the Peregrine did not return to breed one year the geese deserted the site.

When a goose has chosen its site the nest has to be constructed. This is fairly straightforward, a goose's nest is little more than a pile of available material shaped into a circular bowl. In virtually all species it is the female who does most if not all of the building. Both parents have been recorded as building in

the Brent, Barnacle and Greylag, but this seems to be unusual. Certainly it is the female who stands in the nest, pulling and plucking at the vegetation within reach. The male may stand beside her, passing material over his shoulder and dropping it into the nest. The female periodically sits down in the nest and, pressing the nest material together with her breast and feet, slowly rotates, forming the cup.

The nest will be built of whatever is within reach of the bird when standing in the nest or very close by. Thus the final size of the nest will depend on the site where it is built. Arctic tundra nesting species will have at most a small amount of short vegetation and moss to pull together into a rudimentary nest. However, it is quite likely that there is already a well-defined cup present before they start to build, because geese commonly use the same site year after year. The material they use, however slight, combined with the droppings of the sitting female, and of the male if he stands right beside her, as some do, plus the down and eggshells, gradually build into a permanent nest rim. The increased fertility of the rim and surrounding ground encourages vegetation to grow there, and it may even be possible that the presence of the incubating bird for three or four weeks warms the nest cup slightly, even half a degree would make some difference. The vegetation will grow and die back each year, adding a little more to the cup rim. It has been estimated that some nest sites of Pinkfeet in central Iceland may be up to 40 years old and will have been used in most if not all years in that period. The resultant nest cup will have a permanent raised rim up to 10 cm (4 in) in height and as much or more wide.

If the geese are nesting in scrub, or among trees, they make a foundation of twigs and an upper layer of grasses or softer vegetation. Even so, they will only use what is within reach as geese are not able to pick things up and carry them. Exceptionally a goose will stand some way from the nest, plucking material and casting it over its shoulder in the general direction of the nest, then move closer and repeat the operation until the pile arrives at the site. But only a minority of birds do this. In reed-beds and bulrush-stands the nest will, naturally, be built of these plants, often on a base of trampled vegetation that the bird may not have built itself, but found when seeking a good site.

In aerial nest sites, the goose will be able to add little or nothing to what is already there. When Canada Geese nest in old nests of other species, they accept what is already present and can only add to it if twigs or leaves are within their reach from the nest. It is usual to put some kind of nest material in aerial platforms and washtubs, sufficient to make it attractive to the bird. Sawdust, wood shavings or straw are the best. Cliff-nesting geese probably make do with the least material, though if the site is used year after year, droppings, down and eggshells will gradually build up into at least an insulating layer between the eggs and the bare rock. It is doubtful indeed whether the birds would ever lay straight on to the rock, there would have to be some kind of covering of soil in the first place.

Building of the nest is very rapid in arctic nesting species; they have not much time to spare. Greater Snow Geese and Canada Geese have been known to lay eggs within 24 hours of starting to make a nest. Further south the birds may build over a period of several days, though not continuously, spending a short time each day. Greylags with ample material available can take from

TABLE 4: *Nest sites and nest dimensions (in cm)*

	Colony	Dispersed	On ground Mainland	Islets	Cliffs	Ext. Trees	Int. diam.	diam.	Depth
Swan Goose	*						50	30	10
Bean		*	*				40	25	10
Pinkfoot	*		*	*	*		40	22	8
Whitefront (all races)		*	*				40	20	10
Lesser Whitefront		*	*	*			35	15	10
Greylag	*	*	*	*		*	80–110	25–30	13–60
Barhead	*		*	*			40	25	10
Emperor		*	*				33	17	9
Lesser Snow	*		*				40	20	10
Greater Snow	*		*				50	25	12
Ross's	*			*			40	16	8
Canada—large	*	*	*	*	*	*	50–110	25–35	20–45
Canada—small		*	*	*			35	16	9
Barnacle	*			*	*		43	18	7
Brent (all races)	*		*	*			35	20	8
Redbreast	*		*	*	*		35	20	10

three to six days to complete their nests, but a pair of Canada Geese whose first attempt was destroyed, set to and built a completely new nest in four hours. Very shortly afterwards, the female laid her first egg, so there was clearly need to hurry.

Some geese may carry on adding to the nest throughout the incubation period, often adding substantially to the original structure. This is much more likely to happen when the nest is in thick vegetation and there is plenty with which to build. Some geese also seem much more fidgety than others, and spend their time pulling at the nest and anything within reach, rather than just sleeping or sitting still as the majority do. Greylags and large Canada Geese seem most prone to continue building during the incubation period, but then both also nest in thicker vegetation than other species.

The final size and shape of a nest will depend to some extent on the site, whether it is constricting or completely open, on the size of the bird, and on the amount of vegetation available to it. Average dimensions of the nests of most species are shown in Table 4, together with a summary of their usual sites.

Most geese can produce their eggs at the rate of one per day, and in the arctic breeding species this is the general rule, thus shortening the laying period to the minimum. However, even in the smallest species, such as Ross's Goose and the Brent, it is usual for a day to be missed in the sequence, which would seem to indicate that laying a full clutch at this rate is just beyond their

TABLE 5: *Egg dimensions, weights and clutch sizes*

	DIMENSIONS (mm)			WEIGHT (g)			CLUTCH			
	Length	Breadth	Sample	Mean range	Sample	Ref.	Mean or normal range	Extreme range	Sample	Ref.
Swan Goose	82(76–90)	57(53–59)	20	136(120–153)	28	1	5·6	5–10	—	2
Bean	84(74–90)	56(53–59)	75	145(122–164)	53	3	4·6	3–8	—	3
Pinkfoot	78(70–90)	52(48–58)	300	132(111–149)	82	3	4·4	2–8	344	3
European Whitefront	79(72–89)	53(47–59)	120	114(97–126)	51	3	5·6	3–7	—	3
Pacific Whitefront	81(72–90)	54(48–58)	294	estimated 133		4	4·53	1–9	77	4
Interior Whitefront	none apparently recorded						5·7	4–8	—	5
Greenland Whitefront	80	52		117(112–136)	72	1	5·7	3–8	—	3
Lesser Whitefront	76(69–85)	49(43–52)	100	104(82–125)	84	3	4·6	2–8	—	3
Greylag	85(71–98)	59(52–65)	200	165(142–180)	60	6	5·75	2–11	453	7
Barhead	84(75–91)	54(51–59)	140	134(102–149)	45	1	4·56	2–10	110	8
Emperor	79(63–88)	52(45–55)	313	131(118–145)	20	1	4·57	2–10	81	4
Lesser Snow	81(73–88)	54(51–57)	50	121(103–133)	20	9	3·88	2–9	920	10
Greater Snow	81(74–91)	53(50–57)	123	126(102–149)	85	11	4·6	2–9	118	11
Ross's	73(67–80)	48(45–51)	52	estimated 92		12	3·47	1–8	1675	12
Canada—large	86(79–99)	58(54–65)	100	220(173–240)	50	3	5·9	3–10	75	3
—medium	79(72–87)	54(48–58)	90	124(115–132)	12	1	4·2	2–7	21	5
—small	74(63–85)	49(44–54)	3158	91(89–94)	5	4	4·25	1–9	814	4
—Aleutian	77(71–84)	54(51–58)	158	not recorded		13	not recorded			
Barnacle	77(68–82)	50(46–54)	75	105(77–125)	100	3	4·5	3–6	—	3
Dark-bellied Brent	75(73–77)	47(46–48)	9	estimated 85		3	3·5	2–6	—	2
Light-bellied Brent	73(65–83)	47(44–51)	521	79(69–83)	12	14	3·94	1–7	853	14
Black Brant	71(60–80)	47(42–52)	376	85(76–90)	7	4	3·27	1–7	130	4
Redbreast	71(61–72)	49(44–49)	26	74(69–78)	8	1	4·6	3–9	—	2

1, J. Kear; 2, Dementiev & Gladkov (1952); 3, Cramp & Simmons (1977); 4, Mickelson (1975); 5, Palmer (1976); 6, Young (1972); 7, Hudec & Kux (1971); 8, Kydraliev (1967); 9, Ryder (1971); 10, McEwan (1958); 11, Tuck & Lemieux (1959); 12, Ryder (1972); 13, Stephenson & Smart (1972); 14, Barry (1956).

capacity. The most common sequence is for the first three eggs to be laid at one per day, then a day missed, and then the clutch, which is usually four or five, to be completed, again at one per day. Two separate days may be missed if the bird is laying a larger than average clutch of six or seven. The larger geese, breeding further south away from the pressures of a short season, take their time over laying, as they do over nest building. Some of the largest, including the Swan Goose, the Barhead and the large Canadas, lay an average of one egg per two days, or sometimes slightly less. Interestingly, the very small Lesser Whitefront, which also breeds far enough south for the breeding season to be fitted comfortably into the summer, also lays an egg every other day, suggesting that this is the normal rhythm for geese of whatever size, given sufficient time. On the other hand it has been reported that Greylags breeding in western Scotland, lay one egg per day, although others breeding in central Europe lay every other day.

Table 5 shows the average measurements of the different species' eggs together with the ranges. The size of the egg and the number that a female can lay are closely related to the amount of food reserves that she can lay down before the nesting season. In arctic species this means the reserves she has been able to build up prior to arrival on the breeding grounds. As already explained, these same reserves have also had to bring the goose north on migration, and have to last her through the incubation period, perhaps supplemented by a limited amount of feeding during her short spells off the nest. The balancing act that the female has to achieve in order to distribute these reserves of energy between the three requirements is a remarkable physiological performance. The size of the egg and the number in the clutch have been arrived at in the course of evolution and are such that they do not throw too great a strain on the female. Even so, each egg must contain sufficient food reserves to allow the embryo to develop quickly to hatchable size, and at the same time provide a reserve to support the newly-hatched young until they are able to feed themselves, which will be some hours later. Indeed, in an emergency, they may have to live on their remaining yolk for a matter of days.

The overall clutch size has a normal range which is fixed for each species or population. These are shown in Table 5. In some species one has the phenomenon known as 'dump' nesting, where more than one female lays in the same nest to produce abnormally large clutches. The dividing line between what one female is capable of and what must be the output of two or more birds is not known exactly. Dump nesting is most likely to occur in colonies where a pair loses its nest site through territorial strife and the female is forced to lay where she can. The attraction to her of another nest already containing eggs is then usually irresistible. Only one female will carry out the incubation of a dump nest, nearly always the one who built it, but covering more than the normal number of eggs is inefficient and the hatching success will always be low.

Clutch size in arctic nesting geese is affected not only by the condition of the female but by her age and experience. Older, mature birds nearly always lay more eggs than younger ones, particularly if the latter are nesting for the first time at two or three years old. The older birds are probably able to store larger energy reserves. Experienced pairs have a further important advantage over first-time breeders. They can return to the site they used in the previous year which will require the minimum of finding and building, whereas a new pair will have to locate a nest site and then prepare it before they are able to start laying.

The timing of the season will also affect clutch size. In an early season, when the birds can lay almost as soon as they arrive, clutch size will be a little larger than average, whereas in a late spring it will be smaller. Studies of Brent, Snow and Ross's Geese have shown that for every one day's delay in starting to lay, the final clutch will be reduced by one egg. Thus, if the clutch is normally five eggs, and bad weather delays the start of laying by one day, the final clutch will only have four eggs; if delayed for two days, only three eggs may be laid. In this way very tight physiological control is exercised over the time spent laying. The geese must not allow a delay in laying to carry through to a late fledging of the young. Instead the unlaid eggs are resorbed.

Although first-time breeders usually have smaller average clutches than older birds, it is a matter of dispute whether or not the clutch size becomes constant with maturity. Of two studies of nesting populations of large Canada Geese, one concluded that the clutch size continued to increase slightly as the birds grew older, while the other believed that it stayed the same. In colonial species there is a further factor affecting clutch size. Conflicts between densely nesting pairs can cause a decline in the number of eggs actually laid, mostly because of the stress of frequent fights in defence of the nest site. Hatching success may also be reduced.

It can be seen, therefore, that although there may well be a range of clutch sizes that is genetically fixed for that species or population, it is subject to a considerable number of variables which will affect the number of eggs actually laid by a female in a particular year. For this reason, records of clutch sizes should be taken from a large sample of nests spread over a period of several years; and allowance must be made for losses to predators and other causes if the recording is not made as the eggs are actually laid. Clutch sizes are in fact not too meaningful unless it is known at what stage of incubation the figures were gathered, the type of season it was, and so on. Clutch size at laying and clutch size at hatching are of course interesting figures, providing an indication of egg predation, but only large-scale studies will be meaningful.

There is conflicting evidence from different studies concerning the variation in egg size within a clutch. Certainly not all the eggs in a clutch are identical in size or weight, but whereas work on the Lesser Snow Goose colonies on Wrangel Island in the eastern Siberian arctic suggests that the largest egg is laid first, and that there is a successive decrease in size and weight as the clutch progresses, in the Ross's Goose no relationship between egg size and laying sequence could be found. Studies on other species of birds have tended to show that there is no good relationship between size and sequence.

All the species of geese pluck down with which to line the nest, using it as insulation beneath and around the eggs to protect them from rising damp, and as cover for warmth when off the nest feeding. Covering the eggs also conceals them from any predators flying overhead, although the circle of down is usually quite conspicuous because even the dark-bellied species produce light grey or light brown down. Nevertheless, the actual shape of the eggs, which is probably readily recognised by predators as potential food, is hidden from them.

The down comes from the underparts of the female goose and consists of quite small feathers without any flat vane, having instead entirely soft and downy plumules. She plucks an area on either side of her sternum, the keel of a goose, and leaves it virtually bare. This area is then in contact with the eggs in the nest and helps to maintain them at the incubating temperature of about 37·5°C (100°F), or very close to the blood heat of the goose. This bare area is not a true brood patch, such as is possessed by most though not all kinds of birds. Brood patches are completely featherless tracts, normally covered by adjacent areas of feathers. During incubation the blood vessels lying near the skin surface become swollen with blood and therefore more efficient as heat interchangers. The goose does not have this facility, but nor does it want bare areas of skin below the waterline. Instead, it plucks just this area around the sternum, whereupon new feathers begin to grow, so that by the time incubation is complete there is already the beginning of a fresh covering. Among the down in the nest will also be some of the actual body or contour feathers, the outer layer of which conceals the inner down.

Down will first appear in the nest after the laying of the first egg. It is plucked in little clumps by the female, using the tip of her bill. The laying of the second, third and subsequent eggs is signalled by increasing quantities of down but it is not until the clutch is complete that the full amount is plucked. The female will then begin incubation and have ample time to complete the task. With experience one can tell whether a clutch is complete by the quantity of down present.

The Emperor Goose has been reported as not producing the full amount of down until some days after incubation begins, but in any case the total amount in the nests of the Emperor is less than in most other species. The Greylag, too, produces rather little down, though does not add to it after the end of laying. The Ross's Goose plucks very little down until the last egg has been laid, and then quickly produces large amounts. Conflicting reports surround the Whitefront, with some authorities saying that it produces large amounts of down, and others only a little. Such variation may be genuine, but it is also possible that much of the down gets blown away during incubation or becomes wet and bedraggled by rain. This could easily mislead observers into thinking that rather little was produced in the first place. Brent Geese are noted for the large quantity they pluck, a good double handful.

Incubation is by the female goose only. The male may cover the eggs for periods during the laying but thereafter he leaves it entirely to his mate. There is a handful of records, mostly of captive birds, of males taking over the incubation on the death of the female, but these have usually been towards the end of the period, when it begins to matter less if the temperature fluctuates a little. It must be remembered that the male does not supply any down and has no bare skin on his underparts with which to warm the eggs.

The female normally comes off the nest once or, more usually, twice each day for about half an hour in the morning and evening. During these periods she feeds, drinks and bathes. On leaving the nest she pulls the down and nest material over the eggs to keep them warm and to conceal them from predators. When off the nest she is often accompanied by the male. In some species though, the male remains close by the nest, on guard, while the female is feeding. This would seem to be a compromise solution between protecting the female closely while she feeds, and looking after the eggs. The female may feed close to the nest but more usually moves away some distance, to areas where there are no breeding pairs. In bad weather the female will continue to sit in order to protect the eggs from the rain or cold.

Losses of eggs during incubation can be quite high and stem from three main causes. Firstly, there is nest desertion when the female gives up incubating for some reason. Secondly, there is the influence of the weather. Finally, there is predation, the loss of eggs to an animal or bird. It is not possible to rank these in order of importance; each can be of major importance in particular circumstances.

All three causes are, in fact, related to the female's ability to carry out the incubation effectively. In the arctic she can only do this if she has sufficient energy reserves to last her throughout the period. If these begin to run short she will have to spend longer and longer off the nest feeding, allowing cold or wet weather to chill the eggs, and giving predators a much greater chance of finding them. There are two more drastic solutions for a female which runs badly short of reserves; either she will give up incubating altogether and desert the nest, or in extreme cases may lay the eggs but make no attempt at incubation, or she will actually die on the nest, still sitting. This last end to a breed attempt has been recorded a number of times in the large Lesser Snow Goose colonies in the Canadian arctic. In a sample of 20 birds that died in this way, mean weight was 43% below that of females at the start of the breeding season, whereas a more normal weight loss during egg laying and incubation is of the order of 25%. While geese are incubating and have little or no food intake, their loss of weight is directly related to loss of heat. This in turn depends upon the prevailing weather. Adverse conditions, especially low temperatures coupled with strong winds, accelerate the loss of heat and, therefore, of weight.

Arctic weather has already been shown to affect the timing of the start of laying and the number of eggs laid. Low temperatures and precipitation can cause the loss of eggs, and an extreme example is heavy snowfall. There have been cases of falls of a foot or more during the incubation period burying nests and eggs completely and forcing the geese to give up sitting. A more common danger, not only in the arctic, is heavy rain. Birds nesting in marshes will be faced by rising water levels, and those on islands in lakes may be faced with sudden spates, inundating the nests. A slowly rising water level can sometimes be combated by the bird building up the nest to keep it safely out of reach, but this can only be done to a small extent and a sudden flood cannot be resisted.

Another form of flooding is tidal. The only documented cases of severe losses to nesting geese from this cause are in Alaska, in the very low-lying multiple delta of the Yukon and Kuskokwim Rivers. The rivers and numerous smaller streams are tidal for many kilometres inland, and the average height of the land is only a metre or so above sea level. Since the area has been regularly visited by biologists, storms have twice caused tidal surges to sweep inland, completely inundating the land and sweeping nests and eggs before them. Such a wave swept through the area in 1952 and again in 1963 causing great losses. One observer has written of extensive belts of drift and tidewrack at the furthest point reached by the floods, formed of logs, sticks, general debris and thousands of eggs and the new-hatched downy young of Black Brant, whose breeding grounds had been devastated over a wide area.

Predation of eggs is only serious in certain circumstances. Normally, a pair of geese is quite able to defend its nest and eggs against most predators it is likely to encounter. We have already seen how the smaller species meet the problem of arctic foxes by nesting on islands. Island nesting is also common further south where larger mammalian predators, such as racoons and coyotes as well as foxes, occur. Where these sites are in short supply man has come to the aid of, particularly, the Canada Goose by providing artificial sites on poles or in trees. Predation by birds, particularly skuas (jaegers) in the arctic, and members of the crow and gull families both there and to the south, will only occur when the nest is left unattended. This happens during the laying period, when the first egg may be left uncovered and unconcealed in the nest for 24 or even 48 hours; and later, during laying, when the amount of down and nest material may be insufficient to conceal the eggs. It also occurs when the female is off the nest feeding and, as already mentioned this can be in turn affected by the general weather conditions. Blue phase Lesser Snow Geese nesting at the McConnell River on the west shore of Hudson Bay lost about 20% of their eggs to predators, mostly quite late in incubation, when the females were spending increasing periods off the nest.

Studies on Brent, Emperor and small Canada Geese in Alaska showed substantial losses to predators, with Glaucous Gulls and Arctic Skuas (Parasitic Jaeger) causing most damage. Over 50% of Brent Goose eggs were lost out of 425 laid in the study area, mostly to the one or two pairs of Glaucous Gulls actually nesting within the Brent colonies. These birds were evidently able to identify a nest and eggs even when the latter were covered with down. And although the female may only have been off the nest for relatively short periods each day, this would give plenty of opportunity for a bird which knew what it was looking for.

These large gulls can cause great damage in such circumstances. The skuas on the other hand seem more opportunistic, and it cannot be said that goose eggs are their principal diet. Indeed their predation rate on goose nests has been found to be related to the supply of other prey species more commonly taken by skuas. These are mainly lemmings and voles. Both these small mammals are subject to cycles of abundance, swinging from boom to scarcity over a four to seven year period. In years of abundance, predation by skuas on goose nests, and on other species of birds, drops, but when lemmings and voles are scarce the skuas turn their attentions far more to the ground-nesting birds. Predation by all animals and birds on goose nests is increased by disturbance. If something causes the incubating goose to leave the nest in a hurry she may not have time to cover the eggs, thus leaving them exposed for all to see. The worst disturbance undoubtedly comes from man, and even the most careful researcher has to acknowledge an increased predation rate because of his own activities. With experience and care the damage can be reduced to a minimum. The unthinking visitor or photographer has been known to cause enormous havoc.

Geese breeding in temperate latitudes which lose their eggs to a predator are able to lay a second clutch. As the first nest has proved vulnerable, they almost invariably make a new nest in a new site. Renesting will normally take place only if the first clutch is lost early in the incubation period. The ovaries of the female gradually regress after laying and are quite soon beyond the point at which they can be used again that year. In order to lay a second clutch the female has to build up her reserves again by feeding, and an interval of between 12 and 20 days is usual between the loss of the first clutch and the laying of the second. The second clutch is quite often an egg or two fewer than the first, presumably reflecting the amount of energy the female has been able to renew. There seems to be a relationship between the sizes of the first and second clutches, however, and a female which has laid a larger than average first clutch will also lay a relatively large second one.

Renesting in arctic geese is unknown. The main reason being that there is not enough time in the short summer to rear goslings from eggs laid so much later than the normal laying date. Furthermore, the birds are generally rather smaller than those further south and would have great difficulty in finding the reserves to create more eggs, particularly as the feeding would not yet be good at that time. There have been one or two reports of arctic geese apparently laying again immediately after losing their first clutch, but on investigation this has been found to be the female completing her clutch in a new nest, having lost the first two or three eggs as soon as they had been laid.

A too rapid departure of the female from the nest, or perhaps even a flight involving the incubating bird, may cause an egg to roll from the nest. Generally speaking, geese are poor manipulators of objects but they do seem able to roll an egg back into their nests. To do this the female stretches out her head and bill over the top of the egg and pulls it towards her by pressure of the underside of her bill and chin. Experiments on egg-retrieval by Snow Geese showed that they could do this for up to nearly a metre from the nest, walking backwards as they did so. Beyond a metre the egg was generally ignored. Clearly there is a critical radius from the nest for the object to be recognised as an egg belonging to that bird; beyond it the egg becomes just another object and is ignored.

On rare occasions geese have been seen to eat the contents of eggs abandoned outside their nests. There are in fact obvious advantages to the pair if they do this. Firstly, it removes the egg from the vicinity of their nest, where it may otherwise attract predators and so increase the chances of their nest being discovered. Secondly, it undoubtedly provides useful food for the adults at a time when other foods are in short supply. However, it does not seem general practice and it may be that geese would have some difficulty in opening the egg in the first place. Certainly, they have no natural aptitude for using their bills as picks.

There are a number of records of geese sitting on duck eggs, and even one instance of the reverse. Mallard, and occasionally other species, sometimes

TABLE 6: *Hatching and rearing success in certain goose populations*

Species or population	Locality	No. of eggs (e) or clutches (c) in sample	% hatch	No. young (y) or broods (b) in sample	% fledge	Ref.
Pinkfoot	Iceland	1656 e	57·5	952 y	59·7	1
Whitefront	Alaska	349 e	75·9	65 b	88·0	2
		77 c	84·4			
Greylag	Scotland	873 e	87·6	365 y	85·0	3
		147 c	97·2			
Emperor	Alaska	370 e	81·9	139 b	78·0	2
		81 c	88·9			
Lesser Snow	Canada	403 e	69·2			4
		94 c	86·2			
Greater Snow	Canada	239 e	64·0			5
		52 c	67·3			
Ross's	Canada	2235 e	70·3			6
		597 c	77·1			
Canada						
Large	Wyoming	88 c	23·8	21 c	98·0	7
,,	Montana	2471 e	56·0	1390 y	81·2	8
		423 c	85·0			
Medium	Illinois	not given	41·0–73·0	not given	17·0–37·0	9
Small	Canada	119 c	10·0–25·0	not given	10·0–15·0	10
,,	Alaska	3459 e	67·6			2
		814 c	67·3	227 b	86·8	
Barnacle	Svalbard	184 c	54·3			11
Black Brant	Alaska	425 e	40·0			2
		130 c	44·6	72 b	84·9	

1, Gardarsson (1976); 2, Mickelson (1975); 3, Young (1972); 4, Ryder (1971); 5, Lemieux (1959), 6, Ryder (1972); 7, Craighead and Craighead (1949); 8, Geis (1956); 9, Kossack (1950); 10, MacInnes (1962); 11, Ebbinge and Ebbinge (In press—Norsk Polarinstitutt Arbok.)

lay one or more of their clutch in the wrong nest. This generally happens in areas where several pairs are nesting. In at least two cases Canada Geese have been found incubating Mallard eggs, as well as their own. In one instance the Mallard egg hatched before the goose eggs and the duckling attached itself to the female goose. The latter, however, was completely indifferent to this foster child and it subsequently died. The reverse example was noticed in the McConnell River Snow Goose colony where an Eider Duck was found incubating four of its own eggs and one Snow Goose egg. On this occasion they all hatched at roughly the same time and the female Eider led the mixed brood away. However, the gosling perished because the Eider took her brood on to fast-running water. Here the Eider ducklings were completely at home and were able to swim about and find their insect food. The gosling, however, lacked their expert swimming ability and, as a grazing goose, needed fine grasses and other vegetation.

Assuming that the eggs are not lost, incubation proceeds towards the critical moment, the hatch. As this time approaches, the female becomes more attentive, leaving the nest for shorter periods until in the last few days she probably does not leave at all. The male often comes to stand close to the nest too, though this seems variable both individually and among the different species. Barnacle Goose and Pinkfoot are certainly very attentive, but the Emperor and at least some Whitefronts and Brent are less so.

The first outward sign that a goose egg is beginning to hatch is the appearance of a small star-shaped crack near the broad end. A very slight bump is formed, with short radiating cracks. This is generally termed the first star, and the egg is now described as pipping. For up to 12 hours, or even more, before the first star, a faint tapping can be heard if the egg is held close to the ear. At times the gosling in the egg may also call quite audibly. The tapping is caused by the gosling banging steadily with the tip of its bill, where a special 'egg tooth', a small projection, helps its efforts to break through the shell. The egg tooth is shed soon after hatching.

After the formation of the first star, others are made adjacent to it, gradually working round the broad end as the gosling rotates inside the egg. Finally the end of the egg comes away in the form of a cup, and the gosling struggles out into the nest. From first star to hatching usually takes between 24 and 30 hours. Because incubation does not begin until the clutch is complete, all the eggs hatch more or less together, and it is rare for a full clutch to take more than 48 hours to hatch. If it does, it usually means that something delayed the development of the late eggs, perhaps chilling when the female was off the nest.

A number of workers have tried to discover whether there is any relationship between the order in which the eggs are laid and the order in which they hatch. The results are both inconclusive and somewhat contradictory. In one study of Canada Geese it was found that there was a significant correlation between the laying sequence and the order in which the eggs began pipping; and between the order in which they pipped and the order in which they hatched. However, there was no significant correlation between laying and hatching sequences. Work on Snow Geese suggested that there was a relationship between laying order and hatching order but that it was not absolute.

Incubation periods for the different species and populations of geese are set out in Table 7 (p. 142). These are average ranges; rarely, an egg may hatch up to a couple of days earlier or later than shown, but it is of little value to a single egg to do this unless the rest of the clutch behave in the same way. A gosling hatching ahead of the rest of the clutch will need to feed before the others are ready to feed, while one hatching a day or more later will almost certainly be left in the nest when the female leads the brood away. It will be seen from the Table that the northern and smaller geese have shorter incubation periods than the larger species further south.

On hatching, the goslings will stay in the nest until they are dry and capable of leaving. Breaking out of an egg is an exhausting business and the normal reaction is for the gosling to go to sleep. It is also rather wet and slimy and while it sleeps it dries out under the warmth of its mother. Any movement

made by the gosling or the goose helps to rub the protective waxy sheaths from the down, transforming it into a fluffy and charming young bird. The exact time spent in the nest depends to some extent on how long the hatching of the entire clutch takes, and on the weather. If the eggs hatch within a few hours and the weather is warm and dry, the female may lead her young from the nest within only six to ten hours. On the other hand, if cold wet conditions are prevailing, she may keep the young in the nest for up to 24 hours. After that, however, the young must be allowed to feed. They have some energy reserves in their bodies in the form of the yolk sac and in theory they need not eat until this has been fully absorbed, which might take three or four days, but in practice it is better if they can eat as soon as possible.

We now come to the vexed question of how some goslings leave an elevated nest. Most geese nest on the ground and this presents no problem at all to the gosling, which has merely to step over the edge of the nest cup and down the side of the nest mound, if any, to the ground. But a minority, particularly among Canada Geese, Greylags and Barnacle Geese, nest above the ground, high up in trees, or on cliff ledges. How do these goslings descend safely to the ground? The straightforward answer is that they jump, or at least step out into space, and bounce their way down to the ground. This is certainly how ducklings such as Goldeneyes and Buffleheads leave their tree nest holes, or how Mallard ducklings leave a nest box or the crown of a pollard willow. It is also the way that Canada goslings have been seen leaving a cliff ledge 15 metres (50 ft) above an almost sheer drop, and another brood that was in a tree nest even higher. The goslings were called down by their mother who stood at the bottom of the cliff or tree. With some understandable hesitation the goslings one after another took the plunge. Some of those that came down the cliff were temporarily stunned or perhaps winded

by landing on rocky ground, but those that came down the tree fell from branch to branch, their fall being broken in stages so that they landed quite lightly. And certainly a gosling weighing perhaps 120 g (4 oz) and covered in soft down, will not hit anything with very much force even from a height of 15 metres.

Reliance on gravity may be slightly hazardous for the gosling but it seems to work well enough for tree and cliff nesting to continue, with all its attendant benefits of freedom from predators. However, this would seem not to be the only way in which goslings leave the high nest. There is a number of published reports of the parents helping their young down to the ground. The two most detailed accounts refer to Barnacle Geese breeding on cliff ledges in East Greenland. One observer watched a pair of geese flying down from a high cliff each carrying something in its bill. When he next saw them they were on the ground accompanied by two small goslings. The second observer was watching pairs breeding on a cliff about 35 m (110 ft) above the sea. On one occasion an adult, on being disturbed by him from its nest, apparently placed a gosling on its back and flew down with it to the sea.

There are basic objections to be overcome before one can accept either account. In the first case there is the fact that geese seem to be quite incapable of carrying things in their bills. Evidence of this is their method of nest-building described earlier, in which they pick up the material and throw it over their shoulder towards the nest. It would be simpler and quicker if they picked up the material and walked to the nest with it, but this seems beyond their powers. Therefore, to accept that the two geese in the account each picked up a gosling in its bill and flew with it, is to accept a unique and uncharacteristic piece of behaviour that has never been observed before or since. In considering the second instance, it is of course true that a number of birds carry their young on their backs, including three species of swans, the Mute, Black and Black-necked. Grebes do it, too, and it has exceptionally been observed in one or two duck species, including the American Merganser. However, in all these species the young are only carried when the parent bird is swimming, or at rest, never in flight. They snuggle down into the back feathers of the parent, and are often protected by the slightly raised wings. The only bird known to carry its young in flight is the Woodcock which on rare occasions does so for short distances, the young being gripped between the legs and thighs. On the back of a flying bird it is difficult to conceive how a gosling could hang on even though the goose might be flying quite slowly. The published accounts lack important details such as the distance of the observer from the nest, binoculars used, if any, and so on. They are both rather unsatisfactory.

We are left then with the possibility that a gosling might, very rarely, be carried from a high nest by its parents, either in the bill or on its back. These possibilities have been seized upon by more recent writers apparently unable to accept that the alternative, free-fall, or bouncing down by stages, via lower branches or ledges, was possible without killing the gosling. Such an attitude may arise from a mistaken impression of what a nesting cliff and the chosen nest site is really like. As explained earlier, nesting cliffs are often much broken and have at their feet either the sea or steeply sloping rock scree. This scree is often split by tongues of more settled rock and soil, usually vegetated, running up the slopes even to the foot of the cliffs. These would provide an obvious pathway down for the geese and their young. But even in their absence, the rock scree does not present an insurmountable obstacle for an active gosling that can scramble and does not mind the occasional tumble, which is most unlikely to hurt it. It can only land softly. And its greatest advantage is that both parents will be there leading it on, calling constantly and making sure that it does not go off in the wrong direction. There may be some losses of course, perhaps of goslings getting into cracks and holes from which they cannot get out, but they will be small compared with other mortality that will take its toll of the young. There seems no reason to doubt that goslings can safely leave any nest their parents care to choose, and that there has been no need for the parents to develop any special behaviour actions to assist their young down.

The gosling is capable of walking, running, or swimming as soon as it leaves the nest. Both parents look after their brood, and the family will move away from the nest as a unit. The usual order is for the female to lead, followed by the goslings, with the male bringing up the rear. Sometimes they move more or less in line abreast, but the female will still be slightly in front and the male behind. On the first day it is rare for the brood to be taken more than a few hundred metres from the nest, just to the nearest feeding area.

When this is very close to the nest, the young may be brought back to the nest to be brooded at night for the first few days, but this seems uncommon and may be confined to Canada Geese. There is often a steady movement in one direction over a period of days, and a brood can be several kilometres from the nest by the end of the first week. Exceptionally, and especially if the birds have been disturbed by a predator or by man, much longer journeys may be undertaken. During a ringing expedition in East Greenland a pair of Barnacle Geese and their single gosling were caught twice in adjacent valleys. The two valleys opened into the same fjord and the shortest route the geese could have taken was about 20 kilometres (12½ miles). The gosling was about a week old when first caught and three weeks old the second time.

The families of Greylag Geese nesting on the coast of Estonia move steadily outwards through the belt of coastal islands during the first week after hatching, reaching the outermost, which are the least disturbed by man, in about a week. The maximum distance they travel is 30 kilometres (nearly 19 miles). In other species a more usual occurrence is a shift in feeding grounds when the young are older. For example, Canada Geese which breed in scattered pairs on the moorland of Yorkshire, often several kilometres from the nearest water, usually a reservoir, find sufficient early feeding for their young on the banks of the small streams crossing the moor. But in some areas this is a limited food supply and not a very safe place for the adults when they go into their wing moult. They therefore lead their young down the valley of one of the streams to the reservoir of their choice when the latter are some three or four weeks old. Others, however, remain until the whole family can fly. Similarly, Barnacle Geese breeding on small offshore islands in Svalbard have only limited feeding on the islands and when this begins to run short, swim with their goslings to the mainland, perhaps two or three kilometres (1–2 miles) away, and there find suitable marshy grazing areas.

The families of colonially nesting species, or those nesting in loose associations, usually band together into feeding flocks for better protection against predators. A flock also makes more efficient use of the food resources of an area. This grouping does not take place straight away, often being delayed until the goslings are some weeks old. Even within a flock, each family generally keeps together, with the adult birds, particularly the male, defending a kind of moving territory round it against other geese. However, in some species, especially while the young are small, amalgamation of broods may take place. A newly hatched gosling, or any other bird, is susceptible to any stimulus presented to it in its first impressionable hours or days. It will react to the first sights and sounds that it becomes aware of. In particular it will become attached to any large moving object, an attachment that is reinforced if that object makes a frequent and comforting noise. The mother goose provides exactly the right stimuli, with the added advantages of also providing warmth and darkness when the gosling wishes to sleep. It therefore forms an attachment with its mother, and later with its father, by a process called imprinting. However, if a gosling is reared by a human it will become imprinted on that person instead, following it around and responding to its voice.

Imprinting takes place in the first twenty-four hours after hatching, but it is continuously reinforced over the next few days, during which time it is possible for the attachment to be transferred. In particular it can be transferred on to another goose which is clearly the most similar object to the gosling's own mother. In situations where several broods of geese of much the same age are in contact, it is perhaps not surprising that some goslings should become confused as to which is their parent. Indeed, it is a wonder that mixing does not occur more often. In a large Lesser Snow Goose colony, only some 2% of goslings were known to have transferred from one brood to another and only 5% of all broods were involved in such mixing. And it ceased altogether after the first week when the goslings were firmly imprinted. Some parents seem more ready to accept strange goslings than others, which will attack and severely peck any interloper. The strength of the final bond, even while the gosling is still quite young, has been seen after the mass capture of goose families for ringing when there has been every opportunity for mixing and separation. Shortly after one such operation, 95% or more of families were found to have regrouped.

The most marked brood mixing takes place in Canada Geese, among the populations of large birds breeding in the temperate zone. This is perhaps surprising in view of their strong territorial sense when nesting, but brood amalgamation can be very striking. It is not uncommon to see broods of more than a dozen goslings, or even up to 20, sometimes accompanied by two or more pairs of parents but more usually only by one. What does not appear to have been studied closely is how the survival rate of these abnormally large broods compares with that of normal ones. It might be supposed that it would be inferior because the parents would be less able to guard such a large number of young.

During the brood rearing period the male spends a proportion of his time, perhaps as much as a quarter, in keeping watch, standing in the alert posture with his head and neck raised. Because he is on guard the female and the goslings are able to devote most of their time to feeding. This is necessary for the latter in order that they grow to full size and attain the ability to fly as rapidly as possible. In the case of the female, she has to recoup the weight she has lost since the start of breeding. It is therefore important that she should be able to feed for the maximum possible time with few alerts for possible danger. On average, the female will spend only 10% of her time on the alert, but the goslings are almost unaffected and feed for up to 95% of their time.

In the arctic, where there are twenty-four hours daylight throughout June and most of July, and well into August in the far north, the geese spend daily up to 18–20 hours feeding, or even slightly more. The remainder is devoted to washing and preening, and sleeping. The young are brooded under the wings of the female while they are still small, though a large brood will outgrow the available space after they are about two or three weeks old. The female will also shelter them during heavy rain. This brooding is vital to their survival. After about a fortnight they can manage without it, although the brood will often huddle together for mutual warmth.

Losses of young occur particularly in the first two weeks of their life, when they are at their most vulnerable. The weather can take a very heavy toll, when wet, cold conditions happen at or soon after hatching. This can cause a

virtual breeding failure. A relatively short bad spell can be sat out, with the brood protected by the female, but if it persists, then the young must feed or perish, and the attempt to do so may lead to death from exposure. The effect of bad weather diminishes rapidly as the goslings grow, until by the time they are getting their first feathers at about three weeks old there is very little except freak snow storms that can hurt them.

Similarly, predation on goslings is much more likely and more serious whilst they are small. The parent geese will defend their young vigorously against predators, but even so, foxes, crows and large gulls can wreak havoc, particularly when working in pairs as they often do. The most vulnerable period is again while the goslings are very small and especially during any journey between nest site and feeding area. During treks of this sort there is a very great danger of a gosling becoming separated from its parents. Stragglers are very soon picked off by ever watchful gulls or skuas. The published results of some goose studies showing hatching and rearing success are set out in Table 6 (p. 133). Brood sizes may show a fairly rapid decline in the first week or ten days, but thereafter losses are small.

Whilst the young are still growing their parents begin their annual moult, shedding all their flight feathers simultaneously so that they become completely flightless. In some cases the parents do not moult together; one starts well ahead of the other so that the period when both are flightless is reduced. Some observers believe that the female moults first, while others

have found that it is the male which does so. This probably indicates that there is no fixed order, or that it varies between species and populations. The moult is timed so that the parents can fly again by the time their young are on the wing. It takes about three to three and a half weeks for an adult goose to grow a new set of wing feathers, though it can take longer in the larger birds breeding further south. Like all other breeding season activities it takes considerable reserves of energy to produce new feathers. The weight of the birds will stop increasing, which it had been doing ever since the hatch, and will probably decline a little.

The weight of a goose varies considerably during the breeding season. The female's will reach a low point at the time of hatching, maybe as much as 40% below her peak weight which comes just before the spring migration. It rises after the hatch but sinks again during the moult. A male's weight is also at its highest during the period before the spring migration, and although it too loses weight during the first part of the breeding season, it probably falls only about 15–20%. The male's lowest weight is probably reached during the moult. Some recovery is made after the moult and before the autumn migration, but the time available is usually short and the birds will migrate in less good condition than in the spring However, in the former case they were heading to a period of considerable effort and even semi-starvation, whereas on autumn migration they are going to areas of comparatively lush feeding where they can rapidly regain weight before any spells of cold winter weather put a brake on their laying down of reserves. Their weight will probably level out during the winter, or even decline in severe conditions, only to increase again towards the moment of spring departure. A non-migratory goose, or one nesting in temperate latitudes, will probably not show such marked weight variations through the year

The fledging periods of different goose species and populations are set out in Table 7. The exact periods are not known for a few species and it is, in fact, not an easy thing to measure with accuracy. Unless one can observe individual birds closely, from hatching to first flight, one has to calculate the number of days between the hatch and the first observed flight. Nor is it always possible to know whether the flight one sees is the earliest the bird could have flown. The periods are therefore only approximate. In the days immediately prior to fledging the young geese can be seen making attempts to fly, running along with wings outstretched, or standing, flapping their wings vigorously. When doing this latter exercise they may lift themselves off the ground a little, especially in a wind.

Before the autumn migration the geese often exhibit signs of restlessness, taking off and flying round, calling a great deal, before settling back with the rest of the flock. In most arctic populations the geese move when they have to, rather than at a set time. The Pinkfeet breeding in central Iceland are sometimes forced out by early snowfall, as early as mid-September in some years, but in others they stay on well into October. Further north the spread of time is much shorter; winter rarely delays its onset beyond mid-September, and may come as early as the last week of August. If it is exceptionally early, or if some late hatched goslings have not yet fledged, then they will be killed, and perhaps their parents with them. Corpses of young

TABLE 7: *Incubation and fledging periods (days)*

	Incubation	Fledging
Swan Goose	28–30	75–90
Bean	27–29 (25–30)	45–50
Pinkfoot	26–27 (25–28)	45–50
European Whitefront	27–28	40–43
Pacific Whitefront	24–28	40–45
Interior Whitefront	26–28	42–45
Greenland Whitefront	26–27	c. 45
Lesser Whitefront	25–27(–28)	35–40
Greylag	27–28(–29)	50–60
Barhead	28–30	55–60
Emperor	24–27	48–55
Lesser Snow	22–23 (19–24)	42–50
Greater Snow	23–24(–25)	42–50
Ross's	20–21 (19–25)	40–45
Canada—large	26–30	50–60
—medium	26–28	45–50
—small	24–25	40–46
Barnacle	24–25(–26)	40–45
Dark-bellied Brent	24–26	c. 40
Light-bellied Brent	23–25	45–50
Black Brant	22–26	c. 40
Redbreast	23–25	c. 40

Sources: mainly Cramp & Simmons (1977), Dementiev & Gladkov (1952), Palmer (1976).

Brent Geese have been found frozen into the ice on the breeding grounds and it was estimated that they were within five days of fledging.

Although the departure of the geese from the breeding grounds ends the breeding season, the family unit of parents and goslings stays together throughout the following winter and spring. They fly together on migration, the parents showing the young by example the routes to take, the places to stop at and where to feed. On the wintering grounds, too, the family stays together within the larger flock.

At the wintering feeding places, the male parent is still the more vigilant, spending up to 20% of his time with his head up, looking around. The female is more alert than in the summer but still less so than the male. The goslings just feed, secure in the knowledge that they are being looked after, and they may spend up to 98% of their day doing so. They have yet to reach full size. The female no longer leads the brood around, in fact the young usually lead, because they walk faster while feeding. But when walking or swimming, then there is a tendency for one or other parent to lead while the other brings up the rear, the goslings coming in the middle.

The cohesion of the family unit remains well into the spring. The family will leave together on spring migration, but either before they reach the breeding grounds, or on reaching them, the male will cease to treat the young geese as friendly and may try to drive them off his territory, or prevent them coming too close to his mate. There have been rather few observations of this period in the life cycle of geese, except on captive birds which may not be entirely typical, but it seems that the parent–young bond is broken quite readily, although the completeness of the separation varies from species to species. In some species the young do not even go to the breeding grounds, while in others they do so but move away quite soon afterwards, often travelling long distances to a moulting area. Others stay close to the breeding grounds.

Among Lesser Snow Geese, roughly three-quarters of marked families returned entire to the breeding grounds. The great majority of the young left as soon as the adults had begun to nest, that is within a few days, but some stayed on and even visited the territory and the incubating female, being tolerated by the male when they did so. In the event of a successful hatch these young usually left, but if there was a breeding failure they might stay with their parents for the rest of the summer and for much of the following winter. This was noted in as many as 10% of immature Lesser Snow Geese.

Pairing between immature geese takes place towards the end of their second or third winter. Before this occurs, any remaining bond between the young and their parents will have broken, as well as any sibling bond. There seems to be something which prevents, or at any rate greatly reduces, sibling pairings, just as there is in most other birds and animals, including man. As described at the start of this chapter, it is the male which takes the initiative in courtship display, but it is the female which leads the male back to her natal area if it is different from his. Such a procedure will encourage the mixing of genes and keep in-breeding to a minimum. And so the breeding cycle will begin again.

5 Counting, ringing and population dynamics

There are two main techniques used in the study of goose populations; counting, and ringing (or banding). Complete counts of a population are usually termed a census (or an inventory), and may be carried out on the breeding grounds, during migration, or in the wintering quarters. For a very few populations all three are possible, but for most only winter censuses can be carried out. If these can be made regularly they provide information on numbers and distribution, and on changes that may take place in each. There are some populations for which only partial censuses can be achieved, though these are still useful, particularly if the same haunts are counted each time. Several goose populations have never been counted because of geographical or political difficulties.

Information on the numbers of geese in a population is made much more valuable by the simultaneous gathering of data on the relative proportions of old and young birds. Age counts, or age-group counts as they are sometimes called, involve assessing how many young birds are present in the flocks, either as goslings in the summer, or more usually as first-year birds during the autumn or winter. It is also usual and helpful to separate the young into families or broods. The percentage of young birds and the mean brood size together provide a measure of the annual breeding success of the population, both the overall productivity and the number of pairs of geese that have bred successfully. These two parameters make it possible to discover the age structure of the population, which if monitored over a period of years enables one to calculate how many geese die each year in a more meaningful way than by comparing only consecutive censuses. In a stable population the average number of geese that die in a year, the annual mortality, will be balanced by the average number of young geese reared, the annual recruitment. The behaviour of the population, as affected by variations in the annual rates of mortality and recruitment, is termed population dynamics. An understanding of this is essential to any long-term planning for the effective management of a population, whether through conservation or control.

The marking of geese with leg rings, or bands as they are called in North America, also provides information on population dynamics. One can discover how long individual geese live, what kills them, and, by marking sufficient birds, the annual rate at which they die and how this is related to age. This information is an important end-product of ringing but there are others of equal value. The individual goose is identifiable from its leg ring number, and therefore a subsequent recovery (the reporting of the ring number by the person killing or recapturing the goose) provides a direct link between the place of ringing and the place of finding. This may be between breeding grounds and wintering grounds, or vice versa, or between a migration resting area and a haunt at either end of the range. Extensive ringing will show to what extent the range of a species can be divided into more or less discrete populations, the extent of the breeding and wintering areas and migration routes of each population, and whether shifts between populations take place. Counting, by itself, can provide some of this information. Counting taken in conjunction with ringing will mean that the picture is far more complete than if either was used in isolation. Marking of geese can also be extended for use in more detailed studies involving the recognition of the individual in the field, not just in the hand. Observations on social behaviour, the extent to which geese are faithful to particular haunts within the range, and on the life history of each goose, the strength of the pair bond, its annual breeding performance, and so on, have been enormously facilitated in this way.

The descriptions which follow of censusing, and catching and ringing techniques, form a background not only for the discussion on population dynamics which ends this chapter but also for the two following chapters on distribution and status, and on migration.

The distribution of the different species of birds has been of great interest to ornithologists from the earliest days, and as explorers opened up new lands so the ranges of the various geese became more clearly defined. Numbers of birds have been much less well covered until comparatively recent times. Although wild geese have been quarry species for hundreds of years, it is only in this century that there has been concern over the effects of shooting and trapping, and with it a need to find out first how many geese there were in a population, and then to monitor its changes.

Probably the first regular censusing of geese began in 1930 when a group of interested people, organised by James Moffitt of the California Game and Fish Department, started counting the numbers of Black Brant wintering in their State. During the 1930s Moffitt extended his interest to counts of Canada Geese, too. Such pioneering efforts spread as their value became apparent, and before long the United States Fish and Wildlife Service and the Canadian Wildlife Service adopted his ideas widely as standard practice. As more and more knowledge was gained on the range limits of the different species and populations, so it became possible to make more accurate counts. For the last twenty years or more the majority of the important goose populations in North America have been monitored at least once a year, usually on their wintering grounds, while breeding season surveys and migration counts provide less comprehensive additional information.

In Europe, regular goose counting did not really get under way until the 1950s, when organisations in various countries, some Government agencies, but also many voluntary conservation bodies, began to be interested in how many geese they had. For many years they worked in isolation, but as it became to be realised that many goose populations knew no man-made frontiers so cooperation spread, stimulated by the International Waterfowl Research Bureau, an umbrella body concerned with fostering links between countries in the study and conservation of waterfowl.

Surveys of breeding geese have been carried out in a number of areas of North America, rather rarely in Europe, and only a handful of times in the U.S.S.R. There are very great practical and logistical difficulties in making such surveys, particularly the enormous distances to be travelled in getting to the breeding areas and in covering the potential breeding range once there. The use of aircraft has partially solved these problems, but only at considerable cost. It is, therefore, perhaps not surprising that the species which has been censused most regularly and successfully is both the most visible from the air, and the one which breeds in relatively few and concentrated colonies, namely the Lesser Snow Goose. The early counts were, it is true, made from the ground at individual colonies and they extend back over many years. However, when simultaneous counts were required over most of the range, an aircraft was the only practical transport, and air photography the tool that was used. Visual counting by an observer is practicable for small numbers but photographs are essential for large numbers of birds and extensive areas of coverage. White phase Snow Geese show excellent contrast with the ground, and although the blue phase birds are less good they are still readily distinguishable on the photographs.

In the latest and most comprehensive census of breeding Lesser Snow Geese, covering all the colonies in the eastern Canadian arctic, an aircraft was used equipped with a vertically mounted camera producing large format negatives. Black and white film was mainly used after a trial with colour. Two scales of photography were obtained, by high level runs at about 1500 metres (5000 ft) and low level at 450 metres (1500 ft). Even the lower height was sufficiently high not to disturb the geese on their nests. A pattern of parallel flights over each colony ensured complete coverage including overlaps. The analysis of the photographs took place in ideal conditions using light boxes, low-power binocular microscopes, and gridded squares for extremely accurate counting. Some colonies were dealt with completely, for others sample counts were made giving the mean density which, taken with the known area of the colony, produced a total whose limits of accuracy could be calculated. This photographic survey not only gave the first complete census of all the colonies in the eastern arctic, it also provided incidentally an enormous amount of information on the nesting habitat, distribution and behaviour of the geese, detailed nest distribution patterns, and very accurate data on the ratio between white and blue phase birds in each colony, as mentioned in Chapter 1.

Of the other geese nesting in the Canadian arctic, the Brent Geese and the Whitefronts have been covered in a few areas and on some more wide-ranging and exploratory aerial surveys, but not systematically. Canada Geese have been largely ignored as they are too scattered for such techniques. In Alaska the Arctic Slope has been surveyed from the air, but numbers of breeding geese here are comparatively low. The great duck and goose production area of the Yukon–Kuskokwim Delta has been covered on a sampling basis in most years, from which total counts are calculated.

There has been no large-scale survey of breeding geese in Greenland so far, though counts of some species in restricted areas have been made in a few years. Aerial counts of Greylags and Pinkfeet have taken place in Iceland, the former in 1963 and 1964, the latter in 1970. The results neatly demonstrate the relative problems involved in surveying a scattered breeder, and one which is more or less concentrated in colonies or at least in a restricted habitat.

The two surveys of Greylags were done from a light aircraft carrying a pilot and two observers, one covering each side of the aircraft. This species is widely distributed in Iceland, but mainly in the lowland coastal belt, hardly at all in the interior uplands. It is not particularly visible from the air and the only possible technique was to fly low enough to be sure of seeing the birds, which meant not more than 150 metres (500 ft) above the ground. However, the lower one flies the narrower the effective width of the strip of ground which the observers will be able to cover. The habitat for the geese is anything but uniform, so simple transects will not produce an even sampling of the population. Instead it is necessary to try to cover all suitable habitat as thoroughly as possible. The aircraft was therefore flown along the length of rivers, diverting to circle likely looking lakes, and zig-zagging to and fro over large potential areas such as the floors of the broad northern valleys. It has to be admitted that the results of the survey were disappointing when compared with the known size of the population based on winter censuses, thus reinforcing the view that this kind of surveying is very difficult to carry out in a way that ensures good coverage. Information was gained on the distribution of the geese, but neither survey, one in July, the second in the following May, produced anything like satisfactory figures, even for use as a sample from which to make more general deductions. It seems probable that the principal reasons for the undercounting, which was of the order of 50%, was a failure to cover all the potential habitat, and an inability to see scattered pairs or families of geese. Only the relatively large concentrations showed up well enough to be seen and counted.

The 1970 aerial survey of the nesting Pinkfeet in Iceland was completely different in technique and far more successful. However, the technique used was suited to the circumstances and there is no suggestion that it would have succeeded with the Greylags quite apart from the cost. The aircraft this time was a small three-seater helicopter with the pilot sitting centrally and an observer on either side. This method was first used in arctic Canada for counting a single colony of Lesser Snow Geese and it adapted perfectly to the Pinkfeet, even though they did not stand out so well. The latter were known to be nesting in a single large colony in an oasis or marshland set in Iceland's central lava desert. Unlike in Canada, where the helicopter, together with a pilot and an engineer, had operated in the field for weeks at a time, perhaps a thousand kilometres or more from the nearest facilities, the distances in Iceland were much less, only 240 kilometres (150 miles) from the nearest airfield. Even so, fuel had to be provided close to the scene of operations, to avoid much wasted flying.

The oasis containing the colony is roughly triangular in shape and about 16 kilometres (10 miles) across. It has one major and several tributary rivers running through it, and in early June, when the survey was carried out, the

area was more water than land, with innumerable shallow pools of meltwater separated by drier ridges on which the geese place their nests. The first flight over the oasis in the helicopter took the form of a reconnaissance to enable the observers, who had not been there before, to get their bearings and to identify, at least subjectively, the limits of suitable habitat, and the variation in breeding density across the entire area. This done they were better able to plan the actual survey.

One of the observers acted as navigator, plotting the course of the helicopter on a large-scale map and directing the pilot. The other, myself, concentrated on counting the number of goose nests that he could see. At this time all the birds were incubating their eggs. The survey was carried out on the transect method, counting the number of goose nests to be seen within a strip visible from the helicopter as it flew in straight lines across the colony. The width of the strip, 45 metres (50 yards), was kept constant by fixing two marks to the bubble canopy of the helicopter and then flying at a constant height of 60 metres (200 ft). Provided the height did not vary (and the relative flatness of the ground aided the maintenance of a fixed height) the width of ground to be seen between the two marks on the bubble would remain the same. Slight variations would tend to cancel each other out. The observer had to be careful to keep his counting to those nests within the two marks, and to ignore nests even slightly outside them. Thus, for each length of transect flown, a known area of ground was covered and the number of nests within it counted. This produced a density figure for that strip. As the helicopter flew back and forth across the full width of the oasis the navigator-observer identified prominent landmarks such as rivers and the few low gravel hills, and where possible divided each complete transect into several segments, for each of which he obtained a count of goose nests from the observer-counter. It was up to the first observer to make sure that the transects gradually built up to form an even pattern of lines on his map, covering all areas equally, regardless of whether few or many nests were found.

Two complete days were spent on the survey, plus a return visit a few days later to check on some initial results. A further check was also made by counting three areas on the ground as well as from the air. One of the main advantages of a helicopter over a fixed-wing aircraft is that it can be put down almost anywhere at will. When landed, the two observers searched for and counted each nest in a defined area. The results were compared with the transect flights over it. Good agreement was achieved each time. The final answer was obtained by multiplying the mean density of nests obtained from all transects by the total area of nesting habitat. The total of 10,700 pairs will be discussed in its context in the next chapter, on numbers and distribution of goose populations. The total was based on a sample covered by the transects of 1149 nests, or just over 10%, a highly satisfactory fraction of the whole from a sampling point of view. The relatively small size of the oasis, and its compactness, allowed this. A larger area and more dispersed nesting would necessitate the taking of a much smaller sample. However, statistical tests can be used to show that the latter can still be accurate enough for the purpose of measuring the total population.

Even this comparatively small survey cost several hundred pounds sterling in 1970, a reflection of the high cost of using a helicopter, usually three or four times the cost of a fixed wing aircraft. Its advantages often outweigh the cost, however, as they did on this occasion, when a fixed-wing survey would have been much less efficient and would have prevented the very valuable ground checks. Apart from the sheer inaccessibility of this area of Iceland, particularly early in the summer, a survey conducted on the ground would have taken weeks rather than days and would also have caused considerable disturbance to the nesting geese. Contrary to fears that had been expressed beforehand, the Pinkfeet were remarkably unworried by the helicopter. In winter a helicopter normally causes flocks of geese to take off and fly around in an obviously agitated manner. They appear more disturbed by it than by a conventional aircraft. On the breeding grounds the disturbance was minimal, with a majority of pairs remaining by their nests, even though the helicopter was only 60 metres above them, and many of the male geese actually made threat postures towards the machine as it flew over. Most of the geese that did leave their nests could be seen making a circle and coming back to their nests after the helicopter had passed.

There have been no complete counts in Svalbard (Spitsbergen) or in northern Europe, but in most of the central European countries there have been counts or good estimates made of the colonies of Greylags, just as there have been of the temperate breeding Canada Geese in North America. Many colonies of the latter are accessible on the ground or by boat, but aircraft have been used to cover more extensive areas, and some of the regions where there are large numbers of small nesting lakes.

Information from the U.S.S.R. is probably not complete but there appear to have been few if any quantitative surveys from the European arctic, and just a small amount of transect flying from central and eastern Siberia. There the surveys have been aimed at assessing numbers of all species of waterfowl, not just geese, and have been necessarily based on comparatively small samples, bearing in mind the vastness of the country involved. The only exception has been the Lesser Snow Goose whose colonies on Wrangel Island have been counted at irregular intervals. In addition, numbers of breeding Greylags have been estimated for most of southern U.S.S.R.

Counts of geese on migration are made regularly for a few populations, and show good agreement with subsequent counts on the wintering grounds in most cases. To be really useful they should cover either the whole or a significant proportion of a population. This is true, for example, of the Ross's Goose, virtually all of which are to be found in a relatively restricted area of southern Alberta and neighbouring Saskatchewan for a period each autumn. The post-breeding season gathering of Black Brant at Izembek Bay, Alaska, also comes under this heading.

In James Bay and the southern end of Hudson Bay, there is a spring assemblage comprising almost all the Lesser Snow Geese of the eastern Canadian arctic. The geese were censused from the air in May 1973 and 1974. They were found to be concentrated in a narrow strip only four to five kilometres (2½–3 miles) wide, but extending along the coast for over 1600 kilometres (1000 miles). An aircraft was flown down the centre of this strip at about 120 metres (400 feet) above the ground. This caused the geese to take to the wing, when they were counted and photographed by observers on either side of the aircraft. The photographs were used as a check not only on the counting but on the simultaneous estimating of the ratio between white and blue phases of the geese. A detailed statistical treatment showed that although the numbers of birds involved totalled over two million, the percentage error was low, and tended towards underestimation.

In Europe, migration concentrations of geese are few but there are localities around the Baltic and North Sea where most if not all of a population of geese can be found at certain times. The Barnacle Geese wintering in the Netherlands and breeding in the western Soviet arctic can be found in spring on the island of Gotland, off Sweden, and on the west coast of Estonia and its islands. Cooperative counts in recent years have provided a useful check on the winter censuses. There is a similar opportunity in autumn, though the distribution is different and more scattered than in the spring.

Counts of geese actually on migration are sometimes possible but their value is limited unless it is known what proportion of a total population they represent. Counts of Dark-bellied Brent Geese migrating past a promontory in south-west Finland, in the early 1950s, were used as an estimate of the total population in the absence of any winter surveys, but it would have been unrealistic to suppose that the whole population had gone past the observation point during the period of watching. The number seen could only be used as a potential minimum figure.

The actual carrying out of a winter geese census depends very much on the known distribution of the birds. Experience built up over a period of years also affects the way the census is done. In Britain, where bird-watching is an extremely popular hobby, there are large numbers of amateur ornithologists who are prepared to devote some of their spare time to carrying out regular organised bird counts. The largest and longest running of these are the monthly wildfowl counts run by the Wildfowl Trust. On the middle Sunday of each month from September to March, nearly a thousand bird-watchers count the numbers of wildfowl on the local wetland. This may be an estuary, in which case a team of counters is usually taking part, a lake, a stretch of river, or a group of gravel pits. These monthly figures are sent on special forms to the headquarters of the Wildfowl Trust where they are analysed for population trends. Geese figure to some extent in these monthly counts, especially Brent Geese which occur in many estuaries and are present during the day. However, the majority of the farmland feeding geese only come to water at night, to roost, and are dispersed over large areas of farmland during the day. These require a somewhat different technique, though amateurs are still involved.

On a set day of the month, or perhaps a weekend, bird-watchers are asked first to locate and then count the geese in their area. This may involve searching considerable areas of farmland for feeding flocks, or, in many localities, can be done by counting the geese as they leave or return to their roost at dawn or dusk. This latter method is often an easier one because the roosts tend to be well known, whereas the feeding area may extend for several kilometres from the roost in any direction. The larger roosts will require two or more people to make sure that each possible flight-line is covered, with care taken to avoid duplication or omissions. On the whole, dawn flights are easier to count than dusk ones. The different species of geese vary their timing of flight in relation to the light, but on the whole they do not leave in the morning before it is light enough to see them, whereas in the evening they will often return to a roost when it has become too dark for accurate counting. This happens especially where the geese have made a long flight from their feeding area. A dawn count has the added advantage that it grows lighter as each minute passes.

In Britain, at least, censusing the largest number of geese, about 160,000 of two different species, can be done in a weekend with the assistance of about 120 bird-watchers. One professional, myself, spends the week before and after the census, driving round some of the main centres of distribution, filling in with counts in under-covered areas, and carrying out the important breeding success sampling, discovering the proportions of young birds in the flocks and the mean brood size (see below).

Since about 1967, there has been a considerable impetus given to cooperative censuses of geese throughout Europe, following the start of international mid-winter wildfowl counts organised by the International Waterfowl Research Bureau. The European Whitefront and the Dark-bellied Brent Goose were already being counted more or less simultaneously in several different countries, thanks entirely to the interest of individual geese enthusiasts, but now some other species have received attention on a wider scale. Many European countries are less fortunate than Britain in the numbers of bird-watchers that they can call upon to help. For this reason one count each winter may be all that is possible, and there are still some countries where even that is not practicable without considerable efforts by the very few available professionals. In such circumstances, it is important that whatever count is possible should be planned to coincide with the simultaneous censuses in other countries.

Censuses of the type described are only effective when all the geese in the population are readily accessible. This will be the case for the great majority of farmland feeding geese but those that live on the coast may not be easy to count, and geese on offshore islands, particularly uninhabited ones, will require a more specialised technique. Aerial surveys have provided the answer to a number of difficult goose counting problems. The best example in Europe is provided by the populations of Barnacle Geese which live on many of the islands liberally sprinkled along the west coasts of Ireland and Scotland. Of the 170–180 islands involved, only a handful are inhabited, and very few are easy to get to, especially in winter. The only practical way of counting the geese throughout their range in a reasonably short time is from the air, using a small light aircraft. The type chosen is a three or four seater, high-wing monoplane, with a pilot and one or two observers. It approaches each island likely to be holding geese at a height of about 150 metres (400 feet) and at the relatively slow speed of 130–160 kph (80–100 mph). This puts the geese to flight whereupon careful manoeuvring by the pilot bunches them for a quick count by the observer. Photographs are also taken of the flocks but are not relied on in themselves, being used for a subsequent check. It is very difficult to ensure that the entire flock has been photographed and as the surveys may have to be carried out in cloudy dull conditions the quality of the pictures is often poor.

Such an aerial survey can cover maybe fifty small islands scattered along perhaps 150 kilometres (90 miles) of coast in a single flight of a few hours, and the entire survey from south-west Ireland to the north coast of Scotland can in theory be done in four days. However, the shortage of suitable airfields, and above all the difficult weather conditions which often prevail on the Atlantic coasts of Britain and Ireland in winter or spring, mean that surveys always take at least a week and have lasted as long as a fortnight. Several days have to be spent waiting around on the airfield for each day spent flying. Such surveys are not annual affairs, largely because of expense.

Aircraft have been used elsewhere in Europe on an irregular basis but they form a regular and indispensable tool of North American waterfowl counters. The size of area to be covered, and the sheer numbers of birds, virtually preclude any other technique, especially for the great winter concentrations on the Pacific and Atlantic coasts and around the Gulf. Routine survey flights are made during the autumn arrival period and again just before or just after the end of the hunting season, so that kills can be estimated and compared with the results of the bag returns.

The Americans and Canadians have done more than the Europeans in the use of photographs to back up their visual counts. There is plenty of evidence that an experienced observer can count flocks of geese with surprising accuracy. His error may increase with increasing flock size but comparisons with photographs can help him correct for this. Sole reliance on photographs is unusual because of the problems mentioned above. A handy aid to counting geese is a hand tally counter, each press of a button registering another digit. The counter decides beforehand what units he will use, whether tens, hundreds or thousands.

Portable tape recorders are often used as an aid to counting, the observer speaking into a hand-held or, better still, throat microphone. They too, like cameras, are not infallible, and the experience of a blank tape after a survey because of a loose connection or imperfectly pressed start button can be devastating. Frequent tests are advisable.

Counting flocks of geese accurately is a matter of practice. Nearly all counters will improve with experience. There is no hard and fast rule for setting about counting a flock, the circumstances will dictate the method to be used. It depends to a large extent on whether you think you will have only the one opportunity to make a count, or whether repeat counts will be possible. Clearly if you are counting from an aircraft, or counting birds flighting out of a roost at dawn, then you must count quickly the first time, because a check is either difficult or impossible. Each flock or skein of geese must be tallied as fast as possible before the next one appears. It is on these occasions that tally counters are both a boon and a curse. They enable one to count rapidly in selected units without taking one's eyes off the geese in order to write. Doing a roost count, for example, provided one is standing a few hundred metres back from the water, most of the geese will be in long straggling lines or in their typical V-formation by the time they are level with you. And with practice you can quickly run your eyes along the line of birds, counting them off in tens and pressing the tally counter button each time. Problems begin when there is a sudden burst of activity at the roost and several hundred or thousand birds lift off together. It is at such moments that one may have to change the units in which you are counting. To do this the total on the counter must be written down, and the instrument preferably wound back to zero. Valuable seconds can be lost doing this and it is therefore as well to start pressing the button in units that will be suitable right through the count, even though one's mental counting may start off in, say, tens, and increase to hundreds as the pace quickens.

If a flock of geese is feeding quietly in a field and shows no signs of moving elsewhere, and disturbance from whatever source seems unlikely, then there is an opportunity for making more than one count. It is as well to make the first count a rapid one, scanning from one side of the flock to the other, blocking it off in whatever units seem appropriate to its size. If it numbers several hundreds, or a few thousands, then the first count is probably best done in hundreds. The first hundred should be counted with some accuracy, if not individually, then in fives or tens. Having assessed the size of that group of geese it is possible to move more rapidly through the rest of the flock, dividing it visually into segments of the same size as the first. With practice this should give a count accurate to within 10%.

Next comes the opportunity for a more detailed and more accurate count. This may take some time, particularly if the flock is a large one, and so it is best to have somewhere to rest the elbows if using binoculars, or to take up a comfortable position with the telescope on a tripod, or resting it on the lowered window of a car. The latter makes an extremely useful hide in areas where there is a good network of roads. Counting then begins from one side of the flock, moving slowly and unhurriedly through it, usually using the unit of ten. This is a number which most people can estimate quickly and accurately when confronted with any mass of individual items, including geese. Counting in fives would be even better, but with a really large flock accuracy has to be balanced against eyestrain and the possibility of losing the place when moving the telescope very slowly through the flock. Once a firm mental image of ten has been formed it is possible to scan steadily across, clicking up the numbers on a tally counter. Flocks of up to 10,000 can be counted in this way without difficulty, and to an accuracy of within 5%, probably better for a really skilled counter. Having scanned the flock from left to right, the observer should now repeat the count in the reverse direction. Depending on the divergence of his two counts, and on the time available, he may wish to repeat it yet again. The divergence will be one measure of the counter's accuracy; a second observer counting the same flock will provide another; photographs a third.

When carrying out extensive winter counts it is often necessary to accept much less accurate standards of counting and even estimates. The weather is the great bugbear, not just the obvious hazards of poor visibility and heavy rain, but high winds which make telescope work nearly impossible. Under such conditions it is a matter of obtaining the best figure possible, even if this is no more than a guess based on the sound of geese passing overhead in a thick fog!

Counting geese, or any other kind of bird, can be taught to some extent by example. Any beginner will benefit from going out with an already experienced counter and comparing counts of the same flocks, but practice is even better—counting a small flock repeatedly until variation between counts is eliminated, then moving position and counting the flock from a different angle. There is a great deal of difference in the skill needed to count a flock that is helpfully and thinly spread, at right angles to the observer, and one that is densely packed. In the latter case, even the small field of view of the telescope encompasses a large number of birds, and in estimating the fives or tens the eye has to count not only from left to right but from front to back.

It is while counting feeding flocks of geese that the best opportunity arises for monitoring the annual production of the geese. It has already been pointed out that for most species of geese the young of the year are distinguishable in the field from the adults, and that geese go around in family parties within the flocks. Careful observations can, therefore, produce figures for the proportion of young birds present in the flocks, and the mean brood size. Although it is possible to obtain this information from the breeding grounds, there are few populations whose nesting areas are visited regularly enough for this method to be effective. Instead, reliance has to be placed on production surveys, as they are called, carried out in the autumn or winter. It can be done earlier in the season on those populations which have recognised migratory rest areas, like the Ross's Geese in mid-western Canada, and those Whitefronts and Lesser Snow Geese which use the same area. Other populations are surveyed in the late autumn or early winter once the geese have reached more southerly wintering grounds. In several species the characters which enable identification of the young bird in the field become more difficult to distinguish as the winter progresses, as outlined in Chapter 2.

The actual technique of assessing goose production from feeding flocks requires experience in identifying young geese from old, good optical equipment such as a high-powered telescope or spotting scope, plus notebook or portable recorder, perhaps supplemented by hand tally counters. It also requires the skill to put oneself within observation range of the geese, and a lot of luck with conditions of light, distance and disturbance. There is nothing more frustrating than to stalk a flock of geese to within a convenient distance, with the sun in the right quarter, only to have a farm tractor come along and shift them.

Scanning a flock, to obtain the percentage of young and the brood sizes, must take into account the already described tendency of family parties, led by the young birds, to work to the front and edges of a feeding flock. A tally of the birds nearest to the observer will always reveal a higher proportion of young than one made through the middle of the flock from front to back. It is necessary to try to eliminate this bias by taking several samples from different parts of each flock. And again no one flock should be taken as representative of the whole population without sufficient sampling over a period of years to discover whether flocks in different parts of the winter range represent a homogeneous whole, or separate and dissimilar segments. In some populations it is known that birds breeding in one area will traditionally winter in a particular locality, largely separate from birds that have bred in an adjacent nesting area. Weather and other factors may produce differences in breeding success between the two groups. Similarly, non-breeding birds in their second year may have a slightly different winter distribution to the older breeding birds.

Counting the sizes of the broods, from which one calculates a mean, is also fraught with problems. In some geese, notably the Canadas, it is very difficult if not impossible to identify the young birds in the field. In others, identification is straightforward but the geese habitually feed in such dense flocks that it is extremely hard to separate family units. This is often true of Barnacle Geese. It is always a relief to deal with a species such as the Whitefront where the young are readily identified and the birds feed in scattered flocks so that it is easy to pick out each family. From all this it will be obvious that assessments of annual production are liable to error. However, they are useful statistics to have, and there is plenty of evidence that with experience the errors can be reduced to an acceptable level.

The technique used for estimating the proportion of young is to scan with the telescope, slowly through the flock, counting each bird seen and clicking up each young bird on the tally counter. When the count has reached one hundred, the number on the tally counter is read off and written down. Although other sample sizes can be used, this size produces a direct percentage and for calculating the limits of error of the final figure it is convenient to have a standard sample size. Brood sizes require more care than counts of young where it matters little whether families are complete or split. For brood counts it is necessary to make sure that each observation refers to an entire family. As the geese feed over a field, a family party may become extended, and only prolonged watching will reveal which young belong to which pair of adults. It is sometimes possible to pick out obvious families while doing the counts of young, in which case the number of young in the family should be noted by an assistant, or recorded on tape. Even when concentrating solely on brood counts, it is usually possible, if working solo and without a recorder, to scan a small part of the flock, memorise the size of the broods seen, up to four or five perhaps, then write them down before returning to the scanning.

The use made of censuses, age counts and brood sizes in the understanding of population dynamics will be dealt with later in the chapter, after outlining the other major technique used for goose population studies, namely ringing or banding.

Geese have been a quarry of man for many centuries, and although the bow and arrow and later the gun have probably been the main weapons for killing geese away from the breeding grounds, one or two ingenious devices for catching them have also been devised. The principal one, which has been adapted for catching for ringing purposes, is the clap net, used for several hundred years in Europe and still surviving in the Netherlands. Simple snares laid on the ground in favoured feeding areas have also been used widely but the clap net was the only method whereby several birds could be taken at once.

The clap nets still in use in the Netherlands are now devoted almost exclusively to catching geese for ringing and release. But this is a comparatively new development and only twenty years ago the majority of the birds caught were killed for the market. The conversion came when the Dutch conservation agency decided to offer the clap-netters the market price for each goose they caught, ringed and released. Several hundred geese have since been ringed each year, sometimes over a thousand. The main species are Whitefront, with over 10,000 now ringed, and Bean Geese, over 5000, with smaller numbers of Barnacle Geese (2000) and a few hundred Pinkfeet.

Each clap net is about 30 metres long and between five and ten metres wide (33 yards by 6–11 yards). Each end is attached to a pole half the width of the net. The pole is free to swing over in an arc with its bottom end attached to a peg fixed in the ground. The nets are set in favoured goose feeding areas, generally in pairs facing each other so that when sprung they meet in the middle. To set them the nets are furled back into as narrow a strip as possible and camouflaged with vegetation. A strong cord runs from each pair of poles to a hide, perhaps a hundred metres away. When the cord is pulled the angle of pull is such that the poles swing over bringing the nets with them and extending them to their fullest size. Heavy springs are used to provide tension in the poles and cords and so speed the rate at which the nets come over. The nets can be operated independently, in which case it is usual to spring the net which has the wind behind it. This not only makes the net come over faster but disturbed geese will tend to take off into wind towards the net rather than away from it. Pulling the two nets together often results in a better catch as the birds in trying to escape from one net may find themselves caught by the other.

To attract wild geese to within the comparatively small catching area of the nets, the Dutch goose catchers use live decoys. They tether one or more tame geese by a light line round the leg, in a position either close to or actually in the catching area. When a party of wild geese flies over, the catchers release another six or eight tame geese from the baskets which they have beside their hide. These include the mates or young of the tethered birds. On release they therefore fly to their relatives and land beside them. Grain is also spread here as extra bait. The wild geese flying over are attracted by the sight of geese landing in the field and circle down to join them. The presence of geese already on the ground shows them that it is safe to land and that there is food available. With luck the wild birds will land straight into the catching area or feed into it following the bait. When the catchers think they have the optimum number in the catching area they heave on the pull cords. Fewer than 20 goose catchers still work their nets in the Netherlands and the practice seems likely to die out in the future. In the meantime it has shown how a former method of killing geese can be used for their scientific study.

Soon after the last war geese researchers in North America and in Europe were independently developing equipment that would catch geese on their wintering grounds. The Dutch clap nets were found to be too small and limited in scope, and something more effective was sought. The wariness of most geese meant that large cages of wire-netting, which are very successful in catching ducks, waders and many smaller birds, could only be used on relatively tame flocks. In the 1930s cages were used for catching Canada Geese at a migratory resting area in Canada. The traps were very large, and took the form of an open-ended tunnel of string netting about two metres tall, three to four metres wide, and up to eight metres long (6 × 10 × 25 feet). The geese were encouraged by baiting to feed inside this structure, which they soon did because it was permanent and in a well-used feeding area. When sufficient geese were feeding inside the netting tunnel, a cord was pulled releasing two horizontal poles balanced above each entrance. Each pole had netting wound round it. As the poles descended the netting unrolled to form doors to the cage. Many thousands of Canada Geese were caught by this means, but it was never used with any success for other more wary geese which would not come close to, let alone go inside, any man–made structure.

The catching nets that were developed instead of cage traps, are like large clap nets which, instead of being thrown over the birds using a pull–cord and spring–loaded poles, are hurled over them by projectiles. The first kind tried out in Britain, in the late 1940s, used small rockets designed for firing life-saving lines to wrecked ships. They were electrically fired from a hide on the edge of the catching field. Two or three rockets were attached to the leading edge of the net which was furled back into a narrow strip and carefully camouflaged. These early attempts were quite successful and spurred the users, the Wildfowl Trust, to have much more powerful rockets designed and made which would throw a really large area of netting. The final apparatus, which has been in use for over 20 years, was constructed with the help of the Army.

The rockets are modified 25-pounder shells and their propellant a small stick of cordite which is fired electrically via an igniter. Six rockets are spaced down the leading edge of each net which is roughly 55 metres long by 18 metres wide (60 × 20 yards). Two nets are generally used, most often facing each other so that they meet like clap-nets when fully extended, but occasionally end to end. The nets have to be perfectly camouflaged, a simple job on a stubble field, much harder when catching on short grass. The back edge of the net is pegged to the ground via rubber shock absorbers to stop the whole thing taking off when fired. The rockets are placed on ramps set at 45° in holes dug into the ground until their tops are flush. They too are camouflaged. The electric cable is run back to a convenient place of concealment, which can be several hundred metres away if necessary. Although the chosen site will be in regular use by the geese, they can be encouraged by skilful placing of stuffed decoys and the use of grain as bait. Live decoys are not permitted in Britain. If the birds land in the right field but not in the catching area they can sometimes be induced to walk and feed towards the site by someone very carefully showing themselves in such a way that they move away in the right direction. Good judgement is required so that the birds are disturbed enough to walk away but not so much that they take off.

Although the description may make it seem straightforward, the actual catching of the geese is often a long drawn out and extremely tense affair, because one is dealing with very wary birds, prepared to lift off at the slightest sign of something wrong—a cable left uncovered, the wind moving one of the decoys, a passing tractor, a low-flying aircraft, or a bird of prey. Any or all of these things can frustrate a day's catching attempt. After a week of this the tension as the moment of pressing the firing button draws close can be almost unbearable. It is not surprising that for many people catching geese for ringing provides ample satisfaction of the hunting instinct that might otherwise be diverted into trying to shoot them.

The rocket-nets in use in Britain have caught nearly 20,000 geese over the years, not to mention many thousands of waders and other birds. The largest single catch of geese was 490, and there have been several catches of over 300. Over 2000 waders have also been caught at once. Parallel with the developments in Britain was the invention of the cannon-net in North America. This works on a slightly different firing principle to the rocket-nets, though the end result, a net flung over feeding geese, is the same. A rocket carries its fuel on board and so the projectile is quite large and heavy. On the other hand it is very powerful and can pull out up to 20 metres of small mesh netting. A cannon-net works on the mortar principle where a charge is fired under a projectile at the bottom of a barrel, shooting it into the air. In this case the projectile is a cast-iron weight attached to the leading edge of the net. Its power is less than that of a rocket, but so is its size and weight, making for better portability. The most efficient cannon-powered nets are 12 to 15 metres wide (13–16 yards) but are usually of larger mesh than rocket-nets, to reduce the weight. Larger mesh increases tangling of the geese in the netting and makes the job of extracting them longer and more difficult. Both types of net have pocket flaps along the edges to stop any geese from walking out from under the net and escaping.

Although cannon-nets are quite large, the catch of geese increases out of proportion to the width of the netting so that the extra three metres or so of width of the rocket-nets may mean double the catch. This is especially true when the two nets are fired towards each other. The small size of the cannon-nets can, however, be a positive advantage not only because of lightness but for use in confined sites, such as loafing areas on the shores of roosting lakes, and the narrow high-tide strip of dry land where significant numbers of Brent Geese have been caught. In such places the extra width of the rocket-net would be an embarrassment. Most cannon-nets are about 27 metres long (30 yards) and are propelled by three cannons. The two Wildfowl Trust's rocket-nets have remained unique, but cannon nets are widely used in Britain and Europe, and especially in North America where many tens of thousands of geese have been caught. Some of the most successful catching is made at permanent sites which are heavily baited and operated through the winter.

Another method of catching geese originally used by native hunters, and now a much-used technique by goose ringers, is the rounding-up of flightless birds in the summer. The simultaneous moult of all the wing feathers towards the end of the breeding season means that neither the adults nor their as yet unfledged goslings can fly until the new feathers grow. During that time they can only run and swim. Eskimos in Canada and Greenland, and the natives of Siberia, recognised that this was an opportunity to catch the geese and store the bodies for use in the winter. Although it is possible to run down an individual goose, especially with a dog, it is much more efficient to catch a large number together, and it is then a question of guiding a flock of geese into a position from which they cannot escape. Modern goose catchers use corrals of netting but the Eskimos originally made do with interlaced branches of willow, birch and heather. In a few places, U-shaped stone structures have been found. These were permanent corrals and similar ones have been found in the Pinkfoot breeding colony in central Iceland. Their age is not known nor whether they were independently invented by the Icelanders or learnt by them from the Greenland Eskimos.

As a technique for catching geese for ringing, rounding-up of flightless birds was used independently in Iceland in 1951 and 1953, and in arctic Canada in 1952 and the years following. In Iceland the method was worked out by a small party of British and Icelandic ornithologists after they had spent frustrating days running down individual Pink-footed Geese and their goslings, using ponies and hand-nets. The numbers caught were not commensurate with the effort expended. The break-through came when they took advantage of the bunching of the pursued geese and also their tendency to make for the top of one of the low gravel hills in the breeding area. A pen of netting about a metre high (3–4 feet) was erected on stakes on a hill and a flock of geese driven into it. The first catch made in this way numbered 250, compared with the tens and twenties caught per day by the previous method. Two years later a larger team returning to the same Pinkfoot colony made several round-ups, the largest of which caught over 3100 birds. The catchers, on horseback, surrounded a large area of marsh, with a suitable catching hill roughly in the centre; then, on a prearranged signal, slowly closed in, driving the geese before them. With sufficient people it was possible to carry out the drive, and then while holding the birds on the top of the hill, erect the pen of netting nearby and gently herd the flock into it. This had two considerable advantages. Firstly, it meant that there was no need to go onto the selected catching hill before the drive in order to erect the pen and thus alert the geese in the vicinity that people were about. Secondly, because the final drive into the nets could be closely controlled, a much smaller amount of netting was needed. The wings of netting which guided the geese into the corral could be reduced from perhaps 100 metres to 20 or 30.

In Canada the technique of rounding-up flightless geese for ringing was first used on Southampton Island in the north of Hudson Bay, and the species was the Lesser Snow Goose. Here a biologist made use of knowledge of the method still held by one or two of the older Eskimos on the island. They had not practiced it for a great many years but were able to remember how it was done. As with the Pinkfeet, the Snow Geese bunched tightly when surrounded and the flock could be guided quite accurately towards the catching pen. The Eskimos had not the benefit of horses as used in Iceland and their method was therefore slightly different as it had to take into account the slower speed of the catchers relative to the geese. A running goose can easily outpace a running man, and in addition a running flock tends to break up and scatter, so all efforts must be directed to keeping the birds unpanicked, so that they merely walk and stick close together.

The first stage of this method was for a group of catchers to walk slowly past a feeding area where large numbers of geese were known to be. They kept at such a distance that the geese, sensing their presence, walked slowly away and were not scared into running. The catchers gradually encircled the geese, leaving one of their number at intervals to block the retreat in that direction. In due course the geese found themselves surrounded, whereupon they gathered in a bunch, milling around. The catchers might have had to run sometimes to head the geese if they looked like escaping through a gap in the circle but they were always careful to run across the line of the geese and not towards them, so that this would merely turn them in another direction, not send them rushing away. Because transport was lacking it was found easier to take the geese to the pen rather than the other way round. It was also important to have the geese under control as early as possible, rather than advancing over an area in the hope that the geese would move towards and into the catching pen of their own accord.

When the geese had been safely encircled, the catchers closed in on them, all except one, who turned his back on them and walked steadily away towards the pen. The geese, pressed behind and from both sides, and seeing this retreating figure, followed him. One drive on Southampton Island involved walking the geese as much as fourteen kilometres (9 miles), but the Eskimos told of drives lasting several days, until the flock reached the stone corral which had been erected near the camp. The geese and men rested when they got tired. Of course the end result of those drives was meat for the Eskimos; there was no need to consider the well-being of the geese, it was akin to driving cattle to the slaughter. The goose ringing drives on Southampton

Island in the early 1950s resulted in catches of up to 3700, and several in excess of 1000. On two occasions over 15,000 geese were actually surrounded but this was unintentional and far too many for the team to handle, so the majority were allowed to escape.

Since these pioneer goose round-ups the technique has been used widely both in the arctic and further south, indeed it can be used on any flightless geese. In 1955 it was used for the first time in East Greenland when about 300 Barnacle Geese were caught in a series of drives. The drives were repeated with even more success in 1961 and 1963. A slight modification of the technique was adopted on a number of occasions, when it was found that the geese often moved onto the nearest water when disturbed. The encircling movement of the catchers was therefore centred on a convenient small lake, in the same way that a hill was the objective in Iceland. As the catchers closed in the geese were driven from the surrounding marshland onto the lake. Then, while most of the team held the geese on the water, one or two members would erect the pen at one end of the lake. The subsequent drive required boats, unless the water was shallow enough to wade. Two light canoes or inflatable dinghies could be used to drive the geese off the water and into the pen. This method is a little more difficult than a drive confined to dry land but no less successful if carried out carefully. The geese may be likened to a flock of aquatic sheep.

In Svalbard (Spitsbergen), too, Barnacle Geese have been caught and ringed. Several of the catches have been on small offshore islands, but again the geese were first driven onto a small lake, then into the pen. If, as happened on some occasions, the geese were not successfully surrounded on the island, but escaped to the sea, it was found possible to bring them back again by very gently herding them with a boat, powered by an outboard. Just one boat, manoeuvring back and forth behind the geese, could head the flock in the required direction without much trouble. A landing beach was selected close to the chosen pool of water around which the rest of the catchers were concealed, ready to show themselves as soon as the geese came onto the water.

Rounding-up geese has probably reached its ultimate refinement in arctic Canada in the last few years. This has come about with the advent of the helicopter as a regular means of transport for biologists studying the geese. Instead of a long often arduous walk by the catchers, first to surround the birds, then drive them to the pen (an operation that can be done by as few as four or five people but ideally requires a minimum of six or seven), the hard work is all done by the helicopter. The biologists erect a pen in a convenient site near the camp, or not too far from a known concentration of geese, and then conceal themselves beside it. The helicopter pilot takes his machine on a low sweep across the goose feeding area, gently herding the birds in the right direction. This aerial sheep-dog can accomplish with comparative ease what it might take several men many hours to achieve. Skilful piloting can bring a flock of a thousand or more geese right up to the pen, then into it, aided by the well-rested biologists. Not only is there a considerable saving of time and effort but the number of people required is reduced so that there is no need to keep a large team in the field with all the attendant expense. Helicopters are not cheap, of course, but as they are essential for transport it is sensible to make additional use of them in this way.

Although geese round-ups were pioneered in the arctic, they can be carried out just as well on Canada Geese breeding in the temperate United States or Britain. Here the birds are nearly always close to water, large lakes, reservoirs or rivers, and it is merely a question of erecting a pen in a suitable site close to the water's edge, then driving the birds with two or more boats. On the small gravel pits of southern England this is comparatively easy, but on the larger reservoirs, particularly those on which boats are not normally allowed, the geese can be as wary as their arctic counterparts, if not more so, and the driving requires just as much skill.

There is only one species of goose which does not readily allow itself to be caught in this way. Whereas other geese will bunch when scared, then permit themselves to be herded towards and into a catching pen, Greylags show a fierce independence of spirit which makes them extremely difficult to catch. The first step of surrounding a flock, which then moves quickly onto the nearest stretch of water, is no different from other species, but the subsequent driving of the birds into a pen is quite the reverse and often impossible. As the boats press the birds closer to the shore and the waiting pen, the flock begins to spread out instead of bunching like other geese, until the boats find it impossible to keep all the birds moving in the required direction. Geese begin to slip away from the flock at either end, or at the middle if the boats rush to the sides to try to bunch the geese again. As pressure increases, the geese begin to scatter and dive, each goose for itself, with no regard for the apparent protection of being in a flock as favoured by other species. Time and again I have taken part in round-ups of Greylags, organised as for catches of other species and carried out with no less skill and care, but instead of a compact flock of geese swimming over the water, onto the shore and up the bank into the catching pen, one sees with sinking heart the gradual but inexorable dispersal of the birds, their refusal to approach within twenty or so metres of the shore, and the final debacle as they begin diving or threshing over the water to escape the encircling boats. A few birds may land in their panic, and even inadvertently find themselves in the pen, but one is lucky if these number a tenth of the original flock.

The only successful round-ups of Greylags that I am aware of have been in circumstances where the geese were not driven where they did not want to go. Some catches have taken place on lakes in Scotland where the catching pen was concealed in thick vegetation on a small island in the middle of the lake. The geese were used to landing on the island and obviously regarded it as perfectly safe. They were driven by boats, persuaded to land on the island, then as they ran across the island to the water on the other side, found themselves up against a netting fence which guided them into a pen. Similarly, in Denmark, moulting Greylags have been driven through the thick reeds and rushes of the marsh in which they were feeding, into a line of netting erected across their path. The netting was not visible until they were actually up to it, and they were also used to feeding throughout the marshland. Although the Greylags which would not let themselves be driven ashore may have been used to feeding on the areas where the pen has been set

up, and the pen itself out of sight whilst they were on the water, it seems that they have a major resistance to being driven into areas from which they know they have no escape route back to the water. Even this is not the full story, because flocks have refused to land on a low sand spit separating two parts of the same lake, yet they must have been used to walking or running over it. The contrast with, say, Barnacle Geese, which can be held on a pond while a pen is put up in full view and then be driven into it without trouble, is very great.

Two other methods of catching Greylags have been adopted with some success, each suited to the particular circumstances in which they were living. The first is closely akin to a round-up and takes place in some of the parks of Copenhagen where more or less wild Greylags breed. Here they are accustomed to seeing people, including many on bicycles, though without becoming very tame. The catchers wait until a suitable flock of birds is feeding on grass adjacent to one of the park lakes, then they cycle between the geese and the water. They pay out a net, erect it, and catch the geese as they run back to the water. The second method was used off the coast of Norway where Greylags live on some of the offshore islands. In the absence of suitable ponds or lakes on the islands, and finding in any case that the geese retreated to the sea when disturbed, the biologist wishing to ring them pursued the birds individually by boat. He used a small fishing boat which could go much faster than the geese, and though the latter dived when the boat got too close, they could be scooped out of the water with a hand-net. Most geese, particularly when flightless, are good divers and can stay under for up to 40 seconds, during which time they may travel as much as 30 metres.

These two methods apart, it does seem that Greylags have an inbuilt aversion to being herded and driven. Whereas other geese do not seem able to escape from such situations if the goose catchers exercise a certain level of skill and care, Greylags have a well-developed instinct and ability to elude capture. It is tempting to link this with their southerly distribution in the well-populated lands of central and north-west Europe. Although egg-collecting and over-hunting by man has greatly reduced the numbers of breeding Greylags in many areas, particularly southern U.S.S.R., there is no doubt that some special ability has allowed them to survive in close proximity to people over the centuries. Perhaps it is this marked escape reaction when flightless.

Although round-ups of most species of geese have proved very successful there are some dangers associated with them. When the birds are flightless they select an area which has sufficient food to last them until they can fly again, and where they can find a safe refuge, usually an area of water. If this sanctuary is invaded by a team of catchers, and the safety of the water proved illusory, the geese may be deterred from using that area again. A single catch in one year is unlikely to produce this reaction, but catching in successive years has been shown to disturb the geese so much that they desert the area altogether. This is more likely with a flock of non-breeding geese which has moved into an area for the moult, than with breeding birds with their much stronger attachment to the nesting grounds. Non-breeding Canada Geese in the Northwest Territories of Canada shifted their moulting grounds after successive years of catching and clearly a careful balance must be struck between the requirement for marking the birds, and their well-being.

The catching methods for geese have evolved and become more efficient over the years and so have the rings used in marking them. Other forms of marking have been introduced for specific purposes. The earliest rings were of aluminium, a metal that was easy to stamp with a number and address, and to shape into the form of a ring. However, the softness of the ring also meant that it wore easily and became indecipherable after a few years, with the added risk that the ring might fall off altogether. Harder metals were tried until the present alloy, monel, a mixture of nickel and copper, was introduced. Being much harder it requires more sophisticated equipment to stamp it, and also a pair of pliers to close it round the goose's leg. However, once on, there is a fair chance it will last the life of the goose.

Metal rings are necessarily small and the numbers stamped on them smaller still. One can sometimes see that a bird in the field is ringed but further identification is rarely possible without catching the goose or shooting it. A few experiments have been made with larger metal rings bearing larger numbers, but there were various practical problems and it was not pursued with. A less usual use for large metal rings was by the famous Jack Miner in

Canada who made room on the ring for a short Biblical text. He hoped that when the geese, all Canadas, were shot, the hunter, often an illiterate Indian or trapper, would take the ring to the nearest person who could read it for him, hopefully a missionary who would then take the opportunity of trying a little conversion.

Workers wishing to follow the birds' movements more closely first tried coloured rings of metal or plastic with varying success, also coloured dyes applied to the paler parts of the plumage, particularly the white tail coverts. These enabled the identification of groups of birds, perhaps all those of a certain age or caught at the same locality, but there are too few colours for the method to be used for identification of individual geese. Dyes are only satisfactory for short-term studies as most will not survive more than a few months of bleaching or washing. Those that do will disappear with the feathers at the next moult. Other forms of marking have now been developed which will take large contrasting letters or symbols which can be read at a distance. They take one of three forms: large leg rings, neck collars, and nasal saddles or discs.

The last named were actually developed for ducks, and although used with some success on Canada Geese are really only suitable for close range identification, at less than 100 metres. They are made of plastic, either a bent strip (the saddle) or two circular discs, and are fastened to the goose's bill by a thin wire passed through the nostrils in the upper mandible. They appear not to cause any harm or discomfort to the birds, but they certainly look unsightly, and there have been some problems with ice forming on them in very cold weather. Their use has been confined to a few small-scale studies of Canada Geese in North America.

Early neck collars were a simple strip of plastic fastened round the neck but now they are usually 5·0–7·5 cm (2–3 in) broad, of metal or plastic, on which are painted or engraved large numbers or letters. The letters are visible through a telescope at a range of 300 metres or more, and, more important, regardless of whether the goose is on land or water. The collars must be loose enough to be able to slide up and down outside the feathers but not so loose that the bird can get its bill stuck inside. The free movement means that the bird can still preen its whole neck satisfactorily. Such collars have been used mainly on Canada Geese and Lesser Snow Geese, and more recently on

Brent Geese, and have provided detailed information on the behaviour and movements of individuals, the inter-relationships of families and groups of geese, their individual breeding performance and faithfulness to each other and to their breeding and wintering haunts. They do have some drawbacks, particularly the extent to which they may interfere with the natural life and behaviour of the geese. There is much evidence that such interference is either very slight or non-existent but there are a number of observations which suggest that in some circumstances it does occur. The most serious of these indicates a slight reduction in the chances of a collared bird finding a mate, and an increased mortality in times of maximum stress, as for example nesting females in a cold summer. Collars are also prone to icing which can be fatal. However, so far, the information gained from their use seems worth the potential risks imposed.

In Britain, where collars are thought to be unacceptable to the general public, an alternative marking method has been an enlarged leg ring, of a laminated plastic, with a colour, such as yellow or white, over a layer of black. The yellow is engraved away in the shape of numbers or letters, which can be up to 2·5 cm (1 in) high on a ring to fit a Greylag or a Canada Goose, slightly smaller to fit a Brent Goose or a Barnacle. These can be read in good conditions at distances of up to 300 metres, but not of course when the birds are on water or feeding in long vegetation. They are ideally suited to birds which feed on short grass meadow, such as the Barnacle. Their effectiveness can be gauged from the fact that over 90% of 350 Barnacle Geese ringed in Svalbard one summer were identified on their wintering grounds in Scotland the following winter. In another project a similar proportion of some 600 Canada Geese were seen in the winter after ringing.

When geese are caught for ringing it is usual to make a number of checks and measurements. The bird in the hand is an opportunity for accurate ageing and sexing, as described in Chapter 2. It is also usual to weigh and measure them, an operation otherwise only possible on dead birds. The value of such information will already have been apparent from its mention in earlier chapters when considering the division of geese into subspecies, the amount geese eat in relation to their weight, and variations in weight through the year and in the periods of stress such as egg-laying and incubation, the annual moult, and migration. Other checks which may be made on birds in the hand include X-raying to assess the proportion carrying shot, a measure both of shooting pressure and of the ratio of killed to injured geese, and the taking of throat swabs or blood samples in the study of diseases.

When a ringed bird is reported as shot or retrapped one discovers the distance and direction it has moved between ringing and recovery and the time elapsed. If only a few birds are recovered some simple facts are obtained relating to the movements of these particular individuals, the time they have taken to move, and a minimum indication of the age to which they can live. It is only when comparatively large numbers are ringed and then recovered that a realistic picture can be built up that can be assumed to relate to the population as a whole. Some of the information to be gathered from ringing is complementary to that obtained by censusing and age counting. The combination of the two techniques should be the ultimate aim of the comprehensive study.

Counting the proportions of young birds in flocks of geese has been discussed earlier in this chapter. Another way of discovering this ratio is from the samples of birds caught for ringing. However, just as there are biases in the counts of feeding flocks, depending on the location of the sample within the flock, so a rocket-netted or cannon-netted flock of geese may not be representative of the whole population. For example, one tends to fire the nets as soon as sufficient birds have entered the catching area, and if the geese have fed their way there, the leading birds will, as earlier stated, consist of a higher than average proportion of family parties, and the non-breeding birds will be further back in the flock. Regularly baited sites, used for cannon-netting, also produce unrepresentative age ratio samples, with the proportion of adult birds increasing the longer the flock remains on the bait before the nets are fired. This again reflects the fact that family parties are the first to arrive.

The proportion of young birds present in autumn and winter flocks reflects the breeding success of the population the previous summer. Chapter 4 showed how conditions on the breeding grounds could affect the number of young produced each year, even to the extent of preventing the laying of eggs altogether. These failures and their corresponding successes naturally have a marked effect on the size of the population. The majority of the populations of geese, at least in North America and Europe, are harvested through shooting, and at the same time protected from over-exploitation through controls on that shooting and by the provision of protected areas. Successful management of the stocks depends on adequate knowledge of the annual breeding performance and the ability to predict its effect on numbers. In North America, management is by regulated shooting seasons and bag limits in response to annual production counts. Notification of a complete breeding failure can lead to a ban on shooting for the following autumn season. Successive good years may lead to a longer season or larger bag limits. Such sophistication is not yet practised in Europe but longer-term trends in annual reproduction are used here, as also in North America, to predict future changes in total numbers. These in turn will affect decisions on conservation and management practices.

A simple example will demonstrate how the percentage figures of young and mean brood size can be used to discover more about the make up of a goose population, and more about how many birds are breeding and how many dying each year. The addition of knowledge from ringing will provide further relevant data and reinforce some of the results from counting.

We will start with a hypothetical population of 100,000 geese. It was counted during an autumn census before the opening of the shooting season. Production surveys revealed that the percentage of young was 40, and the average brood size 3·2. This means that 40% of 100,000, or 40,000, were young birds, the remaining 60,000 being older birds. Records of percentages in the previous years would enable us to estimate the number of two-year-olds, three-year-olds, etc, in this 60,000, particularly if the population had been extensively ringed. But supposing this was the first year of work on this population; we would have to be content with knowing how many birds were successful parents. This figure is found by dividing the number of young birds by the mean brood size, which gives the total number of families present, 12,500. Taking a figure of two parents to each family (it will actually drop slightly through the winter due to shooting and other mortality), we can state that 25,000 geese were successful parents that year, or about two-fifths of the total 60,000. We have to assume that the remaining 35,000 were either too young to breed, too old, or that they may have attempted it but lost all their eggs or young before the autumn count. Losses can of course occur at various stages in the breeding cycle; eggs and small young to predators or bad weather; older young to starvation; and the latter perhaps failing to complete their first long migration. There is also a component in many goose populations which apparently does not attempt to breed, although they are mature birds.

The reasons for non-breeding by apparently mature geese are not properly understood but are probably related to the condition of the birds in spring, with some females not reaching a high enough weight to enable them to breed. The two mature non-breeding segments of the population, those that have lost their eggs or young, and those that never even start breeding, are the hardest to measure as well as the most interesting, potentially. Only extensive, and expensive summer surveys can help to quantify them and so far no combination of summer surveys with really good winter censuses and production surveys has yet been achieved. Ideally the surveys should be done on a small, closed population with well-defined breeding and wintering ranges.

For some geese populations it is possible to carry out a mid-winter or late winter census which will provide a measure of the losses through the season. These will be mainly from shooting, in all but completely protected populations. Additionally, in North America at least, there are hunters' returns from which to assess the winter's kill. The shooting kill varies greatly from population to population but can be as high as 40% of the total autumn stock. Going back to our imaginary population we will suppose that there was a census held after the end of the shooting season and that the total had fallen to 85,000. The 15,000 birds lost would nearly all have been shot, representing a total mortality of 15%.

The following autumn another census is carried out. On this occasion it is found that the population has dropped further to only 70,000, while there are virtually no young birds at all; there has been a complete breeding failure. Reports from the breeding grounds of a very cold, late spring warned of this likelihood. The further fall in numbers, because there has been no recruitment, represents more deaths, in this case an unusually large number, a further 15,000, which have died since the mid-winter census. The two main possibilities for death outside the shooting season would be starvation during very hard weather in the remainder of the winter, or losses on the nesting grounds, associated in this case with the very late spring and total breeding failure. The total losses between the two autumn censuses held so far come to 30,000, or 30% of the original count of 100,000. This percentage is termed the annual mortality rate.

In the second winter of our imaginary series of counts the population drops to a mid-winter total of 60,000. The shooting losses this year are only 10,000 compared with the previous winter's 15,000. This could be because of a reduced season or bag-limit imposed following the breeding failure, but would be quite likely to happen in any case. Young geese, and their accompanying parents, are easier to shoot and suffer higher mortality than non-breeding birds. This is partly because they are more naive and easier to approach, and partly because as already explained family parties of geese are usually to be found at the fronts of flocks, and will often be the nearest birds to the shooter.

Finally, to complete this example we have a third autumn census following another breeding season. This time the geese have bred rather well, though not as successfully as in the first season. The total count comes to 85,000 and the mean percentage of young is 35%, equal to about 30,000 young birds. The older geese therefore total 55,000. These are the birds which have survived from the 60,000 alive at the end of the previous winter. The drop of 5000 is much smaller than the late winter and summer losses of the year before, and the total losses since the last autumn census come to 15,000, or 21·5%, a lower annual mortality rate than in the first year.

A further difference this year is that the mean brood size is quite low at only 1·5. However, when divided between the number of young birds, 30,000, it shows that in fact there are 20,000 families and therefore 40,000 parents. Thus, in a situation where the breeding success is slightly down on the first year, both the number and particularly the proportion of successful parents are up: 40,000 as a percentage of the 55,000 older geese = 72·7%. Rather more birds have managed to breed in this summer though with a lower overall success per pair. This is in part a reflection of the absence of any one-year-old birds in the non-breeding segment of the population because of the complete breeding failure the year before.

The permutations of breeding success and mean brood size are almost

TABLE 8: *Census and productivity data for an imaginary goose population (see text)*

(a) COUNTS, BREEDING SUCCESS, AND MORTALITY

Period	Total	% young	Total of young	Total of adults	Losses	% mortality
1st autumn	100,000	40·0	40,000	60,000	—	—
1st winter	85,000				15,000	
2nd autumn	70,000	0·0	0	70,000	15,000	30·0/annum
2nd winter	60,000				10,000	
3rd autumn	85,000	35·0	30,000	55,000	5,000	21·5/annum

(b) FAMILY SIZE AND PROPORTIONS OF BREEDERS

Period	Total of young	Brood size	No. of families	Successful parents No.	% of adults	Non-breeders No.	% of adults
1st year	40,000	3·2	12,500	25,000	58·3	35,000	41·7
2nd year	0	0	0	0	0	70,000	100·0
3rd year	30,000	1·5	20,000	40,000	72·7	15,000	27·3

infinite, and each population of geese studied behaves in a slightly different fashion from any other. But I hope the example will serve to show how the more important calculations are carried out. The detailed figures are set out in Table 8. The upper part displays the total counts, percentages and numbers of young birds, number of adults, and the losses, in total and as a percentage. The lower part sets out the breeding success details, showing the numbers and proportions of breeders and non-breeders.

I have taken as an example a mythical goose population which showed wide fluctuations in its annual breeding success, more especially one which sometimes suffered a complete breeding failure. In fact this occurs in only a minority of geese populations, most often in the Light-bellied Brent breeding in arctic Canada and Greenland, and in the Dark-bellied Brent breeding in

TABLE 9: *Census and productivity data for the Icelandic Pink-footed Goose, 1950–76*

(a) COUNTS, BREEDING SUCCESS AND MORTALITY

Winter	Total	% young	Total of young	Total of adults	Losses since previous year	% mortality
1950–1	29,850	48·8	14,570	15,280		
1951–2	34,240	24·9	8,530	25,710	4,140	13·8
1952–3	35,560	23·4	8,320	27,240	7,000	20·4
1953–4	32,490	33·3	10,820	21,670	13,890	39·0
1954–5	36,880	34·9	12,870	24,010	8,480	26·1
1955–6	42,140	17·0	7,160	34,980	1,900	5·1
1956–7	49,610	18·4	9,130	40,480	1,660	3·9
1957–8	36,440	33·6	12,240	24,200	25,410	51·2
1958–9	54,170	25·9	14,030	40,140	(−3,700)	(−10·1)
1959–60	54,210	20·0	10,840	43,370	10,800	19·9
1960–1	57,290	27·6	15,810	41,480	12,730	23·4
1961–2	59,110	37·4	22,110	37,000	20,290	35·4
1962–3	55,980	20·9	11,700	44,280	14,830	25·0
1963–4	56,950	20·2	11,500	45,450	10,530	18·8
1964–5	65,380	26·6	17,390	47,990	8,960	15·7
1965–6	69,140	21·0	14,520	54,620	10,760	16·4
1966–7	76,260	21·6	16,470	59,790	9,350	13·5
1967–8	65,720	10·8	7,100	58,620	17,640	23·1
1968–9	64,920	11·7	7,600	57,320	8,400	12·7
1969–70	73,800	24·4	18,000	55,800	9,120	14·0
1970–1	71,900	23·1	16,600	55,300	18,500	25·1
1971–2	65,000	22·2	14,400	50,600	21,300	29·6
1972–3	72,800	11·4	8,300	64,500	500	0·8
1973–4	82,400	30·5	25,100	57,300	15,500	21·3
1974–5	89,100	17·6	15,700	73,400	9,000	11·0
1975–6	73,200	5·6	4,100	69,100	20,000	22·4
1976–7	71,090	11·3	8,033	63,057	10,033	13·7

Note: 'Adults' is used here to indicate birds one year old or older.

Siberia. The Greater Snow Goose, too, has occasional complete failures and, like the others, breeds in the very far north where conditions are potentially the most severe, whether as late springs or as freak storms during the incubation or fledging periods. Other populations of other species of geese may have very poor breeding seasons, with less than 10% young, sometimes less than 5%, but complete failures are very rare, both because they are breeding further south and because in many cases their range is so great that adverse conditions are unlikely to affect the entire population. A failure in one area may be at least partly counter-balanced by moderate success elsewhere. For example, the Whitefronts of North America have two main populations, based on the Pacific and Central Flyways. Both populations have extensive ranges, with significant proportions in the low arctic where extreme weather

TABLE 9 *(continued)*

(b) FAMILY SIZE AND PROPORTIONS OF BREEDERS AND NON-BREEDERS

Winter	Total of young	Brood size	No. of families	Successful parents		Non-breeders	
				No.	% of adults	No.	% of adults
1950–1	14,570	2·95	4,940	9,880	64·7	5,400	35·3
1951–2	8,530	2·50	3,410	7,820	30·4	17,890	69·6
1952–3	8,320	3·13	2,668	5,320	19·5	21,920	80·5
1953–4	10,820	2·75	3,930	7,860	36·1	13,810	63·9
1954–5·	12,870	3·75	3,430	6,860	28·6	17,150	71·4
1955–6	7,160	2·80	2,560	5,120	14·6	29,860	85·4
1956–7	9,130	2·75	3,320	6,640	16·4	33,840	83·6
1957–8	12,240	2·91	4,210	8,420	34·8	15,780	65·2
1958–9	14,030	2·25	6,240	12,480	31·1	27,660	68·9
1959–60	10,840	3·25	3,340	6,680	15·4	36,690	84·6
1960–1	15,810	2·74	5,770	11,540	27·8	29,940	72·2
1961–2	22,110	2·75	9,940	18,980	51·3	18,020	48·7
1962–3	11,700	2·21	5,290	10,580	23·9	33,700	76·1
1963–4	11,500	4·00	2,880	5,760	12·7	39,690	87·3
1964–5	17,390	2·79	6,230	12,460	26·0	35,530	74·0
1965–6	14,520	2·57	5,650	11,300	20·7	43,320	79·3
1966–7	16,470	2·36	6,980	13,960	23·3	45,830	76·7
1967–8	7,100	1·30	5,460	10,920	18·6	47,700	81·4
1968–9	7,600	1·39	5,470	10,940	19·1	46,380	80·9
1969–70	18,000	2·14	8,410	16,820	30·1	38,980	69·9
1970–1	16,600	2·18	7,610	15,220	27·5	40,080	72·5
1971–2	14,400	1·87	7,700	15,400	30·4	35,200	69·6
1972–3	8,300	1·67	4,970	9,940	15·4	54,560	84·6
1973–4	25,100	2·35	10,680	21,360	37·3	35,940	62·7
1974–5	15,700	2·16	7,270	14,540	19·8	58,860	80·2
1975–6	4,100	1·43	2,870	5,740	8·3	63,360	91·7
1976–7	8,033	1·92	4,184	8,368	13·3	54,689	86·7

Note: 'Adults' is used here to indicate birds one year old or older.

Based on Boyd & Ogilvie (1969) and Ogilvie & Boyd (1976).

is less usual than further north. This is reflected in their annual breeding success, which in the period 1956–1976 has varied from 28·2–42·4%, with a mean brood size from 1·81–2·52 for the birds of the Pacific Flyway, and 19·7–49·7% and 2·04–2·92 mean brood size for the birds of the Central Flyway. On the other hand the population of White-fronted Geese which breeds in north-west arctic Russia and winters in north-west Europe has a more restricted breeding range than either of the others, and also extends further north into the high arctic. Over the years 1946–1975, the proportion of young varied between 8·0–45·2% with a mean brood size of 1·9–2·9.

Fuller details of the annual breeding success of the different geese populations will be given in the accounts in the next chapter. For the purpose of further illustrating the subject of population dynamics I have selected two real-life examples, one of a low-arctic breeding population, the other from the high arctic.

Table 9 sets out the census and productivity data for the population of Pink-footed Geese breeding in Iceland and wintering in Britain. It is a particularly long run of data going back to 1950. My excuse for presenting it in full is that a close study of the figures will tell more about the workings of a geese population than any number of made-up examples. As with Table 8, the first part sets out the population total, the percentage young and mortality calculations, and the second displays the information concerning the number of breeding and non-breeding birds. This is one of the longest and most complete records available for any population of geese. Although there are longer series of counts available, for example, the Black Brant and Light-bellied Brent of North America, these lack production figures and particularly brood counts for the earlier years. The comprehensive inventories and production counts of most North American populations did not appear until the mid-1950s, and for some European populations they are much more recent.

It can be seen from the Table that the Pinkfoot is never subject to complete breeding failures, but some very good years do occur from time to time. The population has been growing steadily over the 25-year period. This has been more the result of a declining mortality rate than because of any improvement in the average breeding success. The latter has in fact also declined, if one compares the average for the later years with that for the earlier ones. This reduction in average breeding success can be linked with a marked increase in the proportion of mature but non-breeding birds, though the reasons for this remain obscure. The declining mortality rate is easier to explain. There has been increased protection for this population over the years through the creation of reserves covering many of the important roosts. There has also been a drop in shooting pressure, largely because a change in habits has taken the geese from roosts on coastal estuaries, where shooting is heavy, to inland reservoirs and lakes where shooting is carefully controlled if allowed at all.

In the last few years the population has ceased its steady upward climb. It took a considerable tumble in 1975 following a particularly bad breeding season; bad by Pinkfoot standards, that is, though still not a complete failure. Predictions for future trends based on recent counts and breeding performance suggest that any further growth will be slow compared with the past as recruitment and mortality come closer to balancing each other. The mortality figures show one anomaly, in 1957, when there was an apparent negative mortality. This probably arose through a counting error, either in the total or in the estimate of breeding success. Such errors are bound to occur from time to time and it is at least satisfactory that only one obvious mistake has been made in all these years. In the earlier part of the period counting was probably less complete than now as the necessary experience was built up. Lesser mistakes may of course be present but the great value of data such as these is the detection of trends and long-term averages, and too much must not be made of any one year's figures.

It is probable that the Pinkfoot is not untypical of many other geese populations in the way that its recruitment and mortality vary. Like many others its dependence on farmland has grown over the years, and improved farming techniques in its main wintering areas in Britain have probably contributed to the reduced winter mortality. Man has thus been helping it on two fronts; deliberately, by the creation of refuges; and unwittingly, by the provision of better feeding. Parallels can be drawn with several other European and North American goose populations.

My second example is also drawn from Europe and deals with the Dark-bellied Brent Geese breeding in central arctic Siberia and wintering in

TABLE 10: *Census and productivity data for the Dark-bellied Brent Goose, 1955–75*

Winter	Total	% young	No. of young	No. of adults and sub-adults	Losses in previous year	% mortality
1955 6	15,500	25·8	3,990	11,510		
1956–7	15,500	6·5	1,008	14,492	1,008	6·5
1957 8	18,500	52·8	9,768	8,732	6,768	43·7
1958–9	18,000	0·4	72	17,928	572	3·1
1959–60	19,500	21·6	4,212	15,288	2,712	15·1
1960–1	21,800	45·0	9,810	11,990	7,510	38·5
1961–2	22,000	5·1	1,122	20,878	922	4·2
1962–3	22,800	0·2	46	22,754	(−754)	(+3·4)
1963–4	23,600	35·0	8,260	15,340	7,460	32·7
1964–5	25,600	34·7	8,883	16,717	6,883	26·9
1965–6	27,300	6·9	1,884	25,416	184	0·7
1966–7	31,500	39·7	12,506	18,994	8,306	30·4
1967–8	31,000	5·6	1,736	29,264	2,236	7·1
1968–9	27,600	0·4	110	27,490	3,510	11·3
1969–70	36,300	49·7	18,041	18,259	9,341	33·8
1970–1	40,800	37·7	15,382	25,418	10,882	30·0
1971–2	34,000	0·7	238	33,762	7,038	17·3
1972–3	51,800	35·5	18,389	33,411	589	1·7
1973–4	84,500	48·5	40,982	43,518	8,282	16·0
1974–5	71,300	0·04	29	71,271	13,529	16·0
1975–6	110,600	46·2	51,097	59,503	11,797	16·5

Ogilvie & St Joseph (1976).

north-west Europe. Neither of the two North American high-arctic breeding populations of geese, the Light-bellied Brent and the Greater Snow Geese, has sufficiently reliable and lengthy records of data. In both cases a serious under-counting in the mid-winter inventories has recently been found, and the spring or autumn monitoring has not been going on long enough for my purpose. There is a serious drawback with the Dark-bellied Brent figures, too, because there are no good samples of brood size until the last couple of years, so it is not possible to calculate the proportion of successful parents each year.

Table 10 sets out the annual counts and percentages of young of the Dark-bellied Brent Geese in north-west Europe, from 1955 to 1975, together with the calculated mortality rates. The breeding success figures show the extreme swings between breeding success and breeding failure which occur in this population. The total numbers grew slowly but steadily between 1955 and 1968, despite alternations of good years and bad, often coming in pairs. The annual mortality, curiously, followed a similar pattern. There are several reasons why mortality should rise in a good breeding year. For example, the young birds are more vulnerable to shooting than older birds, and in years of high numbers of young there will also be a potential strain on the food resources, on the breeding grounds and in the winter. However, the really low annual mortality in years of non-breeding is not so easy to explain, simply because it does go so low. Although it is likely that there are some faulty figures in the Table, largely through counting errors, consistent mortality figures of between 1 and 7% remain puzzling. The apparent negative mortality in 1962 is certainly due to an error somewhere.

In the last seven years, 1969–75, there have been no less than five really good breeding seasons for Dark-bellied Brent and only two failures. This is much better than any earlier period and has been one main reason for the dramatic rise in total numbers. A further contributory factor was the cessation of shooting in Denmark in 1972, leaving only West Germany where the species is regularly shot. It is difficult to apportion the relative effect of this and the good breeding seasons, though incomplete figures from Denmark on the numbers previously shot suggest that it was at least 1000 annually, probably more.

Unfortunately, there are no good brood counts for this population of geese so we are unable to calculate how many pairs are breeding successfully. In other examples of increasing populations it has been found that the proportion of parents gradually drops, as in the Pinkfeet figures in Table 9. This could be brought about by a shortage of nest sites or by some limit to the amount of food available for rearing the young. An increase as dramatic as that of the Dark-bellied Brent Geese would certainly produce a greatly enlarged requirement for both. Unfortunately the breeding grounds are not visited, even by Russian biologists, and we remain in ignorance of what the effect has been of the trebling of the population in the last seven years.

This example is an extremely salutory one for wildlife biologists and managers. For years the population of Dark-bellied Brent was considered dangerously small, and pressures on it likely to increase because of its exclusive use of estuaries under threat of development. Without warning the numbers have grown so much that the simultaneous change of feeding habit to include grazing on farmland has caused problems for farmers. Although protection has been increasing in recent years no-one could have predicted this kind of growth, just as no-one is able to say what would happen if shooting was once more permitted. As with other high arctic breeding populations of geese, the effect of runs of good or bad breeding seasons is quite unpredictable and almost impossible to write into a management plan. Yet the unpredictability must never be forgotten.

So far we have only considered population dynamics as revealed by regular censusing and estimation of annual production. The data obtained from ringing geese can also be used for this purpose though so far the results have not proved very satisfactory. In most cases the annual mortality rates calculated from ringing returns have been higher than the rates obtained from annual censuses. There are inbuilt biases in both kinds of data, particularly ringing, where it is very difficult to mark a really representative sample of the population. There is also the added complication that only a proportion of the rings on birds shot by hunters is reported. There are all sorts of reasons for this: the bird might have been shot out of season and the hunter does not wish to disclose the fact; the hunter may not feel able to afford the postage charge, a genuine problem in less affluent countries in southern Europe or North Africa for example; he may be feeling annoyed about some hunting regulation and unwilling to help the biologist gain any more information which he feels may be used to further restrict his shooting; or he may be shooting close to a ringing site and having already sent back several rings and received virtually the same ringing details for each, feels that sending off any more is not worthwhile. This last difficulty, called 'reporter boredom', is a very considerable one and the minds of the biologists are much exercised to find a way to persuade every hunter that every ring he finds is of equal value, no matter how repetitive the details. The reporting rate has been variously estimated in different studies to under-represent the true recovery rate by anywhere between 30 and 60%. Probably the largest source of error from counts is in the estimation of annual production. The main problem with ringing is catching a sufficient number of birds evenly throughout the population. It may be quite easy to catch a large number of birds at a single trapping site, or in one particular locality, but before applying the results it must be demonstrated that the geese visiting that trapping site are representative of the population as a whole.

The Icelandic Pink-footed Goose population, as well as being counted for the long run of years displayed in Table 9, was ringed intensively on its breeding grounds in Iceland, where about 10,000 were ringed in two summers, 1951 and 1953, and on its wintering grounds in Britain, where some 15,000 geese were marked between 1950 and 1959. One of the first calculations made was an attempt to discover the size of the population by a method other than direct counting. This involves ringing a number of birds in the population, then from the ratio of marked to unmarked geese obtained during subsequent catches one can calculate the approximate size of the total population. However, the Lincoln Index method, as it is called after its inventor, depends upon the complete mixing of the marked and unmarked birds in the population. This was clearly not happening with the Pinkfeet and the results were thus not accurate. In fact, the ringing showed that individual geese were demonstrating strong attachments to traditional wintering haunts. They might visit a number of haunts within the range, at different times of the winter, in response to feeding conditions at the time. But essentially the chances of recapturing or recovering a bird at the site where it was ringed were far higher than of finding it elsewhere. This use of traditional haunts by geese occurs in other populations of geese, too. It has an obvious survival advantage to the individual goose as it will clearly be more likely to find good feeding grounds in an area that it knows, based on a familiar roost. This attachment to particular haunts is not uniform and a proportion of the birds change more freely from one haunt to another. However, it happens sufficiently often to suggest that this is the way in which separate populations with their own discrete wintering areas become established, leading eventually, perhaps, to the evolution of different characteristics and the formation of a new subspecies.

Returning to the British Pinkfeet, it was apparent that if the geese were showing traditional attachments to particular wintering haunts there could not possibly be the random mixing of the population necessary before the Lincoln Index method would become a reliable technique. Only by ringing large samples at each haunt, or in each main wintering area within the total range, could a broad enough sample be marked. This requisite proved impossible to achieve without a vastly disproportionate effort. In fact the ringing programme ceased at about the same time that it was discovered that annual censuses could provide this particular information more reliably and certainly more cheaply.

So the Lincoln Index method failed to work in the case of the Pinkfoot. More recent work on the Lesser Snow Goose, however, has shown some encouraging results when using the method. Certainly it appears that this very much larger population is more amorphous with fewer attachments to wintering haunts, though return to the same breeding colony is probably general.

If the ringing of British Pinkfeet failed to produce mortality rates and population totals as reliable as the censuses it nevertheless has played an important part in our knowledge of this population. In particular, it demonstrated the varying use made of different haunts by different birds. This has a considerable bearing on conservation policy in indicating the relative value of each haunt to the population as a whole. The importance of a single haunt is not necessarily directly related to the numbers of geese visiting it. One particular segment may be using it proportionately more than another; a fact that only ringing could discover.

Each metal ring used on a goose is engraved with a serial number for individual identification, and an address. This latter is usually an abbreviated form of the name and address of the country's ringing organisation or a convenient postal address easy to recognise anywhere in the world, thus: US Fish Wildl. Serv. Washington, DC, or Brit. Museum, London, S.W.7. These are usually preceded by the word Inform or Return. Both addresses are sufficient to enable any letter from the finder of the ring to reach the correct office. It is also to be hoped that the finder not only returns the ring or records the number but states where and when he found it, and how the bird died.

In the case of those geese which are quarry species the principal cause of death reported is shooting, and it is the hunters who return the rings. For a species that may be legitimately shot the percentage of birds so reported is between 90 and 95% of all recoveries sent in. The remaining 5–10% of recoveries may be small in number but they are nonetheless interesting as they, together with recoveries of protected species or populations, throw some light on the ways in which geese die when they are not shot. The picture is incomplete, of course, as there are few if any recoveries from the breeding grounds, particularly those in remote areas. But in the winter months, at any rate, recoveries do occur which describe other fates, although one of the more frequent may also be misleading. Geese are quite often reported as having been eaten by a fox or other predator. While this may be so it cannot be ruled out that the fox killed a goose which was already sick, or injured from shooting, or that the fox had been eating a corpse. It would be much easier for a fox to kill a disabled goose than a healthy one.

Predators take significant numbers of eggs and young, of course, as has already been mentioned in the previous chapter. But there are a few animals or birds which can catch a healthy goose, including Golden, Bald and White-tailed Eagles, all of which have been seen taking a full-grown goose in flight. It is probably not a very common occurrence as there are always likely to be easier prey for the eagles to tackle. However, several reported instances have been of eagles attacking geese that were on migration, when presumably they may be easier to catch, being possibly tired and less able to avoid the attacker. For example, Golden Eagles are known to take Greylags and Pinkfeet migrating over the Cairngorm mountains in Scotland when the geese are at an altitude of over 1200 metres (4000 feet) and flying through the territories of the eagles.

Most other reported forms of death to geese are accidents of one kind or another. The majority of these are connected with man and his artefacts. Geese sometimes fly into overhead wires, radio masts and other obstructions, particularly after dark or in foggy weather. They can also be killed by oil, pesticides and other pollutants, or by ingesting lead shot.

Studies of the mortality of geese, either of causes or annual rates, should take into account the age of the bird. Eggs and goslings are the most vulnerable and suffer the highest percentage losses of any age class. Fledged young birds are also at greater risk than older birds. In most studies it has been found that the mortality rate of geese in their first year is higher than in the second and subsequent years, largely because the birds are less experienced and therefore more likely to be shot, or have accidents. In some cases there is a slight drop in mortality rate between second year and older birds. Once the goose has reached breeding age, usually three years old, the mortality rate levels out, and these and older birds appear to be about equally vulnerable. In unshot populations there may be a slight increase in mortality rates in birds nearing the end of their natural life-span, say after eight to ten years, but the evidence is slight. In quarry species the mortality from shooting appears to affect birds more than one year old about equally.

Table 11 sets out the figures for an imaginary population of geese, starting with 1000 eggs laid, and showing how the numbers decrease at each stage of the life cycle. The mortality rates are average figures based on a number of studies of large Canada Geese, the only populations for which there are good data at every stage, especially through incubation to fledging. Data do exist for some of the arctic breeding species but their annual variability is so great that it is difficult to arrive at an average figure for use in a simplified example such as this.

The mean expectation of life at the different stages, which is based on the mortality rates, is also given in the Table. Individual birds in any population can survive much longer than this, as has been discovered by keeping birds in captivity, protected from predators and most accidents, and adequately fed all the year round. In such circumstances ages of 20–30 years are quite usual. The oldest known goose in the wild is probably not over 25 years, though this is in part a reflection of the fact that sufficiently durable rings have not been in use any longer than this.

Table 12 gives the mean annual mortality rates for adult birds of a number of goose species and populations. The figures are subject to various cautions as already discussed, but they give some idea of the range, particularly between shot and unshot populations. In theory, at least, if the population is stable the overall mortality rate should be balanced by the rate of recruitment, but because of the variation in both rates from year to year, and the variation in mortality with age, one must carefully define the point at which one regards recruitment as having taken place. The most satisfactory is probably the attainment of breeding age by the survivors of each year's brood. In the example given in Table 11, if one takes the average annual clutch size as 4·9 eggs per pair (a reasonable figure for large Canada Geese) this means that 204 pairs or 408 birds, were responsible for laying the 1000 eggs with which we started in the Table. If one applies the average annual mortality rate for adult

TABLE 11: *Mortality rates and life expectancies at different stages in the life cycle of geese, based on data for populations of large Canada Geese*

Stage and period	Mortality suffered	Life expectancy
1000 eggs laid		
670 eggs hatch	33% prior to hatching	
603 goslings fledge	10% prior to fledging	
271 goslings survive to 1 year old	55% during 1st year	1–3 years
176 geese survive to 2 years old	35% during 2nd year	2–4 years
114 geese survive to 3 years old (breeding age)	35% during 3rd year	2–4 years
74 geese survive to 4 years old	35% during 4th year	,,
48 geese survive to 5 years old	35% during 5th year	,,
5 geese survive to 10 years old	35% per annum	,,
1 goose survives to 13 years old	35% per annum	,,

Note: The age of the oldest surviving bird is raised to 18 years if one starts with 10,000 eggs, and to 23 years if one starts with 100,000 eggs.

TABLE 12: *Annual mortality rates of geese*

Species or race	Population or race	All birds	% annual mortality rate Adult	% annual mortality rate 1st winter	References
Pinkfoot	Iceland	18·0			Ogilvie & Boyd 1976
Whitefront	Baltic–North Sea	28·0			Boyd 1962
,,	Interior		31·3	44·1	Miller *et al.* 1968
,,	Greenland	34·0			Boyd 1962
Greylag	Iceland	19·0			Ogilvie & Boyd 1976
,,	West European		33·0	41·0	Paludan 1973
Lesser Snow	Cent. and Miss. Flyways	37·0	25·0	58·9	Boyd 1976
,,	Pacific Flyway		23·7	49·1	Rienecker 1965
Greater Snow		33·0			Boyd 1962
Canada	Large—England	15·6			Thomas (1977)
,,	—South Alaska coast		33·7	57·4	Chapman *et al.* 1969
,,	—New Zealand	30·0			Imber 1968
,,	Medium—Eastern Prairie		27·5	50·0	Vaught & Kirsch 1966
,,	Small—Tall Grass Prairie	27·0			MacInnes *et al.* 1974
Barnacle	Svalbard	14·0			M. Owen (pers. com.)
Brent	Dark-bellied	17·0			Ogilvie & St Joseph 1976
,,	Black Brant		21·8	45·4	Hansen & Nelson 1957

birds of 35% to these 408, after three years their numbers have reduced to 112. This is close enough to the 114 survivors of the 1000 eggs laid that reach three years old, or breeding age, as shown in Table 11, for one to state that the population must be stable. However, a very slight variation one way or the other in any of these factors can cause a decline or an increase. In real-life studies the difficulty lies in identifying which particular factor, or it may be more than one, is having the major effect.

6 Distribution and status

The previous chapter explained how we have arrived at our knowledge of the numbers and distribution of geese. As will be seen in the following species and population accounts, that knowledge varies from relatively complete to fragmentary. Where possible, information on numbers is presented in tables, whereas breeding and wintering ranges are shown on a map or maps. For some populations it has also been possible to indicate some of the more important haunts on the map. Numbers on the map correspond with their use in the text when the particular haunt is mentioned. However, it should be borne in mind that a haunt which is important now may carry very few geese in only a few years' time. Although geese have the reputation of being traditional birds, returning year after year to the same haunt, their numbers are highly variable and the relative importance of any one site can alter radically in only a short period.

In North America, waterfowl populations are divided into four Flyways, Pacific, Central, Mississippi and Atlantic. These are not just migration routes as is sometimes supposed but include the corresponding breeding and wintering ranges at either end of the actual migration path. Geographical features tend to funnel waterfowl migration into comparatively narrow bands, though broad front migration also occurs in some regions. The word 'corridor' is often used for a single migration route followed by one population. There is no similar concept in use in Europe. Attempts to transfer the flyway concept have never been very satisfactory, because of a lack of obvious routes followed by large numbers of different species of birds coming from and going to the same, or at least much over-lapping, breeding and wintering areas. Separation shown by different populations of one species does not justify the use of the word.

The information available on the different species and populations of geese is very variable, and this is reflected in the maps and tables. In some cases it has been possible to map breeding localities and wintering haunts in considerable detail, but in others only the broadest indication of the total range can be given. Because of this, it has been necessary to use several different scales and symbols, therefore care should be exercised before making direct comparisons between maps.

The tables have been assembled from a number of sources and contain as complete a series of population counts and breeding success data as could be managed. It should be stressed, however, that the quality of the counts and of the productivity assessments varies very widely. In many cases it is known that censuses were incomplete or that the breeding success figures obtained may indicate 'impossible' mortality or recruitment. Some cautions on the standard of the figures in the tables are given in the text. Nevertheless, even incomplete counts or imperfect age ratio assessment will still reveal major changes in status, and distinguish between successful breeding seasons and complete failures. Such information is of great interest to the biologist and of value to wildlife managers.

The maps illustrate the normal range of each species, subspecies or population. Because geese are powerful fliers with long endurance, vagrants may turn up almost anywhere. A brief statement attempts to cover this in each case but does not pretend to be exhaustive and it should be borne in mind that many species are commonly kept in captivity from which escapes frequently occur.

MAP 3. Swan Goose *Anser cygnoides*—world range. ⫻ breeding; ////principal breeding
    areas; ⦧wintering.

Swan Goose (Map 3)

We start with a species about which little or nothing is known as to status, and even its distribution map is necessarily sketchy.

The breeding range covers relatively thinly populated, often mountainous, country in the U.S.S.R. and it is perhaps not surprising that there is little definite information on numbers. In Mongolia it is reported as being the third most numerous goose species, after Greylag and Barhead. The remainder of the breeding range and almost all the wintering range lies within the Republic of China and, if Swan Geese have even been counted there, no results have ever been made known. Winter flocks of hundreds have been reported sporadically in the past from southern Japan, but it is now a very rare bird there, though there has been a sighting as recently as January 1976. In the 1930s it was stated that the species was much less common than formerly in many parts of its breeding range. There appears to be no more recent information on changes in its population status.

Bean Goose (Map 4)

The breeding range of this species spans the entire Eurasian continent, overlapping both the tundra and boreal zones. It reaches quite far south into the mountainous region of central Asia. The detailed distribution within this vast range is not well known. The species is not colonial which makes detailed assessments of its distribution much harder. In winter the distribution is much more localised because the birds gather into large flocks in areas close to the Atlantic and Pacific coasts and round the Mediterranean, with comparatively few in between.

Chapter 1 showed that four subspecies of the Bean Goose have been described, and also that it was almost impossible to draw meaningful lines on a map dividing the breeding range between them. This is equally true for the wintering distribution. However, it is possible to divide at least the European wintering birds into a number of seemingly more or less discrete populations. This has been done on the basis of counts plus ringing recoveries, though not many birds have been ringed, except in the Netherlands, while counts are available from only certain regions. Future knowledge may suggest changes in the present divisions.

British population (Maps 4 and 5, Table 13)
This has been generally regarded as a separate population though it seems probable that it is part of the much larger one wintering in the Baltic–North Sea area. Numbers now are very small, under 200 per winter, and have declined from around double that number soon after the 1939–45 war. The pre-war status is obscure, largely because of widespread confusion between the Bean Goose, the Pinkfoot and other grey geese. The Bean Goose appears to have been quite common in northern England and Scotland at the turn of the century, but to have declined steadily ever since. It is not certain why this

MAP 4. Bean Goose *Anser fabalis*—world range. ⫽ breeding; ⧵⧵⧵ wintering.

has happened but one of the more probable causes is the desertion of former breeding areas in Scandinavia whence it is assumed that the British wintering birds come.

There are two regular wintering localities for Bean Geese in Britain. One is on the marshes of the River Yare south-east of Norwich (1). This flock also uses the extensive grazing marshes between Norwich and Great Yarmouth, near Breydon Water. The second locality is in S.W. Scotland in an area of mixed farmland close to Castle Douglas, beside the River Ken (2). In both localities the geese have recently benefited from protection. Voluntary agreements with local wildfowlers prevent their being shot deliberately, and wardening is carried out to reduce disturbance, not least from overkeen bird-watchers.

Small flocks of Bean Geese are seen in at least three other places in Britain, but often only for a short period each winter and there are insufficient records to call these regular wintering sites. One is on the National Nature Reserve at Endrick Mouth, Loch Lomond, the others are in the general area of Holborn Moss, Northumberland, and on Deeside, Grampian. Certainly in these last two areas a flock of, say, 25 Bean Geese could probably spend a whole winter with an excellent chance of going undetected. Greylags winter in Northumberland, and they and Pinkfeet are common in Grampian, so casual observation would easily overlook a small flock of Bean Geese.

Table 13 shows the maximum numbers of Bean Geese recorded since 1950 in Norfolk and Kirkcudbrightshire, with summaries of counts in Norfolk before that. There have been no satisfactory age counts of British Bean Geese,

TABLE 13: *Peak counts of Bean Geese wintering at the two main haunts in Britain, 1941 to 1976–7*

Winter	Norfolk	Kirkcudbright	Winter	Norfolk	Kirkcudbright
1941–45 av.	211	no count	1962–3	47	147
1946–50 av.	124	,,	1963–4	38	3
1950–1	120	,,	1964–5	25	55
1951–2	0	,,	1965–6	36	70
1952–3	75	200	1966–7	46	8
1953–4	0	200	1967–8	48	17
1954–5	0	240	1968–9	40	15
1955–6	101	215	1969–70	66	17
1956–7	54	152	1970–1	73	12
1957–8	78	190	1971–2	67	18
1958–9	102	150	1972–3	77	32
1959–60	80	95	1973–4	109	65
1960–1	30	68	1974–5	102	65
1961–2	52	130	1975–6	91	60
			1976–7	127	82

Compiled from Norfolk and Scottish Bird Reports, from Wildfowl Trust files, and M. J. Seago (pers. com.).

which is perhaps a pity because comparison results from the continent might help to establish the relationship between the two groups. However, the inevitable smallness of the British sample would be a handicap.

Bean Geese rarely arrive in Britain before the New Year, but depart by the end of March. This is a very short wintering season and reinforces the belief that our birds are part of the wintering population across the North Sea. The fluctuations in numbers at the different sites are roughly in parallel, suggesting that all the birds come from some common breeding area. These wintering flocks appear to be entirely composed of rather long- and yellow-billed individuals, which again supports a Scandinavian origin. The Bean Geese, usually from one to four, that appear most winters as stragglers in flocks of other geese in Britain, principally Whitefronts, are often short-billed birds, indicating a more easterly and northerly origin.

Baltic–North Sea population (Maps 4 and 5, Table 14)

This population uses a wintering area which includes southern Sweden, Denmark, East and West Germany, the Netherlands and France, together with an offshoot in Spain. It is by no means certain whether this is a single homogeneous population, but in the absence of any evidence to the contrary it is probably better at this stage to treat it as such. It is difficult to draw an exact dividing line between these birds and the population which winters in central Europe, in particular in Czechoslovakia, Austria and Hungary.

Breeding season counts are almost non-existent. It has been estimated that there are about 1000 pairs of Bean Geese breeding in Finland, but this is not an accurate count. There are no estimates available from Sweden or Norway

MAP 5. Bean Goose *Anser fabalis*—winter haunts of British and Baltic–North Sea populations. ● over 1000; ● under 1000. Numbers indicate haunts referred to in text.

but there are probably no more birds than in Finland. The Nordic countries are beginning a co-operative study of the species in their region and one result of this may be a much better idea of how many pairs breed there. It is known that Bean Geese are much less numerous as breeding birds than formerly, especially in their main stronghold of Finnmark, due to persecution and habitat changes. Although there have been estimates of around 170,000 Bean Geese in the western half of the Soviet arctic and subarctic, it is not known how these can be apportioned between the different wintering groups.

The most easterly wintering area is southern Sweden, in the province of Scania, particularly around the lakes of Vombsjön, Hammersjön and Araslövsjön (3), which the birds use as roosts. Numbers are variable depending on weather conditions. The geese arrive in early October and build up to a peak at the end of the month or in early November. There is then a decline through the rest of November and December, and if there is prolonged hard weather all the geese will leave. However, in the recent mild winters quite large numbers have remained through the winter. Return passage from further south takes place in February and March giving another peak in the latter month before final departure in April. Autumn and spring peaks of several thousand seem to be the rule with a recent maximum of 10,000, or perhaps more, but with many fewer staying through the winter.

Mecklenburg province in East Germany is another important passage area, and numbers of geese also winter there. The principal locality is near Müritz (4), with peak numbers of 10,000–15,000, and another 5000–10,000 geese can be found not far away in the Randow area (5). There are a number of small haunts with a total of over 5000 birds in the Neubrandenburg area. It has been estimated that between 100,000 and 150,000 Bean Geese pass through East Germany in the autumn, but if this is true it is not obvious where they might be going, because this is up to twice the number believed to be in this population. As yet there is no evidence of passage through East Germany south to central Europe (see next population). It is possible that as many as 30,000 Bean Geese have wintered in East Germany, but there has been a

TABLE 14: *Numbers of Bean Geese wintering in the Netherlands, 1960–1 to 1975–6, together with breeding success figures since 1969–70*

Winter	Netherlands peak	% young	Winter	Netherlands peak	% young
1960–1	4,000	no data	1968–9	13,500	no data
1961–2	4,000	,,	1969–70	18,500	30·4
1962–3	4,000	,,	1970–1	25,000	29·0
1963–4	7,000	,,	1971–2	17,000	19·3
1964–5	10,000	,,	1972–3	12,000	17·3
1965–6	7,500	,,	1973–4	20,000	22·3
1966–7	7,500	,,	1974–5	38,000	17·1
1967–8	14,000	,,	1975–6	50,000	21·8

Lebret *et al.* (1976), and Van Impe (1973 and pers. com.).

decline in recent years as numbers have built up in the Netherlands.

In West Germany there are two main Bean Goose haunts, in the north near the mouth of the Elbe (6) where up to a thousand are regular, particularly in spring; and in Emsland, and along the Rhine near the Dutch border (7). About 2000 can be found in each place, with autumn and spring peaks as high as 10,000.

The Bean Goose is a regular wintering species in Denmark and has shown little change since the mid-1960s. They arrive in the last few days of September or during October, then build to a November peak, after which numbers stay relatively steady until February or March when departures begin. In cold weather there may be southward shifts. By far the highest Bean Goose count in recent years was about 8000 in November 1963, but this was exceptional and may have been due to birds straying from their normal migration route from Sweden to Germany, and thence to the Netherlands. There are about a dozen regular Bean Goose haunts in Denmark. Two of these, Tjele in Jutland (8), and Ljungholm on S. Lolland (9), regularly hold from 1000 to 1500 birds, but the remainder have only a few hundreds each. The majority of the haunts are in eastern Denmark, though a few are in northern and western Jutland.

The situation in the Netherlands is more difficult to summarise because of the recent very striking increase in numbers (Table 14). In the late 1960s a mid-winter peak of around 25,000 was usual but in the last four years there has been a sharp rise to about 50,000. The principal areas for Bean Geese are in the south of the country, particularly in the provinces of Zuid Holland and Zeeland, and in Noord Brabant and central Limburg. The geese are also found up the Rhine towards the West German border not far from the haunts in that country. Recently, Bean Geese have been finding new haunts in some of the Ijsselmeer polders. The more important haunts, where numbers regularly reach from 2000 to 5000, include Oostelijk Flevoland (10) in Gelderland Province, the Haringvliet area (11) in Zuid Holland, and the Veersemeer and Wilhelmina polder (12) in Zeeland. However, I would repeat that the recent increase has changed the relative importance of various haunts and it is too early to say which will remain in favour.

Going south from the Netherlands, a few hundred Bean Geese winter in Belgium, mostly on the Zwin reserve (13) in West Flanders. In France, numbers of Bean Geese have been increasing recently, both as wintering birds and on passage through to Spain. The main wintering haunts are in north-east France, especially in the Lorraine and Champagne districts, and in the Rhine valley near the German border. More recently the geese have taken to wintering in the valley of the Somme in north-west France and in the upper Loire in central France. Numbers are nowhere large, with flocks of 200–400 the rule, though around 700 are now wintering in the Loire valley with a maximum count of 1000. Recent mid-winter censuses have just topped 2500 for the whole country, although larger numbers may occur on passage.

The Bean Goose has for long wintered in Spain and it is assumed that the birds there are members of this population. Rather encouragingly, numbers have increased in recent years from about 1500 to the present 4000. The principal locality is in central northern Spain based on lakes near Palencia and

Zamora (14) with about 2500, and just to the south around Valladolid where there are a further 500 birds. There are also some hundreds in the Toledo Province, near Maqueda (15).

There is a number of places in Switzerland, and a few in the extreme south of Germany, where small flocks of Bean Geese, rarely more than 100–200, are found most winters. The birds probably belong to this population as do the handful that winter in the Camargue in the south of France. Stragglers have reached Iceland, Ireland, Portugal, the Azores, Madeira and North Africa.

Counts have not been sufficiently complete to produce a table of annual totals, but regular age counts have been carried out in Zeeland, Netherlands, for the last seven years and these are shown in Table 14. The variation in breeding success between the years is relatively small, typical of a population breeding in regions to the south of the arctic where the summer is longer and the weather less extreme, allowing of a more certain breeding success each year. Even so, the average of just over 22% breeding success suggests that either a significant proportion of adult birds do not breed each year or that there is a considerable loss of eggs and young, perhaps due to predators as well as to weather conditions. The best estimate of a population total is 60,000–70,000.

Central European population (Maps 4 and 6)

As already stated, the separation between this population and that of the Baltic–North Sea is in some doubt, but for want of any other evidence it is treated here as probably discrete. Counts are somewhat fragmentary but the central European population must total at least as many as the Baltic–North Sea population and possibly more, up to 100,000. There are no age counts available nor any good indication of whether numbers are increasing or declining.

There used to be substantial numbers of Bean Geese wintering in eastern Austria but these have decreased, probably, though not certainly, because of a shift over the border into Czechoslovakia. There are two Austrian haunts, both alongside the Danube to the west and to the east of Vienna (1) and together they may hold up to 1000 geese. Further along the Danube and astride the Czechoslovakian–Hungarian border (2) there is a very important wintering area with between 15,000 and 20,000 birds regularly present and a recent peak of 40,000. Precise counts are hard to obtain because the area is large and the geese move freely across the Danube which here forms the state boundary. Sites on the Hungarian side include Tata, a large fish pond, and the Lakes Balaton and Velencei. Hungary has another major wintering area in the south near the town of Szeged (3) where at least 10,000 Bean Geese can be found. However, the relationship between this flock and the geese based on the Kopacki Reserve (4) across the border in Yugoslavia is not fully understood. Since the area was created a reserve, numbers of wintering Bean Geese have increased from 400 in the late 1960s to at least 10,000 in 1972. The two areas are about 160 kilometres (100 miles) apart but it is likely that there may be weather movements from one to the other. Indeed, in very severe weather large numbers of Bean Geese desert these central European states altogether, but so far their destination has not been discovered. Perhaps they

MAP 6. Bean Goose *Anser fabalis*—winter haunts of Central European population.
● over 1000; • under 1000. Numbers indicate haunts referred to in text.

move along the Danube to its delta (5) on the Black Sea, perhaps they head further south. Small numbers, a few hundreds only, appear in northern Greece (6) in most winters but there are no reports of increased numbers in cold winters. Elsewhere in Yugoslavia there are a number of haunts holding a few hundred Bean Geese, including the Split marshes (7) on the Adriatic coast, but none comparing in importance with Kopacki.

Vagrants recorded in southern Greece, Turkey, Malta, Cyprus and Egypt probably belong to this population.

Asian populations

There is virtually no information on numbers of Bean Geese further east, or on separation into populations. There were about 1550 in Japan in January 1973 and about 5000 in January 1976. The species is recorded with some regularity on islands in the Bering Sea including the Aleutians and the Pribilofs. Summer surveys in north-east Siberia and the Chukotski Peninsula show a population of over 250,000 grey geese of which the majority are Whitefronts, but which certainly includes many tens of thousands of Bean Geese.

Pink-footed Goose (Map 7)

In comparison with the Bean Goose this species is straightforward to deal with. There are only two completely discrete populations, both of which have been counted and studied for some years. The breeding grounds lie exclusively within the arctic, in Greenland, Iceland and Svalbard. The wintering grounds are confined to north-west Europe.

Icelandic population (Maps 7, 8 and 9, Table 15)

The breeding area of this population is in Iceland with a small number in East Greenland. There is one principal colony in central Iceland in an oasis of vegetation set in a great lava desert, plus many much smaller groups scattered along river gorges and in other vegetated areas. The wintering grounds are solely in Britain, mainly in Scotland, and in northern and eastern England.

This population has been counted with fair accuracy at least once each winter since 1960, and it has been possible to estimate the total from less complete counts back to 1950. The totals are shown in Table 15 together with the annual breeding success figures. The quite steady increase throughout the period, until the last few years, can be largely attributed to more favourable conditions in Britain, where farming changes have led to an increased food supply, especially in eastern Scotland, and refuges have been established on many of the more important roosts. This has led to a decline in the annual mortality rate which has more than offset a decline in the average breeding success. In the last eight or nine years the totals have fluctuated more widely and it is difficult to be certain whether this is a temporary phenomenon, to be succeeded by further upwards movement, or whether it signals that the population has reached an upper limit.

The breeding success figures shown in Table 15 reveal a certain amount of fluctuation, too, though this population has never had a complete failure, the 5·8% young recorded in 1975 being its lowest. Breeding success and mean brood size have been dropping slowly but steadily over a period of years, a feature noticed in other goose populations. This steady decrease in productivity as the numbers increase may be perhaps due to the operation of a

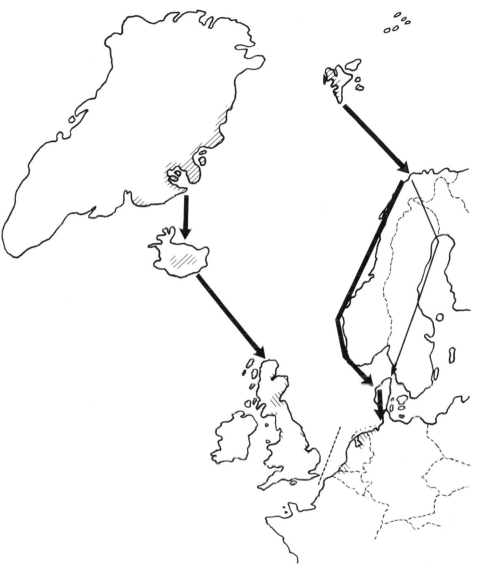

MAP 7. Pink-footed Goose *Anser brachyrhynchus*—world range. ▨ breeding; ▨ wintering. Arrows indicate approximate migration routes. Dotted line divides winter ranges of Iceland and Svalbard populations.

density-dependent mechanism on the breeding grounds where shortage of nest sites or lack of post-breeding supplies may be acting to control numbers. The decline in the annual mortality rate has certainly contributed to the rise in numbers but it may be that mortality and recruitment are now approaching equilibrium.

There is nothing about the wintering grounds to suggest that they are saturated with geese, but if we look at the breeding localities there is some evidence that this may be the case. The detailed breeding range in Iceland is shown on Map 8. Much of this information was produced as a result of a helicopter survey carried out in June 1970. The principal breeding colony in the central oasis of Thjórsárver (1) was first discovered by a small expedition led by Peter Scott in 1951. His visit, and the succeeding one in 1953, had as its main aim the catching and ringing of the geese, of which over 10,000 were marked, but estimates were also made of the size of the colony at between 3000 and 4000 pairs. At that time the total population was around 35,000 birds. No further counts of breeding pairs were carried out, largely because of the inaccessibility of the area until 1970. A threat to inundate the area by damming the river running through it in order to generate electricity produced an urgent requirement for a new survey. When this was carried out in June 1970 it was found that the total of breeding pairs had risen to about 10,700. In the rest of Iceland it was reckoned there were between 1500 and 2000 more pairs, nearly all in scattered small groups and certainly no further major colonies. The only other breeding area for the population is in East Greenland where there has been no survey but for which the best estimates lie between 500 and 1000 breeding pairs. In 1970 the total population was 72,000.

Map 9 shows the principal wintering haunts in Britain. The Pinkfeet formerly roosted mainly on estuaries but the increase of inland reservoirs, where they could roost more or less undisturbed compared with the heavily

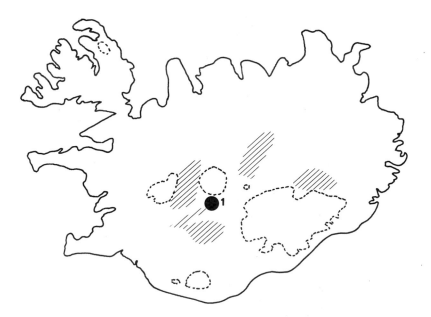

MAP 8. Pink-footed Goose *Anser brachyrhynchus*—breeding haunts in Iceland. Number indicates haunt referred to in text. Dotted lines mark icecaps.

TABLE 15: *Numbers of Icelandic Pink-footed Geese wintering in Britain, 1950–1 to 1977–8, together with annual breeding success. Figures since 1960–1 are from the annual November censuses*

Winter	Total	% young	Brood size	Winter	Total	% young	Brood size
1950–1	30,000	48·8	2·95	1964–5	65,500	26·6	2·79
1951–2	34,000	24·9	2·50	1965–6	69,000	21·0	2·57
1952–3	35,500	23·4	3·13	1966–7	76,500	21·6	2·36
1953–4	32,500	33·3	2·75	1967–8	65,500	10·8	1·30
1954–5	37,000	34·9	3·75	1968–9	65,000	11·7	1·39
1955–6	42,000	17·0	2·80	1969–70	74,000	24·4	2·14
1956–7	49,500	18·4	2·75	1970–1	72,000	23·1	2·18
1957–8	36,500	33·6	2·91	1971–2	65,000	23·2	1·87
1958–9	54,000	25·9	2·25	1972–3	72,500	11·4	1·67
1959–60	54,000	20·0	3·25	1973–4	82,500	30·5	2·35
1960–1	57,700	27·6	2·74	1974–5	89,000	17·6	2·16
1961–2	59,000	37·4	2·75	1975–6	73,000	5·6	1·43
1962–3	56,000	20·9	2·21	1976–7	71,000	11·3	1·92
1963–4	57,000	20·2	4·00	1977–8	69,000	8·5	1·95

Ogilvie & Boyd (1976).

shot coastal haunts, tempted them away and even though a number of estuaries have been made into refuges the geese have not returned in force. A number of important roosts are in fact on small privately owned waters. The landowners normally have some shooting at the geese on their estates but prevent anyone else doing so and, most importantly, treat the roosts as the vital places they are and have few if any shoots at them. This kind of attitude by landowners to the geese makes a considerable difference to the ability of the birds to live in certain areas.

The Pinkfeet arrive in Britain during September from about the middle of the month onwards, depending on the season in Iceland. The breeding birds have mostly left the colony area with their young in late August and move to upland areas where they feed extensively on seeds and berries. There is no fixed period for migration to Britain, shortage of food or suddenly deteriorating weather provide the usual trigger. By the middle of October the entire population has left for Britain. The annual census in Britain is carried out over the first or second weekend in November when the geese are at their peak numbers and still highly concentrated. Thereafter numbers decline slowly through shooting and other mortality, and the birds also disperse as the winter progresses and the excellent feeding provided by barley stubble and harvested potato fields is used up. The geese shift around the country, to some extent responding to weather conditions and food supply. The general tendency is for a movement out of north-east Scotland to the south and south-west, and thence to Lancashire in late November and December. There is a northward movement in late January and February out of Lancashire and a new concentration builds up on the Solway. In March and early April the birds build up strongly in Scotland prior to the departure to Iceland in the second half of April.

The single most important Pinkfoot roost in Britain is a small 28 hectare (70 acre) water just outside Perth (1) where a peak of 27,500 geese has been counted roosting in early November. Numbers fluctuate according to the food supply in the surrounding farmland, the highest counts being in autumns when there has been a lot of grain spillage from gales prior to harvest. When the amount of spilt grain is slight, peak counts may be only half the maximum. The total falls off rapidly through the winter, but several thousand geese continue to use the roost and numbers may increase again in the spring. Other very important roosts where counts of from 5000–10,000, or a little more, are regularly made are: Strathbeg Loch (2) and Meikle Loch, Newburgh (3), both in Grampian; the ponds in Carsebreck north of Dunblane, Perthshire (4); and Loch Leven, Kinross (5). The last site is a noted arrival point for the geese and a peak as high as 15,000 is quite often noted in late September or October, with the birds dispersing to other areas a week or two later.

There are several smaller roosts in central Scotland but the next important area, going south, is in the Lothians south of Edinburgh, where about 15,000–20,000 Pinkfeet are regularly found in the autumn, with most on Gladhouse Reservoir (6) or on a small pool set on a moorland hill at Fala Flow (7). There are several other reservoirs here in the hills and Pinkfeet and Greylags have adopted them in preference to the shallow bays and estuaries on the Forth where they formerly roosted.

In south-west Scotland the Solway Firth (8) has long been an important area, but whereas thirty years ago it was probably the most important haunt in Scotland it has now lost some of its attraction to the geese, perhaps because of the very heavy shooting pressure there. In recent years numbers have built up again though not until after the end of the shooting season, and up to 10,000 are now recorded in late winter and early spring.

Three areas in England now hold Pinkfeet but here, too, there have been some considerable changes over the years. In the 1950s and 1960s there was a general retreat of the geese northwards. As their total numbers increased so they concentrated more and more in Scotland, gradually deserting their former English haunts. This 'short-stopping' seemed to be associated with greatly improved feeding and protection for the Pinkfoot in Scotland compared with the situation in England. The low-lying farmland round the Wash (9) on the east coast used to be a major Pinkfoot haunt before and just after the war, but became virtually deserted by about 1966. However, in the last five or six years the geese have started to return, particularly in the second half of the winter, and totals up to 5000 have been recorded. Further north in the Humber estuary (10) it does not seem that the geese will come back. Farming changes on the feeding grounds in the Yorkshire Wolds have made the area less attractive and where 12,000–15,000 geese fed each autumn twenty-five years ago, there are now barely 1000. Two haunts in southern England have been deserted altogether in recent years. These are in north Norfolk and on the Severn Estuary in Gloucestershire. At the latter site 1500–2000 Pinkfoot were regular before the war but, afterwards, numbers dropped to a few hundreds and then disappeared altogether in the mid-1960s.

In contrast to the other English haunts, the farmland of Lancashire near Southport (11) has seen a striking increase in the last few years. For most of the period since estimates or counts began, a total of up to 4000 was the normal maximum. Then, due in part to the creation of a refuge covering an important secondary roost just inland of their main, estuarine one, there was a tremendous upsurge in numbers, so that in the last five years the peak count, usually in November or December, has gone from 7000 to over 25,000. The geese are taking full advantage of the local habit of leaving barley stubble unploughed through the winter, whereas in other areas of the country it is ploughed in the late autumn. Indeed the farmers do more than leave the stubble, they generally disc harrow it which breaks up the surface and allows any spilt grain to reach the soil where it promptly germinates. The geese thus have not only waste grains to eat but the tender young shoots of barley, which can last them well into the New Year.

As already mentioned, the spring return of the Pinkfoot to Iceland takes place in the second half of April. The main autumn arrival of the geese takes place on the north and north-east coasts of Scotland, but the departure is further to the west with major flight-lines over the west coast and the Outer Hebrides.

Vagrant Pinkfeet known to belong to this population include recoveries of ringed birds on the Azores and the Canaries; stragglers to Spain and Madeira could also belong to this population, but more probably to the next.

Svalbard population (Maps 7 and 9, Table 16)

There has been no complete breeding survey in the Svalbard archipelago where the whole of this population breeds, but the species is widespread all along the west coast and in the interior valleys of the main island of Spitsbergen, and also occurs in small numbers on some of the other islands. Using known breeding distribution and densities, and extrapolating to include all known suitable habitat, good agreement has been found between the present carrying capacity of the archipelago and current winter counts, suggesting that the population is close to or at its maximum.

TABLE 16: *Peak counts of Svalbard Pink-footed Geese wintering in Denmark and the Netherlands, 1965–6 to 1975–6, together with the annual breeding success of Svalbard Barnacle Geese (see text)*

Winter	Total Pinkfeet	% young Barnacles	Winter	Total Pinkfeet	% young Barnacles
1965–6	15,000	no record	1971–2	12,000	15·0
1966–7	15,000	13·3	1972–3	17,700	28·9
1967–8	15,000	27·1	1973–4	18,000	21·0
1968–9	12,200	23·2	1974–5	12,500	15·0
1969–70	13,100	27·0	1975–6	15,000	20·0
1970–1	18,800	47·2	1976–7	16,600	23·0

Fog (1976), Owen & Campbell (1974).

The wintering area lies mainly in the Netherlands with small numbers in north-west Germany, Belgium and north France. Virtually the whole population migrates through Denmark in autumn and in spring, and a few birds remain there in mild winters. It is thought that the majority of the geese migrate down the west coast of Norway, but a scattering of records from Sweden suggests that some geese may go overland from north Norway to the Gulf of Bothnia and then either round or across southern Sweden.

The winter counts of this population do not go so far back as the British ones but there are usually one or two each winter, sufficient to show that in recent years there has been no definite trend. The counts are set out in Table 16, and were made in Denmark, nearly all in October. Counts in the Netherlands in mid-winter have shown good agreement. It is a pity but there do not seem to be any age counts which might explain the fluctuations shown by the counts. What is available, though, is the annual breeding success shown over the same period by the Barnacle Geese breeding in the same Svalbard archipelago. Their ranges do not overlap exactly, the Barnacles are more concentrated on the coast and they may experience slightly different weather conditions because of this. However, there is quite good correlation between the breeding success of the Barnacles and changes in the numbers of Pinkfeet, more noticeable in the period since 1970 than before that year.

The Pinkfeet arrive in Denmark in the last few days of September or the first week of October and rapidly build up to maximum numbers. They are confined to western Jutland, in particular in Vest-Stadil Fjord (12) where the whole population may concentrate briefly before some thousands move on to Tipperne (13) and Fiilsø (14), a little further south. Up to 4000 also call in briefly at Ballum Enge and Højer Enge (15) on the Danish/German border as they move south in early November. Depending largely on the weather for timing, numbers in Denmark drop to about 5000 in mid-November and then to under 1000 in December, these birds being usually in a number of small flocks dispersed between several haunts. Return passage starts in late January, building up through February to 5000–8000 in March and perhaps 12,000, briefly, in April. However, they are more scattered at this time of year than in autumn and it is not certain whether the whole population is within the country at any time. Some may still be in the Netherlands when others have left for Norway. A few more haunts are used in spring than in autumn, including Agger and Harboør Tange (16), and Nissum Fjord (17) in north-west Jutland, to the north of their autumn haunts, all of which are also used.

Pinkfeet in West Germany are confined to the north-west, close to the Danish and Dutch borders, particularly in Emsland (18) and at Jade Busen (19). In former years virtually the whole population wintered here; there was an estimate of 10,000 in Emsland in January 1950, but drainage and associated agricultural changes drove the geese over the border into the Netherlands. They can still be seen in hundreds in Germany, even so, and just occasionally 1000–2000 have stayed through the winter.

Before the desertion of the West German haunts the only places in the Netherlands where Pinkfeet wintered were in the south, principally in Zeeland, but the birds ousted from Germany found suitable places in

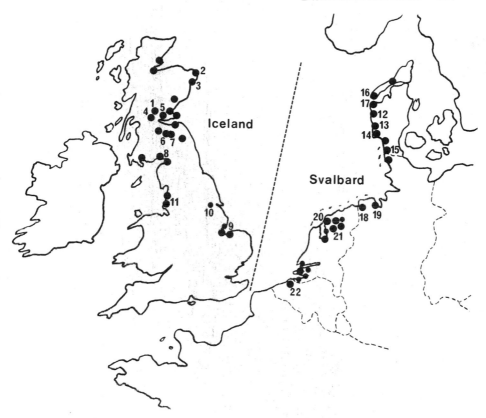

MAP 9. Pink-footed Goose *Anser brachyrhynchus*—winter haunts. ● over 1000; ● under 1000. Numbers indicate haunts referred to in text.

Friesland in the north of the Netherlands and there they have remained. The most important sites are close to the east coast of the Ijsselmeer around Piaam and Workum (20), where between 3000 and 8000 Pinkfeet regularly winter and as many as 12,000, or most of the population, have been seen. Smaller numbers, generally some hundreds, but occasionally a few thousand, are to be seen a little further east around Joure Akmarijp, Terhorne, Oudhof and Brekken (21). A few hundreds have found the new Flevoland polders in the southern Ijsselmeer attractive, and there are still small flocks in the south of the country, mostly scattered tens rather than hundreds, particularly around the many arms of the Rhine–Scheldt delta. If cold weather envelops northern Holland the geese may move south and occupy these haunts in strength for a brief period.

A maximum of 1000 Pinkfeet has been recorded in Belgium, nearly all at the Damme reserve in the north-west of the country (22). More usually from 500 to 800 winter here. Very small numbers winter in France, usually well under 100, except in periods of very severe weather. In 1956 and 1963 large numbers of Pinkfeet moved into France and considerable numbers were shot by the French hunters who could not miss such a good opportunity.

The Pinkfoot has been recorded as a vagrant in Finland, the western U.S.S.R. and several European countries, from Poland south to Italy and east to Romania.

White-fronted Goose (Map 10)

The near-circumpolar distribution shown in Map 10 comprises four named subspecies. The Greenland and Pacific Whitefronts have just one population each, but the European and perhaps the Interior Whitefronts can be split into a number of fairly discrete groups.

European Whitefront

There are five fairly well delimited wintering populations of this sub-species, as indicated on Map 10. Their corresponding summer ranges have not been worked out but are assumed to run correspondingly from west to east through Siberia. European Whitefronts breed almost exclusively in the tundra zone extending south into the scrub zone in only a few areas.

Baltic–North Sea population (Maps 10 and 11, Table 17)
Occupying the most westerly part of the breeding range, this population winters in north-west Europe from East Germany to north France and southern Britain, with the major concentration in the Netherlands. Not surprisingly, it is the best studied of all Whitefront populations, at least in the winter time. There are no counts available from the presumed summer range. Regular and fairly complete winter censuses began in 1959–60 and have continued ever since. The results are set out in Table 17 together with earlier available counts from Britain. These show that until 1970–71 the population was fairly stable, with only minor fluctuations. Then, quite suddenly it doubled in the winter of 1970–71 and has remained on this new higher level and even increased further. The breeding success figures in the last column of the Table show that in that winter the percentage of young was very high, following a quite good season in 1969. However, there have been other runs of good years that have not produced any sudden upsurge in numbers and it is rather puzzling why it should have taken place. One theory is that the increase represents a shift of geese from another population to the east. Unfortunately, counts from there are not complete enough to be able to detect whether even such a large number of birds might have moved.

Another interesting but somewhat depressing fact to be learnt from the Table is that numbers in Britain have actually gone down since the great upsurge in the total. There was a welcome upswing in the late 1960s but then a drop to below previous levels, from which there has been no sign of a recovery. Part of this can be blamed on recent very mild winters, allowing the Whitefronts to stay in the Netherlands and find plenty of food through the

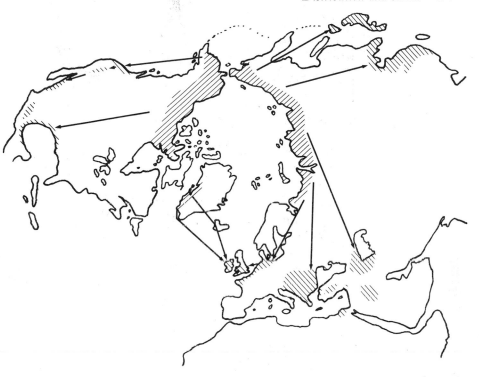

MAP 10. White-fronted Goose *Anser albifrons*—world range. ⦸ breeding; ⦸ wintering. Arrows link breeding and wintering ranges of different subspecies and populations.

winter. But even in past years, when numbers in Britain were higher, it has only been a small proportion of the total that has come on, so this cannot be the whole answer. Another factor of importance has been the steady increase in goose refuges in the Netherlands, of which the Whitefronts have taken full advantage. Again this would tend to allow more geese to stay back in the Netherlands rather than come on west.

The principal Whitefront haunts in Britain only number four, with a handful of subsidiary sites. The New Grounds, at Slimbridge, Gloucestershire (1), has been an important wintering place for this species for centuries, as the shooting records of the estate on which it lies have revealed. Before the 1939–45 war, 20000–3000 were regular, with up to 2000 Pinkfeet. Then, after the war, the Pinkfeet declined gradually until they disappeared altogether, while the Whitefronts increased. Five thousand was the normal maximum from about 1946 to 1967, then in the three following winters the peak rose to give a maximum of 7600 in 1969–70. The following year numbers dropped again and have stayed low ever since, not rising above about 3000 in the last three very mild winters. The first geese arrive early in October but numbers stay low until well into December, increasing quickly to a peak in January. Departures begin in February and are complete by the middle of March.

The second most important British site is in the Towy valley in south Wales (2). The flock here has increased from a few hundreds fifteen years ago to about 2000 in 1970, but like that at the New Grounds it has declined since. It has overtaken in importance the Avon valley, Hampshire (3), where there has been a more steady 600–1200 throughout the period. These two sites are well inland and the geese often roost on riverside floodwater as an alternative to flighting long distances to the nearest estuary. The New Grounds feeding fields are alongside the roost on the Severn estuary. Two neighbouring areas in north Kent (4), the Thames marshes and those on the Isle of Sheppey, traditionally hold some hundreds of Whitefronts each, but the former site has now been virtually lost to development, and it remains to be seen whether the Sheppey marshes can hold all the geese that formerly used both areas. There is still a remnant Whitefront flock on the English/Welsh border near Montgomery (5), where formerly there was a large wintering flock, and small numbers, usually under a hundred, can be found in one or two areas of East Anglia. Essentially this species likes grazed pastures close to a secure, preferably estuarine, roost. Such habitat is not common in Britain and a number of past haunts have been drained or otherwise changed out of existence. However, the existing haunts could certainly hold more geese than

TABLE 17: *Mid-winter totals of the Baltic—North Sea population of the White-fronted Goose, 1946–7 to 1975–6, together with breeding success figures from Britain. Country totals are the highest available for each winter and do not necessarily add up to the population total*

Winter	W. Germany	Netherlands	Belgium	France	Britain	Total	% young	Brood size
1946–53					av. 8,300			
1954–9					av. 8,000			
1959–60	no count	57,000	2,500	1,000	8,400	66,000	34·6	3·05
1960–1	3,600	61,000	2,900	1,000	6,800	72,000	37·1	3·30
1961–2	no count	42,000	3,500	1,000	8,600	51,500	45·4	3·86
1962–3	100	30,000	2,500	44,000	9,800	55,500	10·8	2·79
1963–4	no count	55,000	5,400	2,700	7,400	61,000	22·8	2·84
1964–5	,,	53,000	6,420	1,250	6,000	60,000	27·6	2·30
1965–6	,,	43,000	6,180	1,150	8,400	5ʃ,000	31·0	2·70
1966–7	750	65,000	8,650	750	7,300	47,000	31·3	2·60
1967–8	100	52,500	6,900	500	12,000	61,000	33·9	2·30
1968–9	400	53,000	6,000	500	11,200	64,600	13·2	1·60
1969–70	100	58,500	6,000	500	13,000	81,500	36·8	2·70
1970–1	1,150	90,000	7,700	500	11,000	100,300	45·0	3·50
1971–2	1,050	c. 90,000	3,750	200	6,000	100,000	22·2	1·90
1972–3	1,200	c.110,000	6,100	200	9,000	120,000	42·2	2·70
1973–4	2,700	120,000	6,000	200	8,000	130,000	44·0	2·90
1974–5	2,050	78,500	6,150	200	2,000	100,000	26·8	2·60
1975–6	2,000	110,000	6,000	200	4,000	120,000	44·0	3·10

Ogilvie (1970), Philippona (1972), and data from Wildfowl Trust files.

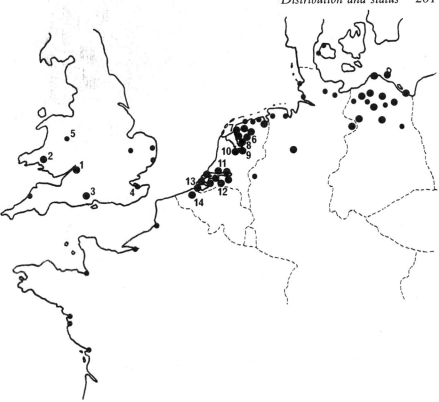

MAP 11. European White-fronted Goose *Anser albifrons albifrons*—winter haunts of Baltic–North Sea population. ● over 1000; ● under 1000. Numbers indicate haunts referred to in text.

they do and it is not very satisfactory that the population should have increased so greatly while short-stopping keeps the geese in the Netherlands and they no longer come to Britain in former numbers.

The Whitefront is widely distributed in the Netherlands with the main haunts in central and western Friesland; on the Ijsselmeer polders, especially the Oostelijk Flevoland; in the west of Noord-Brabant; on the islands at the mouth of the Rhine-Scheldt delta; and in the most southerly part of the country close to the Belgian border. With the recent great increase in numbers it is not always possible to be certain which haunts have received permanent additions to their wintering totals and which the birds are merely visiting temporarily, looking for the more favourable sites. However, a number of localities have recorded peaks of at least 10,000 Whitefronts in the last few years and one or two have topped 20,000. They include farmland around Beetsterzwaag in central Friesland (6), and about four more areas between there and the east coast of the Ijsselmeer, namely Oldeboorn, Joure Akmarijp, Workum and Piaam, and Gaasterland (7). Going south the

Noord–oost Polder (8) and the area around Zwartemeer (9) have both held over 10,000 Whitefronts recently, while the three Flevoland polders (10) held a staggering 54,000 a couple of winters ago, though between 15,000 and 25,000 is a more usual total. In the delta the principal sites seem to be the Oude Land van Strijen (11), the Hollandsdiep area (12), and various sandbanks in the Westerschelde (13), from which the geese flight to feed on the surrounding islands. Clearly, finding Whitefronts to look at in many parts of the Netherlands is not much of a problem, despite the flatness of the land. They are present in strength from December to early March.

The remaining birds of this population are found in Belgium at the Damme reserve (14) just over the border from the Netherlands and close to the most southerly Whitefront haunts in that country. Here there are a regular 3000–6000 Whitefronts while recent increases have brought the peak to close to 10,000. In northern France, in contrast, a former 1000–1500 birds in the late 1960s and perhaps 5000 or even more in the 1950s have dwindled away almost to nothing in the last few years. The recent best sites were the Baie de Somme and the Baie du Mont St Michel, with a few hundreds at each site at the peak. France is still likely to receive larger numbers in very severe winters, as it did in 1963, with birds coming from the Netherlands and Britain extending south down the Atlantic coast. There are records of stragglers as far as Spain and Portugal.

About 20–30 years ago the north German coasts of Schleswig Holstein and Niedersachsen were the best places for Whitefronts in Europe, but drainage and cultivation drove the geese into the Netherlands and it is now exceptional, even with the greatly increased numbers, to find more than a very few thousands there in mid–winter, though much larger numbers can be found during migration periods. Further east, in East Germany, the Whitefront is a common migrant with much smaller numbers staying for the winter. In the recent very mild winters rather more birds have stayed, though relatively few compared with the total population. From counts in October and November it seems that virtually all the Baltic–North Sea population passes through East Germany. For example, it was estimated that 98,000 birds stopped in the country in October–November 1973, in a winter when the total was thought to be about 125,000. The number remaining to winter there has increased from a few hundreds in the 1960s, to nearly 4000 in 1970, and probably 7000 now. This is probably a response to recent mild winters. The principal wintering haunts are in similar areas to those of the Bean Goose, especially in Mecklenburg near the Baltic coast, which is also one of the main passage areas. The return passage through East Germany takes place in late March and April.

Pannonic population (Maps 10 and 12)
This name is taken from an old geographical name for the plain surrounding the middle reaches of the Danube. The population of White-fronts involved winters in Hungary, the western parts of Romania, and in Yugoslavia, with small numbers in Italy, and perhaps Albania. In mild winters they may penetrate no further than Austria and Czechoslovakia, countries they normally pass through on migration. The limits of the

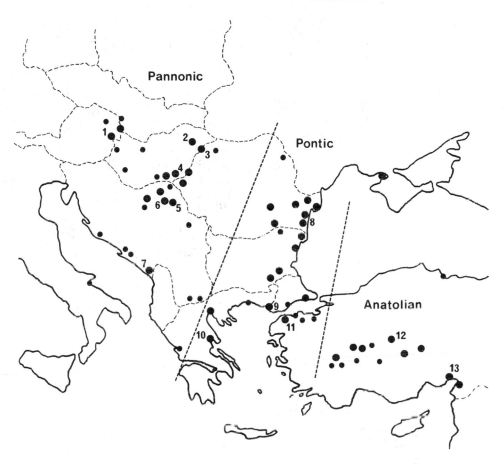

MAP 12. European White-fronted Goose *Anser albifrons albifrons*—winter haunts of Pannonic, Pontic and Anatolian populations. ● over 1000; ● under 1000. Numbers indicate haunts referred to in text. Dotted lines divide wintering ranges of the three populations.

breeding range are not known but are assumed to lie mostly to the east of those of the previous population. Precise counts are also lacking. There are insufficient workers available in the right places for co-ordinated winter counts, but summing what is known for each haunt in average winters it is probable that the total lies between the admittedly fairly wide limits of 60,000 and 100,000, obviously fluctuating over the years as the breeding success varies.

The principal Austrian Whitefront area is round the great lake of Neusiedl See (1) in the east of the country, and the nearby lakes of Seewinkel. Here a few hundreds winter, or thousands in a mild year, but as many as 20,000 may be found on migration. The lowlands along the Danube on the Austrian and

Czechoslovakian borders, hold some hundreds through a mild winter and several thousands on passage. The most famous goose area in Hungary is the Hortobágy (2), once a vast marsh, drained in the second half of the 19th century to become a great waterless plain. When this happened the formerly abundant waterfowl deserted it. But more recently they have returned, following the construction of numerous ponds for the rearing of fish. These provide the vital roosting places and water for drinking and bathing, while the surrounding farmland provides the food. Various agricultural changes have made some areas less attractive than others but the most favoured locality is to the east of the river Tisza, which runs through the Hortobágy. Numbers are very variable and there is probably a lot of movement between here and the fishpond area of Biharugra (3) near the Romanian border. On the Hortobágy there have been recent counts in excess of 8000, while 10,000–15,000 Whitefronts occur throughout the winter at Biharugra. In hard winters numbers may drop to a few thousands, or even just a few hundreds, depending on the severity of the weather. To the south of the Hortobágy there is another important haunt, at Kardoskút (4), where there is a saline lake set in steppe grassland. Up to 25,000 Whitefronts may winter there although a count of around 50,000 was recorded during migration, and a similar one in a different year at Biharugra. There are several other Whitefront roosts in Hungary but records are fragmentary and none seem to hold large numbers regularly, though they may do so temporarily during migration. There are two localities just over the Hungarian border, in western Romania, where several thousand Whitefronts occur, mostly on migration, at Otomani and the Banat.

Yugoslavia is the other principal wintering country for this population, and the three most important haunts are at Belo Blato (5) and Kopački (6) in the north, and at Skadarsko (7) in the south close to the frontier with Albania. Several thousands occur at each haunt. There used to be substantial numbers wintering in Albania but there is no recent information. In Greece, too, the Whitefront was formerly much more common, but the western and northern resorts used by this population are now seldom used, partly as a result of drainage and probably in part because of better conditions further north. Whitefronts occurring in eastern Greece belong to the Pontic population, to be dealt with below. A persistent small flock of Whitefronts on the Adriatic coast of Italy, north of Bari, is presumed to belong to this present population. It now numbers only a few tens of birds, though formerly it reached hundreds, and perhaps occasionally still does so.

Probable stragglers from this population have turned up in Switzerland, Malta, Tunisia and Libya.

Pontic population (Maps 10 and 12)

This is the third European population of Whitefront. Like the others it is not possible to be certain of its breeding area, but the wintering range seems fairly well defined, lying in eastern Romania, particularly round the delta of the Danube, in Bulgaria, eastern Greece and northern and western Turkey. Counts are even more vague than for the Pannonic population. There are very probably at least 100,000 Whitefronts but there may be more. There was a single and staggering count of 500,000 in the Dobrogea, south of the Danube delta area of Romania, in December 1968, and even if this was an overestimate it was obvious from later counts that year that the population was at an exceptionally high level. Such numbers were unlikely to have come solely from a good breeding season and it is more probable that there had been some temporary shift of birds from another population.

The main wintering ground for the whole population is the Dobrogea (8), an area of farmland and shallow lagoons near the mouth of the River Danube. Here, between 10,000 and 50,000 Whitefronts spend the winter. Peaks of 100,000 have been recorded more than once, quite apart from the 500,000 just mentioned. Elsewhere in Romania, Whitefronts occur rather less regularly though flocks of some thousands are likely to appear during migration periods at a number of places. In Bulgaria, recent information suggests that several thousand Whitefronts winter in areas near the Black Sea, though numbers in any one winter are probably affected by conditions in Romania to the north.

North-eastern Greece and north-western Turkey form the southern wintering areas for this population. The Evros Delta (9), which lies astride the border between the two countries, is by far the most important haunt. Several thousands of geese are regularly present and a peak of 25,000 has been recorded. The difficulties of counting in a locality that is divided between two countries is compounded in this case by the rather fraught relations between them in recent years. On the other hand, the presence of a strict security zone on either side of the border may have made access by ornithologists very difficult, but it has undoubtedly reduced the shooting of geese. Other haunts in both countries are all minor, holding a few thousands at the most, with Korla Lake on the Aegean coast of Greece (10) and the Kokabas delta on the Sea of Marmora in Turkey (11) probably the best in each.

Anatolian population (Maps 10 and 12)
The known wintering area of this population is confined to the highlands of Anatolia in central Turkey. Its numbers are not precisely known but are thought to lie in the range of 60,000–100,000 if not more. Counts in this area of Turkey have only been made on a few occasions but a number of lakes, some fresh, some saline, have been found carrying flocks of several thousand Whitefronts. The most important of these is Tuz Gölü (12) where as many as 25,000 have been counted, though 10,000 may be more usual. Neighbouring Whitefront resorts of importance include the Eber Gölü and the Hotamis marshes.

In some years thousands of Whitefronts have been found wintering in the Bay of Iskenderun (13) on the Mediterranean coast of Turkey close to the Syrian border, and there have also been reports of Whitefronts flying south over Cyprus and straggling to Israel. It seems probable that the latter are heading for Egypt, where wintering Whitefronts were formerly numerous, but such recent information as there is suggests that this is no longer true.

Caspian population (Map 10)
An apparently discrete population of Whitefronts has a wintering area on

the southern coasts of the Caspian Sea, in the U.S.S.R. and in Iran. The species used to be numerous in the Tigris–Euphrates marshes of Iraq but there is no recent information. Whitefronts also occur further south in Iran towards the Persian Gulf, and it is assumed that these are part of the Caspian population. The total numbers involved can only be guesswork but upwards of 40,000 seems to be a reasonable estimate.

Asian populations (Map 10)

Virtually nothing is known in detail concerning further populations to the east of the Caspian. There are, or were, wintering areas in Pakistan, northern India, Burma and south-east Asia, as well as in China and Japan. Some thousands of Whitefronts winter in the latter country, for example 5000 were counted in January 1976, about double the total for 1970, but this is many fewer than formerly, partly because of loss of habitat, and partly due to continued persecution on the breeding grounds. These birds are usually referred to the race Pacific Whitefront *frontalis* but I have dealt with them here, being unconvinced that they are separable from other European Whitefronts. Summer surveys in north-east Siberia have shown populations of grey geese in excess of 250,000, of which the majority are Whitefronts but an unknown proportion are Bean Geese.

Greenland White-fronted Goose (Maps 10 and 13, Table 18)

There is only a single population of this subspecies, though there is some evidence that birds from different parts of the breeding range may winter in traditional areas of the wintering range. Separate populations may one day develop in this way but the process has not reached that stage in this case.

The breeding range is shown on Map 10. It extends from about 64°00′–72°30′N up the west coast, an area that is essentially low arctic in type, with a good growth of birch and willow scrub in the valleys, and high heathy plateaus on which the geese are most plentiful. In winter the Greenland Whitefront is found on the west coast of Scotland and in Ireland. This traversing of the North Atlantic from breeding to wintering quarters is a journey undertaken by a number of other species of birds including Brent Goose, Turnstone and Ringed Plover, and is taken as proof that these species spread to this part of the arctic from north-west Europe after the end of the last ice age, and not from North America. They have continued to return to their area of origin for the winter, despite the fact that North America is considerably closer. Reports of Greenland Whitefronts from the Atlantic coast states of America are almost annual but rarely involve more than from one to five birds.

There has never been a complete census of the Greenland Whitefront. The remote and scattered nature of many of its haunts in Scotland and Ireland has made this too difficult and costly a task. However, the two major haunts are counted regularly and there are sufficient counts from some of the other localities to suppose that there are probably about 12,000 birds in the population at present, with some evidence of a slight decline over the last two decades or so. This has not been an overall decline but a contraction of range, with the numbers at the major haunts holding up but many of the minor ones being abandoned as a result of drainage and other disturbances, particularly in Ireland.

By far the most important haunt is the Wexford Slobs (1), flat farmland reclaimed from Wexford Harbour in south-east Ireland. This used to be all grassland, and a proposal to drain it more efficiently and then convert it to arable, about ten years ago, produced many protests. A small area was bought by the Irish Government as a refuge and left unploughed. However, when the remaining much larger area had been cultivated for cereals and potatoes it was found that the geese preferred gleaning these crops after harvest to feeding on the grass. A refuge warden was appointed in 1966 and since then there have been winter counts several times each month. The geese arrive in the last half of October and depart in mid-April. The total has fluctuated slightly but has remained remarkably steady over the last decade (Table 18). There are regular shoots over the area and the average mortality from this and other causes has been found to be about balanced by the annual productivity.

The second most important Greenland Whitefront haunt is on the island of Islay (2) in the Inner Hebrides, Scotland. Here, between 3000 and 4000 birds winter (Table 18), scattered in many small flocks over the island so that the largest number found together is rarely more than 700. Many of the birds use arable farmland, but as many are still using the more traditional bogs and rough pasture. An interesting discovery has been that in most years the annual breeding success of the birds on Islay has been less than on the Wexford Slobs. From ringing recoveries we know that there is some winter segregation of birds from different parts of the breeding range with, curiously enough, those breeding furthest north wintering furthest south. This is called

TABLE 18: *Peak counts of Greenland White-fronted Geese at the Wexford Slobs, Ireland, and Islay, Inner Hebrides, Scotland, 1966–7 to 1976–7, together with breeding success figures recorded at both haunts*

	WEXFORD SLOBS			ISLAY		
Winter	Peak count	% young	Brood size	Peak count	% young	Brood size
1966–7	8,740	no records		4,700	26·1	2·7
1967–8	8,200	no records		3,320	16·0	1·7
1968–9	6,240	32·8	4·1	2,250	16·2	1·5
1969–70	7,280	35·4	3·9	3,050	9·3	2·0
1970–1	7,100	15·5	3·7	2,000	12·5	2·8
1971–2	5,960	14·8	3·4	3,400	7·4	2·0
1972–3	5,380	12·7	3·8	2,580	4·6	2·2
1973–4	5,570	20·5	3·7	4,180	15·1	2·8
1974–5	5,800	17·7	3·6	3,430	18·4	2·9
1975–6	6,020	25·6	3·8	4,150	21·4	3·2
1976–7	6,700	19·6	3·9	4,210	20·8	3·4

O. J. Merne (pers. com.) and own data.

leapfrog migration. The variation in age-counts between Islay and the Slobs confirms this segregation but is somewhat puzzling, because one might expect the more northerly breeding birds to have a lower productivity than those breeding to the south in more favourable conditions. It is possible that the better feeding enjoyed by the birds on the Slobs compared to those on Islay gives them an advantage in condition on arrival on the breeding grounds.

There are few other places in Ireland where more than one or two hundred Whitefronts winter, but still a number where less than a hundred do so. However, it is doubtful whether these tiny groups are really viable over the long term, but it is difficult to see what can be done to encourage them. In Scotland there are two localities on the Mull of Kintyre (3, 4) where some hundreds winter not very far from Islay, and another in Galloway (5). Otherwise, the remaining Scottish haunts hold mere handfuls of birds. It does seem from this, and from the scattered nature of most of the geese on Islay, that this race is considerably less gregarious than most other geese. This may be a reflection of the relatively poorer food supply in bogs and on rough pastures, particularly in terms of density. It is noticeable that where the geese have adapted to arable farmland and improved pasture the average flock size is increased. A former Welsh haunt at Tregaron Bog is now deserted and the remaining flock in Wales, on the Dovey Estuary, has declined in the last five years, and now numbers under 100.

Pacific White-fronted Goose (Maps 10 and 14, Table 19)

This subspecies has only one population and is confined to the Pacific Flyway. The breeding range is restricted to two areas of Alaska, looking comparatively small on the map, but as one of them is the Yukon–Kuskokwim delta, which is probably the largest waterfowl breeding area in the world, the population size is quite respectable. The second breeding area is in Bristol Bay on the north side of the Alaskan peninsula. There are scattered breeding pairs in between, but they make a negligible contribution to the total. Indeed, it is probable that the Bristol Bay area is very minor in comparison with the delta. Sample counts and density estimates for the latter have been combined to suggest a peak of 40,000 breeding pairs of Whitefronts, which, with their young and immature non-breeders, would represent a total of about 200,000 birds. This is closely in line with the largest counts made on the wintering grounds in the last two decades.

The winter counts, together with those for the other North American Whitefronts, to be dealt with next, are set out in Table 19, together with the annual breeding success. The variations in the totals have been considerable and not at all in line with variations in breeding success, which have been comparatively slight. The drop between 1972 and 1973, for example, is very surprising given that 1973 was apparently a good breeding year. A probable explanation is that the accuracy of the counts is low, and also that the breeding success data which are being gathered may not be fully representative. It has recently been suggested that accurate censuses of this population on its

MAP 13. Greenland White-fronted Goose *Anser albifrons flavirostris*—winter haunts. Numbers indicate haunts referred to in text.

wintering grounds are almost impossible, though this rightly has not stopped the biologists trying.

The Pacific Whitefronts migrate down the Pacific coast of North America, making their first stop near the mouth of the Columbia river on the border between Washington and Oregon (1). Thence they move to the Tule–Klamath Basin in southern Oregon and northern California (2).

Virtually the whole population can be found there in October and November, one of the great goose spectacles of North America: over 40,000 hectares (100,000 acres) of marsh, lake and grassland with the four major refuges of Upper and Lower Klamath, Oregon, and Tule and Clear Lakes, California. Several other kinds of geese are there at the same time, together numbering hundreds of thousands, and the ducks can be counted in the millions. The area forms a vital stopping place for migrants out of Alaska heading south for the winter. There is little other water for about 240 km (150 miles) in any direction. The Whitefronts spend some weeks here before moving on in about mid-November, mainly to the great Central Valley of California. A few thousand stay and winter in most years.

The Central Valley lies between the Sierra Nevada mountains and the coastal range. Nearly 800 km long and over 80 km broad (500 by 50 miles) it forms a fertile plain set in an elongated bowl of mountains. Down its centre runs the Sacramento river, giving its name to the Sacramento Wildlife Refuge (3), home not only of the Whitefronts, but of Ross's Geese, small Canada Geese, Lesser Snow Geese and hundreds of thousands of ducks. Here the geese spend the winter, feeding up and down the valley on the extensive rice fields, barley stubbles and on natural marsh plants.

Although the great majority of the Pacific Whitefronts winter in the Central Valley, some thousands make their way further south, heading for the Imperial Valley (4) in the extreme south of California. About 2000 birds stay there but another 7000 or so go still further to the west coast of Mexico, mostly within the Gulf of California. The few hundreds that turn up on the west coast of Guatemala in some winters are usually attributed to this population, but it seems equally likely that they belong to the population wintering in the Gulf, and in east and central Mexico in areas much closer to Guatemala than the west coast haunts. Vagrants from this population have occurred in the Hawaiian Islands including Midway Atoll.

The spring departure starts in the far south of the range in late February but most birds move north in March going to the Klamath Basin area again and staying there during April.

Interior White-fronted Goose (Maps 10 and 14, Table 19)

The Whitefronts that breed in Alaska (other than in Bristol Bay and the Yukon–Kuskokwim delta) and in arctic Canada, form a second North American subspecies. Although the breeding range shown on Map 10 is pretty continuous and the geese may be found breeding within it in suitable habitat almost anywhere, there are in fact twelve distinct areas where they are much commoner than elsewhere. The habitat is of two distinct types: coastal marshy tundra with countless pools and shallow lakes; and upland tundra, up to 200–250 metres (700–800 ft) above sea level, which is drier overall but still has innumerable small waters.

Ringing and observations have indicated a possible division of this population into two subgroups, a western and an eastern. There is much overlap, though, in the breeding range, migration routes, and wintering areas, and so far there is insufficient distinction to make it worth monitoring the two subgroups separately. The breeding range of the western sub-population covers Alaska and western arctic Canada, while the eastern subpopulation breeds in central arctic Canada (Map 14). The most important breeding areas of the former are around the coast of Kotzebue Sound (5), on the inland flats of the Koyukuk, Minto, and Upper Yukon Rivers (6), and on the North Slope (7), all in Alaska, and on the Old Crow Flats (8) and the Mackenzie (9) and Anderson (10) River deltas in western Canada. The eastern subpopulation has its principal breeding areas on the coastal lowlands of Coronation Gulf (11), Queen Maud Gulf (12), and on the south coasts of islands on the north side of these gulfs, namely Victoria Island (13), King William Island (14) and the small Jenny Lind Island lying in Queen Maud Gulf (15). Inland from the latter Gulf there is a breeding area around the headwaters of the Coppermine, Back and Thelon Rivers (16).

Estimates of numbers from the breeding grounds suggest that the population of Alaska may number 50,000–70,000 birds at the end of the summer of which about 50,000 are to be found on the North Slope. The number of breeding pairs in this area is thought to be around 3000 and the large flocks of non-breeders which comprise the majority are believed to have come from inland breeding areas to moult on the coast. Inland breeding numbers are not known, but are almost certainly less than on the North

TABLE 19: *Mid-winter counts of Pacific and interior White-fronted Geese, 1959–60 to 1976–7, together with annual breeding success*

	PACIFIC WHITEFRONT			INTERIOR WHITEFRONT		
Winter	Total	% young	Brood size	Total	% young	Brood size
1959–60	172,368	not recorded		42,000	51·6	2·58
1960–1	185,596	50·4	3·10	42,000	50·4	2·83
1961–2	193,200	36·5	2·33	46,000	19·7	2·04
1962–3	127,690	38·9	2·52	91,692	36·4	2·08
1963–4	171,756	29·8	2·27	99,208	49·7	2·82
1964–5	137,410	31·7	2·29	74,002	28·9	2·37
1965–6	160,000	38·9	2·52	82,000	36·8	2·75
1966–7	185,600	41·8	2·50	93,000	43·8	2·92
1967–8	70,900	31·2	2·49	120,000	36·2	2·57
1968–9	114,200	40·7	2·39	122,000	34·4	2·80
1969–70	206,700	37·2	2·35	136,000	41·2	2·87
1970–1	106,300	28·2	2·21	167,000	44·5	2·72
1971–2	100,600	37·7	2·37	180,000	34·4	2·36
1972–3	54,800	42·2	2·07	174,000	28·4	2·29
1973–4	86,700	38·6	2·47	200,700	42·8	2·70
1974–5	74,500	28·6	1·81	173,500	32·6	2·37
1975–6	83,000	41·2	1·90	180,000	41·9	2·29
1976–7	50,000	n.a.	2·48	254,600	21·2	2·18

Lynch & Voelzer (1974), Voelzer (1976 and pers. com.).

Slope. The Mackenzie and Anderson River deltas also hold large numbers of Whitefronts with estimates for the two, some years ago, of 40,000. The Old Crow Flats to the south-west held about 1400. The Queen Maud Gulf area is probably the most important in the eastern subpopulation's breeding range with at least 10,000 birds there by the end of the summer, plus a further 2000 or more on the islands to the north. The numbers inland are not known but may be substantial.

Counts on the wintering grounds have been plagued by difficulties in finding and censusing all the geese. The best counts nowadays are made in March as the geese gather before heading north. The counts, including both subpopulations, are set out in Table 19. Breeding success figures for the two subpopulations do not usually differ much and a single figure is given. This shows a relatively high level without much variation, which is similar to the Pacific population. The totals show a steady increase, though with significant fluctuations from year to year. Some at least of these fluctuations must be due to counting problems and the overall increase shown may itself be caused in part by an improvement in counting efficiency in recent years. Nevertheless it can be seen that the population is in a more healthy state than that of the Pacific Whitefront.

The western subpopulation mainly follows the Central Flyway, stopping for varying periods in the autumn in northern Alberta and then at the major halting place (17) near Kindersley, Saskatchewan, and on the Souris River in North Dakota just over the border. There they may stay until well into October before heading south again. Many of the geese then appear to make a single nonstop flight to the Gulf coasts of Texas and Louisiana, though some may stop for a time at a number of intermediate localities.

The eastern subpopulation belongs more to the Mississippi Flyway, but there is certainly some joint use with the western group of staging posts in Saskatchewan and North Dakota, as well as more discrete use of haunts in Manitoba around the Saskatchewan river delta (18), and the Whitewater and Oak Lakes. From there they go straight to the Gulf. Ringing has shown that although both subpopulations occur in Louisiana and Texas, there is a far greater proportion of the eastern subpopulation in Louisiana, and of the western subpopulation in Texas. The principal haunts are the great marshes all along the coast from western Louisiana, through Texas and into Mexico. Particular concentrations occur between Galveston Bay (19) and Corpus Christi (20). There are a number of localities on the east coast of Mexico, including the Rio Grande delta (21) and lagoons near Tampico and Veracruz. There are also a number of Whitefront haunts in the northern highlands of Mexico around the larger lakes, though numbers rarely exceed a couple of thousands at any one site. There may be a little mixing there with birds from the Pacific Flyway. However, there are also ringing recoveries which suggest that some birds cross over to the Pacific Flyway from the western subpopulation as they leave Canada, and they may be taking this route before going on to Mexico. Vagrants have reached Cuba.

Northward migration begins in late February and its pace is dictated by weather conditions as the geese follow the spring thaw north. They make use of many of the same stopping places as in the autumn.

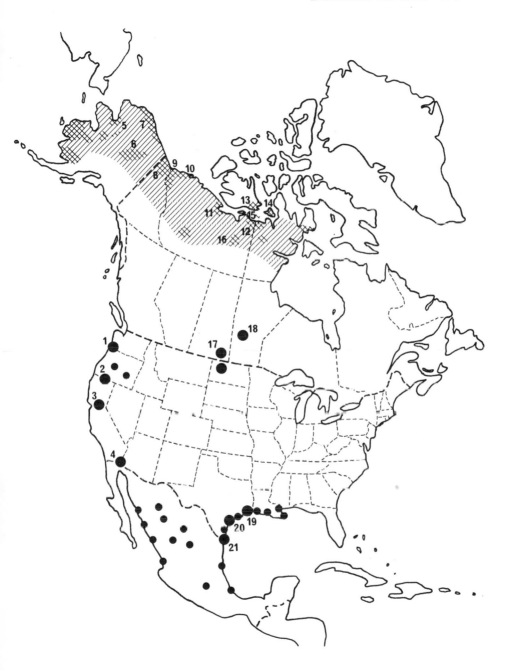

MAP 14. Pacific *Anser albifrons frontalis* and Interior *A.a.gambelli* White-fronted Goose range, and migration and wintering haunts. ⫽ breeding range; ⊞breeding concentrations. Numbered haunts—see text; ● other haunts.

MAP 15. Lesser White-fronted Goose *Anser erythropus*—world range. ⫽ breeding; ⫼ wintering.

Lesser White-fronted Goose (Maps 15 and 16)

The breeding and wintering distribution of this species is shown on Map 15. It is largely a boreal zone breeder, though extending into the tundra in a few regions. The distribution shows the usual division into westerly and easterly wintering areas, but data are completely lacking to show where the corresponding divide in the breeding range might lie.

On numbers, too, there is very little information. It has been estimated that the total population, east and west, might be in the region of 100,000, but there is no information from China, Korea and eastern U.S.S.R. Counts or estimates from the western half of the winter range are not very good, either, and it is uncertain whether there are 20,000–30,000 birds, as some believe, or as many as 50,000 as has been stated. The principal wintering area is around the Caspian Sea, particularly in Russian Azerbaijan (1) on the west coast. There as many as 10,000, or perhaps more, have been reported but recent records are scarce. On the Iranian shores of the Caspian, some hundreds of Lesser Whitefronts have occurred, particularly in Gorgan Bay (2), and elsewhere in Iran there are reports of up to 500 at Lake Rezaiyeh (3) and also at Niriz (4). There are thought to be quite large numbers in the Tigris–Euphrates marshes of Iraq (5), but no counts are available.

Coming westwards the two major haunts are in Hungary where up to 2000 birds have been counted at both the Hortobágy (6) and Kardoskút (7). However, the peak numbers are usually in the autumn, with many fewer remaining for the winter. An exception was in 1972–3, when 5000 were counted in Hungary in December. Over the border in Yugoslavia up to 1000 have been seen at Belo Blato (8). South and east from here, there are just two sites where some hundreds of Lesser Whitefronts appear to be regular, on the Evros Delta (9) on the Greece–Turkey border, and at Burgas in Bulgaria (10) on the Black Sea. At all these haunts the species is less common than it once was.

The Lesser Whitefront is a regular visitor to north-west Europe, with from one to three birds being reported most winters among European Whitefronts in Britain and the Netherlands, and less often among Bean Geese. There have been about 100 occurrences in Britain, the majority at the New Grounds, Slimbridge, Gloucestershire, the home of the largest and best-watched flock

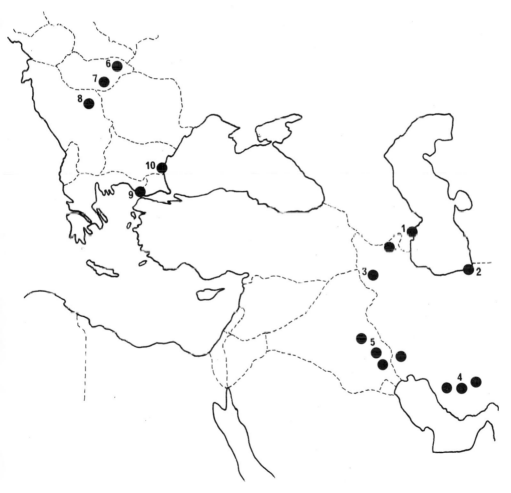

MAP 16. Lesser White-fronted Goose *Anser erythropus*—winter range in south-east Europe and Middle East. ● major haunts. Numbers indicate haunts referred to in text.

of Whitefronts. The second and third records of the species for Britain were at Slimbridge in 1946, but once the Whitefront flock there came under regular and close scrutiny, as it did from that winter onwards, they have been seen in nearly every year. The species has been seen in several other European countries including Denmark, Belgium, France, Austria, Switzerland, and east to Turkey and Egypt.

There is good evidence that the species has declined as a breeder in Scandinavia, though as a very scattered breeding bird it will never be easy to census. There used to be a regular migration of some hundreds through southern Finland, but since the 1960s this has trickled away to a mere handful.

Greylag Goose (Map 17)

The breeding distribution of this species extends further south in Europe than any other goose, while also reaching north to the edge of the arctic (Map 17). It is discontinuous in Europe largely as a result of persecution by man and drainage of natural marshes which formed the Greylag's preferred breeding habitat. It must once have bred throughout Europe and it is known to have done so in England, France and the Netherlands, for example.

Although some birds are wintering within their breeding range the great majority are migratory and it has been possible to divide them into a number of populations that are more or less separate, though interchange between some, particularly in western and central Europe, confuses the picture. As stated in Chapter 1, the usual division into two subspecies is not being followed here as there is no clear way of splitting geographically what is really a cline of variation.

TABLE 20: *Numbers of Icelandic Greylag Geese wintering in Britain, 1952–3 to 1977–8, together with annual breeding success since 1958. Figures since 1960–1 are the annual November censuses*

Winter	Total	% young	Brood size	Winter	Total	% young	Brood size
1952–3	25,000	no records		1965–6	44,500	21·1	3·09
1953–4	29,000	,,		1966–7	58,000	24·9	2·65
1954–5	25,000	,,		1967–8	52,500	11·0	1·78
1955–6	21,000	,,		1968–9	61,000	6·0	1·31
1956–7	24,000	,,		1969–70	62,000	23·8	1·97
1957–8	21,000	,,		1970–1	64,500	25·1	2·36
1958–9	20,000	28·8	2·88	1971–2	64,000	17·5	1·84
1959–60	20,000	34·6	3·44	1972–3	68,000	15·1	1·77
1960–1	26,500	43·5	3·45	1973–4	76,500	30·3	2·56
1961–2	35,000	40·0	3·75	1974–5	69,500	18·8	2·16
1962–3	40,500	31·8	3·13	1975–6	63,000	7·6	1·51
1963–4	32,500	27·5	2·31	1976–7	56,000	13·1	2·13
1964–5	44,000	27·6	3·00	1977–8	62,000	11·2	2·19

Ogilvie & Boyd (1976).

Map 17. Greylag Goose *Anser anser*—world range. ⧵ breeding; ⧵ wintering.

Icelandic population (Maps 17 and 18, Table 20)

This is one of the better studied populations at least on the wintering grounds. Work in Iceland has been confined to aerial surveys in 1963 and 1964, which produced a fairly good map of distribution but did not amount to a full census. The species is confined to the lowland areas, the broad river valleys and the numerous lakes and coastal lagoons, where the habitat is a mixture of farmland and uncultivated heath and scrub. The aerial surveys revealed some areas of concentration but as the total population has roughly doubled since then it is not worth mapping here.

Ringing and other observations have established that the entire Iceland breeding population winters within the British Isles with the exception of a mere handful, a hundred or two, which stay in Iceland, in or around the capital Reykjavik. Since 1960 there has been a reasonably accurate annual autumn census in Britain and the results are set out in Table 20, together with the annual breeding success. The picture closely parallels that for the Icelandic Pinkfoot population (see page 193 and Table 15). The population has been growing steadily, helped by fairly consistent breeding success, though this has been accompanied by an overall decline in the actual number of breeding pairs (again, similar to the Pinkfoot) and a decline in mortality. The recent decrease in numbers is directly related to poor summers in Iceland, particularly in 1975.

The Greylags arrive in Britain later than the Pinkfeet, being able to stay in the lowlands of Iceland longer than the latter can stay in the interior of the country where snow may fall as early as mid–September. The main arrival of

Greylags takes place in the second half of October and is usually complete by early November. The wintering distribution is more widespread in Scotland than that of the Pinkfoot, but there are only very small numbers in northern England, plus a very few in Ireland. Greylags feed almost exclusively on farmland, roosting on inland waters; they use rather few estuaries. Again, like the Pinkfoot, the greatest concentrations are found in autumn when the geese are feeding on stubble and potato fields. The big flocks then break up and the geese become much more dispersed. There is some regrouping in March and a tendency to shift northwards through the country before the main departure for Iceland takes place in mid-April.

The main concentrations are in east central Scotland (Map 18), particularly round Blairgowrie (1) where up to 12,000 congregate in autumn, plus another flock of similar size roosting on Drummond Pond near Crieff (2). At least 5000 are found most years at Strathbeg (3) and Meikle Lochs (4), Grampian, and at Carsebreck, Perthshire (5), and Loch Leven, Kinross (6). There are also several thousands spread between a number of different roosts, mostly reservoirs, in the Lothians south of Edinburgh (7). The considerable overlap with the Pinkfoot will be obvious from this list. The two species co-exist quite happily, often using the same roost, though usually different parts of it, and sometimes feeding in mixed flocks.

Greylags go a little further west in Scotland than the Pinkfoot, with up to 2000 on the island of Bute (8) and near Stranraer in the extreme south-west (9). In addition there are a great many smaller flocks, from 100 to 1000 scattered between the Moray Basin and the Solway Firth. However, numbers in northern England are small, though there used to be several thousands there before the improved feeding and roosting conditions in Scotland held the birds back. There are about 1000 in Northumberland and a handful in the southern Lake District, though most of these are probably descended from feral stock. Greylags have also withdrawn from Ireland in recent decades and there are now barely 200 in all, in two or three localities.

Greylags bred in the Faeroes until about the 1840s, and did so a few times in the early 1940s. A vagrant, probably from the Iceland population, was recorded on Jan Mayen.

North-west Scotland population (Map 18)

There is a small indigenous population of Greylags breeding in the Outer Hebrides and on the north-west Scottish mainland, in Sutherland, Caithness, and Ross and Cromarty. It is very scattered and has proved almost impossible to census or even to map its full distribution (Map 18). It is likely that the population numbers no more than 2000 individuals. Some 60 pairs breed around the shores and on the islands of Loch Druidibeg, South Uist, and form what is probably the largest breeding concentration. A moulting flock of 250 appears each summer on a water in Sutherland, though breeding numbers in that area are small. The birds of this population are clearly the remnants of a much wider distribution that probably covered most of Scotland, northern England and Ireland a few hundred years ago. It has steadily retreated in the face of habitat destruction and over-hunting, the birds being vulnerable throughout the year. Wild Greylags last bred in England in 1831 and in

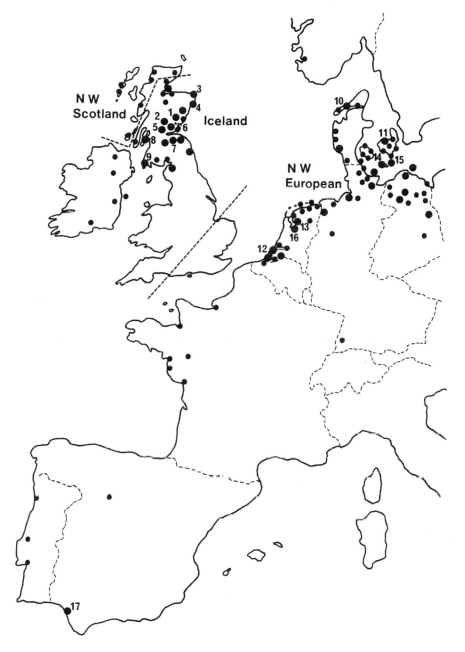

Map 18. Greylag Goose *Anser anser*—major haunts of NW Scotland population, and winter haunts of Iceland and NW European populations. ●over 1000; ● under 1000. Numbers indicate haunts referred to in text. Dotted lines divide the wintering ranges of the three populations.

Ireland sometime in the previous century.

Evidence of migration by this population is slight. A few were ringed on South Uist some years ago, but all winter recoveries have come from that island or neighbouring ones in the Outer Hebrides. Small flocks of wintering Greylags, up to 150, are found on some of the Inner Hebridean islands such as Colonsay and Islay. The annual breeding success of these birds has so often been different from that of the Icelandic birds that it has, plausibly, been suggested that they belong to the north-west Scotland population, instead, though there is no firm proof at present.

Eggs and young taken from the Hebrides in the 1930s were used to establish a feral flock of Greylags on Lochinch, near Stranraer (9). This has since increased and spread on to neighbouring waters up to 80 km (50 miles) away, and the population now numbers over 1000. Apart from some flocking onto favoured haunts in winter, the birds are non-migratory. Eggs and young from this flock have in their turn been used to create feral populations in several places in England.

West European population (Maps 17 and 18)

The breeding area of this population lies in Norway, Sweden and Denmark, with an introduced addition in Belgium. In winter, a small number remains in Denmark but the main wintering grounds lie in the Netherlands and in Spain, plus a few in Belgium and France (Map 18). There have been some useful estimates of the numbers of breeding pairs in each country and some, though incomplete, winter counts.

The number of breeding pairs in Norway is not known for certain but is likely to be at least 2000, possibly more. They are spread all up the west coast including the offshore islands. The Swedish breeding population is much smaller at about 500 pairs, confined mainly to the south-east and east coasts. There were about 100 pairs on the small islands off the larger island of Gotland in 1967. The Norwegian and Swedish breeding stocks have each been increasing in recent years, though some of the Swedish birds belong to the Central European population. In Denmark there are probably about 2500 breeding pairs, well spread through the country in habitats as diverse as the remote Vejlerne marshes (10) in the north where there are up to 200 pairs, and park lakes in the centre of Copenhagen and other conurbations. The Greylag formerly bred in the Netherlands but was driven out at the turn of the century. There has been scattered breeding since, aided by introductions from about 1962. Birds were introduced to the Zwin reserve in northern Belgium in 1956 and this group has since increased to 300 birds, which are joined by some of the migratory population passing through the area each spring and autumn.

Summer concentrations of moulting Greylags occur in Denmark, at Saltbaekvig (11) on the island of Sjaelland (some hundreds) and, formerly, at Vejlerne (10) (up to 3000 in the 1950s); and also in the Netherlands at Haringvliet (12) in the Scheldt delta (several thousands in the 1960s but now only hundreds), and in the Grote Brekken (13) beside the Ijsselmeer (several hundreds). Fuller details of these birds and their possible origins will be given in the discussion on moult migration in the next chapter. It seems that most if not all of these birds are from the Central European population.

The Greylags from Norway and Sweden move into Denmark in the late summer and autumn, to produce a peak of 20,000 in July 1974, and more regular September totals of between 11,000 and 18,000 over the last 12 years. They move quite quickly onwards, taking the Danish breeding birds with them so that October counts have dropped rapidly to only 3000–5000, and less than 1000 Greylags stay through the winter. The more important autumn haunts are in the west of Denmark, two of them, Saltbaekvig (11) and Basnaes (14) on the island of Sjaelland to the west of Copenhagen, the third, Oreby (15), on Lolland to the south. Up to 2000 Greylags can be found regularly at each haunt, with a peak count of 3500 at Basnaes. Much smaller numbers can be seen at several sites in most parts of the country, both in autumn and spring. Total Greylag numbers in spring are much lower, either because the geese take a different route, or because their stay is very brief. The same is true of West Germany, where the main haunts are close to the Danish border, holding up to 4000 in autumn, and 2500 in spring. Only a few hundred birds winter.

The next stopping place for the Greylags is the Netherlands, and there have been fairly complete counts in October and November of what must be virtually the whole population. This has amounted to about 25,000–30,000 birds in recent years, having increased from 10,000 over the last fifteen years. An increasing proportion of the geese stay in the Netherlands through the winter, with perhaps 10,000 in some recent years, even as many as 15,000. The geese are well spread over the country but the main haunts are in the Flevoland polders (16) in the south of the Ijsselmeer, and a group of resorts on the arms of the Scheldt, the Haringvliet (12), Cromstrijen, Strijen, and Hollandsdiep. At each of these haunts the peak occurs at migration time in October and November, with up to 5000 or more, while 2000–3000 birds remain during the winter, though these figures are variable.

Some Greylags winter in northern Belgium, joining the introduced population at the Zwin reserve, but usually less than 1000. Although several thousand Greylags migrate through France to Spain, they stop only rarely on the way and the number actually wintering in France is small, having declined from about 500 in the early 1960s to only 100 in recent years. They are scattered between a number of haunts on the north and west coasts.

The main wintering place in Spain lies in the Marismas, the marshes of the Guadalquivir River mouth, partly in the reserve of Coto Doñana (17). The numbers there have increased roughly in line with the rise in the total population, from up to 12,000 in the early 1960s to a peak of 26,300 in winter 1973–4. In the period 1971–2 to 1974–5, the peak count at the Marismas has been 21,000, 19,000, 26,300 and 19,300. This variation suggests either fluctuating annual breeding success (which is not monitored but is unlikely to vary so much in a temperate breeding population), or because of varying numbers staying back in the Netherlands. Elsewhere in Spain and Portugal there are a few scattered localities where some tens or hundreds of Greylags can be found. The geese reach Spain in force by November and depart again in late February or early March.

Vagrants that can be presumed to belong to this population have reached

Svalbard (including Bear Island), to the north, and the Azores, Madeira, the Canaries and Morocco to the south.

Central European population (Maps 17 and 19)

The breeding area for this population extends from the Baltic to eastern Austria and Czechoslovakia. The boundary between this population and the previous one is not at all clear, but at least some of the Swedish Greylags migrate south to join the Central European population, as do the breeding stocks of Finland (200–250 pairs) and Estonia (750 pairs). South of the Baltic there are about 500 pairs in Poland, and the population of East Germany is put at 2000 pairs and is increasing. Some of the 400 pairs breeding in West Germany may also belong to this population. There are about 300 pairs each in Austria and Czechoslovakia. The picture on the northern and western fringes of this population is confused by the movement of some non-breeding birds to Denmark and the Netherlands for the summer moult, as already mentioned. Even though these birds may return to join the rest of the Central European population in the autumn, this movement into the breeding range of another population gives plenty of opportunity for mixing. Separation between these two populations is therefore not wholly complete and it is difficult to be certain whether or not changes in numbers reflect shifts of birds between populations. However, in recent years both groups have been increasing, which is a healthy sign, and goes some way towards eliminating this possibility.

The wintering grounds lie mainly in North Africa, in Tunisia and eastern Algeria (Map 19). The birds from around the Baltic migrate through Austria, where up to 5000 have been counted at Lake Neusiedl and Lake Seewinkel (1), and then the majority head south-west for Tunisia, where between 5000 and 7000 normally winter, though there was an exceptional count of over 9000 birds in 1973–4. Some hundreds of geese turn south-east and go into Greece and even into Turkey. The main wintering locality in Tunisia is Lake Ichkeul, (2), near Bizerta, which held virtually all the 9000 in 1973–4. Other coastal lakes here and in Algeria hold some hundreds of Greylags. Stragglers have reached Libya and Malta.

On the return migration in spring large numbers of Greylags pass through southern Moravia in Czechoslovakia, with up to 4000 concentrated round an area of fishponds in southern Bohemia (3). This represents a considerable increase in the last twenty years.

There have been no complete counts of the population and no age counts. The best estimate for the total size is 10,000–15,000 birds, though the number of breeding pairs given above would suggest that a slightly higher figure is more probable, or that the overlap with the West European population is greater than is supposed. There have been recent late summer counts in East Germany of up to 15,000, but again it is not certain that all these birds belong to this population.

Pontic population (Maps 17 and 19)

Roughly 10,000–20,000 birds winter in Romania, Greece and north-west Turkey (Map 19). The most important locality is the Evros Delta (14) on the

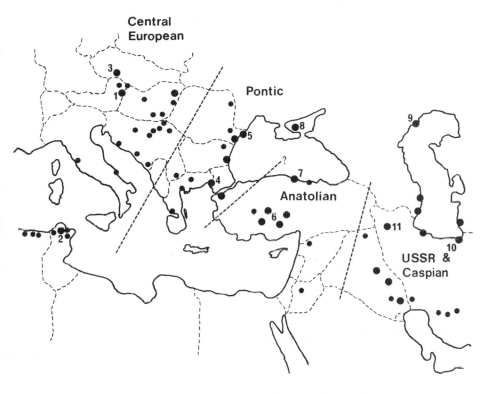

MAP 19. Greylag Goose *Anser anser*—winter haunts of Central European, Pontic, Anatolian, and USSR and Caspian populations. ●over 1000; •under 1000. Numbers indicate haunts referred to in text. Dotted lines divide the wintering range of the four populations.

Greece-Turkey border, where a maximum of 7500 Greylags winter. Some hundreds occur on the Danube Delta (5) in Romania, and on the lakes just to the south, with rare peaks of over 2000.

The breeding range of this population is not precisely known but undoubtedly lies for the most part in the south-west part of the U.S.S.R. Small numbers reach the wintering area from further west, including some from the Central European population, but they probably make only a small contribution to the total. There are about 1000 pairs breeding in Romania itself which almost certainly belong to this population, as do the 50 or so pairs in Bulgaria, and perhaps the 250–300 pairs breeding in Hungary, though these may belong to the Central European population. Some of the 650 pairs breeding in the Ukraine may also belong to the Pontian population though it is perhaps just as likely that they are part of the Anatolian population. The situation can probably only be clarified by extensive ringing, in several different areas, of breeding and wintering birds.

Anatolian population (Maps 17 and 19)

There is an apparently discrete wintering area in Anatolia in central Turkey, with up to 2500 at the Hotamis marshes (6) and the Cavuscu Gölü. There is also a major wintering area on the Black Sea coast of Turkey, at the Kizil Delta (7), where perhaps as many as 5000 winter.

The most probable breeding area for these birds is around the Sea of Azov (8) in the north-west of the Black Sea, and perhaps the Ukraine. Some 3000 pairs breed round the former locality and this would be sufficient to produce a very approximate total of 10,000–15,000 in the wintering range.

Caspian and U.S.S.R. breeding populations (Maps 17 and 19)

The picture to the east of the Black Sea is even less clear than to the west. There are some estimates for the numbers of breeding pairs but it has not been possible to relate these to different wintering areas. Around the Caspian Sea the principal nesting area is the Volga delta (9) and nearby lowlands. There, numbers have increased from about 8200 pairs in 1963 to about 12,000 pairs today. Elsewhere in the U.S.S.R., however, there have been considerable decreases in numbers due to the disappearance of suitable breeding marshes as more land has been drained and cultivated by the expanding human population. Kazakhstan, lying to the north of the Caspian and Aral Seas, has quite large numbers of breeding Greylags, with estimates varying from 18,000 to 23,000, plus a further 15,000–18,000 pairs around the Aral Sea. The total breeding population of the U.S.S.R. in 1967 was put at 50,000–60,000 pairs.

The wintering areas for these birds are not precisely known but extend from the shores of the Caspian, particularly the south, right across Iraq and Iran into Pakistan and India. It has been estimated that about 70,000 Greylags may remain to winter in the western parts of the U.S.S.R. in mild winters, with a concentration of about 10,000 on the south-west coast of the Caspian. There are several haunts for Greylags in Iraq and Iran, though most appear to hold hundreds rather than thousands. The Bay of Gorgan (10) on the Caspian shores of Iran and the Seistan lowlands are exceptions, as up to 2500 have been counted at each site. Lake Rezaiyeh (11) towards the Turkish border, also holds up to 2500 Greylags. The total in Iran may reach 10,000 birds.

Greylags are well distributed in Pakistan, India and Bangladesh, with several thousand in each country. Although the range of the Greylag is shown as extending to the Pacific, numbers are thought to be very small. Their wintering areas are in south-east Asia and nothing much is known about them there.

Bar-headed Goose (Map 20)

This species is as little known, numerically, as the Swan Goose. Likewise, changes in status can only be guessed at. Great declines are reported to have taken place in the last 30 to 50 years but it has not been possible to quantify these. There are three countries in which this species breeds, the U.S.S.R. in the region of Kirghizia, Mongolia, and China in the province of Tibet. Two

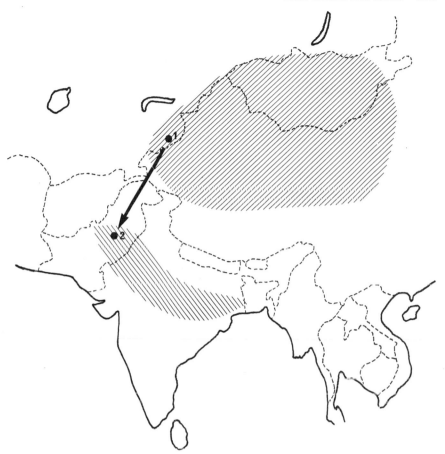

MAP 20. Bar-headed Goose *Anser indicus*—world range. ⧚ breeding; ⧛ wintering. Numbered haunts—see text. Arrow indicates connection between breeding and wintering areas.

breeding sites in Kirghizia, the Son Kul and Chatyr Kul lakes (1) support 40–50 breeding pairs. Two ringing recoveries link this breeding area with a wintering site on the River Indus at the Taunsa Barrage (2) in Pakistan, where up to 300 have been counted. Shooting of them is prohibited but there may well be poaching. Soviet biologists monitoring the breeding grounds remark that a good breeding season does not bring an increase in the following summer, which suggests heavy losses on migration or during the winter.

The Barhead breeds on lakes in most parts of Mongolia but is most numerous in the central and western districts. It is reported that formerly very large flocks could be found but that numbers are now much reduced. There are no actual counts available, but it is still the second most numerous goose after the Greylag.

There certainly used to be many thousands of pairs of Bar-headed Geese breeding in Tibet and the tameness of this and many other species of birds was remarked upon by travellers, right up to the time of the Chinese invasion in 1950. All animal life was regarded as sacred by the Tibetans and so there was practically no taking of wildlife for food, except perhaps of eggs in remote regions. The effect on birds indifferent to man of an invasion by a people who had no qualms about killing them for food can only be imagined. Certainly no information on Barheads or any other birds has come out of Tibet since, but it would be very surprising indeed if the Chinese had not been responsible for a considerable decline. The numerous lakes in some parts of Tibet certainly supported many thousands of breeding pairs in former times.

Apart from the one wintering site in Pakistan mentioned above, there are a number of small flocks to be found in central and eastern India, and a few in lower Assam. There are a handful in Bangladesh. Some apparently used to winter in the Tsangpo valley of Tibet but there is no recent information. The species is seen on migration in some of the valleys leading northwards into Kashmir and Nepal.

There was a free-flying population in southern Sweden in the 1930s but it has died out. Escapes from captivity occur quite frequently in western Europe.

Emperor Goose (Map 21)

Although the breeding and wintering range of this species is very circumscribed, the total numbers are probably in the order of 150,000–200,000 birds. The great majority of these, 95% or more, nest in Alaska, nearly all of them in the Yukon–Kuskokwim delta (1), with very small numbers elsewhere. The latter include about 500 pairs on the Seward Peninsula (2) and a few hundred others at scattered sites on the Bering Sea coasts. The numbers breeding in the Soviet Union are not certainly known but are unlikely to be larger than 1000 pairs. There is a large moulting concentration of up to 20,000 on St Lawrence Island (3) where, however, the species does not breed.

The wintering grounds of the Emperor Goose lie along the entire chain of the Aleutian islands, plus a small flock of up to 300 which winters on the coast of Kodiak Island (4) off the south side of the Alaskan peninsula. There are also some wintering flocks on the Kamchatka peninsula (5) at the western end of the Aleutians. In most winters a small number appear on the Pacific coast of Oregon, and at the two inland goose resorts of Klamath Basin and the Sacramento Valley, California. It can be assumed that these birds have joined the vast numbers of Whitefronts and Canada Geese which breed in the same area of Alaska, and move this way for the winter. Stragglers have reached the Hawaiian Islands.

There has been no long series of age counts of Emperor Geese but it is likely that variation in breeding success is comparatively slight, as it is with the Whitefronts breeding alongside them.

Map 21. Emperor Goose *Anser canagicus*—world range. ● breeding localities; \\\winter range. (After Palmer 1976.)

Lesser Snow Goose (Maps 22 and 23, Table 21)

The breeding range of this goose (Map 22) extends from Wrangel Island, off the north coast of the Chukotski Peninsula, the nearest part of Siberia to Alaska, across the Canadian arctic to Baffin Island. A highly gregarious species, it is confined to some 18 major colonies (of over 1000 pairs) and about the same number or more of minor ones. In winter it is found on the Pacific coast, in the Central Valley of California, in Mexico, on the Gulf coast and a few on the Atlantic coast. There are two separate populations, those of the Pacific Flyway, and those in the Central and Mississippi Flyways, the latter with an offshoot in the Atlantic Flyway.

Lesser Snow Geese are extremely dynamic and over the last twenty years new colonies have been founded, changes have taken place in migration routes, and wintering grounds have been shifted. Individual colonies have also shown striking increases and decreases, the reasons for which are not always obvious. Because they are relatively conspicuous birds and nest in well-defined colonies, quite accurate counts of most of the colonies have been made at regular intervals. The latest survey was by vertical photography and covered all the colonies of the eastern Canadian arctic. Table 21 sets out available counts or estimates for the number of breeding pairs in the principal colonies of the entire range, and gives earlier data where available. The sites of the colonies are shown on Map 23. The obvious changes that have taken place in numbers of breeding pairs will be discussed under the headings of the two populations below.

Pacific Flyway population (Maps 22, 23 and 24, Tables 21 and 22)
The breeding colonies of this population (Map 23) are on Wrangel Island (1), Kendal Island (2) and the Anderson River delta, Mackenzie District (3), and Egg River, Banks Island (4). In addition, there is a small number of scattered breeders on the Arctic Slope of Alaska and along the north coast of the mainland from Bathurst Inlet to the Queen Maud Gulf (5).

Wrangel Island (1) is now the only regular breeding locality in Siberia, but the species was formerly much more widespread and numerous. It was apparently found breeding along much of the Siberian coast as far west as the western side of the Taymyr peninsula, in about 80°–90°E, in the 17th and 18th centuries. Persecution on these breeding grounds, through egg-taking and killing of adults, drove it out and by about 1850 it was virtually extinct to the west of the Kolyma Delta (160°E), and by the beginning of the century it had disappeared completely from the Asian mainland.

Wrangel Island was only discovered in 1849 and little visited thereafter until the Russians established a permanent colony there in 1914. At that time there were certainly huge numbers of Snow Geese nesting, but whether they had always been there, or whether this was the place to which the geese of the mainland had retreated, is not known. Some egg collecting and taking of adults has been carried out on Wrangel Island since it was inhabited but, fortunately, this was always of a limited nature, and since 1960 has been strictly prohibited. The recent sharp decline in the number of pairs on the island is put down to a series of very poor breeding years, and Russian biologists emphasise the adverse effect of arctic foxes on small or declining colonies. One large colony is reported, plus a number of peripheral and, to some extent, ephemeral, smaller ones. The single main colony contained about 130,000 nests out of the total of 200,000 in 1960.

Reports of Snow Geese nesting on the Siberian mainland or on some of the other islands occur from time to time, but the presence of flocks of moulting non-breeding birds confuses the issue. Small numbers of pairs undoubtedly do nest occasionally on the deltas of the Indigirka and Kolyma Rivers. In addition, the Russians have been making various proposals to re-establish the species on the mainland by, among other ideas, artificial rearing and release, and the placing of eggs taken from Wrangel Island in the nests of other species, such as Whitefront, which do breed on the mainland coast. Whether these proposals have yet been put into practice is not clear.

There are no Snow Geese nesting on the west coast of Alaska but a number of pairs breed on the north-facing Arctic Slope, mainly in the western part between Point Barrow and the Colville River. The birds are thinly scattered, using lakes within five kilometres (3 miles) of the coast. One survey found just 19 broods in this area, but also located 5000 moulting non-breeders. It may gain in importance as a breeding place in the future.

Moving into the Canadian arctic there are three very important colonies in

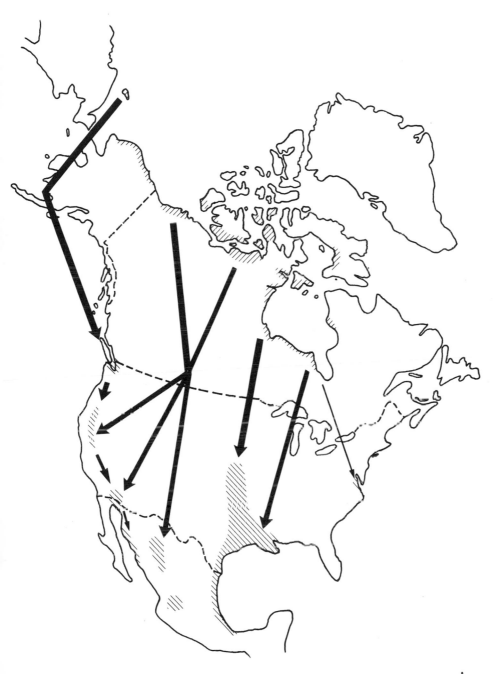

MAP 22. Lesser Snow Goose *Anser caerulescens caerulescens*—world range. ///breeding; ///wintering. Arrows indicate approximate migration routes linking different breeding and wintering areas.

the western part. By far the largest lies along the Egg River on Banks Island (4), an unusual site in that it lies largely inland. As Table 21 shows, it has increased enormously in the last twenty years. Two smaller but increasing colonies are on Kendall Island in the Mackenzie delta (2), and near the Anderson river delta (3). Going west from here, there are scattered small breeding groups perhaps totalling a few hundreds on Victoria, King William and Prince of Wales Islands. Then one comes to an area of the mainland, between Bathurst Inlet and the Adelaide Peninsula (5), where there are up to 30 small colonies scattered inland up the various river systems and on lakes with small islands, as much as 160 km (100 miles) from the coast. Nearly all of

TABLE 21: *Numbers of pairs nesting in Lesser Snow Goose colonies, 1930s to 1970s*

Locality of colony	No. on Map 23	1930s	1940s	1950s	1960s	1970s
Wrangel Island, U.S.S.R.	1	'large'	'large'		200,000	32,000
North Slope, Alaska					20–50	
Kendall Is., Mackenzie Delta	2			3,500	3,500	3,500
Anderson River Delta	3		4,000		2,500	4,000
Egg River, Banks Island	4			60,000	70,000	100,000
Albert Edward Bay, Victoria Is.					750 ⎱	
Bathurst Inlet to Perry R.	⎱ 5				1,700 ⎰ —12,000	
Perry R. to Adelaide Pena.	⎰				5,000 ⎱	
Cape Henrietta Maria	6		100	7,000		29,600
La Perouse Bay	7			15	1,000	2,800
Tha-anne River	8			500	3,000	3,200
South McConnell River						5,900
McConnell River	9		7,000	7,500	15,000	163,000
Wolf Creek				500	1,500	22,500
Maguse River					300	500
Ell Bay					present	200
West Boas River						4,000
Boas River	10	15,000		15,000	30,000	64,800
Bear Cove			present	1,000	1,000	400
South-west East Bay		present		present		1,000
East Bay		present		present	5,000	7,500
Bowman Bay	11 ⎱			82,000	125,000	91,900
Cape Dominion	12 ⎰	100,000		50,000	75,000	36,400
Koukdjuak	13 ⎰			38,000	25,000	95,000

Counts have been drawn from a number of sources, but especially Palmer (1976), Cooch (1963)[1], Ryder (1971)[2], and Kerbes (1975)[1]. The last provided all the 1970s counts, actually 1973, for all colonies between Cape Henrietta Maria and Koukdjuak; these were done by aerial photography and are probably more accurate than any of the other counts.

[1] See Bibliography for Chapter 1.   [2] See Bibliography for Chapter 4.

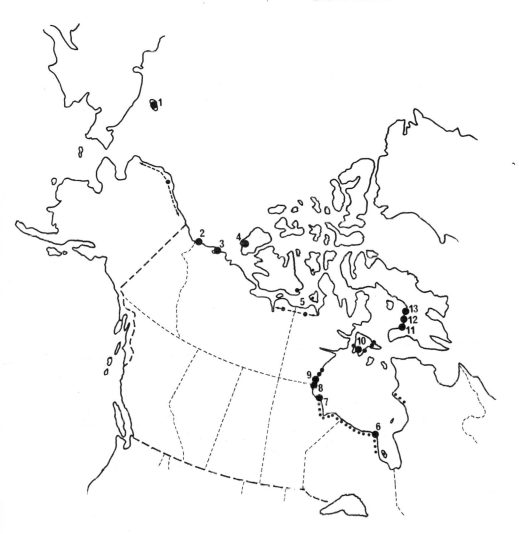

MAP 23. Lesser Snow Goose *Anser caerulescens caerulescens*—breeding colonies. ● major colonies (numbers refer to text and Table 21); ● minor colonies (given in Table 21); ••• scattered breeding.

them are mixed colonies of Lesser Snow and Ross's Geese. The total number of breeding pairs is small but there seems room for expansion at many of the colonies and in other similar areas of habitat in the region. There has certainly been some recent increase even though past records are fragmentary.

Ringing and observations have shown that the above colonies constitute the breeding part of the Pacific Flyway with small numbers of birds entering the Central Flyway. The geese take a number of different migration routes on their way to their wintering grounds, as shown on Map 22. The Wrangel Island birds go mainly via western Alaska where significant numbers of them stay for periods in September, particularly in the Yukon delta. They feed extensively on berries which are rich in nutrients and they are thus able to put on weight, following the summer decrease, prior to the next stage of their migration. This final leg takes them in a long flight over the Gulf of Alaska, not touching land again until they reach the Frazer River delta (1) and Puget Sound (2), Washington and the Columbia River mouth, Oregon (3) (see Map 24). Some follow the coasts of Alaska and British Columbia to the same area. The Puget Sound area holds a wintering population of around 20,000 Lesser Snow Geese, of which about 4000 are in the Frazer River delta. Ringing and other marking has shown that these latter birds may be exclusively Russian in origin, though most Russian birds mingle with Canadian birds at other sites.

From Puget Sound most geese pass inland to Summer Lake, Oregon and the Klamath Basin (4) on the Oregon–California border, arriving in early October. After a period there they move into the Central Valley. About 400,000 Snow Geese can be found there in years of high numbers, with perhaps three-quarters of them in the Sacramento Valley (5). A much smaller number, no more than 15,000 birds, go on to the Imperial Valley (6). There are some other scattered wintering sites in the western states, the largest being at Carson Sink, Nevada (7), where up to 4000 birds have been recorded. A few hundreds appear fairly regularly along the Colorado River in Arizona, and down to the delta in Mexico. Elsewhere in Mexico a few hundred Snow Geese winter along the west coast and there is a flock of up to 1500 on Lake Chapala much further south near Guadalajara. It is assumed that these are from this Pacific Flyway population though, conceivably, they might have crossed over from the Gulf and so belong to that group of geese.

The Central Valley of California is also the wintering area for the breeding Lesser Snow Geese of the western and central Canadian arctic. Their migration routes take them first to gathering grounds in the Mackenzie Delta, then up the Mackenzie River to localities in northern Alberta, particularly Hay Lake (8). The timing depends to some extent on the season, but by early October the major concentrations will have moved on to southern Alberta and Saskatchewan (9), up to 150,000 birds or even more being regularly counted here. Some birds also pause in northern Montana, and then from there a number of routes are followed. The majority of the geese cross the Rockies to the Central Valley, and smaller numbers go on south-south-west via Bear Lake, Utah (10) to the Colorado Delta (11); another group numbering around 25,000 birds heads due south for New Mexico and interior northern Mexico. There are a number of highland lakes in the latter country where flocks of several thousand Lesser Snow Geese occur, but it is likely that they have declined in recent years as, conversely, numbers have increased at the Bosque del Apache National Wildlife Refuge near Socorro, New Mexico (12), to well over 10,000 in recent years, from under 3000 in the late 1960s. The spring migration starts in February and the birds move steadily north, using many of the same halting places as in autumn, pacing their movement according to the advance northwards of the thaw.

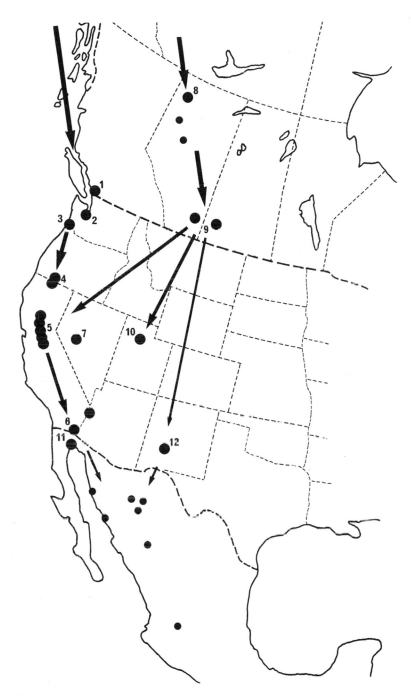

MAP 24. Lesser Snow Goose *Anser caerulescens caerulescens*—migration and wintering haunts of Pacific Flyway population. ●major haunts; ● minor haunts. Numbers indicate haunts referred to in text. Arrows show approximate migration routes.

TABLE 22: *Mid-winter counts of Pacific Flyway Lesser Snow Geese, 1956–7 to 1976–7, together with annual breeding success*

Winter	Total	% young	Brood size	Winter	Total	% young	Brood size
1956–7	351,000	25·5	2·3	1967–8	505,800	16·3	1·7
1957–8	317,000	32·8	2·2	1968–9	413,300	23·5	1·91
1958–9	388,100	20·1	1·9	1969–70	461,700	28·2	2·05
1959–60	360,000	38·2	2·3	1970–1	512,600	37·1	2·17
1960–1	461,000	38·8	2·3	1971–2	436,900	20·4	1·67
1961–2	541,000	20·6	1·8	1972–3	343,200	12·9	1·70
1962–3	482,700	29·5	2·1	1973–4	442,900	39·0	2·16
1963–4	453,900	30·5	2·1	1974–5	424,800	1·0	1·00
1964–5	482,200	23·1	1·8	1975–6	458,900	46·9	2·15
1965–6	440,700	4·7	2·0	1976–7	469,500	n.a.	2·00
1966–7	746,700	49·0	2·6				

Lynch & Voelzer (1974), Voelzer (1976 and pers. com.).

The total population of the Pacific Flyway has been assessed fairly reliably by winter surveys over a long period of years and the results, together with the breeding success data, are set out in Table 22. The totals have fluctuated quite considerably though with no evidence of a long-term or recent decline such as might be suggested by the reported steep decrease of the Wrangel Island breeding population. It would appear that this latter reduction has been offset by the increase of the breeding numbers in the Canadian arctic. There is no direct evidence of an actual shift of birds, just that in one area the geese are doing well, and in another poorly. The variation in annual breeding success is quite large, with occasional years of very low production, for example in 1965 and 1974. In fact, with breeding taking place in such widely separated areas, one would not expect many years in which weather conditions were identical in all colonies. There is some evidence that in recent years the Canadian birds have bred quite well, whereas the Siberian ones have not. The apparent stability of the population is almost certainly concealing quite different fortunes of the two component parts. This makes life hard for those trying to manage the population, in particular those responsible for allocating the annual kill on the autumn migratory rest sites and the wintering grounds. On the one hand, it is apparent that the total stock is bearing up well, on the other there is pressure from the Russians who see their breeding population in decline and would like winter shooting reduced; but there is no certain way of separating the two stocks on their shared wintering range.

Central and Mississippi Flyways population
(Maps 22, 23 and 25, Tables 21 and 23)

The breeding range of this population lies around Hudson Bay, on Southampton Island, and on Baffin Island. There have been cases of dramatic increases in numbers at several colonies and in the last thirty years a number of new colonies have been started, particularly on the south and west coasts of

Hudson Bay, apparently by birds stopping short on their northward migration in spring. The colony at Cape Henrietta Maria in south Hudson Bay (6) (see Map 23) was founded this way, as were those on Akimiski Island, James Bay, and at La Perouse Bay (7). In the last ten years small breeding groups have also become established on the east side of Hudson Bay. A clue to how these colonies were formed came in 1972 when weather conditions on Baffin Island were so bad as virtually to prevent all breeding. Much larger numbers of Snow Geese than usual turned up at Cape Henrietta Maria, and no less than 45,000 pairs bred there. However, the following, more normal, year saw the number drop to 29,600 pairs. It seems as if these extra birds may have gone far enough north to realise that they could not breed in their traditional colony and had returned south to breed where conditions were better. Such adaptability has very obvious survival value and could bring about the founding of new colonies as well as the reinforcement of existing ones.

The McConnell River colony, west Hudson Bay (8, 9), is easily the largest in the Canadian arctic, the Wrangel Island colony having been larger in former years. It is also the fastest growing. Although split into five separate colonies in Table 21, the real divisions are not always clear-cut and the smaller ones can be regarded as offshoots of the main colony. There are five small colonies on Southampton Island and one large one, at Boas River (10). This too has grown considerably though not quite so dramatically as the McConnell River. The third main breeding area is on western Baffin Island in the Great Plain of the Koukdjuak. Three colonies have been identified here though the boundaries between them are a matter of judgement. Those at Bowman Bay (11) and Koukdjuak (13) are about the same size, much larger than the third colony at Cape Dominion (12). Taken together, these colonies have had about the same number of nests since counts began. The lack of growth is probably because they are further north than the others and conditions are consequently more marginal.

A recent aerial survey of all the colonies in the eastern Canadian arctic produced a total of about 500,000 breeding pairs in 1973, plus a further 400,000 non-breeders. This very large figure is in line with aerial counts of the geese made on their northward migration in spring, when virtually the whole population can be found on the shores of James and Hudson Bays. However, these Canadian counts are very much larger than recent winter inventories made in the United States, and although biologists there believed that their winter counts were probably not complete the size of the discrepancy surprised everyone (see below and Table 23).

The autumn migration of the Lesser Snow Geese, from Hudson Bay to their wintering grounds on the Gulf, follows several different routes. There is, first, a considerable accumulation of birds in the south-western part of Hudson Bay and in James Bay. Aerial counts in excess of 300,000 have been made in these two areas in early October. Some birds go direct from there to the Gulf, but considerable numbers fly as far as an area embracing parts of North and South Dakota, and neighbouring areas of Nebraska and Missouri. There is no single take-off point from Hudson Bay for this area, instead a number of corridors converge there, from starting places between the McConnell River and James Bay. The principal haunts in this major resting place are three National Wildlife Refuges, Sand Lake, South Dakota (1) (see Map 25), De Soto, Nebraska (2), and Squaw Creek, Missouri (3). Counts of from 100,000 to 200,000 birds have been made at each of these between late September and late November.

To the east of these western migration corridors smaller numbers of geese move down to resting places in Illinois and then follow the Mississippi Valley to the Gulf, or journey on an even more easterly line over Ohio, Kentucky and Tennessee. There are a number of small stopping places but none normally carrying more than a few thousand geese. The Lesser Snow Goose migration is quite variable from year to year, both in the numbers using any one corridor and in the time spent at the different resting places. This variability must reflect annual differences in the weather during migration and the amount of food available to the geese before they leave and at localities on the way. The majority of the geese in these eastern corridors do not stop anywhere on their migration and fly non-stop from Hudson Bay to the Gulf. Once every ten or so years, however, they interrupt their migration, possibly because of meeting adverse conditions, or because the feeding further north was inadequate, and then spend some weeks at various haunts on the way.

Finally, there is a small group of Lesser Snow Geese, which may one day develop into a discrete population, which has started wintering on the Atlantic coast at Chesapeake Bay (4). This habit only started in the 1930s and fewer than 2000 birds are involved even now. They apparently leave the southern end of James Bay and head south-west to cross western New York State and Pennsylvania.

Apart from the small wintering area on the Atlantic coast, the great bulk of the eastern arctic Lesser Snow Geese winter on the coast of the Gulf of Mexico, in Louisiana and Texas, from the Mississippi Delta (5) to Corpus Christi (6). Though formerly almost entirely restricted to the coastal marshes, the geese have, in the last few years, moved to the extensive rice-growing areas lying a short way inland. Another simultaneous change in habits is the increasing numbers of Snow Geese that are stopping for longer and longer at their Midwest autumn resting places. Even ten years ago only a few tens of thousands could be found at these places as late as December, but in the last few winters as many as 300,000 birds have still been present this far north in the middle of the month. The birds have been responding to the provision of safe roosts on Wildlife Refuges, ample supplies of food on harvested grain fields, and perhaps to a slight trend to milder weather. It has, however, caused problems by allowing the hunters of these States far more shooting than in the past, with a corresponding reduction in the kill allowable on the Gulf coast.

A few thousand Snow Geese winter to the south of the Gulf marshes, down to the Mexico border, and some hundreds along the Mexico coast as far as Veracruz. It is possible that some of this population also reach the Mexican highlands but the majority of the birds there belong to Pacific Flyway population.

The spring departure from the Gulf takes place in early March, with the bulk of the birds having left by the end of the month. The return route follows

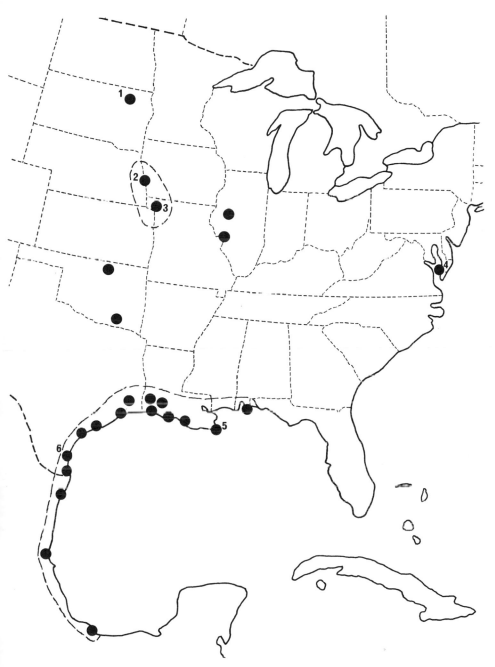

MAP 25. Lesser Snow Goose *Anser caerulescens caerulescens*—migration and winter range of Central and Mississippi Flyways population. ⬤ major haunts. Numbers indicate haunts referred to in text. Dashed line encloses main wintering areas.

a much narrower band than in the autumn, virtually all the birds heading for the stopping places in Missouri and the Dakotas, moving north from there into southern Manitoba, to important haunts to the west of Winnipeg. This is their last stop before James Bay which they reach at the beginning of May.

Winter counts of this population have already been mentioned. Although the recent aerial surveys of the breeding grounds and spring concentrations have revealed a population considerably greater than has been counted in winter, the latter figures are nonetheless of interest because they are likely to reflect trends, even if incomplete. They are set out in Table 23, together with estimates based on the recent aerial counts, and have been extrapolated back to 1964. The latter are calculated with the aid of hunting kill returns and ringing recoveries. Variability in breeding success, also shown in the Table, is not quite so great as in the Pacific Flyway population, though some years have been fairly poor. The difficulties in making a complete winter inventory must be apparent from the enormous area of marshland, and recently rice fields, on the Gulf coast that must be surveyed. Even with aircraft this is a major task. The recent development of birds remaining further north for at least the first part of the winter only compounds the difficulties.

TABLE 23: *Mid-winter counts and estimated autumn totals of the Central and Mississippi Flyway Lesser Snow Geese, 1956–7 to 1976–7, together with annual breeding success*

Winter	Mid-winter count	Autumn estimate	% young	Brood size
1956–7	648,000	no record	35·4	2·03
1957–8	721,000	,,	43·7	2·14
1958–9	527,000	,,	24·2	1·59
1959–60	792,000	,,	50·9	2·49
1960–1	797,000	,,	36·9	2·25
1961–2	576,000	,,	13·2	1·67
1962–3	799,000	,,	31·1	1·93
1963–4	757,000	,,	22·4	2·12
1964–5	796,000	1,512,000	25·8	2·09
1965–6	697,700	1,365,000	33·7	2·11
1966–7	641,600	1,439,000	42·7	2·49
1967–8	633,000	1,311,000	20·2	1·92
1968–9	728,500	1,371,000	12·7	1·88
1969–70	825,600	1,615,000	29·1	1·98
1970–1	1,076,800	2,384,000	26·7	1·84
1971–2	1,340,800	2,490,000	17·2	1·58
1972–3	1,036,900	1,884,000	9·7	1·63
1973–4	1,202,300	2,299,000	37·8	1·94
1974–5	1,123,300	2,109,000	17·6	1·64
1975–6	1,585,000	n.a.	44·6	2·05
1976–7	1,262,700	n.a.	22·7	2·04

Mid-winter counts and breeding success from Lynch & Voelzer (1974) and Voelzer (1976 and pers. com.). Autumn estimates from Boyd (1976).

Vagrant Lesser Snow Geese have been reported from Kashmir and Korea in Asia, the Hawaiian Islands, Cuba (where they may once have wintered), the Antilles and the Azores. In Europe, where Snow Geese have occurred widely from Iceland to Greece, some Greater Snow Geese may also be involved, but in any case escapes probably account for most recent records. Blue phase Snow Geese are almost annual among Greenland Whitefront flocks in Scotland and Ireland, and may be considered as wild.

Greater Snow Goose (Map 26, Table 24)

This subspecies of the Snow Goose breeds in the north-east Canadian arctic, plus a handful in north-west Greenland, and winters on the Atlantic coast of the U.S.A. There is just one population which is more or less separated geographically from the Lesser Snow Goose. The fairly recent development, mentioned above, of small numbers of Lesser Snow Geese wintering on the Atlantic coast produces a slight overlap on the wintering grounds though the migration routes are different. In the breeding range the Greater Snows are almost exclusively to the north of the Lessers, but some pairs of the latter, perhaps adventitious wanderers, or over-shooters, do nest within the Greater Snows' range. There is a possibility of hybridisation between them.

At the southern end of its range the Greater Snow Goose breeds on the north and north-west of Baffin Island (1), and on Bylot Island (2), which lies off the north-east corner. There, about 7500 pairs were nesting in 1957 at a time when the population, which has been steadily increasing, was about 70,000 birds. As 1957 was an excellent breeding season, with about 50% young, one can estimate that the total number of breeding pairs was probably about 15,000, so the Bylot colonies represented about half the breeding pairs in the population. Whether the island still holds this proportion now that the population has shot up to 200,000, is not known. The geese were nesting in small colonies of from 25 to 300 nests, scattered mainly over the south and east part of the island. Going north there are major breeding areas on Ellesmere (3) and Axel Heiberg Islands (4), but rather few in between on Devon Island (5). An aerial survey of north-west Greenland in 1970 gave a probable maximum of 1000 birds, not all of which were breeding.

To the west of Baffin and Ellesmere, breeding has been reported of small numbers of Greater Snow Geese on Somerset, Prince of Wales and Bathurst Islands, and unspecified Snow Geese have been seen on various islands in the Queen Elizabeth Group, including Melville, Prince Patrick and Cornwallis. Although it has been assumed that the northerly locations would make it more probable that these were Greater Snows, it is possible that Lesser Snows moving north from their breeding range might also reach these islands, and without certain identification the matter must remain in doubt.

The Greater Snow Geese begin to leave their breeding grounds in early September and by the middle of the month they are beginning to arrive at their one migration resting haunt, on the St Lawrence River at Cap Tourmente (6). There the whole population spends several weeks, staying

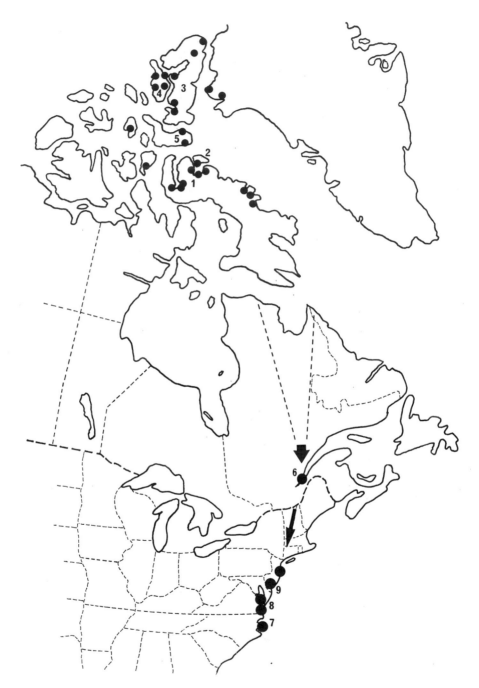

MAP 26. Greater Snow Goose *Anser caerulescens atlanticus*—world range. ● breeding localities; ● major migration and wintering haunts. Numbers indicate haunts referred to in text. Arrows show approximate migration routes.

until the winter snow and ice comes, usually in mid- to late November. It is here that the best annual counts are obtained.

Although a few hundred geese sometimes fly direct to the wintering grounds, arriving in September, the main arrival is not until November. The winter range extends from New Jersey south to North Carolina. Because of the recent great increase in the population, it is not possible to give meaningful counts for the various haunts, but the most important are traditionally the Currituck and Pamlico Sounds of North Carolina (7), with Pea Island in Pamlico Sound a favourite locality. Just to the north, there are further large flocks in Chesapeake and Back Bays, Virginia (8). Only relatively small numbers winter in Maryland and Delaware, but several thousand resort to Delaware Bay (9) and along the New Jersey coast. To the north and south of these areas Greater Snow Geese are comparatively rare.

In February and March the Greater Snows begin to move north up the coast as far as Delaware Bay, and then fly direct to Cap Tourmente where they spend most of April and early May before departing for the breeding grounds.

Table 24 sets out the counts of Greater Snow Geese. The tradition of stopping on the St Lawrence, which may be at least 400 years old, has produced counts from much earlier times than for any other goose population. There may, of course, have been other stopping places in earlier years but, if not, there has been roughly a hundred-fold increase in the population between 1900 and 1975. The run of age counts nicely shows the effect of really good years on the total population, as in 1957, 1970, and then in 1973 and 1975. Aerial counts and, more recently, aerial photography at Cap Tourmente has revealed serious under-counting on the wintering grounds.

TABLE 24: *Numbers of Greater Snow Geese counted on autumn or spring migration at Cap Tourmente, Quebec, and on the wintering grounds in eastern U.S.A., 1956–7 to 1976–7, together with annual breeding success*

Winter	Total Quebec	Winter count	% young	Brood size	Winter	Total Quebec	Winter count	% young	Brood size
1956–7	n.c.	34,790	33·8	3·0	1967–8	75,000	50,500	12·4	1·65
1957–8	70,000	42,700	34·4	2·3	1968–9	68,800	45,700	12·5	1·60
1958–9	47,500	48,250	3·1	2·2	1969–70	89,600	43,730	24·3	2·23
1959–60	n.c.	52,930	42·7	2·6	1970–1	123,330	48,500	46·8	2·89
1960–1	n.c.	67,140	34·1	2·3	1971–2	134,800	81,100	11·3	2·21
1961–2	n.c.	49,700	1·2	1·53	1972–3	143,000	59,100	0·4	—
1962–3	n.c.	64,920	28·4	2·24	1973–4	165,000	95,200	41·1	2·89
1963–4	n.c.	59,700	33·9	2·02	1974–5	199,500	70,300	2·0	2·22
1964–5	n.c.	46,500	20·5	1·71	1975–6	227,900	116,900	34·5	2·88
1965–6	48,500	43,400	2·8	2·16	1976–7	186,730	127,100	9·8	2·40
1966–7	80,000	59,900	37·0	2·37					

Quebec counts from 1968–9 to 1975–6 are spring, remainder autumn.

Mid-winter counts from Lynch & Voelzer (1974), and Voelzer (1976 and pers. com.). Quebec counts from A. Reed (pers. com.).

Greater Snow Geese have straggled to Europe (see under Lesser Snow Goose) and occasionally wander westwards, with ringing recoveries in Texas and Illinois.

Ross's Goose (Map 27, Table 25)

Once thought of as extremely rare and possibly in danger of extinction, this species is now known to have been widely overlooked in the past, and though it has undoubtedly increased in the last two decades it was probably never at serious risk.

There is one major population of Ross's Geese, breeding on the mainland of Canada bordering the Queen Maud Gulf (1). The birds all winter in California. There are tiny but increasing numbers breeding on the west side of Hudson Bay (2), and on Southampton Island (3), which winter on the Gulf coast. It is not known when this separate group was formed but the first reported breeding from Southampton Island was not until the 1950s. However, as they nest in Lesser Snow Goose colonies the Ross's Geese could easily have been overlooked in the past.

The breeding area beside the Queen Maud Gulf extends about 160 km (100 miles) inland and for about 250 km (180 miles) from west to east. There, a survey in the mid-1960s revealed that there were 35 colonies containing from 10 to 6000 pairs. In July 1965 the total of birds found, 32,086, agreed very closely indeed with the February 1965 winter count of 31,880 in California, and with the previous autumn's count at the migration rest area in Alberta and Saskatchewan of 34,300. This is clear evidence that the summer breeding survey had covered the complete breeding range of this population.

The Ross's Geese leave the breeding grounds in early September and move via the Athabaska delta (4), in northern Alberta, to their main staging posts between Macklin and Kindersley (5) in south-west Saskatchewan, and Sullivan Lake (6) over the border in Alberta. The next stop is at Freezeout Lake (7) in the Great Falls area of Montana, then, turning south-west, the geese fly over the Rockies to the Klamath Basin (8) on the Oregon–California border, reaching there in mid-October. By November they are moving south to the Central Valley (6) where a sizeable proportion winter. The bulk of the population moves on further, however, to the San Joaquim Valley (7) where the Merced National Wildlife Refuge provides a sanctuary. Small numbers may occur a little further south. The spring return starts in March and takes in the Malheur Refuge in Oregon on the way to the southern Alberta and northern Montana haunts where they spend most of April. Northern Alberta is reached in May. The movement northwards closely follows the 0°C (32°F) isotherm marking the start of the spring thaw.

Counts of Ross's Geese for the last twenty years are shown in Table 25, together with breeding success data. There was a significant increase in the 1960s compared with the 1950s, though some of this may have been due to more reliable counts based on a better understanding of the distribution, and to improved identification of the species, separating it from the hundreds or thousands of Lesser Snow Geese also wintering in central California. Total

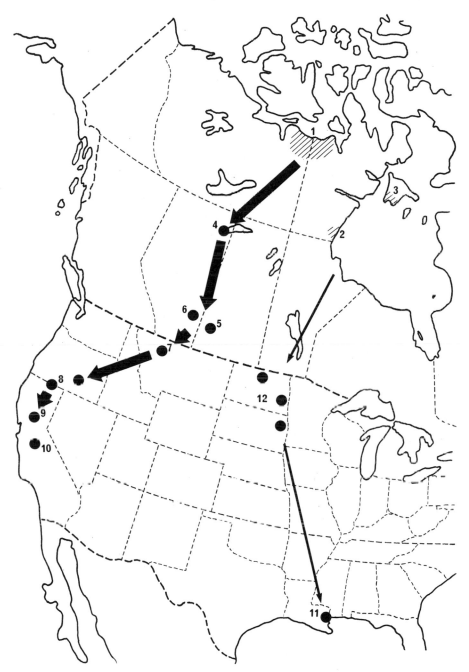

MAP 27. Ross's Goose *Anser rossii*—world range. ⫽breeding; ●major migration and wintering haunts. Numbers indicate haunts referred to in text. Arrows show approximate migration routes.

TABLE 25: *Mid-winter counts of Ross's Geese, 1954–5 to 1976–7, together with annual breeding success*

Winter	Count	% young	Brood size	Winter	Count	% young	Brood size
1954–5	6,000	no records		1966–7	31,400	53·2	2·87
1955–6	11,000	,,		1967–8	38,980	27·1	2·59
1956–7	7,925	,,		1968–9	19,700	32·4	2·56
1957–8	12,800	,,		1969–70	21,700	00·0	0·00
1958–9	15,600	,,		1970–1	32,380	00·0	0·00
1959–60	18,000	,,		1971–2	30,700	0·4	2·55
1960–1	23,050	51·3	2·70	1972–3	18,800	00·0	0·00
1961–2	27,920	3·3	2·26	1973–4	27,260	45·1	2·71
1962–3	25,250	n.r.	2·22	1974–5	21,790	13·7	1·79
1963–4	32,450	47·4	2·77	1975–6	28,230	41·5	2·73
1964–5	31,850	46·1	2·72	1976–7	37,800	n.a.	n.a.
1965–6	30,400	00·0	0·00				

Dzubin (1965), Lynch & Voelzer (1974), Voelzer (1976 and pers. com.). Counts since 1969–70 made in February.

failures to breed are rare, that in 1972 being part of a very widespread failure of geese in the Canadian arctic following an extremely cold, late spring.

The small numbers wintering on the Gulf coast (11) have only recently been estimated. 441 were counted in 1967–68, increasing to 1135 the following year, and it is likely that the total is still growing. This parallels the increase in numbers breeding at the McConnell River, west Hudson Bay. These birds migrate through North and South Dakota (12).

Ross's Geese have turned up in Europe, particularly in Britain, but none have been shown to be wild rather than escapes. A pair of the latter bred unsuccessfully two or possibly three years running in Iceland in the early 1960s, spending each winter in Scotland with Greylags.

Canada Goose (Map 28)

This species breeds throughout most of Canada, except the extreme northern arctic islands, and over much of the U.S.A. north of about 35°N and to the west of the Allegheny Mountains. It is the most numerous goose species and has increased greatly in the last 30 years.

The confused taxonomic status of this species was discussed in the first chapter. It is now the turn of the population status to come under scrutiny. The Canada Goose is one of the most intensively studied quarry species in North America and a large part of the work has been aimed at a better understanding of the various populations so that they can be managed more efficiently, providing the hunters with good sport while maintaining overall numbers. One of the basic facts that has arisen from detailed work on wintering populations is that many of them contain birds of different sizes and colouring, normally described as separate subspecies. A reduction in

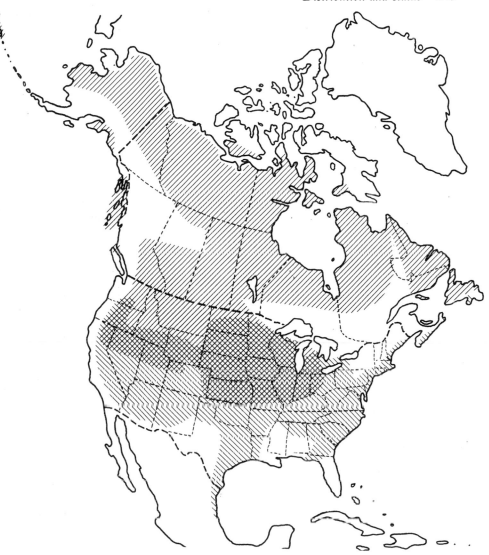

MAP 28. Canada Goose *Branta canadensis*—world range, excluding introduced populations in Europe and New Zealand. ▨ breeding; ▨ wintering.

wintering habitat over the centuries, plus the recent great increase in the total number of geese, has led to extensive overlap and mixing of birds coming from different breeding grounds. Where once populations may have been separated, allowing morphological differences to evolve, much is now back in the melting pot.

Canada Goose populations have been changing in numbers and composition quite markedly over the years. Recent knowledge leads to the suspicion that many earlier assumptions as to status and distribution of some populations were based on inadequate knowledge. In the case of the Canada Goose, especially, statements on numbers and distribution are liable to become rapidly out of date.

In the treatment which follows, I start with the four main North American flyways as my primary division. Within these it is possible to identify a number of populations that have been shown to be reasonably discrete, though this is not to say that further work will not produce further subdivisions or some amalgamations. I will also be referring to my groupings of the named subspecies outlined in Chapter 1. Numbers of some Canada Goose populations are not as well documented as for other North American geese and a further problem is that it is very difficult, if not impossible, to age them satisfactorily in the field. Consequently, annual production figures do not exist and population fluctuations cannot be readily linked with variations in breeding success.

PACIFIC FLYWAY (Map 29)

This flyway embraces five identifiable populations of Canada Geese. One, restricted to the separable race the Aleutian Canada Goose *leucopareia*, is very small both in range and numbers. Another made up of the small Canadas breeding in Alaska and wintering mainly in Oregon and California, covers a large range and contains up to a quarter of a million geese. The other three are both intermediate in numbers and consist of larger birds. Censusing is very difficult in most cases and the available counts must be treated with caution.

Aleutian population (Map 29)

The Aleutian Canada Goose is the rarest known race of any goose species. In 1974 the total population was thought to number no more than 790 birds. It is confined as a breeding bird to Buldir Island (1), one of the outer islands of the Aleutian chain, though it formerly bred on many of the other islands in the chain, as well as islands in the Bering Sea and as far east as the Kuriles, north of Japan. The introduction of foxes to these islands was followed by the extermination of the goose as a breeding species. Probably because Buldir was comparatively small, less than 18 square kilometres (7 square miles), foxes were never brought there, and a breeding population survived.

The Aleutian Canada Goose was formerly much more numerous, though no quotable figures are available. The race was thought to be migratory, with its main wintering grounds in the Central Valley of California, with another component going to Japan where it became extinct in the 1920s. Until recently, though, it was considered that the remnant population had become more or less sedentary, staying within the Aleutian chain throughout the year. Now, however, it is believed that the birds are still migrating, certainly along the length of the nearly 1500 km (900 miles) Aleutian chain to Izembek Bay, Alaska (2), at its mainland end, while it is quite likely that they are continuing all the way to California. The insignificant numbers of this race would be easily overlooked among the extremely large flocks of small Canada Geese from mainland Alaska which make the journey to the same wintering grounds.

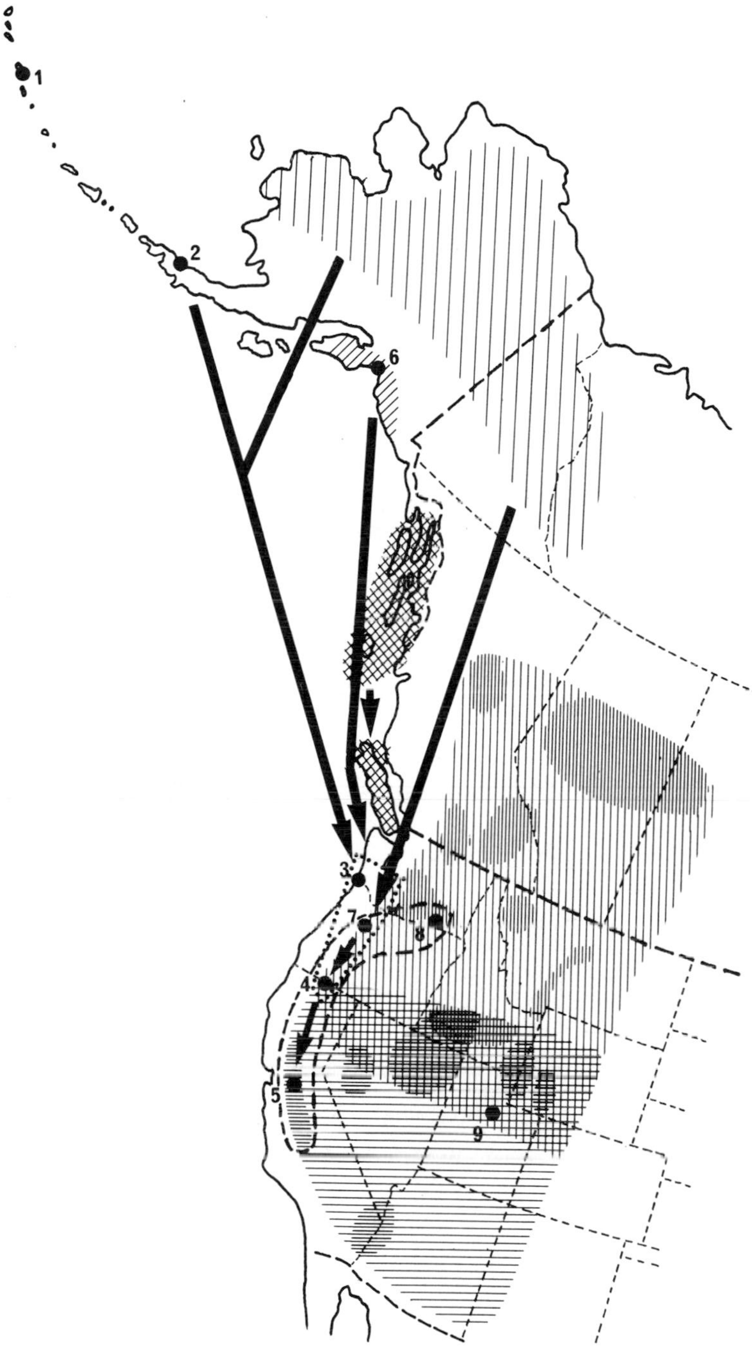

MAP 29. Canada Goose *Branta canadensis*—breeding and wintering ranges in the Pacific Flyway. Alaska population: |||| breeding; dashed line encloses wintering. South Alaska Coast population: //// breeding; dotted line encloses wintering. NW Coast population: ✕✕ breeding and wintering. Great Basin population: |||| breeding; ≡ wintering; |||| ≡ major concentrations. Numbered haunts—see text. Arrows connect breeding and wintering areas of different populations.

There have been some recent attempts to reintroduce the Aleutian Canada Goose to other islands in the chain by transplanting and using captive reared birds, but so far this seems not to have been successful.

Alaska population (Map 29, Table 26)

The Canada Geese breeding in Alaska form part of the Northern Group of smallish arctic breeders described in Chapter 1. They are of small to medium size and include dark and pale birds as well as some intermediates. The small dark birds are usually called Cackling Geese *minima*, while the others are variously termed Taverner's or Lesser Geese *taverneri* or *parvipes*. As mentioned in Chapter 1 the latter two races are not separable and intergrading between them and *minima* undoubtedly takes place.

Although racial separation of the coastal and interior Alaskan Canada Geese may be over-stated, there are undoubtedly two sub-populations of geese involved, each having more or less separate breeding grounds and initial migration routes but extensively overlapping wintering grounds. The great majority of the geese nesting on the coastal delta migrate across the neck of the Alaskan peninsula, some stopping at Bristol Bay, but the remainder going straight across the sea to the Columbia River (3). From there they pass to the Klamath Basin (4), on their way to the Central Valley, California (3), where they spend the winter.

A small number of coastal breeding Canadas make their way in autumn to Izembek Bay, Alaska (2), where they join the majority of the geese from the interior of Alaska. From there this sub-population, too, makes an over-sea flight to Washington State, passing up the Columbia River then turning south through Oregon, the Klamath Basin, and finally reaching, with the other Canadas, the Central Valley. The totals of the two sub-populations have been monitored with fair regularity on their wintering grounds, and are set out in Table 26. The return route in spring takes them up the coast, even well inland, not directly across the sea.

Vagrant small Canada Geese, probably from this population, have occurred in Japan, the Hawaiian Islands and south to Mexico.

TABLE 26: *Mid-winter counts of the two sub-populations of the Alaskan population of Canada Geese, 1959–60 to 1976–7*

Winter	Coastal	Interior	Total	Winter	Coastal	Interior	Total
1959–60	156,170	41,390	196,560	1968–9	104,030	30,600	134,630
1960–1	165,930	135,810	301,740	1969–70	96,540	66,620	163,160
1961–2	190,780	146,630	337,410	1970–1	113,960	58,520	171,480
1962–3	238,330	77,150	315,480	1971–2	102,130	108,200	210,330
1963–4	109,000	96,300	205,300	1972–3	54,440	101,060	155,500
1964–5	131,940	92,430	224,370	1973–4	85,870	64,450	150,320
1965–6	66,190	69,990	136,180	1974–5	40,790	153,410	194,200
1966–7	123,980	122,000	245,980	1975–6	51,250	101,960	153,210
1967–8	63,640	59,780	123,420	1976–7	56,360	116,420	172,780

J. Chattin (pers. com.).

South Alaska Coast population (Map 29)

The geese of this population breed on the south coast of Alaska and are fairly large in size and generally dusky in colour. They have usually been treated as a separate subspecies, the Dusky Canada Goose *occidentalis*, distinct from the similarly coloured if slightly larger birds further south along the coast, termed Vancouver Canada Geese *fulva*. As Chapter 1 made clear, this is overstating the differences between them and that at most there is a slight cline in decreasing size from south to north. If one must give them a subspecific name, Dusky *occidentalis* will do for both. Together they form the Pacific Coast Group.

The geese of this population have their breeding headquarters in the delta of the Copper River (6), with the range reaching west along the south Alaskan coast to Cook Inlet and east to the Bering Glacier, a total of about 440 km (275 miles). The Copper River area was drastically affected by the Alaskan earthquake of 1964, when parts of it were lifted as much as 2 m (6 ft) and many low-lying wet areas became almost literally high and dry. However, the effects on the geese seem not to have been too serious.

The wintering area of these birds lies in Washington, Oregon and northern California, with the largest concentration in the Willamette Valley (7), north-west Oregon, where between 15,000 and 23,000 geese are regular migrants. Much smaller numbers are found along the coasts of south-west Washington and northern California. Between 1000 and 1500 birds remain within the breeding range, among the islands of Prince William Sound. A further 2000 stop off at the Queen Charlotte Islands and Vancouver Island which are on their migration route. The total population was estimated at 34,750 in autumn of 1966, but shooting and other losses reduced it to not more than 20,500 birds by the time of the mid-winter census. It has fluctuated but not greatly changed since.

North-west Coast population (Map 29)

This population is sometimes included with the South Alaska Coast population under the present name, but separation seems justified on the basis of their distribution and migration patterns, though not, as already stated, taking it as far as subspecies. These birds are normally described as Vancouver Canada Geese *fulva* but are here lumped with Dusky Canada Geese *occidentalis*. At its extreme north-west limit the breeding range of this population reaches to Glacier Bay, Alaska, and so is separated by about 480 km (300 miles) from the nearest birds of the South Alaska Coast population. From Glacier Bay it extends south down the coast through the many islands of the Alexander Archipelago, the Queen Charlotte Group and Vancouver Island.

The majority of the geese winter within their breeding range, though some thousands move south as far as Washington, at least, and a few are known to reach northern Oregon. However, ringing has shown that movements of over about 150 km (90 miles) are the exception. The total population is thought to be of the order of 80,000–90,000 birds, based on early autumn aerial surveys in coastal Alaska in the late 1960s. Before this, however, it was widely held that the population was much smaller, somewhere between

15,000 and 20,000 birds, of which about 7000 were on the Queen Charlotte and Vancouver Islands. With a range covering nearly a thousand kilometres and hundreds of islands it may be some time before this conflict in numbers is satisfactorily resolved. It is likely, however, that the aerial counts are more accurate and that the earlier, much lower figures were due to inadequate surveying of the large and complex range.

Great Basin population (Map 29, Table 27)

This is a convenient umbrella name for what is a complex mixture of overlapping subpopulations, some of them probably discrete, many of them almost certainly not. To add to the confusion there has been much expansion and infilling of the breeding range in recent years, some of it by transplanting of birds, but most of the expansion has arisen naturally as the geese have discovered and colonised the many stock ponds and impoundments created in the region. Additionally, although some of the subpopulations are normally non-migratory, they will move if the winter is very severe, usually to places already being used by other Canada Geese from separate breeding areas.

This population is generally said to consist solely of the Western or Great Basin Canada Goose *moffitti* and certainly the birds within it are all much of a size and colouring, being generally large and pale, and showing rather less variation than some of the other named subspecies. However, the same authorities confine *moffitti* to the Great Basin region and this is certainly much less valid. There is, as already stated, virtually no difference between *moffitti* and the Giant Canada Goose *maxima* which breeds to the east across the plains and into the Midwest. They all form part of the Southern Group of large, mostly pale Canada Geese.

The breeding range of the Great Basin population extends from the southern parts of Alberta and British Columbia, through Washington, Oregon, Idaho, western Montana and western Wyoming, into north-east California, Nevada, Utah and north-west Colorado. There was a survey of breeding pairs in the late 1950s and early 1960s. There were about 2000 pairs in British Columbia and Alberta, with the Columbia and Okanagan Valleys of the latter province particularly favoured. Washington State had about 1500 pairs, nearly all in the Columbia and Snake River basins (8). The Snake River on its course through Idaho held the majority of the 1000 pairs in that state. Western Wyoming held about 150 pairs, Utah about 1000 pairs, over half of them on the Bear River (9), and Nevada had just over 300 pairs. The largest numbers of breeding pairs were in California, with 3500 pairs, of which about 1500 were on and around Tule Lake in the Klamath Basin (4), and Oregon, which had around 5500 pairs, mostly in the south. The total was estimated at around 15,000 pairs with the autumn population put at about 100,000. It has fluctuated around this level since the late 1950s survey, though with some tendency to increase, see Table 27.

A large proportion of the geese winter within the breeding range though there is a tendency to move south and west in autumn, producing concentrations of about 20,000 in the Columbia Basin, and up to 40,000 in California, mostly in the Central and Imperial Valleys and at Honey Lake.

TABLE 27: *Mid-winter counts of the Great Basin population of Canada Geese, 1959–60 to 1976–7*

Winter	Count	Winter	Count	Winter	Count
1959–60	140,658	1965–6	113,550	1971–2	117,303
1960–1	144,072	1966–7	166,480	1972–3	101,000
1961–2	115,420	1967–8	111,890	1973–4	111,380
1962–3	126,820	1968–9	112,210	1974–5	133,530
1963–4	121,340	1969–70	112,500	1975–6	218,210
1964–5	106,820	1970–1	108,470	1976–7	143,320

Totals may include some birds of the South Alaska Coast population as the wintering grounds overlap.

J. Chattin (pers. com.).

There are smaller but still significant numbers on the Snake River plain in Idaho, and in Nevada and Arizona.

CENTRAL FLYWAY (Map 30)

Four populations have been described for this flyway, two comprising small Canada Geese breeding in the arctic and subarctic and wintering well south in America, one of them reaching the Gulf, and two populations of large Canadas. All four populations number several tens of thousands. The small Canadas have been censused fairly regularly, and the figures are shown in tables. The counting of the larger birds has not produced a good series of counts. In addition there are a number of mainly resident flocks of large Canada Geese that do not fit into any single population, and are managed separately. They are found in North and South Dakota, Nebraska, western Minnesota and Iowa. Many of the flocks have been artificially established.

Highline population (Map 30)

This name is taken from the Highline Plains which border the east side of the Rockies. The birds involved are all large and rather pale, belonging to the Southern Group and generally given the name Great Basin Canada Geese *moffitti*. They lie on the eastern flank of the Great Basin population. The breeding areas are in the extreme southern portions of Alberta and Saskatchewan Provinces (a few hundred pairs in each during surveys in 1955–65), eastern Montana (about 1200 pairs), eastern Wyoming (150–200 pairs) and the western parts of North and South Dakota (under 100 pairs in each). These figures are already rather out of date as the population has been increasing and expanding its range in recent years, utilising the many new small reservoirs and farm impoundments that have been built.

Distances travelled on migration are comparatively short; the most northerly wintering area lying on the North Platte River in Wyoming (1), with up to 10,000 geese, and the bulk of the remaining birds, up to 30,000, on reservoirs in northern Colorado. A few thousand go further south to the Bosque del Apache National Wildlife Refuge (2) in central New Mexico.

The total population has increased steadily from fewer than 10,000 in the early 1960s to nearly 20,000 in the mid-1960s to around 50,000 in the last few years.

Short Grass Prairie population (Map 30, Table 28)

The name given to this population derives from its occupation of the rather arid western part of the Great Plains, contrasting with the lusher eastern part which has given its name to another population, the Tall Grass Prairie. The geese of the Short Grass Prairie are mostly small to medium in size and usually described as Lesser Canada Geese *parvipes*, but there are usually some Richardson's Canadas *hutchinsii* and a few larger Great Basin Canadas *moffitti* mixed with them. The smaller geese form part of the continuous cline which I have called the Northern Group, while the larger birds may be intergrades between the small Northern Group and the large Southern Group geese.

The Short Grass Prairie population has been sub-divided into western and eastern segments having adjacent, indeed overlapping, breeding and wintering areas and migration routes, but sufficiently distinct to permit separate monitoring and management practices. The breeding range of the western segment extends from about 58°N in Alberta and Saskatchewan north through the District of Mackenzie to within about 10–15 km (5–10 miles) of the arctic ocean, and between about 110°W and the border with the Yukon Territory. They are very scattered breeders, preferring the neighbourhood of fast-flowing water and generally avoiding the coast. The eastern segment seems rarely to stray far from the coast, not more than perhaps 80 km (50 miles) and it breeds between about 110°W and 100°W, round the shores of the Queen Maud Gulf and on the southern part of Victoria Island. In this region there is some overlap and probable mixing with birds from the Tall Grass Prairie population which will be dealt with below.

The two population segments begin to leave their breeding grounds in the first part of September and arrive at a major staging area in eastern Alberta

TABLE 28: *Mid-winter counts of the Short Grass Prairie population of Canada Geese, 1947–8 to 1976–7*

Winter	Count	Winter	Count	Winter	Count
1947–8	24,250	1957–8	60,300	1967–8	125,400
1948–9	23,450	1958–9	76,000	1968–9	73,900
1949–50	26,000	1959–60	77,700	1969–70	106,900
1950–1	27,800	1960–1	103,350	1970–1	150,200
1951–2	44,700	1961–2	80,150	1971–2	148,700
1952–3	44,050	1962–3	123,000	1972–3	153,000
1953–4	52,600	1963–4	112,000	1973–4	138,200
1954–5	44,100	1964–5	128,450	1974–5	103,200
1955–6	38,300	1965–6	100,750	1975–6	217,300
1956–7	48,800	1966–7	92,900	1976–7	103,600

Counts prior to 1962–3 made in January, since then in mid-December.

Grieb (1970 and pers. com.), and H. Miller (pers. com.).

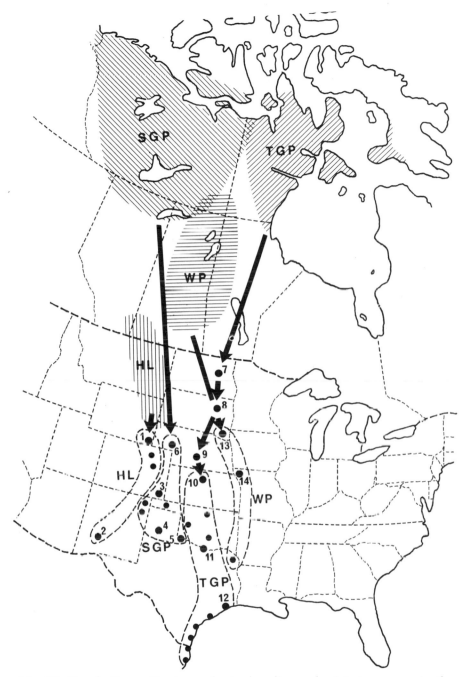

Map 30. Canada Goose *Branta canadensis*—breeding and wintering ranges in the Central Flyway. Breeding ranges: ▨ Short Grass Prairie population (SGP); ▨ Tall Grass Prairie population (TGP); ▤ Western Prairie population (WP); ▥ Highline population (HL). Dashed lines enclose respective winter ranges, and arrows connect breeding and wintering ranges of different populations. Numbered haunts—see text; ● other haunts.

and western Saskatchewan. To some extent the western segment keeps to the former province and the eastern segment to the latter, but the geese do not respect administrative boundaries and there is some mixing of the two stocks. The staging area they use is more or less continuous suitable habitat right across the province boundary, extending for about 250 km (150 miles) into Alberta and 150 km (90 miles) into Saskatchewan, and for about 320 km (200 miles) from north to south. It contains numerous lakes, several rivers and has extensive wheat-growing areas providing ample stubbles on which the geese can feed. The same staging area is used by Whitefronts, Lesser Snows and Ross's Geese as already mentioned under those species. The geese remain in this area until forced south by approaching winter, migrating en masse, usually some time in November.

The next stage of the autumn migration is a direct flight to the wintering area, although the geese of the two segments probably follow much the same route across Montana, Wyoming and western Nebraska, they diverge in the winter quarters. The principal wintering haunt of the western segment is the Two Buttes reservoir (3) in south-west Colorado. Up to 60,000 birds, approximately two-thirds of the total, winter there, and on other reservoirs in the valley of the Arkansas River. The remaining third go further, about 25,000 flying due south to Buffalo Lake, Texas (4), and about 5000 south-west to several lakes in north-east New Mexico.

Almost all of the eastern segment make for the Waggoner Ranch area of Texas (5), perhaps 250 km (150 miles) from Buffalo Lake. There is a number of roosting lakes here, particularly Santa Rosa Lake. A proportion of the geese stop off on migration each autumn on the North Platte River in Nebraska (6) and some may remain throughout the winter, if conditions stay suitable. The northward movement of both segments begins in late February or March and takes in the same southern Canada resting area as in the autumn.

Total counts of this population and its two segments have been made for many years and the figures are given in Table 28. They show a steady increase in the eastern segment but a striking one in the western segment, with the former roughly trebling in nearly thirty years but the latter growing five-fold. Some of the ups and downs may be due to poor breeding or perhaps, sometimes, to shifts of birds from one segment to the other. The overall increase is not in doubt, however, and is in part due to successful management. There are no age counts of these Canada Geese, but data gathered from hunters and from cannon-netted birds caught for marking have shown that there is a high annual breeding success, ranging from about 19–57%, with no really bad years in the period examined.

Tall Grass Prairie population (Map 30, Table 29)
The geese of this population belong to the same Northern Group as the previous population. Whereas the latter are said to comprise mainly Lessers plus a small proportion of Richardson's, the reverse is the case here. In fact, all this means is that the Tall Grass population is drawn from the more easterly part of the breeding range of the small Canada Goose cline, where the birds tend to be smaller than further west, though individuals representing the complete size range are present.

TABLE 29: *Mid-winter counts of the Tall Grass Prairie population of Canada Geese, 1961–2 to 1976–7*

Winter	Count	Winter	Count	Winter	Count
1961–2	97,750	1967–8	129,950	1973–4	160,500
1962–3	68,650	1968–9	61,070	1974–5	133,525
1963–4	98,930	1969–70	86,765	1975–6	179,500
1964–5	74,825	1970–1	133,220	1976–7	158,800
1965–6	70,670	1971–2	160,940		
1966–7	69,940	1972–3	148,400		

Hine & Schoenfeld (1968), and H. Miller and C. Schroeder (pers. com.).

Counts prior to 1969 in late October; since then in December.

The breeding range extends east from about 102°W and north of about 60°N. It thus overlaps with the Short Grass Prairie population around the boundary between the Mackenzie District and the District of Keewatin. From there it extends to the west coast of Hudson Bay and then takes in Southampton Island, the Boothia and Melville Peninsulas, and the western part of Baffin Island. Scattered breeding of small Canadas to the north and east of Baffin Island, and on Bylot Island and, rarely, West Greenland, may be presumed to belong to this population.

The autumn migration takes place in a series of hops, from staging post to staging post down the North American continent, to wintering quarters from southern Kansas to the Gulf coast in Texas and Mexico. Not all the geese use all the staging areas, leap-frogging takes place with only part of the population using any one of them, then perhaps over-flying others direct to the winter range. The first group of haunts they use is in southern Manitoba and at Devil's Lake, North Dakota (7), and Sand Lake, South Dakota (8). Peaks here are in late September and October. Further south there is a staging area in southern Kansas and northern Oklahoma, in particular at the Quivira (9) and Salt Plains (10) National Wildlife Refuges. Peaks of several tens of thousands are reached in mid-November. In mild winters some thousands may stop and winter here, but the great majority move on to their true wintering areas centred on Lake Texoma, Texas (11), and along the coast of Texas from Houston (12) west and south into Mexico.

Counts of this population began in 1960 and have continued each year since. The counts to date are shown in Table 29. The considerable increase in recent years may be due, in part, to better censusing methods.

Western Prairie population (Map 30)

There are two Prairie populations, the Eastern and the Western. The latter is placed in the Central Flyway while the former, although adjoining and even overlapping with it in places, is more correctly assigned to the Mississippi Flyway and will be dealt with under that heading. The bulk of the birds in both populations are usually termed Interior Canada Geese *interior*, though larger birds designated as Giant Canada Geese *maxima* are also stated to be present. Clearly, all are members of the Southern Group of pale birds with a considerable range of size. The situation is further confused because there is a very large overlap in migration and wintering areas between the Western Prairie population and the Tall Grass Prairie population, so that during censuses there are some problems in distinguishing which birds belong to which population.

The Western Prairie population breeds to the west of 100°W in Manitoba and across Saskatchewan to near the Alberta border. In the south the limit is thought to be around Yorkton, Saskatchewan, and Dauphin, Manitoba, while in the north the birds reach the southern part of the Northwest Territories. The overlap with the Eastern Prairie population comes around the 100° meridian.

After a short migration the first wintering area is reached in southern South Dakota, particularly on and around the Fort Randall Reservoir (13) and Lake Andes, where between 25,000 and 30,000 stay. Another 10,000 geese move further south to Missouri and winter near Squaw Creek (14) and some thousands go as far as eastern Texas. The total population fluctuated between 25,000 and 40,000 during the 1960s, then increased sharply to 60,000–90,000 in the early 1970s, but the problems of overlap with other populations makes accurate assessment difficult.

MISSISSIPPI FLYWAY (Map 31)

The Canada Geese of the Mississippi Flyway have been divided into three populations. They overlap to a certain extent but are censused and managed separately. Total numbers are very large, with over 60,000 geese counted in recent winters. The available breakdown of counts is shown in Tables 30–32. All three populations are made up of birds referred to as Interior Canada Geese *interior* plus a proportion of larger birds, usually termed Giant Canada Geese *maxima*. It is more satisfactory to treat all as part of the Southern Group, showing considerable size variation (and there is complete intergrading) but all predominantly pale in colour. As in the Central Flyway, there are also many resident, often introduced, flocks of large, pale birds which do not belong to any single population. They are usually managed individually.

Eastern Prairie population (Map 31, Table 30)

The breeding range extends from about 100°W, where it overlaps with the Western Prairie population, eastwards through central Manitoba and north-west Ontario to the south-west coast of Hudson Bay, where there is overlap with the Mississippi Valley population. The autumn migration takes the birds south through Minnesota and the eastern Dakotas to Swan Lake National Wildlife Refuge, Missouri (1), the principal wintering haunt. There an average of over 125,000 Canadas have wintered in recent years out of a total population of around 180,000. The highest count was 166,000 in winter 1973–4. Formerly, Swan Lake was only an autumn resting place and although the counts at this time of year were very high, with 133,000 in 1955, the wintering numbers were only 20,000–30,000. Since the mid-1960s there has been an increasing tendency to winter there, producing considerable management problems due to the changes in hunting pressure. The

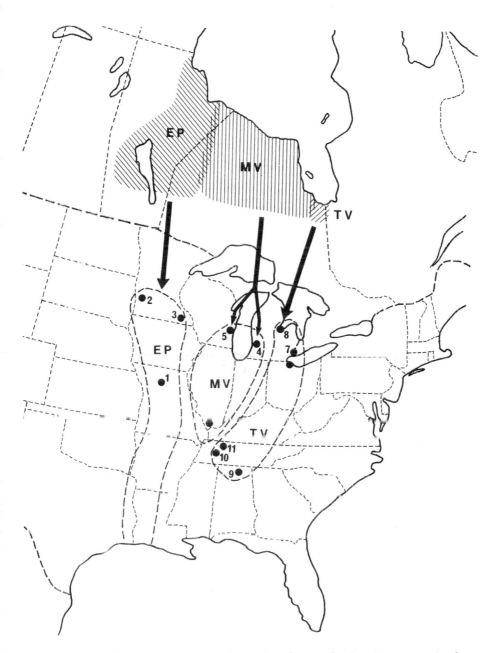

MAP 31. Canada Goose *Branta canadensis*—breeding and wintering ranges in the Mississippi Flyway. Breeding ranges: ⫻Eastern Prairie population (EP); ‖‖ Mississippi Valley population (MV); ⫽Tennessee Valley population (TV). Dashed lines enclose respective winter ranges and arrows connect breeding and wintering ranges of different populations. Numbered haunts—see text.

TABLE 30: *Mid-winter counts of the Eastern Prairie population of Canada Geese, 1960–1 to 1975–6*

Winter	Count	Winter	Count	Winter	Count
1960–1	57,100	1966–7	159,850	1972–3	181,420
1961–2	53,500	1967–8	151,570	1973–4	205,790
1962–3	99,480	1968–9	130,920	1974–5	197,150
1963–4	96,400	1969–70	106,600	1975–6	204,440
1964–5	73,060	1970–1	111,100		
1965–6	141,820	1971–2	157,320		

Circulated reports of inventories in the Mississippi Flyway.

remaining wintering areas are in Minnesota at Lac Qui Parle (2) and Rochester (3), and in Iowa, Arkansas and Louisiana. The last named states used to carry much larger numbers but have lost out because of the increasing preference shown by the geese for the Swan Lake area. Recent total counts are shown in Table 30.

Mississippi Valley population (Map 31, Table 31)

This population has increased strikingly in the last thirty years and it has also redistributed itself on its winter quarters in response to the creation of Refuges. The breeding range lies close to the south coast of Hudson Bay and the west coast of James Bay. There the birds overlap with the previous population but seem not to breed further inland than about 150 km (90 miles), whereas the Eastern Prairie population extends two or three times that distance from the coast. On leaving the breeding grounds the geese split to go either side of Lake Michigan. In recent years about one-third of the total, around 100,000, take the east bank, stopping at a number of localities on the way, the main one being Swan Creek, Michigan (4). They then head for the wintering areas in southern Illinois. The remaining two–thirds fly down the west side of Lake Michigan and make a stop of several weeks, from late September to the end of November, at the Horicon National Wildlife Refuge (5) not far from Milwaukee. This refuge was actually created in 1940 specifically to protect ducks, particularly Redheads, but lying astride the

TABLE 31: *Mid-winter counts of the Mississippi Valley population of Canada Geese, 1960–1 to 1975–6*

Winter	Count	Winter	Count	Winter	Count
1960–1	174,700	1966–7	208,920	1972–3	295,770
1961–2	146,000	1967–8	215,200	1973–4	277,710
1962–3	175,950	1968–9	287,740	1974–5	304,300
1963–4	184,420	1969–70	324,450	1975–6	304,940
1964–5	200,780	1970–1	292,070		
1965–6	161,860	1971–2	293,890		

Circulated reports of inventories in the Mississippi Flyway.

Canada Goose migration route it was perhaps inevitable that the geese would discover it, and make use of it. This happened on a large scale in the late 1940s and early 1950s, and now anything up to 200,000 geese may be there for periods in the autumn.

The final destination of both flights of Canada Geese is the Horseshoe Lake Refuge (6) in the extreme south of Illinois. Formerly, the birds went further south to areas along the Mississippi River in Mississippi and Louisiana but the creation of good conditions further north has resulted in yet another case of short-stopping. There is now a cluster of refuges in Illinois and neighbouring Kentucky and Tennessee attracting a total of over 300,000 Canada Geese. These include Horseshoe Lake, Union County, Crab Orchard, Ballard County and Reelfoot Lakes. Recent counts are given in Table 31.

Tennessee Valley population (Map 31, Table 32)

This is the third and smallest population in the Mississippi Flyway. There is overlap with the Mississippi Flyway to the west and with the adjacent Mid-Atlantic population of the Atlantic Flyway to the east. The breeding grounds lie around the southern coast of James Bay and on Akimiski Island in the Bay. It was formerly thought to extend well up the east coast of Hudson Bay but these birds are now attributed to the Atlantic Flyway. The geese have migratory stopping places in Michigan and near the head of Lake Erie before they fly to wintering areas in Alabama and Tennessee. As with the other

TABLE 32: *Mid-winter counts of the Tennessee Valley population of Canada Geese, 1960–1 to 1975–6*

Winter	Count	Winter	Count	Winter	Count
1960–1	78,300	1966–7	96,590	1972–3	101,240
1961–2	84,100	1967–8	88,200	1973–4	135,930
1962–3	57,890	1968–9	73,900	1974–5	102,970
1963–4	82,210	1969–70	106,850	1975–6	115,600
1964–5	97,030	1970–1	105,450		
1965–6	86,970	1971–2	117,640		

Circulated reports of inventories in the Mississippi Flyway.

populations in this flyway there has been an increasing tendency for the birds to stay further north in recent winters, and substantial numbers now do so, with up to 20,000 still at the Jack Miner Sanctuary, Ontario (7), and a further 10,000 at the Shiawassee Refuge, Michigan (8), as late as mid-December. The main southern wintering haunts are the Wheeler Refuge, Alabama (9), where about 30,000 can be found, and the Tennessee (10) and Cross Creeks (11) Refuges in Tennessee, with about 30,000 and 5000 respectively. There are several lesser haunts in both states. The overall pattern has been for population increase, helped initially by the creation of refuges covering the wintering areas, and later by management and control of hunting. Census totals for recent years are given in Table 32.

ATLANTIC FLYWAY (Map 32)

This easternmost Flyway takes Canada Geese from breeding areas between Hudson Bay and the Labrador coast and funnels them down the east of the Alleghenies to wintering areas close to the Atlantic Seaboard. All the geese are medium to large pale birds, usually divided between Interior and Atlantic Canada Geese *interior* and *atlanticus*. There is clearly considerable overlap and mixing between the two described forms and it is more realistic to regard them as part of the Southern Group of Canada Geese, perhaps separating along the lines of the two populations in this flyway, but certainly including intergrades. One of the populations, the North Atlantic, is quite small, but the other, the Mid-Atlantic, is easily the largest of them all.

Mid-Atlantic population (Map 32, Table 33)

The Ungava Peninsula in northern Quebec forms the breeding area for this population. The birds are thinly spread throughout much of the tundra and boreal forest south to about 50°N, but there are some areas of high density, particularly on the east coast of Hudson Bay and around the shores on Ungava Bay in the north. Small numbers also breed on the southern part of Baffin Island and rather larger numbers on the Belcher Islands in Hudson Bay.

Staging posts for this population are rather few and, after gathering on the shores of Hudson and James Bays, the birds can and do fly direct to the wintering grounds on the Atlantic Coast. However, a great deal of effort has been expended in recent years into trying to persuade at least some of the birds to stop off at places on the way, if only for a few weeks. This has been successfully achieved at sites along the St Lawrence Seaway in southern Ontario, and at Refuges in New York and Pennsylvania, though only a few thousand geese are involved to date.

The winter range extends from New York State to Florida but the

TABLE 33: *Mid-winter counts of Canada Geese in the Atlantic Flyway, 1959–60 to 1976–7, and of the Mid-Atlantic and North Atlantic populations, 1969–70 to 1976–7*

Winter	Atlantic Flyway Total	Winter	Mid-Atlantic population	North Atlantic population	Atlantic Flyway Total
1959–60	386,400	1969–70	751,400	23,800	775,200
1960–1	544,380	1970–1	649,500	25,500	675,000
1961–2	418,900	1971–2	640,500	59,700	700,200
1962–3	480,820	1972–3	679,300	32,700	712,000
1963–4	528,200	1973–4	728,800	31,400	760,200
1964–5	482,500	1974–5	777,500	41,800	819,300
1965–6	600,200	1975–6	732,400	52,100	784,500
1966–7	604,000	1976–7	883,400	40,200	923,600
1967–8	615,200				
1968–9	678,800				

USFWS Annual Waterfowl Status Reports, and E. Ferguson (pers. com.).

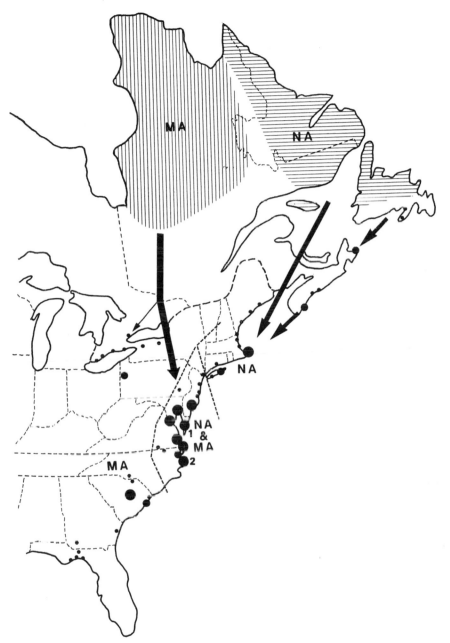

MAP 32. Canada Goose *Branta canadensis*—breeding and wintering ranges in the Atlantic Flyway. Breeding ranges: ||| Mid-Atlantic population; ≡ North Atlantic population. Dashed lines indicate division and overlap of the two populations and arrows indicate approximate migration routes. ● over 10,000; ● 5000–10,000; ● other haunts. Numbers indicate haunts referred to in text.

numerical distribution shows an enormous concentration in Delaware and Maryland, in particular on the Delmarva peninsula (1). Here over 500,000 geese have been counted in recent winters, an incredible concentration which has taken advantage of the unique combination of abundant food supplies in this major corn-growing area, plus adjacent wetlands along the shores of the peninsula and a considerable degree of protection in both Government and private refuges. To the north of Delmarva there are only some 35,000 geese, mostly in Pennsylvania, and a few in New York; to the south there are about 60,000 each in Virginia and North Carolina, and perhaps 10,000 in South Carolina. Small numbers still reach Florida, mostly crossing to the Gulf coast, but this is a remnant of the former 20,000–30,000 Canadas that used to winter there. The birds, yet again, are not bothering to fly so far south.

The total population is now in the region of 750,000, having risen from around 200,000–300,000 in the late 1940s. The growth rate slowed a little as this level was reached in the late 1960s, but the population is certainly healthy enough. Counts are shown in Table 33.

North Atlantic population (Map 32 and Table 33)

This population breeds on the island of Newfoundland, where there are between 5000 and 6000 pairs, and along the Labrador coast, and inland into the interior of Ungava where it overlaps with the previous population. The migration route is entirely coastal and, as the birds pass south, flocks stop off at a number of places for the winter; the furthest south is around Pea Island, North Carolina (2). Between 1000 and 2000 remain in the south of Newfoundland and perhaps twice as many stay in the southern part of Nova Scotia. Up to 7000 winter in Massachusetts, about 3000 in New York, including Long Island, 3000 in New Jersey, and perhaps 10,000 at Pea Island. It seems probable that there are some in the Maryland–Delaware area among the enormous concentrations of birds belonging to the previous population, but it has not proved possible to sort them out.

The total population is presently around 30,000–50,000 and has probably not changed much in recent years (see Table 33). The picture is somewhat confused because within its wintering area a number of resident flocks of Canada Geese have become established, particularly in the north-eastern states. They now total several thousand birds.

Canada Geese outside North America

Canada Geese have been introduced into a number of countries. As early as the last half of the 17th century the first birds were sent to Britain from the Canadian or American colonies. There has been considerable discussion as to which race they belonged, but apart from the fact that, today, they are mostly rather large and pale, it seems unlikely that any conclusions can be reached at this distance in time, and doubtful if much would be achieved by doing so. The original birds were clearly from the Southern Group of large pale Canada Geese.

The geese were originally brought over, in part at least, as ornamental birds and were released on the lakes created in some of the landscaped gardens of Britain's new stately homes. Whether it was hoped to utilise the geese for food or for sport is not known. Little, too, is known of their subsequent history of spread around the country, except that it appears that the majority of the birds were, or quickly became, sedentary and that such colonisation of new waters as there was, took place more by man's movements of pairs from place to place rather than by natural means.

The first ever census of the Canada Geese in Britain was in July 1953. The total was found to be about 3500, though with the rather wide limits of 2200–4000 birds. The geese were still largely concentrated on private lakes but were beginning to live on reservoirs and gravel pits as well. During the 1950s an extensive programme of transplanting was undertaken, partly to relieve landowners whose flocks had grown too large for comfort, and partly to establish new flocks where it was hoped some sport shooting would result. The effect was not entirely as desired because the flocks which had had their numbers reduced quickly increased again in the absence of any continuing control, while neither they nor the newly established flocks provided much sport, being too tame and accustomed to man to fly more than absolutely necessary. If these geese can walk from their roosting water to the feeding fields they will do so, and even when flying they often stay close to the ground.

The consequence of dispersing the birds, coupled with their colonisation of the rapidly growing number of shallow and attractive gravel pits, particularly in southern England, was a great increase in the number of geese. The next census was carried out in July 1967 and 1968. By now the population had risen to around 10,500. Complaints of agricultural damage began to increase although total numbers were still small by any standards, but British farmers are not used to having even a hundred geese eating their crops and grass through the spring and summer. Another census held in the summer of 1976 showed a further substantial increase to around 19,500 birds. There are major concentrations of over 1000 in the lower Thames valley near Reading, in parts of the Midlands, to the north-west and north-east of Birmingham, in north Shropshire and Cheshire, and in Yorkshire. Movements of birds between areas are slight, and it has proved possible to split the geese into some 25 to 30 subpopulations, which should make for much easier management and control. The Yorkshire group is unique in having a moult migration of immature birds to northern Scotland, which will be dealt with in more detail in the next chapter.

There are almost annual records of Canada Geese being seen in winter, mainly in Scotland and Ireland, and mainly in company with Greenland Whitefronts, and occasionally with Greenland Barnacle Geese. They vary from large pale birds, through medium pale and dark, to small pale and thus include birds from the Northern and Southern Groups of North America. Although escapes of some of these forms occur there seems no reason to doubt the wild origin of these birds.

Elsewhere in Europe, Canada Geese were introduced into Sweden in 1929, and into Norway in 1936. The latter population has remained small but in Sweden the total population increased from a few hundreds in the 1930s to around 3500 in 1966 and perhaps to as many as 15,000 in 1975. Some of these birds migrate south and west to winter in southern Norway, Denmark, East and West Germany and the Netherlands, but up to 3500 have remained to winter in southern Sweden in the last few, mild years, especially around Lake Hammersjön. Canada Geese were introduced into south-west Finland in 1964 and have bred each year since 1966. They migrate in autumn, presumably to Germany. There are now some hundreds of birds.

Fifty Canada Geese were taken from America to New Zealand in 1905, and some more in 1920. Like the European birds these were predominantly large and pale, and have been variously attributed to the Giant and Atlantic races. The geese increased and spread very rapidly as the habitat was ideal and they had no competitors and few predators among the native fauna. In recent years the total has been put at 15,000–20,000, and some control has been necessary to reduce agricultural damage.

There are a number of recent records of Canada Geese from Kashmir, but all have been based on descriptions supplied by hunters, and no skin has been preserved. It is difficult to think where these birds might be coming from.

Barnacle Goose (Map 33)

There are three populations of Barnacle Geese, their breeding grounds located in three separated parts of the European arctic. Their wintering grounds all lie in north-west Europe; they are separate, but by comparatively short distances only. The three populations are all quite small, the largest about 50,000 birds, the smallest only 7,000, but all have been increasing steadily in recent years and are in much healthier condition than twenty years ago.

Greenland population (Maps 33 and 34, Table 34)

The breeding range of this population is confined to the ice-free coastal areas of East Greenland, from Scoresby Sound at about 70°N to Germania Land at 78°N. This considerable area has been very poorly surveyed for geese and although breeding colonies have been located they only account for part of the known number of breeding pairs as assessed by autumn age counts. The discovered colonies are all either on cliff ledges or on small islands in the many large fjords. They range from about 5 to 50 pairs and, clearly, this lack of really large colonies plus the inaccessibility of much of the land until after the geese have hatched their eggs, due to the presence of ice in the fjords and offshore, has prevented a greater knowledge of the breeding distribution.

The geese are forced to leave Greenland in early September by the onset of snow and freezing conditions and they move to Iceland, concentrating in the broad northern valleys and also on some of the southern uplands. There the whole population spends from four to six weeks before heading for the British Isles, where they spend the winter. The arrival time in Britain is usually in the third week of October but the sudden onset of winter in Iceland can bring them earlier than this. Conversely, good conditions there, or sometimes adverse winds, can delay the arrival into the first week of November.

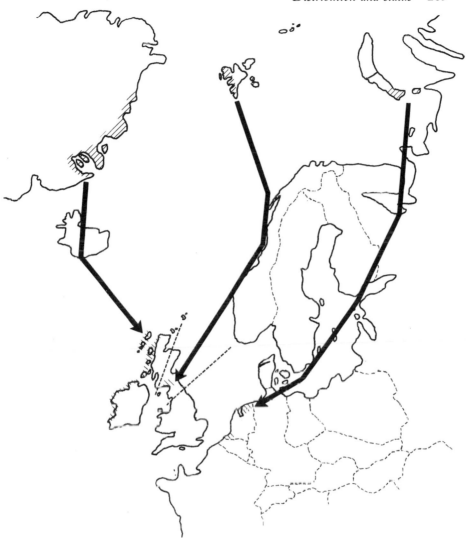

MAP 33. Barnacle Goose *Branta leucopsis*—world range. 𝄕 breeding; ⦚wintering. Arrows indicate approximate migration routes. Dotted lines divide winter ranges of the three populations.

In winter the geese of this population are virtually confined to islands, scattered from County Kerry in the extreme south-west of Ireland, to the north coast of Sutherland in northern Scotland (Map 34). In between, they inhabit about 170 islands plus a very few headlands. The majority of the islands are small and uninhabited, though most are grazed by sheep, at least in summer, helping to produce sufficiently short grass to attract geese. About

30% of the geese flocks are under 50, and nearly three-quarters of them are under 250. Many of the flocks are not confined to a single island but range between several in a group.

Although, in the past, it is probable that the whole population was thus scattered and split, a steady concentration has taken place over the past twenty years on to one island, Islay (1) in the Inner Hebrides. This is a large, inhabited island but through protection by the major landowners the geese have been able to settle and adapt to feeding on farmland instead of rough grazing. From around 3000 in the 1950s the population on Islay rose slowly to about 8000 in the mid-1960s. In the same period the total for this population rose from about 11,000 to 18,000 birds. Since then there has been a much faster rate of increase on Islay to no less than 24,000 in 1976, when the population total was about 35,000. There has been little or no change in numbers at any of the other haunts, just a steadily increasing number and proportion on Islay. The birds on Islay live in a number of flocks spread through several feeding areas. There are two main roosts in sheltered arms of the sea. The next largest flock of Barnacle Geese is that on the Inishkea islands (2) in Co. Mayo, Ireland, where an average 2500 are found. Only one other flock, on the Monachs, Outer Hebrides (3), has reached four figures.

Although it has been possible to count the flock on Islay at least once every winter, and on the Inishkeas in most winters, the rest of the range can only be surveyed from the air. Because of expense and difficulty, this has only been done occasionally. The counts that have been made, plus the more regular ones on Islay, are set out in Table 34. The increase on Islay, not paralleled by the rest of the population, suggests that the Islay birds form a sub-group, and

TABLE 34: *Total counts of Greenland Barnacle Geese wintering in the British Isles, together with annual peak counts on Islay, Scotland, 1952–3 to 1977–8, and annual breeding success figures from Islay, 1959–60 to 1977–8*

Winter	Total count	Peak count	% young	Brood size	Winter	Total count	Peak count	% young	Brood size
1952–3		3,000	no record		1965–6	20,000	9,000	11·2	1·7
1953–4		2,750	,,		1966–7		10,500	13·0	1·4
1954–5		9,000	,,		1967–8		16,500	17·1	1·8
1955–6		3,000	,,		1968–9		13,300	9·5	1·3
1956–7	11,800	3,000	,,		1969–70		14,300	20·0	1·9
1957–8		7,500	,,		1970–1		15,100	19·4	2·5
1958–9		5,600	,,		1971–2		17,100	13·6	1·8
1959–60	8,800	7,100	14·1	2·5	1972–3	23,600	17,200	12·1	2·1
1960–1	13,900	6,800	9·7	1·9	1973–4		18,300	17·4	2·5
1961–2	14,000	8,000	10·7	2·1	1974–5		19,400	13·0	2·2
1962–3		8,700	7·6	2·5	1975–6		20,200	13·9	1·9
1963–4		10,400	30·6	2·8	1976–7		24,000	22·4	2·5
1964–5		8,300	7·5	n.r.	1977–8		19,600	4·9	1·8

Note: Only five complete counts have been attempted.

Boyd (1968), Ogilvie & Boyd (1975), and own data.

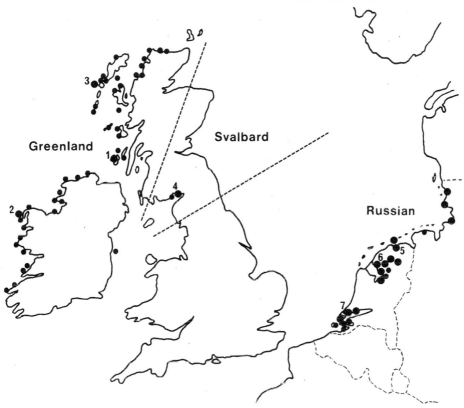

MAP 34. Barnacle Goose *Branta leucopsis*—winter range. ●over 1000; ●under 1000.
Numbers indicate haunts referred to in text. Dotted lines separate wintering
range of the three populations.

this is confirmed by their breeding success which is regularly better than for
the birds on the Inishkeas, the only other locality where age counts have been
done. It seems probable that the better feeding on Islay enables them to breed
more successfully than birds elsewhere. Breeding success is variable but total
failures seem to be rare. Separation into populations is not complete,
however, as a certain amount of ringing has shown. It is at least to be
welcomed that there has not been a wholesale influx to Islay of birds from
other parts of the range. The concentration there is already large enough to
cause some conflict with farming without the added worry of the aban-
donment of the rest of the range.

The northern return begins in mid-April and once again Iceland is used as a
staging post on the way to East Greenland. Most of the month of May is spent
here. Stragglers probably (or certainly) from this population provide many
records in North America, mostly on the east coast from Baffin Island to
North Carolina. Escapes are frequent, though, and probably account for

reports from central and southern states. A bird ringed in Greenland was recovered on the Azores.

Svalbard population (Maps 33 and 34, Table 35)

The island archipelago of Svalbard includes, as its largest island, Spitsbergen, the name that used to be applied to the whole island group. A small population of Barnacle Geese has been known to breed here since the turn of the century, and has probably been there much longer, though never large. It was not until 1963 that it was finally established that the whole of the Svalbard breeding population wintered only on the Solway Firth (4), which forms the boundary on the west coast between England and Scotland. It had been suspected that this might be so some years earlier when a few birds ringed in Svalbard appeared in the wintering flock of the Solway, but in the winter of 1962–3 over 90 birds ringed the previous summer in Svalbard were recaught on the Solway, whereas none of the several hundred birds ringed in East Greenland were captured. The separation of the two populations is only 175 kilometres (110 miles), from the Solway to the major winter haunt of the Greenland birds, Islay.

Barnacle Geese have long wintered on the Solway and old records suggest that in the first part of this century several thousands were present. Even as late as the 1930s there may have been large flocks there though the records are not wholly reliable. What is more certain is that by the end of the 1939–45 war, during which several airfields had been built around the Firth and disturbance had been severe, there were only a few hundreds. Protection was

TABLE 35: *Numbers of Svalbard Barnacle Geese wintering on the Solway, Scotland, 1946–7 to 1976–7, together with annual breeding success since 1958–9*

Winter	Total count	% young	Brood size	Winter	Total count	% young	Brood size
1946–7	400	no records		1962–3	3,400	5·3	2·0
1947–8	400	,,		1963–4	4,250	42·8	2·8
1948–9	300	,,		1964–5	3,400	9·6	1·9
1949–50	700	,,		1965–6	3,700	15·6	2·0
1950–1	550	,,		1966–7	3,700	12·0	2·4
1951–2	600	,,		1967–8	3,700	27·2	2·1
1952–3	720	,,		1968–9	4,200	23·2	2·0
1953–4	1,200	,,		1969–70	4,000	27·0	2·6
1954–5	1,000	,,		1970–1	3,200	47·2	3·0
1955–6	810	,,		1971–2	3,700	15·0	2·3
1956–7	1,000	,,		1972–3	4,400	26·0	2·0
1957–8	1,150	,,		1973–4	5,100	21·0	1·6
1958–9	1,350	49·2	2·7	1974–5	5,200	15·0	1·8
1959–60	1,650	14·6	2·6	1975–6	6,050	20·6	2·2
1960–1	2,800	38·6	3·0	1976–7	7,200	23·0	2·6
1961–2	2,800	19·1	2·5	1977–8	6,750	3·5	2·0

Ogilvie (1970), Owen & Campbell (1974), and Wildfowl Trust files.

given to the geese in 1954 and a National Nature Reserve created at the favoured wintering haunt on the north shore at Caerlaverock in 1956. The population responded very well to this measure as the figures set out in Table 35 show. There were some setbacks to the growth of the population in the 1960s but there has been at least a tenfold increase in the last thirty years. The breeding success is quite variable though really bad years are uncommon. However, the variation in numbers suggests that there is occasionally a high mortality, perhaps on the breeding grounds. In 1970–1 the total was actually lower than the previous year despite a very high breeding success. The failure to increase in the 1960s also indicates a higher mortality than at any time in the last five years.

The breeding range has been fairly well mapped though some new areas may remain to be discovered. The first nests that were found were mainly on inland cliffs, but the bulk of the population now nests in small colonies on offshore islands. These are often too tiny to provide much food for the goslings, which are therefore taken by their parents to marshland on the adjacent mainland. The known nesting areas are nearly all on the west coast of the main island of Spitsbergen with some in the inland valleys which open out to the west. A few pairs have been found breeding on some of the easterly islands of the group but surveys there have not been very complete and more may be found in future, particularly as the population is expanding. There is a puzzling discrepancy between the large flocks of Barnacle Geese reported from the Solway Firth fifty or more years ago and the very small numbers of breeding birds known in Svalbard before the recent increase. It suggests that geese from somewhere other than Svalbard were wintering on the Solway in those days.

The geese leave Svalbard in mid–September and fly to northern Norway. They then move down the Norwegian coast, using some of the very many small islands to be found there. Recent observations suggest that they have traditional favourite islands on which flocks may spend most of their time, rather than island–hopping day by day southwards. The first arrivals on the Solway are usually in the last week of September and the bulk of the population is present by mid–October. Most years a few birds are seen on the north-east coast of England in Northumberland, pausing as they make their landfall after crossing the North Sea. On the Solway the geese use the extensive saltmarsh of the Caerlaverock National Nature Reserve, and an area of adjacent farmland which is also a refuge, run by the Wildfowl Trust. They stay there for most of the shooting season as, although shooting of the geese is prohibited, the surrounding area is heavily shot for other species of wildfowl and disturbance is therefore considerable. Later in the winter they move to Rockcliffe, another large saltmarsh at the head of the estuary. Some also use farmland a short distance west of Caerlaverock at Southerness. The geese depart in mid- to late April, and spend most of the month of May on islands off the Norwegian coast, mainly in an area close to the arctic circle.

Russian population (Maps 33 and 34, Table 36)

This population of Barnacle Geese, too, has increased greatly in the last two decades, producing a somewhat curious situation because although the winter counts are quite reliable and show an increase from around 20,000 in the 1950s to about 50,000 now, Russian biologists have not increased their estimate of the number of breeding pairs in their country. Sufficient ringing has been carried out on the Dutch wintering grounds to show that there is no mixing with the other two populations, with the only summer recoveries coming from the known breeding range in the north-west part of arctic Russia. Published maps of their breeding distribution show the geese as

TABLE 36: *Numbers of Russian Barnacle Geese wintering in the Netherlands, 1960–1 to 1975–6, together with breeding success since 1969–70*

Winter	Total	% young	Winter	Total	% young
1960–1	20,000	no records	1968–9	29,000	no records
1961–2	23,000	,,	1969–70	29,000	14·5
1962–3	27,000	,,	1970–1	34,000	38·7
1963–4	16,000	,,	1971–2	33,000	4·5
1964–5	26,000	,,	1972–3	46,000	44·2
1965–6	25,000	,,	1973–4	54,000	36·1
1966–7	24,000	,,	1974–5	45,000	11·7
1967–8	33,000	,,	1975–6	50,000	32·9

Counts from Lebret *et al.* (1976). Breeding success figures from J. Van Impe (pers. com.).

confined to the islands of Novaya Zemlya and Vaigach, where they nest in rather small colonies on cliff ledges. It would appear that there has been no recent attempt by the Russians to update their knowledge of the breeding numbers and distribution of this species in their arctic. Perhaps they would get a pleasant surprise if they did so.

The autumn migration routes have been monitored through the Baltic in some detail. It is not known whether the geese stop in the Soviet Union before they reach the Baltic but it seems probable as they would have to leave their breeding grounds in early September, yet many are still arriving at their first Baltic stopping place in northern Estonia in October. From there the geese fly via southern Sweden and Denmark, or through northern Germany, to reach their wintering grounds in the Netherlands in November. Their principal haunts lie in the north of the country, particularly on the new polders created from the Lauwersmeer, a former tidal bay opening into the Waddensee (5). Practically the whole population may be found here at times. There is a low-lying island just offshore, Schiermonnikoog, which also carries several thousand birds. Localities further south and west in Friesland are also used during the winter, for example, between Oldeboorn and the Ijsselmeer (6), where peaks of 15,000 have been recorded, especially during hard weather which pushes the birds out of the Lauwersmeer area. Several thousand Barnacle Geese normally reach the south of the Netherlands, using haunts in the Rhine–Scheldt Delta (7), particularly Haringvliet and Hollandsdiep, and the flocks there will be greatly increased during spells of severe weather, up to 20,000 or more.

Barnacle Geese formerly wintered almost exclusively in West Germany and did not reach the Netherlands, but extensive drainage and disturbance in the former country, and the creation of vast areas of new grazing land in the Lauwersmeer, produced a shift in the centre of gravity of the population. This was no doubt encouraged by the protection given to them by the Dutch, whereas the Germans continue to shoot them. Numbers of Barnacle Geese still occur in West Germany but mostly on migration. However, in recent mild winters a few thousands have been staying in the major migration resting areas of the Hamburger Hallig and Franzosenland, on the west coast of Schleswig Holstein, and in Niedersachsen.

The spring departure from the Netherlands and Germany takes place in March and April and the geese use two main stopping places in the Baltic before going further north and east. These are the island of Gotland, Sweden, and on the west coast of Estonia and the associated islands. These two areas are used more intensively than in the autumn and may simultaneously hold about 10,000–15,000 birds each, for periods during May.

Counts of the population are not so comprehensive as for the other two but are set out in Table 36, together with the breeding success data which is available. The steady increase shows no signs of slowing and, all in all, one must rate the Barnacle Goose as an extremely successful species during the last twenty years.

Vagrant Barnacle Geese, which may, however, include some escapes, have been reported widely in Europe east to Romania and south to the Mediterranean, with scattered records from Morocco and Egypt.

Dark-bellied Brent Goose (Maps 35 and 36, Table 37)

There is only one population of this race, breeding along the most northerly coast of mainland Siberia between about 72° and 95°E on the Taymyr Peninsula. From there the geese make a long migration to winter on the shores of the North Sea, in Britain and the Netherlands, and down the west coast of France. Little is known about detailed distribution or densities on the breeding grounds, though it may be assumed that as with other Brent Geese they are mainly on low-lying tundra areas close to freshwater lakes or the sea.

Their autumn migration takes them along the north coast of Russia and then across the White Sea to the Baltic. It is also stated that some birds fly round the north coast of Scandinavia and down the Norwegian coast, or across the Gulf of Bothnia, but evidence for this is slight and there may also be confusion with the Light-bellied Brent Geese coming south from Svalbard. There seem to be few resting places in the Baltic, and the first arrivals in western Europe are in October in Denmark, particularly in south-west Jutland and in the Dutch and German Waddensee, around the islands on the seaward edge.

TABLE 37: *Mid-winter totals of Dark-bellied Brent Geese wintering in north-west Europe, 1955–6 to 1976–7, together with annual breeding success*

Winter	Britain	France	Netherlands	W. Germany	Denmark	Total	% young
1955–6							
1956–7	7,400	3,700	1,500	2,200	1,700	16,500	28·0
1957–8							
1958–9	no count						
1959–60	no count						
1960–1	14,800	6,500	200	a few	300	21,800	45·0
1961–2	no count						
1962–3	15,200	6,800	100	a few	700	22,800	0·2
1963–4	12,300	10,000	c. 1,000	c. 100	c. 200	23,600	35·0
1964–5	10,800	13,500	c. 1,000	c. 100	c. 200	25,600	34·7
1965–6	17,600	8,500	c. 1,000	c. 100	c. 200	27,300	6·9
1966–7	15,800	11,500	4,000	a few	c. 200	31,500	39·7
1967–8	18,900	8,600	3,000	300	c. 200	31,000	5·6
1968–9	18,200	8,200	1,000	100	100	27,600	0·4
1969–70	18,800	13,300	3,450	300	500	36,300	49·7
1970–1	23,800	13,300	2,300	800	600	40,800	37·7
1971–2	22,500	9,600	1,100	c. 500	c. 300	34,000	0·7
1972–3	29,300	18,400	2,200	c. 1,000	900	51,800	35·5
1973–4	41,200	32,900	7,100	c. 3,000	300	84,500	48·5
1974–5	31,400	21,500	12,700	c. 8,000	400	74,000	0·04
1975–6	50,000	41,000	18,000	c. 10,000	600	119,000	46·2
1976–7	48,200	43,200	13,400	c. 2,600	400	107,800	11·6

Ogilvie & St Joseph (1976).

MAP 35. Brent Goose *Branta bernicla*—world range. 🌿breeding; 🌊wintering. Arrows link breeding and wintering ranges of different subspecies and populations.

By mid–October the geese are arriving at the most important haunt in the entire range, Maplin Sands, off Foulness Island, Essex (1). Recent November counts have reached 18,000, taking in the adjacent much smaller haunt of Leigh Marsh. By November, too, other localities in Britain and France are gaining birds rapidly while in December and January numbers in the Netherlands, Denmark and West Germany drop to a minimum. In recent mild winters this minimum has been as high as 15,000 birds, two-thirds of them in the Netherlands, split between the Waddensee (2) and the Rhine–Scheldt Delta (3). Numbers at Foulness drop through the winter as the birds disperse to other haunts, but the total in all the Essex estuaries remains high, at about 30,000, while the two adjacent south-coast harbours of Chichester and Langstone (4) build to a mid-winter peak of about 15,000 birds. Other important localities include the Blackwater Estuary, Essex, the Wash (5), with a recent maximum of 6000, the North Norfolk Harbours (6) (5000 at peak), and much smaller numbers in north Kent and along the south coast as far as the Exe Estuary. The principal French haunt is in the Golfe du Morbihan, Brittany (7), where up to 20,000 winter, or between 40 and 60% of the French total.

There is quite a lot of movement throughout the winter, but it has been possible to carry out at least one annual census and many individual haunts are counted much more frequently. The results are set out in Table 37, together with the annual breeding success. The latter figures show an enormous variation, with highly successful years alternating with complete failures. Not unnaturally this 'boom or bust' situation produces sharp changes in the total numbers, though there has been a steady upward trend since counting began, helped by the granting of increased protection throughout the wintering range. In the last six years, a series of good breeding seasons has contributed to a sudden and striking population explosion so that there are currently about six times as many geese of this race as there were twenty years ago.

The return migration begins quite early, with the bulk of the geese clear of Britain and France by the end of March. However, they do not move far, and large concentrations build up in the Waddensee area of the Netherlands, West Germany and Denmark, with perhaps two-thirds of the population present during much of April and well into May.

Brent Geese have occurred in most European countries and south to North Africa, including Morocco and Egypt, and in the Azores.

Light-bellied Brent Goose (Map 35)

There are three populations of this race of Brent Goose, two wintering in north-west Europe and one in eastern North America, although the breeding grounds split the other way, with one in the Old World and two in the New. One population is quite large, though subject to considerable variation, but the other two are small.

Atlantic Seaboard population (Maps 35 and 37, Table 38)

This population breeds in arctic Canada and winters on the Atlantic coast of the United States. Its exact breeding range is difficult to determine because of intergrading on the western side with Black Brant, which anyway fly west and south-west to winter on the Pacific Coast, and the unknown dividing line between this population and the birds which also breed in arctic Canada but winter on the other side of the Atlantic in Ireland. However, from such evidence as there is, including some recent ringing and colour marking, the Atlantic population certainly breeds to the south of the Irish birds, on Southampton Island and Baffin Island, and on some of the islands to the south of Melville Sound. North of the Sound it becomes more problematical, and Melville Island birds and those on Prince Patrick Island probably all winter on the Pacific coast, and their plumage is intermediate between Light-bellied and Black Brant. Further south there are some Light-bellied Brent Geese breeding on the shore of the Queen Maud Gulf but there is another intergrading area west of the Gulf.

The Light-bellied Brent gather in James Bay in the autumn, at the southernmost part of Hudson Bay, and there the bulk of the population may stay through late September and the first part of October. The birds then have an overland migration direct to their wintering grounds on the Atlantic coast.

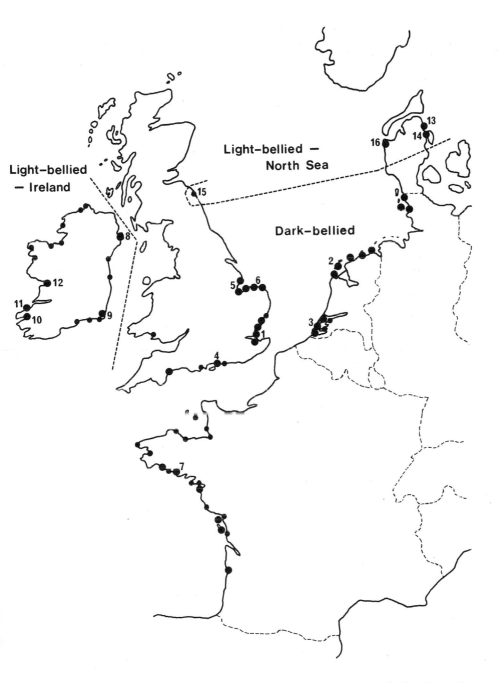

MAP 36. Dark-bellied and Light-bellied Brent Goose *Branta bernicla bernicla* and *hrota*—winter haunts of Dark-bellied Brent, and of Ireland and North Sea populations of Light-bellied Brent. ● over 1000; • under 1000. Numbers indicate haunts referred to in text. Dotted lines divide the three populations.

There was, formerly, a second migration route from Ungava Bay, via the St Lawrence estuary and then down the New England coast, but this route seems to have become less and less used in recent years, although there is still a small spring passage.

The wintering grounds lie along the Atlantic coast from Massachusetts to North Carolina, with very small numbers sometimes reaching South Carolina. The principal haunts are along the coast of New Jersey, and on south-west Long Island, New York (1). In recent years, 90% of the population, or from 50,000–150,000 birds will be found there, predominantly on the coast south of Barnegat (2) and in Grassy Sound and Absecon Bay. Much smaller numbers, a few thousands only, occur in Delaware (3) and Chesapeake (4) Bays, and in Back Bay, Virginia (5). The North Carolina haunts are at Currituck (6) and Pamlico (7) Sounds.

The spring return begins in March, the geese moving up the coast before heading inland direct to James Bay. Most of the month of May is spent there before the final northward leg to the breeding grounds.

There have been regular counts of this population of Brent Geese since the 1930s when there was a crash in numbers, attributed to the decimation of their food plant *Zostera* by the disease in the 1930s. However, there may have been other, perhaps associated, causes, such as a run of bad breeding seasons. The population recovered from the crash, and throughout the 1950s and 1960s seemed to be on a fairly even keel, despite fluctuations caused by variation in breeding success. Then, in the early 1970s, there was a sudden steep decline as shown in Table 38. This was started by a bad breeding season and followed by a much heavier shooting kill than usual in 1971. It was made worse by a second and completely disastrous breeding attempt in 1972, when it appears that large numbers of adults may have perished. A ban on shooting in 1972 helped to save the situation and the population is now beginning to climb to previous levels. The effect of the heavier than normal shooting and the two consecutive breeding failures were, however, a salutory warning to those who thought that the current management had everything under control.

TABLE 38: *Mid-winter counts of the Atlantic Seaboard population of Light-bellied Brent Geese, 1959–60 to 1976–7, together with annual breeding success since 1969–70*

Winter	Count	% young	Brood size	Winter	Count	% young	Brood size
1959–60	238,420	no records		1968–9	130,900	no records	
1960–1	266,000	,,		1969–70	106,500	30·4	2·39
1961–2	124,600	,,		1970–1	151,000	39·0	2·40
1962–3	167,400	,,		1971–2	73,300	5·7	2·14
1963–4	182,900	,,		1972–3	41,900	0·08	—
1964–5	181,600	,,		1973–4	87,600	59·1	3·22
1965–6	165,400	,,		1974–5	88,400	12·1	2·58
1966–7	219,200	,,		1975–6	127,000	37·9	2·89
1967–8	213,500	,,		1976–7	115,400	10·1	2·06

Lynch & Voelzer (1974), Voelzer (1976).

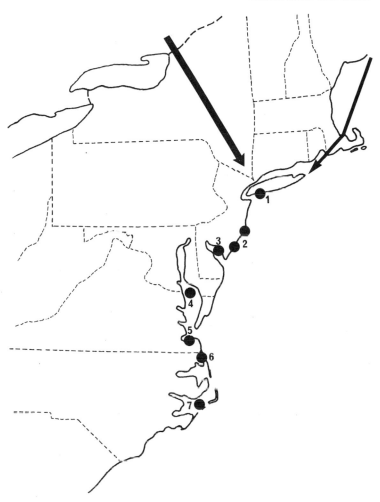

MAP 37. Light-bellied Brent Goose *Branta bernicla hrota*—winter range of Atlantic Coast population. ● major haunts. Numbers indicate haunts referred to in text. Arrows show approximate migration routes.

Shooting will not now be restarted until the population is safely above 100,000 again. This time has been further delayed by catastrophic losses during the very severe winter of 1976–7, when large numbers of geese starved. The population in the spring of 1977 was below 40,000.

Irish population (Maps 35 and 36, Table 39)

As already mentioned, the breeding range of this population overlaps with that of the previous one. However, it is known that Light-bellied Brent Geese breeding in north-east and northern Greenland belong to this population, and recent ringing suggests the inclusion of those breeding on Ellesmere and Axel

Heiberg Islands, and perhaps on some of the smaller islands in the north and east of the Queen Elizabeth archipelago. The migration route by which these birds reach Ireland has not been established. Flocks of some thousands occur in western Iceland each autumn and spring and it has been assumed that these birds reach Iceland either via northern Greenland and down the east coast, or else straight over the icecap from north-west Greenland. Another theory is that the breeding birds from the Canadian islands go down the west coast of Greenland and then either turn north again to Iceland or fly direct to Ireland.

The geese arrive in Ireland in October, some at least having spent the last part of September and the first part of October in Iceland. There is a major autumn concentration in Strangford Lough (8) in Northern Ireland (Map 36) before geese disperse to other haunts, including Wexford Harbour (9) on the east coast, and Castlemaine Harbour (10), Tralee (11) and Galway (12) Bays, among others, on the west coast. November counts have been carried out in several winters and are presented in Table 39; but in several years a second count in February has almost always shown a sizeable decrease, by as much as 6000 in 1973, or 40%. This has seemed inexplicable in this protected species on the basis of natural mortality, and no further wintering grounds have been found which would explain the drop. It may be that, by February, the birds are in much smaller flocks than in the autumn and in many more haunts, and the counting is incomplete. Certainly, the theory that the birds have a later winter movement across the Atlantic to join the population in North America is hardly tenable.

North Sea population (Maps 35 and 36)

This is by far the smallest of the three populations of this race and is, indeed, so small and, apparently, declining as to cause concern for its continued existence. The breeding range is thought to be restricted to the Svalbard archipelago but may also include the Franz Josef Islands further east. Most breeding pairs have been found on small offshore islands scattered through the archipelago, but as the numbers have declined so the information has become more fragmentary. Localities with several breeding pairs even ten years ago are now being deserted. There may be a possible correlation with

TABLE 39: *Numbers of Light-bellied Brent Geese of the Irish population counted in early winter, 1960–1 to 1974–5, together with annual breeding success*

Winter	Count	% young	Winter	Count	% young
1960–1	11,910	no records	1968–9	7,770	no record
1961–2	12,050	,,	1969–70	12,950	47·0
1962–3	no count	,,	1970–1	12,000	no record
1963–4	,,	,,	1971–2	no count	26·0
1964–5	,,	,,	1972–3	11,170	v. poor
1965–6	7,350	,,	1973–4	16,140	v. good
1966–7	8,060	,,	1974–5	11,600	<1·0
1967–8	8,310	,,			

Irish Bird Reports.

the increase of the Barnacle Goose and its adoption of the same islands for breeding.

The wintering areas for this population lie in northern Denmark and on the north-east coast of England. It is thought that the birds fly down the coast of Norway or the Baltic coast of Sweden, and the bulk of the population can be found in Mariager (13) and Randers (14) Fjords in north-east Jutland by October. Most stay there through the winter but a varying proportion fly across the North Sea to the Lindisfarne National Nature Reserve (15) in Northumberland, where recent peaks have been in the order of 500 birds. Total counts are hard to come by, partly through difficulty in separating these birds from the Dark-bellied Brent Geese also wintering in Denmark. It seems that the population has declined from around 4000–5000 in the 1950s and early 1960s, to less than 2500 now. On the spring passage through Denmark, the most favoured haunt is Nissum Fjord (16). Map 36 shows the mid-winter situation, when the Light-bellied and Dark-bellied Brent are well separated. In autumn and spring both races occur at the same localities in Denmark and, until the recent Danish ban on shooting Brent, the rarer race was at risk.

Black Brant (Map 35)

There are two populations of this race, one well documented and studied, the other very little known. They have well separated wintering grounds but the dividing line between their breeding range is less well defined.

Far Eastern population (Map 35)

Small numbers of Brent Geese winter in Japan, on the adjacent coast of eastern U.S.S.R., and possibly in Korea and China. The breeding range lies in northern Siberia, between that of the Dark-bellied Brent and the other population of this race which winters on the Pacific coast of North America. The approximate boundaries are 120° and 150°E. The situation is made more complicated by the presence within this general area of moulting birds from the Pacific population. The Novosibirsk Islands are thought to be part of the breeding range together with neighbouring coasts of the mainland, from the Lena Delta eastwards.

To reach the winter quarters the geese apparently migrate overland to the Sea of Okhotsk, or continue to the Sea of Japan, or even the Yellow Sea. Distances to the last area are very large without an intermediate stop, in excess of 3200 km (2000 miles), and one of the shorter overland routes seem more likely, followed by coasting movements.

There is virtually no information on numbers of this population, nor indeed on its true taxonomic status, though it seems probable that the birds are closer to Black Brant than to Dark-bellied Brent, perhaps intergrades. There was a count from Japan of 256 birds in January 1973, but in January 1976 fewer than 100 were found.

Pacific Coast population (Maps 35 and 38, Table 40)

This population of geese probably has the distinction of being the first to be regularly censused. James Moffitt, after whom one of the races of Canada Geese was named, conducted the first count along the Pacific Coast in the winter of 1930–31. The principal breeding area lies in the great waterfowl production region of the Yukon–Kuskokwim Delta, Alaska, and a 1968 estimate of around 35,000–40,000 pairs suggests that over half the total breeding pairs in the population nest there. The north slope of Alaska is also important with several thousand pairs, and eastwards there are Black Brant in hundreds, or low thousands, in the Mackenzie Delta, on Banks and Victoria Islands, and on the coasts of Queen Maud Gulf. These places and the islands to the north of Banks Island are close to the western edge of the range of the Light-bellied Brent and an area of intergrading exists. Extensive marking and observations are essential if the true dividing line is to be established, always supposing that it is constant. Numbers of breeding pairs in the region are quite small.

The breeding range of this population extends across the Bering Sea to the northern coast of Siberia and the Chukotski Peninsula. Wrangel island had between 1000 and 2000 breeding pairs in the early 1960s together with several thousand moulting non-breeders. At some point to the west of Wrangel Island lies the dividing line between this population and the last.

In late summer almost all the Black Brant of Alaska move to Izembek Bay (1) at the western end of the Alaskan Peninsula. There they are joined by the birds from Siberia and from western Canada in a great autumn concourse numbering between 100,000 and 150,000 birds, or close to the total population. It has been stated that approximately 250,000 Black Brant gather there but this is considerably in excess of the winter inventories and, unless the latter are omitting large numbers of birds, it must be an over-estimate.

The departure from Izembek Bay is a mass one, the birds leaving within a

TABLE 40: *Mid-winter counts of the Pacific Coast population of Black Brant, 1950–1 to 1976–7, together with annual breeding success*

Winter	Count	% young	Brood size	Winter	Count	% young	Brood size
1950–1	168,300	no records		1963–4	185,300	no records	
1951–2	167,100	,,		1964–5	165,700	,,	
1952–3	154,600	,,		1965–6	156,900	21·0	n.r.
1953–4	132,300	,,		1966–7	179,700	40·3	2·86
1954–5	135,200	,,		1967–8	154,300	17·5	2·58
1955–6	109,700	,,		1968–9	143,200	17·6	2·55
1956–7	132,500	,,		1969–70	141,700	26·0	2·66
1957–8	126,000	,,		1970–1	149,200	38·0	3·10
1958–9	68,500	,,		1971–2	124,700	35·7	2·43
1959–60	136,200	,,		1972–3	124,900	38·7	n.r.
1960–1	168,100	,,		1973–4	129,600	29·4	2·83
1961–2	170,250	,,		1974–5	123,500	4·6	2·25
1962–3	139,600	,,		1975–6	112,050	36·7	3·07
				1976–7	146,470	35·3	2·84

Lynch & Voelzer (1974), Voelzer (1976 and pers. com.).

MAP 38. Black Brant *Branta bernicla nigricans*—breeding and wintering ranges.
⁄⁄⁄ breeding range. Dashed lines enclose region of intergrading with Light-
bellied Brent Goose. ●major haunts; •minor haunts. Numbers indicate
haunts referred to in text. Arrows show approximate migration routes.

very short time, usually in the first half of November. They make a long over-sea flight to a landfall on the coast of Baja California. Until about 20 years ago the Brant were split on the wintering grounds, with roughly half in California and to the north, and half on the Baja California coast. More recently, however, there has been a shift southwards and now only about 10% are left in the United States, with the vast majority in Mexico. A few hundreds remain in Izembek Bay for the winter. There is then a large gap to the next group of perhaps a hundred Black Brants in Puget Sound, British Columbia (2). Numbers in Washington and Oregon are much reduced from earlier years to about 6000 and 2000, respectively, in mid-winter. The coast of California holds still fewer birds, only some 1000, in Humboldt (3) and other Bays. The population of Mexico has grown from about 80,000 in the 1950s to the present 100,000–130,000 and whereas they were almost all on the Baja California coast (4), they are now divided more or less equally between there and the mainland coast of Mexico (5), within the Gulf of California. Stragglers have reached the Hawaiian Islands.

On the spring migration there is a steady movement up the Pacific Coast, producing considerable concentrations in some of the California Bays, particularly Humboldt Bay where up to 40,000 Black Brants may occur at peak during March and April, and up the coast of Oregon and Washington, and into British Columbia. From there the geese continue up the coast on migration and may then cross over the Yukon Territory to the north Canadian coast. Others continue to Izembek Bay, arriving in early May, and are joined by many more which have flown more directly across the Gulf of Alaska from British Columbia, or even from further south. From Izembek the geese disperse to their various breeding grounds having first spent most of May feeding on the enormous growth of *Zostera* there. At least some of the birds that will breed in the Canadian arctic do not go there direct but make the long detour to Izembek. The Alaskan breeders can leave for their breeding grounds before the end of May but the Canadian birds' nesting areas are not snow-free until early June and the geese delay their departure from Izembek accordingly.

As already stated, the first count of this population was in 1930–31. Since then there has been an annual census and the figures since 1950 are given in Table 40, together with breeding success data. The latter show much less variability than other Brent Goose populations, largely because most of these Black Brant breed much further south, away from the harsher conditions affecting the others. Although the more northerly segments of this population, breeding in north-west Siberia, on Wrangel Island and in the Canadian arctic islands, may suffer alternate breeding successes and failures the effect of this will be swamped by the much larger numbers breeding in the relatively stable conditions of western Alaska. There, variation is known to be slight, as shown by studies of Canada Geese and Whitefronts breeding in the same area. Only very occasionally does disaster occur, as in 1963, when a storm sent a tidal surge sweeping through the low-lying breeding areas carrying nests, eggs and young goslings before it. But even this did not produce a very poor production year overall.

Red-breasted Goose (Map 39)

The precise status of this species is not clear at present. Until recently, it was thought that it had declined drastically in the last twenty years and should be regarded as in danger of extinction. Now, however, it seems that although there has been a serious drop in numbers, and that this may be continuing, it has not been as severe as had been thought. The breeding range is concentrated on the Taymyr Peninsula in central arctic Siberia, with much smaller numbers on the adjacent Yamal and Gydan Peninsulas. As described in Chapter 4, the geese nest on the ground on low hummocks or the tops of riverbank cliffs, virtually always in small colonies and close to the nest of a Peregrine or other bird of prey. Peregrines have decreased in this region, as in so many other parts of their range, largely through pesticide poisoning which they take in during the winter when they are living in agricultural areas. The dependence of the Redbreasts on the falcons is apparently so great that a decrease in the number of breeding pairs of the latter is bound to affect the geese adversely.

The Redbreasts formerly wintered almost exclusively on the coast of the Caspian Sea in Russian Azerbaijan. Their headquarters was the Kyzyl Agach Forest Reserve (1). This was their traditional haunt, at least until the early 1960s, and it was here in winter 1956–7 that the largest single count was made. Unfortunately, the actual figure has been variously reported as 40,000 and 60,000, a somewhat disturbing discrepancy. However, whichever is thought to be correct, there has undoubtedly been a decline since then. Azerbaijan has been largely deserted and there are now fewer than 2000 birds wintering there. The crash is thought to have been largely brought about by agricultural changes, including the growing of cotton on a massive scale instead of cereals. The Redbreasts feed on stubble fields and grass, and sometimes on sprouting wheat. The marshland edges of the Caspian, which they used, have also been drained.

The extent of the present wintering range is not fully known and is one of the more intriguing mysteries in the field of goose distribution. One of the major areas is, undoubtedly, Romania. Although it is often stated that this is a completely new area for the geese, they have been recorded there in small numbers for forty years or more. However, it was not until 1968 that it was realised that the Dobrogea (2), a farmland area south of the Danube delta, was of such major importance. In December of that year it was estimated that there were about 25,000 Red-breasted Geese present. Such a total has not been approached since, and in subsequent winters the highest count has ranged between 4000 and 9000. Accurate counts are rarely made more than once or twice each winter, and there is no way of knowing whether the peak is present at that particular time, nor how many geese may be passing through. Certainly the peak of 25,000 has never been approached since, and this not unnaturally gave rise, in the absence of any other known wintering areas, to the belief that there might have been a catastrophic decline, in addition to that in Azerbaijan, from the count of not less than 40,000 twelve years earlier. The possibility remained, however, that there might yet be some hitherto undiscovered wintering place. The 25,000 geese seen in December 1968 were with the half-million White-fronted Geese mentioned earlier in this chapter. The latter are assumed to have been involved in some large-scale shift of populations, and it could be that some of the Redbreasts, too, were displaced from somewhere else. The great question has always been, and remains, where?

Very recently it has been revealed that up to 6000 Redbreasts have been found in Bulgaria, just over the border from the Danube Delta in Romania. Formerly, it was believed that only a few hundreds were present in the whole country. However, these large numbers have so far only been recorded in November and December, and it is not known, firstly, whether they remain there through the winter, or secondly, whether they are indeed completely different birds from those in Romania. There have been insufficient counts in Romania to be certain that the geese there remain through January and February. Searches elsewhere in Europe have revealed under a hundred birds in Greece and none anywhere else. If the geese are moving on from the Black Sea, then they must be moving south to Turkey, or possibly Iraq. Both countries have considerable wetland areas and Turkey in particular holds large numbers of White-fronted Geese. But so far, surveys in Turkey have not come up with any Redbreasts, and attempts to carry out comprehensive waterfowl surveys in Iraq have not yet been successful and we have to content ourselves with a general statement that has emerged to the effect that 'several hundred regularly winter there'. Small numbers (up to 500) have been found at Lake Rezaiyeh (3) and the Bay of Gorgan (4) in northern Iran, but none further south.

A final twist to the story has come from the U.S.S.R. There, a biologist working on the east coast of the Black Sea, not far from the Turkish border, has reported seeing substantial numbers of Red-breasted Geese, up to 20,000, migrating south in autumn. He does not know where they go, except that he is certain they leave the Soviet Union. Again, one can only turn one's eyes to Turkey and Iraq, and possibly Iran, though the wetlands of this last country are fairly well known.

The difficulty in getting good coverage of even the known haunts of the species, plus the recent major shift in wintering quarters from the Caspian to the Black Sea, plus some as yet unknown areas, makes the compiling of meaningful totals extremely difficult. Apart from the very recent 20,000 Redbreasts migrating to the east of the Black Sea, plus not less than 6000 (and perhaps many more) in Romania and Bulgaria, there appears to have been a considerable decline from the 40,000, or perhaps 60,000, seen in Azerbaijan in 1956–7. But can one go further than that, or even that far? The only corroboration comes from the breeding grounds, where surveys in the summers of 1972 and 1973 suggested a total of about 25,000 geese, while more recently still it has been estimated that there are about 12,000 full-grown birds present on the breeding grounds, and that they may rear up to 8000 young in a good year. The method by which these figures were arrived at has not been fully disclosed, but it appears to have been by sampling the numbers found along certain river systems and then extrapolating on the basis of the total of suitable habitat available. Using all the figures we have, it does not

MAP 39. Red-breasted Goose *Branta ruficollis*—world range. ⧄ breeding; ● major winter haunts; • minor winter haunts. Numbers indicate haunts referred to in text. Arrow shows observed migration route (see text).

seem unreasonable to say that the population has halved in the last twenty years. Quite what to do about arresting the decline, assuming it is continuing, and helping the species to recover to more healthy levels, is easier to decide than to put into practice. Currently, it is still legal to shoot Redbreasts in all the European countries in which it regularly winters, as it is in Iraq. Clearly this needs changing. Peregrines breeding in the Taymyr Peninsula can only be restored to their former numbers by the cessation of the use of persistent agricultural pesticides in their wintering areas. The areas are not precisely known but probably include large areas of southern U.S.S.R. and, perhaps, further south.

The Red-breasted Goose has occurred as a vagrant in many European and Mediterranean countries, including about 25 records in Britain. However, some reports involve escapes from captivity.

SUMMARY

This survey of geese populations around the northern hemisphere has revealed a comparatively cheerful picture overall. The numbers of most geese in Europe and North America are either stable or increasing, some of them

TABLE 41: *Average totals of geese in the different populations during the 1960s and 1970s. Where available, totals are averages of counts given in Tables 13 to 40. Estimates are preceded by "c.". Guesses are shown in brackets*

Species or race	Population	1960s	1970s
Swan Goose			(10,000)
Bean Goose	British	100	150
	Baltic–North Sea		c. 70,000
	Central Europe		c. 100,000
	Asian		(100,000)
Pinkfoot	Icelandic	65,000	75,000
	Svalbard	14,000	16,000
European Whitefront	Baltic–North Sea	61,000	110,000
	Pannonicum		c. 80,000
	Pontic		c. 100,000
	Anatolian		c. 80,000
	Caspian		c. 40,000
	Asian		(200,000)
Greenland Whitefront		c. 12,000	c. 12,000
Pacific Whitefront		155,000	79,000
Interior Whitefront		90,000	190,000
Lesser Whitefront			(100,000)
Greylag Goose	Icelandic	45,000	66,000
	NW Scotland		c. 2,000
	West Europe	c. 15,000	c. 30,000
	Central Europe		c. 13,000
	Pontic		c. 10,000
	Anatolian		c. 12,500
	Caspian		c. 200,000
	Asian		(100,000)
Bar-headed Goose			(10,000)
Emperor Goose			c. 175,000
Lesser Snow Goose	Pacific Flyway	500,000	440,000
	Cent. & Miss. Flyways	1,400,000	2,150,000
Greater Snow Goose		72,000	168,000
Ross's Goose		27,000	28,000

rapidly. Only in Asia are there several species or populations which appear to be declining, but information in some cases is so scanty that it would be rash to make any positive statements about them. Table 41 brings together the current estimated total for those populations for which figures are available, giving where possible, the total ten years ago. No-one comparing these totals could be left in much doubt that despite mistakes and mismanagement, or even the total lack of management, wild geese are much more numerous than they were even a decade ago. Perhaps if the figures were obtainable it would be more salutory to compare the present-day totals with those for a few hundred, or even a few thousand years ago, before man had such a drastic effect on natural habitats or had begun slaughtering geese on the scale reached at the turn of the last century. But it is likely that some populations have never

TABLE 41 continued

Species or race	Population	1960s	1970s
Canada Goose	Aleutian		790
	Alaska	215,000	172,000
	South Alaska Coast	c. 35,000	c. 35,000
	North-west Coast	c. 80,000	c. 80,000
	Great Basin	110,000	133,000
	Highline	c. 20,000	c. 50,000
	Short Grass Prairie	104,000	145,000
	Tall Grass Prairie	84,000	155,000
	Western Prairie	c. 35,000	c. 75,000
	Eastern Prairie	106,000	175,000
	Mississippi Valley	204,000	290,000
	Tennessee Valley	83,000	110,000
	Mid-Atlantic	c. 540,000	730,000
	North Atlantic		38,000
	British	c. 11,000	c. 19,500
	New Zealand		c. 18,000
	Scandinavian	c. 3,500	c. 15,000
Barnacle Goose	Greenland	16,000	30,000
	Svalbard	3,000	4,700
	Russian	25,000	43,000
Dark-bellied Brent		26,000	65,000
Light-bellied Brent	Atlantic Seaboard	170,000	97,000
	Ireland	9,500	12,500
	North Sea	c. 3,500	c. 2,500
Black Brant	Far Eastern		(10,000)
	Pacific Coast	155,000	130,000
Red-breasted Goose		(40,000)	(30,000)
Totals of populations counted in 1960s and 1970s		4,534,600	5,963,350
Total of all populations in 1970s			7,432,640

been larger than they are today if only because of the almost unlimited food supply now available to them from farmland.

Many populations of geese may have increased despite, rather than because of man's management and conservation, but the critics of current practices in these fields would be hard put to attribute all of such growth to natural causes, even though the amelioration in the arctic climate that occurred in the 1940s and 1950s must have helped. The lack of any significant downturn despite the recent apparent climatic cooling owes at least something to active steps taken in the wintering areas to help the geese by restricting shooting and increasing refuges. Longer-term effects of climatic change cannot be foretold, apart from the general thought that further arctic cooling must be harmful to the geese. Managers and conservationists will just have to be prepared to work harder for their aims of providing ample stocks of geese.

7 Migration

Information on migration routes and timing was included in the previous chapter as they form a vital link in any account of breeding and wintering ranges. The mechanics of migration and of flight, the stimuli which geese require to start migrating, and the weather conditions they prefer, have received considerable attention but remain difficult to study in an objective way. Moulting concentrations of geese were also mentioned in the previous chapter under the appropriate population headings, but the subject of special moult migrations which are undertaken by many waterfowl, and in particular by geese, was not discussed.

One of the best-known features of the flight of geese is their adoption of a V-formation. There is such a strong connection between this habit and geese in the public's mind that the average person is always surprised to be told that other species of birds, especially gulls, often fly in Vs too, and that some species of geese rarely if ever do so. The Wildfowl Trust at Slimbridge, Gloucestershire, frequently receives letters and telephone calls from people living nearby reporting flocks of geese heading towards its refuge. Several thousand geese do in fact winter there but investigation of the reports virtually always reveal that they refer to Common Gulls, of which there is a major roost of some 50,000 birds on the estuary mudflats adjacent to the goose refuge. These gulls disperse during the day to feed on farmland up to 25 km (15 miles) or even more distant, flighting back in late afternoon in long straggling lines and, very often, V-formations.

Confusion and argument concerning the V-formation flight of geese is not confined to the general public however. There has been considerable debate among scientists as to whether the V-formation confers any aerodynamic benefit on the geese, or whether it is purely for convenience as the easiest method of avoiding each other yet keeping in visual contact. Another point much discussed is whether the same bird leads the V throughout the particular flight or whether different birds take over from time to time.

Those who believe that there is a positive physical advantage to V-formation flying argue strongly that it has evolved to enable the geese to fly further using less energy than they otherwise would. This makes considerable sense for a large bird which, as explained in Chapter 4, is only able to put on a comparatively small amount of extra weight prior to migration. Even a small gain in efficiency during the actual flight would help. One study which went into the theoretical aspects of V-formation flying suggested that there might be a gain of as much as 70%. The main benefit came in the reduction of drag. Contrary to many previous conclusions, this particular study showed that the lead bird also gained by being in a V, though less than the birds behind him. It was further suggested that the angle of the V was close to the theoretical optimum and that the birds would have little difficulty in maintaining this angle. As well as the reduction in drag it is also thought that each bird except the leader receives a small, but significant amount of lift from the air wave caused by the wing-beat of the bird in front of it.

Both these theoretical advantages would seem to require really accurate station keeping by the geese relative to each other, firstly in angle and distance and, secondly, particularly for distance and even phase of wing-beat. However, analysis of cine-film and careful observation has shown that these conditions are not fulfilled. Canada Geese are among the species in which V-formation is usual, but a breakdown of formation-type among a sample of just over 100 flocks of migrating Canada Geese showed that only 17% were in a pure V-formation, with a further 16% in the shape of a J, which could be considered similar. The greatest number (40%) were in a diagonal line which might still give benefit from wing-beat lift but would not be nearly so efficient at reducing drag as a full V. About 20% of the flocks were in no definable formation, just flying in clusters or even line-abreast, which would certainly require equal effort from each bird.

Analysis of cine-film of Greylags, Whitefronts and Bean Geese showed no phase relationship whatever of wing-beats between the birds. Individuals within a V-formation varied their own frequency of wing-beats without any relation to those of the bird in front of them. Each individual had its own mean frequency of beating its wings. In addition the formations studied showed great variation in the angle of the V and in the individual distance maintained between any two birds. Wing-beat synchrony would also require that the birds were in the same horizontal plane, as would a reduction in drag, but individuals in a flock often rise or fall relative to each other. The investigators concluded that these latter variations, coupled with the lack of any wing-beat synchrony, could not be explained by any theory which assumed that there was some gain in aerodynamic efficiency.

There seems little doubt that this is not the end of the controversy. Newer and more sophisticated theoretical models will be produced to prove that V-formation is of direct benefit to the birds, but these theories will remain, like their predecessors, very difficult to prove by practical experiment. While it is possible to train single birds (nothing much bigger than a pigeon so far) to fly in a wind tunnel, no-one has attempted to persuade a flock of birds to do so, and it seems improbable that final proof can be forthcoming without some such experiment. In the meantime, it appears more satisfactory to leave aerodynamic efficiency to the realms of speculation and merely to state that it must be of advantage to the geese to fly in such a way that they can maintain close visual contact, vitally necessary where the young have to accompany their parents in order to learn the migration routes and best wintering places. It is certainly no accident that all but three of the goose species have white upper and under tail coverts, contrasting with darker back and dark tail, which will act as an excellent visual signal to a following bird. The exceptions are the Snow Goose and Ross's Goose, which are sufficiently visible in their white plumage (the blue phase Lesser Snow Goose having whitish tail coverts), and the Emperor Goose which has a pure white tail to contrast with its dark body. At the same time, flying in a V, a J, or a diagonal line, reduces the possibility of collisions between the birds, and avoids the turbulence they would meet if they flew directly behind other geese.

The question of whether one goose leads a formation, of whatever shape, for the duration of that flight, is almost impossible to answer. It has been widely assumed that because geese habitually stay together in family parties, the male, the dominant bird of the family, will lead when the family takes to the air. And because any flock of geese is composed of several families, pairs and individuals flying together, the male of the largest family is, perhaps, the bird most likely to be in the lead. This is almost beyond proof. One small argument against it is that the male often brings up the rear when a family is feeding on the ground, with the quicker walking young and the female ahead of him. Visual evidence as to whether the lead changes during a flight is contradictory, with at least one experienced goose researcher stating that he has never seen this happen even though he has followed a great many flocks of migrating geese by car and aeroplane. My own experience is that the lead changes quite often, and the formation adopted by any particular flock also changes shape at intervals. No-one has been able to follow a flock of geese for a really long distance and for many hours at a time, and without this kind of evidence the situation must remain unresolved.

The V-formation of geese is commoner among the larger species, especially when they are making longer flights. When flitting from one field to another no particular formation is adopted. Those in favour of the theory that the birds gain from being in a V, use both points as arguments in their favour; and certainly the larger the bird, and the further it is flying, the more it has to gain. On the other hand, on short flights the need for visual contact is also much reduced as all the birds are likely to be in familiar surroundings. The smaller species, particularly the Brent Goose and the Barnacle Goose, rarely adopt a V-formation, but commonly fly in straggling lines or bunches. Both species will sometimes fly in tight-packed flocks, performing mass aerial evolutions much like a flock of starlings or waders. This has only been seen on the wintering grounds and, as with the other kinds of birds, has an obvious role to play as a reaction to an avian predator, but often takes place without any such stimulus being present.

The height and speed of migration is another topic on which there are many scattered observations but little detailed investigation, for obvious reasons. However, the use of radar, particularly in North America, and reports of aeroplane pilots, has produced a certain amount of information on the heights of migrating geese and it is possible to make some general statements on this and the average speed. The latter has been timed by direct observation between two points, by following birds in a vehicle or even an aeroplane, and by calculations based on migration departures and arrivals at different localities.

There are few advantages to be gained from flying very close to the ground and except in poor weather geese follow the general rule among migrating birds of climbing to a height that will avoid most ground-based obstructions and the turbulence that they and other surface features produce. Observations of migrating Canada Geese by pilots in North America showed that about three-quarters of all flocks were flying between about 230 and 1050 metres (750–3500 feet) above the ground. Flocks flying below about 200 metres were generally doing so in poor weather, low cloud with or without rain. The high-flying birds, some as high as 2500 metres (8000 feet), may have been avoiding areas of high ground, or seeking better conditions. Geese certainly have no difficulty in flying higher than this if they have to cross mountain ranges; up to 3500 metres (11,000 feet) or more for some stretches of the Rocky Mountains crossed by geese. In Asia, Bar-headed Geese regularly migrate between their wintering grounds in India across the Himalaya range to breed in Tibet and beyond. Most of Tibet lies at a height of around 4000 metres (13,000 feet) and the majority of the passes over the mountains are higher than this. Migrating Barheads have been seen at heights in excess of 6000 metres (20,000 feet), an altitude also equalled by Lesser Snow Geese in North America, although they had not the same ground heights to clear. The Barheads have to reach such heights as a matter of necessity, but the Snow Geese do not, and it may be that the Snow Geese were getting an unusual amount of lift from the prevailing weather conditions, or perhaps finding better tail winds by going higher.

Geese migrating over the sea are thought to fly lower than over land, but observations are few and probably not representative. Certainly there are not the obstructions over the sea, but on the other hand there is some air turbulence near the surface and it is likely that for the longer flights the geese would climb to be clear of it.

The speed of a bird's flight over the ground is the result of three component forces, its own forward speed powered by its wings, and the speed and direction of the wind. A goose flying at 50 km per hour (31 mph) with a wind directly behind it of 40 kph (25 mph) will be moving relative to the ground at 90 kph (56 mph). If the wind were directly opposed to it, its actual speed over the ground would be only 10 kph (6 mph). Thus, any direct observations of the speed of a goose in flight must take account of the wind speed and direction, but few do, and accurate recordings of just how fast a goose will fly, when neither aided nor impeded by the wind, are rare. Some observations of Canada Geese using two theodolites suggested a mean speed in level flight, in calm conditions, of almost 50 kph (30 mph). It would seem from this and other records that speeds of between 40 and 60 kph (25–37 mph) are normal for migrating geese, though they are capable of higher speeds than this over short distances—when escaping from danger for example. With wind assistance, high speeds are possible and there is plenty of evidence that geese prefer to fly with a following wind, thus increasing their ground speed and reducing the overall flying time.

A detailed study has taken place on the migration of Lesser Snow Geese through southern Manitoba, and in particular past Winnipeg Airport where there have been accidents involving aircraft and migrating geese. The airport lies on the route for very large numbers of geese, especially in the spring. The first aim of the study was to discover the main factors governing the timing and duration of the heaviest movements of geese. Many of the geese were using a staging locality about 160 km (100 miles) south-west of the airport, but others passed through directly from areas further south. Detailed weather observations were made at the airport and at the staging post, and the movements of the geese were monitored with the aid of radar.

The strongest correlations between the migration of the Lesser Snow Geese and the weather were found to be related to wind direction and speed. The geese showed a strong preference for a tail wind, or one from at least some direction behind them. Side winds, and particularly head winds, were avoided and, if such winds got up after the geese had started, could even turn them back or force them to land. Contrary to expectation the geese avoided very strong tail winds, preferring those of lower than average speed. It is not clear why this should be so, except perhaps that, unless it was blowing exactly in the direction they wished to go, a strong wind would tend to drift them off course more quickly and further than a weaker one.

The geese demonstrated a considerable ability for selecting favourable conditions for their migrations. They would move in the clear period ahead of a warm front, which generally brings dense cloud and rain, on the west side of a high-pressure area or on the east side of an occluded front. In both the latter situations the winds are generally light and southerly in direction, giving an ideal tail wind. Rain was avoided and prolonged periods of rain would delay take-off. Clear skies in themselves were not preferred, though often present, particularly near high-pressure areas. Temperature made little difference, but other studies have shown that there is a general correlation between the movement of geese northward up the continent and the retreat northwards of the 35°F isotherm, which is roughly equivalent to the temperature required to produce the spring thaw. The geese move steadily north until they reach the major staging area of James Bay. Then, after feeding there for a while the most northerly breeders set off on a single long hop north to their nesting colony, overtaking the 35°F isotherm on the way, arriving well ahead of it, and laying their eggs while snow and ice are still present.

The second main aim of the Winnipeg Airport study was to predict major movements as a way of giving advance warning to air traffic controllers and pilots so that the risk of collision between aeroplanes and geese could be reduced. In the first season, when knowledge was still limited, only about a quarter of the duration of heavy migration was predicted. On the other hand, virtually all the predicted periods of heavy migration did in fact take place. In the following two years the forecasters had the experience of the previous springs to build on and were able to identify a number of important factors. Chief among these was, firstly, the date, which was most likely to lie between the 2nd and 17th of May; secondly, the weather at the staging post, 160 km south-west, two hours before a movement over the airport was to be expected. This had to be a tail wind, or one mainly from behind, plus less than normal precipitation; and, finally, the weather at Winnipeg Airport, which had to show either a tail wind or very light side or head winds, similar winds at a higher level, up to about 1000 metres (3300 feet) above the ground, and lower than normal precipitation. Provided these factors could be identified successfully, the forecasts were quite accurate. The proportion of actual heavy migration correctly predicted rose to 65% in the second year, and a very satisfactory 85% in the third year. However, the number of hours of predicted heavy migration which actually occurred fell from 100% in the first year, to between 75% and 80% in the following years. The whole system of predicting the really heavy movements of Lesser Snow Geese over Winnipeg Airport proved quite successful in terms of general warning to pilots and controllers, but more detailed work involving data on flock size and density of flocks, important factors affecting the likelihood of collisions, proved impossible to turn into realistic forecasts.

These Lesser Snow Geese studies are the only really detailed ones concerned with the proximate factors triggering goose migration. A number of less intensive observations have shown a general tendency to depart from a wintering area or staging post in more or less favourable conditions. Over a number of years geese leaving the British Isles for Iceland have been observed passing the Outer Hebrides off the west of northern Scotland. There was a definite correlation between the sighting of flocks and the presence of a high-pressure area over northern Scotland, giving calm and sunny conditions. However, there are two main types of high pressure that can cover this region, one with a southerly origin, coming from the Azores, the other a northerly one, based on Greenland. When the latter is present there is normally clear weather stretching between northern Scotland and Iceland, giving the geese good conditions all the way. But the Azores high rarely if ever reaches as far north as Iceland, and the usual pattern is for there to be a depression over Iceland with the associated fronts extending southwards. If the geese left Scotland in an Azores high they could be expected to run into cloud and rain before making their landfall in Iceland 800 km (500 miles) away. This could, perhaps, lead to losses of disorientated birds. However, the observations, though spread over several years, involved relatively few geese—about 8000, which represents only a small fraction of the number of geese flying between Scotland and Iceland in a single year. The majority may not have been moving on those particular days, or in those weather conditions.

The timing of any migratory flight seems more dependent on weather conditions than time of day, but there does seem a preference, observed in a number of different populations, for a departure in daylight, though with some tendency for the afternoon or early evening. Clearly, the geese can navigate satisfactorily by either the sun or the stars and, as many of their flights last for more than twelve hours, may often use both in a single journey. The apparent preponderance of daytime departures may be because they are more readily seen.

The distances travelled non-stop by migrating geese vary as much as the overall distances travelled by different populations. Probably the longest-distance flyers are the Black Brant going from Wrangel Island to Mexico, a distance of about 6500 km (4000 miles). The Lesser Snow Geese, from the same place to California, the Light-bellied Brent Geese from eastern Arctic Canada to Ireland, and the Dark-bellied Brent Geese from Siberia to France, all make journeys in excess of 4800 km (3000 miles). The longest non-stop flights are probably those of the Black Brant from Izembek Bay, Alaska, to the Mexican coast, and the Lesser Snow Geese flying from James Bay to the Gulf Coast. The former is much the longer, about 4800 km (3000 miles), but rather more is known about the latter as it takes place over land and between two regularly monitored areas. The straight-line distance is about 2700 km (1700 miles) and is covered by the geese in under 60 hours, perhaps considerably less. This would be an average of just under 50 kph (30 mph) without allowing for any wind resistance, whereas the prevailing weather in James Bay at the time of departure in autumn includes a steady ground wind of about 56 kph (35 mph). It is believed, from radar and other observations, that the geese fly high, to a maximum of 3000 metres (10,000 feet), when making this flight.

It is usual for geese to have one or more stopping places on their migration route, though the position of these relative to the breeding and wintering regions is variable. In many cases autumn staging areas are only comparatively short distances south of the actual breeding range, though sufficiently far south to give the birds a further month or more of feeding before wintry weather sets in. In this period the adults can feed intensively to restore weight lost during the breeding season and the subsequent moult, and the young can continue to grow. Long before the end of this time the breeding grounds to the north will be frozen up. Such areas have been mentioned in Chapter 6 and include: Izembek Bay, Alaska (Black Brant and Canadas); Klamath Basin, Oregon/California (Whitefronts, Snow Geese, Ross's Geese and Canadas); the southern parts of Saskatchewan and Alberta (Whitefronts, Ross's Geese and Canadas); James Bay, Ontario/Quebec (Lesser Snow Geese, Canada Geese and Light-bellied Brent); and Cap Tourmente, Quebec (Greater Snow Geese); all in North America. Iceland plays this part for Light-bellied Brent Geese, Greenland Whitefronts, Pinkfeet and Barnacle Geese coming from Greenland; and the islands on the coast of Norway also hold migrant Barnacle Geese and Pinkfeet from Svalbard. In the northern U.S.S.R. there are some equivalent areas on the arctic mainland coast used by White-fronted Geese and Barnacles breeding on the more northerly islands, or coming from further east, like the Dark-bellied Brent.

The geese leave these staging areas when the weather or the food supply deteriorates, and the next stage of their journey may take them directly to their wintering quarters or to another intermediate stop, depending on the local geography and on the routes and distances involved. Some fortunate populations can move steadily in a series of short hops, but others have at least one long flight to make.

Much the same happens on the spring return, with nearly all migratory populations having a major feeding area between the wintering and breeding grounds. All the areas mentioned above are used once more, but one region where the situation is different between autumn and spring is in north-west Europe and north-west U.S.S.R. There the autumn staging posts of the Whitefronts, Barnacles and Dark-bellied Brent were on the arctic coast and this is still frozen up in late April and May when it is needed, so the geese stay further back along the migration route, much closer to the wintering grounds. The Dark-bellied Brent Geese that have wintered in Britain and France move east as far as the Netherlands, West Germany and Denmark, concentrating in the great shallow Waddensee that runs along the south-east corner of the North Sea. There they spend most of April and well into May before leaving on a non-stop flight for the north coast of the U.S.S.R., thence east to their breeding grounds. The Barnacle Geese go as far east as the island of Gotland, off Sweden, and the coastal islands of Estonia. The Whitefronts that have wintered in the Netherlands and Britain have a different ploy. They migrate in autumn south-west from their north-west U.S.S.R. breeding grounds on the shortest route to their wintering area, but in the spring they set off eastwards until they reach the region of Moscow due south of their breeding range. When they have spent some weeks there through April and early May they move north, thus putting a right-angle bend into their spring migration route. Different routes in spring and autumn are not uncommon among the geese, though this is one of the more marked examples. Others include the Black Brant on the Pacific Coast, the Lesser Snow Geese and some of the small Canada Goose populations.

It will be apparent from the maps in Chapter 6 that some of the routes flown by the geese present considerable potential hazards. The long sea crossings are an obvious example, but perhaps the most spectacular journey is that undertaken by Greenland Whitefronts and Light-bellied Brent Geese over the Greenland icecap. For a long time this was not thought possible and even now there are sceptics. However, the evidence is strong and the feat by no means beyond the powers of the geese. Flocks of each species appear in western Iceland in spring and autumn, and although it is conceivable that they have reached there by flying round the south of Greenland, or in the case of the Brent, the north, there are many observations of them heading in a north-westerly direction in spring, which would take them across the icecap. The shortest probable distance is just under 1500 kilometres (900 miles), of which, about 800 km (500 miles) is icecap, the rest sea or land. The icecap rises to a maximum height of about 3500 metres (11,000 feet) which, as we have seen, is no higher than some other geese regularly fly. This is not to underestimate the hazard faced in the event of meeting bad weather. When flying over land the birds can, if necessary, come down almost anywhere, as in theory they can on the sea, though there are no observations to prove that they ever do. However, even descending close to the waves will allow them to orientate with reference to the wind direction as shown by the wave pattern. Over the Greenland icecap there is little purpose in descending. It may well be that losses do occur on this journey from time to time, but clearly the benefits of a much shorter route are worth the hazards.

The normal influence of weather on migration has been dealt with earlier and it has also been mentioned that in many cases the geese wait for the onset of freezing conditions or snowfall before leaving autumn migration staging areas and moving south. This could be risky if, for example, winter came suddenly, with blizzards lasting for days. But this rarely happens and the normal fall in temperature is usually sufficient to send the geese on their way. Some mass departures of geese take place apparently without direct weather influence, as for example the 200,000 or more Black Brant which leave

Izembek Bay, Alaska, in late October within a matter of hours. Temperature may be the cause, it certainly is not a shortage of food such as may occur in some other areas, as the *Zostera* crop in Izembek Bay is many times greater than is required by the geese.

An example of geese being forced to move and then running into trouble took place in autumn 1963. A heavy snowfall on the autumn feeding areas of the Pink-footed Geese in central Iceland obliged them to leave. They then found themselves heading for their Scottish wintering areas with a very strong westerly wind drifting them to the east of their normal landfall in Scotland and out over the North Sea. Many were able to reorientate and observers on the east coast of Scotland saw flocks of Pinkfeet flying towards the coast low over the sea, beating against the wind. At the same time reports were received from southern Norway and Denmark of flocks of some hundreds of Pinkfeet in areas where they were not normally seen, or not until the Svalbard Pinkfeet come through later in the season. Recoveries of some ringed birds soon confirmed that these were Icelandic Pinkfeet that had been drifted up to 500 km (300 miles) off their course.

Another example of the reaction of geese to severe weather comes from southern Sweden, where several thousand Bean Geese pause on migration in autumn. Most move on further south and west but up to 2000 stay through the winter if it is mild enough. Often, however, spells of cold weather occur and the geese may have to leave. It has been found that cold temperatures by themselves will not usually stimulate them, nor will snowfall in calm conditions. The geese just sit it out, resting on the ice of their roost lake, or sitting in the snow on the feeding fields, conserving their energy. If the snow and ice remain for more than about three days the geese leave, but often it thaws before this time has elapsed and they are able to stay. If, on the other hand, the snow comes not with a calm but there are strong winds and blizzards, then the geese leave the moment there is a slight lull, or even before the storm comes, though it is not known how they foretell its approach.

If unusually severe conditions come to a traditional wintering area, one at the furthest point of the normal migration, the birds are forced to leave or to remain, in which case they may starve. Instinctively, they seek to escape by flying in their usual migratory direction, thus taking themselves pre-dominantly south, eventually to warmer areas. However, these regions will be unknown to the geese and they may have difficulty in locating adequate roosting and feeding places. In addition, they may have to run the gauntlet of heavy shooting by delighted hunters for whom wild geese are a rarity. In 1962–63, a prolonged and very cold spell of weather occurred throughout north-west Europe, and several populations of geese were forced out of their normal haunts. Whitefronts, Barnacle Geese and Pinkfeet wintering in the Netherlands were largely pushed into northern France. Whitefronts win-tering in Britain moved away south and west, moving in large numbers to Cornwall where the freeze-up was not so total. Others crossed the Channel to northern and even western France. In all these areas the geese were heavily shot as the shooters made the most of a once-in-a-lifetime chance. However, these risks apart, the value of onward migration in severe weather is obvious.

A different type of migration also has survival value for geese, although in this case the birds that do not migrate may do better than those that do. Many species of waterfowl make a special migration prior to the annual summer moult. This moult migration, as it is known, occurs in several geese populations. It involves the non-breeding immature birds and also failed breeders. Instead of spending the summer on or near the breeding grounds they go to special areas at which they shed their wing feathers and become flightless for a period of three to four weeks while new feathers grow. On regaining their ability to fly they generally spend a little more time in the area putting on weight prior to their autumn migration.

There are examples of moult migration in nine of the fourteen species of geese; Map 40 displays the principal ones. A feature that nearly all of them share is that moult migration is northwards from the breeding grounds, with an easterly or westerly component in some cases. The arrows on the map join the area of origin of the moult migrating geese, mainly though not always the breeding area, with their destination, the moulting ground. There appear to be two explanations for this northward migration, though it is not possible to say which is right, though perhaps both play a part. Firstly, northward is in most cases the major direction of the spring migration, allowing for additional easterly or westerly tendencies as the case may be. The geese are therefore continuing in the direction which is instinctive to them. The second reason takes into account the fact that whereas the breeding range cannot extend further north than the latitude which allows sufficient time to complete the breeding cycle in the available summer period, the length of time needed to moult is much shorter. Therefore the geese can carry out their moult in areas well to the north of their breeding range, exploiting habitat and food resources that would not otherwise be utilised. A possible third reason is that the essential requirement for a moulting locality is a large area of suitable water and marsh as free from danger as possible, with a minimum of disturbance by predators or man, and these conditions are more likely to be found to the north than in any other direction.

The principal explanation for a moult migration of immature non-breeding geese is that it relieves the pressure on the breeding birds. There is some advantage to the migrating geese themselves in that they are enabled to spend the summer in an area with ample food and are not in competition with the parents and young on the breeding grounds. Against that they have the hazards of a further migration. However, the main benefit must go to the breeding pairs and their goslings. For them the need for sufficient food is paramount, both for the growth of the goslings and for the restoration of the parents, particularly the female. The removal from the breeding grounds of large numbers of competitors for this food must greatly increase the potential productivity of the breeding population. However, despite this advantage there are several species and populations of geese which have not evolved this mechanism nor any equivalent one.

There are two main types of moult migration by geese. The first and commonest type is of immatures returning to the breeding area, or in one case never leaving it, because the population is sedentary apart from the moult migration, and then moving north to their moulting places. In the second type the immatures set off on the spring migration towards the breeding

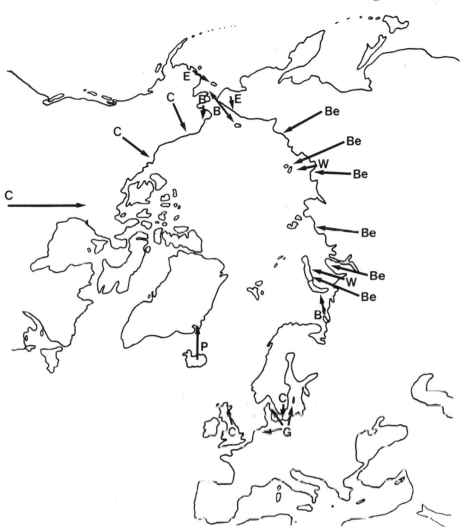

MAP 40. Moult migration. Arrows indicate direction and approximate distances of movements. Bean Goose (BE); Brent Goose (B); Canada Goose (C); Emperor Goose (E); Greylag Goose (G); Pink-footed Goose (P); White-fronted Goose (W).

grounds but never reach them. Instead, they stop short at a suitable moulting area or turn off the route and head north to their selected site. The first kind of moult migrators may be joined by adults which have tried but failed to breed, birds which never laid or birds which lost their eggs before the hatch.

No moult migration has been detected in either of the purely Asian geese, the Swan Goose and the Barhead, though this may be as much a reflection of our lack of knowledge concerning them as the fact that no such migration exists. Nor have moult migrations been found in the Barnacle, the Redbreast, or in Ross's Goose. In all these species the immature non-breeding birds stay within the general breeding range, flocking together on suitable marshes. These latter may be adjacent to the breeding sites, or some distance away, but there is no exodus that could be termed a migration. Several of the Ross's Goose moulting areas are also feeding places for the breeding birds and their young.

In two other species, Lesser White-fronted Goose and Snow Goose, both Lesser and Greater, moult migration is a very local affair, or one involving comparatively short distances. The only instance reported for the Lesser Whitefront is in Scandinavia where non-breeding birds were said to move away from the lowland breeding areas into uplands, to moult in large flocks. However, little is known of the actual numbers of birds or distances moved, and the species is in any case much rarer in that region now than it was at the time of the observations, fifty or more years ago. No such migration has been recorded elsewhere in the range.

Lesser Snow Geese immatures return to the colonies with their parents, and a proportion of them, perhaps the majority in most cases, stay on the fringes of the colony to moult. However, some do move away, mainly northwards, and may travel considerable distances. On Banks Island there is a moulting concentration in the Thomsen River area on the north coast, about 250 kilometres (150 miles) from the Egg River colony on the island. In this case it is thought that the one-year-old birds move away to moulting sites whereas the older immatures, two- and perhaps three-year-olds, stay close to the colonies. However, this conflicts with evidence from the largest Lesser Snow Goose colony at the McConnell River mouth, Hudson Bay, where one-year-old birds are quite frequently seen with their parents, even while the latter are nesting. There is a small northward movement of non-breeding birds away from this colony, too, but the location of the moulting site remains unknown. Moulting flocks of Greater Snow Geese have been found in a number of places within the general range of the subspecies, though some may be quite a distance from the nearest colony.

The map shows six arrows denoting northward moult migration of Bean Geese. They are, to some extent, schematic. Moulting concentrations have been found in the areas indicated, namely Novaya Zemlya (both islands), the central Yamal peninsula, the western Taymyr peninsula, the Lena Delta, the New Siberian Islands, and the Indigirka Delta, but a single arrow pointing to each concentration should, probably, be replaced by a fan of arrows coming from a much enlarged area to the south. In at least some cases the moulting birds belong to the larger-billed, longer-bodied Bean Geese of the forest zone, which are therefore migrating into the breeding range of the short-billed, round-bodied tundra Bean Geese. Some of the latter have a moult migration, particularly to northern Novaya Zemlya and to the New Siberian Islands, but many of the immatures gather in small flocks within the breeding range. The overlap of the two populations in the summer could contribute to the mixing that has taken place, blurring the suggested subspecific differences, as discussed in Chapter 1.

Only one of the two populations of Pink-footed Geese has a moult migration. There is a particularly well-marked example in the Icelandic population, but none has been discovered in the Svalbard population. As related in Chapter 6, the principal breeding area in Iceland is a marsh in the centre of the country, where perhaps three-quarters of the breeding pairs are located, with much smaller numbers scattered through other parts of interior Iceland, plus some hundreds of pairs in East Greenland. We now know that almost all of the immature birds perform a moult migration to East Greenland, but the first observations which demonstrated this were made as recently as 1952. In the middle of June of that year a British ornithologist saw large flocks of Pinkfeet migrating north over one of Iceland's northern valleys. The date was too late for them to have been birds on their way to breed in East Greenland and the ornithologist rightly concluded that they were non-breeding birds from the main colony heading for a moulting area. Further, if negative, evidence for the existence of a moult migration came from the two expeditions to the main breeding colony in 1951 and 1953, when hardly any non-breeding geese were seen.

Since 1952 there have been many more observations confirming the moult migration of Pinkfeet though their distribution within East Greenland is not at all well known. The birds probably frequent the many coastal and fjord areas which extend for over a thousand kilometres, many of them relatively inaccessible. It seems unlikely that there is any single locality holding all or even the greater part of the geese. Instead, they are probably split into a great many smaller flocks. The largest flock that has been seen to date is about 1700. In recent years the non-breeding segment of the population has totalled as many as 40,000 birds. Recent aerial surveys have failed to find more than two or three thousand moulting in Iceland, so it has to be assumed that the remainder are in East Greenland, but only a small proportion of the potential areas have been looked at. This particular moult migration does not take the immatures completely clear of the breeding range as there are some breeding birds in East Greenland, but they are a scattered and relatively unimportant part of the total breeding population, and the migration removes the immatures from competing for the food resources of the really vital main colony in Iceland.

White-fronted Geese in Eurasia have a number of moulting concentrations, several of them in the same areas as the Bean Geese, including the northern island of Novaya Zemlya, to which birds from the southern island breeding areas move, and the New Siberian Islands, which act as a moulting ground for immatures from the arctic coastal region between the Lena and Yana rivers. Other large gatherings occur in the central Yamal and western Taymyr peninsulas, and on the delta of the Indigirka. These, however, are really within the breeding range whereas few if any breed on the northern islands.

There is no known moult migration of the Greenland Whitefront, nor a long distance movement of any Whitefront in North America, though some large concentrations of moulting birds do occur within the breeding range, for example, up to 20,000 in the Anderson River Delta region of the Northwest Territories, Canada.

Small moult gatherings of Greylags have been known in north-west Europe for many years but it is only comparatively recently, after some of the birds had been caught and ringed, that recoveries showed some to be moving several hundred kilometres to moult. A moulting flock of several hundred birds was known to occur in the 19th century on the island of Hallands Väderö off the west coast of Scania, southern Sweden. The island was not inhabited until 1844, and thereafter the numbers of geese gradually decreased until they finally disappeared about 1910. The main cause was shooting by the islanders.

In the early 1930s a moulting flock of some 300 Greylags was first noticed in the extensive freshwater marsh of Vejlerne in northern Jutland, Denmark. Vejlerne is about 6000 ha (15,000 acres) in extent, consisting of shallow lakes, reed-beds and grass meadows. Its size, food resources and the inaccessibility of the reed and marsh areas, combined to make it a most suitable goose moulting area. The moulting Greylags increased slowly from about 500 in 1934 to no less than 3000 in 1955. Although Greylags breed in Denmark, including small numbers at Vejlerne itself, it was apparent that the moulting birds must be coming from outside the country. Several hundred were caught and ringed during the 1950s and recoveries duly came from northern Germany, Poland, Austria and Czechoslovakia. It was thus made clear that these birds belonged to the Central European Population and not to the West European Population which breeds in Scandinavia, including Denmark, and migrates through Denmark to winter in the Netherlands and Spain.

In the late 1950s the Vejlerne moulting population began to decrease, and by about 1965 had virtually disappeared. Quite why this happened is not certain but it is distinctly possible that catching the geese for ringing had something to do with it as there is evidence from elsewhere that, if done too often, it destroys the sense of safety so essential to the moulting birds. At any rate the decline at Vejlerne coincided with the establishment of a completely new moulting site at Grote Brekken, a remote area of wet grassland on the east coast of the Ijsselmeer, in the Netherlands. The Greylags were first seen in 1957, and around 400 birds were present in 1959 and subsequently. In 1964 a second moulting flock was discovered in the Netherlands, at Haringvliet, in Zuid Holland, an area of saltings and adjoining grassland in the Rhine Delta. Their numbers fluctuated considerably, reaching a peak of several thousands in the late 1960s then dropping to 1100 in 1969, and to only 400 in 1971. At the same time other moulting areas had appeared including another in Denmark, at Saltbaekvig in Sjaelland, where some hundreds arrived to moult in 1964 and years since, and in Sweden on the island of Gotland. There are about 110–150 breeding pairs on Gotland but the moulting flock now numbers between 3000 and 5000 birds. Some have been ringed, producing recoveries from Poland south to Austria and Czechoslovakia as did those ringed at Vejlerne.

The breeding range of the Central European Population of Greylags extends from Finland through Poland and East Germany to Austria and Czechoslovakia. Thus, of the different moulting sites, Gotland lies almost wholly to the north of the breeding range but the two Danish localities lie between north-west and west, while those in the Netherlands are, if anything, to the south of at least some of the range, though still north-west of the more southerly parts of it. Observations in northern Germany have shown a westerly passage in June of Greylags moving, presumably, to Denmark and the Netherlands for the moult. So these birds are an exception to the theory that moult migrating geese continue northwards as an extension of their normal migration direction. The birds of this population migrate on a line slightly east of north between their North African wintering grounds and their breeding localities.

Moulting concentrations of Greylags occur within the breeding ranges of the Icelandic and the North-west Scottish Populations but actual moult migrations are either non-existent or very short. A flock of about 250 Greylags moulting on a lake in eastern Sutherland is on the very edge of the Scottish breeding range. It represents a sizeable fraction of the total population of about 2000. Up to 2500 Greylags moult in the Ranafjord area of western Norway, based on two groups of small islands, the Vegas and the Viknas. Ringing recoveries show that these are part of the Norwegian breeding population. There is a large moulting flock, too, in the Volga Delta on the Caspian Sea, which forms part of the breeding population of the southern U.S.S.R. Other moulting flocks have been found in southern U.S.S.R. particularly in Kazakhstan which has the largest numbers of breeding pairs.

Emperor Geese have one large-scale moult-migration and possibly another smaller one whose destination is as yet unknown. Moulting flocks of between 10,000 and 20,000 have been found on the extensive marshland areas on the south side of St Lawrence Island, lying midway between Alaska and Siberia. Some at least, and probably all, of these birds come from the Alaskan breeding grounds of the species which lie almost completely to the south, or rather south-east. The species is not known to nest on St Lawrence Island and this is therefore a true moult migration, taking the geese between 250 and 500 kilometres (155–310 miles) north from their breeding area. Birds from the Siberian breeding range, lying around the Chukotski Peninsula at the eastern extremity of Asia, have been seen gathering in late June at Ukouge Lagoon on the north coast. A peak of 200 Emperors was recorded but the geese then left the Lagoon while they could still fly and their ultimate destination remains unknown.

There are several moulting concentrations of Canada Geese in northern Canada, some of which are within the population's breeding range, but others involve a moult migration of one population into the range of another. The small Canada Geese breeding in the interior of Alaska have a moult migration to the Arctic Slope along the north coast of the State. There are virtually no breeding Canada Geese in this area but at least 15,000 moulters. Further east there is a concentration of up to 25,000 small Canadas in the coastal area between the Mackenzie and Anderson River deltas. This is on the northern fringe of an extensive breeding area for this, the Short Grass Prairie Population.

The most significant moulting area for Canada Geese is centred round the Aberdeen and Beverly Lakes region of the Thelon River in the Keewatin District. The lakes lie about equidistant between Hudson Bay and the Queen Maud Gulf in an area where there are almost no breeding Canada Geese. About 30,000 birds have been found moulting here and ringing has shown that they belong to a number of populations. The majority are large Canada Geese from breeding areas lying up to 3000 kilometres (1800 miles) to the south. Recoveries have identified them as belonging to the Great Basin, Highline, Western and Eastern Prairie Populations. There are also many small Canada Geese moulting here which presumably belong to either or both of the Short and Tall Grass Prairie Populations, whose breeding ranges lie either side of the moulting area. As with the Bean Geese, this meeting of birds of different forms during the moult may well contribute to inter-breeding and therefore intergrading.

Moult migration by small Canada Geese seems to be uncommon. Nothing is known among the breeders of the west coast of Alaska, for example, nor have any moulting areas been found for the majority of the Tall Grass Prairie Population which breeds round northern Hudson Bay and on Southampton and Baffin Islands. Birds have been seen moving north in summer on the west side of Hudson Bay but it is not known where to. Considerable numbers do moult on Southampton Island well within the breeding range. To the east of Hudson Bay there are several moulting concentrations within the breeding range of the Mid-Atlantic Population of large Canada Geese on the Ungava peninsula, and of the North Atlantic Population in Labrador. There is a tendency for them to be more numerous in the north which would make them at least partial moult migrants.

It is of considerable interest that a moult migration has developed among the introduced Canadas in Britain, and possibly among the Swedish breeding population. The first Canada Geese were brought to Britain in the second half of the 17th century and established as ornamental waterfowl on lakes in cities and on private estates. Not much attention was paid to them by ornitholog-ists until the 1950s, and it was about this time that the first birds were noticed summering on the Beauly Firth, a broad shallow estuary in northern Scotland. For ten years or more, numbers there remained very small, hardly more than 50 birds. Then, during the 1960s, the total rose sharply to reach over 300 by 1969. After levelling out at this figure for a few years they nearly doubled their number to about 600 in 1973 and 1974, and increased again to 800 in 1975 and 900 in 1976. The first of these moulting geese to be ringed was in 1963, since when there have been five more catches. In the first catch there were two geese ringed in Yorkshire in previous years, and the link between this moulting flock and a breeding population inhabiting a considerable area of central Yorkshire was firmly established in succeeding years. In the last catch, about 600 geese were caught in July 1975 and marked with individually lettered plastic rings. Over 90% of these were sighted in Yorkshire in the following winter. The total population in Yorkshire is now of the order of 2700 birds having roughly doubled in the last 10 years. The proportion moving to moult in Scotland has thus increased relative to the total number in the population.

Apart from catching the moulting birds there has been extensive ringing of the breeding birds in Yorkshire, together with their goslings, from which it has been found that not all the non-breeding immatures make the moult migration. Indeed, the proportion of one-year-olds making the journey can be as low as 20%, yet this should be the most eligible age group. Furthermore, immature non-breeders, that is one- and two-year-olds, have made up only about 50% of some of the catches. Thus, half the birds migrating are three years old or more and therefore in theory old enough to breed. Either these are birds which have failed in their breeding attempt or for some reason, perhaps a shortage of nesting sites, have not bred at all. The breeding season starts quite early in Yorkshire, in April, so there is plenty of time for a bird that has failed to breed to make up its mind to migrate north for the moult. At some of the breeding sites the number of geese is controlled by taking or pricking eggs, which would tend to increase the number of failed breeders going on the migration.

The distance between Yorkshire and the Beauly Firth is about 480 kilometres (300 miles), and the moulting area is about the most northerly suitable site that the geese could have found before reaching the north coast. It is puzzling that they should bother to go so far when there are other apparently suitable moulting areas closer to Yorkshire. The geese actually call in at some of them on their way north or south. But perhaps the biggest puzzle is why they go at all. Yorkshire is particularly well endowed with waters, including the private estate lakes where the geese were originally established and drinking water reservoirs. The geese breed on and around these waters and gather in moulting flocks, some of which are almost entirely of non-breeding birds. It is difficult to say for certain that there is or is not room for several hundred more to stay and moult but there must definitely have been room in the 1950s when only some 50 geese migrated away.

The Yorkshire–Beauly Firth moult migration is still the only one known among the Canada Geese of Britain. Counts and ringing have shown that the Canada Geese are split into a large number of more or less discrete sub-populations, and movements between them are uncommon. For example, a handful of geese ringed in the south of Yorkshire, in the adjacent counties of Nottinghamshire and Derbyshire, have migrated to the Beauly Firth, but this is out of a total population in these counties in excess of 2000, most of them ringed. There may be short distance movements of non-breeding birds to moult gatherings but none appear to take geese beyond the normal range of their sub-population. It has been suggested that the moult migration is the result of an ancient adaptation based on hereditary factors. The exact origin of the British Canada Geese is in doubt but it has been widely assumed that they come from stocks of large Canada Geese that were caught in eastern parts of the United States or Canada by settlers from Europe. There has been some argument over the subspecies involved, most of it in favour of the Atlantic and Giant races, which I have treated together. However, in the eastern half of their range, moult migration is not very well developed in these birds, the only movements recorded being within the breeding range. The re-emergence of long-suppressed instinctive tendencies remains of very great interest even if we cannot know why or how it took place.

Finally, a small gathering of moulting Canada Geese has recently been reported from the island of Hiddensee on the Baltic coast of East Germany. They are assumed to be birds from the Swedish population, some of which winter in East Germany. This moulting area lies due south of the breeding area and is in this respect unique.

The last species to be dealt with in this catalogue of moult migration is the Brent Goose. This exhibits both types of moult migration already mentioned. Some birds make a northward movement from the breeding grounds, but a proportion of the immatures never reach the breeding area but divert from their spring migration route to the moulting localities. The picture is somewhat confused by a mixture of these two types in widely separated areas, the Alaskan–east Siberian breeding range of the Black Brant, and the west Siberian breeding range of the Dark-bellied Brent.

The exact situation regarding movements of non-breeding Black Brant has yet to be resolved. However, a number of facts are known, or appear to be. Firstly, considerable flocks of non-breeding birds moult on the Yukon–Kuskokwim Delta of western Alaska, which is also where enormous numbers breed. However, ringing recoveries of these non-breeders include some from eastern Siberia, in subsequent summers, when it may be assumed that they were breeding. The simplest explanation is that these birds, having wintered with the rest of the population on the Pacific coasts of Mexico and California, did not bother to return as far as their natal areas, in Siberia, but stopped off short in the undoubtedly excellent moulting habitat of western Alaska. Nevertheless, there are observations from Siberia which suggest that some, at least, of the Siberian non-breeders do return all the way to the breeding grounds, and then head back to Alaska to moult.

There are records going back nearly a hundred years of Brent Geese flying north in summer from the New Siberian Islands. As there was no known land lying to their north this, with other bird observations, was taken as evidence of the existence of undiscovered land in the arctic basin. However, it is now clear that the birds are, in fact, embarking on a great circle course, the shortest possible route over the globe, although appearing otherwise on a flat map, which will take them to Alaska. So at least some Brant do apparently return to Alaska to moult having passed it on their spring migration. They may have attempted to breed in Siberia and failed. Thus, their moult migration takes them at least part of their way along their usual autumn route. There is a further confusing factor in that at least some Brent Geese breeding on the mainland south of the New Siberian Islands are thought to belong to the population that winters on the Asiatic side of the Pacific, migrating overland to reach the arctic coast. However, ringing in Alaska has not yet produced any recoveries in this wintering area.

Up to 10,000 Black Brant have been found in Wrangel Island in eastern Siberia, where, in addition, between 1000 and 2000 pairs breed. On the Arctic Slope of Alaska around 25,000 moulting Brant were found concentrated on a series of lakes in the Cape Halkett area. Scattered pairs breed throughout this area and all along the Slope, but clearly most of the moulting birds had come from elsewhere. It is not certain whether they have come north from the main breeding area in western Alaska, or stopped short on the migration route of geese going to breed in the western Canadian arctic islands. As mentioned in the previous chapter, large numbers of Brant breeding on those islands fly right round Alaska on their spring migration.

Elsewhere in North America most moulting Brent Geese seem to stay in the vicinity of the nesting colonies, as has been observed on Southampton

Island, for example. There are no reports of moult migration among the Light-bellied Brent of the eastern arctic archipelago, nor in Greenland, nor in Svalbard, but this may in part be due to the general lack of detailed information concerning these birds.

Many immature Dark-bellied Brent Geese do not complete their migration in spring but stop off instead on the Kanin Peninsula, or on Kolguev Island, or divert northwards off their route to the Novaya Zemlya Islands. Very large numbers have been recorded as moulting there during the last hundred years or more. The natives of the area have traditionally taken a toll of these flocks. For example, in one drive on Kolguev Island in 1894 over 3000 geese were caught and killed for food. On the breeding grounds further east other immature Brent appear to moult close to the nesting colonies.

Looking at the geese as a whole, moult migration is an incomplete adaptation, with many species and populations not taking part. In some of the latter cases this may be as much geographical as anything else, there being a lack of any other suitable localities for the purpose. In others it seems that the advantage which some populations gain from moult migration is not universal. It is possible that the immature birds are literally forced out of the breeding areas in some cases by a combination of parental aggression and sheer pressure on the available resources, but data to support this is lacking. Indeed, in the case of the Iceland Pinkfeet, observation of the nesting grounds suggests that the parents take little notice of their previous year's young and certainly do not attack them at any time. Really intensive studies of the phenomenon are difficult to carry out, not least because any catching and ringing of the moulting birds must be carefully done if it is not to have an adverse effect. The disappearance of the moulting Greylags from the Vejlerne haunt has already been mentioned in this context, and some of the flocks of Canada Geese in the Thelon River area of Canada also changed their moulting area after round-ups in successive summers.

The Canada Geese that move between Yorkshire and the Beauly Firth in Britain are currently one of the best-studied moult-migrating populations because it has been possible to carry out regular ringing and make observations on both the migratory and non-migratory segments. Nevertheless, great care has been taken to limit the number of catches in the moulting locality. So far there have been six catches in fourteen years since the ringing began. The temptation to catch more often had to be resisted even though in the short term quite a lot of knowledge might have been gained. A particularly interesting result already thrown up by the study is that the moult migrators suffer a higher mortality than birds of the same age which remain within the breeding area. This is, in one way, perhaps to be expected as the moulters are making a double journey which must entail more risk than staying at home. The risks are increased because some of the moulters are still on their way south at the beginning of September when the shooting season begins and many break their journey at coastal haunts where shooting pressure is high. However, when considering a phenomenon that apparently has a positive, if obscure, advantage to one part of a population, the breeding birds and their young, it is a little surprising to find that there is a small but distinct adverse effect on the birds whose action brings that advantage. The difference in mortality rate is quite significant, 23% for the moult migrators compared with only 10% for the non-migratory geese.

The Yorkshire–Scotland study has also confirmed observations on other moulting geese, namely that the journey to the moulting place is completed quickly, often in one flight if the distance permits, whereas the return trip is more leisurely, and may indeed take place some weeks after the geese have regained flight. The duration of flightlessness is between three and four weeks for all species, with a natural tendency for the smaller geese to take less time. However, this is a very difficult measurement to make precisely unless one can follow individual geese, otherwise one can only take an average value. Captive birds do not necessarily give a true picture, because lifestyle and location are vastly different. There is probably individual variation among wild geese, and the circumstances in which the first flight after the moult is made will also have a bearing on the period of flightlessness. A strong wind will obviously aid flight and the need to escape from a predator could also induce premature flight. It is generally agreed that a goose can fly when its wing feathers have reached about 75% growth.

The remaining question frequently asked about a goose's wing moult is how do the birds know when to stop flying? And there is a corollary as to whether a goose ever takes off and finds itself moulting in mid-air. The answer to both would seem to be that the goose is aware of the first loosening of its feathers, indicating that moult is imminent. How long the warning is I do not know, but once this point has been reached the goose will make very sure not to fly. If forced to fly, in order to escape from some threatening situation, the feathers usually come out as it makes its take-off. With maximum-power wing-beats, the thrust proves too much for the loosened feathers. I have seen this happen many times with geese which still have their old feathers when being rounded up for ringing. They make a frantic attempt to escape but the result is disastrous, with quills coming out at each flap of the wings. I once saw a goose come down from about 3 m (10 ft) up in the air when it suddenly started to lose feathers, but it was able to make a more or less graceful landing. A goose that has been released after a round-up will often make its first flight since the moult as it tries to get away as fast as it can from the catching pen. A slight downhill run to the water, perhaps, or a strong wind, will just enable it to maintain height, brushing the water, maybe, with its new wing-tips as it tries to keep airborne.

8 Exploitation and conservation

Wild geese have been the quarry of man ever since he found ways of catching them. Eggs, young and flightless adults would always have been available to people living near breeding sites. Domestication of geese followed naturally on the habit, still prevalent today in some areas, of taking a few eggs or goslings and rearing them to eat at a later date. The killing of wild geese in winter relied on ingenuity in snaring, trapping or shooting, first with arrows, later with guns. While the geese were more numerous than man it is unlikely that they would have been significantly reduced except in very local situations. And whilst man's sole requirement was food, and methods of killing primitive, the same was probably true. But as the numbers of people increased and spread, as more accurate firearms became widely available, and especially as the idea of shooting for pleasure caught hold among the masses rather than the privileged few, so many populations of geese came under threat.

The geese which probably suffered most from the increase in human population were those breeding in the temperate latitudes, like the large Canada Geese of North America and the Greylag of Europe. Their vulnerability not only to winter shooting and trapping but also to depredations during the breeding season led to extinction over wide areas. The fact that they survived at all is due to the inaccessibility of at least some of their haunts, followed by protective measures in the nick of time.

Certain wintering populations of geese, particularly those living in restricted habitat close to well-populated areas, went through a period of heavy over-shooting in the last half of the 19th century and the first part of the present one. Reserves for geese were unknown and although the number of people involved in the shooting was probably not high by present-day standards, restrictions were few or nonexistent and incentives, in many cases, great. Some wildfowlers shot birds in order to make a living, selling them to the market. It was not always an easy living, but they sometimes achieved very large kills, using punt guns of enormous bore, or a combination of baiting and decoys. Others who shot geese did so purely for sport but became obsessed by their determination to attain ever larger bags.

This period of wildfowling may have resulted in unjustifiably large kills of geese but it left behind it a legacy of another sort for the enjoyment of future generations. A few of the keenest wildfowlers and sportsmen were sufficiently inspired by the aesthetic pleasure derived from the geese themselves, and from the killing of them, that they wrote down their experiences in diary or book form. Others found expression in drawing or painting; a few in both. Many of the books now rate highly as works of considerable literary power, and even a reader who has never attempted or wanted to shoot a goose can derive great enjoyment from them. The writers included a minority who had the interest and the ability to add to the sum of knowledge concerning their quarry. Weights, measurements, drawings and descriptions were made in great and meticulous detail. The contents of the gut were analysed to produce the first clear evidence of what the geese ate. Detailed observations were recorded that have not been bettered to this day. Yet, for all the information that they amassed, few paid much attention to the well-being of the geese, or questioned their own or other shooters' activities, and whether they might not be excessive. As a result some wintering populations of geese were completely exterminated from traditional haunts, and total numbers were much reduced.

An awakening consciousness of the dangers of over-shooting came slowly, particularly in European countries. The slaughter of geese and other birds was at least as great in North America but the realisation of the excesses being committed came earlier. The two most destructive factors were spring shooting, and the very ready sale of shot birds. Shooting for money, known as market hunting, was very prevalent and some gross excesses were committed. Bags of several hundred geese in a day were achieved. The first Act of Congress which did much towards curbing this destruction was the Lacey Act passed in 1900. Its main provision affecting geese prohibited the shipment of illegally taken game birds from one state into another. Previously it was not possible for the first state to prosecute in such cases. The Lacey Act made it a Federal offence. The states were thus given much more effective powers to enable them to exercise their own protective legislation.

However, the Lacey Act did not stop market hunting and spring shooting, and evasions of its provisions were commonplace. Shooting of wildfowl rose to a peak in the first decade of this century following the introduction of automatic shotguns and more reliable and effective ammunition, and in the virtually complete absence of any close seasons. However, opposition was growing and in 1913 the Weeks–McLean Act was passed which stated that all wildfowl and other game birds which were not resident in any single state, in other words any migratory bird, were regarded as a Federal responsibility, to be controlled by the Department of Agriculture which issued regulations to give threatened species adequate protection. This Act aroused a lot of hostility from hunters but before long a much more powerful Act was passed, which gave Federal authorities a weapon for wildlife conservation against which the diehards were virtually powerless.

Nowadays we take for granted co-operation between countries in the management and conservation of wildlife, but looking back sixty years the Migratory Bird Treaty of 1916 between the governments of the United States and Canada to regulate the taking of migratory birds was indeed a revolutionary step and years ahead of its time. It is indeed ironic that the Treaty was with Great Britain, Canada being then one of its dominions. It was only in 1975 that Britain signed on its own behalf its first international convention dealing with the conservation of wetlands and waterfowl.

The Migratory Bird Treaty Act was passed by Congress in 1918, thus ratifying the Treaty, and it laid down, among other things, closed seasons for shooting and also led directly to the setting up of the Bureau of Biological Survey under the U.S. Department of Agriculture. This was, of course, the forerunner of the U.S. Fish and Wildlife Service. Two great steps taken in subsequent years were, firstly, the passing of the Migratory Bird Conservation Act in 1929, which strengthened the Federal ability to regulate hunting seasons and bag limits, and also authorised the creation of a network of wildfowl refuges; secondly, the passing in 1934 of the Migratory Bird Hunting Stamp Act. The idea of earmarking revenue for specific projects is alien to the thinking of many governments, including the British, but not in the U.S.A. The Act required every hunter over the age of 16 to purchase, annually, a special Federal Hunting Stamp, widely known as the Duck Stamp, at any post office, and to keep it on his person while out shooting. The initial cost was one dollar, but this has been successively raised and is currently $7.50. The income from this source has been used both for land purchase and for management of existing refuges. Between two and three million stamps are now bought each year. Not surprisingly, with this basic income very great achievements have been made.

A great deal of money and effort goes into trying to perfect the ideal goose-shooting situation in relation to as many separate goose populations as possible. This ideal would allow all the hunters, at the various migratory resting stations and wintering areas of a particular population, to shoot geese in proportion, firstly to the available surplus, secondly to the numbers of hunters, and thirdly to the period that the geese stay in each area. The calculation of the harvest must be based on the known population level, the success or otherwise of the current breeding season, and the desired level of numbers, or population objective. This last, in turn, should be related to the carrying capacity of the habitat used by the birds, and should make allowances for the influence of short-term weather effects and longer-term trends brought about by climatic or habitat changes.

Needless to say, such an ideal has yet to be reached in many cases but good progress towards it has been made despite criticism, valid in part, that there is not a sufficient understanding of how goose populations are naturally regulated and that present-day management is at least as much a matter of luck as of judgement. The fact that three countries are involved (Mexico signed a Migratory Bird Treaty with the United States in 1936) makes for some friction and it is easy to point to individual cases where obvious mistakes have been made. In the last few years the Canadians have been conducting comprehensive surveys of some of their goose populations, including Greater and Lesser Snow Geese, and Light-bellied Brent, and have found substantially greater numbers than have been recorded during the mid-winter inventories on their United States wintering grounds. On the debit side there have been some recent discrepancies in the apparent kills recorded in different areas, and there is much still to sort out so that hunters in different areas have equal opportunities. Only in the last few years have the Canadians appreciated the importance of the hunting of geese by the Indians in the James Bay and southern Hudson Bay area, not only to the geese but also to the Indians, for whom this is a vital source of food. However, the fact that most goose populations in North America have shown healthy increases in recent years is a sign that at least the management has erred on the cautious side, which can only be a matter of praise. The main tools that wildlife managers have at their disposal are annual inventories and production surveys, purchase and management of refuges, including the provision of feeding areas (often specially planted crops) and control of hunters through a system of flexible response. Seasons, bag limits and, in some areas, shell limits, and hunters' returns, are used to balance the requirements of the hunting community with the available surplus in the goose populations.

In Europe, in contrast with the North American situation, each country has developed its own pattern of shooting regulations and wildfowl refuges, and only in the last 10 years has any attempt been made to bring some kind of coherence to the prevailing muddle. Nor has any country yet applied the same degree of management or control of hunters as in North America. This is no place to review the history of goose conservation in every European country but it is worth summarising what has happened in Britain, as well as noting the current state of affairs throughout Europe.

Acts of Parliament in Britain controlling the taking of game birds and animals date back to the fifteenth century. They were mostly directed at protecting the privileges of royalty and big landowners. Wild ducks and geese were not classed as game and did not receive any kind of legal protection until the first Wild Birds Protection Act of 1880. Under this Act, a close season was fixed for the first time, running from March 2nd to July 31st. 'Fixed' is a misnomer as County Councils were given powers to extend or curtail the close season in part or all of their county. Many of them made use of these powers and ridiculous anomalies occurred. For example, many county boundaries follow rivers to their mouths and situations arose where it was permissible to shoot for several days longer on one side of the estuary than on the other. The 1880 Act also included a Schedule of species which landowners and occupiers might not kill during the closed season, even on their own land. However, this Schedule did not include any species of goose and con-sequently they could still be shot at any time of the year on private land if the owner wished to indulge or allow someone else to do so. It might seem an extraordinary loophole that any close season should not apply equally all over the country, but it must be remembered that the Parliament which passed the Act was composed largely of the land-owning class who were naturally reluctant to see their own privileges curtailed. County Councils, too, typically included a high proportion of landowners at that time, and their own interests were bound to rank large in their consideration of the Act. Nevertheless, many such people were only too aware of the dangers of over-shooting and exercised rigid control over wildfowling on their land.

Various additions and amendments were made to the 1880 Act over the years, but it was not until 1939 that a major new Act came into being that greatly affected wildfowl. This Act was called the Wild Birds (Ducks and Geese) Protection Act. Its most significant new step was the extension of the close season, reducing the shooting period to August 12th to January 31st, thus creating a longer close season than the open period. An extra shooting period was allowed on the foreshore to February 20th. County Councils still retained powers to vary seasons, but only to the extent of reducing the open season, they were no longer allowed to extend it. Thus, for the first time, the same minimum close season was in force throughout the country. In the same Act, all species of wild geese were placed on the Schedule, prohibiting landowners to shoot them on their own land outside the open season.

At about the time the 1939 Act was going through Parliament there was a concerted attempt to learn more about the status of wild ducks and geese throughout Europe. Earlier moves had come in the 1920s when the Swedish Government, largely stimulated by one man, Professor Einar Lönnberg, suggested to other European governments that they should co-operate in establishing international laws to protect wildfowl populations which migrated through several different countries. In 1926 it was proposed at the quadrennial International Ornithological Congress that each country should draw up a report on the subject and that a conference should then be convened to consider the matter further. Although the conference duly took place, nothing of much use followed from it.

Renewed interest came in the mid-1930s, following startling reports from North America that they were instituting severe limitations on shooting, in view of the drastic decline in wildfowl numbers that had been recorded. The main impetus came from the International Committee for Bird Preservation, an independent, largely voluntary, organisation of interested individuals and organisations. The British Section of this Committee was mainly responsible for promoting the 1939 Act, and it also set up a Wildfowl Inquiry sub-committee as a contribution to the resurrected idea of European-wide action on wildfowl conservation. The members of the sub-committee included scientists, ornithologists and sportsmen. They came together and pooled their knowledge to produce two books devoted to what was currently known about the status of wildfowl in Britain and the factors affecting them.

In one of the books produced by the sub-committee there is a table showing the shooting seasons then in force in other European countries. This was given as a comparison with the British season which had just been reduced to August 12th to January 31st, and February 20th on the coast. The variation in timing and duration of seasons was very great, with commencing dates for shooting as early as the middle of July in several countries, including Belgium, France and Germany, through various dates in August in the Netherlands, Italy, Norway and Greece, to September 1st in Sweden and Switzerland. Very clearly, these starting dates had nothing to do with the timing of migration of the wildfowl through the various countries, for which the rational response would have indicated earlier dates in the more northern and eastern countries, and later dates in those further south and west towards the end of the migration routes. The open season finishing dates were equally variable, with a few in February, most in March, but some, including Belgium (one of the first to start), not until mid-April.

The 1939–45 war put a brake on further measures to improve the law on wildfowl conservation in Britain and had a mixed effect on the birds themselves. Although there were many fewer shooters pursuing their sport, both because many were called-up and because cartridges were in short supply, professional wildfowlers found an eager market for the birds they shot and were therefore encouraged to shoot more than before and to ignore seasons. In some areas restrictions on access led to the creation of virtual sanctuaries for the birds, while in others, military activities, particularly the establishment of airfields, brought about enormous increases in disturbance. There are lurid tales from more than one area of 'wildfowling' being carried out with high-powered rifles and sub-machine guns by off-duty servicemen.

After the war, it took several years before a further Bird Protection Act was passed, in 1954. It was preceded by some fairly acrimonious debate between wildfowlers and conservationists, who mistook each other's intentions. However, before too long they found that their aims were the same, the preservation of sufficient stocks of wildfowl to enable a properly regulated harvest to be taken by shooting, and nowadays all work together harmoniously. The 1954 Act gave complete protection to the Brent Goose, following the realisation that its numbers had been seriously depleted. It also banned shooting of the Barnacle Goose, largely because numbers on the Solway Firth, the only mainland haunt, were also severely reduced since before the war. The open season was further curtailed (September 1st to January 31st), but the extension to February 20th on the coast remained. Only the Government Minister responsible now had powers to vary the season, this power being removed from County Councils. They retained the right to ban shooting on Sundays within their counties, which a few did, and this was also instituted in Scotland.

At about the time of the passing of the 1954 Act, a committee which included members from the wildfowling and conservation bodies, and involved the Government conservation body, the Nature Conservancy, began making recommendations for the setting up of a network of wildfowl refuges covering important haunts throughout the country. Some of these were given statutory protection as National Nature Reserves, others relied on local co-operation between landowners and wildfowling clubs. Many of them were particularly important for geese, covering as they did some of the principal roosts.

Compulsory acquisition of land for nature reserves is virtually unknown in Britain, and great reliance has to be placed on the willingness of landowners to allow their land to be declared a reserve, and thus to give up some of their rights to shooting and access. Fortunately, this co-operation has rarely been refused. For hundreds of years many landowners have done more for wildfowl conservation than many of the Acts of Parliament. By protecting the birds of their estates, prohibiting shooting except by small groups of friends and relatives, and voluntarily restricting the number of shoots held each year, they have successfully protected many otherwise very vulnerable goose roosts and feeding areas.

Recent modifications to the law as it affects geese in Britain have been slight. In 1955, shooting of Barnacle Geese was permitted on islands off the west coast of Scotland, for a two-month season, but the small Solway flock retained full protection. Perhaps the most important change was the banning of the sale of dead wild geese in 1968. This followed a campaign against the rather small number of commercial goose shooters, particularly those in

Scotland. There was little of the element of sport in their activities. They did not even confine their shooting to the coastal marshes and estuaries as did the professional wildfowlers, for whom an annual bag of two or three hundred was reckoned as very good indeed. These latter professionals had virtually died out before the war, though a few lingered on, acting more as wildfowling guides than trying to make a living out of shooting and selling their kill, an activity that received a boost during the war but petered out soon afterwards. The commercial goose shooters, on the other hand, were operating on the feeding fields, shooting over decoys and doing so purely in order to sell the birds they shot to hotels and game dealers. Bags of up to a hundred a day were not uncommon and, perhaps not surprisingly, some revulsion was felt against this slaughter and its lack of any element of sport. The ban on the sale of dead geese put an effective stop to the practice.

  The law in Britain is now quite adequate so far as the protection of wildfowl is concerned, but it lacks flexibility. Changing the law takes many years of hard effort, and even when changes in the regulations are permitted the process can take several months, by which time the reason for doing so may have passed. This has been particularly apparent in the context of trying to reduce the impact of geese on farm crops. The present law permits a farmer or landowner to shoot or kill geese outside the open season, provided he can prove to a court of law that his action was necessary to prevent damage to his crops. In practice this is too cumbersome and long-winded a procedure to cope with a situation that can occur at any time. One interpretation that can be placed on the law is that the birds have to be killed while actually doing the damage. Most farmers would regard this as too late, and the strongest comments come from those who have experienced damage in one year and wish to prevent it being repeated the next. What is needed, and what the law does not at present provide, is some system of licencing whereby a farmer or landowner who could prove that damage had occurred in the past or was very likely to occur could be permitted to kill the geese to prevent such damage. Certain safeguards would be required, including the proof by the farmer that vigorous scaring of the geese had been tried and failed. In this way it would be possible to respond very quickly to specific complaints of damage or impending damage. Permission to kill the birds would be restricted to as small an area as necessary, perhaps to one farm only. At present an extension of the shooting season or the removal of a bird from a protected schedule to a shooting schedule, or vice versa, can only take place after the publication of the intention to do this in the press, followed by a statutory period for objections to be entered, and then time for consideration of these by the Minister concerned. Not unnaturally, this takes some months to achieve, and although this procedure, with its built-in safeguards, should still be followed for any major changes in the regulations, a much more flexible and speedier response is necessary for the limited number of annual cases where damage may occur.

  An example of the present cumbersome law, and of the necessity for such safeguards as prior publication and the receiving of objections, occurred as recently as 1974 when the Secretary of State for Scotland, the Minister responsible for administering the Protection of Birds Acts in Scotland, published a Proposal in the press to transfer the Greylag and Pink-footed Geese to the Second Schedule of the Act. The Second Schedule contains those species of birds, generally considered to be pests, which may be shot at any time of the year. These include crows, starlings, the larger gulls, woodpigeons and the like. The Proposal covered six whole counties of central Scotland and was aimed at alleviating alleged damage to a comparatively small number of farms. Unfortunately, it is necessary for areas to be specified which correspond to administrative boundaries, and the intention was to take in a wide enough area to cover all complaints. The Proposal came with almost no warning to the conservation bodies in the country, and even the government conservation agency seemed to be taken unawares. The Minister was acting on the advice of his Advisory Committee on Wild Birds for Scotland, a body of appointed people not fully representative of all interests, and not as well informed in this instance as might have seemed necessary.

The Proposal aroused a storm of protest, and not solely from the voluntary conservation bodies, who saw in it a horrifying backward step at a time when Britain and other traditionally conservation-minded European countries were doing their best to persuade the remaining countries to reduce their shooting seasons. In particular, they were encouraging such countries to close the seasons earlier than the dates in February, March and even April, which many still held to. The wildfowlers, too, were indignant. It raised spectres of untold damage to the populations of the two goose species and the other wildfowl likely to be disturbed, and perhaps shot as well, in the spring months when pairing and the initial stages of the breeding season were under way. In their defence the Advisory Committee clearly saw it as the only way open to them under the existing law to allow continued shooting of geese in those areas where damage was likely to be caused to farm crops, and at those times of year, February to April, when such crops were most at risk and damage most probable. It was a good demonstration of the inadequacy of the options open to the Committee under the law as it stood, and still stands.

The conservationists and wildfowlers, including the Wildfowl Trust, a voluntary body but in receipt of government funds for research into wildfowl, were further upset at an apparent lack of consultation between the Advisory Committee and themselves, and one hoped-for benefit from this episode is that it should not be able to occur again. When the Secretary of State bowed to the weight of the opposition and rescinded his Proposal, a working party was set up to look into the problem of the two geese species and their potential threat to agriculture, and at the very least this will create a procedure to be followed in the future.

The shooting of geese and other wildfowl in Europe still lacks any coherence, although some progress is now being made in the right direction. In 1969, the International Waterfowl Research Bureau set up a Hunting Rationalisation Research Group, whose main tasks have been to gather data on the existing shooting laws in all European countries and then to try to introduce uniformity, based on knowledge of numbers and timing of migration of the different waterfowl populations.

The latest available survey of current shooting restrictions was made in 1975–76. Regrettably, the progress since the 1939 information, referred to above, has not been very great. The latter did not include full details of which species were protected in the different countries, but in 1975–76 no species of goose was fully protected throughout Europe, though taking into account the normal ranges of the different species, the Brent Goose and the Barnacle Goose were protected over the greater part of their ranges, with West Germany allowing shooting of both, and Norway and Britain permitting shooting of the Barnacle Goose in certain areas. Nearly every country in northern Europe protected at least one species of goose all the time, sometimes more, but Poland and West Germany allowed shooting of all species, as did several countries of central and southern Europe, including Switzerland, Austria, Portugal, Spain and Italy.

The timing and duration of shooting seasons in Europe have improved slowly over the last thirty-five years and only two countries, France and East Germany, start in July, the middle of the month and last week, respectively, compared with six countries in 1939; and twelve countries delay their opening until at least September 1st, compared with two in 1939. There is even better improvement in the closing dates, with only three countries continuing after the middle of March, Poland, France and Italy, compared to eight countries that closed after that date in 1939. The average length of season in the 21 countries surveyed on both occasions has fallen from seven and a half months to five and a half. Clearly there is still a long way to go in rationalisation of seasons, but although a lack of control over shooting may have driven geese out of some countries altogether, and greatly reduced numbers in others, there is not much evidence of serious decline of whole populations that can certainly be attributed to over-shooting.

Not only is Europe a long way behind North America in the matter of shooting seasons and their regulation, it has even further to go towards control by bag limits. Only in the east European countries is this commonly practised with daily bag limits of one to three geese in, for example, the U.S.S.R. and Bulgaria. A number of western European countries have shooting clubs or organisations who impose voluntary bag limits on their members, but this has only a limited effect.

The methods and practices of hunting or shooting which are allowed in different countries are also highly variable. The majority of countries, though not Britain, forbid shooting after dark, while allowing it to begin a stated time before sunrise, usually an hour, and to extend a similar time after sunset. Some, including Britain, do not allow shooting from motor-boats, but a few actually permit shooting from aircraft! Other regulations cover shotgun calibre, the use of punt-guns, live decoys, artificial light, and so on. The differences between countries are far greater than the similarities. Rationalisation has a long way to go.

Finally, only a minority of European countries have a mechanism for gathering data on how many wildfowl are shot each season. In North America each hunter is required to send in a return giving details of his bag. This is carried out in relatively few countries in Europe, though some send out selective questionnaires to a sample of hunters and assess the annual kill in that way. The fact that a single population of geese may be found in ten or a dozen different countries in the course of a year, each with its own shooting laws, makes realistic management, based on a flexible response to changes in the numbers, whether through varying breeding success or shooting, extremely hard to achieve. But if geese stocks in Europe are to be conserved, and a reasonable harvest of each permitted, much closer co-operation will be needed.

There is really very little knowledge of how many geese are shot in Europe each year, or even in any individual country. Denmark publishes annual figures of the total of geese, of all species, shot each year, and these range from about 8000 to 12,000. The picture for Britain is hardly known. One can make estimates based on known mortality rates for the different species of geese but can come no nearer than to say that between twenty and thirty thousand geese are shot each winter. We happen to be in the fortunate position that nearly all our geese populations are in a reasonably healthy state, and some at least of their main haunts are no-shooting refuges, either statutory or private. But clearly the ability to gather reliable shooting statistics would be of considerable value in discovering more about the part that shooting plays in the annual mortality of different populations. It has been possible to discover something of this from ringing recoveries but apart from a large-scale programme of Pinkfoot ringing in Britain and Iceland in the 1950s, and the ringing of Whitefronts and Bean Geese in the Netherlands, relatively few geese have been marked in Europe.

In North America annual hunting statistics are gathered as a matter of course and published in considerable detail. The numbers of geese killed are very high, but then so are both the stocks available and the number of hunters wishing to shoot them. There are nearly three million waterfowl hunters in the United States and over 400,000 in Canada. Although ducks are their main quarry, with around 17 million shot each year, geese also figure largely, with the following totals for the autumn and winter of 1972–73, a below-average year after a very poor arctic breeding season: 1 million Canada Geese, 360,000 Snow Geese, 160,000 Whitefronts, and 16,000 Brent Geese. The number of Snow Geese was well below earlier years because of a closed season on the Atlantic coast that autumn. In addition to these totals, the native Eskimos and Indians are believed to take 100,000–200,000 geese of all species annually, as well as considerable numbers of eggs.

The figures above have been adjusted to take account of the estimated number of geese that were killed but not retrieved. The normal allowance for this, based on direct observation and hunters' returns, is about 15%. It varies slightly from area to area and for different species. This 'crippling loss', as it is termed, has been the subject of much effort in the United States, aimed at reducing it as much as possible. Closely related to it is the proportion of birds which are hit by shot pellets but not killed. The most accurate method of measuring this is by X-ray or fluoroscope. An examination of over 1000 Canada Geese in Missouri, and a similar number of Pink-footed Geese in Britain, found that on average between 40 and 45% of adult birds carried one or more pellets in their bodies. These pellets were mostly lodged in the muscle where they remained inert and appeared not to cause the birds any permanent discomfort. Certainly the weights of birds with pellets were not significantly different from those without. The number of pellets carried by

individual geese varied from one to no less than 23. The latter was an extreme case, however, and over 90% of the geese with shot were carrying between one and four pellets. As might be expected, only a small percentage of geese in their first autumn were carrying pellets; about 5% of Pinkfeet, which were checked shortly after their arrival in Britain from Iceland where there is little or no shooting; and over 20% in young Canada Geese, which were not X-rayed until after several weeks of the shooting season.

It is thought that the majority of birds carrying lead pellets get them from shooters firing at too great a distance, rather than aiming badly. A restricted study done in the United States kept a number of shooters under observation and measured the distances at which they fired at both ducks and geese. For 175 shots fired, the average quarry distance was about 64 metres (71 yards), with a range from as close as 22 metres (24 yards), to an astonishing 220 metres (240 yards). No less than 20% of all shots fired were at birds more than 82 metres (90 yards) away. The results of the shooting showed that the mean distance for a killing shot was 52 metres (57 yards), while for a shot which was known to wound but not kill the bird, it was 64 metres (70 yards). Shots which missed the birds altogether had a mean distance of 75 metres (82 yards). In all cases the hunters were using 12-bore guns, and size 4 shot or larger.

Crippling loss, and by implication the numbers of birds wounded but not killed, was dramatically reduced on the Horicon National Wildlife Refuge in Wisconsin, where controlled shooting is allowed from hides (blinds). In the first years of shooting on the refuge in the mid-1950s it was estimated that it took 40 shots to account for each goose killed, and the crippling loss stood at a horrifying 42%. As the hunters gained in experience both figures fell markedly. However, over the years there was an increasing tendency for shooting at extreme ranges, and firing far more shells than was necessary.

Consequently, after a year's intensive observation and monitoring in 1962, a limit of six shells per hunter per day in the hide was introduced in 1963. In both years the bag limit was fixed at one goose per hunter per day. Continued monitoring, which included asking hunters how many shells they had expended, and checking from places of concealment, found that the number of shots per hunter fell from about 6·7, for both successful and unsuccessful hunters, to only 2·6. The average number of shots per goose killed also fell, from 9·7 to 6·4. The overall rate of kills was down, however, from 69% to 56% of those hunters who shot at geese. A satisfactory statistic was the proportion of hunters who killed their goose with only one shot, which went up from 10% to 18%. This reflects greater restraint on the part of the hunters, who having only six shells in all, held their fire until they were more certain of getting their bird. The crippling loss fell from about 21% to 14%. Before the introduction of the shell limit, some hunters were taking 25 shells or more to bag one goose, while a few were firing as many as 35 shells without success.

Various other measures are used at controlled goose-shooting refuges in North America. Among the more important are the siting of hides, which must not be too close to each other (at least 180 metres (200 yards) is recommended); restrictions on the size of gun and shot used; bag limits; and the use of decoys, normally silhouettes or plastic moulds, which encourages shooting within reasonable range. By exercising these various controls it is found that the shooting is improved and the goose population benefits through fewer wounded birds; and, generally, because the refuge managers have a better control over what is happening to the stocks under their management. One problem which has yet to be satisfactorily resolved, however, is the ever-growing demand for goose shooting in areas where it is considered that the stocks cannot stand any more hunting than at present. Various methods have been tried to make the opportunities for shooting equal for all and the issue of tags to the hunters seems to have been the most favourably received by all sides. For this a seasonal limit is set of, say, six geese per hunter. Six special tags are then issued with each annual license and a tag has to be fixed round the leg of the dead goose immediately it is retrieved. It is an offence to be in possession of a goose without such a tag or to move it anywhere before tagging it. The tags are not reusable and the hunter must complete a return for each tag used.

Management of goose stocks in North America does not stop at control of the hunter through bag and season limits. There is also an extensive programme of creating and managing refuges. The refuge system has built up over the years until there are now over 1000 major wildlife refuges, totalling over 7,500,000 hectares (18,500,000 acres), used by a very significant proportion of the continent's geese. Some of the refuges are federal-owned, others state-owned, but a number are private, and may be owned by gun clubs who nonetheless regard themselves as wildlife conservers as well as shooters. Wetlands purchased for refuges cannot be left to themselves; they invariably require considerable management, particularly in the control of water levels and the improvement of the habitat for the geese. The latter may involve planting of food plants, or ploughing and reseeding grassland based on an analysis of the birds' food preferences, reduction of disturbance and, in the breeding range, the provision of nesting islands or artificial sites.

In some ways the system of refuges and their active management has turned out to be too successful in certain areas of the United States. There has been an increasing tendency, both in the Atlantic and Mississippi Flyways, for the Canada Geese to winter further north than formerly. The birds have almost certainly been finding all their needs satisfied in the more northerly haunts which they traditionally visited on migration, and no longer feel the necessity of moving on south for the winter. This contraction of range has often been accompanied by an increase in total numbers, so clearly the population is not suffering from it. However, the shooters in the more southerly areas are not unnaturally upset when their quarry disappears through no fault of their own. The attempted solution to this problem has been the programme of transplanting geese from the northerly sites back to the more southerly ones in the hope that this would re-establish the full migratory range.

In the period 1953 to 1965 no less than 20,700 Canada Geese were caught from flocks wintering in Illinois and Missouri and transplanted south to the four south-eastern states of Louisiana, Mississippi, Arkansas and Florida. The average distance that the birds were moved was about 850 kilometres (530 miles). Three main techniques were used in trying to establish the geese. Firstly, a comparatively small number were released directly on arrival, with no constraints. Secondly, the primary feathers of one or both wings would be pulled out. It takes about six weeks for new feathers to grow during which time it was hoped that the birds would become acquainted with the area and might find it suitable for a permanent home. This was the commonest method. Thirdly, some immatures were penned on the release site for two years, until they were old enough to breed. It was hoped that when they migrated to breed they would return bringing their young with them. These geese were feather-cut to stop them flying during their confinement. The results of all this effort, and not inconsiderable expense, was extremely disappointing. At only one of the nine release localities, all of them on national wildlife refuges, was there any success.

Although transplants to increase or restore a wintering range have proved very difficult to achieve, use of the method to establish breeding flocks has been comparatively successful with large Canada Geese in the United States and in Europe, and to a lesser extent with Greylags in Europe, too. Indeed, there have been many successful establishments of breeding stocks of Canada Geese in America. The entire European population stems from transplanted birds, and the considerable increase and spread of the species in Britain during the 1950s and 1960s was achieved by catching and relocating birds. Only to a comparatively small extent have the geese pioneered new areas for themselves, except in Sweden where, after initial releases, flocks have become established and have then spread of their own accord.

The catching and moving of Canada Geese in Britain began in the early 1950s, largely in response to requests from farmers and landowners whose flocks had got too large. It was felt that removing some birds was an easy solution to the problem, while at the same time enabling a landowner, or sometimes a wildfowling club, to obtain some geese to put on their water. It was not for several years that the dangers inherent in this policy became apparent. The flocks which had been reduced in number quickly multiplied again in the absence of any other form of control, and the relocated flocks settled readily and began breeding. Before long the inevitable happened, there were more requests for the removal of surplus birds than there were landowners who still wanted them. Complaints of damage, or alleged damage, from farmers became more widespread and frequent.

One of the problems attached to Canada Geese in Britain is the difficulty in encouraging sporting shooting of them. In general they are far too tame! Instead of performing dawn and dusk flights between roost and feeding grounds, and being wary enough to fly sufficiently high to provide difficult shooting, many flocks of Canada Geese rarely fly at all, just walking out of their roosting lake to feed; or if they do take to the air, they stay at little more than hedge height. Although many of the introductions were intended to provide sport, few shooters were prepared to take advantage of such habits and so the geese remained tame and continued to increase. Some landowners now take steps to control the numbers breeding on their property, mostly ineffectively by taking eggs. This is attacking at the wrong end of the population pyramid, as only a small proportion of the eggs laid will result in full-grown geese, and so the control takes many years to have any useful effect on numbers. Repeat layings by the geese can quickly make up the numbers if these eggs, too, are not removed. A slightly better alternative is to pierce or shake the eggs and then leave them in the nest. The goose will not usually desert until after the normal incubation period, by which time it is probably too late for her to make another attempt. Other control measures have been adopted; some are, like egg taking or piercing, technically illegal, though the slightly ambiguous British law probably allows them if they can be shown to prevent damage to farm crops. Certainly there have been no prosecutions, nor are there likely to be.

The best solution to too many Canada Geese would seem to be much heavier shooting of the birds, which could be done quite legally during the normal open season. Wholesale slaughter is possible, and has occurred, of some of the tame flocks, but if the numbers genuinely are too high, and agricultural damage is resulting, then it must be deemed necessary. If a particular flock was first reduced to an acceptable level by shooting and its numbers prevented from growing thereafter by regular shoots, the geese might eventually become much more wary than they are, and thus provide the sport shooting which has so long been desired. Because counts and ringing have shown that the British population is split into numerous discrete groups, with little wandering or mixing, it should be possible to devise a satisfactory control for each group, based on its numbers, distribution and the level of complaints against it. The situation is not helped, however, by the widely differing reactions of afflicted farmers. Some are content until their local flock exceeds 200–300, while others start complaining bitterly when numbers top 20.

The other species that has been transplanted with some success in Europe is the Greylag. Greylags have died out in a number of breeding localities, largely through human pressure, and have successfully been reintroduced by release of adults and young. On the continent of Europe the reintroductions have been with birds taken from its existing migratory population. In Britain, however, the Wildfowlers Association has been establishing flocks of sedentary Greylags, mainly with eggs and young birds taken from the feral population in south-west Scotland. This stock itself stems from the equally sedentary Hebridean Greylag population. The wildfowlers have been successful with introductions in several areas, notably the Lake District and south-east England. Although hopes have been expressed that the latter group might link up with migratory Greylags across the North Sea in Belgium and the Netherlands, there is no sign of this happening, nor much likelihood of it while the geese can have such favourable conditions by remaining where they are. Numbers are still low, but those responsible for the Greylag programme seem not to appreciate that they may be creating a problem exactly paralleling that of the Canada Geese. Present flocks are in good farmland and the non-migratory geese are only too likely to become a nuisance, as well as becoming too tame to provide good shooting. A few wildfowlers are also trying to establish other species of geese in different parts of the country, including Barnacle Goose, Whitefront and Bean, which have no place in the breeding avifauna of Britain. The Canada Goose is surely a sufficiently obvious example of the dangers of introducing an alien breeding species into a country and encouraging it. Must it be repeated and must the same problems arise before the process is halted?

The Canada Goose is one of the species which induces most complaints of agricultural damage, perhaps the majority from areas where there are resident flocks and so crops are under attack at all times of the year. However, migrating and wintering flocks of this and other species can also arouse farming opposition in certain circumstances as was related in Chapter 3. A considerable amount of attention has been paid to this question in recent years because not only have the numbers of geese been rising in many areas, but the standards of farming have been improving, with individual farmers and landowners out to get the best from their land. The more they invest the less they like to see their potential returns apparently going into geese. Many farm pests can be tackled on the basis that they are an unmitigated nuisance to be got rid of by whatever means, and with no regrets. Geese on the other hand cannot be dismissed so lightly. Shooters, bird watchers and conservationists all have their point of view, and none can agree to regard geese purely as an agricultural pest.

It is not easy to assess alleged damage to farm crops. So much can happen to a field of winter-sown cereal between the time the shoots are eaten off by a flock of geese until the harvest. A reduced yield may or may not have been wholly or partially the fault of the geese. Extensive trials have been carried out using captive geese penned on to plots of various crops to produce the effect of a flock of geese on a field. The plots were then harvested at the right time and the yields measured. Results confirmed that grazing of winter wheat, even two or three times in a winter, grazing of grass throughout the winter, or grazing of spring barley, had no measurable effect even when done to a degree never likely to be reached in the wild. Neither grass nor grain yields were adversely affected. Loss or damage can be caused to grass that has been fertilised to bring on an 'early bite', and to any newly sprouting cereal crop where the ground is unusually wet and the geese 'puddle' the surface into liquid mud, which then sets hard as it dries. Other damage can be caused by geese stripping unharvested cereals, though this is confined to rather few areas and to those seasons when the geese arrive early or the harvest is very late. It is most unusual in Europe though more frequent in North America.

The answer to goose damage takes various forms. The best, from the goose's point of view, is to farm for the geese, a policy adopted widely in North America. This involves the provision of extensive areas of crops for the birds to eat. It has been found preferable to provide food for the geese in this way in areas on or adjacent to existing wildlife refuges, rather than have the birds dispersing at will to feed over far larger areas and on farmers' crops. By concentrating the geese it is easier to control the shooting of them, while at the same time preventing or at any rate greatly reducing the potential damage to farm crops. The crops grown include grazing or browse plants such as clover and grass, as well as wheat, barley and maize which may be left standing at harvest time or cut and left lying in the fields. In some areas the potential yield is in excess of requirements by the geese present, and so the surplus can be harvested and sold to defray expenses. The scale of operations is large, as might be expected, but overall costs have been kept surprisingly low.

The alternative to providing food for the geese is to compensate farmers who suffer losses. This is regarded by some administrators as a much easier option without the need for the federal or state wildlife agency to become farmers themselves. However, there is, perhaps not surprisingly, much argument as to the proper way of assessing compensation, with many saying that far too much is paid out and that it would be far cheaper to grow the crops instead. The farmers on the other hand say they are not getting enough. Whichever side one is on, one thing is clear, that money is available in North America on a large scale to be devoted towards lessening the impact of the geese on the farming community. The money comes from state or federal funds, and ultimately from the shooter who is thus paying directly for his sport and towards its improvement.

In Europe we are far behind in this respect. Only in the Netherlands is there a fund for compensating farmers for damage caused by geese and other wildfowl, and like the American system the money comes from the shooters' license fees. In Britain there is no method of obtaining compensation for damage caused by geese or any other kind of pest, and the farmer is usually only given advice, not practical help. The idea of growing crops specially for the geese has not so far gone further than trying to improve areas of grassland on refuges used by them, both by ploughing and reseeding with preferred mixtures, and by restricting stock grazing to leave plenty available for the geese.

There is no doubt that it is possible to prevent a flock of geese from damaging crops, but it takes time and therefore money. Geese are essentially wary birds and except in areas where they have become unusually tame, as for example many Canada Geese flocks in Britain, it is normally possible to scare them from a particular field. Carbide bangers, rotating orange and black 'flashers', hydrogen-filled balloons, strips of coloured plastic, and the old-fashioned scarecrow all act up to a point. But as many farmers have learnt the hard way, if the attraction of the food is strong enough the geese will get used to almost any kind of scare. It is no good putting out some scarecrows and expecting them to work effectively for several weeks. Even wary geese soon learn that this object, though perhaps flapping in the wind, is otherwise harmless. Loud bangs may emanate at intervals from apparatus in the field but, so long as nothing more damaging occurs, after a few days the geese will be feeding unconcernedly. To scare geese effectively it is not enough to acquire a device and place it in the field. It should be moved every few days, or changed completely for another type of scare. This may take more time, money, or manpower than the farmer can willingly spare but he should balance this against the possible loss he may otherwise suffer.

Some farmers take more drastic action and shoot the birds, but as most damage is probable in the spring, after the end of the shooting season, they have a problem of whether or not to break the law. There has not been a prosecution brought against a farmer who took the law into his own hands in this way, but it has to be said that shooting is not particularly effective unless it is carried out extensively. And a farmer who can afford to do that can afford to use adequate scaring methods instead.

It has, not unreasonably, been argued that the farmers in Britain ought to get compensation for damage to crops. Alternatively, if the conservation bodies who make objection to geese being shot out of season really care then they should take upon themselves the duty of either scaring the geese or providing compensation. Unfortunately, the way the voluntary conservation bodies in Britain are financed virtually precludes such action except on a small scale. The government agency, the Nature Conservancy Council, has carried out a limited amount of scaring on farms adjacent to refuges in order to encourage the geese to use the refuge instead, but there is no system by which they can pay farmers, nor any money. It is a vexed problem, aired each time a new case of damage or alleged damage comes to light; then, if there are no complaints for a year or so the whole subject is put away until the next time.

Geese are perhaps less prone to natural and man-made hazards than some other waterfowl. Serious outbreaks of disease, such as botulism, more readily affect ducks, with their more frequent use of shallow water and mud where this particularly lethal bacterium flourishes. Pollution of water, particularly by oil but also by other chemicals, is again more likely to affect more aquatic birds, though there have been some cases where several thousand geese have been oiled after a spillage in an estuary used as a roost. There have also been some recent incidents of poisoning of Greylags and Pinkfeet in Britain after the birds had eaten newly sown grain that had been treated with a pesticide. The chemical is an organophosphorous compound introduced after organochlorines had been banned. It is necessary to protect the crop from attacks by wheat bulb fly which is very prevalent in certain areas of the country. Unfortunately, it appears that the geese are particularly susceptible to the chemical, which seems to have a higher toxicity among grey geese than it does among other birds and animals. Normally, when the grain is sown in drills it is harmless to the geese, which cannot dig down for it. However, a certain amount is always spilt on the surface, and in one case the geese had pulled up the newly sprouting wheat after wet weather had loosened the soil. Measures have since been taken to try to restrict the use of the chemical in areas where geese are present, though this is not easy and there is no alternative chemical that is so effective. There is also the possibility that one or two of the poisonings have been deliberate.

Reviewing the state of goose populations across the world, the situation does not appear too gloomy, at least in western Europe and North America. Some populations in central and eastern Europe, and in Asia, are in a less healthy state. The following species accounts summarise the present situation and prospects so far as they are known. Although man's effect, good or bad, gets the most emphasis, it must always be borne in mind that the large number of arctic-breeding populations of geese are very vulnerable to any deterioration in the climate. Even a short period of colder summers in the arctic could have disastrous consequences.

SWAN GOOSE

Such knowledge as we have suggests a serious decline in the last few decades with no evidence that much has or can be done about it. Until there is co-operation in such matters between the Russians and the Chinese the goose will continue to suffer.

BEAN GOOSE

Apart from the relict British wintering population, numbers in north and west Europe are generally increasing, despite a recorded decrease in the breeding population of Scandinavia. It would seem that the numbers breeding in Russia must be increasing. There is insufficient data to report on changes in the size of populations further east in Europe or Asia, but the former at least appear to be holding their own. Wintering conditions in Europe are quite satisfactory.

PINK-FOOTED GOOSE

The Svalbard breeding population appears to be relatively stable though it may have increased over the last twenty years. Conditions in the Netherlands are as good as they have ever been but it is not known whether the breeding grounds can accommodate more.

The Icelandic population has undergone a long period of increase since counts began in 1950, more than doubling its total before apparently levelling out in the last few years. A period of stability seems probable, or one of slight growth, but there is still one major threat hanging over the population. In 1969, Icelandic hydro-electric engineers put forward plans to flood virtually the whole of the marshland in central Iceland where about three-quarters of the breeding pairs are located. The plan has been strenuously opposed both in Iceland and in Britain, and the Iceland government postponed any decision while research was undertaken into the geese and other aspects of the natural history of the area. Economic considerations, as so often, seem likely to weigh more heavily than conservation arguments, and the project is probably more than Iceland can currently afford, even with substantial loans.

However, the engineering reasons for building the dam will remain and so the idea may be revived in the future. If it goes ahead it will have a drastic effect on the population unless the birds are able to find alternative breeding areas. Using known criteria, no alternatives appear to exist in Iceland, and small numbers breeding in East Greenland suggest that this area is not wholly suitable for many more.

WHITE-FRONTED GOOSE

The four European populations all seem healthy enough, with the north-west population having greatly increased in recent years, though possibly at the expense of some of the others. Little or nothing is known about the Asian birds. In North America, numbers in both major populations are large and the Central Flyway birds have increased quite substantially in recent years. The Pacific Flyway population has been more stable. The Greenland Whitefront is the only subspecies to give cause for concern. Its numbers are comparatively small and several minor haunts have been deserted in recent years. Whether the population is actually declining is hard to assess but it is certainly not increasing and the concentration onto two major haunts is not a good thing, especially as shooting is fairly heavy at each.

LESSER WHITE-FRONTED GOOSE

Little is known of the status of this species but breeding numbers in Scandinavia are said to have declined. Nothing is known of numbers in Asia.

GREYLAG GOOSE

The Icelandic breeding population has been through a very good period in the last fifteen years and has more than doubled its numbers. It has recently declined a little but this may only be a temporary setback. Complaints of agricultural damage in Scotland are increasing but seem unlikely to lead to any drastic measures. The north-west Scotland population seems to be holding its own but information is scant.

The Western European population has undoubtedly increased over the last decade, as has the Central European population, but both were much more numerous in past centuries and some of their breeding areas are still vulnerable. Further east, numbers were once greater than they are now but it does seem that measures to protect the birds have been taken in time in most countries, particularly in eastern Europe and in the U.S.S.R.

BAR-HEADED GOOSE

Like the Swan Goose this Asian species is reported to have declined greatly in the last fifty years or more, and conditions for it in Tibet have certainly worsened since 1950. Conservationists in India, Pakistan and the U.S.S.R. are beginning to co-operate in looking after the flocks in their countries.

EMPEROR GOOSE

This species seems to be at a reasonably high and stable level with few threats to its continued well-being.

LESSER SNOW GOOSE

This subspecies has increased greatly in the eastern Canadian arctic in the last thirty years, and though there have been periods when the numbers were thought to be levelling out or declining, it is now clear that counting techniques were imperfect. Whether continued counting will be good enough to monitor the population remains to be seen, but prospects appear quite good despite very heavy shooting pressure. Although they are feeling their way and have incomplete data, the people responsible for managing the wintering stocks have been successful thus far.

The Lesser Snow Geese of the central and western Canadian arctic are also doing well, but one breeding group, that on Wrangel Island in eastern Siberia, has apparently declined very sharply in the last fifteen years. This has been attributed to deteriorating summer weather and to arctic fox predation. Presumably something could be done about the latter. Requests from the Russians for the Americans to restrict shooting in the wintering areas are difficult to comply with because of the problems of identifying the Wrangel Island birds from the other Snow Geese with which they mix.

GREATER SNOW GOOSE

The total population was probably some 3000 geese in 1900. There are now around 200,000. There seems little that can seriously threaten this population although there are now complaints from farmers against it.

ROSS'S GOOSE

There was a period not many years ago when Ross's Goose was thought to be a rare, even an endangered, species, but it is now known that many birds had been overlooked. The present population fluctuates quite a lot but seems sufficiently under control for its relatively small size to be safe.

CANADA GOOSE

Of all the groups and populations of this species, only the tiny numbers of the Aleutian Canada Goose give cause for concern. Virtually all the others have increased substantially in the last twenty years, even though several still have some way to go to reach the population objectives which have been set for them. Some are under very heavy pressure from shooters but it seems that the people in charge have so far got their sums right.

BARNACLE GOOSE

All three populations have been increasing since counts began in the 1950s. The smallest population, breeding in Svalbard, has shown the largest percentage increase and though it is still vulnerable, wintering as it does in just one locality, it is adequately protected and, short of a natural disaster, it seems secure. The Greenland population is running into trouble from farmers on Islay, and the concentration of three-quarters of the population on this one island is unsatisfactory. However, overall it is in a healthy state. The Russian breeding population, too, gives every sign of continued increase.

DARK-BELLIED BRENT GOOSE

It is only a few years since this population was at around the 30,000 level and its principal wintering area in eastern England, where as many as 6000 birds could be found at peak, was designated as the site of London's third airport. When that threat was removed, for economic reasons, not because of the well-presented case of the conservationists, there followed a population explosion by the geese. One of the strongest arguments used against the airport was that if that wintering site was removed the displaced geese would have nowhere to go as all other haunts were full. Our knowledge was not as good as we thought, because the population is now nearly four times the size it was then and could well continue to increase. Only the general threat to estuarine and coastal habitat through drainage and reclamation threatens it now, provided any future shooting is carefully controlled.

LIGHT-BELLIED BRENT GOOSE

The very small Svalbard population has been declining for several years and although the most serious adverse factor of shooting in Denmark has now ceased it shows no signs of recovery. It may be that its breeding islands in Svalbard are no longer so attractive following their take-over in many cases by the expanding Barnacle Goose population.

The birds wintering in Ireland have increased slowly in the last ten years but the population is still small in view of the enormous variation in breeding success. Few of its wintering haunts are adequately protected though none are seriously threatened at the moment.

The population wintering on the Atlantic coast of North America was at a very low ebb in the 1930s but, following full protection, increased to a point in 1951 when shooting could restart. Strict control of seasons and bag limits enabled shooting to continue through to 1971–72. There was then an exceptionally large kill followed by a total failure to breed and an associated loss of adults. The population crashed from about 150,000 to under 50,000 in two years. Shooting was immediately stopped but the recovery is taking time and has emphasised the vulnerability of this species to arctic weather and to over-shooting. This makes future control harder to exercise, though even more necessary. In 1976–77, severe winter weather caused heavy losses, adding yet another dimension to the problem.

BLACK BRANT

The Pacific coast population has been relatively stable in recent years; a considerable proportion breeds in the low arctic of western Alaska and it is much less vulnerable to variations in breeding success than the other Brent Goose subspecies.

RED-BREASTED GOOSE

This species has declined sharply in the last twenty years, though there are now indications of a levelling out. Much needs doing, first to discover the wintering grounds and then to protect it there, and to investigate its breeding biology more fully, and to assess conditions in the summer.

And so what of the future? In North America and Europe nearly all goose populations are in a reasonably healthy state with a good proportion of them increasing steadily during the last twenty years. Pressures on their habitats are also increasing, however, and it is only through constant monitoring and management that the present state of affairs has been attained and is being held. There are some populations, though, that are in a parlous state and it has to be admitted that there is often a lack of knowledge concerning them and this only makes their rescue that much the harder. One cannot afford to make mistakes with a population numbering only a few thousands, or even hundreds, and time is rarely on our side. Some other populations, particularly in North America, are well below the target sizes which, it is believed, should insure against sudden crashes from natural causes, but provide shooting for hunters in all parts of the autumn and winter range. There are other populations whose management is still in an embryo state or based on inadequate information. Yet despite criticism, there is little danger of any North American goose populations, with the possible exception of the Aleutian Canada Goose, becoming extinct through any preventable causes.

In Europe the picture is not quite so bright. The Svalbard Light-bellied Brent Geese and the Red-breasted Geese are declining and look like continuing to do so. Other populations are perilously small or excessively concentrated into a few haunts. However, the majority of geese in Europe seem to be flourishing, and with far less interference than in North America, though this is not suggested as a good thing. Only in Asia are most goose populations giving cause for concern, but information is woefully inadequate and nothing much seems likely to be possible, either to improve the state of knowledge or the lot of the geese, in the present political climate.

A major step forward on the international front came in 1971 with the agreement of the Ramsar Convention on the protection of wetlands of international importance, especially as waterfowl habitat. This Convention requires ratifying countries to attach a list of wetlands of international importance when signing and to undertake to protect them. It is the first international agreement which affects national planning of land-use. So far (1977), 19 countries have signed or ratified and no less than 169 wetlands have been attached, totalling some 5,500,000 hectares of wetland habitat safeguarded. Although aimed at protecting the vital wetland habitat and all birds which live there, geese naturally benefit from this to a considerable degree. With this sort of international interest in their well-being, with such concern and financial involvement at all levels in North America, and with slow but steady steps being taken in Europe towards rationalisation of protection and hunting laws, the prospects for geese can be summed up as good.

The appeal of geese is to the senses of man, to his eyes, his ears, and to an inner feeling of aesthetic pleasure. That pleasure can come from the thrill of seeing a goose fall to one's gun, a fitting climax to a battle of wits between the geese and yourself. Alternatively it can stem from an emotion that combines the sheer delight to be gained from watching and hearing them, with something less tangible yet somehow deeply gratifying, the sense of contact with the wildest of all wild birds, wild geese.

Bibliography

The reader wishing to check a statement in the text, and every reviewer, no doubt, will have noticed that I have omitted all citations of references in the text, though not from the Tables. The average reader will, I hope, have shared the satisfaction I find in a book that has a text uninterrupted by such citations. Their value to the few is in my opinion heavily outweighed by their general encumbrance to the many. I have taken my curtailment of references a stage further by giving here a highly selected bibliography, though one that nonetheless contains over 200 titles. Even so, this is barely one-fifth of the works I consulted and it would be unrealistic to expect the necessary space and expense to be devoted to listing them all. I have tried to select all the more important papers and books, seeking where possible the most recent publication of a particular author so that his bibliography will help the really interested reader. For those completely frustrated in their search for an authority for a statement in this book, I will endeavour to reply to letters of enquiry.

This bibliography is arranged by chapters, thus offering as much help as I can to the searcher after sources, preceded by a handful of more general works. In addition, a few papers are cited more than once where their relevance to more than one chapter is too great to ignore.

GENERAL WORKS

BELLROSE, F. C. 1975. *Ducks, Geese and Swans of North America*. Harrisburg, Pa.: Stackpole Books.

CRAMP, S. and SIMMONS, K. E. L. (Eds). 1977. *The Birds of the Western Palearctic*, Vol. 1. Oxford: Clarendon Press.

DEMENTIEV, G. P. and GLADKOV, N. A. 1952. *The Birds of the Soviet Union*, Vol. 4. Moscow.

GODFREY, W. Earl. 1966. *The Birds of Canada*. Ottawa: National Museum of Canada.

HINE, R. L. and SCHOENFELD, C. (Eds). 1968. *Canada Goose Management*. Madison, Wis.: Dembar Educ. Inc.

HUDEC, K. and ROOTH, J. 1970. *Die Graugans* (Anser anser). Wittenberg Lutherstadt: A. Ziemsen Verlag.

JOHNSGARD, P. A. 1975. *Waterfowl of North America*. Bloomington: Indiana Univ. Press.

331

LINDUSKA, J. P. (Ed.). 1964. *Waterfowl Tomorrow*. Washington: U.S. Dept. of Interior.

PALMER, R. S. (Ed.). 1976. *Handbook of the Birds of North America*, Vol. 2. New Haven: Yale Univ. Press.

PHILIPPONA, J. 1972. *Die Blessgans*. Wittenberg Lutherstadt: A. Ziemsen Verlag.

CHAPTER 1: INTRODUCTION AND CLASSIFICATION

CHOATE, E. A. 1973. *The Dictionary of American Bird Names*. Boston: Gambit.

COOCH, F. G. 1963. Recent changes in distribution of color phases of *Chen c. caerulescens. Proc. Int. Orn. Cong.* 13:1182–94.

COOKE, F. and COOCH, F. G. 1968. The genetics of polymorphism in the goose *Anser caerulescens. Evolution* 22:289–300.

COOKE, F., MIRSKY, P. J. and SEIGER, M. B. 1972. Color preferences in the Lesser Snow Goose and their possible role in mate selection. *Can. J. Zool.* 50:529–36.

COUES, E. 1890. *Key to North American Birds*. Boston: Estes & Lauriat.

DELACOUR, 1951. Taxonomic notes on the Bean Geese, Anserfabalis Lath. *Ardea* 39:135–42.

DELACOUR, J. and MAYR, E. 1945. The family Anatidae. *Wilson Bull.* 57:3–55.

KERBES, R. H. 1975. The nesting population of Lesser Snow Geese in the eastern Canadian Arctic: a photographic inventory of June 1973. *C.W.S. Rep. Ser.* No. 35.

MACLEOD, R. D. 1954. *Key to the names of British Birds*. London: Pitman.

SWANN, H. KIRKE, 1913. *A dictionary of English and Folk-names of British Birds*. London: Witherby.

TRAUGER, D. L., DZUBIN, A. and RYDER, J. P. 1971. White geese intermediate between Ross' Geese and Lesser Snow Geese. *Auk* 80:856–75.

CHAPTER 2: IDENTIFICATION

BOYD, H. 1954. Notes on the belly-markings of White-fronted Geese. *Wildfowl Trust Ann. Rep.* 6:79–81.

COOKE, F. and COOCH, F. G. 1968. The genetics of polymorphism in the goose *Anser caerulescens. Evolution* 22:289–300.

HANSON, H. C. 1967. Characters of age, sex and sexual maturity in Canada Geese. *Ill. Nat. Hist. Surv. Div. Biol. Notes,* No. 49.

HIGGINS, K. F. 1969. Bursal depths of Lesser Snow and small Canada Geese. *Jour. Wildl. Mgmt.* 33:1006–8.

HIGGINS, K. F. and SCHOONOVERML, J. 1969. Ageing small Canada Geese by neck plumage. *Jour. Wildl. Mgmt.* 33:212–4.

KUYKEN, E. 1970. Melanisme, albinisme en andere kleurafwijkingen bij wilde ganzen. *Gerfaut* 60:3–25.

LYNCH, J. J. and SINGLETON, J. R. 1964. Winter appraisals of annual productivity in geese and other water birds. *Wildfowl Trust Ann. Rep.* 15:114–26.

OGILVIE, M. A. and WALLACE, D. I. M. 1975. Field identification of grey geese. *Brit. Birds* 68:57–67.

VAN IMPE, J. 1970. Het voorkomen van een gele oogring bij Kolganzen, *Anser a. albifrons* Scopoli. *Gerfaut* 60:224–6.

CHAPTER 3: ECOLOGY, FOOD AND FEEDING

EBBINGE, B., CANTERS, K. and DRENT, R. 1975. Foraging routines and estimated daily food intake in Barnacle Geese wintering in the northern Netherlands. *Wildfowl* 26:5–19.

HARWOOD, J. 1974. The grazing strategies of Blue Geese *Anser caerulescens*. Unpub. Ph.D. Thesis. Univ. of Western Ontario.

HUDEC, K. 1973. Die Nahrung der Graugans, *Anser anser*, in Südmähren. *Zool. Listy* 22:41–58.

KEAR, J. 1963. The history of potato-eating by wildfowl in Britain. *Wildfowl Trust Ann. Rep.* 14:54–65.

KEAR, J. 1966. The food of geese. *Int. Zoo Yrbk.* 6:96–103.

KOERNER, J. W., BOOKHOUT, T. A. and BEDNARIK, K. E. 1974. Movements of Canada Geese color-marked near southwestern Lake Erie. *Jour. Wildl. Mgmt.* 38:275–89.

LOOSJES, M. 1974. Over terreingebruik, verstoringen en voedsel van Grauwe Ganzen *Anser anser* in een brak getijdengebied. *Limosa* 47:121–43.

MATTOCKS, J. G. 1971. Goose feeding and cellulose digestion. *Wildfowl* 22:107–13.

NEWTON, I. and CAMPBELL, C. R. G. 1970. Goose studies at Loch Leven in 1967–68. *Scot. Birds* 6:5–18.

NEWTON, I., THOM, V. M. and BROTHERSTON, W. 1973. Behaviour and distribution of wild geese in south-east Scotland. *Wildfowl* 24:111–22.

OWEN, M. 1971. The selection of feeding site by White-fronted Geese in winter. *J. Appl. Ecol.* 8:905–17.

OWEN, M. 1972. Some factors affecting food intake and selection in White-fronted Geese. *J. Anim. Ecol.* 41:79–92.

PHILIPPONA, J. and MEULEN, H. T. v. de. 1969. De ganzen in het midden en zuiden van Friesland. *Limosa* 42:139–55.

POLLARD, D. F. W. and WALTERS-DAVIES, P. 1968. A preliminary study of the feeding of the Greenland White-fronted Goose *Anser albifrons flavirostris* in Cardiganshire. *Wildfowl* 19:108–16.

RANWELL, D. S. and DOWNING, B. M. 1959. Brent Goose winter feeding pattern. *Anim. Behav.* 7:42–56.

RAVELING, D. G., CREWS, W. E. and KLIMSTRA, W. D. 1972. Activity patterns of Canada Geese during winter. *Wilson Bull.* 84:278–95.

ROCHARD, J. B. A. and KEAR, J. 1970. Field trials of the reactions of sheep to goose droppings on pasture. *Wildfowl* 21:108–9.

YELVERTON, C. S. and QUAY, T. L. 1959. Food habits of the Canada Goose at Lake Mattamuskeet, North Carolina. *Game Div. N. Ca. Wildl. Res. Comm.* March 1959.

CHAPTER 4: BREEDING

BARRY, T. W. 1956. Observations of a nesting colony of American Brant. *Auk* 73:193–202.

BARRY, T. W. 1962. Effect of late seasons on Atlantic Brant production. *Jour. Wild. Mgmt.* 26:19–26.

BOYD, H. 1953. On encounters between wild White-fronted Geese in winter flocks. *Behaviour* 5:85–129.

BRAKHAGE, G. K. 1965. Biology and behavior of tub-nesting Canada Geese. *Jour. Wildl. Mgmt.* 29:751–71.

COOCH, F. G., STIRRETT, G. M. and BOYER, G. F. 1960. Autumn weights of Blue Geese *(Chen caerulescens)*. *Auk* 77:460–5.

CRAIGHEAD, F. C. and CRAIGHEAD, J. J. 1949. Nesting Canada Geese on the Upper Snake River. *Jour. Wildl. Mgmt.* 13:51–64.

CRAIGHEAD, J. J. and STOCKSTAD, D. S. 1961. Evaluating the use of aerial nesting platforms by Canada Geese. *Jour. Wildl. Mgmt.* 25:363–72.

FLATH, D. L. 1972. Canada Goose–Osprey interactions. *Auk* 89:446–7.

GARDARSSON, A. 1976. Population and production of the Pink-footed Goose *(Anser brachyrhynchus)* in Thjórsárver, 1971–1974. Mimeo Report, Reykjavik.

GEIS, M. B., 1956. Productivity of Canada Geese in the Flathead Valley, Montana. *Jour. Wildl. Mgmt.* 20:409–19.

HANSON, H. C. 1962. The dynamics of condition factors in Canada Geese and their relation to seasonal stresses. *Arctic Inst. N. Amer. Tech. Paper* 12.

HANSON, W. C. and BROWNING, R. L. 1959. Nesting studies of Canada Geese on the Hanford reservation, 1953–56. *Jour. Wildl. Mgmt.* 23:129–36.

HARVEY, J. M. 1971. Factors affecting Blue Goose nesting success. *Canad. J. Zool.* 49:223–34.

HUDEC, K. 1971. The breeding environment of the Greylag Goose *(Anser anser)* in Czechoslovakia. *Zool. Listy* 20:177–94.

HUDEC, K. and KUX, K. 1971. The clutch size of the Greylag Goose *(Anser anser)* in Czechoslovakia. *Zool. Listy* 20:365–76.

INGLIS, I. R. 1976. Agonistic behaviour of breeding Pink-footed Geese with reference to Ryder's hypothesis. *Wildfowl* 27:95–9.

JOHNSGARD, P. A. 1965. *Handbook of Waterfowl Behavior.* Ithaca: Cornell Univ. Press.

JONES, R. N. and OBBARD, M. 1970. Canada Goose killed by Arctic Loon and subsequent pairing of its mate. *Auk* 87:370–1.

KISTCHINSKI, A. A. 1971. Biological notes on the Emperor Goose in north-east Siberia. *Wildfowl* 22:29–34.

KONDLA, N. G. 1973. Canada Goose goslings leaving cliff nest. *Auk* 90:890.

KOSSACK, C. W. 1950. Breeding habits of Canada Geese under refuge conditions. *Amer. Mid. Nat.* 43:627–49.

KRECHMAR, A. V. and LEONOVITCH, V. V. 1967. (Distribution and biology of the Red-breasted Goose during the nesting period.) *Probl. Severa* 11:229–34. (In Russian.)

KYDRALIEV, A. 1967. (The Bar-headed Goose in Tian Shan.) *Ornitologiya* 8:245–53. (In Russian.)

LeFEBVRE, E. and RAVELING, D. G. 1967. Distribution of Canada Geese in winter as related to heat loss at varying environmental temperatures. *Jour. Wildl. Mgmt.* 31:538–46.

LEMIEUX, L. 1959. The breeding biology of the Greater Snow Goose on Bylot Island, Northwest Territories. *Canad. Fld. Nat.* 73:117–28.

LEIFF, B. C. 1969. Eider hatching goose eggs. *Wilson Bull.* 81:465–6.

McEWEN, E. H. 1958. Observations on the Lesser Snow Goose nesting grounds, Egg River, Banks Island. *Canad. Fld. Nat.* 72:122–7.

MacInnes, C. D. 1962. Nesting of small Canada Geese near Eskimo Point, Northwest Territories. *Jour. Wildl. Mgmt.* 26:247–56.

MacInnes, C. D., Davis, R. A., Jones, R. N., Lieff, B. C. and Pakulak, A. J. 1974. Reproductive efficiency of McConnell River small Canada Geese. *Jour. Wildl. Mgmt.* 38:686–707.

Mickelson, P. G. 1975. Breeding biology of Cackling Geese and associated species on the Yukon–Kuskokwim Delta, Alaska. *Wildl. Monog.* 45.

Munro, D. A. 1960. Factors affecting reproduction of the Canada Goose *(Branta canadensis)*. *Proc. Int. Orn. Cong.* 12:542–56.

Norderhaug, M., Ogilvie, M. A. and Taylor, R. J. F. 1965. Breeding success of geese in west Spitsbergen 1964. *Wildfowl Trust Ann. Rep.* 16:106–10.

Nyholm, E. S. 1965. Ecological observations on the geese of Spitsbergen. *Ann. Zool. Fenn.* 2:197–207.

Ogilvie, M. A. 1976. *The Winter Birds*. London: Michael Joseph.

Prevett, J. P. and Prevett, L. S. 1973. Egg retrieval by Blue Geese. *Auk* 90:202–4.

Ryder, J. P. 1969. Egg-eating by wild Lesser Snow Geese *(Anser caerulescens)*. *Avic. Mag.* 75:23–4.

Ryder, J. P. 1971. Size difference between Ross' and Snow Goose eggs at Karrak Lake, Northwest Territories, in 1968. *Wilson Bull.* 83:438–9.

Ryder, J. P. 1971. Distribution and breeding biology of the Lesser Snow Goose in central Arctic Canada. *Wildfowl* 22:18–28.

Ryder, J. P. 1972. Biology of nesting Ross's Geese. *Ardea* 60:185–217.

Salomonsen, F. 1972. Zoogeographical and ecological problems of arctic birds. *Proc. Int. Orn. Cong.* 15:25–72.

Sherwood, G. A. 1967. Behavior of family groups of Canada Geese. *32nd N. Am. Wildl. Conf. Trans:* 340–55.

Stephenson, J. D. and Smart, G. 1972. Egg measurements for three endangered species. *Auk* 89:191–2.

Syroechkovskii, E. 1975. (Egg weight and its effect on mortality of young Snow Geese on Wrangel Island.) *Zool. Zh.* 54:408–12. (In Russian.)

Tristan, D. F. and Zveskin, A. G. 1960. (The biology of the Bar-headed Goose in Tian Shan.) *Zool. Zh.* 39:145–7. (In Russian.)

Tuck, L. M. and Lemieux, L. 1959. The avifauna of Bylot Island. *Dansk Orn. Foren. Tidsskr.* 53:137–54.

Uspenski, S. M. 1964. Die Weisswangengans in der Sowjetunion. *Falke* 11:7–10.

Will, G. C. and Crawford, G. I. 1970. Elevated and floating nest structures for Canada Geese. *Jour. Wildl. Mgmt.* 34:583–6.

Wood, J. S. 1965. Some associations of behavior to reproductive development in Canada Geese. *Jour. Wildl. Mgmt.* 29:237–44.

Young, J. G. 1972. Breeding biology of feral Greylag Geese in south-west Scotland. *Wildfowl* 23:83–7.

CHAPTER 5: COUNTING, RINGING AND POPULATION DYNAMICS

Ankney, C. D. 1975. Neckbands contribute to starvation in female Lesser Snow Geese. *Jour. Wildl. Mgmt.* 39:825–6.

BOYD, H. 1962. Population dynamics and the exploitation of ducks and geese. *Brit. Ecol. Soc. Symp.:* 85–95.

BOYD, H. 1976. Mortality rates of Hudson Bay Snow Geese. *CWS Prog. Notes,* No. 61.

BOYD, H. and OGILVIE, M. A. 1969. Changes in the British-wintering population of the Pink-footed Goose from 1950–1975. *Wildfowl* 20:33–46.

CHAPMAN, J. A., HENNY, C. J. and WIGHT, H. M. 1969. The status, population dynamics, and harvest of the Dusky Canada Goose. *Wildl. Monog.* 18.

COOCH, C. G. 1957. Mass ringing of flightless Blue and Lesser Snow Geese in Canada's eastern Arctic. *Wildfowl Trust Ann. Rep.* 8:58–67.

CURTIS, S. G. 1976. Estimating numbers of Lesser Snow Geese. *CWS Biometrics Section, MS Reports,* No. 14.

EYGENRAAM, J. A. 1960. Goose-netting in the Netherlands. *Wildfowl Trust Ann. Rep.* 11:77–79.

IMBER, M. J. 1968. Sex ratios in Canada Goose populations. *Jour. Wildl. Mgmt.* 32:905–20.

HIGGINS, K. F., LINDER, R. L. and SPRINGER, P. F. 1969. A comparison of methods used to obtain age ratios of Snow and Canada Geese. *Jour. Wildl. Mgmt.* 33:949–56.

HUDEC, K. and FORMANEK, J. 1970. Ringing results of the Greylag Goose *(Anser anser)* in Czechoslovakia. *Zool. Listy* 19:145–61.

KERBES, R. H. 1975. The nesting population of Lesser Snow Geese in the eastern Canadian Arctic: a photographic inventory of June 1973. *CWS Rep. Ser.* No. 35.

KERBES, R. H., OGILVIE, M. A. and BOYD, H. 1971. Pink-footed Geese of Iceland and Greenland: a population review based on an aerial survey of Thjórsárver, Iceland. *Wildfowl* 22:5–17.

LUND, HJ. M-K. 1965. Marking of 240 Greylags *(Anser a. anser L.)* in Norway. *Trans. Cong. Int. Union Game Biol.* 6:267–70.

LYNCH, J. J. and SINGLETON, J. R. 1964. Winter appraisals of annual productivity in geese and other water birds. *Wildfowl Trust Ann. Rep.* 15:114–26.

MILLER, H. and DZUBIN, A. 1965. Regrouping of family members of the White-fronted Goose *(Anser albifrons)* after individual release. *Bird-Banding* 36:184–91.

OGILVIE, M. A. and BOYD, H. 1976. The numbers of Pink-footed and Greylag Geese wintering in Britain: observations 1969–1975 and predictions 1976–1980. *Wildfowl* 27:63–76.

OGILVIE, M. A. and ST. JOSEPH, A. K. M. 1976. The Dark-bellied Brent Goose in Britain and Europe, 1955–76. *Brit. Birds* 69:422–39.

PALUDAN, K. 1973. Migration and survival of *Anser anser* ringed in Denmark. *Vid. Medd. Dansk Natur. Foren.* 136:217–32.

RIENECKER, W. C. 1965. A summary of band returns from Lesser Snow Geese *(Chen hyperborea)* of the Pacific Flyway. *Calif. Fish & Game* 51:132–46.

SCOTT, P. and FISHER, J. 1953. *A Thousand Geese.* London: Collins.

VAUGHT, R. W. and ARTHUR, G. C. 1965. Migration routes and mortality rates of Canada Geese banded in Hudson Bay lowlands. *Jour. Wildl. Mgmt.* 29:244–52.

VAUGHT, R. W. and KIRSCH, L. M. 1966. Canada Geese of the eastern prairie population, with special reference to the Swan Lake flock. *Mo. Dept. Conserv., Tech. Bull.* 3.

CHAPTER 6: DISTRIBUTION AND STATUS

BOFENSCHEN, G. and KRAMER, H. 1969. Überwinterungsplätze der Wildschwäne und Wildgänse im bereich der Nordsee und der westlichen Ostseeküste. *Dechiana* 122:87–116.

BOYD, H. 1968. Barnacle Geese in the west of Scotland, 1957–1967. *Wildfowl* 19:96–107.

BOYD, H. 1976. Estimates of total numbers in the Hudson Bay population of Lesser Snow Geese, 1964–1973. *CWS Prog. Notes*, No. 63.

DAAS, H. D. J. 1967. De Kleine Rietgans *(A. f. brachyrhynchus)* als Wintergast in Nederland. *RIVON* 1963:1–100.

DZUBIN, A. 1965. A study of migrating Ross Geese in western Saskatchewan. *Condor* 67:511–34.

DZUBIN, A., BOYD, H. and STEPHEN, W. T. D. 1975. Blue and Snow Goose distribution in the Mississippi and Central Flyways, 1951–71. *CWS Prog. Notes*, No. 54.

FOG, M. 1971. Haunts in Denmark for White-fronted Goose *(Anser albifrons)*, Bean Goose *(Anser fabalis* non *brachyrhynchus)* and Pink-footed Goose *(Anser fabalis brachyrhynchus)*. *Dan. Rev. Game Biol.* Vol. 6, No. 3.

FOG, M. 1976. Gåsetaellinger 1975–76. *Dansk Vildt.* 1975–76: 15–16.

GRIEB, J. R. 1970. The Shortgrass Prairie Canada Goose population. *Wildl. Monog.* 22.

HANSEN, H. A. 1962. Canada Geese of coastal Alaska. *Trans. N. Amer. Wildl. Conf.* 27:301–20.

HANSEN, H. A. and NELSON, U. C. 1957. Brant of the Bering Sea: migration and mortality. *Trans. N. Amer. Wildl. Conf.* 22:237–56.

HEYLAND, J. D. and BOYD, H. 1970. Greater Snow Geese in northwest Greenland. *Dansk Orn. Foren. Tidsskr.* 64:198–9.

IMBER, M. J. 1971. The identity of New Zealand's Canada Geese. *Notornis* 18:253–60.

ISAKOV, Y. 1972. (Distribution and numbers of the Greylag Goose population in the Soviet Union.) Pp. 9–12 in *Geese in the USSR* (Ed. E. Kumari). (In Russian.)

JONES, R. D. 1963. Buldir Island, site of the remnant breeding population of Aleutian Canada Geese. *Wildfowl Trust Ann. Rep.* 14:80–83.

JONES, R. D. 1970. Reproductive success and age distribution of Black Brant. *Jour. Wildl. Mgmt.* 34:328–33.

JOHNSON, A. and HAFNER, H. 1970. Winter wildfowl counts in south-east Europe and western Turkey. *Wildfowl* 21:22–36.

KACZYNSKI, C. F. and CHAMBERLAIN, E. B. 1968. Aerial surveys of Canada Geese and Black Ducks in eastern Canada. *U.S. Fish & Wildl. Sci. Rep.* 118:1–29.

KING, J. G. 1970. The swans and geese of Alaska's Arctic Slope. *Wildfowl* 21:11–17.

KISTCHINSKI, A. A. 1973. Waterfowl in north-east Asia. *Wildfowl* 24:88–102.

KORHONEN, S. 1972. Tuloksia Kanadanhanhen istutuskokeilusta. *Suomen Riista* 24:52–6.

KUMARI, E. 1971. Passage of the Barnacle Goose through the Baltic area. *Wildfowl* 22:35–43.

LEBRET, T., MULDER, TH., PHILIPPONA, J. and TIMMERMAN, A. 1976. *Wilde Ganzen in Nederland*. Zutphen: Thieme.

LEMIEUX, L. 1959. Histoire naturelle et aménagement de la Grande Oie Blanche *Chen hyperborea atlanticus*. *Nat. Canad.* 86:133–92.

LYNCH, J. J. and VOELZER, J. F. 1974. 1973 productivity and mortality among geese, swans and brant wintering in North America. *US Fish & Wildl. Serv. Prog. Rep.*

MILLER, H. W., DZUBIN, A. and SWEET, J. T. 1968. Distribution and mortality of Saskatchewan-banded White-fronted Geese. *Trans. N. Amer. Wildl. Conf.* 33:101–119.

MORZER-BRUIJNS, M. F. 1966. Pleisterplaatzen van Wilde Ganzen in Nederland. *Het Vogeljaar* 14:235–60.

MORZER-BRUIJNS, M. F., PHILIPPONA, J. and TIMMERMAN, A. 1973. Survey of the winter distribution of Palaearctic geese in Europe, Western Asia and North Africa. *IWRB Goose Research Group Rep.*

MORENO, A. S. 1975. Censos de aves acuaticas en las Marismas del Guadalquivir inviernos 1967–68 y de 1972 a 1975. *Ardeola* 21:133–51.

NELSON, U. C. and HANSEN, H. A. 1959. The Cackling Goose—its migration and management. *Trans. N. Amer. Wildl. Conf.* 24:174–87.

OGILVIE, M. A. 1968. The numbers and distribution of the European White-fronted Goose in Britain. *Bird Study* 15:2–15.

OGILVIE, M. A. 1969. The status of the Canada Goose in Britain 1967–69. *Wildfowl* 20:79–85.

OGILVIE, M. A. 1970. The status of wild geese in Britain and Ireland. Pp. 249–57 in *The New Wildfowler in the 1970s* (Ed. N. M. Sedgwick, P. Whitaker and J. Harrison). London: Barrie and Jenkins.

OGILVIE, M. A. and BOYD, H. 1975. Greenland Barnacle Geese in the British Isles. *Wildfowl* 26:135–47.

OGILVIE, M. A. and BOYD, H. 1976. The numbers of Pink-footed and Greylag Geese wintering in Britain: observations 1969–1975 and predictions 1976–1980. *Wildfowl* 27:63–76.

OGILVIE, M. A. and ST. JOSEPH, A. K. M. 1976. The Dark-bellied Brent Goose in Britain and Europe, 1955–76. *Brit. Birds* 69:422–39.

OWEN, M. and CAMPBELL, C. R. G. 1974. Recent studies on Barnacle Geese at Caerlaverock. *Scot. Birds* 8:181–93.

PAAKSPU, V. 1972. (Present-day studies of the Greylag Goose population in the Matsalu Bay.) Pp. 13–19 in *Geese in the USSR* (Ed. E. Kumari). (In Russian.)

PALUDAN, K. 1965. Grågåsen traek og faeldningstraek. *Dansk Vildt.* 12.

PENKALA, J. M., APPLEGATE, J. E. and WOLGAST, L. J. 1975. Management of Atlantic Brant: implications of existing data. *Trans. N. Amer. Wildl. Conf.* 40:325–33.

PHILIPPONA, J. 1976. Waardering van ganzenpleisterplaatsen. *Het Vogeljaar* 24:10–13.

PREVETT, J. P. and MACINNES, C. D. 1972. The number of Ross' Geese in central North America. *Condor* 74:431–8.

ROOTH, J. 1971. The occurrence of the Greylag Goose *Anser anser* in the western part of its distribution area. *Ardea* 59:17–27.

ROUX, F. and TAMISIER, A. 1969. Size of the populations and extent of world distribution of Anatidae wintering in France. *Oiseau* 39:121–39.

RUTSCHKE, E. 1964. Bless *(Anser albifrons)* und Saat *(Anser fabalis)* gans auf Rast- und Überwinterungsplätzen im Gebiet der Mark. *Beitr. Vogelk.* 9:420–6.

SMITH, R. H. and JENSEN, G. H. 1970. Black Brant on the mainland coast of Mexico. *Trans. N. Amer. Wildl. Conf.* 35:227–41.

SOIKELLI, M. 1973. Decrease in numbers of migrating Lesser White-fronted Geese *Anser erythropus* in Finland. *Riistatiet Julk* 33:27–30.

STERBETZ, I. 1976. (Development of wild-geese migration on the Hungarian gathering-places.) *Aquila* 82:181–94. (In Hungarian.)

USPENSKI, S. M. 1965. *Die Wildgänse Nordeurasiens.* Wittemberg Lutherstadt: A. Ziemsen Verlag.

USPENSKI, S. M. 1965. The geese of Wrangel Island. *Wildfowl Trust Ann. Rep.* 16:126–8.

VAN IMPE, J. 1973. Bepaling in het veld van leeftijdsklassen bij de Rietgans *Anser fabalis. Limosa* 46:192–8.

VERTSE, A. 1967. Ecological problems of White-fronted Geese passing the winter in Hungary. Presence of White-fronted Geese in the last century. *Aquila* 73–74:11–32. (In Hungarian.)

VOELZER, J. F. 1976. Productivity and mortality among geese, swans and brant wintering in North America 1974. *U.S. Fish & Wildl. Serv. Prog. Rep.*

YOCOM, C. F. 1965. Estimated populations of Great Basin Canada Geese over their breeding range in western Canada and western United States. *Murrelei* 46:19–26.

CHAPTER 7: MIGRATION

ANDERSSON, Å. 1969. Hallands Väderö som ruggningsplats för Grågås *Anser anser* under 1800-talet. *Vår Fågelvärld* 28:116–23.

BERGER, M. 1972. Formationsflug ohne Phasenbeziehung der Flügelschläge. *J. Orn.* 113:161–9.

BLOKPOEL, H. and GAUTHIER, M. C. 1975. Migration of Lesser Snow and Blue Geese in spring across southern Manitoba. Part 2: Influence of the weather and prediction of major flights. *CWS Rep. Ser.* No. 72.

BLURTON JONES, N. G. 1972. Moult migration of Emperor Geese. *Wildfowl* 23:92–3.

HAACK, W. and RINGLEBEN, H. 1972. Über den Mauserzug nichtbrütender Graugänse *(Anser anser)* im nord- und mitteleuropäischen Raum. *Die Vogelwarte* 26:257–76.

HOLGERSEN, H. 1958. Pinkfeet in Europe: the effect of the cold weather of February 1956 on the distribution of Pink-footed Geese in north-west Europe. *Wildfowl Trust Ann. Rep.* 9:170–4.

LEBRET, T. and TIMMERMAN, A. 1968. Een concentratie van ruiende Grauwe Ganzen *(Anser anser)* in Nederland. *Limosa* 41:2–17.

LISSAMAN, P. B. S. and SHOLLENBERGER, C. A. 1970. Formation flight of birds. *Science* 168:1003–5.

LUND, Hj. M-K. 1971. Ringing of *Anser anser* in Norway. *Sterna* 10:247–50.

MARKGREN, G. 1963. Migrating and wintering geese in southernmost Sweden. *Acta Vert.* 2:295–418.

OUWENEEL, G. L. 1969. Ruiende Grauwe Ganzen *(Anser anser)* in het Haringvliet in de zomer van 1969. *Limosa* 42:206–23.

SALOMONSEN, F. 1968. The moult migration. *Wildfowl* 19:5–24.

STERLING, T. and DZUBIN, A. 1967. Canada Goose molt migrations to the Northwest Territories. *Trans. N. Amer. Wildl. Conf.* 32:355–73.

TAYLOR, J. 1953. A possible moult-migration of Pink-footed Geese. *Ibis* 95:638–42.

WALKER, A. F. G. 1970. The moult migration of Yorkshire Canada Geese. *Wildfowl* 21:99–104.

WILLIAMS, T. C., KLONOWSKI, T. J. and BERKELEY, P. 1976. Angle of Canada Goose V flight formation measured by radar. *Auk* 93:554–9.

WILLIAMSON, K. 1968. Goose emigration from western Scotland. *Scot. Birds* 5:71–89.

CHAPTER 8: EXPLOITATION AND CONSERVATION

BELL, R. Q. and KLIMSTRA, W. D. 1970. Feeding activities of Canada Geese in southern Illinois. *Trans. Ill. State Acad. Sci.* 63:295–304.

BRAKHAGE, G. K., REEVES, H. M. and HUNT, R. A. 1971. The Canada Goose tagging program in Wisconsin. *Trans. N. Amer. Wildl. Conf.* 36:275–95.

DAVENPORT, D. A., SHERWOOD, G. A. and MURDY, H. W. 1973. A method to determine waterfowl shooting distances. *Wildl. Soc. Bull.* 1:101–5.

ELDER, W. H. 1955. Fluoroscopic measures of shooting pressure on Pink-footed and Grey Lag Geese. *Wildfowl Trust Ann. Rep.* 7:123–6.

FRILEY, C. E. 1959. Controlled goose shooting at Michigan's Swan Creek Highbanks. *Trans. N. Amer. Wildl. Conf.* 24:245–60.

HAMILTON, G. A. and STANLEY, P. I. 1975. Further cases of poisoning of wild geese by an organophosphorous winter wheat seed treatment. *Wildfowl* 26:49–54.

HANSON, H. C. and CURRIE, C. 1957. The kill of wild geese by the natives of the Hudson–James Bay region. *Arctic* 10:211–29.

KEAR, J. 1963. The protection of crops from damage by wildfowl. *Wildfowl Trust Ann. Rep.* 14:66–71.

KEAR, J. 1970. The experimental assessment of goose damage to agricultural crops. *Biol. Conserv.* 2:206–12.

KLEIN, D. A. 1966. Waterfowl in the economy of the Eskimos on the Yukon–Kuskokwim Delta, Alaska. *Arctic* 19:319–36.

LAMPIO, T. 1974. Bag limits, sale, export, import and recolonisation of waterfowl. *Finn. Game Res.* 34:51–6.

LAMPIO, T. 1974. Protection of waterfowl in Europe. *Finn. Game Res.* 34:15–33.

LAMPIO, T., VALENTINCIC, S. and MICHAELIS, H. K. 1974. Methods and practices of waterfowl hunting rationalisation. *Finn. Game Res.* 34:36–46.

OWEN, M. 1975. Cutting and fertilising grassland for winter goose management. *Jour. Wildl. Mgmt.* 39:163–7.

TAUTIN, J. and Low, J. B. 1975. Harvest trends of Canada Geese in Utah. *Trans. N. Amer. Wildl. Conf.* 40:334–45.

Index

Numbers in italics refer to colour plates

343

Approaching Multivariate Analysis

Approaching Multivariate Analysis

A practical introduction

2nd edition

Pat Dugard, John Todman and Harry Staines

Routledge
Taylor & Francis Group

LONDON AND NEW YORK

Published in 2010
by Routledge
2 Park Square, Milton Park, Abingdon, Oxfordshire OX14 4RN

Simultaneously published in the USA and Canada
by Routledge
711 Third Avenue, New York, NY 10017

First issued in paperback 2014

Routledge is an imprint of the Taylor & Francis Group, an informa business

Copyright © 2010 Psychology Press

Typeset in Times by RefineCatch Limited, Bungay, Suffolk
Cover design by Jim Wilkie
Cover artwork by Amy Todman

British Library Cataloguing in Publication Data
A catalogue record for this book is available from the British Library

Library of Congress Cataloging-in-Publication Data
Dugard, Pat.
    Approaching multivariate analysis : a practical introduction / Pat Dugard,
    John Todman, and Harry Staines. – 2nd ed.
        p. cm.
    Includes bibliographical references and index.
    ISBN 978–0–415–47828–1 (hbk)
    ISBN 978–0–415–64591–1 (pbk)
    1. Psychometrics.   2. Psychology—Statistical methods.   3. Multivariate
    analysis.   I. Todman, John B.   II. Staines, Harry.   III. Title.
    BF39.T57 2009
    150.1'519535—dc22   2009024732

To friends

Contents

Preface to the second edition

The ink was scarcely dry on the first edition before one of our medical friends said we should do a version for doctors, and this is the result. We have added three chapters on topics that are of special interest to medical researchers, though they could be useful to psychologists also, as our examples demonstrate. We have updated to SPSS version 16 and made some revisions to earlier chapters, especially Chapters 1 and 10. Chapters 2–14 have examples drawn from psychology fully demonstrated in the text, as in the previous edition, but we have added corresponding examples from medicine. In the text the medical examples are summarized in Example Boxes, but the full demonstrations are available, along with all the datasets, on the book website (www.psypress.com/multivariate-analysis).

The medical and psychology examples are exactly matched, and none uses very technical information, so in fact any scientist could read and understand them. However we think that, for most people, it is easier to see how unfamiliar statistical techniques could be applied if the demonstration examples are drawn from a familiar field of study.

This time we have provided an Appendix with some notes on using SPSS syntax. For selected analyses from the book, we show both the SPSS syntax and also the corresponding SAS syntax. The latter is for the benefit of those medical researchers who are required to provide their results in SAS for official bodies such as the FDA or EMEA. In this edition we have used SPSS 16.0, AMOS 16.0 and SAS 9.

Before we could finish work on this edition, our friend and co-author John Todman died. He was a great inspiration to many students and researchers and he is greatly missed. He enjoyed working with us until close to the end and hoped that readers would be empowered by his work.

As always, we are grateful to John Morris of the University of Dundee Department of Psychology, who gave us excellent technical support. We were helped in finding suitable medical examples by several medical friends, especially Suzy Duckworth. Chandru and Sadhana Chandrasekar, Margaret Crocker and Sue Povey also contributed their expertise. David Clark-Carter's careful review prompted us to make some clarifications and corrections. We are grateful to all of them but of course any errors are our own.

Once again we have found it extremely enjoyable working on this project, trying to share our enthusiasm and make some statistical methods that may be unfamiliar more accessible. We hope you will enjoy trying out methods you may not have used before. When you have gained some confidence, you should be ready to learn more about these techniques and, as before, we have provided some recommended further reading.

Preface to the first edition

Both of us have spent many hours teaching students statistics and working with researchers to help them to understand their data. In our youth we taught many students to do analysis of variance on a calculator, but all that changed with the advent of statistical software such as SPSS, which would do all the calculations in what seemed like an instant. The downside for students was that they were expected to understand quite complex datasets at a much earlier stage in their careers, often around the third year of an undergraduate course. Our experience suggests that once more than two variables are involved, most people find understanding and using appropriate methods pretty daunting. So the ease of doing the calculations is offset by the difficulty of deciding what should be done and understanding the results. This book is an attempt to give students and researchers a way into this area, which will show them how to get started and where to go for more detailed information once some confidence has been gained. The level here is introductory and there is much more to learn about all of the methods we describe. For two methods that many readers will have already encountered, analysis of variance and regression, we give a more extended account, but even for those we have omitted much that will be found in more advanced texts.

The methods are explained using intuitive and geometrical ideas and diagrams; there is no mathematical justification. The uses of each method described are illustrated using extended examples that are analysed using SPSS (or, in two cases, another SPSS product called AMOS). We show how to set the analyses up and how to understand the output. At the end of each chapter we briefly illustrate how the results might be written up for a journal article. At the end of the book is a list of books that give more extended treatments of the methods and a grid to show for which chapters they are most useful. We have kept references to a minimum in the text, but a few chapters do have references to a paper or advanced text and these are listed at the end of those chapters.

We have greatly enjoyed working on this project and we hope to convey something of our enthusiasm to our readers. It is hard work for any scientist to learn to use statistics effectively, but the rewards are great. Your data are trying to tell you a story, perhaps an exciting story that no previous investigator has heard; you owe it to yourself and your team to learn enough to hear it clearly, and then tell it to others in words they can understand. About 100 years ago the great German mathematician David Hilbert said that if you cannot explain it to the next person you meet in the street, you have not understood it properly. This rather overstates the case, but we do believe that we can make hard ideas accessible, though it takes a lot of effort. We have tried to do that here, and we hope our readers will be empowered and share that power with their own readers and students.

1 Multivariate techniques in context

Using this book

In this book we aim to help students and researchers who have experimental or observational multivariate data to understand and make best use of them. Your data have a story to tell: first you must listen carefully to that story yourself, then tell it as clearly as you can to your readers. We describe 13 types of multivariate technique and show how they can be used in the following chapters. Many readers will have already encountered two of the methods, analysis of variance (ANOVA) and regression, so we take our description of these further than the introductory level that we use for all the others. If you are encountering ANOVA for the first time, you may wish to try out a one-way analysis before returning to the rest of the chapter. If you have not met regression before, you may prefer to try out some examples before proceeding to hierarchical regression.

In the final chapter, we briefly outline some approaches to the very large topic of longitudinal data. There is a list of 'Further reading' at the end of the book, which gives suggestions for exploring further the topics in each of the chapters. The Appendix shows the SPSS syntax for selected analyses. For the benefit of those medical researchers who are required to provide results in SAS we show, when possible, the corresponding SAS syntax.

In this chapter we briefly describe the methods for dealing with multivariate data that we introduce in Chapters 2–14. If you do not want to read the whole book but just want to identify a method to help you with your current problem, the rest of this chapter may help you to decide where to start looking. Or, since each of the following chapters begins with an introductory section that describes the sort of problem for which the method is useful, you could read each of these until you find one that seems promising If you want to start learning about multivariate methods more generally, then the following summary of how the methods are related will provide a useful context. However, you could just plunge right in at Chapter 2, and perhaps return to this when you have already started to see how some of the methods work.

We show how to use SPSS to apply all but two of the methods we consider, with most of the dialog boxes shown along with the output. Some of the methods have many options and facilities, and we do not demonstrate all of them. One way to find out about those we do not discuss is to right click on any item in a dialog box. This opens a small information window. The Help file is also useful: click **Help** then **Topics** on the menu bar to get an index that you can scroll through. You can also search for key words. Some Help pages offer a tutorial that can be accessed by clicking **Show me** at the bottom of the page.

Two of the methods we introduce, confirmatory factor analysis and path analysis (both being aspects of structural equation modelling), are not covered adequately by SPSS, so we give a very brief introduction to AMOS, which is a statistical package designed for these analyses (it is also an SPSS product).

Many of the datasets we use are fabricated so that particular points can be demonstrated, but they are always described in the context of realistic experiments. For each dataset we have described two experiments, one in psychology and another in medicine. The analysis is fully described in the text for the psychology experiment. The medical experiment is summarized in an Example Box in the text, and the full analysis is on the book website. The homepage is www.psypress.com/multivariate-analysis, and you can go straight to the medical examples at www.psypress.com/multivariate-analysis/medical-examples, or straight to the datasets at www.psypress.com/multivariate-analysis/datasets. The medical examples are listed by chapter, and the datasets just by name.

We use real data where we have a set that exactly matches our requirements. Small datasets are also printed in the text, but for larger ones we usually just show a few lines to demonstrate the layout. All of the datasets used can be obtained in full from the book website. The website names of all datasets appear at the end of the table captions.

Statistics in research

The primary objective of any research project is to improve understanding of some process or phenomenon, or to assist in the solution of some practical problem. Almost always, it will involve collecting and interpreting data. Elementary statistics provides methods for summarizing and displaying observations on one or two variables, and for testing some hypotheses. Graphical displays such as histograms, boxplots, scatterplots and cross-tabulations make effective use of the two dimensions of the page to expose important features of the data. The familiar t and χ^2 tests, and simple regression, are useful when we are ready to go beyond description and attempt explanation or prediction. Generally, understanding our data may involve any of the following activities (often more than one of them): generating and testing hypotheses, prediction, classification or grouping, investigating dependence among variables, looking for structure, or seeking ways to simplify, reduce or summarize them.

In many research projects, we collect data on several variables, sometimes on many variables, either because we are not sure what will turn out to be important or because we already know or suspect that our problem has several dimensions. At the exploratory or descriptive stage we need ways to look at our data that will enable us to begin to see relationships and patterns of dependence, or identify groups of cases or variables so that some structure can be discerned. Visual displays are very helpful but for more than two variables we need some new approaches. By the time we are in a position to attempt explanation or prediction we already know a lot about the problem. For this stage we need extensions of the familiar methods for testing hypotheses and also a multivariate version of regression.

The techniques described in this book include extensions of elementary methods for hypothesis testing and regression, exploratory methods to assist in discerning important features of datasets with more than two variables, methods for analysing survival data and counts that may depend on covariates, and longitudinal data. In this introductory chapter we shall briefly show how the methods for dealing with three or more variables that are considered in later chapters are related to more familiar methods used with one or two variables, and also to each other.

Terminology and conventions

A variable is *continuous* if it is measured on a scale like length, time or weight, where any values between points on the scale are possible. A variable is *discrete* if only certain values are possible, for instance a COUNT of interactions can take only whole number values and so is discrete.

A *categorical* variable takes just a few values, which need not be numerical: an example would be POLITICAL AFFILIATION, with values 'labour', 'conservative', 'liberal democrat', 'other' and 'none'. There is often room for debate about exactly what values a categorical variable should take: should we for instance include values 'communist' and 'green' rather than put these in with 'other'? Care is needed also to make sure that the categories are mutually exclusive and exhaustive, in other words, that each case belongs to exactly one category. A catch-all category such as 'other' will make sure that every case belongs somewhere. However we also have to be sure that no case can belong to more than one category, as would happen if we grouped ages as 'up to 20', '20–30', '30–40', etc. The values of a categorical variable may be given numerical *codes*, such as 1 to denote 'labour', 2 for 'conservative', and so on.

Any categorical variable is necessarily discrete. A discrete variable with only two values, such as GENDER with values 'male' and 'female', is often called *binary* or *dichotomous*.

Variables may also be described as *quantitative* or *qualitative*. Quantitative variables are counts or measurements and so may be continuous or discrete. Qualitative variables are those such as political affiliation, where any number attached to them can only be a coding. Qualitative variables can only be categorical and so are discrete. In this paragraph we have introduced a convention we use throughout the book: variable names (including those of latent variables, as in factor analysis) appear in small capitals.

Both continuous and discrete variables may be on an *interval* scale, where differences have the same meaning at different parts of the scale. Temperature is measured on an interval scale: a rise of 10 degrees has the same meaning whether it occurs near freezing or on a hot summer day. A *ratio* scale has a real zero: the statement 'I am twice as heavy as you are' makes sense because the weight scale has the same zero whether you use kilograms or pounds. Temperature has only an arbitrary zero, set at the freezing point of water on the Celsius scale but set at 32 degrees below the freezing point of water on the Fahrenheit scale. The statement 'It is twice as hot in this room as it is outside' does not make sense. If it is 10 °C outside and 20 °C inside, then on the Fahrenheit scale the temperatures are 50 °F and 68 °F. Any ratio scale is also an interval scale. A categorical variable is usually only *nominal*: the values have names but not numerical values. Categories may be *ordered*, as for instance in those for the variable FREQUENCY: 'daily', 'weekly', 'monthly', 'less than once a month'. If ordered categories are given numerical codes, care must be taken not to treat the numbers so assigned as belonging to an interval scale.

In this book we abbreviate *dependent variable* to DV and *independent variable* to IV. An IV is a variable that is manipulated for the purposes of an experiment, and a DV is a variable believed to be at least partly determined by the IV(s). A *covariate* is a variable that we cannot manipulate but is recorded because it may influence the DV. IVs and covariates are often jointly referred to as IVs. This is especially the case in the context of regression analysis, where predictor or regressor variables that are really covariates are referred to as IVs.

Some authors describe problems as multivariate only if there are at least two DVs, but we use the term for any problem where we have data on more than two variables. These may be a DV and several IVs or covariates, two or more DVs and several IVs, or we may not know enough to say that some variables are IVs and others depend on them, so all the variables have the same status in the investigation. We refer to the individuals on whom we have measured the variables as *cases*. Usually the cases are individual people, especially when our investigations are in psychology or medicine. But cases can be animals, organizations or other entities. A variable is a property of a case, so it may be a property of a person, or of an animal, organization or other entity. In the SPSS datasheet, cases form the rows and variables are the columns. The set of data, arranged with cases as rows and variables as columns, is referred to as the *dataset, datasheet* or *data matrix*. A matrix is just a rectangular array of numbers.

A *population* denotes all members of some category of interest, which may be people, other entities or a reference set of potential observations. It is often very large or potentially infinite: all children who could be taught to read using our new method, all NHS hospitals in the UK, all pilots who will be trained on our simulator, all present and future psychology students in our university, or even all possible scores that could be obtained with numerous repetitions of a test. Whether we do an experiment or an observational study, we have to use a *sample* from the population of interest. If we want to be able to infer something about a population from work we do with our sample, we need to draw a *random sample* from the population. In a random sample, every member of the population of interest has an equal chance of being included in the sample. This is an ideal that is seldom achieved; the best we can usually manage is a random sample from some part of the population, such as a random sample from this year's psychology students. But if we are doing an experiment, it is essential to use *random assignment* of participants to experimental conditions. This can be achieved with the help of SPSS: just put the ID numbers of the participants in the first column of the datasheet and use **Data**, then **Select Cases** from the menu bar. In the resulting menu, click on the radio button for **Random sample of cases** and then on the box marked **Sample**. On the next menu you can specify the percentage or number of cases you wish to select in your random sample. In this book we use **bold** for SPSS menu items and choices in dialog boxes.

Other conventions we have used include an asterisk (*) to denote multiplication, as is usual when using a computer keyboard, and italics the first time technical terms are used. Brief explanations of many of the technical terms are provided in a Glossary. In the 'Reporting results' sections we have quoted probabilities as given by SPSS rather than giving significance levels, since the actual probabilities are more informative. Where SPSS shows a probability as $p = .000$, this should be interpreted as meaning $p < .001$, and generally this is how we report it.

Testing hypotheses

We use the familiar language of hypothesis testing when we extend our methods to three or more variables. The *null hypothesis* is the one we test, and it usually takes a form such as 'there are no differences among the population means', 'all population variances are equal', 'there is no association among the variables'. A *Type I error* occurs when we reject a null hypothesis that is in fact true. When we say a result is *significant at the 5% level*, we mean we reject the null hypothesis with the probability of a Type I error set at 5% or .05. Even this statement is shorthand: it means 'If the null hypothesis is true then the probability of observing a result at least as extreme as ours because of random variation is .05 or less'. In fact, when we obtain a significant result, *either* the null hypothesis is true and we have observed by chance a rare event, *or* the null hypothesis is not true and we have observed a common event. We usually just say the result is significant at the 5% (or 1% or whatever) level, and we do not always state the null hypothesis explicitly.

When we have only one IV and one DV the available hypothesis tests depend on whether the variables are discrete or continuous, and this is also true when we move to more than one IV or more than one DV. If we do an experiment to compare two groups, we have an IV that has just two values describing the groups, perhaps 'treatment' and 'control', or 'training method A' and 'training method B'. So in this case we have a discrete IV. The DV could be continuous (a measurement of some outcome variable) or discrete (a count of the number of successes in each group perhaps). An experiment may have a continuous IV but this is less common: we might give participants 1, 2, 5 or 10 hours on a training program and measure their performance on a standard task at the end. Observational studies often have continuous IVs (which are really covariates): perhaps we measure heights and IQ scores for some 10-year-old children to see whether intellectual development might be related to physical development. An observational study can also have a discrete IV: we could investigate whether the study hours of students differ in the faculties of arts, science, medicine and law. We will briefly review the methods available for testing hypotheses with one DV and one IV, each of which may be discrete or continuous, and we will indicate how each method may be extended to the multivariate case.

Continuous DV and discrete IV

If we have a discrete IV with two levels and a continuous DV, we can test the hypothesis that the two population means are equal using the *t*-test (Student's *t*), provided that the DV has the same variance in the two populations and is approximately normally distributed. These two assumptions, of normality and equal variance, are called the *parametric assumptions*. If the DV does not satisfy them, the Mann-Whitney test provides an alternative to the *t*-test for independent samples and the Wilcoxon signed rank test can be used for related samples. These are called *non-parametric tests* and the assumptions needed for these are less restrictive.

For a discrete IV with more than two values, analysis of variance (ANOVA, Chapter 2) provides the extension to the *t*-test that we need. This is often referred to as *one-way* ANOVA. Like the *t*-test, it makes the parametric assumptions. ANOVA easily extends to allow more than one discrete IV: this is a *multifactorial* ANOVA (usually just referred to as a *factorial* ANOVA). If we have more than one continuous DV we can use multivariate analysis of variance (MANOVA, Chapter 3). There are non-parametric alternatives but we do not discuss them in this book (see the list of 'Further reading' at the end of the book).

Both DV and IV continuous

Simple linear regression gives us a method for dealing with some problems where both the IV and DV are continuous. It is not suitable for all such problems: a scatter plot with the IV on the horizontal axis and the DV on the vertical axis will suggest whether the two variables are related and, if so, whether the relationship is approximately linear over the range of our observations. Regression also makes parametric assumptions similar to those needed for the t-test and ANOVA: the DV should have an approximately normal distribution whatever the value of the IV, and the variance of the DV should be constant for all values of the IV.

Multiple regression (Chapter 4) extends the method to include several IVs. Even discrete IVs can be included, though usually not more than one or two, and even then only if they have just a few values. Multiple regression can be further extended to include more than one (continuous) DV, but we do not go that far. ANOVA and multiple regression can be combined in analysis of covariance (ANCOVA, Chapter 5), and in Chapter 6 we show how regression and correlation analysis can be used to examine some specific kinds of hypotheses about ways in which variables may be related to one another. Specifically, we consider the use of partial correlation analysis and regression to explore how the effect of one variable on another may be mediated or moderated by another variable.

The particular case where the DV is a survival time is discussed in Chapter 14. The IVs may be discrete (different treatments or conditions) or continuous (often covariates such as age, weight or score on a personality scale).

Both DV and IV discrete

If we have one discrete IV and one discrete DV, then we can display the results in a cross-tabulation, and test the hypothesis that there is no association between the IV and the DV using the χ^2 test of association (sometimes called Pearson's χ^2 test). The same test can be used for an observational study where the two variables have the same status rather than being an IV and a DV. Once we have more than two variables we can no longer use a simple display, and in fact extending the idea of the χ^2 test proves unexpectedly difficult. Loglinear models (Chapter 12) provide an approach to this problem.

Discrete DV and continuous IV

We may have a discrete DV and continuous IV in a situation where we would like to predict group membership from an easily available measurement: perhaps some success has been claimed in predicting whether a tumour is malignant or not from a psychometric test, before a biopsy result is available. We may also hope to manipulate group membership by controlling an IV: an example might be if we could predict membership of the pass/fail categories for our students from number of hours of study, then we may be able to persuade them to adjust their study hours to improve their chance of being in the pass category. Problems like these can be tackled with discriminant analysis or logistic regression. It is possible to use them with just one IV and one DV as in these examples, but they are more commonly used with more than one IV, and we describe this in Chapter 9. They are often used as part of a more exploratory approach.

Poisson regression (Chapter 13) tackles another set of problems; here the DV is a count of the times an event (often adverse, such as a bad reaction to a drug) occurs during an observation period. This count may be influenced by one or more IVs. The IVs can be discrete (different drugs or treatments perhaps) or continuous (length of time a person has smoked, age or other covariates).

The model and prediction

To summarize then: For problems where we are ready to test hypotheses or attempt predictions for continuous DVs we can consider using ANOVA, MANOVA, regression, ANCOVA or survival analysis; for cases where the DV is discrete, loglinear models, discriminant analysis or Poisson regression may be useful. The basic idea with all of these methods is to attempt a *prediction* of the DV for each set of values of the IVs. For methods such as the *t*-test, where we test a null hypothesis of equal means, the null hypothesis predicts that the difference between the means will be zero. In regression, we attempt an explicit prediction of the DV for each value of the IVs. In factorial ANOVA we test whether the level of each IV makes a difference to the predicted mean of the DV. In survival analysis we test whether the level of an IV affects the predicted mean survival time. The method of predicting the DV is called the *model*. IVs that turn out not to be useful in predicting the DV are dropped from the model. ANOVA, MANOVA, regression and ANCOVA are examples of the *General Linear Model* (GLM), a term you will find in the SPSS menus. The loglinear model, Poisson regression and survival analysis are examples of the *Generalized Linear Model*, which is an extension of the GLM. We will discuss these in later sections.

Power

We can set the level of significance (the alpha level) for a hypothesis test (we usually use 5% or 1%). This is the probability of a Type I error, or the probability of rejecting the null hypothesis when it is in fact true. It is easy to choose this probability or level of significance because the null hypothesis is simple: it says something like 'the means are equal' or (in regression) 'the slope is zero' (which is the same as saying the DV does not depend on the regressor variable). The null hypothesis is said to be simple because if the means are equal there is only one possible value for the difference between them (zero). The alternative hypothesis is usually not simple: it says something like 'the means are not equal'. This is not simple because if the means are not equal then the difference between them may be anything. If the null hypothesis is not true we may fail to reject it, and this is called a *Type II error*. We may be especially likely to fail to reject an untrue null hypothesis if it is not *very* untrue, in other words if the means, though unequal, are not very far from equal. If the means are enormously different we are quite unlikely to fail to reject the null hypothesis. So if the null hypothesis is false, the probability of a Type II error depends on by how much it is false. Of course, we do not know by how much it is false; if we did we would not be doing the test. But the probability of a Type II error also depends on the number of observations we have, and of course we do know this, and we might want to manipulate it to reduce the probability of a Type II error.

The *power* of a test is the probability that we do reject a false null hypothesis (so it is 1 – the probability of a Type II error). Whatever our chosen level of significance, we would like the power to be as high as possible. One approach is to set the required power for the smallest effect size that would be of practical interest. We might perhaps say, 'If the means differ by at least 5 units, we want the power to be at least .8'. If we can specify the direction of the change (e.g., an increase in the average test score or a decrease in the time to undertake a task) then we perform a one-tailed test and, other things being equal, the power will be increased. We describe this and alternative approaches to estimating the effect size required, and show how, given the effect size, it is possible to decide on the sample size needed using a dedicated power analysis package such as SPSS SamplePower. It is also possible to use tables to decide on sample sizes: Clark-Carter (2009) provides an excellent introduction to these.

A useful option offered by SPSS for some tests is to display the *observed power*. To calculate this, SPSS assumes that the means observed for the samples used are the actual means of the populations they represent, and finds the probability that the null hypothesis will be rejected with the sample sizes and inherent random variation we have.

By increasing the number of observations sufficiently, we can increase the power of our test to reject the null hypothesis even if the difference between the means is very small. In other words, even the smallest departure from the null hypothesis can be detected with high probability by using sufficient observations. If a study involves collecting data on an enormous number of participants (as genetic studies sometimes do), then the power of a test to detect minute departures from the null hypothesis may be very high. In such cases it is particularly important to report not just the significance of the results but also the estimated size of any differences (*effect size*).

The General Linear Model

Some of the most familiar statistical methods that we use for just one IV and one DV, including the *t*-test and simple linear regression, can be seen as special cases of the General Linear Model (GLM). The IV can be a continuous variable measured on an interval or ratio scale, as in regression, or it can take just two values to indicate group membership, as in the *t*-test. If we use x to denote a value of the IV, the mean value of the DV is predicted to be a simple function, $a + bx$, where a and b are just numbers that have to be estimated. In regression, b is the slope or regression coefficient and a is the intercept. In the *t*-test, the IV would be coded as $x = 0$ for one of the groups and $x = 1$ for the other group, so a is the mean for one of the groups (where $x = 0$) and $a + b$ is the mean of the other group (where $x = 1$). This kind of function, where the IV is just multiplied by a number, is called a *linear function*, hence the General *Linear* Model. The numbers a and b are called the *model parameters*. The reason for including this explication is to indicate the essential unity of some statistical procedures that are often presented as being quite distinct. If you find this confusing, do not worry; it will not prevent you from making use of the GLM!

To apply the *t*-test, or to test whether the regression coefficient is zero, we need to assume that the DV has an approximately normal distribution about its mean and a constant variance for any value of the IV. But this simple scheme, a DV with constant variance approximately normally distributed about a mean that is a linear function of the IV, is easily extended to include analysis of variance (ANOVA), both one-way and multifactorial, and also regression with more than one IV (multiple regression). To see the essential unity of these methods, mathematicians express them in terms of matrix algebra, and when this is done it is easy to see that ANOVA with more than one DV (multivariate ANOVA, or MANOVA) can also be included in the GLM. This also applies to cases where the DV is influenced by both continuous IVs, as in regression, and group membership, as in ANOVA; such cases are known as analysis of covariance (ANCOVA) models. Thus all of the problems that can be dealt with using ANOVA, MANOVA, simple or multiple regression or ANCOVA are cases of the General Linear Model. Though the details may differ, in each of them we are estimating the values of or testing hypotheses about the model parameters. These problems occupy Chapters 2–5 in this book. We use them to work on problems that we already know quite a lot about: enough to set up an experiment or organize an observational study designed to resolve rather specific questions.

Generalized Linear Models

Generalized Linear Models, as you might guess, extend further the idea of the General Linear Model. The loglinear models that are the subject of Chapter 12 provide one example of the Generalized Linear Model. In the loglinear model it is the *logarithms* of the cell probabilities (and not the cell probabilities themselves) that are linear functions of the DVs. In the General Linear Model, we try to predict the DV using a linear function of the IVs. In the General*ized* Linear Model, it is some function, such as the log, of the DV that we try to predict with a linear function of the IVs. Although this does not sound like a very big step from the GLM, in practice most people find it a serious challenge to their intuition, so do not be surprised if you find Chapter 12 hard work. Chapters 13 and 14 also deal with Generalized Linear Models, and they too are harder work than the earlier chapters. We left these topics to the later chapters even though a natural place might be immediately following the GLMs. However, as well as being more difficult for most people than the preceding chapters, these topics are also less general in their application.

Chapter 12 deals entirely with categorical or discrete data, whereas Chapters 2–11 all deal with continuous data or a mixture of continuous and categorical data. Problems with just categorical data are not so common in psychology or medicine, but when you do have one, none of the previous methods is much help. As with the GLMs, the loglinear model is concerned with hypothesis testing, so deals with problems where we are beyond the exploratory stage. Chapter 12 is just an introduction to a large topic, but if this is what you need we think it will enable you to find your way in.

Chapter 13, on Poisson regression, provides an extension of the ideas used in linear regression to problems where the DV is a count of events that occur randomly at a rate that may be influenced by IVs we can manipulate or by covariates that we merely observe. As you will see, events that occur at random but may nevertheless be of great importance are extremely common, so this extension to our usual regression methods is very useful.

Survival analysis, the topic of Chapter 14, is used wherever the time until some event occurs is of interest. The event can be recovery or death of a patient but equally it can be the failure of a component, an error in a process or dropping out of a training program. Because not all cases reach the event by the end of the study (some components are still operational or some participants are still in the training program at the end), survival analysis has to be able to deal with these so-called *censored* observations.

Logistic regression (which is considered in Chapter 9 on discriminant analysis) is also an example of a Generalized Linear Model, but we have used it only as a way to solve some discriminant problems: those with just two groups to distinguish and a mixture of continuous and categorical data on the cases. You will not find logistic regression used in this limited way any more difficult than discriminant analysis.

Exploratory methods

Exploratory methods for one or two variables include frequency tables, cross-tabulations, histograms, dotplots, boxplots, scatterplots, side-by-side boxplots and all the descriptive statistics such as mean, standard deviation and range.

None of these extend easily to more than two dimensions because they rely on displays on the two-dimensional page or on our limited ability to appreciate numerical values. But the ideas are still useful: we need to look for ways to display the data that show up important features and enable us to understand them more easily. Some of the most interesting problems are at this earlier stage of investigation. Our variables are often all of the same status rather than being IVs and DVs. We may be trying to understand whether there is some structure in our dataset that is too subtle to be easily seen or is obscured by variables we have yet to see are irrelevant. We may be hoping to find that there are subgroups in the data, or that some of the variables we have recorded are measuring different aspects of the same thing. Or we may be hoping to find a way of sorting cases into groups using easily recorded measurements. For these problems we may find help in the exploratory methods described in Chapters 7–11.

Among the exploratory methods, we have: factor analysis and path analysis, which are usually used in attempts to group variables; discriminant analysis and cluster analysis, which are concerned usually with grouping cases; and multidimensional scaling, which may allow us to produce a useful visual display of cases or, occasionally, variables.

Path analysis is an extension of multiple regression that focuses on the pattern of relationships among a set of variables rather than just on which IVs predict a DV and how strongly. It may be used as a confirmatory technique to check the fit of a proposed model for the patterns of influence among the variables, but it is also often used in an exploratory manner, trying out several plausible sets of relationships.

Factor analysis is used a lot in psychology, either in an exploratory way, as in attempts to identify an underlying factor that cannot be measured directly but influences scores on several variables, or in a confirmatory manner, as in testing a model that specifies particular relationships among *latent variables* (that cannot be measured directly) and their measurable *indicator variables*. To set up a factor analysis we need a score or measurement on each variable we are interested in for each case in the study. The method attempts to identify disjoint subgroups of variables so that each variable in a subgroup is strongly associated with one factor but not with any other factors. In exploratory mode, we would hope to find a smaller number of factors than we have variables, so that we can see a relatively simple structure to the problem through what may have seemed like a mass of data. In confirmatory mode, on the other hand, the goal is to test the goodness of fit of a hypothesized factor model to the data.

So factor analysis and path analysis, respectively, represent the *measurement modelling* and *structural modelling* components of *structural equation modelling*. Factor analysis models relationships among the measurements (called *indicator variables* in the context of structural equation modelling), and path analysis compares different models of causation. These may provide ways to group variables and to examine the nature of influences among variables or groups of variables, but how about grouping cases? If we already know there are subgroups of cases, perhaps groups who improve with different types of treatment, or tumours that turn out to be malignant or benign, we may still find it a problem deciding to which group a particular case belongs. Of course it will eventually become obvious when the treatment helps or fails, or when the nature of the tumour is revealed by a biopsy. But often it would be really useful to have a way to sort cases into groups at an early stage, especially if nothing as clear as a biopsy is available for the problem but some decision about treatment must be made. This is the problem addressed by discriminant analysis and logistic regression.

A less clear-cut problem arises when we have measurements on a number of variables for a set of cases and we suspect that the cases fall naturally into subgroups. However, if there are subgroups, we do not know how many there are or how to distinguish them. If we could identify subgroups then we could simplify our problem by considering them one at a time, perhaps thereby getting a better understanding of causes or finding effective methods of treatment or support. So cluster analysis addresses this problem, putting together cases that are most alike according to the variables we have recorded and attempting to find a small number of natural subgroups. The same method can be used to look for clusters of variables, but most often it is cases that we try to group in this way.

A cluster analysis begins by calculating a *similarity* or *distance* between each pair of cases, using their scores on all the recorded variables. The distance may be, and usually is, a conceptual distance rather than a distance in space. Multidimensional scaling also works on the distances between pairs of cases, but instead of looking for subgroups it just draws a map of the cases, like drawing a map of the towns in an atlas from the triangle of intercity distances at the front of the atlas. Whether or not the cases do fall into natural subgroups, this pictorial representation can be quite revealing.

So, in summary, this group of exploratory methods can be used in combination. A multidimensional scaling might hint at the existence of subgroups of cases and a cluster analysis may increase our confidence in this. A discriminant analysis might then give us a fairly effective way to place new cases in one of the groups. A cluster analysis or multidimensional scaling applied to variables might suggest the existence of groups of variables that could be the expression of underlying factors, and a factor analysis might confirm this. In general, exploratory analyses may lead to the use of confirmatory techniques. For example, a path analysis might investigate the nature of relationships among variables identified in exploratory factor analysis. Structural equation modelling may combine a measurement model (confirmatory factor analysis) and a structural model (path analysis) to investigate the influences among measured (indicator) variables and latent variables, and this may be supplemented by specific procedures to test hypotheses about mediation and moderation effects on DVs.

Reference

Clark-Carter, D. (2009). *Quantitative psychological research: A student's handbook* (3rd ed.). Hove, UK: Psychology Press.

2 Analysis of variance (ANOVA)

Introduction and terminology

The ANOVA technique tackles essentially the same problem as the t-test but, instead of being limited to dealing with the difference between two sample means, there is no restriction on the number of means among which differences may be examined. In fact, the t-test is exactly equivalent to an ANOVA applied to the special case of just two means; the square of the t value obtained will be equal to the value of F obtained in the corresponding ANOVA. The other important feature of the ANOVA is that it can deal with two or more independent variables (IVs) simultaneously. It can be used to examine the effect of each IV independently and, very importantly, the effects of *interactions* among them.

ANOVA is the method most often used for analysing data from a classical experiment, in which one or more IVs are controlled at a small number of values and a DV is observed at each combination of the IV values. A typical example would be an experiment in which three methods of teaching students to work with data were compared. Each method was tried with three levels of practice, and after the training the students performed a task on which they were marked out of 25 (the score is the DV). The IVs are the TRAINING method (which takes the three values 'means-ends analysis', 'hypothesis generation' and 'rule application') and the number of practice TRIALS (which takes the three values 5, 10 and 15). There were 27 participants who were randomly assigned to the nine combinations of IV values, three to each. This is one of the experiments that we will discuss further when we show how to perform an ANOVA with more than one factor in SPSS.

Factors

The dependent variable (DV) in an ANOVA is referred to in the usual way – in fact, there can be more than one DV, but that case will be covered in the next chapter. The IVs, on the other hand, are usually referred to as *factors*. When there is only one IV, the ANOVA is described as a *one-way* analysis or design. When there is more than one IV, we speak of a *factorial* analysis, with each IV being a factor in the design. Each factor can have two or more discrete values, referred to as *levels*. These may be numerical levels, for example, when the IV is STIMULUS EXPOSURE TIME, with levels of, say, 100, 200, 300 and 400 milliseconds. Alternatively, the levels can be qualitative labels, for example, when the IV is MODALITY, with levels of, say, 'visual', 'auditory' and 'tactile'. In each case, these are the values of the factors that the researcher has chosen to use, either by manipulation (allocation of levels to participants or occasions) or classification (labelling of participants; e.g., POLITICAL AFFILIATION, with levels such as, 'labour', 'conservative', 'other' and 'none'). The number of factors and the number of levels in each is often indicated in the description of a factorial design as, for example, a 2 × 3 × 3 factorial for a design with three factors, the first having two levels and the second and third each having three levels. Sometimes, a design is summarized by specifying just the number of factors. The previous example would then be described as a three-way factorial. In a one-way analysis, a level of the factor is the same as a *condition* in the experiment, so we could refer to a 100 ms condition or a visual condition. However, and this seems to be confusing for some students initially, when there is more than one factor, levels of factors and conditions of the experiment are not the same. Consider this example: we will present stimuli in either a visual or auditory modality, in a quiet or noisy environment. So, we have a two-way factorial design or, more informatively, a 2 × 2 factorial design. The DV might be REACTION TIME. There are two levels of each factor and the total number of conditions is 2 × 2 = 4. The conditions are visual/quiet, visual/noisy, auditory/quiet and auditory/noisy. An ANOVA is *balanced* when we have the same number of observations for each condition. The reason for one being *unbalanced* is often a missing observation due to some unforeseen event such as illness of a participant.

Between- and within-subjects designs

Each factor in an ANOVA can be either a *between-subjects* (*unrelated, independent groups*) factor or a *within-subjects* (*related, repeated measures*) factor. A between-subjects factor is one in which each level is allocated (in most cases, randomly) to a different group of participants, or participants are classified into different groups on the basis of their pre-existing level on the factor of interest (e.g., POLITICAL AFFILIATION; AGE; INCOME). A within-subjects factor is one in which all levels are allocated to all participants. Thus, if MODALITY were a within-subjects factor, all participants would receive both visual and auditory presentations and, just as in a repeated measures design to be analysed using a related *t*-test, counterbalancing (or separate randomization of the order of multiple presentations for each participant) would be necessary to deal with order effects. If all of the factors in a design are between-subjects, the design is referred to as a *between-subjects* (*between groups*; *independent groups*; *between participants*) design. As the use of the rather dehumanizing term 'subjects' is gradually being replaced by the term 'participants', you may choose to use alternative descriptors for the designs. We will continue to use the between- and within-subjects terms because these compound terms have become part of the conventional language of experimental design and analysis. If one or more factors is between-subjects and one or more is within-subjects, the design is referred to as a *mixed* design. If all factors are within-subjects, then we have a *within-subjects (repeated measures) design*.

A full description of an ANOVA design will include reference to the type of design and the nature of each factor. An example might be:

> We used a mixed (2 × 3 × 3) factorial design, with the first factor (GENDER: male; female) being between groups, and with repeated measures on the second factor (MODALITY: visual; auditory; tactile) and repeated measures on the third factor (INTENSITY OF STIMULUS: high; medium; low). The DV was simple REACTION TIME.

Main effects

When a factorial ANOVA is carried out, the number of statistics calculated, and therefore the number of effects tested, will depend on how many factors there are. For each factor, there will be a test of the null hypothesis that there are no differences among the means for levels of that factor, ignoring the distinctions between levels of the other factors. This is called a test of the *main effect* of the factor. The means that are being considered in a test of the main effect of MODALITY in a 2 × 2 factorial design, in which GENDER is the other factor, are illustrated in Figure 2.1. For a test of the main effect of MODALITY, it is the visual mean and the auditory mean (the two shaded cells) that are considered. For a test of the main effect of GENDER, the male mean and female mean are considered (on the right of Figure 2.1).

		Modality: visual	Modality: auditory	
Gender	male	male/visual mean 200 ms	male/auditory mean 350 ms	male mean 275 ms
	female	female/visual mean 300 ms	female/auditory mean 150 ms	female mean 225 ms
		visual mean 250 ms	auditory mean 250 ms	grand mean 250 ms

Figure 2.1 Conditions and main effects in a factorial ANOVA (equal numbers in conditions assumed)

Fisher's F *statistic*

The test of the null hypothesis that (for example) there is no difference between the visual and auditory means is based, like the *t*-test, on comparing the observed difference between the means with the variability within each treatment group. In this example, we would be considering the variability within each of the four treatment groups: male/visual, female/visual, male/auditory and female/auditory. Since the treatment received by all members of a group is the same, the variability within the group must be due to random and individual effects. The bigger the difference between group means compared to this inherent variability, the more likely it is to be due to treatment effects and not just another manifestation of inherent variability. If we have more than two factor levels to consider, visual, auditory and tactile perhaps, we have to use the variability among the means rather than a difference, but the idea is the same: compare variability among the means to inherent variability within a treatment group. The statistic used for the test is Fisher's F (we owe the idea to R. A. Fisher, a geneticist, statistician and polymath who developed it for use in agricultural experiments). Something about F that puzzles many students is the degrees of freedom or *df* (remember the degrees of freedom for *t*?). F has two lots of degrees of freedom; the second one quoted is analogous to the *df* for *t*, and refers to the number of observations within each treatment group and the number of treatment groups. Usually you can calculate this as $k(n-1)$, where k is the number of treatment groups and n the number of observations per treatment group. The first *df* quoted for the F is one less than the number of levels of the factor being tested. If you do your ANOVAs in SPSS, the *df*s as well as the F values and probabilities all appear in the output.

An intuitive explication of the meaning of F

What we are doing in any ANOVA is decomposing the total variance into components attributable to the factor(s) in the design (and the interactions among them, if there is more than one factor) and a component attributable to uncontrolled random error. The sum of squared deviations of factor-level means from the grand mean (divided by its *df*s to give an average value: the *Mean Square (MS) Between Groups*, as it is often referred to) provides an *estimate* of the variance that could be due to the effect of the factor and/or the effect of 'error' (uncontrolled within-group variation). The squared deviations of individual scores from their own group means (divided by their *df*s), on the other hand, can only be an estimate of error variance (or *MS Error*), since all participants within the same group receive the same experimental treatment. F then equals the ratio of these two estimates. Thus:

$$F = MS \text{ Between Groups} / MS \text{ Error}$$

which is in fact

$$F = \text{Estimate of (variance due to factor} + \text{variance due to error)} / \text{Estimate of variance due to error}$$

So, if most of the total variance is due to the factor, the ratio will be high (F takes a high value), whereas if most of the total variance is due to error, the ratio will approach 1. You might take a minute to satisfy yourself that the preceding statement is true. Tables (or SPSS output) tell us how much greater than 1 F needs to be to make it improbable (e.g., $p < .05$) that such a value would be obtained when the null hypothesis is true.

Fixed and random factors

Factors are either *fixed* or *random*. Fixed factors are by far the most common, and those we analyse in this book are fixed. Here is an example of the sort of situation where you might need to use random factors (and read about them in one of the books in 'Further reading' at the end of the book). An experiment to find out about the productivity of two types of machine that make widgets has two factors: MACHINE with two levels (Type A and Type B) and OPERATOR with four levels (Jones, Smith, Brown and

Green). Any inferences we draw from the experiment about differences between the machines and among the operators refer to the machines and operators used, and whereas we are specifically interested in the two machines (a fixed factor), the four operators were just chosen at random from all the operators who work at the widget factory. So we may be more interested in how much the means will vary across the whole population of operators than how much they vary among these particular four. In this case it would be appropriate to say that OPERATOR is a random factor.

Interaction effects

In addition to the main effects, an ANOVA will also test for interaction effects for each combination of factors (e.g., A × B, B × C, A × C, A × B × C in a three-way factorial). These interactions are spoken as 'A by B', 'B by C', etc.

An interaction effect exists when the pattern of differences among levels of one factor is different at the various levels of one or more other factors. For example, if we consider the means of the four conditions in Figure 2.1, shown again in Table 2.1, that would suggest an interaction between gender and modality, such that males have faster reaction times to visual stimuli, whereas females have faster reaction times to auditory stimuli. In other words, we could not just conclude that females are, in general, faster than males (the main effect of gender) even if the difference between overall female and male means (females: (150 + 300)/2 = 225 ms; males: (350 + 200)/2 = 275 ms, assuming equal numbers of participants in each of the four conditions) were statistically significant, because that is clearly not true for visual stimuli. There is a very important lesson here.

Table 2.1 Condition means in a factorial ANOVA

Gender	Modality	
	Visual	*Auditory*
Male	200	350
Female	300	150

Simple effects

If there is a significant interaction between two factors, any significant main effects of those factors need to be interpreted with great care. This is particularly so when there is a *crossover* interaction, that is, when the effect of one factor is in the *opposite* direction for different levels of another factor, as in our example. The effect of a factor at a particular level of another factor is called a *simple effect*. In order to get a better understanding of a significant interaction, it is usual to test the significance of at least some of the simple effects. In the above example, we would be interested in whether females reacted significantly faster than males to auditory stimuli and whether males reacted significantly faster than females to visual stimuli. We could also, of course, test the simple effects of modality for males and for females. The gender by modality interaction is illustrated in Figure 2.2, where the means involved in testing two of the four possible simple effects are indicated.

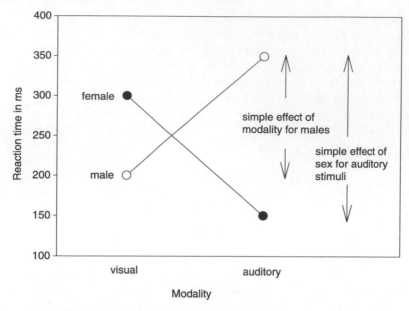

Figure 2.2 Testing for simple effects when there is a significant interaction.

Ceiling and floor effects

It may still be worth carrying out tests of simple effects when there is an interaction that is not a crossover. A non-crossover interaction can be seen if, when the interaction is plotted, the lines on the graph are non-parallel but do not cross, but it also becomes important to consider the possibility that the interaction is an artefact of the measurement scale used. There may have been a *ceiling effect* or a *floor effect*. A ceiling effect may occur, for example, when the mean score for one condition cannot go much higher than that for another condition because the former is already near the top of the scale. There is then very little scope for improvement on that particular scale. It is then possible that, if the scale extended further, the mean for that condition would be higher, making the lines on a plot of the interaction more nearly parallel (i.e., removing the interaction). A floor effect is just the same but at the bottom end of the scale. Figure 2.3 illustrates a situation where a possible ceiling effect may have created a significant, but spurious, non-crossover interaction. In this example, the DV was the number of logic problems, out of 20, solved correctly in a given time. Males were close to the maximum score of 20 in the noisy surroundings, so they may have been able to solve more logic problems in quiet surroundings (as the females were) if more problems had been presented.

Assumptions and transformations

The arbitrariness of scales

Even when there are no ceiling or floor effects, non-crossover interactions still need to be handled with caution. Sometimes, when the choice of scale for the DV is arbitrary, which is often the case, *transformation* of the scale (e.g., by using the square root

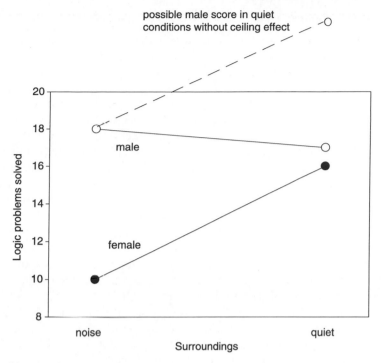

Figure 2.3 A possibly spurious interaction due to a ceiling effect.

or logarithm of raw data values) may remove a significant interaction, leaving more readily interpretable main effects. The notion of scale arbitrariness may best be understood from some examples. If we wanted to measure estimates of sizes of discs at different distances, we might choose to use the diameter or the area estimates as our DV. In this case the transformation from diameter to area is a function of the square of the diameter: $\pi(\frac{d}{2})^2$. Who is to say which is correct? Again, should we use time taken on a writing task or writing speed, where one is the reciprocal of the other? How about using physical energy or decibels, a logarithmic transformation, to measure loudness? So, how should we decide on which scale an ANOVA should be carried out?

Meaningfulness of effects

The first consideration must be meaningfulness of interpretation of a significant effect. If a difference among means of transformed data will be difficult to interpret, as with a log transformation of IQ for example, you should think twice about doing it. In other cases, such as choice reaction time (CRT), a transformation may enhance interpret-ability. CRT has a curvilinear relationship with number of choices, which becomes a linear relationship when CRT is transformed to log CRT. In some areas of research, a particular transformation is routinely carried out. For example, in psycholinguistic studies, it is very common to use a log transformation of reaction time (RT) data. Because the transformation is so familiar, there tend not to be problems with the interpretation of effects on the log of RT data in this field.

Meeting parametric assumptions

Another reason for considering a transformation of the data is to make them conform to the assumptions that we make when we quote probabilities in the results (sometimes called the *parametric assumptions*). The first is the *normality assumption*: we assume that the observations for any condition in the experiment have a normal distribution, at least approximately. In practice it is not easy to be sure whether this is true or not, but any normal distribution is symmetrical, and we can often check at least on this. In fact even if the distribution is not really normal but is symmetrical, the probabilities from the ANOVA will be a good approximation to the truth. RT data are frequently positively skewed: their distribution has a long tail for higher values on the right of the distribution. This occurs because there is a limit to how much faster than the average it is possible to respond to a stimulus (the absolute limit is zero, of course), but there is no obvious limit to how much slower than average it is possible to respond. So, RT data frequently violate the assumption of normality by being very asymmetric. Typically, applying a square root or logarithmic transformation will make the distribution more symmetrical and so closer to normal. This is an obvious benefit, given that probabilities associated with asymmetric non-normal distributions are often inaccurate, especially if sample sizes are small and/or there are very unequal sample sizes in the various conditions.

The second assumption is that the variance of observations is the same for any condition, at least approximately. This is called the *homogeneity of variance* assumption. Often a transformation of the raw data that increases the normality of the distributions will also make the variances more similar. Particular types of transformation are often recommended for particular types of violation of parametric assumptions, though there is nothing wrong with trying out several and seeing which does best in terms of meeting parametric assumptions. This is quite different from trying out several, doing the analysis on each transformed dataset and reporting the one that produces the result you like best, which is definitely not acceptable.

To transform or not to transform?

Some researchers feel quite uneasy about transforming data; it feels like cheating. Provided that you keep in mind the first consideration – that the interpretation of the results needs to 'make sense' – there is nothing inherently wrong with doing ANOVAs, or other analyses, on transformed data. Remember that there is rarely one obviously correct measurement scale for a construct. What would be the choice of measurement scale for a construct such as stress, for example? A transformed scale will not necessarily be more arbitrary than a scale initially chosen from a considerable number of possibilities. It makes sense to use a transformation to make data conform more closely to parametric assumptions provided that interpretability is not sacrificed. Much has been written elsewhere about the use of transformations and our intention is, as usual, to tell you enough to give you the confidence to turn to more detailed discussions. References for texts that contain useful and accessible additional information about transformations, as well about ANOVAs in general, are given in the 'Further reading' at the end of the book. An example dataset where the parametric assumptions are not satisfied and a transformation is helpful is given in the next chapter, where we show some of the diagnostics available to help in deciding whether assumptions are satisfied, and also give some advice about missing data and observations with outlying values.

Effect size and power

Factors affecting power

When contemplating the collection of data to test one or more hypotheses, an important consideration is the smallest size of effect that you would not want to miss, that is, one that would avoid the occurrence of a Type II error. Another way of looking at it is to consider the power of a test to reject a null hypothesis that is in fact untrue. The probability of a Type II error is β and the power of a test is denoted by $1 - \beta$. There are various ways in which the power of a test can be increased. Perhaps the most obvious ways of increasing power are to maximize effect size (e.g., by making the levels of a factor more extreme) and to exercise greater experimental control (reduction of random nuisance effects), but the way that is most focussed on once the design has been settled is the number of participants per condition. Other things being equal, the more participants there are, the greater will be the power of the test. In order to find out how many participants per condition are needed to achieve the desired power (a minimum power of .8 is frequently chosen), you need to decide what is the smallest effect size that you do not want to miss, what a level (probability of a Type I error) you intend to test at (e.g., $p < .05$) and whether you will be using a one- or two-tailed test. A test with a larger a level is more powerful than one with a smaller a level, so a test at the 5% level is more powerful than a more conservative one at the 1% level. If no attempt is made to estimate the number of participants needed to stand a reasonable chance of finding an effect when one exists, it is entirely possible that an experiment may be an expensive waste of time and resources.

Estimating effect size

It is fairly straightforward to decide on the a level, and usually it is clear whether a one-tailed test could be used. It is also not difficult to decide on a minimum acceptable power (many researchers accept .8). However, deciding what is the smallest effect size at which you want your minimum power to apply takes a little more work, because you need to know not only the difference between the level means that would be sufficiently useful that you do not want to miss it, but also you need an estimate of the intrinsic variation (error variance) that will be found in your experiment. There are three approaches that can be adopted for choosing an effect size: an approximation can be based on the findings from prior research involving similar variables; an estimate can be made of the smallest effect size that would have practical or theoretical usefulness; or conventions (similar to those for selecting an a level) can be used. Cohen (1988) proposed a set of conventions that have been widely adopted. For the two-sample case and a one-tailed test he used a measure of effect size (which he called d) based on the difference between the group means. To calculate d you also need an estimate of the common standard deviation (sd) of the measure in the two populations, and then $d = (m_a - m_b)/sd$. He suggested that $d = .2, .5$ and $.8$ be taken as small, medium and large effects, respectively. This measure of effect size can be understood as indicating the percentage of overlap between the two distributions, with the percentages of overlap being 85%, 67% and 53% for small, medium and large effects, respectively.

When there are more than two means, as in ANOVA, this measure of effect size is not applicable. The oldest measure of the strength of an experimental effect is denoted by eta squared (η^2), and is the proportion of total variance accounted for by the effect variance, that is, η^2 = Effect SS/Total SS. A measure of effect size that is analogous to Cohen's d is $f = \sqrt{\eta^2/(1 - \eta^2)}$. The values of f designated as small, medium and large effects are .10, .25 and .40, respectively. The conventional values for different effect sizes may be summarized as follows:

Small effect size:	$d = .2$ (85% overlap)	$f = .10$	$\eta^2 = .01$
Medium effect size:	$d = .5$ (67% overlap)	$f = .25$	$\eta^2 = .06$
Large effect size:	$d = .8$ (53% overlap)	$f = .40$	$\eta^2 = .14$

Estimating sample size required

Once you have decided on the required power, the a level, whether the test is to be one or two tailed and whether you want your chosen minimum power to apply to a small, medium or large effect, then you can proceed to estimate the number of cases needed for each combination of factor levels (each combination of factor levels is often called a *cell*) of your ANOVA. It used to be the case that, in order to determine the sample size needed to achieve a given power, it was necessary to refer to extensive sets of tables of the kind provided in Cohen (1988). Clark-Carter (2009) provides an excellent introduction to these.

Things are much simpler now. There are statistical packages, such as SamplePower (supported by SPSS), dedicated to that end. You just have to select the appropriate design, then follow the guidance provided to indicate the power (e.g., .8) and the a level (e.g., .05, two-tailed) required, and either enter an estimated effect size directly or provide the necessary information for the program to compute it (e.g., estimated common within-condition sd). The program will then indicate the requisite number of participants per cell.

Retrospective (observed) power

A related, but somewhat separate, issue is that of *observed* or *retrospective power*, that is, power that is calculated after the experiment has been completed. Retrospective power (SPSS calls it observed power) tells us what the power would be if the values of the population (i.e., true) means and variances were equal to those found in the experiment. One reason for being interested in retrospective power is that the power estimated from the current experiment may guide us in the determination of sample size for our next experiment, perhaps a partial replication. Retrospective power, along with effect size, is also useful for *meta-analysis*, which involves evaluation of studies in the literature, and for that reason in particular it is becoming the norm to include this information in journal publications of experimental studies. If you are thinking of using retrospective power to explain your results, however, you should read Howell's discussion of this suspect practice first (Howell, 2007, p. 226). SPSS provides estimates of effect size and power for ANOVAs when the General Linear Model option is selected. SPSS actually calculates partial eta squared: Effect SS/(Effect SS + Error SS).

A one-way ANOVA

We will begin with an example of the simplest (one-way) design, which we will also use to explain the use of follow-up tests, because the concepts involved are easier to explicate in that most simple case and the understanding gained can be readily applied to the more complex, factorial, designs. We will then go on to demonstrate analysis of the three most common factorial designs: balanced (equal numbers in each condition) between-subjects, within-subjects and mixed designs, all with fixed factors. As with all designs, a power analysis to determine sample size should have been carried out prior to commencement of the experiment.

A psychology example of a one-way design

The data from a one-way between-subjects design are shown in Table 2.2. There are five levels of the IV, which is DEPTH of processing. It is suggested that the more deeply people process stimuli, the more likely they will be able to recall them. Thus, if people are given the task of counting the letters in a list of words that they are shown, they should be expected to recall fewer of the words than if the task was to think of an adjective to go with each word. This would be so because in order to think of an appropriate adjective it is necessary to access the meaning of the word, whereas this is not necessary in order to count the letters. So, the depth of processing is considered to be greater the more attention is paid to the meaning of stimuli. The specific hypothesis was that depth of processing, and therefore RECALL (the DV), would show an upward trend from the task of counting letters in each word, through thinking of a rhyming word, thinking of an adjective to go with each word, to forming a mental image of each word. A fifth (intentional) condition was when the task was to actively try to remember each word, in which case it was expected that participants would use an effective strategy involving the meaning of each word. Fifty participants were randomly assigned, 10 to each condition, and the data are shown in Table 2.2. We note here that when we carried out a power analysis using the SamplePower software, we found that for a two-tailed test at $\alpha = .05$ and with a 'large' effect specified, 16 participants per condition would be required to achieve a power of .8. In this example experiment with fabricated data, the 10 participants per condition gave power equal to less than .6 for the same α level and effect size, which in a real experiment would be on the low side.

Table 2.2 Recall data from a one-way between-subjects design

Counting	Rhyming	Adjective	Imagery	Intentional
9	7	11	12	10
8	9	13	11	19
6	6	8	16	14
8	6	6	11	5
10	6	14	9	10
4	11	11	23	11
6	6	13	12	14
5	3	13	10	15
7	8	10	19	11
7	7	11	11	11

A one-way design: Setting it up in SPSS

Because this is a between-subjects design, the data need to be entered in just two columns, one for the IV (DEPTH) and one for the DV (RECALL), so that each participant occupies a single row. Thus, in the RECALL column, the data for the counting condition would be entered first and the data for the other conditions would be entered in turn below that. The DEPTH column would contain ten 1s, followed by ten 2s, ten 3s, ten 4s and ten 5s. The first and last few rows showing the data organized for entry into SPSS can be seen in Table 2.3 (the full dataset can be found on the book website as psy.anova.oneway.sav).

Table 2.3 First and last few cases of data from a one-way between-subjects design set out for the SPSS datasheet (the full dataset can be found as psy.anova.oneway.sav on the website)

Depth	Recall
1	9
1	8
1	6
1	8
⋮	⋮
5	14
5	15
5	11
5	11

In fact, the output will be easier to read if the five levels of training are given their names rather than the codes 1–5. We can easily arrange this once the data are in the datasheet. At the bottom of the datasheet, click the **Variable View** tab. Now we see each of the variables listed with their properties. Each of these properties can be altered: for instance we may want to specify that zero decimal places are displayed (the default is two) for our factor levels, and perhaps for other data when we have only whole numbers. Click in the **Values** cell for DEPTH and a button appears: clicking this opens SPSS Dialog Box 2.1, and here we can assign labels to each of the five levels of DEPTH. Type 1 in the **Value** box, type counting in the **Value Label** box and click **Add**. Repeat with 2 and rhyming, and so on, to 5 and intentional. The dialog box is shown just before we click **Add** for the last time. Then click **OK**. To see the labels displayed in the datasheet, return to **Data View** using the tab at the bottom, then click **View** on the menu bar, then **Value Labels**, which toggles between displaying code numbers and labels. If your output tables do not show the value labels, go to **Edit** in the menu bar, then **Options**. Click the **Output Labels** tab at the top, and make sure all of the boxes display **Values**. It may also be helpful to give the DV an extended label to be used in the output. To do this, select **Variable View** at the bottom tab, click **Label** in the DEPTH row and write 'depth of processing' in the highlighted cell.

SPSS offers great control over the way variables are defined, including different ways to deal with missing data. To see the full range of options click **Help** on the menu bar, then **Topics**. This gives an index, and you can scroll down or get to the right part of it more quickly by typing a word or part of a word in the box. From the index choose **variables** and the subentry **defining**. As well as a page of information there is an excellent tutorial that can be viewed by clicking **Show me**.

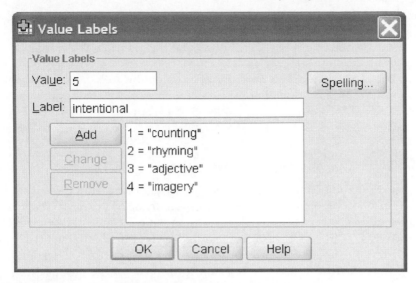

SPSS Dialog Box 2.1 Assigning factor-level labels.

A one-way design: Requesting the analysis in SPSS

Once the data are entered, select **Analyze** from the menu bar, then **Compare Means**, then **One-Way ANOVA**, to get SPSS Dialog Box 2.2. Select RECALL from the variable list and use the arrow to put it in the **Dependent List** box. Then put DEPTH in the **Factor** box in the same way, so the dialog box appears as shown.

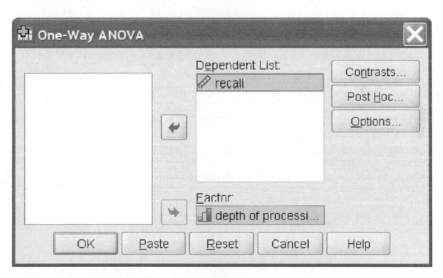

SPSS Dialog Box 2.2 Starting a one-way between-subjects ANOVA.

Click the **Options** button to get a list of statistics for optional printing. Click the **Descriptives** box to get means, etc., then **Homogeneity of variance test** for Levene's test of equality of group variances and **Means Plot**. Either the Brown-Forsythe or Welch test can be used instead of the *F* test if the assumption of equal variances is not met.

The **Options** dialog box also offers a choice of methods for dealing with **Missing Values** but you will usually want to accept the default, **Exclude cases analysis by analysis**. We will ignore the **Contrasts** and **Post Hoc** buttons for the moment. When we have looked at the output for the main analysis, we will return to these buttons to carry out *follow-up* tests. **One-Way ANOVA** in SPSS does not offer an option to request a calculation of effect size or retrospective power, but the former is easily calculated from the output by hand (i.e., Effect SS/Total SS), and the latter can then be obtained using a power analysis package such as SamplePower. Click **OK** to get the main analysis.

A one-way design: Understanding the output

If you are using version 16 of SPSS you will find that at the start of the output is a list of the syntax (SPSS commands) resulting from your dialog box choices. Version 15 and earlier did not provide this. (If you wish, you can turn it off. Click on **Edit**, then **Options** and the **Viewer** tab. Untick **Display commands in the log** at the bottom left.) The syntax can be useful, for example if you plan to carry out a series of similar analyses on different datasets, but we will not refer again to this part of the output except in the Appendix, where we provide the syntax for selected analyses.

SPSS Output 2.1 shows the output tables. The first table gives the means, standard deviations, etc. for each level of the IV. Next comes the test of homogeneity of variance. We may note, however, that some authors have questioned the legitimacy of Levene's test. In any case, ANOVA is quite robust to moderate departures from homogeneity unless treatment groups are small and unequal in size. In our example we see that the Levene statistic is not quite significant (the probability is .054, look at the Sig column), though if we had smaller and/or unequal group sizes we might consider using the

Descriptives

recall

	N	Mean	Std. Deviation	Std. Error	95% Confidence Interval for Mean		Minimum	Maximum
					Lower Bound	Upper Bound		
counting	10	7.00	1.826	0.577	5.69	8.31	4	10
rhyming	10	6.90	2.132	0.674	5.38	8.42	3	11
adjective	10	11.00	2.494	0.789	9.22	12.78	6	14
imagery	10	13.40	4.502	1.424	10.18	16.62	9	23
intentional	10	12.00	3.742	1.183	9.32	14.68	5	19
Total	50	10.06	4.007	0.567	8.92	11.20	3	23

Test of Homogeneity of Variances

recall

Levene Statistic	df1	df2	Sig.
2.529	4	45	.054

ANOVA

recall

	Sum of Squares	df	Mean Square	F	Sig.
Between Groups	351.520	4	87.880	9.085	.000
Within Groups	435.300	45	9.673		
Total	786.820	49			

SPSS Output 2.1 Results of the one-way between-subjects ANOVA.

Brown-Forsythe or Welch test instead of the *F* test (these are available in the **Options** dialog box). Then we get the ANOVA summary table, with the *F* statistic quoted and its *df*, and we see that the difference among the five conditions is highly significant: $F(4,45) = 9.085$, $p < .001$. From the summary table we can easily compute effect size as $\eta^2 = 351.52/786.82 = .447$, which is equivalent to an *f* value of .90 (see formula above). This is a very large effect size and, when it is entered in the SamplePower package, together with $a = .05$, two-tailed and $n = 10$ per cell, the power analysis indicates that retrospective power = 1.

Finally, the plot we requested is shown in SPSS Output 2.2.

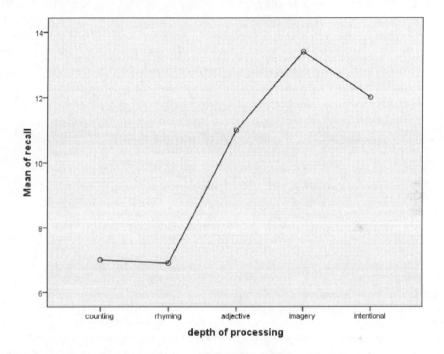

SPSS Output 2.2 Plot of means for the one-way between-subjects data.

Example Box 2.1

An alternative medical example for the same one-way design

The full analysis for this example can be found at www.psypress.com/ multivariate-analysis/medical-examples (click on Chapter 2).

A pilot study is designed to investigate dosages for a new ACE-inhibitor in the treatment of hypertension. The new drug is believed to have fewer side effects than the currently favoured ACE-inhibitor. Fifty patients with systolic blood pressure (SBP) in the range 150–170 mmHg are randomly allocated to one of five conditions. The IV is drug dosage (DOSAGE), with levels being 4, 6, 8 and 10 mg for the new drug and 10 mg for the old drug, which is known to be an effective level for that drug. The DV is the drop in SBP 1 week after administration (SPBDROP).

Outcomes

It is clear from the plot that the reduction in SBP does not increase steadily as the dosage of the new drug increases. However there is a significant linear trend in the drop in SBP over drug dosages, and post hoc comparisons among pairs of conditions show dosages of 4 and 6 mg of the new drug to differ significantly from dosages of 8 and 10 mg of the new drug and a dosage of 10 mg of the old drug. Within these two groupings, the conditions do not differ significantly. Therefore, the new drug at dosages of 8 and 10 mg is as effective as the old drug at a dosage of 10 mg, but with fewer side effects. It seems possible that the new drug has an effectiveness threshold between dosage levels of 6 and 8 mg, which is supported by the significant difference found between the first two and the last three conditions using a post hoc Scheffé test. Another pilot study to locate the threshold of effectiveness for the new drug should be carried out prior to a full trial of the new drug.

Alternative variables for use in SPSS
The full dataset, med.anova.oneway.sav, can be found on the book website

Variable	Psychology	Medicine
IV	DEPTH Depth of processing 1=counting 2=rhyming 3=adjective 4=imagery 5=intentional	DOSAGE ACE-inhibitor dose 1=new4mg 2=new6mg 3=new8mg 4=new10mg 5=old10mg
DV	RECALL Mean recall	SBPDROP SBP drop (mg)

A one-way design: Post hoc *tests*

It is obvious from the plot that there is not a steady increase from counting to imagery. There are now several strategies available to us. We could carry out *post hoc* tests on the differences between all pairs of conditions, in which case we would need to deal with the problem of *multiple testing*. It would not be okay to just do a series of *t*-tests. Briefly, if we were to carry out 20 tests with α (the probability of a Type I error) set at .05 and the null hypothesis was true in every case, just by chance we might expect to find one difference significant at $p < .05$ (i.e., 1 in 20 Type I errors). There are a variety of procedures designed to set α for the *family of tests* at .05, and these differ in how conservative they are. One of the most commonly used is Tukey's Honestly Significant Difference (HSD) test. We will use that. We now re-do our analysis and ask for the Tukey HSD test at the same time. As before, select from the menu bar **Analyze**, then **Compare Means**, then **One-Way ANOVA**, but this time click the **Post Hoc** button to get a choice of post hoc tests. Select **Tukey**, then click **Continue** and **OK** to get the results of the Tukey test.

Another commonly used option, which is slightly less conservative than the Tukey test, is the Student-Newman-Keuls (**S-N-K**) test. If you wanted to compare each experimental condition with a control condition you could choose the **Dunnett** test, and if the assumption of homogeneity of variance is not met then several alternative post hoc tests are provided. Of these, we recommend the **Games-Howell** test. Further discussion of post hoc tests is beyond the scope of this book, but an excellent discussion is provided by Howell (2007).

The results of the post hoc tests are provided in two forms, of which the first is the simplest to follow. This is shown in SPSS Output 2.3. You can see that each level of DEPTH of processing, starting with counting, is compared with every other level. Counting is first compared with rhyming: the mean difference between these levels was 0.100 with a *confidence interval* from −3.85 to 4.05. Since this confidence interval overlaps zero, the null hypothesis that the mean difference is zero would not be rejected. The probability (look in the Sig. column) is 1.000, so it is virtually certain that the observed difference between these two levels is just random variation.

Multiple Comparisons

recall
Tukey HSD

(I) depth of processing	(J) depth of processing	Mean Difference (I-J)	Std. Error	Sig.	95% Confidence Interval	
					Lower Bound	Upper Bound
counting	rhyming	0.100	1.391	1.000	-3.85	4.05
	adjective	-4.000*	1.391	.046	-7.95	-0.05
	imagery	-6.400*	1.391	.000	-10.35	-2.45
	intentional	-5.000*	1.391	.007	-8.95	-1.05
rhyming	counting	-0.100	1.391	1.000	-4.05	3.85
	adjective	-4.100*	1.391	.039	-8.05	-0.15
	imagery	-6.500*	1.391	.000	-10.45	-2.55
	intentional	-5.100*	1.391	.006	-9.05	-1.15
adjective	counting	4.000*	1.391	.046	0.05	7.95
	rhyming	4.100*	1.391	.039	0.15	8.05
	imagery	-2.400	1.391	.429	-6.35	1.55
	intentional	-1.000	1.391	.951	-4.95	2.95
imagery	counting	6.400*	1.391	.000	2.45	10.35
	rhyming	6.500*	1.391	.000	2.55	10.45
	adjective	2.400	1.391	.429	-1.55	6.35
	intentional	1.400	1.391	.061	-2.55	5.35
intentional	counting	5.000*	1.391	.007	1.05	8.95
	rhyming	5.100*	1.391	.006	1.15	9.05
	adjective	1.000	1.391	.951	-2.95	4.95
	imagery	-1.400	1.391	.851	-5.35	2.55

* The mean difference is significant at the .05 level.

SPSS Output 2.3 Results of Tukey *post hoc* tests.

This output tells us that counting and rhyming did not differ significantly and also that adjective, imagery and intentional did not differ significantly from one another. On the other hand, each of counting and rhyming differed significantly ($p < .05$) from each of adjective, imagery and intentional. The same information appears in the next output table, headed 'Homogeneous Subsets', which we have not shown.

A one-way design: Planned comparisons

Another strategy would be to carry out planned comparisons (i.e., based on hypotheses that motivated the research). One such hypothesis might be that there would be a linear trend across the five conditions. This can be tested by re-doing the one-way ANOVA, but this time click the **Contrasts** button to get SPSS Dialog Box 2.3. Click the **Polynomial** box, and use the drop-down arrow to put **Linear** in the **Degree** box. We are selecting the first (linear) polynomial contrast or comparison. If we wanted to test for a quadratic trend (a single curve) we would tick **Polynomial** and select **Quadratic** in the **Degree** box. In the same fashion we could select a **Cubic** (a double curve) or **4th** polynomial in the **Degree** box. It is only possible to test up to a polynomial one less than the number of conditions (i.e., $5 - 1 = 4$, in this case). In fact, if you select the 4th polynomial, you will get tests of all of the lower polynomials as well. We will do that because, as well as testing the linear trend, we can make a point about the cubic trend. So, the dialog box is as shown.

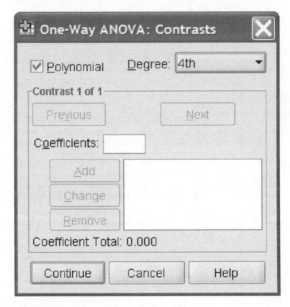

SPSS Dialog Box 2.3 Testing for trend: linear, quadratic, cubic and 4th order polynomials requested.

Click **Continue** and **OK** to see the results of the trend tests. The output is in SPSS Output 2.4 shown opposite. In the first row, the results of the test of differences among the five conditions are repeated, then the results of the four trend tests are given. The one we were initially interested in is the *planned contrast*; the *a priori* hypothesis of a linear trend. We see that, even though the plot did not appear to be very close to a straight line, the linear trend is highly significant: $F(1,45) = 28.144$, $p < .001$. In the following row, we learn that the deviation from the linear trend, that is, the non-linear component of the trend remaining, approaches significance ($p = .055$). There are three *df*s for the non-linear part of the trend, so the near significance of the *p* value suggests that a particular non-linear component of trend taking one of these *df*s may also be significant. In fact, the cubic trend is significant ($p = .013$), which is not surprising given

ANOVA

recall

			Sum of Squares	df	Mean Square	F	Sig.
Between Groups	(Combined)		351.520	4	87.880	9.085	.000
	Linear Term	Contrast	272.250	1	272.250	28.144	.000
		Deviation	79.270	3	26.423	2.732	.055
	Quadratic Term	Contrast	13.207	1	13.207	1.365	.249
		Deviation	66.063	2	33.031	3.415	.042
	Cubic Term	Contrast	64.000	1	64.000	6.616	.013
		Deviation	2.063	1	2.063	0.213	.646
	4th-order Term	Contrast	2.063	1	2.063	0.213	.646
	Within Groups		435.300	45	9.673		
	Total		786.820	49			

SPSS Output 2.4 Results of trend tests: linear, quadratic, cubic and 4th order polynomials.

that the plot in SPSS Output 2.2 shows a double (S-shaped) curve. Even though the cubic trend is significant, we would not see any point in reporting it unless we could think of some plausible (post hoc) explanation for it. In this case, a possible explanation does exist. Neither counting nor rhyming requires any necessary accessing of meanings of words in the stimulus list, and it could be for that reason that RECALL does not differ between them. It could also be that, while both adjective and imagery require that meaning is accessed, imagery promotes the accessing of more detailed meaning than adjective. Finally, although participants in the intentional condition are likely to use a reasonable recall strategy, some of their strategies may well be less effective than the use of imagery. Now, we need to be clear that, if we report the cubic effect, we would not be *confirming* a hypothesis – we would be *generating* a hypothesis from inspection of our data. This hypothesis would need to be tested in a new experiment.

A one-way design: Complex post hoc comparisons

There is a further situation concerning follow-up tests that we will raise. This is when we look at our data and generate a complex post hoc hypothesis that requires more than testing differences between all pairs of means (Tukey) or testing each experimental mean against a control mean (Dunnett). For example, we might generate the hypothesis that tasks that 'demand' that meaning be accessed will result in higher recall than tasks that can be carried out without accessing meaning. Specifically, we would be hypothesizing that the last three conditions (adjective, imagery, intentional) would show higher recall than the first two conditions (counting, rhyming). We can use the *Scheffé* procedure to test complex post hoc hypotheses. For the example just suggested, we would compare the mean of the first two conditions with the mean of the last three. To do this we define a *contrast*, which multiplies each level mean by a suitably chosen *coefficient*, which is just a number. For our example we compare the mean of the first two levels (counting and rhyming) with the mean of the last three (adjective, imagery and intentional). To find the difference we need to subtract one mean from the other. The steps for assigning coefficients to the levels are:

(1) Mean of first two levels: (counting + rhyming)/2 = $\frac{1}{2}$ counting + $\frac{1}{2}$ rhyming

(2) Mean of last three levels:

$$\text{(adjective + imagery + intentional)}/3 = \frac{1}{3}\text{ adjective} + \frac{1}{3}\text{ imagery} + \frac{1}{3}\text{ intentional}$$

(3) $\text{Contrast} = \frac{1}{3}\text{ adjective} + \frac{1}{3}\text{ imagery} + \frac{1}{3}\text{ intentional} - \frac{1}{2}\text{ counting} - \frac{1}{2}\text{ rhyming}$

(4) Coefficients for contrast (in the same order as the levels): $-\frac{1}{2}, -\frac{1}{2}, +\frac{1}{3}, +\frac{1}{3}, +\frac{1}{3}$

The coefficients must sum to zero, and those for the means in the first set that are assumed not to differ are identical, and those for the means in the other set are also identical. You can easily see that this holds in the above case. However, SPSS does not allow us to enter fractions, and many, such as 1/3 in our example, do not have an exact decimal version. So it is best to find a version of the contrast that uses small whole numbers. Thus, there is a final step:

(5) Multiply by the lowest common denominator (the smallest number that can be divided without a remainder by the two denominators 2 and 3, i.e., 6) to get all whole numbers −3, −3, 2, 2, 2.

The contrast we end up with is six times the one we wanted, but we shall be testing whether it is zero, so six times the original is just as good.

To do this in SPSS return to SPSS Dialog Box 2.2 and click the **Contrasts** button to get SPSS Dialog Box 2.4. Enter the first coefficient (−3) in the **Coefficients** box and click **Add**. This is repeated for successive coefficients. The dialog box is shown just before **Add** is clicked for the last time. Click **Continue** and **OK** to obtain the output. The result of the comparison is shown in SPSS Output 2.5.

SPSS Dialog Box 2.4 Weighting the means with coefficients to make the desired comparison.

Contrast Coefficients

Contrast	depth of processing				
	counting	rhyming	adjective	imagery	intentional
1	-3	-3	2	2	2

Contrast Tests

		Contrast	Value of Contrast	Std. Error	t	df	Sig. (2-tailed)
recall	Assume equal variances	1	31.10	5.387	5.773	45	.000
	Does not assume equal variances	1	31.10	4.826	6.445	37.829	.000

SPSS Output 2.5 Coefficients creating the contrast and the result of the contrast.

The first output table just displays the coefficients we entered. The second table gives the result of the comparison. We select the first or second row, depending on whether or not the Levene test indicated that we could assume equal variances. The Levene statistic was not significant, so we look at the first row. We find a t value that is highly significant, but we do not accept the significance level given because we need to allow for the fact that we decided on the comparison after looking at our data, which is equivalent to testing all possible contrasts before looking at the data (a rather extreme form of multiple testing). Instead, we use the Scheffé correction. As the Scheffé correction works with F rather than t, we square the t value to get $F = 33.33$ with 4 and 45 degrees of freedom. Now comes the adjustment. If we look up the critical value of $F(4,45)$ in a statistical table for α set at .001, we get $F_{crit} = 5.56$. The adjustment involves multiplying this critical value by the number of levels of the factor minus one (i.e., 4). So the adjusted critical value of F is $4 \times 5.56 = 22.24$, which is still less than our obtained value of $F = 33.33$, so the two sets of means differ significantly using a Scheffé correction for post hoc multiple testing: adjusted $F(4,45) = 33.33, p < .001$.

A one-way design: Multiple planned comparisons

Before leaving the topic of follow-up tests, we make one further point concerning the testing of planned comparisons (i.e., comparisons arising from a priori hypotheses). If you test more than two or three planned comparisons you run into the same issue of multiple testing that arose in connection with post hoc tests, especially if the various comparisons are not *orthogonal* (independent of one another). A convenient adjustment for multiple testing in this situation is provided by the *Bonferroni t*-test. We do not explain how to determine whether planned comparisons are independent, or why it matters, in this book. There is an excellent chapter in Howell (2007) that we recommend if you want to understand more about these topics.

In SPSS the p value reported from the *Bonferroni* correction for multiple testing is the original p value multiplied by the number of possible tests (with a maximum reported value of 1.000). So if you had a factor with five levels, then the p value reported from the Bonferroni t-test would be multiplied by 10 (because of the 10 pairs). Note that in general if you have k levels then there will be $k(k - 1)/2$ pairs and so each Bonferroni p value will be multiplied by this value. This is unnecessarily conservative and would lead possibly to failing to reject a hypothesis if you only wanted to test, for example, two pairs.

A factorial between-subjects design

A psychology example of a between-subjects design

The data from a 3 × 3 between-subjects design are shown in Table 2.4. In this experiment three methods of teaching students to work with data were compared. Each method was tried with three levels of practice and after the training the students performed a task on which they were marked out of 25 (their SCORE). The factor TRAINING has three levels: 'means-ends analysis', 'hypothesis generation' and 'rule application'. The factor TRIALS also has three levels: 5, 10 and 15 practice trials. The 27 participants were randomly assigned to the nine conditions, 3 to each condition, so each condition, or *cell in the table*, has three *replicates*. Each observation in the table represents one participant. As usual, if this were a real experiment, the number of participants per cell should be justified by a power analysis.

Table 2.4 Data from a factorial between-subjects design

Training procedure	Number of practice trials		
	5	10	15
Means-ends analysis	6	12	18
	4	9	25
	8	10	22
Hypothesis generation	14	19	15
	20	24	14
	17	13	22
Rule application	9	14	10
	14	12	12
	12	19	20

A between-subjects design: Setting it up in SPSS

The SPSS datasheet should be arranged with each participant occupying a row and each variable occupying a column, so we need three columns for our variables SCORE, TRAINING and TRIALS. The order is not important but we list all the scores for 5 practice trials followed by all those for 10 trials and finally all those for 15, making a column of length 27, which is one observation for each of the 27 participants. The next column gives the training method (coded 1, 2 or 3) for each observation, so there are three 1s followed by three 2s and then three 3s, and the whole list of nine is repeated twice more. The next column has nine 5s, then nine 10s and finally nine 15s. The order in which the variables are placed does not matter as long as it is the same for every participant. The first 11 rows of our datasheet appear as Table 2.5 (the full dataset can be found on the book website as psy.anova.between.sav).

Table 2.5 First few cases of data from a factorial between-subjects design set out for the SPSS datasheet (the full dataset can be found as psy.anova.between.sav on the website)

Score	Training	Trials
6	1	5
4	1	5
8	1	5
14	2	5
20	2	5
17	2	5
9	3	5
14	3	5
12	3	5
12	1	10
9	1	10

A between-subjects design: Requesting the analysis in SPSS

Once the datasheet is complete with its 27 rows and 3 columns, choose from the menu bar **Analyze**, then **General Linear Model**, then **Univariate**, to get SPSS Dialog Box 2.5. Select SCORE from the variable list and use the arrow to put it in the **Dependent Variable** box. Then put TRAINING and TRIALS in the **Fixed Factors** box, so the dialog box appears as shown. We shall not be considering random factors, and covariates are considered in

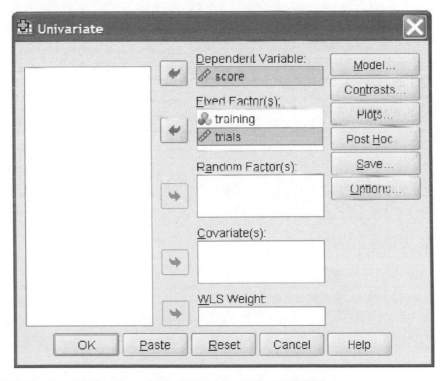

SPSS Dialog Box 2.5 Starting a factorial between-subjects ANOVA.

Chapter 5, 'Analysis of Covariance (ANCOVA)'. The **WLS Weight** box allows you to apply weights to the observations, but again this is something we do not consider. If you click **OK** now you will get the ANOVA, but we will look at some of the extra information available from the other buttons.

First click the **Model** button to get SPSS Dialog Box 2.6. The **Full factorial** radio button is the default, and we could accept this. This will include the main effect for each of our IVs and also the interaction between them. However, we will take this opportunity to demonstrate how to build the required model yourself. It might be useful to be able to do this if, for example, the interaction turned out not to be significant and we decided to remove it in order to improve the power of the ANOVA to detect significant main effects. So we click the **Custom** radio button and build up the model terms ourselves. From the **Build Term(s)** menu select **Main effects**, then use the arrow to put both factors into the **Model** box. Then select either **Interaction** or **All 2-way** from the menu, select both factors and use the arrow to put the interaction in the **Model** box. Here, because we have only two factors, there is only one interaction between them, so **All 2-way** will just give us one two-way interaction, the same as if we selected **Interaction**. However, in an experiment with three factors, there would be three two-way interactions (and one three-way), so we could enter all of the two-way interactions by selecting **All 2-way** and all three factors before clicking the arrow. If we want to enter just one of the two-way interactions though (perhaps after finding that the other two are not significant), it is useful to have **Interaction** available on the menu to do this.

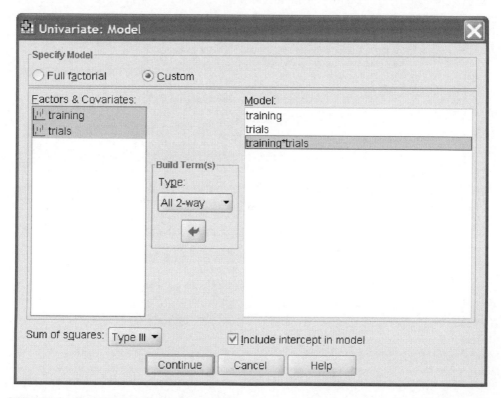

SPSS Dialog Box 2.6 Specifying the model.

Near the bottom of the dialog box is a menu offering different choices for **Sum of squares**. Type III is the default, and almost always the one we want. Chapter 5 on ANCOVA gives a brief discussion of a situation where a different choice may be appropriate. Make sure **Include intercept in model** (the default) is ticked, otherwise we shall be assuming that the overall mean is zero.

Click **Continue** to return to SPSS Dialog Box 2.5, and click the **Plots** button to get SPSS Dialog Box 2.7. Select TRIALS and use the arrow to put it in the **Horizontal Axis** box. Then put TRAINING in the **Separate Lines** box. Click **Add** and TRIALS * TRAINING appears in the **Plots** box. This will allow us to see a graph shown in SPSS Output 2.8. We could have reversed the roles of the two factors. In fact you can request both these plots if you wish, since when you click **Add**, the **Horizontal Axis** and **Separate Lines** boxes empty, so you can now put TRAINING in the **Horizontal Axis** box, TRIALS in the **Separate Lines** box and click **Add** again. Click **Continue** to return to SPSS Dialog Box 2.5.

SPSS Dialog Box 2.7 Requesting a plot of the effects.

Now click the **Options** button to get a list of statistics for optional display. Since we have requested a visual display of the means in the plot, leave the **Display Means for** box empty. If we decide later that means for the nine conditions, or those for each of the three levels of TRAINING, and for each of the three levels of TRIALS, might be useful, we can always re-run the analysis and request them. We could also request a table of means for the interaction, which would give us a table of means for each of the nine conditions in the experiment: remember that we had three observations (replicates) for each condition. But for now, omit all these. In the **Display** group click **Homogeneity tests**, which will provide a check on the assumption that variances are equal in all conditions. The **Residual plot** provides a check on the assumption of approximate normality, so click this as well. The **Estimates of effect size** should be reported if our factors turn out to be significant, though you should be aware that SPSS provides *partial* estimates of effect size (the proportion of factor plus error variance accounted for by the factor) and that may not be what you want. If you want full estimates of *eta squared* (that is, the proportion of total variance accounted for by the factor), you will need to divide SS(factor) by SS(total) yourself. The Sums of Squares (SS) are given in SPSS ANOVA summary tables. The **Observed power** will be potentially useful for planning future experiments and should be reported in order to facilitate any future meta-analyses. So, we select **Estimates of effect size, Observed power, Homogeneity tests** and **Residual plot**, then click **Continue** to return to SPSS Dialog Box 2.5.

The **Save** button allows us to keep the values of the DV that are predicted by the model (they can be added to the datasheet). There are other statistics that can also be saved, but we will not use this facility. We also ignore the **Post Hoc** button. We considered post hoc tests in connection with the one-way example. The same principles apply in relation to factorial designs but, if you want to use them there, you are advised to consult more detailed treatments of the topic (see 'Further reading' at the end of the book).

We also introduced the use of the **Contrasts** option for follow-up tests in our one-way example. Again, the principles apply to factorial designs as well, but you probably need to read further before using **Contrasts** in factorial designs. In fact, we have found that it is often simpler to do these contrasts by hand, making use of some of the standard output from the SPSS analysis, but we are not going to embark further on this rather big topic. The buttons at the bottom are mostly self-explanatory (**Paste** allows you to paste the SPSS commands and so use the command language; the Appendix tells you how you can use this). Press **OK** to get the analysis.

A between-subjects design: Understanding the output

The first table in the output (not shown here) just lists the factors, their levels and the number of observations at each level. Each of our factors has three levels, and there were 27 observations, 9 at each level of each factor, or 3 at each of the nine combinations of factor levels. Next is a test for the equality of variances, that is, a check on the homogeneity of variance assumption, shown as the first table in SPSS Output 2.6.

Levene's Test of Equality of Error Variances[a]

Dependent Variable:score

F	df1	df2	Sig.
1.069	8	18	.426

Tests the null hypothesis that the error variance of the dependent variable is equal across groups.

a. Design: Intercept + training + trials + training * trials

Tests of Between-Subjects Effects

Dependent Variable:score

Source	Type III Sum of Squares	df	Mean Square	F	Sig.	Partial Eta Squared	Noncent. Parameter	Observed Power[b]
Corrected Model	537.852[a]	8	67.231	4.867	.003	.684	38.933	.974
Intercept	5749.481	1	5749.481	416.182	.000	.959	416.182	1.000
training	122.074	2	61.037	4.418	.027	.329	8.836	.685
trials	162.074	2	81.037	5.866	.011	.395	11.732	.811
training * trials	253.704	4	63.426	4.591	.010	.505	18.365	.870
Error	248.667	18	13.815					
Total	6536.000	27						
Corrected Total	786.519	26						

a. R Squared = .684 (Adjusted R Squared = .543)

b. Computed using alpha = .05

SPSS Output 2.6 The test for the homogeneity of variance assumption and the ANOVA summary table.

Below the table is a reminder of the terms we included in our analysis. In our example, $F(8,18)$ is only 1.069 and the probability of this (look at the Sig column) is well above .05, so the assumption of homogeneity of variance is satisfied.

Next comes the ANOVA table, the second in SPSS Output 2.6. The Intercept, or grand mean, is significantly different from zero (look in the Sig column opposite Intercept) but this is rarely of any interest. Below that we see that the main effect of TRAINING is significant at the 5% level: $F(2,18) = 4.42$, $p = .027$, <.05, with an effect size of partial $\eta^2 = .33$ and retrospective (observed) power = .69. The main effect of TRIALS is also significant at 5%: $F(2,18) = 5.87$, $p = .011$, <.05, with an effect size of partial $\eta^2 = .40$ and power = .81. The interaction is just significant at the 1% level: $F(4,18) = 4.59$, $p = .010$, with an effect size of partial $\eta^2 = .51$ and power = .87.

Since the interaction is significant, as we saw earlier we must interpret the main effects with care. We will return to this after we have looked at the remainder of the output. We consider next our Residual plot, shown as SPSS Output 2.7. A reminder of the model used is at the bottom. The useful plot from here is in the centre of the bottom row. This one shows the predicted values of the DV from the model on the X-axis, and the residuals on the Y-axis. The residual of an observation is the difference between the observation and the value predicted by the model. Here the residuals have been standardized so they have a mean of zero and a standard deviation of 1. If our normality assumption is correct, the standardized residuals are standard normal random variables, and this plot should show a shapeless cloud of points. Our plot is indeed a shapeless cloud of points and we can take it that, for our data, the normality assumption is satisfied.

Dependent Variable: score

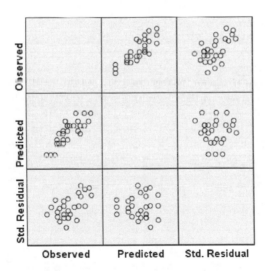

Model: Intercept + training + trials + training * trials

SPSS Output 2.7 Residual plots.

The graph at centre left shows the predicted versus the observed values: a perfect fit would give a straight line, but of course there are always bits of random variation. The three graphs at upper right are just mirror images of those at lower left. The graph of standardized residuals versus observed values is of no interest since the residuals are always correlated with the observed values.

So we consider next our plot, which appears at the end of the output, and is shown as SPSS Output 2.8. Here we see that the TRAINING methods 'hypothesis generation' and 'rule application' show similar patterns: an increase in the SCORE when we increase the

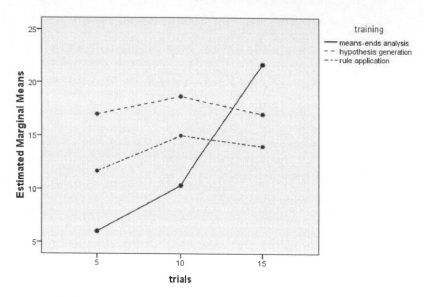

SPSS Output 2.8 A plot of the means.

number of TRIALS from 5 to 10, and a slight decrease when the number of TRIALS is increased again to 15. The hypothesis generation method scores between about three and five higher than the rule application method at every level of TRIALS. The pattern for the means-ends analysis TRAINING method is quite different, with the SCORE being very much higher at 15 TRIALS than at 10. This difference in patterns will account for the significance of the interaction.

Example Box 2.2

An alternative medical example for the same between-subjects design

The full analysis for this example can be found at www.psypress.com/ multivariate-analysis/medical-examples (click on Chapter 2).

A pilot study is designed to investigate the efficacy of three drugs at three dosages in the preventative treatment of migraine. The selection criterion for 27 patients is at least 20 moderate or severe migraines in the past 12 months, based on an annual migraine diary in which occurrences of mild, moderate and severe migraine are recorded (a mild migraine is one that does not interfere with usual activities, a moderate migraine is one that inhibits but does not wholly prevent usual activities and a severe migraine is one that prevents all activities). Nine patients are randomly allocated to each of three drug types and, within each drug type, three are randomly allocated to each of three dose levels (low, medium and high). The factors are thus drug type (DRUG) with three levels (drug 1, drug 2 or drug 3) and drug dose (DOSE) with three levels (low, medium and high). The DV is reduction in the number of moderate or severe migraines within the following 12 months.

Outcomes

We can see from the plot that drugs 2 and 3 show a similar pattern: an increase in the effect when we increase the dose from the first to the second level, then a slight decrease at dose level 3. Drug 2 scores higher than drug 3 at each dose. The pattern for drug 1 is different, with a sharp increase in effect at the highest dose. (See SPSS Output 2.8 for the plot.) This difference in patterns accounts for the significant interaction. There are significant main effects of drug type (drug 2 > drug 3 > drug 1) and drug dose (dose 3 > dose 2 > dose 1), and a significant interaction between the two factors, as referred to above. In view of the significant interaction, tests of simple effects are carried out and it is found that there are significant simple effects of drug type at low and medium dosages. A subsequent full study will involve low levels of drug types 2 and 3 and a placebo.

Alternative variables for use in SPSS
The full dataset, med.anova.between.sav, can be found on the book website

Variable	Psychology	Medicine
Factor 1	TRAINING Training method 1=means-ends analysis 2=hypothesis generation 3=rule application	DRUG Drug type 1=drug 1 2=drug 2 3=drug 3
Factor 2	TRIALS 1=5 practice trials 2=10 practice trials 3=15 practice trials	DOSE 1=low dose 2=medium dose 3=high dose
DV	SCORE Mean recall	SCORE Reduction in migraine frequency

A between-subjects design: Simple effects following a significant interaction

As we have already mentioned, because the interaction is significant, we really need to compare TRAINING methods at each level of the TRIALS variable, that is, we need to examine the simple effects of TRAINING. The simplest way to do this is to split the data into three, with a set for each level of TRIALS. Then we carry out a one-way ANOVA on each of the three datasets. To split the data into three sets, while in the SPSS datasheet, select **Data** from the menu bar and then **Split File**. Click on the radio button **Organize output by groups** and use the arrow to move TRIALS into the **Groups Based on** box. Check that **Sort the file by grouping variables** is selected and click **OK**. Then proceed to request a one-way analysis just as in the previous one-way example. In the dialog box that is like SPSS Dialog Box 2.2, move SCORE into the **Dependent List** box and TRAINING into the **Factor** box and click **OK**. SPSS will do three one-way analyses, one for each level of TRIALS. The results – an ANOVA of SCORE for each level of TRIALS – are shown in SPSS Output 2.9.

ANOVA[a]

score

	Sum of Squares	df	Mean Square	F	Sig.
Between Groups	181.556	2	90.778	14.086	.005
Within Groups	38.667	6	6.444		
Total	220.222	8			

a. trials = 5

ANOVA[a]

score

	Sum of Squares	df	Mean Square	F	Sig.
Between Groups	104.667	2	52.333	3.438	.101
Within Groups	91.333	6	15.222		
Total	196.000	8			

a. trials = 10

ANOVA[a]

score

	Sum of Squares	df	Mean Square	F	Sig.
Between Groups	89.556	2	44.778	2.264	.185
Within Groups	118.667	6	19.778		
Total	208.222	8			

a. trials = 15

SPSS Output 2.9 One-way ANOVAs to test for simple effects following a significant interaction.

These results suggest that only the simple effect of TRAINING at the 5-trial level of TRIALS is significant: $F(2,6) = 14.086$, $p < .01$. However, it is legitimate to use all of the data (i.e., from all levels of TRIALS) to get a better estimate of the error (within groups) variance, provided that variances are homogeneous across conditions. As this is a reasonable assumption in this case, we will adopt that strategy. To do this, replace the within-groups MS in each one-way table with the within-groups MS (13.815, labelled Error in SPSS Output 2.6) from the main 3×3 ANOVA. Then use that value in the formula $F = \text{MS(training)}/\text{MS(error from main ANOVA)}$ to obtain a new F value for each simple effect. The values are: $F(5 \text{ trials}) = 6.57$, $F(10 \text{ trials}) = 3.86$, $F(15 \text{ trials}) = 3.24$, all with 2 and 18 dfs (from the main ANOVA table). We refer to tables for the F distribution and find that, with 2 and 18 dfs, the critical value with α at .05 is $F_{\text{crit}} = 3.55$, and that with α at .01 is $F_{\text{crit}} = 6.01$. So, we find the simple effect of training at the 5-trial level to be significant at $p < .01$ and that at the 10-trial level to be significant at $p < .05$. So, that little bit of extra work was quite worthwhile.

You may note that, having found significant simple effects of TRAINING, we may still want to find out whether pairs of training levels differed from one another at the given level of TRIALS. This is a question that can be addressed with a Tukey post hoc test, for example. Finally, it would be perfectly feasible to examine the simple effects of TRIALS at each level of TRAINING as well as, or instead of, the simple effects of TRAINING at each level of TRIALS. Which we choose to look at is just a matter of the focus of our interest: in this case, probably on TRAINING more so than on TRIALS.

A factorial within-subjects design

A psychology example of a within-subjects design

In this experiment ten participants had to decide whether two objects were identical when they were presented at different orientations. To see whether they were identical, one of the objects needed to be rotated through an angle of 30°, 60° or 90°. The objects were either letters or abstract shapes. The DV was the time in milliseconds to make the decision, identical or not. Each of ten participants did a letter and a shape at each angle, so we have two within-subjects variables. The data are shown in Table 2.6. As usual, for a real experiment, the sample size would have been based on a power analysis.

A within-subjects design: Setting it up in SPSS

We will call our two within-subjects variables MODE (with two levels, 'letter' and 'shape') and ANGLE (with three levels, 30, 60 and 90). Notice that the two levels of MODE are both used within each level of ANGLE, giving the two within-subjects variables a hierarchical structure. As always we need one row of the SPSS datasheet for each participant and we need a variable name for each of the six columns of observations. The easiest way might be just to call the observations TIME1, TIME2, . . . TIME6, or we might prefer to call them A1M1, A1M2, . . . A3M2 (where 'A' stands for ANGLE and 'M' stands for MODE), which reflects the meaning of the six conditions. This is what we have done, so the SPSS datasheet contains the six columns of data arranged as in Table 2.6, with the six variables named A1M1, A1M2, . . . A3M2.

Table 2.6 Data from a design with two within-subjects variables (psy.anova.within.sav)

| Participant | Amount of rotation required | | | | | |
| | 30 | | 60 | | 90 | |
	Letter	*Shape*	*Letter*	*Shape*	*Letter*	*Shape*
1	240	261	251	266	259	264
2	290	288	300	293	306	318
3	326	342	328	350	334	363
4	255	268	262	267	270	278
5	260	284	324	290	313	321
6	292	264	322	292	320	329
7	279	266	301	284	332	326
8	289	260	293	309	306	297
9	301	264	335	283	320	268
10	292	317	302	313	307	309

A within-subjects design: Requesting the analysis in SPSS

Once we have the datasheet with 10 rows and 6 columns, we select from the menu bar **Analyze, General Linear Model** and **Repeated Measures**, and we get SPSS Dialog Box 2.8. We have two within-subjects factors to enter and we need to do it in the correct order, with ANGLE first, since that is the one that contains each level of MODE. So type ANGLE in the **Within-Subject Factor Name** box, 3 in the **Number of Levels** box and click **Add**. Then repeat the process with MODE and 2. There is no need to type anything in the **Measure Name** box, but if you like you could type TIME for the DV to give us SPSS Dialog Box 2.8 as shown. Click **Define** to get SPSS Dialog Box 2.9 (shown opposite).

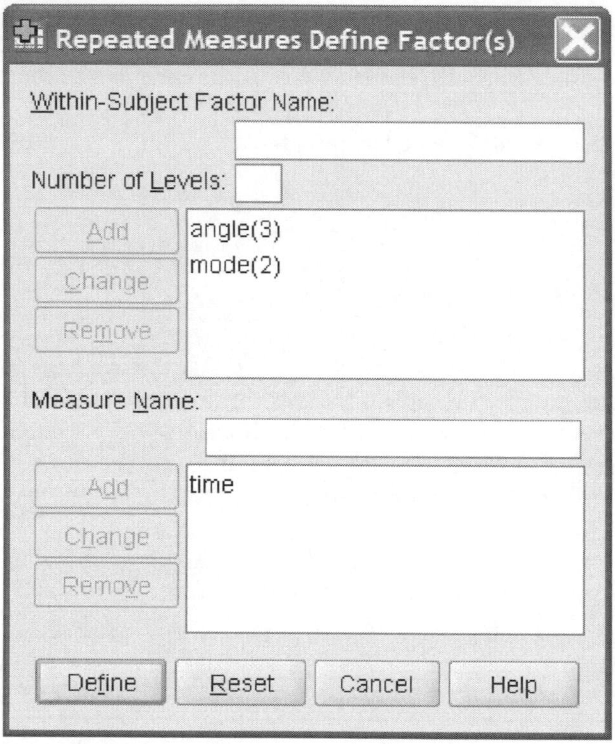

SPSS Dialog Box 2.8 Defining the within-subjects factors.

All we have to do is use the arrow to put the variables into the **Within-Subjects Variables** box in the correct order, so the result is as shown. You can check that the factors were entered in the correct order: see that the first column, A1M1, is labelled (1,1), both factors at level 1; the second column, A1M2, is labelled (1,2), where factor 1 (ANGLE) is at level 1 and factor 2 (MODE) is at level 2. This is correct for our first two columns of data. You can easily check that the entries are correct for the remaining four columns. We have no between-subjects factors or covariates.

If we click the **Model** button we get a dialog box like SPSS Dialog Box 2.6. We can either accept the default (**Full Factorial**) or click the **Custom** radio button and enter the main effects for MODE and ANGLE and their interaction, as we did for TRIALS and TRAINING in SPSS Dialog Box 2.6. The results are exactly the same, so we may as well accept the default.

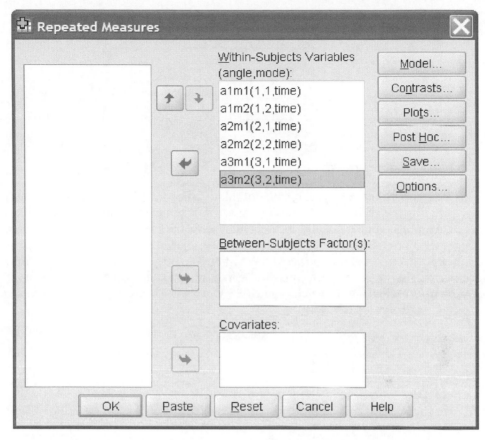

SPSS Dialog Box 2.9 Defining the factor levels for the within-subjects factors.

In the **Plots** dialog box (like SPSS Dialog Box 2.7), put ANGLE in the **Horizontal Axis** box and MODE in the **Separate Lines** box.

In the **Options** dialog box, click **Estimates of effect size** and **Observed power**. Homogeneity tests are not available for within-subjects factors. You can get **Residual plots** but there will be one for each of the variables A1M1–A3M2, each with 10 points on it (one for each subject). The 10 points on the A1M1 plot all have ANGLE at level 1 and MODE at level 1, so they all have the same predicted value. This means that, in a plot of predicted values on the horizontal axis against residual values on the vertical axis, all 10 points will lie on a straight vertical line. All you can observe, therefore, is whether any of the points lie a long way from the others, indicating a poor fit for the corresponding observation. The same is true for each of the plots for the rest of the variables A1M2–A3M2. None of the plots show such an effect and we do not reproduce them here. Now all that remains is to click **Continue** and **OK** to get the analysis.

A within-subjects design: Understanding the output

The first table in the output is a summary of the data, which is a useful check on the way the factors were defined (SPSS Output 2.10). Here you can see that we entered our two factors in the correct order, with our six columns of data corresponding in pairs to the three levels of ANGLE.

Within-Subjects Factors

Measure:time

angle	mode	Dependent Variable
1	1	a1m1
	2	a1m2
2	1	a2m1
	2	a2m2
3	1	a3m1
	2	a3m2

SPSS Output 2.10 Data summary.

This summary is followed by the tables of multivariate tests. These provide an alternative procedure to the repeated measures analysis. The multivariate analysis requires fewer assumptions, but is usually more conservative than the conventional repeated measures (within-subjects) analysis. Discussion of the multivariate solution will be held over to the next chapter on MANOVA. For our purposes here, we will confine ourselves to the within-subjects analysis. First, we need to look at the result of the Mauchly sphericity test, which is in SPSS Output 2.11. We see that the result is

Mauchly's Test of Sphericity[b]

Measure:time

Within Subjects Effect	Mauchly's W	Approx. Chi-Square	df	Sig.	Epsilon[a] Greenhouse-Geisser	Huynh-Feldt	Lower-bound
angle	.749	2.315	2	.314	.799	.945	.500
mode	1.000	0.000	0	.	1.000	1.000	1.000
angle * mode	.912	0.737	2	.692	.919	1.000	.500

Tests the null hypothesis that the error covariance matrix of the orthonormalized transformed dependent variables is proportional to an identity matrix.

a. May be used to adjust the degrees of freedom for the averaged tests of significance. Corrected tests are displayed in the Tests of Within-Subjects Effects table.

b. Design: Intercept
Within Subjects Design: angle + mode + angle * mode

Tests of Within-Subjects Effects

Measure:time

Source		Type III Sum of Squares	df	Mean Square	F	Sig.	Partial Eta Squared	Noncent. Parameter	Observed Power[a]
angle	Sphericity Assumed	6492.633	2	3246.317	14.711	.000	.620	29.423	.996
	Greenhouse-Geisser	6492.633	1.598	4061.885	14.711	.001	.620	23.515	.987
	Huynh-Feldt	6492.633	1.889	3436.407	14.711	.000	.620	27.795	.994
	Lower-bound	6492.633	1.000	6492.633	14.711	.004	.620	14.711	.925
Error(angle)	Sphericity Assumed	3972.033	18	220.669					
	Greenhouse-Geisser	3972.033	14.386	276.107					
	Huynh-Feldt	3972.033	17.004	233.590					
	Lower-bound	3972.033	9.000	441.337					
mode	Sphericity Assumed	93.750	1	93.750	0.159	.699	.017	0.159	.065
	Greenhouse-Geisser	93.750	1.000	93.750	0.159	.699	.017	0.159	.065
	Huynh-Feldt	93.750	1.000	93.750	0.159	.699	.017	0.159	.065
	Lower-bound	93.750	1.000	93.750	0.159	.699	.017	0.159	.065
Error(mode)	Sphericity Assumed	5300.417	9	588.935					
	Greenhouse-Geisser	5300.417	9.000	588.935					
	Huynh-Feldt	5300.417	9.000	588.935					
	Lower-bound	5300.417	9.000	588.935					
angle * mode	Sphericity Assumed	165.100	2	82.550	0.680	.519	.070	1.361	.147
	Greenhouse-Geisser	165.100	1.838	89.815	0.680	.508	.070	1.251	.142
	Huynh-Feldt	165.100	2.000	82.550	0.680	.519	.070	1.361	.147
	Lower-bound	165.100	1.000	165.100	0.680	.431	.070	0.680	.115
Error(angle*mode)	Sphericity Assumed	2184.233	18	121.346					
	Greenhouse-Geisser	2184.233	16.544	132.026					
	Huynh-Feldt	2184.233	18.000	121.346					
	Lower-bound	2184.233	9.000	242.693					

a. Computed using alpha = .05

SPSS Output 2.11 Mauchly test of sphericity and within-subjects analysis.

non-significant for ANGLE and for the interaction (ANGLE * MODE). There is no test for MODE because it has only two levels. The result of the within-subjects analysis is also in SPSS Output 2.11.

As the Mauchly test of sphericity was non-significant, we can look at the 'Sphericity Assumed' rows of the table, where we see that only the effect of ANGLE is significant: $F(2,18) = 14.71, p < .001$, with partial $\eta^2 = .62$ and power $= 1.00$. Had the sphericity test been significant, we would have needed to look at one of the other rows, which make various adjustments to the *df*s to allow for the violation of the sphericity assumption. We consider these in the next chapter on MANOVA. For ANGLE, it makes sense to ask whether the linear trend was significant, since the time taken to reach a decision could depend on how large the necessary angle of rotation was. That information is provided in the next (Tests of Within-Subjects Contrasts) table. We do not reproduce that table but we can report that the linear trend was significant: $F(1,9) = 19.09$, $p < .01$. The final table (Tests of Between-Subjects Effects) is of no interest when we have no between-subjects factors, as all it does is test the hypothesis that the overall mean is not zero, so it also is not reproduced here.

Finally we find the plot we requested (see SPSS Output 2.12) showing the effects. Here we can see that the decision TIME increases steadily with the rotation ANGLE, for both 'letter' (MODE level 1) and 'shape' (MODE level 2), with the values for 'shape' similar to those for 'letter' at ANGLE $= 30°$ and $90°$ and somewhat lower than those for 'letter' at ANGLE $= 60°$. However, our ANOVA tells us that neither the difference between the two levels of MODE nor its interaction with ANGLE is significant: with this number of observations, a difference of this size could just be due to random variation.

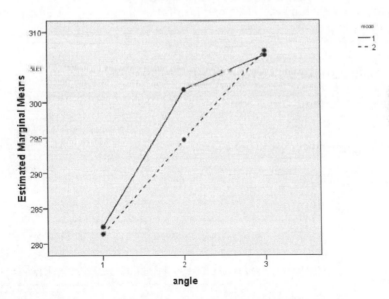

SPSS Output 2.12 Plot showing the effects of two within-subjects factors.

Example Box 2.3

An alternative medical example for the same within-subjects design

The full analysis for this example can be found at www.psypress.com/multivariate-analysis/medical-examples (click on Chapter 2).

A study is designed to determine whether choice reaction time (CRT) might serve as a marker of neurological function that could be used to assess the impact of experimental therapies on presymptomatic gene carriers for Huntington's disease. Ten presymptomatic gene carriers, identified through family history investigations followed by genetic testing, are recruited. They complete a CRT task on three occasions at intervals of 1 year. The CRT task involves making a left or right touch response on a touch-sensitive screen to a visual or auditory stimulus presented to the individual's left or right. The visual and auditory stimuli are presented in blocks, with order of modality balanced across participants. So we have a 3×2 factorial design with two within-subjects (repeated measures) factors: YEAR (year 1, year 2, year 3) and modality (MODE: 1 = visual, 2 = auditory). The DV is mean CRT for 30 trials in each of the 6 conditions.

Outcomes

There is a significant main effect of year (year 3 > year 2 > year 1), and the linear trend is significant. There is no significant effect for modality or for its interaction with year. As CRT increases regularly over years during the presymptomatic period, a test of this kind has potential as a marker for the progression of the disease following therapeutic interventions during the period when no obvious symptoms are apparent.

Alternative variables for use in SPSS
The full dataset, med.anova.within.sav, can be found on the book website

Variable	Psychology	Medicine
Factor 1	ANGLE Angle of rotation 1=30 degrees 2=60 degrees 3=90 degrees	YEAR Year of test 1=year 1 2=year 2 3=year 3
Factor 2	MODE 1=letter 2=shape	MODE 1=visual stimulus 2=auditory stimulus
DV	TIME Choice reaction time (ms)	TIME Choice reaction time (ms)

A mixed factorial design

A psychology example of a mixed design

Here we have an experiment where nine 10-year-olds were each presented with word lists in both blocked and unblocked modes (METHOD). The children were in three ability groups (IQ), with three in each group. The order in which they tackled the blocked and unblocked modes was randomized for each child. The DV is the score on free RECALL of the word lists. The data appear in Table 2.7. Once again, we remind you that, for a real experiment, the sample size should be justified by reference to a power analysis.

Table 2.7 Data from a mixed design (IQ between-subjects and presentation METHOD within-subjects) (psy.anova.mixed.sav)

Participant	IQ	method	
		Recall (blocked)	*Recall (unblocked)*
1	High	15	14
2	High	18	12
3	High	12	11
4	Medium	14	10
5	Medium	12	8
6	Medium	15	12
7	Low	13	6
8	Low	11	9
9	Low	14	5

A mixed design: Setting it up in SPSS

To set up the ANOVA in SPSS we need, as usual, a row of the datasheet for each participant. We shall need one column for the between-subjects variable, IQ, and two columns for the within-subjects variable, METHOD, one for each level of that variable (i.e., blocked and unblocked). Notice that the DV, the score on free RECALL, must be recorded as a variable for each level of the METHOD variable, which is the one that is within-subjects, so that each participant occupies one row of the datasheet. The SPSS datasheet is set out just like Table 2.7, except that we do not need the first column giving the participant number, nor do we need the heading METHOD, so we have nine rows and three columns of data, and we have called the variables IQ, RECALL1 and RECALL2 in the datasheet. The levels of IQ could be coded 1, 2 and 3 and labels assigned similarly to the example in SPSS Dialog Box 2.1.

A mixed design: Requesting the analysis in SPSS

Once the datasheet is ready, from the menu bar select **Analyze, General Linear Model** and **Repeated Measures** to get a dialog box like SPSS Dialog Box 2.8. First we must define the within-subjects factor. Type the factor name, which is METHOD in our example, in the **Within-Subject Factor Name** box. Then type 2 in the **Number of Levels** box and click **Add**. We have no more within-subjects factors. The **Measure Name** is the

DV, in our case RECALL, so type this into the box and click **Add**. Click **Define** to move on to a dialog box like SPSS Dialog Box 2.9.

Now use the arrow to put first the variable BLOCKED and then the variable UNBLOCKED into the **Within-Subjects Variables** box. The first variable that we enter becomes the value of the DV RECALL at level 1 of the within-subjects factor METHOD, and the next becomes the value at level 2. The small up and down arrows can be used to reverse the positions of the two levels of METHOD if necessary. Use the arrow to put IQ in the **Between-Subjects Factors** box.

Clicking the **Model** button gives us a dialog box like SPSS Dialog Box 2.6. This time there are separate boxes for **Within-** and **Between-Subjects** factors, and as we have only one of each we may as well accept the default **Full factorial** model. We could click the **Custom** radio button as we did in the between-subjects design, but all we can do is put METHOD in the **Within-Subjects Model** box and IQ in the **Between-Subjects Model** box. We could specify the interactions to include if we had more than one variable in a category, but the interactions between within-subjects and between-subjects variables to be included will be determined by the mixed nature of the design. The default sum of squares, Type III, is the one usually needed. If your design is balanced then all the different types give the same answer. For Type I, the sums of squares are found sequentially, allowing for variables already in the model so that the order of the variables in the model matters. For Type II, the sum of squares for a main effect is not adjusted for any interactions containing it. Type III gives the reduction in the residual sums, assuming that the effect was the last one entered into a model containing all the other variables. Type IV is a variation of Type III developed for designs with a combination of factor levels with no observations. Click **Continue** to return to the main dialog box.

The **Plots** button gives us a dialog box just like SPSS Dialog Box 2.7. This time, we request a plot with METHOD on the horizontal axis and separate lines for IQ. Remember to click **Add** and then **Continue**. In the **Options** dialog box, once again request **Estimates of effect size, Observed power, Homogeneity tests** and **Residual plot**. Then press **Continue** and **OK** to get the analysis.

A mixed design: Understanding the output

First in the output come two tables (not shown here) summarizing the levels of the within-subjects factor and showing the number of observations at each level of the between-subjects factor. This summary is followed by the tables of multivariate tests. In this case we have just one within-subjects factor and it has only two levels. In these circumstances the multivariate and univariate tests are equivalent and we just show the within-subjects analysis (we discuss the multivariate tests in the next chapter on MANOVA). In SPSS Output 2.13 we see the ANOVA table for the within-subjects effects. We see that METHOD is judged significant: $F(1,6) = 21.06$, $p = .004$, $< .01$, for sphericity assumed and also for all of the three adjusted methods (which will be discussed in the next chapter), and with an effect size of partial $\eta^2 = .78$ and power = .97. The interaction of METHOD with IQ is not significant: $F(2,6) = 1.22$, $p > .05$.

Since METHOD has only two levels, only the linear contrast is possible, and the table of within-subjects contrasts that follows the ANOVA table just repeats the information that METHOD is significant and its interaction with IQ is not.

Next is the test we requested to check the homogeneity of variance assumption, here done separately for the RECALL scores at the two levels of METHOD. Both probabilities

Tests of Within-Subjects Effects

Measure:recall

Source		Type III Sum of Squares	df	Mean Square	F	Sig.	Partial Eta Squared	Noncent. Parameter	Observed Power[a]
method	Sphericity Assumed	76.056	1	76.056	21.062	.004	.778	21.062	.966
	Greenhouse-Geisser	76.056	1.000	76.056	21.062	.004	.778	21.062	.966
	Huynh-Feldt	76.056	1.000	76.056	21.062	.004	.778	21.062	.966
	Lower-bound	76.056	1.000	76.056	21.062	.004	.778	21.062	.966
method * IQ	Sphericity Assumed	8.778	2	4.389	1.215	.360	.288	2.431	.178
	Greenhouse-Geisser	8.778	2.000	4.389	1.215	.360	.288	2.431	.178
	Huynh-Feldt	8.778	2.000	4.389	1.215	.360	.288	2.431	.178
	Lower-bound	8.778	2.000	4.389	1.215	.360	.288	2.431	.178
Error(method)	Sphericity Assumed	21.667	6	3.611					
	Greenhouse-Geisser	21.667	6.000	3.611					
	Huynh-Feldt	21.667	6.000	3.611					
	Lower-bound	21.667	6.000	3.611					

a. Computed using alpha = .05

Tests of Within-Subjects Contrasts

Measure:recall

Source	method	Type III Sum of Squares	df	Mean Square	F	Sig.	Partial Eta Squared	Noncent. Parameter	Observed Power[a]
method	Linear	76.056	1	76.056	21.062	.004	.778	21.062	.966
method * IQ	Linear	8.778	2	4.389	1.215	.360	.288	2.431	.178
Error(method)	Linear	21.667	6	3.611					

a. Computed using alpha = .05

Levene's Test of Equality of Error Variances[a]

	F	df1	df2	Sig.
recall1	0.598	2	6	.580
recall2	0.176	2	6	.842

Tests the null hypothesis that the error variance of the dependent variable is equal across groups.

a. Design: Intercept + IQ
Within Subjects Design: method

Tests of Between-Subjects Effects

Measure:recall
Transformed Variable:Average

Source	Type III Sum of Squares	df	Mean Square	F	Sig.	Partial Eta Squared	Noncent. Parameter	Observed Power[a]
Intercept	2473.389	1	2473.389	549.642	.000	.989	549.642	1.000
IQ	48.111	2	24.056	5.346	.046	.641	10.691	.609
Error	27.000	6	4.500					

a. Computed using alpha = .05

SPSS Output 2.13 ANOVA table for within-subjects factors, test for homogeneity of variance and ANOVA table for the between-subjects factor.

in the Sig column are well above .05 so we need have no concern about this assumption. The ANOVA table for the between-subjects factor follows and we see that the main effect of IQ is significant at the 5% level: $F(2,6) = 5.35$, $p = .046$, with an effect size of partial $\eta^2 = .64$ and power = .61. These results are all shown in SPSS Output 2.13.

Right at the end of the output is our plot (SPSS Output 2.14), where we see these results illustrated. The high IQ group performs best with both methods, followed by the medium IQ and then the low IQ groups. For all IQ groups, RECALL scores were higher using the BLOCKED METHOD. The differences among the group means were a little greater when the UNBLOCKED METHOD was used (but this difference was not great enough to cause a significant interaction effect).

Finally, the residual plots (one for RECALL scores at each level of METHOD) are not very informative in this analysis (because there are so few points in each) and we do not reproduce them here.

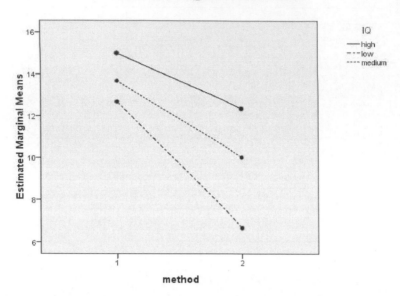

SPSS Output 2.14 Plot showing mean RECALL scores for three IQ groups for each of two methods of presentation, BLOCKED (Method 1) and UNBLOCKED (Method 2).

Example Box 2.4

An alternative medical example for the same mixed design

The full analysis for this example can be found at www.psypress.com/ multivariate-analysis/medical-examples (click on Chapter 2).

A study is designed to compare the effectiveness of top-of-the-range analogue and digital hearing aids in a wide range of acoustic environments for adults with mild to moderately severe sensorineural hearing loss. Nine adults aged between 50 and 60 years are recruited, three in the mid-range of each of three levels of hearing loss, based on the pure tone average of hearing thresholds at 500, 1000 and 2000 Hz. The three levels of hearing loss (LOSS) are defined as 60–65 dB (moderately severe), 45–50 dB (moderate) and 30–35 dB (mild). None of the participants has used a hearing aid before. Participants use either an analogue or digital hearing aid (TYPE), customized to their requirements, for a period of 2 months before its effectiveness is assessed. They then use the other type of hearing aid, again customized to their requirements, for 2 months before its effectiveness is assessed. The order of use of type of hearing aid is balanced across participants. Level of hearing LOSS is a between-subjects factor and TYPE of hearing aid is a within-subjects factor. The DV is a hearing difficulty score on the assessment test (DIFFIC). The test involves the presentation of 30 samples of speech recorded in environments ranging from quiet to extremely noisy and the participant reports 'difficulty' or 'no difficulty' in understanding each sample. The hearing difficulty score is the total number of samples for which difficulty is reported.

Outcomes

As expected, there is a significant main effect of level of hearing loss (moderately severe > moderate > mild) on difficulty experienced. Of greater interest, the other main effect, type of hearing aid, is also significant (analogue > digital). As there is no interaction between the two factors, the results suggest that a choice between these two types of hearing aid for adults in this age range with sensorineural loss anywhere in the mild to moderately severe range should favour the digital type.

Alternative variables for use in SPSS
The full dataset, med.anova.mixed.sav, can be found on the book website

Variable	Psychology	Medicine
Factor 1 (between-subjects)	IQ Intelligence test score 1=high 2=medium 3=low	LOSS Degree of hearing loss 1=moderately severe 2=moderate 3=mild
Factor 2 (within-subjects)	METHOD 1=BLOCKED 2=UNBLOCKED	TYPE 1=ANALOGUE 2=DIGITAL
DV	RECALL Free recall score	DIFFIC Hearing difficulty score

Reporting results

When reporting an experiment and an ANOVA it is not necessary to include the tables of SPSS output as we have done here. They can be summarized, quoting the values of the *F* statistic with the degrees of freedom and the probabilities, together with effect sizes and retrospective power. However, graphs that help you to understand the data will also help your readers, so include them if space permits. Also, report on any checks you did on the assumptions of normality and homogeneity of variance. For instance, we could summarize the results for our mixed design like this:

As described in the Method section, we had a mixed design with one within-subjects factor, METHOD, with levels 'blocked' and 'unblocked', and one between-subjects factor, IQ, so we performed a repeated measures ANOVA. The main effect of METHOD was significant: $F(1,6) = 21.06$, $p = .004$, with an effect size of partial $\eta^2 = .78$ and retrospective power = .97. The main effect of IQ was also significant: $F(2,6) = 5.35$, $p = .046$, with an effect size of partial $\eta^2 = .64$ and retrospective power = .61. The interaction was not significant: $F(2,6) = 1.22$, $p = .360$. Tests for the homogeneity of variance were applied to observations at each level of the within-subjects factor, and in each case the hypothesis of equal variances was not rejected. Residual plots gave no reason to suppose that the normality assumption was unjustified. A plot of the means of each level of METHOD (blocked and unblocked) for each IQ group is shown in Figure A (*this is our SPSS Output 2.14*).

It can be seen that the high IQ group performs best with both methods, followed by the medium IQ and then the low IQ groups. For all IQ groups, RECALL scores were higher using the blocked METHOD. The differences among the IQ group means were a little greater when the unblocked METHOD was used (but this difference was not large enough to cause a significant interaction effect).

References

Clark-Carter, D. (2009). *Quantitative psychological research: A student's handbook* (3rd ed.). Hove, UK: Psychology Press.

Cohen, J. (1988). *Statistical power analysis for the behavioural sciences* (2nd ed.). Hillsdale, NJ: Lawrence Erlbaum Associates, Inc.

Howell, D. C. (2007). *Statistical methods for psychology* (6th ed.). Pacific Grove, CA: Duxbury.

3   Multivariate analysis of variance (MANOVA)

Introduction

Multivariate ANOVA, with more than one DV, is a natural extension of ANOVA and is used in similar situations. Just as with ANOVA, the IVs can be between- or within-subjects, or we may have both in a mixed design. If we record several aspects of the outcome then we have several DVs and a multivariate ANOVA (or MANOVA). There are three specific uses of MANOVA that you are likely to encounter if you regularly analyse experimental data. The first two are the analysis of between-group data when there is more than one DV (e.g., REACTION TIME and ERRORS) and the analysis of within-group data when there is more than one DV, whether or not there are any between-group factors in the design. In these cases, MANOVA is used to test for effects (just as in ANOVA) using a *weighted combination* of the DVs that maximizes the differences among conditions. If this test yields significant effects, we know that experimental conditions differ on some combination of the DVs and this legitimizes a search for the effects in each of the DVs individually in a series of ANOVAs. There are really no new concepts to learn, but the setting up of MANOVAs and interpretation of the SPSS output often seem quite complex initially.

The remaining use of MANOVA is as an alternative to a repeated measures analysis when there is only one DV. Instead of the repeated measures being treated as levels of an IV, they are treated as a set of DVs (different measures on the same participants). The MANOVA solution does not need the assumption of sphericity, which is a reason for preferring it to the more familiar repeated measures ANOVA. The sphericity assumption is that the standard deviations of the within-subject differences between all the pairs of levels are equal. For example, if 10 subjects were measured three times then we could find the difference for each subject between their measurements at times 1 and 2, 1 and 3 and 2 and 3. Sphericity would be confirmed if the standard deviation of these three sets of 10 differences were approximately equal. More formal tests exist, which we will meet later in this chapter. Although MANOVA does not require the sphericity assumption, it does tend to be more conservative.

To perform a MANOVA we need to design our experiment so that participants are randomly assigned to treatment groups, just as in simpler experiments. In addition, MANOVA makes parametric assumptions that are the multivariate analogues of those made for ANOVA: the DVs are from a multivariate normal distribution for each treatment group, and these distributions have a common covariance matrix. A covariance matrix is an array of the variances and covariances of a set of variables, with the variances down the diagonal and the covariances in the upper and lower triangles. Here, for instance, is the covariance matrix for three variables X, Y and Z:

$$\begin{pmatrix} \text{var}(X) & \text{cov}(X, Y) & \text{cov}(X, Z) \\ \text{cov}(X, Y) & \text{var}(Y) & \text{cov}(Y, Z) \\ \text{cov}(X, Z) & \text{cov}(Y, Z) & \text{var}(Z) \end{pmatrix}$$

The matrix is symmetric, with the lower triangle mirroring the upper triangle.

In addition to illustrating the three uses of MANOVA we have referred to above, as this extension to ANOVA involves no new concepts we also use this chapter to demonstrate some *diagnostics*, that is, ways to check on the assumptions of ANOVA and MANOVA. When our data fail one of the diagnostic tests, we show how to try out *transformations* that may help. We also include here a brief discussion of *missing data* and *outliers*.

A between-subjects design with two DVs

A psychology example and (fabricated) data for a MANOVA (between-subjects) design

For our experiment we are testing training methods for recruits to a call centre dealing with travel queries. There are two training methods (METHOD): one uses part of the first session to describe the network using a map and the paper timetables available to the public; the other goes straight to the online information system that successful trainees will be expected to use when responding to queries. Both methods are tried with one, two and three training SESSIONS, so we have six experimental conditions. Thirty new recruits are randomly assigned, five to each of the conditions. After completing the training session(s) each recruit does a test in which they must respond to a standard set of queries put to them over their phones by the trainers. The number of queries they answer correctly in the test time (CORRECT) is recorded, and also the average delay in seconds before they begin their responses (DELAY). The data appear in Table 3.1 (ignore for the moment the fifth column, labelled TIME). Note that it is necessary to have more cases than DVs in every combination of factor levels (each combination of factor levels is often called a *cell*). This is a minimum requirement and, as in ANOVA, if this were a real experiment the sample size should have been based on a power analysis. One way to tackle this is to consider the DV for which you want to be able to detect the smallest effect and base your sample size on the number needed for acceptable power for that one. Sample sizes for the other experimental designs in this chapter should also be decided using a power analysis.

A between-subjects design with two DVs: Setting it up in SPSS

This is a between-subjects design, since each participant experiences just one of the six training conditions, so the first four columns of Table 3.1 are arranged exactly as required for the SPSS datasheet, with each participant occupying one row and with a column for each of the variables (IVs in the first two columns, DVs in columns 3 and 4).

Table 3.1 Data from a between-subjects experiment to compare training programs (psy.manova.between.sav)

Method	Sessions	Correct	Delay	Time
1	1	7	19	0.1429
1	1	7	17	0.1429
1	1	8	19	0.1250
1	1	9	18	0.1111
1	1	9	18	0.1111
1	2	11	16	0.0909
1	2	10	17	0.1000
1	2	12	18	0.0833
1	2	11	15	0.0909
1	2	8	16	0.1250
1	3	15	13	0.0667
1	3	9	12	0.1111
1	3	12	13	0.0833
1	3	15	11	0.0667
1	3	10	13	0.1000
2	1	10	15	0.1000
2	1	9	15	0.1111
2	1	11	15	0.0909
2	1	13	13	0.0769
2	1	9	17	0.1111
2	2	15	14	0.0667
2	2	22	14	0.0455
2	2	19	13	0.0526
2	2	13	13	0.0769
2	2	28	15	0.0357
2	3	21	10	0.0476
2	3	21	10	0.0476
2	3	16	12	0.0625
2	3	32	11	0.0313
2	3	43	11	0.0233

A between-subjects design with two DVs: Requesting the analysis in SPSS

From the menus choose **Analyze**, then **General Linear Model**, then **Multivariate**, to get a dialog box just like SPSS Dialog Box 2.5, except that the box at the top is labelled **Dependent Variables** instead of **Dependent Variable**. Using the arrows, put METHOD and SESSIONS into the **Fixed Factor(s)** box and CORRECT and DELAY into the **Dependent Variables** box. We could just click **OK** to get the analysis, but we will use the buttons on the right to get some extra information. If we click the **Model** button we get a dialog box just like SPSS Dialog Box 2.6, and just as with univariate ANOVA we can accept the default full factorial model or we can build a **Custom** model with the main effect of each of our factors and their interaction. The result will be the same, so we will just accept the default. As before, the default **Type III Sum of Squares** is also appropriate since we have a balanced design (the same number of participants in each condition).

Clicking the **Options** button gives us SPSS Dialog Box 3.1. This time we will request displays of **Homogeneity tests**, **Spread vs level plots** and **Residual plots**. Click **Continue** to return to the main dialog box, then ignore the other buttons for now and click **OK**.

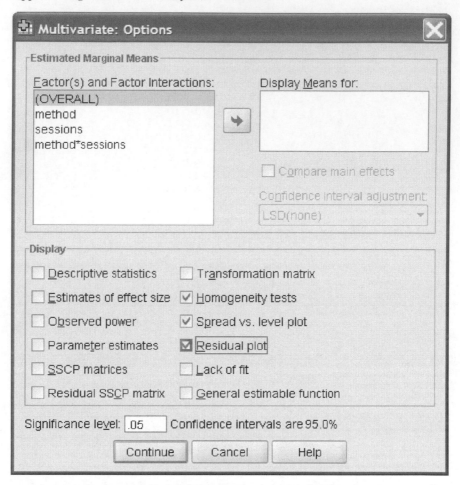

SPSS Dialog Box 3.1 Displaying some diagnostics.

These displays will allow us to check on the model assumptions, and since we shall find that our data do not conform to the assumptions we will turn now to consider the output, leaving consideration of the other buttons until later.

A between-subjects design with two DVs: Understanding the diagnostics output

First in the output is a table (not shown here) that summarizes the data, telling us how many cases were at each level of each factor. Next comes the first table in SPSS Output 3.1, Box's test of equality of covariance matrices. For univariate ANOVA we need to assume that the DV has the same variance for all combinations of factor levels (the homogeneity of variance assumption). The analogous assumption for MANOVA is that the DVs have the same covariance matrices for all combinations of factor levels. We can see that our data fail this test, since the F calculated from Box's M is significant at the 1% level (probability = .005 from the Sig row in the table). We reject the hypothesis that the covariance matrices are equal.

Box's Test of Equality of Covariance Matrices[a]

Box's M	42.317
F	2.213
df1	15.000
df2	3150.554
Sig.	.005

Tests the null hypothesis that the observed covariance matrices of the dependent variables are equal across groups.

a. Design: Intercept + method + sessions + method * sessions

Levene's Test of Equality of Error Variances[a]

	F	df1	df2	Sig.
correct	7.669	5	24	.000
delay	0.137	5	24	.982

Tests the null hypothesis that the error variance of the dependent variable is equal across groups.

a. Design: Intercept + method + sessions + method * sessions

SPSS Output 3.1 Tests of homogeneity of variances.

Ignoring the next table (Multivariate Tests) for the moment, we find below it the second table in SPSS Output 3.1. Here we have the homogeneity of variance test applied separately to each DV. For DELAY we would accept the hypothesis of equal variances (probability in the Sig column is .982), but for CORRECT we would reject it. Most likely it is only our DV CORRECT that is causing the problem. Since our data do not conform to the MANOVA homogeneity of variance assumption we will ignore the MANOVA tables and look at the plots we requested: perhaps these will suggest a possible remedy. SPSS Output 3.2 overleaf shows the first two Spread vs. Level plots. For the first plot, the standard deviation (*sd*) of CORRECT has been calculated for the five observations in each of the six combinations of factor levels. Each *sd* has been plotted against the mean value of CORRECT for that combination of factor levels. We can see that there is a clear relationship: the bigger the mean, the bigger the *sd*.

The plot for DELAY does not show such a relationship, although we can see some variation in the *sd*s for delay. With only five observations used to calculate each *sd*, we expect some variability due to random sampling, even if the *sd*s would be the same if we could observe the populations of all possible recruits receiving each of the six training schedules. For DELAY, the largest *sd* is less than twice the smallest, but for CORRECT, the largest is more than 10 times the smallest. Two more Spread vs. Level plots (not shown here) plot the variance instead of the *sd* against the mean. Turn now to the residual plots shown in SPSS Output 3.3 on page 61.

The centre plot on the bottom row of each matrix is the one we want. If the normality and homogeneity of variance assumptions are met, then the residuals will just be a random sample from a standard normal distribution, and the plot of residuals against predicted values will show a shapeless cloud of points. For DELAY, this is just what we do see. However, for CORRECT we see the range of the residuals expanding as we move from left to right, from lower to higher predicted values. The variance is not the same for all values of the IVs, reinforcing what we already know from the Spread vs. Level plots.

A between-subjects design with two DVs: Trying out transformations

There are several transformations we could consider for a variable where the variance increases with the mean, as is the case for CORRECT. A log, a square root or a reciprocal

Spread vs. Level Plot of correct

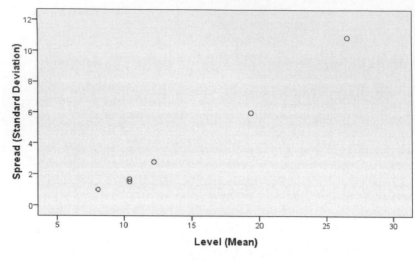

Groups: method * sessions

Spread vs. Level Plot of delay

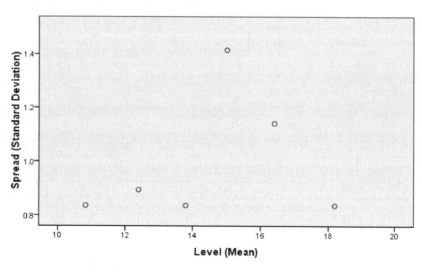

Groups: method * sessions

SPSS Output 3.2 Spread vs. Level plots show *sd* of CORRECT increases with mean.

Dependent Variable: correct

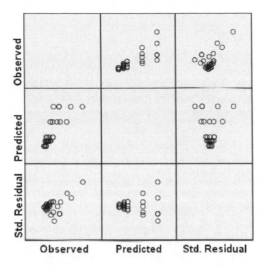

Model: Intercept + method + sessions + method * sessions

Dependent Variable: delay

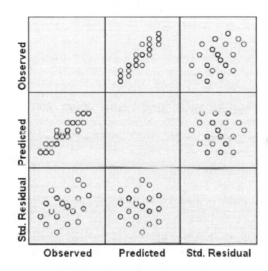

Model: Intercept + method + sessions + method * sessions

SPSS Output 3.3 Residual plots show variance of residuals increasing with predicted value for CORRECT, but not for DELAY.

transformation would tend to reduce the variance at higher values of the mean. To apply a transformation, use **Transform**, then **Compute** from the menu bar, to get SPSS Dialog Box 3.2. In the **Target Variable** box, type a suitable name for the transformed variable: here we use LOGCORRECT for the transformed variable log(CORRECT).

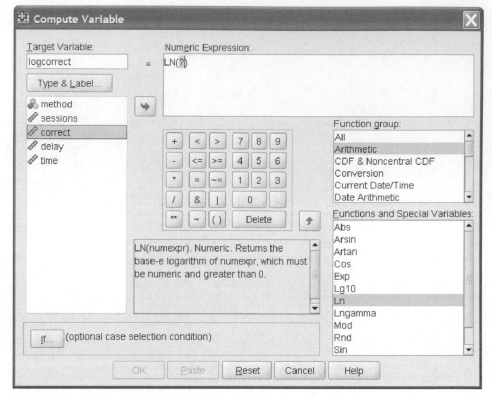

SPSS Dialog Box 3.2 Making a transformed variable.

Then choose a function group (here we want the **Arithmetic** group) to open up a list of functions in the **Functions and Special Variables** box. From this list, find the one you want and use the up arrow to put it in the **Numeric Expression** box. There are two log functions, Lg10 gives log to the base 10 and Ln gives natural logs: either will do but we chose Ln here. Now we use the right arrow to put CORRECT in the **Numeric Expression** box where the **?** is, and click **OK**. We now have a new variable in the datasheet called LOGCORRECT. For some transformations you need the arithmetic buttons instead of the function list. For instance, to get the reciprocal, click the 1, then / for divide, then use the arrow to enter CORRECT, so the **Numeric Expression** reads 1/CORRECT.

We used these methods to make two more transformations of CORRECT, the square root (called SQUROOT) and the reciprocal (called TIME). Using these as the DVs in a MANOVA we obtained the Spread vs. Level plots shown in SPSS Output 3.4. For LOGCORRECT and SQUROOT we see the same kind of dependence of the *sd* on the mean that we saw for CORRECT. However, if you compare these graphs with the one for CORRECT in SPSS Output 3.2 you will see from the vertical scale that the largest *sd* for CORRECT is about 11 times the smallest. For LOGCORRECT, the largest *sd* is about four times the smallest, and the same is true for SQUROOT. So both of these transformations have made the increase in *sd* with the mean less extreme. The reciprocal transformation, TIME, has removed the dependence of the *sd* on the mean, though the *sd* still shows some variation.

Spread vs. Level Plot of logcorrect

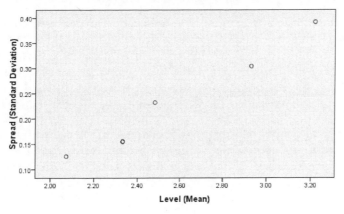

Groups: method * sessions

Spread vs. Level Plot of squroot

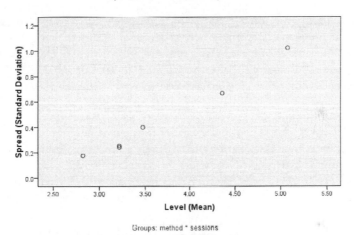

Groups: method * sessions

Spread vs. Level Plot of time

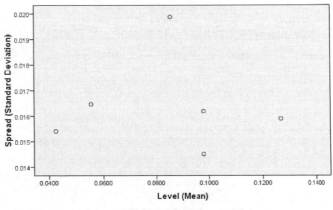

Groups: method * sessions

SPSS Output 3.4 Spread vs. Level plots for three transformations of CORRECT.

A between-subjects design with two DVs: Meaningfulness of transformed data

If we transform a variable to make it conform better to our assumptions, we also need some sensible interpretation of the transformed variable. Of our three trial transformations, the one that does the best job on the homogeneity of variance assumption is the reciprocal (which we called TIME). But does the reciprocal of CORRECT have any meaning? Yes it does. Our participants did a test where we counted the number of queries answered correctly in a fixed time, so the reciprocal of this count is proportional to the average TIME they spent on each query, which is just as good a measure of their speed as the CORRECT count was. The log and square-root transformations, on the other hand, have no obvious interpretation. Happily in this case we have a transformation that gives a new sensible variable that also conforms better with our assumptions than the original did. So using TIME instead of CORRECT, we will repeat our MANOVA.

A between-subjects design with two DVs: Requesting a reanalysis in SPSS

Now to include the extra column TIME in our datasheet, all we have to do is choose **Analyze, General Linear Model and Multivariate** again, and then the variable list in the dialog box also includes TIME. Put TIME and DELAY in the **Dependent Variables** box instead of CORRECT and DELAY. In the **Options** dialog box (SPSS Dialog Box 3.1) click **Estimates of effect size** and **Observed power** as well as the items already selected.

Clicking the **Plots** button gives a dialog box just like SPSS Dialog Box 2.7. Put SESSIONS into the **Horizontal Axis** box and METHOD into the **Separate Lines** box using the arrows, then click **Add**. Click **Continue** to return to the main dialog box.

The **Contrasts** button gives us SPSS Dialog Box 3.3, and we could use this to obtain contrasts between the last level of SESSIONS (three sessions) and each of the two lower levels (one and two). This could be useful in helping to decide how many training sessions to use if the SESSIONS factor is significant. Change the **Contrast** to **Simple** using

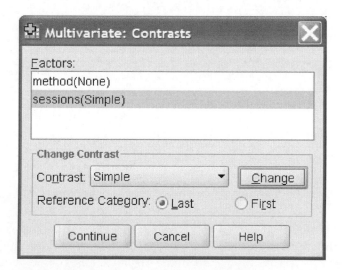

SPSS Dialog Box 3.3 Requesting contrasts for the SESSIONS factor.

the arrow and the **Change** button. Check that the **Reference Category** is **Last**. Click **Continue** and **OK** to get the analysis. Using the simple option, as here, tests each of the other levels of the chosen factor against the specified reference level (here, the last level). The Helmert option tests each level against the mean of the subsequent levels. The mirror image is difference, which tests each level against the mean of the previous levels. The repeated option tests each level against the next level.

A between-subjects design with two DVs and transformed data: Understanding the multivariate output

With our transformed DV TIME replacing CORRECT, we find that Box's test of equality of covariance matrices is not significant (probability = .915, but we do not show the table this time). Levene's tests for the equality of variance for the individual DVs are also not significant. The Spread vs. Level plot for TIME was shown in SPSS Output 3.4 and was satisfactory. The residual plot for TIME is not shown but is similar to that for DELAY shown in SPSS Output 3.3. So, we are satisfied that our data conform to the assumptions needed for MANOVA and we will now look at the analysis.

Multivariate Tests[d]

Effect		Value	F	Hypothesis df	Error df	Sig.	Partial Eta Squared	Noncent. Parameter	Observed Power[b]
Intercept	Pillai's Trace	0.996	3.136E3	2.000	23.000	.000	.996	6272.072	1.000
	Wilks' Lambda	.004	3.136E3	2.000	23.000	.000	.996	6272.072	1.000
	Hotelling's Trace	272.699	3.136E3	2.000	23.000	.000	.996	6272.072	1.000
	Roy's Largest Root	272.699	3.136E3	2.000	23.000	.000	.996	6272.072	1.000
method	Pillai's Trace	0.766	37.550[a]	2.000	23.000	.000	.766	75.101	1.000
	Wilks' Lambda	.234	37.550[a]	2.000	23.000	.000	.766	75.101	1.000
	Hotelling's Trace	3.265	37.550[a]	2.000	23.000	.000	.766	75.101	1.000
	Roy's Largest Root	3.265	37.550[a]	2.000	23.000	.000	.766	75.101	1.000
sessions	Pillai's Trace	1.128	15.524	4.000	48.000	.000	.564	62.094	1.000
	Wilks' Lambda	.099	25.135[a]	4.000	46.000	.000	.686	100.542	1.000
	Hotelling's Trace	6.849	37.872	4.000	44.000	.000	.774	150.686	1.000
	Roy's Largest Root	6.495	77.945[c]	2.000	24.000	.000	.867	155.890	1.000
method * sessions	Pillai's Trace	0.167	1.092	4.000	48.000	.371	.083	4.368	.317
	Wilks' Lambda	.835	1.093[a]	4.000	46.000	.376	.086	4.332	.314
	Hotelling's Trace	0.195	1.071	4.000	44.000	.382	.089	4.286	.309
	Roy's Largest Root	0.182	2.178[c]	2.000	24.000	.135	.154	4.356	.401

a. Exact statistic

b. Computed using alpha = .05

c. The statistic is an upper bound on F that yields a lower bound on the significance level.

d. Design: Intercept + method + sessions + method * sessions

SPSS Output 3.5 The MANOVA table.

SPSS Output 3.5 shows the MANOVA table. The intercept or grand mean is rarely of interest: the null hypothesis that it is zero is rejected but we should be very surprised if it were not. For each of the two main effects and the interaction we have four test statistics. Wilks' lambda is the matrix analogue of the ratio of the residual sum of squares to the total sum of squares, so for METHOD it compares the within-treatment variability with the total variability. So the Wilks statistic falls between zero and 1. The total variability will always be greater, but the bigger the difference between the two METHOD means, the more of the total this accounts for, and the closer to zero is Wilks' ratio. If the two METHOD means are almost the same, the ratio will be almost 1. Our value for METHOD is .234. The other three statistics use different combinations of residual and between-group variances and each of the four statistics is converted to an approximate *F*. The degrees of freedom are shown and the probability of an *F* this large if the null hypothesis of equal group means is true is given. The four statistics may not all agree about whether or not a result is significant. Tabachnick and Fidell discuss the power and robustness of these statistics in various circumstances (see 'Further reading' at the end of the book). SPSS also offers some advice: if Hotelling's trace and Pillai's trace are nearly equal then the effect is likely to be non-significant, and if Roy's largest root and Hotelling's trace are equal or nearly equal then the effect is due mainly to just one of the DVs, or else there is a strong correlation between the DVs, or else the effect does not contribute much to the model.

For the main effect of METHOD we see in the Sig. column that the null hypothesis is rejected by all the test statistics (probability < .001 in every case): there is a significant difference between the two training methods on our pair of DVs TIME and DELAY. However, the fact that Roy's and Hotelling's statistics are equal tells us that probably this effect is mainly due to just one of the DVs, or else the DVs are rather highly correlated. We can easily check the correlation using **Analyze, Correlate, Bivariate** from the menu bar and entering TIME and DELAY into the **Variables** box. We find that the correlation is .74, which is indeed rather high: our two DVs are measuring rather similar things. If we design further experiments to assess these training programs we could look for other aspects of performance to measure in order to obtain a more complete picture.

The results for SESSIONS are similar: this main effect is also highly significant. Roy's and Hotelling's statistics are similar but not equal, but we already know the correlation of the DVs is high. The interaction METHOD * SESSIONS is not significant: the probabilities in the Sig. column are all much greater than .05.

Partial eta squared and observed power were requested and their values are shown at the right of the MANOVA table. As always, the closer the value of partial eta squared is to 1, the more important the effect is in the model. It is a matrix analogue of the ratio of the variance accounted for by the effect to the sum of this and the variance due to error. For the main effects, all of the partial eta squared values exceed .5, while for the interaction the highest is .154. For each of the two highly significant main effects the retrospective power is 1.00 (you would be unlikely to miss an effect of these sizes in a replication using the same sample size) and for the non-significant interaction the highest value for power (Hotelling's Trace) is .38.

A between-subjects design with two DVs and transformed data: Understanding the univariate output

The Tests of Between-Subjects Effects table (SPSS Output 3.6) shows the univariate ANOVA for each of the DVs. If you requested a univariate ANOVA of DELAY with METHOD and SESSIONS as fixed factors, you would get exactly the results printed in the DELAY rows of this table, and similarly for TIME. Generally speaking, however, the correct procedure is to carry out the MANOVA first and to only proceed to univariate ANOVAs if effects on the linear combination of DVs are significant. Looking at this table we can see that both main effects are significant for each of our DVs, and the interaction is significant for neither. The partial eta squared and retrospective (observed) power values are similar for both DELAY and TIME to those found in the multivariate output.

Tests of Between-Subjects Effects

Source	Dependent Variable	Type III Sum of Squares	df	Mean Square	F	Sig.	Partial Eta Squared	Noncent. Parameter	Observed Power[b]
Corrected Model	time	0.024[a]	5	0.005	17.491	.000	.785	87.453	1.000
	delay	180.567[c]	5	36.113	34.948	.000	.879	174.742	1.000
Intercept	time	0.213	1	0.213	786.244	.000	.970	786.244	1.000
	delay	6249.633	1	6249.633	6048.032	.000	.996	6048.032	1.000
method	time	0.011	1	0.011	40.056	.000	.625	40.056	1.000
	delay	45.633	1	45.633	44.161	.000	.648	44.161	1.000
sessions	time	0.013	2	0.006	23.074	.000	.658	46.148	1.000
	delay	131.667	2	65.833	63.710	.000	.841	127.419	1.000
method * sessions	time	0.000	2	0.000	0.624	.544	.049	1.249	.142
	delay	3.267	2	1.633	1.581	.227	.116	3.161	.301
Error	time	0.007	24	0.000					
	delay	24.800	24	1.033					
Total	time	0.244	30						
	delay	6455.000	30						
Corrected Total	time	0.030	29						
	delay	205.367	29						

a. R Squared = .785 (Adjusted R Squared = .740)

b. Computed using alpha = .05

c. R Squared = .879 (Adjusted R Squared = .854)

SPSS Output 3.6 The table of univariate ANOVA results.

If you find a significant MANOVA result, as we did here, you may wish to determine which variables are the most important in producing the significance. You might be tempted to use the univariate ANOVA above for this purpose, but this is not recommended for two reasons. First, by performing a series of univarate ANOVAs you are ignoring the correlation between the DVs. Second, when you perform a number of tests each at the 5% significance level, you encounter the problem of multiple testing as described in the previous chapter (see 'A one-way design: Post hoc tests'). This effectively increases above 5% the chance of rejecting the null hypothesis when it is actually true. One way to avoid the latter problem is the step-down MANOVA or the Roy-Bargman *F* test. This ensures that the overall significance level remains at a specified level (e.g., 5%) irrespective of how many tests are performed. You must first order the DVs in decreasing order of importance prior to any data collection. Test the first DV using a univariate ANOVA (as shown in Chapter 2). Then test the next most important DV in a model that also contains the first DV using analysis of covariance, which we consider in Chapter 5. Continue in the same way, adding the DVs one at a time in order of importance, keeping the previous ones in the model. This allows you to gauge the relative importance of the DVs. Although this procedure ensures that you do not increase the chance of rejecting the null hypothesis when it is true, the results are heavily dependent on the ordering of the DVs. To implement this technique you need to use the command language. The syntax is given by Tabachnick and Fidell (see 'Further reading' at the end of the book).

In SPSS Output 3.7 we show just one of the plots: for each method the mean time spent per query reduces as the number of training sessions goes from one to two and then three. The lines are nearly parallel because there is no significant interaction between METHOD and SESSIONS. The plot for DELAY is similar.

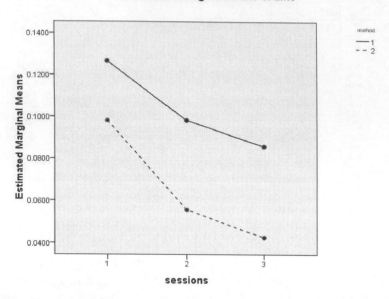

SPSS Output 3.7 Plot showing the effect on TIME of SESSIONS for each METHOD.

Example Box 3.1

An alternative medical example for the same MANOVA between-subjects design

The full analysis for this example can be found at www.psypress.com/multivariate-analysis/medical-examples (click on Chapter 3).

Neuropsychological investigations have found that early dementia often includes decline of recent memory, such that everyday tasks are forgotten, even though the individual remains capable of performing them. A study is conducted to compare the effectiveness of two electronic devices designed to help people with Alzheimer's dementia to remember to carry out everyday tasks. Thirty people are recruited who have dementia that includes the symptom of recent memory decline sufficient to necessitate prompts for everyday tasks to get done. Each recruit has a partner who is keen to help by acting as the recorder for the trial. There is a list of daily tasks such as washing, dressing, getting breakfast, making tea, checking cooker/kettle is switched off, etc. Factor 1, with two levels, is the electronic METHOD used to prompt recall (time- and location-sensitive prompt using geophysical location technology; time-sensitive prompt). In each case, the prompt is delivered in the form of a prerecorded spoken message via a device worn on the wrist. Factor 2 (TRAINING), with three levels, is the type of training given to the patient and partner before the trial starts. Level 1 gives a full day of practice for the patient, with the partner there throughout and the occupational therapist (OT) supervising and instructing at frequent intervals. Level 2 also has a day of practice but the OT, after instructing the partner, only joins them to supervise for a few minutes four times during the day. At level 3 (the cheapest option) the OT instructs the partner and then leaves them unsupervised for the practice day, only checking on them at the end. During each day of the trial week the partner records each task on the list that is successfully completed following a prompt, and the total is the DV COMPLETE. The partner is also trained to record the time in seconds between the prompt and commencement of each task. The mean of these processing times for completed tasks is the other DV, PROCESS.

Outcomes

The homogeneity of variance assumption for PROCESS is not met, so various transformations of that DV are tried and the reciprocal results in the homogeneity assumption being met. The data are re-analysed using that reciprocal, which we call SPEED. As in the psychology example, we note that the reciprocal of PROCESS does have a meaning: we could interpret it as speed of processing. In the multivariate analysis using the transformed data, both prompt method and number of practice days have significant effects on our pair of DVs and there is no interaction between the two factors. The univariate analyses on each of the DVs show main effects of prompt METHOD (time- plus location-sensitive prompt > time-sensitive prompt) and TRAINING type (OT supervises closely > OT supervises loosely > OT instructs partner) on the SPEED of processing and also on the number of tasks successfully completed (COMPLETE).

Alternative variables for use in SPSS
The full dataset, med.manova.between.sav, can be found on the book website

Variable	Psychology	Medicine
Factor 1	METHOD Training method 1=map & paper 2=online	METHOD Electronic prompt 1=time/location sensitive 2=time sensitive
Factor 2	SESSIONS 1=1 training session 2=2 training sessions 3=3 training sessions	TRAINING 1=OT supervises closely 2=OT supervises loosely 3=OT instructs partner
DV 1	CORRECT Number correct in test time	PROCESS Mean time before starting tasks (s)
DV 2	DELAY Response delay (s)	COMPLETE Mean number of tasks completed
Reciprocal of DV 1	TIME Mean time per response (reciprocal of CORRECT)	SPEED Mean processing speed (reciprocal of PROCESS)

A within-subjects design with two DVs

A psychology example and (fabricated) data for a MANOVA (within-subjects) design

Having looked at the diagnostics for our between-subjects example in some detail, we will present an example of a within-subjects MANOVA much more briefly. We will imagine an experiment, similar to the repeated measures experiment in the ANOVA chapter, where the two IVs are MODE (letter, shape) and angle (30°, 60° and 90°). As in Chapter 2, the two levels of MODE are both used within each level of ANGLE. Again, the number of participants is 10, but we have introduced a second DV. In addition to measuring RT (time to decide whether two stimuli were identical when placed in the same orientation), we now measure amount of head movement as well.

A within-subjects design with two DVs: Setting it up in SPSS

We can show the way the data are entered most clearly by adopting a systematic code for the 12 variables entered in the SPSS datasheet. The DV used to obtain the score for each condition is represented by v1 or v2. We represent the three levels of the first repeated measures IV (ANGLE) with A1, A2 and A3, and the two levels of the second repeated measures IV (MODE) with M1 and M2. So, for example, the 30°/shape condition is represented by A1M2 and the amount of head movement in the 30°/shape condition is represented by v2A1M2. The data are shown in Table 3.2.

Table 3.2 Data from a within-subjects experiment to compare effects of angle of orientation and stimulus mode on mental rotation time and physical head movement in a same/different decision task (psy.manova.within.sav)

v1a1m1	v1a1m2	v1a2m1	v1a2m2	v1a3m1	v1a3m2	v2a1m1	v2a1m2	v2a2m1	v2a2m2	v2a3m1	v2a3m2
240	261	251	266	259	264	17	25	23	25	26	24
290	288	300	293	306	318	21	20	18	18	15	17
326	342	328	350	334	363	20	19	23	23	18	23
255	268	262	267	270	278	20	19	12	21	25	21
260	284	324	290	313	321	20	20	20	20	17	19
292	264	322	292	320	329	23	20	20	20	20	18
279	266	301	284	332	326	20	21	19	19	19	17
289	260	293	309	306	297	21	21	20	17	21	20
301	264	335	283	320	268	20	17	23	21	16	22
292	317	302	313	307	309	18	23	23	19	19	20

As this is a within-subjects design in which each participant experiences all six of the ANGLE/MODE conditions, the columns of Table 3.2 are arranged exactly as required for the SPSS datasheet, with each participant occupying one row and with a column for each of the conditions for each DV.

A within-subjects design with two DVs: Requesting the analysis in SPSS

From the menus choose **Analyze**, then **General Linear Model**, then **Repeated Measures**, to get a dialog box like SPSS Dialog Box 2.8. Put ANGLE into the **Within-Subject Factor Name** box and 3 into the **Number of Levels** box and click **Add**. Repeat for MODE and 2. Then put names for the two DVs (e.g., RT and HEADMOVE) in the **Measure Name** box. The result is shown in SPSS Dialog Box 3.4.

Click **Define** to get SPSS Dialog Box 3.5. Next, move all of the IVs into the **Within-subjects Variables** box in the correct order, just as for a repeated measures ANOVA (if the IVs were entered in SPSS columns as in Table 3.2, they will be in the right order and can be moved as a block), so that the dialog box looks like SPSS Dialog Box 3.5.

In **Options**, select **Estimates of effect size** and **Observed power** as usual and, assuming you do not want to select any of the other **Options** or **Plots**, click **OK**, and the analysis will be done.

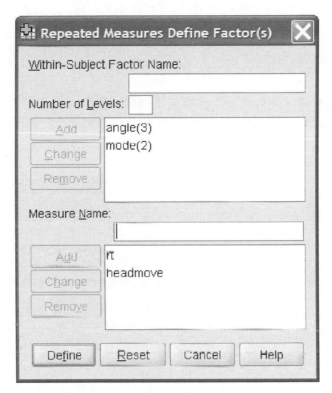

SPSS Dialog Box 3.4 Defining factors and DVs for repeated measures MANOVA.

A within-subjects design with two DVs: Understanding the multivariate output

SPSS often generates more output than you know what to do with and it is important to be able to pick out the bits you need. On this occasion, therefore, we will show you the complete output (SPSS Output 3.8) of the within-subjects MANOVA and just draw your attention to the relevant bits.

The first table, Within-Subjects Factors, just provides a check on the variables entered: that they are in the correct order. Then comes the Multivariate Tests table. Ignore the between-subjects effect (which only refers to the intercept since we have no between-subjects factors) and go straight to the within-subjects effects. The four alternative test statistics were discussed in detail for the between-subjects example earlier in the chapter. We see that, whichever test we use, only ANGLE reaches significance: $F(4,6) = 4.93, p < .05$, with partial eta squared $= .77$ and retrospective power $= .68$. The pattern of test statistics suggests that the effect may only be significant for one of the DVs (see earlier discussion of these test statistics in relation to the between-subjects example). Next, we see that Mauchly's test of the assumption of sphericity is non-significant, which tells us that we can refer to the 'Sphericity Assumed' rows in the Univariate Tests table. Before that, however, we have another Multivariate table and

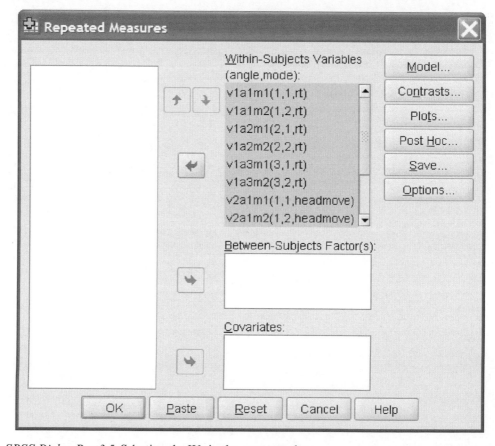

SPSS Dialog Box 3.5 Selecting the IVs in the correct order.

Within-Subjects Factors

Measure	angle	mode	Dependent Variable
rt	1	1	v1a1m1
		2	v1a1m2
	2	1	v1a2m1
		2	v1a2m2
	3	1	v1a3m1
		2	v1a3m2
headmove	1	1	v2a1m1
		2	v2a1m2
	2	1	v2a2m1
		2	v2a2m2
	3	1	v2a3m1
		2	v2a3m2

Multivariate Tests[c]

Effect			Value	F	Hypothesis df	Error df	Sig.	Partial Eta Squared	Noncent. Parameter	Observed Power[b]
Between Subjects	Intercept	Pillai's Trace	0.998	2.429E3	2.000	8.000	.000	.998	4858.037	1.000
		Wilks' Lambda	.002	2.429E3	2.000	8.000	.000	.998	4858.037	1.000
		Hotelling's Trace	607.255	2.429E3	2.000	8.000	.000	.998	4858.037	1.000
		Roy's Largest Root	607.255	2.429E3	2.000	8.000	.000	.998	4858.037	1.000
Within Subjects	angle	Pillai's Trace	0.767	4.928[a]	4.000	6.000	.042	.767	19.711	.879
		Wilks' Lambda	.233	4.928[a]	4.000	6.000	.042	.767	19.711	.879
		Hotelling's Trace	3.285	4.928[a]	4.000	6.000	.042	.767	19.711	.879
		Roy's Largest Root	3.285	4.928[a]	4.000	6.000	.042	.767	19.711	.879
	mode	Pillai's Trace	0.193	0.956[a]	2.000	8.000	.424	.193	1.912	.163
		Wilks' Lambda	.807	0.956[a]	2.000	8.000	.424	.193	1.912	.163
		Hotelling's Trace	0.239	0.956[a]	2.000	8.000	.424	.193	1.912	.163
		Roy's Largest Root	0.239	0.956[a]	2.000	8.000	.424	.193	1.912	.163
	angle * mode	Pillai's Trace	0.176	0.320[a]	4.000	6.000	.855	.176	1.279	.086
		Wilks' Lambda	.824	0.320[a]	4.000	6.000	.855	.176	1.279	.086
		Hotelling's Trace	0.213	0.320[a]	4.000	6.000	.855	.176	1.279	.086
		Roy's Largest Root	0.213	0.320[a]	4.000	6.000	.855	.176	1.279	.086

a. Exact statistic

b. Computed using alpha = .05

c. Design: Intercept
Within Subjects Design: angle + mode + angle * mode

Mauchly's Test of Sphericity[b]

Within Subjects Effect	Measure	Mauchly's W	Approx. Chi-Square	df	Sig.	Epsilon[a] Greenhouse-Geisser	Huynh-Feldt	Lower-bound
angle	rt	.749	2.316	2	.314	.799	.945	.500
	headmove	.986	0.117	2	.943	.986	1.000	.500
mode	rt	1.000	0.000	0	.	1.000	1.000	1.000
	headmove	1.000	0.000	0	.	1.000	1.000	1.000
angle * mode	rt	.912	0.737	2	.692	.919	1.000	.500
	headmove	.971	0.236	2	.888	.972	1.000	.500

Tests the null hypothesis that the error covariance matrix of the orthonormalized transformed dependent variables is proportional to an identity matrix.

a. May be used to adjust the degrees of freedom for the averaged tests of significance. Corrected tests are displayed in the Tests of Within-Subjects Effects table.

b. Design: Intercept
Within Subjects Design: angle + mode + angle * mode

Tests of Within-Subjects Effects

Multivariate[d,e]

Within Subjects Effect		Value	F	Hypothesis df	Error df	Sig.	Partial Eta Squared	Noncent. Parameter	Observed Power[a]
angle	Pillai's Trace	0.632	4.159	4.000	36.000	.007	.316	16.635	.881
	Wilks' Lambda	.371	5.461[b]	4.000	34.000	.002	.391	21.843	.954
	Hotelling's Trace	1.690	6.760	4.000	32.000	.000	.458	27.041	.984
	Roy's Largest Root	1.686	15.171[c]	2.000	18.000	.000	.628	30.341	.997
mode	Pillai's Trace	0.193	0.956[b]	2.000	8.000	.424	.193	1.912	.163
	Wilks' Lambda	.807	0.956[b]	2.000	8.000	.424	.193	1.912	.163
	Hotelling's Trace	0.239	0.956[b]	2.000	8.000	.424	.193	1.912	.163
	Roy's Largest Root	0.239	0.956[b]	2.000	8.000	.424	.193	1.912	.163
angle * mode	Pillai's Trace	0.072	0.335	4.000	36.000	.853	.036	1.340	.117
	Wilks' Lambda	.928	0.322[b]	4.000	34.000	.861	.037	1.289	.113
	Hotelling's Trace	0.077	0.309	4.000	32.000	.870	.037	1.237	.110
	Roy's Largest Root	0.077	0.695[c]	2.000	18.000	.512	.072	1.390	.149

a. Computed using alpha = .05

b. Exact statistic

c. The statistic is an upper bound on F that yields a lower bound on the significance level.

d. Design: Intercept
Within Subjects Design: angle + mode + angle * mode

e. Tests are based on averaged variables.

SPSS Output 3.8 The complete output of the within-subjects MANOVA. (*Continued overleaf*)

Univariate Tests

Source	Measure		Type III Sum of Squares	df	Mean Square	F	Sig.	Partial Eta Squared	Noncent. Parameter	Observed Power[a]
angle	rt	Sphericity Assumed	6492.633	2	3246.317	14.711	.000	.620	29.423	.996
		Greenhouse-Geisser	6492.633	1.598	4061.885	14.711	.001	.620	23.515	.987
		Huynh-Feldt	6492.633	1.899	3436.407	14.711	.000	.620	27.795	.994
		Lower-bound	6492.633	1.000	6492.633	14.711	.004	.620	14.711	.925
	headmove	Sphericity Assumed	1.900	2	0.950	0.129	.880	.014	0.258	.067
		Greenhouse-Geisser	1.900	1.971	0.964	0.129	.877	.014	0.254	.067
		Huynh-Feldt	1.900	2.000	0.950	0.129	.880	.014	0.258	.067
		Lower-bound	1.900	1.000	1.900	0.129	.728	.014	0.129	.062
Error(angle)	rt	Sphericity Assumed	3972.033	18	220.669					
		Greenhouse-Geisser	3972.033	14.386	276.107					
		Huynh-Feldt	3972.033	17.004	233.590					
		Lower-bound	3972.033	9.000	441.337					
	headmove	Sphericity Assumed	132.767	18	7.376					
		Greenhouse-Geisser	132.767	17.743	7.483					
		Huynh-Feldt	132.767	18.000	7.376					
		Lower-bound	132.767	9.000	14.752					
mode	rt	Sphericity Assumed	93.750	1	93.750	0.159	.699	.017	0.159	.065
		Greenhouse-Geisser	93.750	1.000	93.750	0.159	.699	.017	0.159	.065
		Huynh-Feldt	93.750	1.000	93.750	0.159	.699	.017	0.159	.065
		Lower-bound	93.750	1.000	93.750	0.159	.699	.017	0.159	.065
	headmove	Sphericity Assumed	2.400	1	2.400	0.970	.350	.097	0.970	.143
		Greenhouse-Geisser	2.400	1.000	2.400	0.970	.350	.097	0.970	.143
		Huynh-Feldt	2.400	1.000	2.400	0.970	.350	.097	0.970	.143
		Lower-bound	2.400	1.000	2.400	0.970	.350	.097	0.970	.143
Error(mode)	rt	Sphericity Assumed	5300.417	9	588.935					
		Greenhouse-Geisser	5300.417	9.000	588.935					
		Huynh-Feldt	5300.417	9.000	588.935					
		Lower-bound	5300.417	9.000	588.935					
	headmove	Sphericity Assumed	22.267	9	2.474					
		Greenhouse-Geisser	22.267	9.000	2.474					
		Huynh-Feldt	22.267	9.000	2.474					
		Lower-bound	22.267	9.000	2.474					
angle * mode	rt	Sphericity Assumed	165.100	2	82.550	0.680	.519	.070	1.361	.147
		Greenhouse-Geisser	165.100	1.838	89.815	0.680	.508	.070	1.251	.142
		Huynh-Feldt	165.100	2.000	82.550	0.680	.519	.070	1.361	.147
		Lower-bound	165.100	1.000	165.100	0.680	.431	.070	0.680	.115
	headmove	Sphericity Assumed	0.300	2	0.150	0.020	.981	.002	0.039	.053
		Greenhouse-Geisser	0.300	1.943	0.154	0.020	.979	.002	0.038	.052
		Huynh-Feldt	0.300	2.000	0.150	0.020	.981	.002	0.039	.053
		Lower-bound	0.300	1.000	0.300	0.020	.891	.002	0.020	.052
Error(angle*mode)	rt	Sphericity Assumed	2184.233	18	121.346					
		Greenhouse-Geisser	2184.233	16.544	132.026					
		Huynh-Feldt	2184.233	18.000	121.346					
		Lower-bound	2184.233	9.000	242.693					
	headmove	Sphericity Assumed	137.033	18	7.613					
		Greenhouse-Geisser	137.033	17.488	7.836					
		Huynh-Feldt	137.033	18.000	7.613					
		Lower-bound	137.033	9.000	15.226					

a. Computed using alpha = .05

Tests of Within-Subjects Contrasts

Source	Measure	angle	mode	Type III Sum of Squares	df	Mean Square	F	Sig.	Partial Eta Squared	Noncent. Parameter	Observed Power[a]
angle	rt	Linear	mode	6300.100	1	6300.100	19.095	.002	.680	19.095	.972
		Quadratic	mode	192.533	1	192.533	1.728	.221	.161	1.728	.218
	headmove	Linear	mode	1.600	1	1.600	0.219	.651	.024	0.219	.070
		Quadratic	mode	0.300	1	0.300	0.040	.845	.004	0.040	.054
Error(angle)	rt	Linear	mode	2969.400	9	329.933					
		Quadratic	mode	1002.633	9	111.404					
	headmove	Linear	mode	65.900	9	7.322					
		Quadratic	mode	66.867	9	7.430					
mode	rt	angle * mode	Linear	93.750	1	93.750	0.159	.699	.017	0.159	.065
	headmove	angle * mode	Linear	2.400	1	2.400	0.970	.350	.097	0.970	.143
Error(mode)	rt	angle * mode	Linear	5300.417	9	588.935					
	headmove	angle * mode	Linear	22.267	9	2.474					
angle * mode	rt	Linear	Linear	6.400	1	6.400	0.067	.802	.007	0.067	.056
		Quadratic	Linear	159.700	1	159.700	1.080	.326	.107	1.080	.154
	headmove	Linear	Linear	1.137E-13	1	1.137E-13	0.000	1.000	.000	0.000	.050
		Quadratic	Linear	0.300	1	0.300	0.038	.849	.004	0.038	.054
Error(angle*mode)	rt	Linear	Linear	862.100	9	95.789					
		Quadratic	Linear	1322.133	9	146.904					
	headmove	Linear	Linear	68.500	9	7.389					
		Quadratic	Linear	70.533	9	7.837					

a. Computed using alpha = .05

Tests of Between-Subjects Effects

Transformed Variable:Average

Source	Measure	Type III Sum of Squares	df	Mean Square	F	Sig.	Partial Eta Squared	Noncent. Parameter	Observed Power[a]
Intercept	rt	5246900.817	1	5246900.817	1720.545	.000	.995	1720.545	1.000
	headmove	24240.600	1	24240.600	2165.772	.000	.996	2165.772	1.000
Error	rt	27446.017	9	3049.557					
	headmove	100.733	9	11.193					

a. Computed using alpha = .05

SPSS Output 3.8 (Continued)

footnote 'e' says it is based on averaged variables. In fact this is the table you would get if you treated the 10 subjects as levels of a factor, so that instead of a repeated measures design you treat it as a **GLM Multivariate** design with three IVs: angle, mode and subject. This would not normally be of interest, so ignore this table and press on to the table of Univariate Tests.

A within-subjects design with two DVs: Understanding the univariate output

Univariate tests on the ANGLE factor are justified by the significant multivariate effect of ANGLE reported in the first multivariate table. The Univariate Tests table confirms that the effect of angle is significant for the DV RT: with sphericity assumed $F(2,18) = 14.71$, $p < .001$, with partial eta squared = .62 and retrospective power = .996. The Within-Subjects Contrasts table tells us that the linear effect of ANGLE is also significant for the DV RT: $F(1,9) = 19.09$, $p < .01$. Finally, the Tests of Between-Subjects Effects table can safely be ignored since we have no between-subjects factors.

If the test for sphericity suggested that this assumption was not justified, then the probability values from the other three rows of the Univariate Tests table should be considered. These are obtained by multiplying the numerator and denominator degrees of freedom for F by the corresponding value of epsilon from the right of Mauchly's Test of sphericity table. The most conservative is the last of the three values, the lower bound. Greenhouse-Geisser is also conservative, especially for small sample sizes. The Huynh-Feldt value for epsilon may be calculated as greater than 1, but if so the value 1 is used (so no adjustment is made).

Example Box 3.2

An alternative medical example for the same MANOVA within-subjects design

The full analysis for this example can be found at www.psypress.com/ multivariate-analysis/medical-examples (click on Chapter 3).

The study reported as a medical example (Huntington's disease) for a within-subjects ANOVA is repeated with a minor variation. Instead of the CRT response being made on a touch-sensitive screen, it is made on one of two pressure-sensitive pads to the right and left of the participant's midline. The pads are connected to a timer, which records the CRT (DV 1). In addition, the pressure-sensitive pads record the strength of response, which constitutes a second DV. The two within-subjects factors are again YEAR of test and stimulus MODE.

Outcomes

The multivariate effect of year of test on the two DVs is significant (year 3 > year 2 > year 1), which justifies univariate tests on that factor. The only univariate effect of year of test that is significant is that on CRT (DV 1), and for that DV the linear effect is also significant.

Alternative variables for use in SPSS
The full dataset, med.manova.within.sav, can be found on the book website

Variable	Psychology	Medicine
Factor 1	ANGLE Angle of rotation 1=30 degrees 2=60 degrees 3=90 degrees	YEAR Year of test 1=year 1 2=year 2 3=year 3
Factor 2	MODE 1=letter 2=shape	MODE 1=visual stimulus 2=auditory stimulus
DV 1	TIME Choice reaction time (ms)	TIME Choice reaction time (ms)
DV 2	HEADMOVE Extent of head movement	STRENGTH Strength of response

Extension to a within- and between-subjects (mixed) design with two DVs

If you had a multivariate *mixed* design – one in which there were one or more between-subjects IVs as well as one or more within-subjects IVs and more than one DV – the MANOVA would be carried out as for the all within-subjects design we have described above, except that in SPSS Dialog Box 3.5 the between-subject IVs would be moved into the **Between-Subjects Factor(s)** box before **OK** is clicked. The output would be similar, except that between-subjects effects and interactions involving between- and within-subjects factors would be included.

MANOVA and repeated measures ANOVA compared

We now consider the situation in which there is a between-subjects IV, a within-subjects IV and only one DV, as the design is initially conceived. It may be possible to conceptualize levels of the within-subjects IV as comprising different measures (i.e., DVs). In this situation, it is possible to carry out a between-subjects MANOVA instead of a mixed (one between, one within) factorial ANOVA.

A psychology example of a design that can be analysed using ANOVA or MANOVA

To illustrate the difference between these analysis options, we return here to the data from the mixed design shown in Table 2.7. Each subject belongs to one of three IQ groups (the between-subjects IV) and does two RECALL tests, one each using the blocked and unblocked METHODS. METHOD was the within-subjects IV, and the data were analysed in Chapter 2 using ANOVA. We could, however, regard the two RECALL tests as a pair of DVs and subject the data to a MANOVA to test the effect of IQ. In this case, IQ would be the only IV, so we would not be able to use the MANOVA to compare the two METHODS.

The ANOVA carried out in Chapter 2

When we carried out the ANOVA for the mixed design on these data in Chapter 2 we focussed on the univariate output, in which only one DV was assumed. The same analysis commands also generated a multivariate solution, though the solutions are identical when there are only two levels of the within-subjects factor.

When we examined the output of the univariate analysis in Chapter 2 we found that the effect of IQ was significant: $F(2,6) = 5.35$, $p < .05$. We now repeat the analysis of these data using MANOVA.

Requesting the MANOVA in SPSS

We will label blocked and unblocked scores as RECALL1 and RECALL2 as before. Select **Analyze**, then **General Linear Model**, then **Multivariate**. Using the arrows, put IQ into the **Fixed Factor(s)** box and RECALL1 and RECALL2 into the **Dependent Variables** box. Click the **Options** button and request **Homogeneity tests, Estimates of effect size** and **Observed Power**, then click **Continue** to return to the main dialog box and click **OK**.

The SPSS output for the MANOVA

The Box test (not shown here) was not significant, and the Levene tests were identical to those shown in SPSS Output 2.13. The Multivariate Tests and Between-Subjects Effects tables are shown in SPSS Output 3.9. The results from the Multivariate Tests

Multivariate Tests[d]

Effect		Value	F	Hypothesis df	Error df	Sig.	Partial Eta Squared	Noncent. Parameter	Observed Power[b]
Intercept	Pillai's Trace	0.989	2.302E2	2.000	5.000	.000	.989	460.428	1.000
	Wilks' Lambda	.011	2.302E2	2.000	5.000	.000	.989	460.428	1.000
	Hotelling's Trace	92.086	2.302E2	2.000	5.000	.000	.989	460.428	1.000
	Roy's Largest Root	92.086	2.302E2	2.000	5.000	.000	.989	460.428	1.000
IQ	Pillai's Trace	0.717	1.678	4.000	12.000	.219	.359	6.710	.368
	Wilks' Lambda	.289	2.147[a]	4.000	10.000	.149	.462	8.588	.434
	Hotelling's Trace	2.432	2.432	4.000	8.000	.133	.549	9.727	.442
	Roy's Largest Root	2.422	7.267[c]	2.000	6.000	.025	.708	14.534	.745

a. Exact statistic

b. Computed using alpha = .05

c. The statistic is an upper bound on F that yields a lower bound on the significance level.

d. Design: Intercept + IQ

Tests of Between-Subjects Effects

Source	Dependent Variable	Type III Sum of Squares	df	Mean Square	F	Sig.	Partial Eta Squared	Noncent. Parameter	Observed Power[b]
Corrected Model	recall1	8.222[a]	2	4.111	0.902	.454	.231	1.805	.144
	recall2	48.667[c]	2	24.333	6.844	.028	.695	13.687	.719
Intercept	recall1	1708.444	1	1708.444	375.024	.000	.904	375.024	1.000
	recall2	841.000	1	841.000	236.531	.000	.975	236.531	1.000
IQ	recall1	8.222	2	4.111	0.902	.454	.231	1.805	.144
	recall2	48.667	2	24.333	6.844	.028	.695	13.688	.719
Error	recall1	27.333	6	4.556					
	recall2	21.333	6	3.556					
Total	recall1	1744.000	9						
	recall2	911.000	9						
Corrected Total	recall1	35.556	8						
	recall2	70.000	8						

a. R Squared = .231 (Adjusted R Squared = -.025)

b. Computed using alpha = .05

c. R Squared = .695 (Adjusted R Squared = .594)

SPSS Output 3.9 Results from a MANOVA with IQ as the IV and RECALL1 and RECALL2 as the DVs.

table suggest that IQ has no significant effect: for example, from Wilks' lambda $F(4,10) = 2.15$, $p = .15$. However, tests on the individual DVs in the Between-subjects Effects table suggest that IQ has a significant effect on RECALL2 (probability in the Sig column = .028, partial eta squared = .70, retrospective power = .72) but not on RECALL1 (probability = .454).

The SPSS multivariate output for the ANOVA in Chapter 2

Now we look again at the repeated measures ANOVA of the mixed design data in Table 2.7 reported in the previous chapter. We did not show the Multivariate Tests table and this is now shown in SPSS Output 3.10.

Multivariate Tests^c

Effect		Value	F	Hypothesis df	Error df	Sig.	Partial Eta Squared	Noncent. Parameter	Observed Power^b
METHOD	Pillai's Trace	0.778	21.062^a	1.000	6.000	.004	.778	21.062	.966
	Wilks' Lambda	.222	21.062^a	1.000	6.000	.004	.778	21.062	.966
	Hotelling's Trace	3.510	21.062^a	1.000	6.000	.004	.778	21.062	.966
	Roy's Largest Root	3.510	21.062^a	1.000	6.000	.004	.778	21.062	.966
METHOD* IQ	Pillai's Trace	0.288	1.215^a	2.000	6.000	.360	.288	2.431	.178
	Wilks' Lambda	.712	1.215^a	2.000	6.000	.360	.288	2.431	.178
	Hotelling's Trace	0.405	1.215^a	2.000	6.000	.360	.288	2.431	.178
	Roy's Largest Root	0.405	1.215^a	2.000	6.000	.360	.288	2.431	.178

a. Exact statistic

b. Computed using alpha = .05

c. Design: Intercept + IQ
   Within Subjects Design: mode

SPSS Output 3.10 Multivariate Tests table from a repeated measures ANOVA.

This gives just the same information as the Within-Subjects Effects table shown in SPSS Output 2.13, but not at all the same as the Multivariate Tests table from the MANOVA.

Example Box 3.3

An alternative medical example of a design that can be analysed using ANOVA or MANOVA

The full analysis for this example can be found at www.psypress.com/multivariate-analysis/medical-examples (click on Chapter 3).

   The ANOVA analysis of the medical example of a mixed design is compared with a MANOVA on the same data. Here, we regard the two hearing difficulty scores (TYPE) as a pair of DVs, which we re-label as DIFFIC1 and DIFFIC2 instead of ANALOGUE and DIGITAL to emphasize their change of status to DVs. The MANOVA tests the effect of degree of hearing loss – the between-subjects factor (LOSS) – on the pair of DVs. The effect of type of device (TYPE) cannot be tested in the MANOVA, of course, because it is no longer an IV.

Outcomes

The ANOVA found a significant effect of loss of hearing, whereas the MANOVA did not find a significant effect of that factor on the pair of DVs. However, there was a suggestion of an effect of loss of hearing on DV 2, the DIFFIC2 (digital) scores. It is clearly important to consider which analysis approach is appropriate.

Alternative variables for use in SPSS MANOVA
The full dataset, med.anova.mixed.sav, can be found on the book website

Variable	Psychology	Medicine
Factor 1 (between-subjects)	IQ Intelligence test score 1=high 2=medium 3=low	LOSS Degree of hearing loss 1= moderately severe 2=moderate 3= mild
DV 1	RECALL1 Recall score (blocked)	DIFFIC1 Hearing difficulty (analogue)
DV 2	RECALL2 Recall score (unblocked)	DIFFIC2 Hearing difficulty (digital)

Repeated measures ANOVA and MANOVA options compared

In moving from the MANOVA to the repeated measures ANOVA we have moved from a pair of DVs to regarding the two conditions under which the DVs were obtained as a within-subjects factor, so we have two IVs instead of one. Which is the right way to do it? Is there a right way? Well, if we are interested in the effect of the METHOD, we have to treat that as an IV. MANOVA does not give a way to compare the elements of the DV vector. If our concern is with the effects of IQ, we can do the analysis either way. If the assumptions required for a within-subjects ANOVA are reasonable, that analysis might be preferred because the test is generally more powerful (less conservative). The ANOVA analysis found a significant effect of IQ: $F(2,6) = 5.35$, $p = .046$, $< .05$ (see SPSS Output 2.13 in the Tests of Between-Subjects Effects table). The MANOVA analysis failed to do so: $F(4,10) = 2.15$, $p = .15$, $> .05$ (see SPSS Output 3.9). If the assumptions are in doubt, however, the more conservative MANOVA, which makes less stringent assumptions, should be preferred.

Before leaving our discussion of MANOVA, we draw your attention to two related issues that create problems in many large studies but can be especially annoying in the context of ANOVA and MANOVA. These are the issues of missing data and outliers, and we address them in the following two sections.

Missing data

Even one missing observation can destroy the balance of our carefully thought out design. However, even in an observational study with no tidy, balanced design to mess up, the problems caused by missing data are similar, and what we say here applies throughout the book. For further reading see Tabachnick and Fidell.

Missed observations: Random or associated with the DV?

The main problem with missing data is that the reason observations are missing may be associated with the DV. Here is an example: If all the customers calling at a bank branch during one week are asked to complete a service satisfaction questionnaire before they leave, many will not do it, either because they are in a hurry or because they see no need to bother. Which customers *will* bother? Perhaps those who are dissatisfied and want to complain will do it, and maybe also those whose lives are rather leisurely. These customers are unlikely to be typical of all those using the branch and results cannot be generalized. This is an extreme case where we would collect no data at all on many customers. More often we have data on several (or many) variables on many cases, but for some cases the record is incomplete because they did not answer all questions, did not attend for all tests or dropped out before the end because they became bored, ill or disenchanted. Then the first problem is to decide whether the reasons for the missed observations are random or associated in some way with the DV. If there are many cases and very few (less than 5%) with missing data, which seem to occur at random (perhaps because a question was missed by mistake, or a participant was prevented from attending on one occasion for some reason unrelated to the experiment), then you may consider omitting cases with incomplete records. However, if many cases have missing data or if there is some pattern to the omissions, then you need to consider other solutions.

Possible solutions when missing observations are not random

First decide whether most missing data are confined to one or two variables. Perhaps there was some problem with wording that made a question confusing, or perhaps an extreme weather event kept many participants away from one session. In this case, if the variable is not critical to the study or if it is closely related to another variable with nearly complete data, then the problem variable may be abandoned.

Sometimes it can be revealing to compare cases with missing data on some variables to cases with complete records on those variables. This may provide helpful ideas on how to deal with the problem but also may throw some unexpected light on the incomplete variables. Ideas about what can and cannot be asked or discussed change with time and vary among cultures, so perhaps some subgroup of respondents found some questions intrusive and did not answer. Such a finding could be quite useful and perhaps also suggest how to deal with the data that were obtained.

Many studies focus on subsets of the data for different parts of the investigation, in which case it is possible to consider the missing data problem separately for each subset, and for most subsets it may turn out to be only a minor problem.

Missing observations are sometimes replaced by the mean or median value for the variable, or else the group mean for the variable. This is not an option for categorical data: the nearest equivalent would be to replace the missing value with the most commonly occurring category. A disadvantage of this method is that variability is reduced.

Where a method (such as factor analysis) uses a correlation matrix, it can be calculated using only cases that are complete on all variables. This ensures that the resulting correlation matrix is internally consistent. The alternative strategy calculates each correlation using all cases that are complete on the variables in that correlation, even if they have missing data on other variables. This uses all available data, but may compromise the internal consistency of the correlation matrix. If only a few data are missing in a large dataset then this effect will be negligible, but if many observations are missing it can cause problems with the analysis.

All methods of dealing with missing data have associated disadvantages, and whatever the study it is worth investing a lot of effort to ensure that as few observations as possible are missed.

Outliers

A related problem is that of observations with values far away from all the rest. Such observations are referred to as *outliers*.

Outliers: Due to errors?

There may be a case with a very extreme value on just one variable, or else a case where the combination of values on several variables makes them extreme. Here is a simple example of the latter: In our dataset we have a man whose height is recorded as 198 cm (very tall but not out of range) and whose weight is recorded as 56 kg (very light but not out of range). If our records are correct, this man is light enough to be a jockey and tall enough to bang his head when he goes through a door, which makes him very extreme, and on a plot of heights and weights he would be far from all the other points. Such observations are suspect: Did we record the data correctly? Did we write a 9 instead of a 7, or a 5 instead of an 8? Sometimes examination of the original records can reveal a transcription or other error, or make it clear that a decimal point was misplaced, so that correction is easy. More often, we may suspect an error but be unable to check.

Outliers: When not known to be due to errors

An outlier need not be in error: we may have a genuine observation that is very different from all the rest. This may have something useful to tell us, or it may just increase the intrinsic variation in our experiment and make it less sensitive. There are circumstances where it makes sense to remove an outlier and examine the results without it, but if you do this you should always report what you did and why, since it could be a temptation to remove an outlier to make the results more impressive. This issue is discussed further in the chapter on regression, where it can be a particular problem, but questions about the integrity of your dataset, the possibility of errors and the reasons for missing data apply to any investigation, whatever methods of analysis are used.

Reporting results

Just as when we report the results of an ANOVA, we do not need to include the tables produced by SPSS; it is sufficient to quote the *F* values and probabilities together with effect sizes and retrospective power values. If you performed checks on assumptions, or performed transformations of the data, include a brief account of these. Any graphs that helped you to understand your data will also help your readers, so include them if space permits. We could describe our first example, the between-subjects design, like this:

As described in the Method section, we had a between-subjects design in which training METHOD and number of SESSIONS were the IVs, and we recorded two outcomes for each participant: number of CORRECT answers and DELAY before starting. Box's test ($p < .01$) showed that the assumption of equal covariance matrices was not justified, and Levene's tests suggested that the problem lay with CORRECT. Plots showed that the *sd* of CORRECT increased with its mean, so a reciprocal transformation was considered. Since the reciprocal of the number of correct responses will be proportional to the average time taken to respond, using this transformed variable, which we called TIME, makes sense. When we replaced CORRECT with TIME, Box's test was not significant ($p = .91$) and neither were the Levene tests on individual DVs, so we used TIME and DELAY in our analysis. Both METHOD and SESSIONS were significant and the interaction was not. The F values derived from Wilks' statistic were: $F(2,23) = 37.55$, $p < .001$ for METHOD (partial eta squared = .77, retrospective power = 1); $F(4,46) = 25.13$, $p < .001$ for SESSIONS (partial eta squared = .69, retrospective power = 1); and $F(4,46) = 1.08$, $p = .376$ for the interaction. Probabilities obtained from the Pillai, Hotelling and Roy statistics were similar. However, the Hotelling and Roy statistics were equal for METHOD and nearly equal for SESSIONS, so it is likely that the significant result for the main effects is mainly due to just one of the DVs, or else that the DVs are highly correlated. A check showed that TIME and DELAY had a correlation of .74, which is indeed high. So although we have demonstrated that both the number of training sessions and the method used have a significant effect on the outcome for the trainees, the two measures of outcome that we used were highly correlated, and in any future study we shall look for a way to measure aspects of the outcome that are more different.

4   Multiple regression

Introduction and intuitive explication

Regression is used for three purposes: *explanation, prediction* and *control*. We shall not be much concerned with the last, which occurs mainly in the chemical industry, but both of the first two are common in the social sciences. Here we will show how to use regression and also how to avoid some pitfalls.

Simple regression

You will probably be familiar with the basic concepts used in simple regression (i.e., with only one IV), as discussed briefly in Chapter 1. We will recapitulate briefly here. Suppose we were interested in predicting how a cohort of psychology students would perform in exams in their 3rd year from their performance in 1st year exams. The regression of 3rd year scores on 1st year scores for a fabricated dataset is illustrated in Figure 4.1. The IV (or *predictor* or *regressor* variable) is the score in the 1st year and is on the *X*-axis. The DV (or *criterion* variable) is the score in the 3rd year and is on the *Y* axis. The solid line from lower left to upper right, through the data points, is the regression line (line of best fit). This is the line from which you would obtain the best prediction of the 3rd year mark from the 1st year mark. For example, if the 1st year mark is 40, hold a ruler vertically from 40 up to the regression line, then read the corresponding value on the *Y*-axis (it is about 75).

The residual for a data point is the difference between the actual *Y* value and that given by the regression line. The residuals for two data points are shown.

We have extended the *Y*-axis to −50 in order to show the *intercept* (or the *regression constant*, where the regression line cuts the *Y*-axis when *X* = zero), which is approximately −43.

We also illustrate the calculation of the *slope* (the *regression coefficient* or *b*) of the regression line. To see this, look at the triangle marked below the regression line on Figure 4.1. The vertical side of the triangle covers about 75 units and the horizontal side about 25 units. So for each unit increase on the *X*-axis, there is an increase of about 3 units on the *Y*-axis. This is the slope, so in this example *b* is about 3.

The values of the intercept and slope define the linear regression line (*Y* = Intercept + *b* * *X*). Thus, given the values of the intercept, the regression coefficient (*b*) and an individual student's score on the 1st year exam, we can use the regression equation instead of the graph to compute his or her predicted score on the 3rd year exam. For example, for an individual who scored 55 on the 1st year exam, his or her predicted

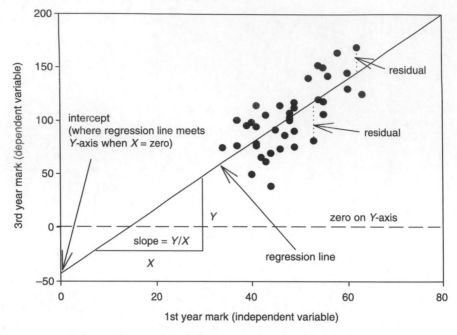

Figure 4.1 Regression of 3rd year marks (DV) on 1st year marks (IV).

score on the 3rd year exam would be –43 + 3 * 55 = 122. For a student who scored 40 on the 1st year exam, the value would be –43 + 3 * 40 = 77. Reading from the graph, especially if there are no grid lines as here, will not be quite as exact, and when we used a ruler and the graph to read the predicted 3rd year value from a 1st year value of 40 we got 'about' 75.

Of course, we also need to know how reliable our prediction is. We can calculate a *t* statistic and the level of statistical significance of the regression coefficient (we have not shown this here), and in this case it turns out that $p < .001$. The fact that the regression is highly significant gives some reassurance that the prediction is useful, but we discuss this in more detail when we get to multiple regression below.

Multiple regression

Multiple regression uses the same concepts, and extends them to the case where there is more than one IV. The basic idea is that a DV can be expressed as a linear function of one or more IVs, which are assumed to be free from random variation, plus some random variation. The linear regression equation can be expressed as:

$$Y = a + b_1(x_1) + b_2(x_2) + \ldots + b_k(x_k)$$

where Y is the predicted value of the DV, a is the regression constant (the intercept value), $b_1, b_2, \ldots, b_k$ are the *partial regression coefficients*, and k is the number of IVs in the equation. In addition to the prediction of an individual's score on the DV, when there are several IVs the relative contribution of each of these to the prediction of the DV becomes an important issue.

The restriction to linear functions

It may be thought that confining attention to linear functions would be a severe limitation to the usefulness of regression analysis, as many relationships among variables are unlikely to be strictly linear. However, restricting ourselves to linear functions is less restrictive than at first appears, because even a relationship that is more complex may be approximately linear over part of the range of the variables considered (hopefully, the part we are interested in). If this is not the case, then it may be possible to use a simple transformation of one or more variables (perhaps a log or reciprocal of the scores on the variable) that will give an approximately linear relationship over the range of interest. Towards the end of the chapter, we will show you a very striking example from astronomy to demonstrate this.

Data requirements

The dependent variable must be at least a good approximation to an interval scale, and so must the majority of the independent variables. However, some categorical variables can be included and we discuss this towards the end of our example statistical analysis.

Sample size

Regression is a method where you usually need a large dataset, though the size depends as usual on the required power, the strength of the relationships between the IVs and the DV, the intrinsic variability of the DV and whether there are relationships among the IVs. Tabachnick and Fidell (see 'Further reading' at the end of the book) suggest the following rule of thumb: as a minimum you probably need about $50 + 8k$ cases (where k is the number of IVs) to test for the significance of the overall regression. For testing the significance of individual IVs, about $104 + k$ would be a minimum. In our example below we have five IVs, though we do not use all of them in our first attempt at prediction. But if we think they may all be useful we need enough cases to be able to attempt a regression with all five IVs included. This suggests that we could do a useful investigation with 110 cases ($50 + 8 * 5 = 90$ but $104 + 5 = 109$). Once again, SPSS SamplePower may be used to provide more specific guidance. In this case we find that in order not to miss an effect that accounts for a modest 15% of the variance ($R^2 = .15$), a sample size of $N = 80$ would be sufficient to give power $= .8$, and a sample size of $N = 110$ would give power $= .93$.

You are more likely to get a useful prediction if you can find a small set of IVs, with each related to the DV but unrelated to each other. If you just collect data on all the variables you think may contribute to predicting a DV and try pouring them all into a regression, you will need a very large dataset to have any hope of identifying the best set of predictors. As always, careful thought and planning before you start will help to make your investigation more focussed.

Assumptions: Independence of data points

There are two important assumptions about the data and we shall look at some ways of checking up on them. The first assumption is that the data points are independent. If each data point represents a case, then this is most likely true, but there are some situations where it may not be true. The most common is when observations have been collected sequentially in time. Then it is possible that there will be correlations between pairs that were close together in time. For example, if we were interested in predicting a baby's weight (the DV), we might expect its weight to increase from week to week and we might also expect it to increase if it ate more. So, the IVs would be TIME and AMOUNT, but for times that were close together (e.g., T1 and T2, T2 and T3, . . ., T9 and T10, etc.) the baby would tend to have similar weights. If weights for these times were paired in two columns as below:

T1	T2
T2	T3
T3	T4
⋮	⋮
T9	T10

it is likely that they would be correlated, indicating that they were not independent. This is referred to as *autocorrelation* and is easily checked. There are special methods for dealing with autocorrelated time series (see Todman & Dugard, 2001).

Assumptions: Constant variance and normal distribution

The second assumption is that the variance of the DV is constant over the range of values of the IVs covered by the dataset. This is analogous to the homogeneity of variance assumption for ANOVA. There are plots (to be introduced later in the chapter) to help with deciding if this is true.

If these two assumptions are correct, then the fitted regression equation is the best linear function of the IVs for predicting the DV: best in the sense of minimizing the sum of squared residuals – recall that residuals are the deviations of DV scores from the regression line. However, if you want to test hypotheses about the regression, you also need to assume that the DV is approximately normally distributed at any set of values of the IVs. Plots can help with checking this too, and they will also be introduced later in the chapter.

In addition, if there are linear or nearly linear relationships among the IVs, there can be computational problems that make parameter estimates unreliable. There is a way to check for this, which we will demonstrate. If the problem is identified, then at least one of the IVs is redundant and should be removed.

Outliers

If one value of a predictor variable lies well beyond the range of most of the other values, this observation may have a very large *influence* on the resulting regression. Here is an extreme example. Suppose we try to predict the effect on reaction time of drinking alcohol. We observe reaction times (Y) in a controlled environment for 10 participants who have all refrained from alcohol for at least 24 hours (so $X = 0$ for all of them). Then we give another participant 2 units of alcohol ($X = 2$) and after 15 minutes test his or her reaction time under the same conditions. It is possible to fit a regression to these data to predict reaction time (Y) from alcohol intake (X), but the single observation with $X = 2$ would have an inordinate influence on the result since all the other observations are at $X = 0$. Also our entire estimate of random variation in reaction time would be based on what happens at $X = 0$. No-one would do anything as extreme as just described but, especially if we have several predictor variables, it is worth checking that each takes a set of values spread over the full range, rather than being mostly clustered rather close together with just one or two distant values.

SPSS offers influence statistics (in the **Save** dialog box in regression) to assist in identifying observations with a large influence. We briefly outline a selection of those available here. The DfFit column for a row shows the change in the predicted value if that observation had been removed from the data and the model recalculated. The standardized version (SDfFit) can be used to identify influential observations. These are defined as those with an absolute value greater than 2 divided by the square root of $(k + 1)/n$, where k is the number of variables in the model and n is the number of observations. The DfBeta columns for a particular row show the equation of the regression model that would be obtained if that observation had been excluded (the one used to generate DfFit). The standardized versions can also be generated, which can be used to identify influential points. These are values for which the absolute value of the standardized DfBeta is greater than 2 divided by the square root of n. Cook's distance is also used to measure the influence of a point on the model. Observations with a Cook's distance greater than 1 should be examined carefully.

An *outlier* in the context of regression is an observation with a large positive or negative residual. This means that the predicted value (for Y) is a long way from the observed value. There can be many reasons for an outlier: the recorded value of Y or one of the predictors may be in error. Sometimes it is possible to check if an error is a possible explanation, but it may be that we have not been very successful in predicting for this case because there are variables we do not yet know about and have not measured that influence the value of Y. In future, when we try to predict from new data we may well encounter other cases for which our predictions will be similarly poor, so the presence of an outlier may be a useful indication that, even if we can often predict quite well, we may sometimes be a long way off. However, prediction of most cases may be improved if an outlier is removed from the regression (prediction for the outlier will then be even worse). So in some circumstances where it is important to predict as well as possible for the majority of cases, even if an occasional one is a long way off, it may be right to remove an outlier. Be careful though, you may be accused of removing an awkward case to make your results look more impressive, and also you may lose an opportunity to learn something unexpected. Often a parallel 'sensitivity analysis' is performed where results are compared with and without outliers. This can be very useful in determining the effect on any predictions of retaining or excluding outliers.

A psychology example of a multiple regression problem

A large IT company is looking for a better way to predict which job applicants will be successful trouble-shooters. The problem is that many of those who are best at the technical parts of the job seem unable to listen to the clients or discuss their needs. So the company is looking for a way to identify people who will communicate with their clients as well as be able to deal with technical problems. They already use, with mixed results, two aptitude tests, which we will call APT1 and APT2. They have spent some months collecting data on 110 of the staff who trouble-shoot for staff or clients as part of their job, and these now have a success score for this type of task, which we will call SUCCESS. All of them have also taken a personality test that gives some measure of intro-version/extraversion, and which we will call EXTRAVER. The idea is that if SUCCESS can be well predicted from some combination of these variables, staff can be deployed more effectively and be expected to spend more of their time doing tasks at which they excel, and new applicants can be recruited specifically for these roles. This is an example of an attempt to use regression for prediction. Of course it may also contribute to an explanation, and even in a small way to control. If it turns out that you can predict how well people do this kind of task using a personality scale, it may be that this kind of ability is hard-wired and not very susceptible to change. On the other hand, if this is not the case, you may be able to exercise some control by helping them to perform better by providing more appropriate training, and a further study could investigate this possibility.

Multiple regression: Some (fabricated) data

The first few rows of data are shown in Table 4.1 (the full dataset can be found as psy.regression.stepwise.sav on the book website). Also in Table 4.1, we have two cat-egorical variables, ITDEGREE and OTHERIT, that record part of their educational back-ground and will be used later, but for the moment we will ignore these and consider only the first four columns. They should be entered into the SPSS datasheet in the usual way, one row for each case, so we have six columns, including the two variables we use later.

Table 4.1 The first few rows of data on task success, aptitude, personality scores and education for 110 computing staff (the full dataset can be found as psy.regression.stepwise.sav on the website)

SUCCESS	APT1	APT2	EXTRAVER	ITDEGREE	OTHERIT
68	117	104	27	**0**	**0**
36	93	90	43	0	0
25	101	96	48	1	**0**
36	116	108	59	0	0
35	103	92	45	1	0
35	101	95	38	**0**	1

Multiple regression: Inspecting the correlation matrix

The usual starting point for a regression analysis is inspection of the correlation matrix for all of the variables. This gives you an initial idea of the relationships among the variables, but not everything of interest is necessarily apparent from the pattern of correlations. Sometimes plotting the DV against the IVs one at a time can suggest when a relationship may exist but be non-linear and may give you a better indication of whether a regression analysis will be helpful. However, we need to be careful about drawing conclusions based on plots involving one IV at a time because, unfortunately, with several independent variables, looking at them one at a time gives little indication of how effective they may be as predictors together. Look at Figure 4.2, which shows SUCCESS plotted against APT2. This graph does not look promising: it seems unlikely that APT2 will be a useful predictor of SUCCESS. Nevertheless, it turns out that, in the presence of APT1, it does make a significant contribution to predicting SUCCESS.

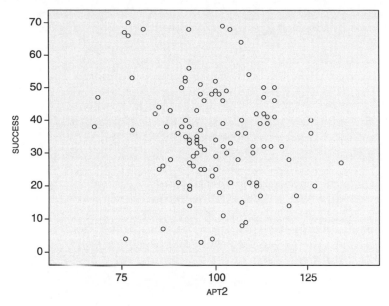

Figure 4.2 Dependent variable plotted against one of the IVs.

Multiple regression: Statistical analysis

It is not hard to do a regression analysis – in fact if you only have one IV you can easily do it on a calculator – but deciding whether your regression model is a good enough fit or whether it is of any practical use is more difficult. If it does look useful, then users must remember that it should not be applied outside the range of values of the IVs that was covered in the original dataset. Also it can be tempting to fall into the trap of assuming that successful prediction implies causation. Every scientist knows that association does not imply causation, but somehow a neat regression analysis that results in successful prediction sometimes seems to lure people into believing they have identified causes and not just predictors. SPSS provides many ways to check on the fit, and we will look at several of them, but only your good scientific sense will keep you from the other errors.

Standard multiple regression: Requesting the analysis in SPSS

From the menu bar choose **Analyze**, then **Regression**, then **Linear** to get SPSS Dialog Box 4.1 (overleaf). Select the DV (SUCCESS in our case) from the list on the left and use the arrow to put it in the **Dependent** box. Then put the IVs (APT1, APT2 and EXTRAVER) into the **Independent(s)** box in the same way. You may want to try out regressions on each IV one at a time before you get into multiple regression, but here we will proceed straight to using all our IVs. Make sure the **Method** box reads **Enter** (we look at a stepwise alternative later). The dialog box now looks like SPSS Dialog Box 4.1, and you could accept all the defaults and click **OK**. However, we will make use of the buttons at the side to get some extra information.

First click the **Statistics** button and get SPSS Dialog Box 4.2 (overleaf). The default settings will show the estimated regression coefficients (**Estimates**) and the **Model fit** in the output window. **Confidence intervals** for the regression coefficients may also be

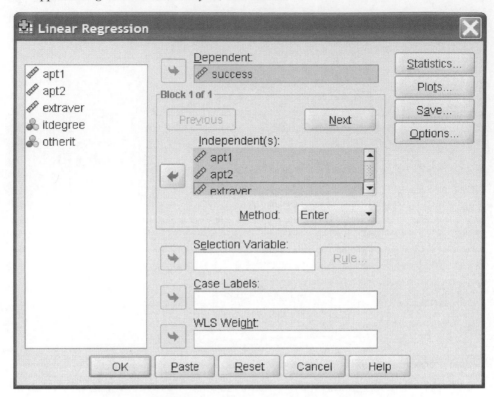

SPSS Dialog Box 4.1 First dialog box for regression.

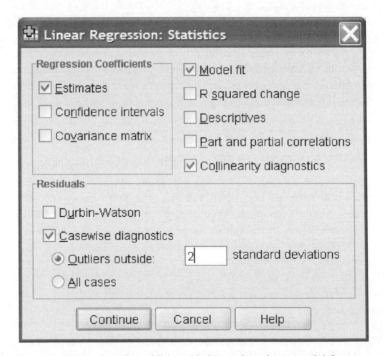

SPSS Dialog Box 4.2 Dialog box for additional information about model fit.

useful (wide ones indicate that the estimates are rather imprecise). The **Durbin-Watson** test for serially correlated residuals is useful if data have been collected sequentially over time, so that they may not be independent observations. **Casewise diagnostics** (selected here) enables you to identify any cases that are badly fit by the model. Outliers outside two standard deviations should occur by chance in only about 5% of our cases, and larger deviations should be even more rare. Here we have requested a list of cases where the residuals exceed two standard deviations. The **R squared change** is one way of judging the effectiveness of each IV in the regression. It is, however, unnecessary to select it in this case because the information will be in the default output since we are entering all our IVs together. In later analyses where we enter IVs in stages you need to select this statistic. The **Descriptives** and the **Part and partial correlations** give information about the IVs, and the **Collinearity diagnostics**, selected here, indicates if there are linear relationships among the IVs that would make the estimates of the regression coefficients unreliable. Click **Continue** to return to SPSS Dialog Box 4.1.

Now click the **Plots** button to get SPSS Dialog Box 4.3. A plot of the residuals against the fitted values is useful for checking the assumption that the variance of the DV is constant over the range of values of the IVs. This can also alert us to other failures of the model, as we will see when we look at the astronomy example later. The **ZRESID** and **ZPRED** are just the residuals and predicted values, each standardized by subtracting the mean and dividing by the standard deviation, so select them for plotting as **Y** and **X**, respectively. The **Normal probability plot** will give us a check on the assumption of normality that we need for hypothesis tests. SPSS Dialog Box 4.3 shows these selections.

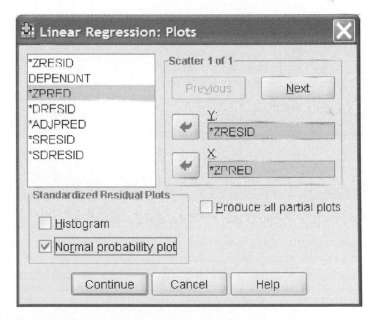

SPSS Dialog Box 4.3 Selecting plots from a regression analysis.

Click **Continue** to return to SPSS Dialog Box 4.1. The **Save** button can be left for later and the **Options** button applies when we do a stepwise regression, again later. Click **OK** to get the analysis.

Standard multiple regression: Understanding the main analysis output

First in the output is a table (not shown) that lists which variables are in the regression and shows whether a stepwise method was used. We just entered all our independent variables so this table is of little interest. We consider later the version obtained when we do a stepwise regression.

Next come the Model Summary and ANOVA tables shown in SPSS Output 4.1. Under the Model Summary table are listed the independent and dependent variables, and in the table we see the value of R^2, which tells us that in our example .302, or 30%, of the variance of SUCCESS was explained by the regression on APT1, APT2 and EXTRAVER. R^2 always increases with the inclusion of additional predictor variables. Adjusted R^2, which is also given, takes account of the number of predictor variables and also the number of cases. This statistic is intended to allow comparison between different regressions or even regressions fitted to different sets of data, and may be useful as an initial rather rough indicator for this purpose. Normally it is the unadjusted R^2 that is reported. The ANOVA table shows that for the overall regression $F = 15.29$ with 3 and 106 degrees of freedom, with a probability (in the Sig. column) well below .05. So the regression is significant.

Model Summary[b]

Model	R	R Square	Adjusted R Square	Std. Error of the Estimate
1	.550[a]	.302	.282	12.776

a. Predictors: (Constant), extraver, apt2, apt1
b. Dependent Variable: success

ANOVA[b]

Model		Sum of Squares	df	Mean Square	F	Sig.
1	Regression	7486.951	3	2495.650	15.289	.000[a]
	Residual	17302.540	106	163.232		
	Total	24789.491	109			

a. Predictors: (Constant), extraver, apt2, apt1
b. Dependent Variable: success

SPSS Output 4.1 Model summary and ANOVA tables.

Example Box 4.1

An alternative medical example of a multiple regression problem

The full analysis for this example can be found at www.psypress.com/multivariate-analysis/medical-examples (click on Chapter 4).

One hundred and ten patients diagnosed as having the eating disorder bulimia are recruited to a study designed to evaluate potential predictors of SUCCESS of a 10-week course of treatment using cognitive behavioural therapy (CBT). The DV is a success score based on responses to patient and GP post-treatment question-naires. The potential predictors include scores on three variables that may be regarded as providing good approximations to interval scales: (1) score on a self-esteem inventory (SELFEST), (2) SEVERITY of the eating disorder based on family and patient interviews and questionnaires, and (3) score on a DEPRESSION inventory. In addition, there is a categorical variable with three unordered levels (referral initiated by GP; referral initiated by a family member; referral by the patient). This categorical variable is used to form two dummy variables (GP: GP = 1, other = 0; FAMILY: family member = 1, other = 0).

Outcomes

Using only the interval predictors in a stepwise regression, SELFEST is the best predictor of SUCCESS, followed by SEVERITY, with DEPRESSION contributing little. When the two dummy variables are added to the stepwise regression, SELFEST is again the best predictor of SUCCESS, followed next by GP and then by SEVERITY. An increase of 1 in SELFEST results in an increase of 0.52 in predicted SUCCESS, whereas being coded 1 for GP (referral initiated by GP) reduces predicted SUCCESS by 10.19 and an increase of 1 in SEVERITY reduces predicted SUCCESS by 0.25. The best prognosis for success of CBT arises when the patient scores relatively high on self-esteem, when the referral is not initiated by a GP and when the self-reported severity of the illness is relatively low. Depression score and whether the patient or a family member initiates referral are irrelevant to the prediction of success. Using cross-validation (the variable XVAL indicates which cases are in the training set and which form the validation set), there are only two validation cases and two training cases outside the 95% confidence interval for predicted SUCCESS.

Alternative variables for use in SPSS
The full dataset, med.regression.stepwise.sav (or med.regression.crossvalidation.sav with the addition of the variable XVAL), can be found on the book website

Variable	Psychology	Medicine
Dependent variable	SUCCESS Trouble-shooting success	SUCCESS CBT success
Predictor variable 1	APT1 Aptitude measure 1	SELFEST score on self-esteem
Predictor variable 2	APT2 Aptitude measure 2	SEVERITY Severity of eating disorder
Predictor variable 3	EXTRAVER Extraversion score	DEPRESSION Depression score
Dummy variable 1	ITDEGREE IT degree/other (other = tech. training or none)	GP GP referral/other (other = patient or family)
Dummy variable 2	OTHERIT Tech. training/other (other = IT degree or none)	FAMILY Family referral/other (other = GP or patient)
Cross-validation variable	XVAL Training vs. validation set	XVAL Training vs. validation set

Next is a table of coefficients, shown in SPSS Output 4.2. This (in the column labelled 'B') gives the estimated values of the regression coefficients and then their standard

Coefficients[a]

Model		Unstandardized Coefficients		Standardized Coefficients	t	Sig.	Collinearity Statistics	
		B	Std. Error	Beta			Tolerance	VIF
1	(Constant)	15.570	13.397		1.162	.248		
	apt1	0.595	.097	.512	6.151	.000	.952	1.051
	apt2	-0.342	.100	-.285	-3.430	.001	.956	1.047
	extraver	-0.142	.112	-.103	-1.267	.208	.994	1.007

a. Dependent Variable: success

SPSS Output 4.2 Regression coefficients and collinearity check.

errors. From this we see that we can calculate the predicted value of SUCCESS for any case as:

Predicted SUCCESS = 15.570 + 0.595 * APT1 − 0.342 * APT2 − 0.142 * EXTRAVER

Higher scores on APT1 predict higher scores on SUCCESS (the coefficient is positive), but higher scores on the other two variables predict lower scores on SUCCESS.

In the *t* and Sig. columns we see the results of testing, for each coefficient, the null hypothesis that it is zero, assuming that the other variables are included in the regression. The probability of this value of the *t* statistic if the null hypothesis is true is also given. We can see that for our example APT1 and APT2 are significantly different from zero but EXTRAVER is not.

Standard multiple regression: Understanding the diagnostic output

Because we requested collinearity diagnostics in SPSS Dialog Box 4.2, we have two extra columns on the right. The first column, Tolerance, gives a value between zero and 1, which is the proportion of a variable's variance not accounted for by the other independent variables in the regression. Values close to zero show that there are linear relationships among the independent variables that will cause computational problems. In that case, one or more of the independent variables should be removed. All our values are close to 1, so the independent variables do not depend linearly on each other. The VIF (or variance inflation factor) is just the reciprocal of the tolerance. There is another table (not reproduced here) with further details on collinearity but the tolerance values in SPSS Output 4.2 will usually suffice.

Since we requested casewise diagnostics in SPSS Dialog Box 4.2, we get a table listing cases where the residual is more than two standard deviations (shown in SPSS Output 4.3). There are three of these, with the largest (in absolute value) just under 3, which is no cause for concern with 110 cases. We would expect about 5% as large as 2, just by chance. SPSS can calculate a variety of transformations of the (raw or unstandardized) residuals. The **standardized residual** is the residual divided by its standard error. Hence observations with residuals with more than two standard deviations are those with a standardized residual greater than 2. The **studentized residual** is similar to the standardized residual but it is more sensitive to departures from the model. This is because its scaling factor takes into account how far the observation is from the mean. The deleted and studentized residuals for an observation are found as above but from the model that excludes that observation.

Casewise Diagnostics[a]

Case Number	Std. Residual	success	Predicted Value	Residual
67	-2.903	4	41.09	-37.094
84	2.056	64	37.74	26.262
97	2.095	69	42.23	26.771

a. Dependent Variable: success

Residuals Statistics[a]

	Minimum	Maximum	Mean	Std. Deviation	N
Predicted Value	11.61	60.33	35.51	8.288	110
Residual	-37.094	26.771	0.000	12.599	110
Std. Predicted Value	-2.883	2.994	0.000	1.000	110
Std. Residual	-2.903	2.095	0.000	0.986	110

a. Dependent Variable: success

SPSS Output 4.3 Information about residuals and predicted values.

The next table is also shown in SPSS Output 4.3, and gives descriptive statistics for the predicted values and residuals, and the versions of them standardized to Z values.

The normal probability plot we requested in SPSS Dialog Box 4.3 is shown in SPSS Output 4.4. If the assumption of normality is correct, then the residuals form a random sample from a standard normal distribution, and the plot shown will be a straight line from the origin (0,0) to top right (1,1). Our residuals are quite a good approximation to that, which means we can have confidence in the ANOVA and *t*-tests on the regression coefficients.

SPSS Output 4.4 Normal probability plot of residuals.

The residual plot that was also requested in SPSS Dialog Box 4.3 appears last and is shown in SPSS Output 4.5. If the assumption of constant variance is true and if the linear regression model is a reasonable fit, the residuals should not show any dependence on any of the independent variables, and so not on the predicted values either. In fact if

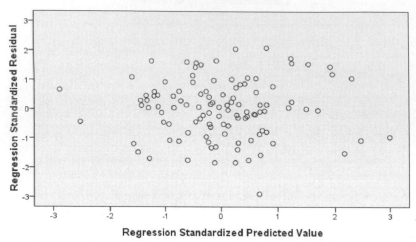

SPSS Output 4.5 Residual plot: Standardized residuals against standardized predicted values.

our assumptions about the data are correct the residuals form a random sample from a normal distribution and so this plot should show a shapeless cloud of points: any discernible pattern is bad news for our model. But ours looks good. We will show you one later that displays the inadequacy of a regression model.

Using a stepwise method

We have already seen that the *t*-test on the coefficient of EXTRAVER suggested that this variable contributes nothing to predicting SUCCESS. We could try the regression again, omitting this variable, and see whether the proportion of the variance of SUCCESS accounted for by the regression is significantly reduced. But SPSS offers a way to deal with this as part of the analysis. This may be useful if you have a longer list of independent variables, some of which may be useful predictors but some of which are almost certainly useless. What you want is the best subset to do the job of prediction as well as possible with as few variables as possible. Trying out all possible subsets yourself would not only be tedious and time consuming, but at the end you would have difficulty sorting out the best from your long list. Even with only three possible independent variables, there are seven possible subsets containing at least one of them. One solution is to use a stepwise method, and SPSS offers three. We would, however, like to include a note of caution here. The stepwise methods we are about to describe select a subset of variables entirely by statistical criteria. One variable may be included and another excluded when the difference between their ability to predict the DV is very small and perhaps there is an effect of random variation in the sample data. It is always best to select variables for possible inclusion in a regression on the basis of theoretical or practical considerations. Of course, when you try the regression you may have to reject some of these: your theory may not be as good as you hope and the relationships it proposes may be weak or even non-existent. But choosing a subset of variables for which you have no coherent theoretical underpinning is unlikely to be a very fruitful strategy. Nevertheless, a stepwise method may be a useful way to identify some promising candidate variables for further consideration, so we explain how to do it in SPSS. There are three methods.

Forward selection

Forward selection starts with the independent variable that is the best predictor of the dependent variable and checks that the coefficient is significantly different from zero, at the 5% level. Then it adds the one that improves the prediction the most, subject to a criterion, usually that the coefficient is significantly different from zero at the 5% level. The process continues until no more variables pass the criterion. SPSS allows adjustment of the criterion so you could add variables that are significant at, say, 10%, or else only those that are significant at 1%.

Backward elimination

Backward elimination starts with all independent variables in the regression, then removes the one with the smallest t statistic, provided that its p value is at least .10. The process continues until no more variables are removed. Again, the criterion can be adjusted.

Stepwise regression

Stepwise regression combines forward selection and backward elimination. At each step the best remaining variable is added, provided it passes the significant at 5% criterion, then all variables currently in the regression are checked to see if any can be removed, using the greater than 10% significance criterion. The process continues until no more variables are added or removed. This is the one we shall use. It is not guaranteed to find the best subset of independent variables but it will find a subset close to the best.

Stepwise regression: Requesting the analysis in SPSS

In SPSS Dialog Box 4.1, in the **Method** box, replace **Enter** with **Stepwise**. You will also find in the list of methods one called **Remove**. This allows you to remove some variables from the equation as a block. You can also control the entry of successive IVs or blocks of them, rather than allowing statistical criteria to determine what gets entered and in what order. This is achieved with the **Enter** method selected and using **Next**, between the **Dependent** and **Independent(s)** boxes. We will consider this sequential method later.

The statistical criteria for adding and removing variables can be modified in a dialog box that is opened by clicking on the **Options** button, but we can accept the defaults (enter if significant at 5% and remove if not significant at 10%, as described above). You can also force the regression equation to pass through the origin by not including the constant, but this is rarely required, and the default is to include the constant. There are also different ways to deal with missing values, but again we can accept the default.

Stepwise regression: Understanding the output

When we use a stepwise method, the first table in the output, shown in SPSS Output 4.6, is more interesting. In our example it shows that APT1 was the best

Variables Entered/Removed[a]

Model	Variables Entered	Variables Removed	Method
1	apt1	.	Stepwise (Criteria: Probability-of-F-to-enter <= . 050, Probability-of-F-to-remove >= .100).
2	apt2	.	Stepwise (Criteria: Probability-of-F-to-enter <= . 050, Probability-of-F-to-remove >= .100).

a. Dependent Variable: success

Model Summary

Model	R	R Square	Adjusted R Square	Std. Error of the Estimate
1	.460[a]	.212	.204	13.453
2	.540[b]	.291	.278	12.812

a. Predictors: (Constant), apt1

b. Predictors: (Constant), apt1, apt2

SPSS Output 4.6 Model summary for stepwise regression.

predictor of SUCCESS and was entered first. Then APT2 was entered and neither was removed. No more variables were entered or removed and so the final model has just APT1 and APT2 to predict SUCCESS. The proportion of the variance of SUCCESS explained by this model is .291 (R^2 for Model 2 – the final model – in the second table in SPSS Output 4.6), which is almost the same as the .302 achieved with EXTRAVER included as well.

Because EXTRAVER contributed so little to the regression, the diagnostics are similar to those we have already looked at. Only the table of coefficients, shown in SPSS Output 4.7, has any more to tell us. This gives the coefficients for the new regression model (Model 2) with only APT1 and APT2 as IVs.

Coefficients[a]

Model		Unstandardized Coefficients		Standardized Coefficients	t	Sig.	Collinearity Statistics	
		B	Std. Error	Beta			Tolerance	VIF
1	(Constant)	-18.343	10.087		-1.819	.072		
	apt1	0.535	0.099	.460	5.383	.000	1.000	1.000
2	(Constant)	9.225	12.460		0.740	.461		
	apt1	0.605	0.097	.520	6.249	.000	.957	1.045
	apt2	-0.347	0.100	-.289	-3.474	.001	.957	1.045

a. Dependent Variable: success

SPSS Output 4.7 Coefficients for new regression.

Categorical variables

So far we have only used variables on at least interval scales, but you can incorporate categorical variables as independent variables.

Creating dummy variables

To use a categorical variable in a regression analysis you need to create *dummy variables*. As well as the aptitude and personality data on our computer staff, we have a record of part of their educational background, namely whether they have a degree in IT or computing, IT technician training not involving a degree or neither.

This educational information gives us a categorical variable with three unordered levels. We can only use this in a regression by forming two dummy variables (one less than the number of categories). The first dummy variable, which we have called ITDEGREE, is coded 1 for people with a degree in IT or computing and zero for the others. The second, which we have called OTHERIT, is coded 1 for those with IT technician training without a degree and zero for the others. Those with neither a computing nor IT degree, and no IT technician training, will be coded zero on both of these dummy variables. No case can be coded 1 on both dummy variables, since they represent mutually exclusive categories on the original categorical variable. Table 4.2 shows the codings for the two dummy variables and illustrates the application of the codes to three cases from the dataset (shown in bold in Table 4.1): case 1 with no IT degree and no technical training: case 3 with an IT degree and case 6 with technical training. We could have used any two of the three levels of the original categorical variable to define the two dummy variables, then those cases in the unused level would have been coded zero on both dummies. For a binary variable, you only need one dummy. If you have several categorical variables each with three or more levels, you can see that you can easily end up with an unwieldy set of dummies.

Table 4.2 Codings for two dummy variables to represent three categorical variables

Dummy variable	Degree	Tech. training	Neither	Case 1	Case 3	Case 6
1. ITDEGREE	1	0	0	0	1	0
2. OTHERIT	0	1	0	0	0	1

Stepwise regression with a categorical variable: Requesting the analysis in SPSS

Now we will try our regression again, this time including the dummy variables that code for education. They can be added to the **Independent(s)** box using the arrow in exactly the same way as the other independent variables (see SPSS Dialog Box 4.1). Before starting the stepwise regression it is good to perform a multiple regression with all candidate predictor variables and check that the collinearity statistics give no cause for concern, since collinearity may affect the stages in the process. If we do that for our data we find that the lowest Tolerance is .76, which tells us that, for each independent variable, the proportion of variance not accounted for by other independent variables in the equation is high enough for us to continue with our stepwise regression. Make sure this is selected in the **Method** box.

Stepwise regression with a categorical variable: Understanding the output

The model summary is shown in SPSS Output 4.8. You can see that APT1 was entered, then ITDEGREE, then APT2. None was removed and no more variables were entered. The resulting model has an R^2 of .394, so just under 40% of the variance of SUCCESS is explained by APT1, ITDEGREE and APT2, which is a little better than the 30% explained by APT1 and APT2 (see SPSS Output 4.6).

Variables Entered/Removed[a]

Model	Variables Entered	Variables Removed	Method
1	apt1	.	Stepwise (Criteria: Probability-of-F-to-enter <= .050, Probability-of-F-to-remove >= .100).
2	itdegree	.	Stepwise (Criteria: Probability-of-F-to-enter <= .050, Probability-of-F-to-remove >= .100).
3	apt2	.	Stepwise (Criteria: Probability-of-F-to-enter <= .050, Probability-of-F-to-remove >= .100).

a. Dependent Variable: success

Model Summary[d]

Model	R	R Square	Adjusted R Square	Std. Error of the Estimate
1	.460[a]	.212	.204	13.453
2	.595[b]	.354	.342	12.236
3	.627[c]	.394	.377	11.907

a. Predictors: (Constant), apt1

b. Predictors: (Constant), apt1, itdegree

c. Predictors: (Constant), apt1, itdegree, apt2

d. Dependent Variable: success

SPSS Output 4.8 Stepwise regression summary with education variables included.

The ANOVA shown in SPSS Output 4.9 tells us that the final regression model (Model 3) was significant at the 0.1% level. The regression coefficients are also shown in SPSS Output 4.9. You can also see there that the collinearity check gives no cause for concern, as the tolerance for all variables included is close to 1. From the B column we can see that an increase of 1 in the APT1 score increases the estimated SUCCESS score by 0.52. Being coded 1 for ITDEGREE (which means having a degree in IT or computing) *reduces* the estimated SUCCESS score by 10.19 (the coefficient is negative). This means that on these particular tasks, those staff with a degree in computing or IT perform worse than those without such a degree. An increase of 1 in the APT2 score also decreases the estimated SUCCESS score (by 0.25). Judging by these results, the best people to tackle the trouble-shooting tasks are those with high APT1 scores, no IT or computing degree and low APT2 scores.

The last table in SPSS Output 4.9 shows that the new model has three cases with standardized residuals greater than 2. However, none is very large and they still comprise less than 3% of 110 cases. The residual plot and normal probability plot (not shown here) are very similar to those we obtained with the previous model, and we conclude that the model with SUCCESS predicted by APT1, ITDEGREE and APT2 is somewhat better than the previous one with APT1 and APT2.

Estimating the success of predicting new cases

The example we have been considering is typical of the way an attempt to predict scores on a DV using regression often turns out. Our regression is significant but it only explains about 40% of the variance of the variable we want to predict. As in our case here, this may give a useful general indication for action: we shall probably get more satisfied clients if we deploy staff with high APT1 scores, low APT2 scores and who do not have degrees in computing or IT, and when recruiting we should remember that those who do not hold the best computing qualifications may be particularly useful in the trouble-shooting area. However, if we were hoping to get

ANOVA[d]

Model		Sum of Squares	df	Mean Square	F	Sig.
1	Regression	5243.584	1	5243.584	28.973	.000[a]
	Residual	19545.907	108	180.981		
	Total	24789.491	109			
2	Regression	8768.588	2	4384.294	29.282	.000[b]
	Residual	16020.903	107	149.728		
	Total	24789.491	109			
3	Regression	9760.179	3	3253.393	22.946	.000[c]
	Residual	15029.312	106	141.786		
	Total	24789.491	109			

a. Predictors: (Constant), apt1
b. Predictors: (Constant), apt1, itdegree
c. Predictors: (Constant), apt1, itdegree, apt2
d. Dependent Variable: success

Coefficients[a]

Model		Unstandardized Coefficients		Standardized Coefficients			Collinearity Statistics	
		B	Std. Error	Beta	t	Sig.	Tolerance	VIF
1	(Constant)	-18.343	10.087		-1.819	.072		
	apt1	0.535	0.099	.460	5.383	.000	1.000	1.000
2	(Constant)	-5.986	9.521		-.629	.531		
	apt1	0.460	0.092	.395	5.012	.000	.971	1.029
	itdegree	-11.602	2.408	-.383	-4.852	.000	.971	1.029
3	(Constant)	12.495	11.605		1.077	.284		
	apt1	0.520	0.092	.447	5.644	.000	.912	1.097
	itdegree	-10.190	2.410	-.334	-4.228	.000	.918	1.089
	apt2	-0.252	0.095	-.210	-2.645	.009	.905	1.105

a. Dependent Variable: success

Casewise Diagnostics[a]

Case Number	Std. Residual	success	Predicted Value	Residual
18	2.101	52	26.98	25.018
67	-2.563	4	34.52	-30.516
97	2.060	69	44.47	24.532

a. Dependent Variable: success

SPSS Output 4.9 ANOVA and regression coefficients with education variables included, and cases with large residuals.

good predictions of actual SUCCESS scores we shall probably be disappointed. For this we probably need a regression with about two-thirds of the variance accounted for, or even more if we hope for fairly precise results. Recall that for a standard normal distribution, 95% of values lie within 1.96 of the mean (zero). So for values with an approximately normal distribution, 95% of values lie within about two standard deviations of the mean. Now look back to SPSS Output 4.3 and see that the standard deviation of the residuals is 12.599, so about 95% of predicted values will be within about 2 * 12.599, or about 25, of the actual value. The full range of observed success values is only 67 (from 3 to 70), so although using the regression as a predictor is certainly better than just guessing (the fact that it is significant tells us that), it may not be of much practical use. You could not, for instance, confidently use it to predict scores at employment interviews and select only those with a predicted value above some threshold.

In addition to the common problem discussed above, prediction on new cases will be a little less successful than for those used to calculate the regression coefficients. Every dataset will have some random variation, and the calculated regression coefficients are optimal for this dataset, including its random components. New data will have different random components and the regression coefficients will be slightly less than optimal. There are two ways to estimate how well your regression will predict for new cases, both of which are used in practice.

Checking prediction success: Waiting for actual DV values

One way is to predict for new cases using the regression equation, and then to wait until you can get the actual DV values for these new cases and calculate the standard deviation of the residuals (the lower the standard deviation, the closer cases will be to the multiple regression prediction). This approach is only a problem if your prediction causes you to make some decision, perhaps about training, that makes it impossible to get a realistic actual value later because the decision you made will have influenced the result (e.g., those predicted to be good at trouble-shooting are given extra training to do that job). This is sometimes referred to as *criterion contamination*.

Checking prediction success: Using training and validation sets

Another approach is to randomly assign your cases to two datasets. The first, called the *training set*, is used to calculate the regression. The second is called the *validation set*. The predicted score is calculated for all the cases in the validation set, but as we already have their actual scores we can find the residuals and their standard deviation. It is quite tedious to do this with a calculator but SPSS will do it easily if we use the **Selection Variable** box in the first regression dialog box.

First, we need an extra variable to indicate which cases are in the training set and which in the validation set. We could call this variable xval, for cross-validation, and code 1 for the training set and code 2 for the validation set. It is best to assign cases randomly to the two sets, but to make it easy for you to reproduce our results we have assigned alternate cases, starting with the first, to the training set, so our extra variable is a column of alternating 1s and 2s. The dataset with this added column can be found on the website as psy.regression.crossvalidation.sav. In SPSS Dialog Box 4.1, select the new variable xval and use the arrow to put it in the **Selection Variable** box. Then click the **Rule** button and enter **equal to 1** in the box. Now the regression will be calculated using only those cases for which xval = 1, our training set. The dialog box now looks like SPSS Dialog Box 4.4. Leave all the IVs in the **Independent(s)** box and leave the **Method** as **Stepwise**.

Even though the regression will be calculated using only those cases selected by the **Selection Variable**, we can use the **Save** button to keep the values predicted by the regression for all of the data in the datasheet, the training set (xval = 1) and the validation set (xval = 2). Click the button and get the dialog box shown in SPSS Dialog Box 4.5 (on p. 104). Save the **Unstandardized Predicted Values** and their **Residuals**, so that we have these in the datasheet as two new columns. You may be interested in the 95% confidence intervals for the predicted values and, if so, tick **Individual** in the **Prediction Intervals** box as shown. Click **Continue** and **OK**.

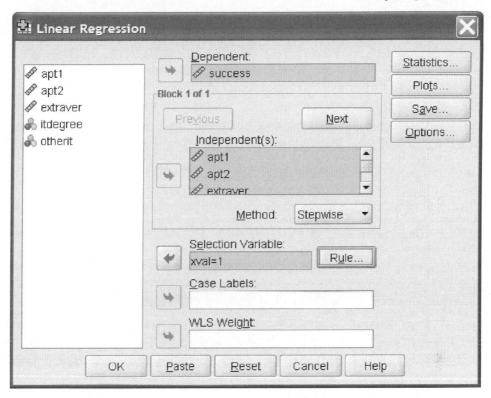

SPSS Dialog Box 4.4 Using the variable xval to select validation set cases for the regression.

Training and validation sets: Completing the analysis and understanding the output

In addition to the output already described, which now refers only to the 55 cases in the training set, we have extra columns in the datasheet giving predicted values, residuals and confidence intervals for all of the cases in both datasets. You may want to sort the list on the xval variable and look to see how many of the validation cases have a success score inside the 95% confidence interval for the predicted value (select **Data** from the top menu bar, then **Sort Cases**). (If you assign alternate cases to the training and validation sets as we did, you should find all but two of the validation cases inside the 95% confidence interval. The training set also has two cases falling outside the confidence interval.) A simple way to compare results on the training and validation sets is to look at the standard deviations of the residuals. Choose **Analyze**, then **Compare means**, then **Means** from the menu bar. Put unstandardized residual in the **Dependents List** and xval in the **Independents List**. The result is the table shown in SPSS Output 4.10. You can see that the standard deviation of the residuals for the validation set (13.04) is about 10% larger than that for the training set (11.87), and this suggests that prediction for new cases will be correspondingly less precise. After splitting your dataset like this to estimate precision in future prediction, it is best to use as the predictor the regression calculated on the full dataset.

Linear Regression: Save

Predicted Values
- ☑ Unstandardized
- ☐ Standardized
- ☐ Adjusted
- ☐ S.E. of mean predictions

Residuals
- ☑ Unstandardized
- ☐ Standardized
- ☐ Studentized
- ☐ Deleted
- ☐ Studentized deleted

Distances
- ☐ Mahalanobis
- ☐ Cook's
- ☐ Leverage values

Influence Statistics
- ☐ DfBeta(s)
- ☐ Standardized DfBeta(s)
- ☐ DfFit
- ☐ Standardized DfFit
- ☐ Covariance ratio

Prediction Intervals
- ☐ Mean ☑ Individual
- Confidence Interval: 95 %

Coefficient statistics
- ☐ Create coefficient statistics
  - ◉ Create a new dataset
    - Dataset name:
  - ○ Write a new data file
    - File...

Export model information to XML file
- Browse...
- ☑ Include the covariance matrix

Continue   Cancel   Help

SPSS Dialog Box 4.5 Saving predicted values.

Report

Unstandardized Residual

xval	Mean	N	Std. Deviation
1	0.0000000	55	11.86713931
2	-1.6144827	55	13.04430323
Total	-0.8072413	110	12.43875039

SPSS Output 4.10 Comparison of standard deviations of residuals for training (1) and validation (2) sets.

Predicting for new cases

The **Selection Variable** box can also be used to calculate predicted values for any new cases. Just add the new cases to the bottom of the dataset already in the data window. Of course their SUCCESS scores will be missing. You need a variable to select the original cases for the regression. You could make a new variable called CHOOSE, and code all the original cases as 1 and the new cases as 2. Then put CHOOSE = 1 in the **Selection Variable** box. Do not forget to use the **Save** button to save the predicted values for all cases, including the new ones, to the data window.

Hierarchical regression

An intuitive rationale

As should be clear from our example stepwise analyses, the criteria for entry and removal of IVs are strictly statistical (see the section on 'Using a stepwise method' if you need a reminder). Sometimes, the researcher has theoretical or empirical reasons for deciding on the order in which IVs, or blocks of IVs, are entered. Several variables may be selected for entry as a block because they are conceptually linked, as with a group of personality variables, or because one IV or block of IVs is conceptually prior to another (e.g., weight might be considered prior to training when predicting success as a sumo wrestler). Another possible reason for entering variables as a block might be because they are relatively inexpensive to measure, so we would like to enter them first in the hope that they will provide good enough prediction without needing to include subsequently entered, more expensive variables in the prediction equation.

Order of entry

You may wonder whether there are any general guidelines for determining an order of entry. Well, IVs that are accorded greater theoretical (or practical) importance are often entered first, in order to see whether other theoretically related IVs add anything to the prediction of the DV as they are added. On the other hand, more theoretically import-ant IVs may be entered last, in order to see whether they add anything to the prediction over and above earlier entered nuisance variables. We shall see in the next chapter, on analysis of covariance (ANCOVA), another method that offers an approach to the statistical control of nuisance variables: there we meet the same problem in a different form. In the end, it comes down to the researcher having a logical or theoretical reason for preferring one order over others. Recall that in the stepwise method the criteria for ordering the IVs are purely statistical and the purpose of the analysis is therefore necessarily limited to finding the best prediction equation with as few IVs as possible, or else to exploration and hypothesis generation. This is so because the order of entry of IVs can have a profound effect on their apparent importance, and which of two vari-ables comes first can depend on a decimal place. In hierarchical regression, on the other hand, effectively the researcher will be testing hypotheses about how much variance in the DV can be attributed to some IVs after that due to earlier IVs has been accounted for.

A psychology example of a hierarchical regression problem

So, the question being asked concerns the proportion of variance in the DV that is accounted for by one IV (or block of IVs) when other IVs (or blocks of IVs) have been controlled. Let us consider an example that follows on from our previous IT trouble-shooting analyses. Recall that we found that APT1, ITDEGREE and APT2 were the best predictors of SUCCESS, whereas the personality variable EXTRAVER and the non-degree technician training variable OTHERIT contributed little. We might wonder whether EXTRAVER, in the presence of another personality variable, locus of CONTROL, would be more predictive. More importantly, given the rather low proportion of the DV variance accounted for (less than 40%), we might hypothesize that targeted training will improve trouble-shooting performance. Specifically, we might want to know how well SUCCESS2 (a re-measure of success) is predicted by an on-line training program (TRAINING) after we have controlled (allowed for) the effects of personality variables, such as EXTRAVER and locus of CONTROL (Block 1), followed by control of the aptitude variables APT1 and APT2 (Block 2) and the educational background variables ITDEGREE and OTHERIT (Block 3). To test the hypothesis, we enter the variables one block at a time, ending with the variable of primary interest, TRAINING (Block 4). Our rationale for this order of entry is that we are looking first at influences that are relatively 'hard-wired' (personality block followed by aptitude block), then at experiential variables (the educational background block), before assessing how much additional variance is accounted for by targeted training. The data for this analysis can be found as psy.regression. hierarchical.sav on the book website. Notice that we now have two extra IVs, and applying the rule of thumb mentioned earlier suggests we need about four extra cases. We have neglected this requirement here.

We decide to use on-line training because that way we can minimize disruption of the work of the company and, at the same time, randomly allocate different amounts of training to our 110 staff. One hundred and ten individual work schedules are prepared, with 0–10 hours of training included in the schedules. The schedules are then distributed randomly to IT staff.

So, at each step of entry of a variable or block of variables, the increase in the proportion of variance (increase in R^2) in SUCCESS2 that is accounted for is computed. In fact, the computational procedures are the same as for stepwise regression. Hierarchical regression differs only in that the researcher decides on the order in which IVs are entered and in that more than one IV can be entered at a time. It is the change in R^2 statistic that is often of most interest when you have a reason for adding IVs, or blocks of them, in a particular order. After showing you how to do the hierarchical analysis, we will therefore only show you the Model Summary output table, which will contain the R^2 Change information.

Hierarchical regression: Requesting the analysis in SPSS

To do the above hierarchical regression, you would need to choose **Analyze**, then **Regression**, then **Linear** to get SPSS Dialog Box 4.1. Select the DV (SUCCESS2 in our example) from the list on the left and use the arrow to put it in the **Dependent** box. Make sure that the **Method** selected is **Enter**, then select the first IV (or block of IVs) – EXTRAVER and CONTROL, in our example – and move it to the **Independent(s)** box and click **Next**. This will cause '**Block 2 of 2**' to replace '**Block 1 of 1**' to the left of **Next**.

Select the next IV (or block of IVs) – APT1 and APT2, in our example – and move it to the **Independent(s)** box. Click **Next**, which will cause **'Block 3 of 3'** to be displayed. Select the next IV (or block of IVs) – ITDEGREE and OTHERIT, in our example – and move it to the **Independent(s)** box. Click **Next**, which will cause **'Block 4 of 4'** to be displayed. Select the IV of primary interest – TRAINING, in our example – and move it to the **Independent(s)** box. The dialog box will now look like SPSS Dialog Box 4.6. Because there are no more IVs to enter, ignore the **'Block 4 of 4'** that is displayed and click the **Statistics** button and select **R Squared Change**. Then, either click **Continue** and **OK** or, if you want diagnostics, etc., first click any of the buttons at the side (see 'Standard multiple regression: requesting the analysis in SPSS', where we discussed some of the available choices in relation to our first example).

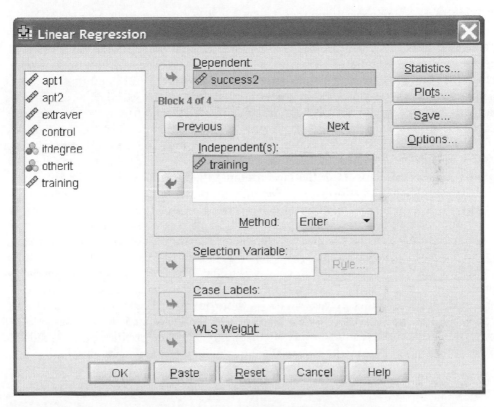

SPSS Dialog Box 4.6 Hierarchical regression dialog box following entry of four blocks of IVs.

Hierarchical regression: Understanding the output

The output includes the following tables: Variables Entered/Removed, Model Summary, ANOVA (testing regression for all four models), Coefficients (includes collinearity statistics such as Tolerance if **Collinearity** diagnostics was selected), Excluded Variables (at each step – includes tolerance statistics) and Collinearity Statistics (if selected). We will only reproduce the Model Summary (SPSS Output 4.11), which includes R^2 change, the statistic that is probably of most interest when entry of IVs is controlled to test a hypothesis. The interpretation of content in the other output boxes has been discussed in previous sections.

Model Summary

Model	R	R Square	Adjusted R Square	Std. Error of the Estimate	Change Statistics				
					R Square Change	F Change	df1	df2	Sig. F Change
1	.470[a]	.221	.206	12.200	.221	15.180	2	107	.000
2	.663[b]	.439	.418	10.449	.218	20.429	2	105	.000
3	.728[c]	.530	.503	9.659	.091	9.948	2	103	.000
4	.805[d]	.647	.623	8.407	.117	33.945	1	102	.000

a. Predictors: (Constant), control, extraver

b. Predictors: (Constant), control, extraver, apt2, apt1

c. Predictors: (Constant), control, extraver, apt2, apt1, itdegree, otherit

d. Predictors: (Constant), control, extraver, apt2, apt1, itdegree, otherit, training

SPSS Output 4.11 R Square and R Square Change statistics for hierarchical regression.

Look at the R^2 change column in SPSS Output 4.11 (it is generally safe to ignore the adjusted R^2 values). You will see that when the first block of IVs (EXTRAVER and CONTROL) is entered, R^2 Change is .221 (which, for the first block, is the same as R^2 of course) and this is significant at the 0.1% level ($p < .001$). The addition of the second block (APT1 and APT2) results in a substantial increase in R^2 of .218 and this increase is highly significant (i.e., in excess of an additional 20% of the variance in SUCCESS2 is accounted for). The addition of the third block (ITDEGREE and OTHERIT) adds relatively little (about 9%) to the variance accounted for. However, addition of the fourth block (the single IV, TRAINING) adds a highly significant 12%, bringing the total proportion of explained variance to .647 (column 3 in the table). Thus, we are able to conclude that our hypothesis was supported: the more training the IT staff received, the better was their trouble-shooting performance. Over and above the influence of personality variables, aptitude variables and educational variables, on-line training accounted for an additional 12% of the variance in the DV. The training was very effective.

We have not shown the Coefficients table here, but from it we can see that APT2 and EXTRAVER have coefficients that do not differ significantly from zero. The personality variable CONTROL has a coefficient that does differ from zero: it was a much better predictor of success than EXTRAVER. If we repeat the hierarchical analysis without APT2 and EXTRAVER, the results are very similar to those described in the previous paragraph, and we still get nearly 64% of the variance of SUCCESS2 explained. As always, we must bear in mind that different measures of personality, aptitude or education (or, indeed, other categories of IVs) might have resulted in a different picture emerging.

Example Box 4.2

An alternative medical example of a hierarchical regression problem

The full analysis for this example can be found at www.psypress.com/multivariate-analysis/medical-examples (click on Chapter 4).

Following on from the stepwise regression, the possibility was considered that DEPRESSION might be more predictive of SUCCESS in the presence of another state variable such as social isolation (ISOLATION). More importantly, as only about 40% of the variance in SUCCESS is accounted for by the variables in the stepwise analysis, we speculate that we might be able to get a better prediction of SUCCESS2 (a later re-measure of success 10 weeks later) if we follow up the CBT treatment with a DIARY intervention, in which patients are asked to keep a record of their thoughts and feelings every day for the 10 weeks following CBT. The measure for the DIARY variable is the number of weeks for which entries were made on all 7 days. The rationale is that the more patients keep rehearsing CBT-induced changes in the way they think and feel about their lives, the more their maladaptive behaviour is likely to change. Specifically, we want to know how well SUCCESS2 is predicted by the diary intervention after we have controlled (allowed for) the effects of state variables (DEPRESSION and ISOLATION entered in Block 1), followed by control of the theoretically related variables (SEVERITY and SELFEST in Block 2) and the dummy variables for referral initiation (GP and FAMILY in Block 3). The variables are entered a block at a time, ending with the intervention variable of primary interest (DIARY in Block 4).

Outcomes

When Block 1 (DEPRESSION and ISOLATION) is entered, a significant amount of variance ($R^2 = .22$) in SUCCESS2 is accounted for. The addition of Block 2 (SELFEST and SEVERITY) results in a substantial and significant increase in R^2 of .218. The addition of Block 3 adds relatively little (about 9%) to the variance accounted for, though this addition is still significant. The single variable in Block 4 (DIARY) adds a significant 12%, bringing the total proportion of explained variance to .647. Thus, we conclude that adding the predictor variable ISOLATION and following CBT with a diary intervention is well worthwhile. If the hierarchical analysis is repeated without the variables SEVERITY and DEPRESSION the results are very similar, with about 64% of the variance of SUCCESS2 explained, confirming that those two variables have little predictive value with respect to SUCCESS2.

Alternative variables for use in SPSS
The full dataset, med.regression.hierarchical.sav, can be found on the book website

Variable	Psychology	Medicine
Dependent variable	SUCCESS2 Re-measure of success	SUCCESS2 Re-measure of success
Predictor variables Block 1	APT1 Aptitude measure 1 APT2 Aptitude measure 2	SELFEST Score on self-esteem SEVERITY Severity of eating disorder
Block 2	EXTRAVER Extraversion score CONTROL Locus of control	DEPRESSION Depression score ISOLATION Social isolation
Block 3	ITDEGREE IT degree/other (other = tech. training or none) OTHERIT Tech. training/other (other = IT degree or none)	GP GP referral/other (other = patient or family) FAMILY Family referral/other (other = GP or patient)
Block 4	TRAINING Amount of training	DIARY Number of full weekly entries

Non-linear relationships

We have already mentioned that confining attention to linear relationships is not as restrictive as first appears, either because we may be interested in only part of the range where linearity approximately applies, or else because there is some simple transformation of one of the variables that turns a non-linear relationship into an approximately linear one.

A striking example from astronomy

In this section we make a short diversion into astronomy, which provides the most striking example we know of a non-linear relationship that can be turned into an approximately linear one with a simple transformation. Table 4.3 shows the distances from the sun of the planets in the solar system. Column 1 gives the number of the planet counting outwards from the sun, so Mercury is number 1, Earth is number 3 and Neptune is number 9. Pluto, with slightly ambiguous status at the time of writing, is number 10. The asteroid belt between Earth and Mars is given the number 4, and an average distance for the asteroids is given. The distances are in astronomical units to avoid very long numbers. One astronomical unit is the distance of the Earth from the sun, so from the table you see that Pluto is nearly 40 times as far from the sun as Earth is.

Table 4.3 Planetary distances for the solar system
(regression.nonlinear.sav)

Number	Distance
1	0.39
2	0.72
3	1.00
4	1.52
5	2.77
6	5.20
7	9.50
8	19.20
9	30.09
10	39.50

Of course, since we have counted the planets outwards from the sun, the distances obviously increase as the number goes from 1 to 10. But why would the distances increase in the extremely regular way that the scatterplot in Figure 4.3 shows? This mysterious relationship was first observed nearly 250 years ago, and many attempts have been made to establish the exact form of the relationship and to explain why it occurs. As far as we know, these problems remain unsolved but they give plenty of scope for trying out various features of regression analysis.

A badly fitting straight line

Plotting the data as in Figure 4.3 should warn us not to try to fit a straight line. Nevertheless, it is still *possible* to calculate the best straight line, even though the fit is

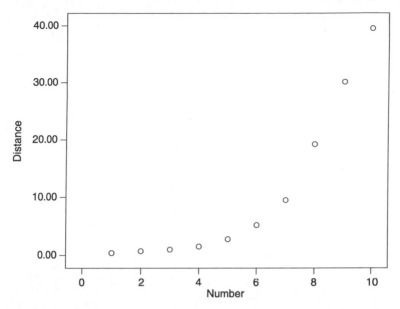

Figure 4.3 Distances of planets in the solar system plotted against their numbers counted outwards from the sun.

terrible. It is worth noting that although the model is clearly incorrect, the regression is significant at the 1% level and the proportion of variance accounted for is nearly 80%, as you can check for yourself if you perform a linear regression on the data in Table 4.3. This illustrates one of the ways in which regression can so easily be misused: you can perform the calculations successfully even on data for which linear regression is hopelessly inappropriate. As well as looking at the significance of the regression and the proportion of variance explained, it is also necessary to perform some checks on the fit of the model, as outlined in the section 'Standard multiple regression: understanding the diagnostic output'. If you plot the residuals against the fitted values in this case, instead of a shapeless cloud of points like we got in SPSS Output 4.5, we get the U shape seen in Figure 4.4 overleaf. This is an extreme example of a case where the residual plot shows that the fitted model (a straight line) is a very poor fit. For the residual plot, we hope to see a shapeless cloud of points, since, if the model is a good fit, the residuals are just random variables with a normal distribution.

Transformation to a linear relationship

The attempt to understand the planetary distances by looking at the log of the distances dates to 1913. The plot of LOG(DISTANCE) against NUMBER is shown in Figure 4.5 overleaf. (We used the natural logarithm, but using log to the base 10 is just as good.) A simple transformation, the log, of one of the variables, has produced what looks like a nearly perfect straight line. Wonderful! If only all regression analyses were as easy! This time more than 99% of the variance of LOG(DISTANCE) is explained by the linear regression on NUMBER. You will probably never see a regression that explains this much of the variance again.

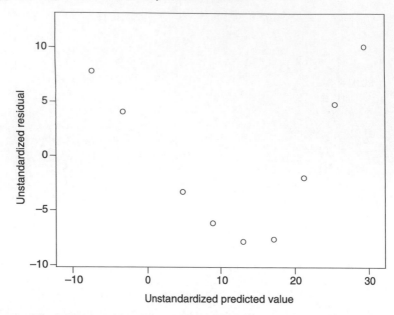

Figure 4.4 Residual plot for data where a straight line is a very poor model.

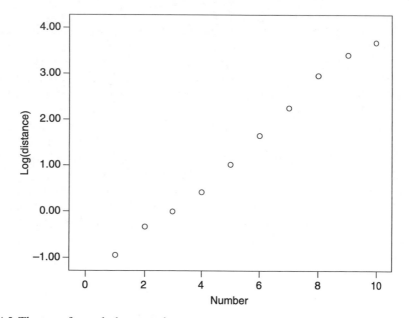

Figure 4.5 The transformed planetary data.

Proportion of variance is not everything!

But look at the residual plot in Figure 4.6. Do these residuals form a shapeless cloud of points? Alas no, they form a slightly irregular wave. Only a tiny part of the variance of LOG(DISTANCE) is not explained by the regression, but that remaining tiny part is not random.

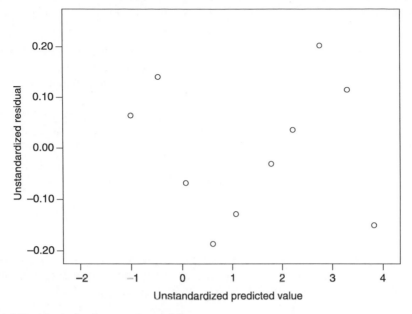

Figure 4.6 Residual plot for transformed data.

Look at Figure 4.7, where the transformed data are plotted along with the fitted straight line, and you can see the points forming a shallow wave, starting from the left, above the line, then below it, then above again, then finally below it for the last point. The residual plot just exaggerates this wave and makes it easier to see.

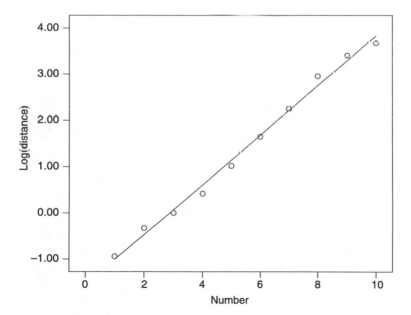

Figure 4.7 Transformed data and the fitted line.

A cautionary tale

Although we still do not know the correct form of the relationship between DISTANCE and NUMBER or LOG(DISTANCE) and NUMBER, the investigations we outlined here have inspired much fruitful inquiry into how planetary systems might form around stars. Like any other investigation, a regression analysis may produce as many questions as answers, but may be fruitful nonetheless.

In this section we have used an example with only one independent variable to illustrate how a simple transformation may make a non-linear relationship nearly linear. But the example also shows that even if a regression is significant and explains a large proportion of the variance, it is still important to check on the fit of the model. By going back to the case of a single independent variable we can see all of this very clearly in graphical displays.

Reporting results

When reporting a regression analysis you should always include some information on your checks on how the model fits, for the reasons illustrated in the astronomy example. The following paragraphs illustrate how you might report the results of attempting to predict the SUCCESS score from the aptitude test scores, the personality test and the educational information, using the stepwise method. We will include here a residual plot and a normal probability plot for the final model, which we omitted earlier. We will also provide an interpretation of the results that might be appropriate for inclusion in a Discussion section of a report.

> We performed a stepwise regression of the SUCCESS scores on the independent variables APT1, APT2, EXTRAVER, ITDEGREE and OTHERIT described in the Method section. The criterion for entry was prob(F) ≤ .05 and for removal was prob(F) ≤ .10. The first variable entered was APT1, followed by ITDEGREE and then by APT2. None was removed and no more were entered, so the final model was:

> Predicted SUCCESS = 12.495 + 0.520 * APT1 − 0.252 * APT2 − 10.190 * ITDEGREE

> This shows that higher SUCCESS scores are predicted for those with higher APT1 scores, lower APT2 scores and who do not have a degree in computing or IT (since those who do have one, coded 1, will have 10.19 subtracted from their predicted SUCCESS score). This regression was significant: $F(3,106) = 22.94$; $p < .001$, accounting for 39.4% of the variance of SUCCESS ($R^2 = .394$).

> The tolerances for the three variables in the regression all exceeded .9, so there was no evidence of collinearity in the independent variables. Three cases (less than 3% of the 110) had standardized residuals that exceeded 2. The (absolute) values were 2.101, 2.563 and 2.060. We do not consider that these values indicate any lack of fit.

> The normal probability plot of the residuals and the plot of standardized residuals against fitted values are shown in Figures A and B. These support our view that the model is a good fit.

Dependent variable: Success

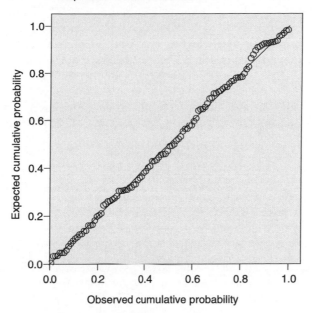

Figure A Normal probability plot of residuals.

Dependent variable: Success

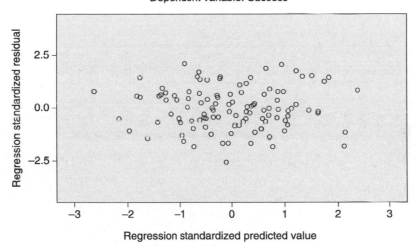

Figure B Standardized residuals plotted against standardized fitted values.

Interpretation of the results is normally presented in the Discussion section of a report and something along the lines of the following paragraph might be included there in this case.

Although the regression was significant and the model was a good fit, we consider that with only about 40% of the variance explained we cannot usefully apply our results to predicting SUCCESS scores for new cases. However, the results do suggest that we should deploy those members of staff with high APT1 scores, low APT2 scores and who do not have a degree in computing or IT as our main trouble-shooters, as these are likely to be the most effective. The results also suggest that when advertising for and selecting new staff, we should remember that those without the best qualifications in IT and computing may be especially useful as trouble-shooters if they score well on APT1. Finally, although the scale we used measures only one aspect of the extremely complex concept of personality, the fact that our personality variable was not a useful predictor makes us optimistic that we can improve performance with appropriate training. This is a subject for future research.

A training extension was in fact described, but does not feature in the above report, so it is reasonable to consider that as a possible issue for future research in the discussion section of the report.

Reference

Todman J. B. & Dugard P. (2001) *Single-case and small-n experimental designs: A practical guide to randomization tests*. Mahwah, NJ: Lawrence Erlbaum Associates, Inc.

5 Analysis of covariance (ANCOVA)

Introduction and intuitive explication

Analysis of covariance (ANCOVA) is a most useful technique for exploring differences among treatment groups when the DV we are interested in is influenced not just by our treatments but also by at least one other variable that we can measure but may not be able to control. It combines the ANOVA technique to examine the effect of different levels of a treatment factor (the IV) with the regression technique to allow for the effect of a random nuisance variable (NV), called a *covariate*, on the outcome. We use some examples to convey the general idea, before going on to illustrate in detail how to use the technique.

A design with a covariate: Example 1

Suppose you were designing an independent groups experiment to test the hypothesis that people will recall more items from a list of noun pairs, when prompted with one word from each pair, if they are instructed to form an interactive mental image linking each word pair than if they are instructed to just keep repeating the word pairs to themselves. For example, consider the word pair, 'shoe–donkey'. In the imagery condition, a participant might form a mental image of a donkey with a shoe on one of its ears and, when prompted with the word 'shoe', that participant is expected to try to recall the mental image in order to retrieve the word 'donkey'. However, we know that individuals differ greatly in their self-reported ability to form vivid mental images. Some participants in the imagery condition may therefore be unable to follow the instruction effectively, while some participants in the control condition may find it hard to suppress their normal image-forming activity. The result may be that much variability is introduced into the data because of the effect on the DV of the random NV, IMAGERY ABILITY. Such variability will make it harder to see the effect of the IV on the DV if the null hypothesis is in fact false. It makes sense, therefore, to try to assess the difference between the experimental and control means after having allowed for ('taken out') any effects of the NV (i.e., the covariate). This can be achieved in an ANCOVA, provided that a measure of the covariate has been obtained, for example, by conducting a pretest, preferably well before running the experiment. This might involve asking participants to form mental images of nouns and then obtaining their ratings of the vividness of their images.

A design with a covariate: Example 2

Consider another example. Suppose someone has come up with a new method of teaching children to read and you want to test it against the current method employed in a school. Let us assume that you can randomly assign the children who are due to be taught to read to NEW and CURRENT method groups (levels of the IV) and that a standardized test of reading skills is available as the DV. If the children's scores on an intelligence test were available, it would be a good idea to use them as a covariate, because individual differences in intelligence are likely to have an effect on the attainment of reading skills. If there happened to be a preponderance of brighter children in the NEW group, we might be led to conclude, possibly erroneously, that the new method was indeed superior. If, on the other hand, there happened to be a preponderance of brighter children in the CURRENT group, any real superiority of the new method might be masked by the effect of intelligence on the DV. The risk of making a Type I error (finding a significant effect when the null hypothesis is true) or a Type II error (failing to find a significant effect when the null hypothesis is false) can be reduced by using a random NV as a covariate, provided that there really is a correlation between the covariate and the DV.

ANCOVA: A graphical illustration

Focussing on a graphical representation of the correlation between a covariate and the DV may help in gaining an intuitive idea of what an ANCOVA does. Considering the example just given, the correlation between the covariate (INTELLIGENCE TEST score) and the DV (READING SKILLS score) can be represented in a scattergram in the manner illustrated in Figure 5.1, where a regression line of READING SKILLS score (*Y*-axis) on

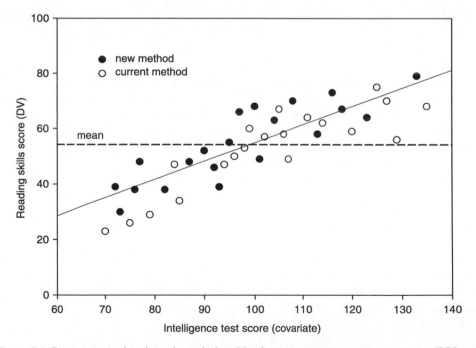

Figure 5.1 Scattergram showing the relationship between READING SKILLS score (DV) and INTELLIGENCE TEST score (covariate) for two treatment conditions (IV).

INTELLIGENCE TEST (*X*-axis) has been drawn through the points and a horizontal broken line has been added at the level of the mean READING SKILLS score (mean = 53.6). Suppose that the filled dots represent children in the NEW group and the unfilled dots represent children in the CURRENT group. Now, if we were ignoring the covariate, we might look at the number of filled (NEW) dots above and below the mean (i.e., above and below the broken line), hoping to find a preponderance of them above the mean. Similarly, we would hope to find a preponderance of unfilled (CURRENT) dots below the mean. If you count them up, you will find that for the filled dots there are 10 above and 10 below the broken line and for the (unfilled) dots there are 11 above and 9 below the broken line. Obviously, this is not encouraging!

If we now take the covariate into account, instead of asking whether the filled and unfilled dots are distributed unevenly above and below the broken line (the mean of the DV), we can ask whether the *regression line* has a preponderance of filled dots above it and a preponderance of unfilled dots below it. Counting them up, you will find that, for the filled dots, there are 12 above and 8 below the regression line and, for the unfilled dots, there are 6 above and 14 below the regression line. Even though there are roughly as many dots of both kinds above and below the DV mean, they are distributed quite unevenly above and below the regression line. So, having allowed for the correlation between READING SKILLS scores (the DV) and INTELLIGENCE TEST scores (the covariate), things look much more promising for our hypothesis. If the slope of the regression line were to be less steep, indicating that INTELLIGENCE TEST scores were less predictive of scores on the DV, the distribution of the dots around the broken line (DV mean) and the regression line would become more similar. With zero slope, the two lines would coincide of course, meaning that, for all values of the intelligence test score, the best predictor of the DV would be its own mean. So, it should be obvious that as the regression line becomes less steep, we would expect less gain by using the covariate.

ANCOVA: Towards a formal account

The foregoing discussion was offered as an informal explication rather than as a formal treatment of ANCOVA. For a start, it completely ignored the *size* of the residuals (distance from the regression line). Also, in a formal account, the focus is not exclusively on the single regression line for the totality of cases, but also on the separate regression lines for each level of the IV. The question then becomes whether there is statistical support for the hypothesis that the filled and unfilled dots represent samples drawn from two populations with different regression lines, rather than samples drawn from a single population with a single regression line. Figure 5.2 shows the two regression lines, the upper one for the filled dots and the lower one for the unfilled dots. The greater the separation between the two lines and the more tightly the filled and unfilled dots cluster around their own regression lines, the more likely that the null hypothesis of a single regression line sufficing will be rejected in the ANCOVA.

We are now ready to embark on a formal discussion of how to use the ANCOVA technique. First, you should be aware that, as in ANOVA, more than one treatment factor (the IV) can be included and, as in multiple regression, more than one measured variable (covariate) can be included. However, to make it possible to illustrate the method graphically, we shall begin with a single treatment factor (the IV) at three levels and a single additional measurement (the covariate). We use fabricated data to enable us to illustrate the use of this powerful technique in easy stages.

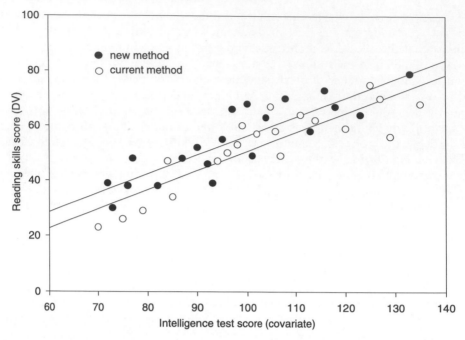

Figure 5.2 Scattergram showing the relationship between READING SKILLS score (DV) and INTELLIGENCE TEST score (covariate) with separate regression lines for two treatment conditions (IV).

ANCOVA: A psychology example of a pretest–posttest control group design

The design example that we will use is one for which ANCOVA is highly appropriate but it is often neglected in favour of less satisfactory alternatives. The design is a pretest–posttest control group design, which is frequently analysed with an ANOVA of gain scores or with a two-factor repeated measures ANOVA, in which the interaction between the IV (treatment) and test occasion (pre/post) tests the hypothesis that treatments have no effect. Dugard and Todman (1995) have shown why the ANCOVA should be preferred to both of these alternative analyses.

We consider an experiment where we are testing two possible training programs, which are intended to improve people's ability to solve spatial manipulation problems. We shall also have an untrained control group. So our IV, TRAINING, has three levels: methods A and B, and none for the controls. Of course people's ability to solve spatial manipulation problems varies whether they are trained or not, so we shall use two parallel tests that have been developed for assessing this ability, and all participants will take the first test at the start of the experiment. Then, after the training, or the lapse of the same time for the controls, they will all take the second test. We will recruit 60 volunteers and assign them at random, 20 to each of the two training groups and the control group.

The (fabricated) data

The two sets of test scores are recorded as PRETEST and POSTTEST. Actually, we have fabricated three versions of the data for this experiment in order to show the full power

Table 5.1 The first four rows of each training method for the three datasets (the full dataset can be found as psy.ancova.sav on the website)

Training	Dataset 1		Dataset 2		Dataset 3	
	Pretest 1	Posttest 1	Pretest 2	Posttest 2	Pretest 3	Posttest 3
None	106	110	136	128	119	141
None	110	87	74	56	111	139
None	85	76	95	107	145	166
None	104	96	105	120	92	128
Method A	110	96	118	164	114	153
Method A	101	77	93	129	94	138
Method A	129	118	88	143	131	172
Method A	79	63	99	120	86	133
Method B	111	112	74	127	96	161
Method B	102	121	86	162	64	131
Method B	130	126	121	162	76	144
Method B	124	105	111	163	86	158

of the ANCOVA approach. Table 5.1 shows the first four rows of each training method for all three datasets; each has a set of PRETEST and POSTTEST scores, but the TRAINING levels are only listed once. The full dataset, along with an extra variable called TIME that we use later, can be found on the book website (psy.ancova.sav).

Graphical considerations: Dataset 1

A first step in the analysis of the data, and one that is quite informative, is to plot POSTTEST (DV) against PRETEST (covariate) scores for all treatment (IV) groups on a single graph, in the same way as in our informal example illustrated in Figure 5.1. On the plot, the three treatment groups are distinguished by different symbols. We begin by looking at a plot for the first dataset, shown in Figure 5.3(a). You can see that the POSTTEST scores increase with the PRETEST scores in an approximately linear way, with some random variation. However, the symbols for the three TRAINING levels are thoroughly mixed together on the graph, with no discernible separation. For this dataset, as we shall see when we proceed to the analysis, neither of our two training methods had any effect: all three groups had similar POSTTEST (DV) results, which depended only on the PRETEST (covariate) scores.

Graphical considerations: Dataset 2

Now consider the second dataset, and the graph of POSTTEST against PRETEST scores, which is shown in Figure 5.3(b), again with the TRAINING levels distinguished by different symbols. This time we can see that the points representing method A mostly lie above those for the controls, and points representing method B mostly lie above those representing method A. For all groups, we can still see that POSTTEST scores increase linearly with PRETEST scores, allowing for some random variation. Careful scrutiny of the graph shows us something else: if we were to fit regression lines of POSTTEST on PRETEST scores for each of the three TRAINING levels, the lines would be approximately parallel.

(a) Graph of dataset 1

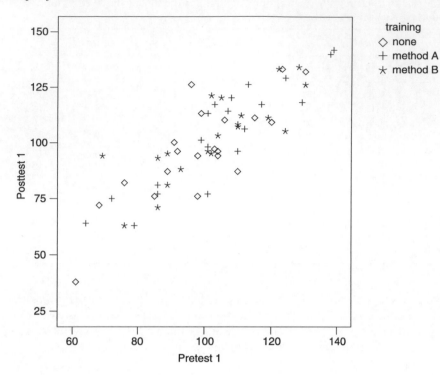

(b) Graph of dataset 2

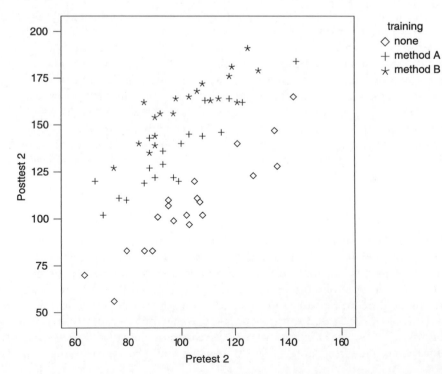

(c) Graph of dataset 3

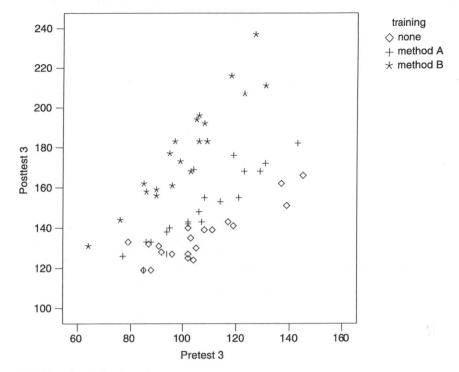

Figure 5.3 Graphs of the three datasets.

Graphical considerations: Dataset 3

Now turn to the last dataset, graphed in Figure 5.3(c). Once again we can see the separation of the three TRAINING levels, with method B higher than method A, and this higher than the controls. This time, however, if we were to fit regression lines of POST-TEST on PRETEST for each treatment group the lines would not be parallel. The line for method B would be steeper than that for method A, which in turn would be steeper than the one for the controls.

Graphical considerations: Comparison of the three datasets

Figure 5.4 is a diagrammatic representation of our three datasets. In the first version of our experiment (dataset 1) the POSTTEST scores do not show any difference among the treatment groups (T1, T2 and T3), as in Figure 5.4(a). In the second version (dataset 2) the graph makes it obvious that there are differences among the treatments, but the effect is quite simple: each training method has raised the regression line of POSTTEST on PRETEST but the lines are parallel, as in Figure 5.4(b). Here, applying T3 (method B) instead of T1 (no training, the control group) would just add a constant amount to the POSTTEST scores (except for random variation). Similarly for T2. In the terminology used in many statistics texts, this is referred to as *homogeneity of regression slopes*.

(a) A diagrammatic representation of dataset 1, showing no differences among the treatment groups

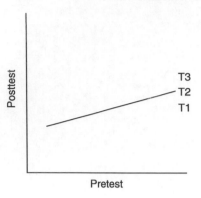

(b) A diagrammatic representation of dataset 2, showing parallel lines for the three treatment groups

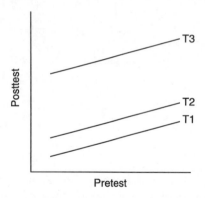

(c) A diagrammatic representation of dataset 3, showing lines for the three treatment groups that are not parallel

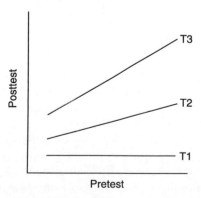

Figure 5.4 Diagram of the three datasets (adapted from Dugard & Todman, 1995).

In the last version (dataset 3), we see in Figure 5.4(c) that for T3 the difference in POSTTEST scores resulting from unit difference in PRETEST scores is greater than is the case for T2 (the line is steeper). For T2 the difference in POSTTEST scores resulting from unit difference in PRETEST scores is greater than is the case for T1 (the controls). The two training programs spread the POSTTEST scores across a wider range as well as raising them on average, that is, there is an interaction between treatment levels (the IV) and PRETEST scores (the covariate). This is referred to as *non-homogeneity of regression slopes*.

ANCOVA: Assumptions

The analysis of covariance allows us to quantify the above observations. Before we begin, two assumptions are needed, and both are easily checked by looking at the graphs. First, we assume that the relationship between the DV (POSTTEST) and the covariate (PRETEST) is approximately linear within each level of the IV (TRAINING). If this is not the case, then almost certainly complex processes are at work and these will require careful investigation within each level of the IV before any attempt is made to compare these levels. The other assumption is that the variance of residual POSTTEST scores is approximately the same over the full range of PRETEST scores and in each IV level. In other words, the points do not become more widely scattered about their lines as we move from left to right, nor as we move from one level of the IV to another.

In addition to the assumptions that are specific to ANCOVA, we need the same assumption of random allocation to treatments as is needed for any analysis at all. It is not uncommon for statistics texts to refer to the requirement of an assumption of homogeneity of regression, but this is not, in fact, necessary, as can be seen from our analysis of dataset 3 illustrated in Figure 5.3(c).

Power considerations

As usual, in a real experiment the sample size should be based on considerations of expected effect size and required power. For a regression analysis with just one IV, the rule of thumb suggested for that would give a sample size of about 58 (50 + 8 * 1), since testing for the significance of the model as a whole is the same as testing for the (only) individual IV. However, what we have here is a design that combines ANOVA (with one factor at three levels) and regression. SPSS SamplePower gives the power as just below .8 (.77 in fact) with 20 cases per level of the factor and one covariate, if the effect size is large. This is sufficient for our purpose in this example.

ANCOVA: Requesting the analysis for dataset 1 in SPSS

We begin by considering dataset 1. From our graphical analysis we expect that there will be no significant differences among TRAINING levels, but we expect that the covariate (PRETEST) will have a significant effect. The most general model fits a regression of POSTTEST on PRETEST for each level of TRAINING without applying any constraints to the parameters. This allows the slopes to be different, as in Figure 5.4(c). It is usually best to begin by fitting this most general model, then we can progressively eliminate higher order terms if they are non-significant. We will follow this approach with dataset 1. On the menu bar choose **Analyze**, then **General Linear Model**, then **Univariate**. We need a univariate analysis because we have only one DV or outcome (POSTTEST). We get the same dialog box as the one used for starting an ANOVA, SPSS Dialog Box 2.5. We are looking at the first dataset here, so our **Dependent Variable** is POSTTEST1, our **Covariate** is PRETEST1 and our **Fixed Factor** is TRAINING (fixed and random factors were discussed in Chapter 2 on ANOVA). Insert the variables in appropriate boxes using the arrows.

Once the variables are entered we need to click the **Model** button to specify the model to be used, and again we get the same one as we used in ANOVA. This time look at the bottom to where **Sum of Squares** is set at the default, **Type III**. If we accept this, in the analysis each term will be considered in relation to all of the other terms listed in the model. This is usually what we want, but may not be appropriate if we have a clear idea of the order or hierarchy in which the terms can be expected to contribute to an explanation of the IV. In our experiment we do have – we are pretty sure the PRETEST score is important. The variation in the POSTTEST scores not explained by this may be explained by TRAINING, and any remaining variation after we allow for that may be explained by the interaction term. With this order quite clear in our case, we opt for **Type I** sum of squares, which considers each term in relation to those already considered (above it in the list).

Now we must choose the **Custom** model, so that we can get the terms in the correct order, so click the radio button. To build the terms in the correct order, enter the covariate, PRETEST1, into the **Model** box first using the arrow, then the factor, TRAINING, and finally the interaction term. To get this last one, select both the factor and the covariate together and use the arrow to get the interaction term, TRAINING * PRETEST1, into the model. The result of all this is SPSS Dialog Box 5.1. Click **Continue**, then as

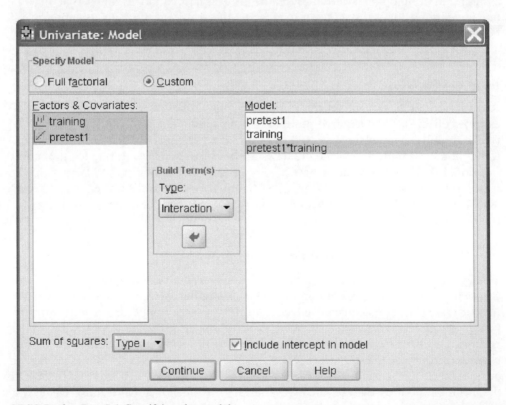

SPSS Dialog Box 5.1 Specifying the model.

usual we can use the **Options** button to request **Estimates of effect size** and **Observed power**. We can accept the defaults for all other choices, so click **OK**.

ANCOVA: *Understanding the output for dataset 1*

The output appears in SPSS Output 5.1. The first table (not shown here) just confirms that we had 20 participants at each level of TRAINING. The second is the ANCOVA table. The column at the right of *F* shows the significance of each term in the model. First we note that the interaction term, TRAINING * PRETEST1, has a large probability (.672) of occurring by chance, so this term is not significant. The estimate of the effect size (partial eta squared) is also small. If this term is omitted from the model, we shall have a more powerful test of the main effects of TRAINING and PRETEST1, so our next step is to go back to the model dialog box and remove the TRAINING * PRETEST1 term. This gives the output shown in SPSS Output 5.2.

Tests of Between-Subjects Effects

Dependent Variable:posttest1

Source	Type I Sum of Squares	df	Mean Square	F	Sig.	Partial Eta Squared	Noncent. Parameter	Observed Power[b]
Corrected Model	20453.195[a]	5	4090.639	28.846	.000	.728	144.229	1.000
Intercept	611858.017	1	611858.017	4314.605	.000	.988	4314.605	1.000
pretest1	20304.245	1	20304.245	143.178	.000	.726	143.178	1.000
training	35.184	2	17.592	0.124	.884	.005	0.248	.068
training * pretest1	113.766	2	56.883	0.401	.672	.015	0.802	.112
Error	7657.788	54	141.811					
Total	639969.000	60						
Corrected Total	28110.983	59						

a. R Squared = .728 (Adjusted R Squared = .702)

b. Computed using alpha = .05

SPSS Output 5.1 Analysis for dataset 1 with interaction term included.

Tests of Between-Subjects Effects

Dependent Variable:posttest1

Source	Type I Sum of Squares	df	Mean Square	F	Sig.	Partial Eta Squared	Noncent. Parameter	Observed Power[b]
Corrected Model	20339.429[a]	3	6779.810	48.854	.000	.724	146.561	1.000
Intercept	611858.017	1	611858.017	4400.905	.000	.987	4408.905	1.000
pretest1	20304.245	1	20304.245	146.308	.000	.723	146.308	1.000
training	35.184	2	17.592	0.127	.881	.005	0.254	.069
Error	7771.555	56	138.778					
Total	639969.000	60						
Corrected Total	28110.983	59						

a. R Squared = .724 (Adjusted R Squared = .709)

b. Computed using alpha = .05

SPSS Output 5.2 Analysis for dataset 1 without the interaction term.

Now we can look at the significance of the main effects. We see that the IV, TRAINING, has a high probability (.881) of occurring by chance: the different methods had no significant effect (and the estimated effect size is small). This is what we expected after looking at the graph in Figure 5.3(a). The covariate (PRETEST1) has a very small probability, less than .001, so this certainly has a significant effect. Again, this is what we expected from our graphical analysis. The Corrected Model and Intercept terms are usually of no interest and can be ignored at this stage.

Reducing the model and understanding the new output

If we now omit the IV, TRAINING, our model will be reduced to the familiar simple regression of POSTTEST1 on PRETEST1, putting all the data from set 1 together. Of course SPSS offers simpler ways to do this, but to follow our model reduction process to its conclusion we will do it with **General Linear Model** again. Just remove the factor (TRAINING) from the **Model** box. This time click the **Options** button again and check the box for **Parameter estimates**, as well as those for effect size and observed power already ticked. The results are shown in SPSS Output 5.3.

Tests of Between-Subjects Effects

Dependent Variable:posttest1

Source	Type I Sum of Squares	df	Mean Square	F	Sig.	Partial Eta Squared	Noncent. Parameter	Observed Power[b]
Corrected Model	20304.245[a]	1	20304.245	150.850	.000	.722	150.850	1.000
Intercept	611858.017	1	611858.017	4545.786	.000	.987	4545.786	1.000
pretest1	20304.245	1	20304.245	150.850	.000	.722	150.850	1.000
Error	7806.739	58	134.599					
Total	639969.000	60						
Corrected Total	28110.983	59						

a. R Squared = .722 (Adjusted R Squared = .718)

b. Computed using alpha = .05

Parameter Estimates

Dependent Variable:posttest1

Parameter	B	Std. Error	t	Sig.	95% Confidence Interval		Partial Eta Squared	Noncent. Parameter	Observed Power[a]
					Lower Bound	Upper Bound			
Intercept	-3.049	8.602	-0.354	.724	-20.267	14.169	.002	0.354	.064
pretest1	1.021	0.083	12.282	.000	0.855	1.188	.722	12.282	1.000

a. Computed using alpha = .05

SPSS Output 5.3 Analysis for dataset 1 using only PRETEST1 as regressor.

Here we see that the probability for the covariate is less than .001 and the estimated effect size is large. As expected, the POSTTEST1 scores are significantly dependent on the PRETEST1 scores, and the second table gives us the regression coefficient, 1.021. The intercept does not differ significantly from zero and the slope is close to 1, so in our first dataset the POSTTEST scores would be well estimated just from the PRETEST scores.

ANCOVA: Requesting the analysis for dataset 2 in SPSS

Now we turn our attention to our second dataset, where we expect to find that the different treatments have a significant effect. Once again set up the model exactly as in SPSS Dialog Box 5.1, except that PRETEST1 and POSTTEST1 are replaced by PRETEST2 and POSTTEST2.

ANCOVA: Understanding the output for dataset 2

The result is shown in SPSS Output 5.4. All we need to note from this is that the interaction term is not significant, with a probability of .427 and a small estimated effect size. We do not reject the null hypothesis that the three regression lines all have the same slope (i.e., they are parallel). For this dataset we do not need the most general model illustrated in Figure 5.4(c): the simpler model with parallel lines illustrated in Figure 5.4(b) adequately describes these data, as we had already guessed from looking

Tests of Between-Subjects Effects

Dependent Variable:posttest2

Source	Type I Sum of Squares	df	Mean Square	F	Sig.	Partial Eta Squared	Noncent. Parameter	Observed Power[b]
Corrected Model	50182.693[a]	5	10036.539	114.724	.000	.914	573.619	1.000
Intercept	1078164.150	1	1078164.150	12324.074	.000	.996	12324.074	1.000
pretest2	20074.203	1	20074.203	229.460	.000	.809	229.460	1.000
training	29957.162	2	14978.581	171.214	.000	.864	342.429	1.000
training * pretest2	151.328	2	75.664	0.865	.427	.031	1.730	.191
Error	4724.157	54	87.484					
Total	1133071.000	60						
Corrected Total	54906.850	59						

a. R Squared = .914 (Adjusted R Squared = .906)

b. Computed using alpha = .05

SPSS Output 5.4 Analysis for dataset 2 with the interaction term included.

at our graph in Figure 5.3(b). Because the regression lines are parallel, we know that the effects of the treatments are the same for all values of the PRETEST. Estimating the TRAINING effect is just equivalent to estimating the vertical separation of the regression lines, and testing for significant differences among TRAINING levels is equivalent to testing the hypothesis that the distances between the lines are zero.

Testing the training effect and understanding the output

This, of course, is what we want to do next. We can fit the model with parallel lines by removing the interaction term from the model. Use the **Options** button to request **Parameter estimates** again. The results are in SPSS Output 5.5.

We can see at once from the first table in SPSS Output 5.5 that the covariate (PRETEST2) is significant and has a large estimated effect size. This tells us that we can reject the hypothesis of no linear relationship between PRETEST2 and POSTTEST2. Also, the significant TRAINING effect tells us that, with POSTTEST2 scores adjusted to take account of

Tests of Between-Subjects Effects

Dependent Variable:posttest2

Source	Type I Sum of Squares	df	Mean Square	F	Sig.	Partial Eta Squared	Noncent. Parameter	Observed Power[b]
Corrected Model	50031.365[a]	3	16677.122	191.554	.000	.911	574.662	1.000
Intercept	1078164.150	1	1078164.150	12383.832	.000	.995	12383.832	1.000
pretest2	20074.203	1	20074.203	230.573	.000	.805	230.573	1.000
training	29957.162	2	14978.581	172.045	.000	.860	344.089	1.000
Error	4875.485	56	87.062					
Total	1133071.000	60						
Corrected Total	54906.850	59						

a. R Squared = .911 (Adjusted R Squared = .906)

b. Computed using alpha = .05

Parameter Estimates

Dependent Variable:posttest2

Parameter	B	Std. Error	t	Sig.	95% Confidence Interval		Partial Eta Squared	Noncent. Parameter	Observed Power[a]
					Lower Bound	Upper Bound			
Intercept	52.231	7.120	7.335	.000	37.967	66.495	.490	7.335	1.000
pretest2	1.054	0.067	15.815	.000	0.921	1.188	.817	15.815	1.000
[training=1]	-54.049	2.951	-18.314	.000	-59.961	-48.137	.857	18.314	1.000
[training=2]	-19.285	2.969	-6.496	.000	-25.232	-13.338	.430	6.496	1.000
[training=3]	0[b]	.	.	.	.	.	.	.	.

a. Computed using alpha = .05

b. This parameter is set to zero because it is redundant.

SPSS Output 5.5 Analysis for dataset 2 without the interaction term.

PRETEST2 scores, the hypothesis of no difference between training methods can be rejected (the parallel lines have non-zero separations and the estimated effect size is large).

Using parameter values to obtain differences among training methods

The table of parameter estimates tells us that the slope of each of the (parallel) regression lines is 1.054. To get the intercepts for each of the regression lines we have to add the parameter called 'Intercept' in the table to the value given for each level of TRAINING. So, for the controls (TRAINING 1) the intercept is

$$52.231 + (-54.049) = -1.818$$

and to predict the POSTTEST2 scores for the controls using this model we need the equation

$$\text{POSTTEST2} = -1.818 + 1.054 * \text{PRETEST2}$$

Similarly, to get the intercept for the method A (TRAINING 2) group we need

$$52.231 - 19.285 = 32.946$$

and the prediction equation for this group is

$$\text{POSTTEST2} = 32.946 + 1.054 * \text{PRETEST2}$$

For the method B (TRAINING 3) group the intercept is $52.231 + 0$, so the prediction equation is

$$\text{POSTTEST2} = 52.231 + 1.054 * \text{PRETEST2}$$

Thus the first training program (method A) increases POSTTEST2 scores by an estimated $32.946 - (-1.818) = 34.746$ (the difference between their intercepts) at all PRETEST2 levels. The second training program (method B) increases POSTTEST2 scores by an estimated $52.231 - (-1.818) = 54.049$ at all PRETEST2 levels.

Note that statistics packages do not all present parameter estimates in the same way, so if you use one other than SPSS you may have to spend a few minutes working out how to interpret them.

There are two simpler models but both would be rejected for this dataset. The first assumes no difference among treatments (a single regression line will do for all 60 observations, as in Figure 5.4(a)). This model would be rejected because of the significant TRAINING effect in SPSS Output 5.5. The other simpler model assumes there is no dependence of POSTTEST2 on PRETEST2 so that the analysis of the data would reduce to a one-way ANOVA of POSTTEST2 by TRAINING, ignoring PRETEST2 scores. This model would be rejected because of the significant covariate in SPSS Output 5.5.

Using SPSS to obtain differences among training methods

We have already shown how to find the regression lines for the treatment groups from the table of parameter values, and this tells us how far apart the lines are (just compare their intercepts). However, we can obtain comparisons among treatments directly from SPSS by requesting specific contrasts. Suppose we want to compare each of the two training methods with the control condition. We can use the **Contrasts** button to get the comparisons that interest us. To compare the two training methods with the control, set the **Contrasts** dialog box as in SPSS Dialog Box 5.2. Click the **Change** button after selecting **Simple** from the **Contrast** list and **First** as the reference category. Then click **Continue**. Using the simple option, as here, tests each of the other levels of the chosen factor against the specified reference level (here, the first level). The Helmert option tests each level against the mean of the subsequent levels. As a mirror image, the difference option tests each level against the mean of the previous levels. The repeated option tests each level against the next level.

SPSS Dialog Box 5.2 Contrasts dialog box.

The results can be seen in SPSS Output 5.6 overleaf. Training method A (TRAINING level 2) raises scores by nearly 35 points. Training method B (TRAINING level 3) raises scores by just over 54 points.

ANCOVA: Requesting the analysis for dataset 3 in SPSS

We turn now to consideration of dataset 3. Once again we begin by fitting the most general model, setting it up as in SPSS Dialog Box 5.1, but with PRETEST3 and POSTTEST3 replacing PRETEST1 and POSTTEST1.

ANCOVA: Understanding the output for dataset 3

This results in the analysis summary shown in SPSS Output 5.7, in which we are again interested in the line of the first table giving the values of the sum of squares, *F* and

Contrast Results (K Matrix)

training Simple Contrast[a]		Dependent Variable posttest2
Level 2 vs. Level 1	Contrast Estimate	34.763
	Hypothesized Value	0
	Difference (Estimate - Hypothesized)	34.763
	Std. Error	2.976
	Sig.	.000
	95% Confidence Interval for Difference Lower Bound	28.802
	Upper Bound	40.725
Level 3 vs. Level 1	Contrast Estimate	54.049
	Hypothesized Value	0
	Difference (Estimate - Hypothesized)	54.049
	Std. Error	2.951
	Sig.	.000
	95% Confidence Interval for Difference Lower Bound	48.137
	Upper Bound	59.961

a. Reference category = 1

SPSS Output 5.6 Contrasts for dataset 2.

probabilities for the interaction term TRAINING * PRETEST3. With $F(2,54) = 16.863$, this term is highly significant. This time the estimated effect size for the interaction is also much larger, though only about half those for the main effects. So this time we reject the null hypothesis that the three lines all have the same slope. There is no simpler model for this dataset. Looking now at the main effects we see that the TRAINING factor is highly significant: $F(2,54) = 197.792$ and $p < .001$. The covariate

Tests of Between-Subjects Effects

Dependent Variable:posttest3

Source	Type I Sum of Squares	df	Mean Square	F	Sig.	Partial Eta Squared	Noncent. Parameter	Observed Power[b]
Corrected Model	39106.436[a]	5	7821.287	123.548	.000	.920	617.741	1.000
Intercept	1439021.067	1	1439021.067	22731.370	.000	.998	22731.370	1.000
pretest3	11928.716	1	11928.716	188.431	.000	.777	188.431	1.000
training	25042.704	2	12521.352	197.792	.000	.880	395.585	1.000
training * pretest3	2135.015	2	1067.508	16.863	.000	.384	33.726	1.000
Error	3418.498	54	63.306					
Total	1481546.000	60						
Corrected Total	42524.933	59						

a. R Squared = .920 (Adjusted R Squared = .912)

b. Computed using alpha = .05

Parameter Estimates

Dependent Variable:posttest3

Parameter	B	Std. Error	t	Sig.	95% Confidence Interval		Partial Eta Squared	Noncent. Parameter	Observed Power[a]
					Lower Bound	Upper Bound			
Intercept	32.299	11.120	2.905	.005	10.005	54.592	.135	2.905	.814
pretest3	1.462	0.109	13.415	.000	1.244	1.681	.769	13.415	1.000
[training=1]	39.398	15.441	2.552	.014	8.441	70.356	.108	2.552	.707
[training=2]	16.003	15.876	1.008	.318	-15.826	47.833	.018	1.008	.168
[training=3]	0[b]								
[training=1] * pretest3	-0.858	0.148	-5.796	.000	-1.154	-0.561	.384	5.796	1.000
[training=2] * pretest3	-0.511	0.151	-3.375	.001	-0.815	-0.207	.174	3.375	.912
[training=3] * pretest3	0[b]								

a. Computed using alpha = .05

b. This parameter is set to zero because it is redundant.

SPSS Output 5.7 Analysis for dataset 3 with the interaction term included.

PRETEST3 is also significant, with a very large F and $p < .001$. However, we recall that interpreting significant main effects is not straightforward when there is a significant interaction.

Obtaining prediction equations for each of the treatment groups

To get the prediction equations for each of the treatment groups we have to combine the parameter values listed in the second column of the table of estimates. The intercept for the controls is

$$32.299 + 39.398 = 71.697$$

and the slope for the controls is

$$1.462 + (-0.858) = 0.604$$

so the prediction equation for the controls is

$$\text{POSTTEST3} = 71.697 + 0.604 * \text{PRETEST3}$$

Similarly, for method A the equation is

$$\text{POSTTEST3} = 32.299 + 16.003 + (1.462 - 0.511) * \text{PRETEST3}$$

or

$$\text{POSTTEST3} = 48.302 + 0.951 * \text{PRETEST3}$$

For method B the equation is

$$\text{POSTTEST3} = 32.299 + 1.462 * \text{PRETEST3}$$

Focussing on the differences among slopes

It is easy to see from Figure 5.3(c) or Figure 5.4(c) that the effect of TRAINING is not the same at all levels of the PRETEST3. For low PRETEST3 values (on the left of the figures) the differences among treatments are smaller than for the high PRETEST3 values (on the right). For method B (TRAINING 3), the POSTTEST3 scores increase by 1.462 for each unit increase in PRETEST3, but for method A (TRAINING 2), POSTTEST3 scores increase by only 0.951 for each unit increase in PRETEST3. Another way of saying this is that we have a significant interaction between PRETEST3 and TRAINING. This being the case, there is little point in trying to discuss differences among training methods in terms of the mean (or adjusted mean) effects. The important difference among training methods found here is the difference among the slopes of the regressions of POSTTEST3 on PRETEST3. The increase in POSTTEST3 per unit increase in PRETEST3 is greatest for method B (TRAINING 3) and least for the controls (TRAINING 1).

Focussing on the individual slopes

Once we reject the hypothesis of parallel regressions, as we have done here, we may want to test other hypotheses about the slopes. For example, we may want to test the hypothesis that the slope is zero (i.e., POSTTEST3 does not depend on PRETEST3) for each level of TRAINING. So far, all we know is that, since the slopes are not equal, they cannot all be zero. We may also want to test whether the slopes for method A and method B are significantly different, or compare the slopes of either with that for the controls.

Testing the differences between pairs of slopes

From the list of parameter estimates shown in SPSS Output 5.7 we found the intercepts for the three regression lines, but these are rarely of interest when the lines are not parallel. If you want to test whether the slope of the reference level is different from another level, consider the interaction terms in the output from the second table in SPSS Output 5.7. For example, if you wished to test if the slopes for TRAINING = 2 and TRAINING = 3 (the reference level) are different, consider the TRAINING = 2 * PRETEST3 line. The difference between the slopes is −0.511, with its standard error in the next column of 0.151. The value of t is the difference divided by its standard error, giving

$$t = \frac{-0.511}{0.151} = -3.384$$

The Sig. column shows that this has a p value of .001. Clearly, in this case the slopes for methods A and B do differ significantly.

If you want to compare two slopes and neither of them corresponds to the reference level, the easiest way is to change the code for one of the levels so that it becomes the reference level. For example, to compare the slopes for TRAINING = 2 and TRAINING = 1, just recode TRAINING = 1 as level 4 and re-run the analysis. Level 1 of TRAINING, now coded 4, will be the reference level and you can get the difference, its standard error, t and its p value from the TRAINING = 2 * PRETEST3 line of the table once again.

In the above examples using datasets 2 and 3, the differences among treatment groups are so large that even a one-way ANOVA of POSTTEST scores will reject the null hypothesis that the mean POSTTEST scores do not differ between treatment groups. Even in these cases, however, the covariance analysis reveals important features of the data.

Example Box 5.1

ANCOVA: An alternative medical example for the same pretest–posttest control group design

The full analysis for this example can be found at www.psypress.com/multivariate-analysis/medical-examples (click on Chapter 5).

Normal adults have a platelet count in the range 150–400 * 10^9/l blood. Aplastic anaemia is a serious illness that causes a drop in all blood cells, including platelets. A platelet reduction is life threatening when the count drops below 20. The condition can be treated with platelet transfusion, but this usually has only a short-term effect. The illness is not curable but can usually be successfully treated to provide long or permanent remission. Patients normally receive a short course of antithymocyte globulin (ATG), to be followed by further treatment in the long term. A study is carried out to investigate how best to get the initial treatment started. Sixty patients are recruited to the study, which is designed to compare the effect on platelet count 1 week after treatment (POSTCOUNT) with (1) transfusion, (2) a short course of ATG or (3) transfusion followed immediately by ATG, after 'taking out' any initial differences in the count by treating the pretreatment count (PRECOUNT) as a covariate. Twenty patients are allocated at random to each of the three treatment conditions (TREAT). A second factor, gender (SEX), is introduced to illustrate ANCOVA with more than one treatment factor.

Outcomes

Three datasets are fabricated in order to illustrate important features of the ANCOVA approach. Each dataset comprises pretest (before treatment) and post-test (1 week after treatment) platelet counts for patients in the three treatment conditions. The posttest count is the IV of interest and the pretest count is treated as a covariate in order to evaluate the treatment effect on the posttest count after allowing for initial differences in the pretest count. For dataset 1, the covariate (the pretest) has a significant effect on the posttest count but there is no difference among treatments. For dataset 2, the covariate (pretest) is again significant and there is a significant treatment effect (ATG and transfusion > ATG > transfusion alone) that does not differ at different values of the pretest count (i.e., parallel slopes). For dataset 3, as well as significant covariate and treatment effects, there is a significant treatment × pretest interaction (i.e., slopes differ). This tells us that the treatment effect is bigger when pretest values are higher. Introduction of the second factor, gender, finds neither a main effect nor any interaction involving that factor.

Alternative variables for use in SPSS
The full dataset, med.ancova.sav, can be found on the book website

Variable	Psychology	Medicine
IV (Factor 1) Main factor of interest	TRAINING Method of training 1=control 2=method A 3=method B	TREAT Method of treatment 1=transfusion 2=ATG 3=transfusion + ATG
IV (Factor 2) Subsidiary factor	TIME Time of day (am/pm)	SEX Gender (m/f)
Covariates	PRETEST Test before training	PRECOUNT Count before treatment
DV	POSTTEST Test after training	POSTCOUNT Count after treatment

ANCOVA with more than one treatment factor

Adding another factor

So far we have considered data that can be well understood using graphs. With more variables involved, graphical analysis can only give a series of partial pictures. Here we introduce an extra factor into our experiment (extra covariates can also be used). We now reveal that in order to get our experiment completed in a reasonable time, we had to use both morning and afternoon sessions for testing. It is possible that the time of day could influence scores: people may be less alert and less able to solve spatial manipulation problems after lunch. So, the 20 participants in each of our groups were assigned at random, half to morning and half to afternoon testing sessions. Both tests for each participant took place at the same time of day. In the data list of Table 5.1, we have arranged the data so that the first 10 in each training group were tested in the morning. The extra column of data can be seen in the dataset psy.ancova.sav on the book website.

Requesting the ANCOVA to include all interactions

We refer to this new factor as TIME, and include it in the model for an analysis of dataset 2. The model is set up as in SPSS Dialog Box 5.1, adding the terms in the order PRETEST2, TRAINING, TRAINING * PRETEST2, TIME, PRETEST2 * TIME, TRAINING * TIME, TRAINING * PRETEST2 * TIME, so we have all second-order and third-order interactions included. We enter the terms in the model in the order we believe is correct, and again use Type I sum of squares.

Making sense of the output

The results appear in SPSS Output 5.8. We can see at once that the third-order interaction TRAINING * TIME * PRETEST2 is not significant, and neither are the second-order interactions TRAINING * TIME, TIME * PRETEST2 and TRAINING * PRETEST2. Removing these interaction terms from the model will give us more power to detect the main effects. If we do this we get the second table in SPSS Output 5.8, in which we see that the main effect of TIME is also non-significant (and has a small estimated effect). We are back to the model we found before: training methods represented by parallel regression lines of POSTTEST2 on PRETEST2 scores.

Reporting results

The example we used here to illustrate ANCOVA was simpler than some you might want to investigate yourself, but the ideas will be useful even in complex problems. There is no substitute for looking at and thinking about your data. Graphs will help you to understand relationships even if they can only give partial pictures, as is the case when you have more variables than in our example. Looking at your data carefully before you get to work on the analysis will help you to consider the possible models and understand the results, so that you can explain them clearly to your own readers when you come to write them up. Graphs that help you to understand will also help your readers, and if space permits, include them. If you decide to use the Type I sum of

Tests of Between-Subjects Effects

Dependent Variable: posttest2

Source	Type I Sum of Squares	df	Mean Square	F	Sig.	Partial Eta Squared	Noncent. Parameter	Observed Power[b]
Corrected Model	50556.975[a]	11	4596.089	50.717	.000	.921	557.886	1.000
Intercept	1078164.150	1	1078164.150	11897.325	.000	.996	11897.325	1.000
pretest2	20074.203	1	20074.203	221.515	.000	.822	221.515	1.000
training	29957.162	2	14978.581	165.286	.000	.873	330.571	1.000
training * pretest2	151.328	2	75.664	0.835	.440	.034	1.670	.185
time	36.139	1	36.139	0.399	.531	.008	0.399	.095
time * pretest2	15.786	1	15.786	0.174	.678	.004	0.174	.069
training * time	72.091	2	36.046	0.398	.674	.016	0.796	.111
training * time * pretest2	250.266	2	125.133	1.381	.261	.054	2.762	.283
Error	4349.875	48	90.622					
Total	1133071.000	60						
Corrected Total	54906.850	59						

a. R Squared = .921 (Adjusted R Squared = .903)

b. Computed using alpha = .05

Tests of Between-Subjects Effects

Dependent Variable: posttest2

Source	Type I Sum of Squares	df	Mean Square	F	Sig.	Partial Eta Squared	Noncent Parameter	Observed Power[b]
Corrected Model	50068.130[a]	4	12517.032	142.277	.000	.912	569.106	1.000
Intercept	1078164.150	1	1078164.150	12255.105	.000	.996	12255.105	1.000
pretest2	20074.203	1	20074.203	228.176	.000	.806	228.176	1.000
training	29957.162	2	14978.581	170.256	.000	.861	340.512	1.000
time	36.765	1	36.765	0.418	.521	.008	0.418	.097
Error	4838.720	55	87.977					
Total	1133071.000	60						
Corrected Total	54906.850	59						

a. R Squared = .912 (Adjusted R Squared = .905)

b. Computed using alpha = .05

SPSS Output 5.8 Analysis for dataset 2 with TIME as an additional factor.

squares, as we did here, you should explain the order in which the terms are entered into the model. It is not necessary to include the tables of SPSS output as we have done here. They can be summarized, quoting the values of the *F* statistics with the degrees of freedom and the probabilities. For instance, we could summarize the results for our dataset 2 like this:

An ANCOVA was conducted, using the Type I sum of squares since we wanted each term considered allowing for those previously added to the model, rather than allowing for all other terms in the model (Type III sum of squares). For the reasons explained in our description of the experiment, we expected that the POST-TEST scores would be influenced by the PRETEST scores, whether or not participants received any training. The covariate PRETEST was therefore the first term entered in our model. We also hypothesized that the training method, if any, would influence the POSTTEST scores, so the factor TRAINING was entered next. If there were a TRAIN-ING effect, and if this effect were not the same at all values of the PRETEST, then the regression lines of POSTTEST on PRETEST would not be parallel for the three training methods and there would be an interaction between the factor TRAINING and the covariate PRETEST. This interaction term was therefore the final one added to our model. The interaction was not significant: $F(2,54) = .87$; $p = .427$. Hence the null hypothesis of parallel lines for the regression lines in our model was not rejected. Removing the non-significant interaction term from the model allowed more residual degrees of freedom for estimating parameters. In this reduced model, we found the effect of TRAINING to be highly significant: $F(2,56) = 172.05$; $p < .001$.

The estimated effect size (partial eta squared) was also large at .86. As expected, the covariate (PRETEST scores) also had a highly significant effect, with $F(1,56) = 230.57$ ($p < .001$) and a large estimated effect size (partial eta squared $= .81$). Method A increased POSTTEST scores by an estimated 34.75 (95% CI 28.8–40.7) at all PRETEST levels. Method B increased POSTTEST scores by an estimated 54.05 (95% CI 48.1–60.0) at all PRETEST levels.

Reference

Dugard, P., & Todman, J. (1995). Analysis of pretest–posttest control group designs in educational research. *Educational Psychology*, *15*(2), 181–198.

6 Partial correlation, mediation and moderation

Introduction

The problems considered in this chapter are closely related to those discussed in Chapter 4, and we use regression again as part of the solution. However, here the emphasis is on exploring relationships among several variables, whereas previously we were focussed on trying to predict one variable from several others. In our Chapter 4 examples, the variable of interest was SUCCESS (and, subsequently, SUCCESS2). We wanted to discover the 'best' selection and weighted combination of IVs for predicting SUCCESS. We were also interested in evaluating the fit of the model and in establishing how much of the variance of SUCCESS was explained by the model, and how much additional variance in SUCCESS2 could be attributed to a training procedure when the other IVs were controlled. In many research situations, however, we are more interested in understanding a relationship among variables than in predicting one of them. Then, partial correlation analysis and specific regression techniques for looking at the mediation or moderation of relationships among variables are of interest.

We have already used partial correlation coefficients: the statistical criteria used to determine the order of entry and removal of IVs into a stepwise regression are based on partial correlation analysis. But partial correlation analysis can be more than a technique used within regression analysis to determine the order of entry and removal of IVs, and we now consider partial correlation coefficients in a bit more detail and look at an example where partial correlation analysis throws some light on relationships among four variables.

Partial correlation

Antecedent variables

There are two different complicating issues that may arise about an observed relationship between an IV and a DV. First, there may be an *antecedent* variable that has both a direct and an indirect influence on the DV, the indirect influence being via its relationship with the IV. In this case, if that part of the variance of the DV that is attributable to variance common to the antecedent variable and the IV is removed, the remaining part of the relationship between the IV and DV that is unique may be non-significant. The Venn diagram in Figure 6.1 illustrates this. The various areas represent shared variance (squared correlations). The squared correlation between the IV and the DV is represented by their area of overlap ($a + b$), b represents what is common to all three

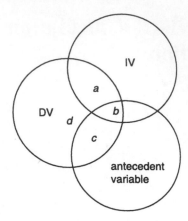

Figure 6.1 Venn diagram with areas representing shared variance among an IV, a DV and an antecedent variable.

variables, and $(b + c)$ represents the squared correlation between the antecedent variable and the DV. If the IV is given precedence over the antecedent variable, the IV is credited with all of $(a + b)$, and what remains of the DV after removal of the unique influence of the antecedent variable is $(a + b + d)$. Then $(a + b)/(a + b + d)$ is the square of the partial correlation between the IV and the DV, with the contribution of the antecedent variable controlled. The partial correlation between the IV and the DV, with the antecedent variable controlled, may be written as $r_{XY.A}$, where A stands for the antecedent variable.

Another way of illustrating the relationships involved is shown in Figure 6.2(a).

(a) IV–DV relationship with antecedent variable

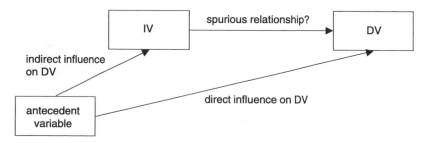

(b) IV–DV relationship with intermediate variable

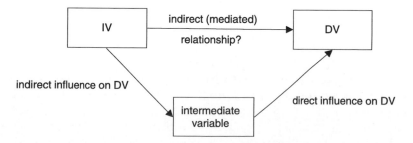

Figure 6.2 Questioning the IV–DV relationship: Spurious, indirect or direct.

If the correlation between the IV and DV disappears when the direct and indirect influences of the antecedent variable are removed, we can infer that the relationship between the IV and DV is *spurious*.

Intermediate (mediating) variables

The second kind of complicating issue arises when there is an *intermediate* or *mediating* variable – one that is influenced by the IV and in turn influences the DV. The Venn diagram (Figure 6.1) and its explication are equally applicable to this situation. You just need to substitute 'intermediate' or 'mediating' variable for 'antecedent' variable. In fact, antecedent and intermediate variables are often referred to jointly as *nuisance* variables or *covariates*. We prefer the label 'covariate' because it is more neutral: it would be a mistake to regard mediating variables as necessarily a nuisance rather than as theoretically interesting. The type of complication arising from consideration of a mediating variable is illustrated in Figure 6.2(b). In this case, if the correlation between the IV and DV disappears when the correlations of the intermediate variable with the IV and with the DV are removed, we can infer that the relationship between the IV and DV is *indirect* via the intermediate variable (or *mediated* by the intermediate variable). The partial correlation between the IV and the DV, with the intermediate variable controlled, may again be written as $r_{XY.A}$, where A stands for the intermediate variable this time. Note that the letter A does not stand exclusively for 'antecedent' variable. It stands for the first variable to be controlled in an attempt to better understand the relationship between the IV and DV.

'Order' of correlations

The usual bivariate correlation is sometimes referred to as a *zero-order* correlation. A partial correlation with one variable controlled is a first-order correlation. The logic of the control of an antecedent or intermediate variable extends to the control of more than one such variable. If there were two antecedent variables, for instance, the (second-order) partial correlation could be written as $r_{XY.AB}$, and the computational procedures are as for a first-order partial correlation (control of a single variable) but with an additional step to deal with the second variable.

A psychology example suitable for partial correlation analysis

A relationship between computer anxiety (CA) and gender has been found in a number of studies, with females generally scoring higher than males (i.e., more computer anxious). Findings are variable, however, and biological gender does not adequately account for this variability. It is possible that *psychological gender* (masculinity score minus femininity score, based on an adjective checklist questionnaire) may provide a more satisfactory account. There is also evidence that students in different faculties differ on CA.

Partial correlation: The data

Self-report questionnaire measures of CA and psychological gender were obtained for 138 first-year undergraduate students in two departments, one in an Arts and Social Sciences faculty and one in a Science and Engineering faculty, in order to investigate the relationship between biological gender (SEX) and CA, taking into account the effects of psychological gender (PSYGEN) and FACULTY (Todman & Day, 2006). A power analysis using SPSS SamplePower indicated that a sample size of $N = 80$ would be sufficient to provide power = .8, assuming that $r = .3$ was the smallest correlation we wanted to avoid missing with $\alpha = .05$, two-tailed. We have therefore taken the data from the first 80 students to provide an example of partial correlation. The first few rows of data are in Table 6.1 (the full dataset can be found as psy.partial.sav on the book website). The data should be entered in an SPSS worksheet in four columns, just as in Table 6.1.

Table 6.1 The first few rows of data on biological gender, computer anxiety, psychological gender and faculty for 80 students (the full dataset can be found as psy.partial.sav on the website)

SEX[1]	CA	PSYGEN	FACULTY[2]
1	2.06	−0.15	1
2	3.65	−1.38	1
2	2.06	−0.35	1
2	1.24	−0.50	1
2	2.29	−0.85	1
1	1.24	−0.55	2

1 Sex: 1 = male, 2 = female.
2 Faculty: 1 = Arts and Social Sciences, 2 = Science and Engineering.

Partial correlation: The relationships tested

We carried out a partial correlation analysis to clarify the relationship between SEX and CA, controlling for PSYGEN and FACULTY. This analysis was carried out to determine whether the biological gender – CA relationship could be construed as direct or indirect (i.e., mediated by psychological gender and/or faculty). Additional partial correlation analyses, controlling for PSYGEN and FACULTY one at a time, could also be carried out to further clarify the relationship, but these analyses are not reported here.

Partial correlation: Requesting the analysis in SPSS

First, it is a good idea to look at the bivariate (zero-order) correlations among the variables. To do this, choose **Analyze**, then **Correlate**, then **Bivariate**. Select the four variables and use the arrow to put them in the **Variables** box. Accept all of the defaults and click **OK** to get a Pearson correlation matrix with two-tailed p levels, with significant values indicated by asterisks.

To do the partial correlation analysis, choose **Analyze**, then **Correlate**, then **Partial**. Use the arrows to move SEX and CA into the **Variables** box and PSYGEN and FACULTY into the **Controlling for** box. Accept the defaults and click **OK**.

Partial correlation analysis: Understanding the output

The bivariate correlation matrix, which is not reproduced here, confirms that correlations between all pairs of variables, with the exception of that between PSYGEN and

FACULTY, were significant at $p < .05$ or lower. This suggests that it makes sense to proceed with the partial analysis. The result of the partial correlation analysis is shown in SPSS Output 6.1.

Correlations

Control Variables			sex	ca
psygen & faculty	sex	Correlation	1.000	.065
		Significance (2-tailed)		.572
		df	0	76
	ca	Correlation	.065	1.000
		Significance (2-tailed)	.572	
		df	76	0

SPSS Output 6.1 Partial correlation between biological gender (SEX) and computer anxiety (CA) with psychological gender and faculty controlled.

The bivariate correlation between SEX and CA was r $(df = 78) = .31$, $p < .01$, two-tailed. This indicates that the female students (coded 2) had higher scores on CA than the male students (coded 1). However, you can see in SPSS Output 6.1 that when PSYGEN and FACULTY were controlled the correlation dropped to r $(df = 76) = .06$, $p = .57$, two-tailed. We can infer that the relationship between biological gender and CA is mediated by psychological gender and/or faculty. We have not reproduced the analyses here, but we can tell you that partialling out psychological gender and faculty one at a time suggested that psychological gender was the principal mediator.

This result leads to the question of whether psychological gender is directly related to CA when biological gender and faculty are controlled. In passing, we suggest that biological gender is an antecedent variable (prior to psychological gender) and faculty is probably an intermediate variable (i.e., established subsequent to biological gender and prior to CA, if we assume that psychological gender influences choice of faculty rather than the reverse). You may note here that it makes no difference to the analysis whether a covariate is antecedent or intermediate, but it may make a difference to your interpretation of the result of the analysis. The procedure for this partial correlation analysis is the same as before, except that PSYGEN and CA go in the **Variables** box and SEX and FACULTY go in the **Controlling for** box.

The result of this analysis is shown in SPSS Output 6.2. The bivariate correlation between PSYGEN and CA was $r(df = 78) = -.45$, $p < .001$, two-tailed. Recall that psychological gender was computed as 'masculinity' minus 'femininity' scores, so high scores mean higher masculinity and the negative correlation tells us that students with higher masculinity scores showed less CA. You can see in SPSS Output 6.2 that the relationship

Correlations

Control Variables			ca	psygen
faculty & sex	ca	Correlation	1.000	-.406
		Significance (2-tailed)		.000
		df	0	76
	psygen	Correlation	-.406	1.000
		Significance (2-tailed)	.000	
		df	76	0

SPSS Output 6.2 Partial correlation between psychological gender (PSYGEN) and computer anxiety (CA) with biological gender (SEX) and faculty controlled.

remained strong when SEX and FACULTY were controlled: $r(df = 76) = -.41$, $p < .001$, two-tailed. It seems that if students self-report a preponderance of stereotypically 'feminine' characteristics such as 'gentle' and 'sympathetic' over 'masculine' characteristics such as 'assertive' and 'willing to take risks' (i.e., low scores on PSYGEN) they will be more likely to have relatively high levels of CA, regardless of sex or faculty membership.

Example Box 6.1

An alternative medical example suitable for partial correlation analysis

The full analysis for this example can be found at www.psypress.com/ multivariate-analysis/medical-examples (click on Chapter 6).

Family history, measured as a binary variable, is a predictor for depression. It may be, however, that a family history of depression is related to a familial tendency towards anxiety, but there is a distinction here between anxiety as a relatively stable personality trait (trait anxiety) and anxiety as a temporary state (state anxiety) in response to stressful internal or external events. The balance between state and trait anxiety, measured as state anxiety minus trait anxiety (ANXIETY), may provide a better predictor of depression than the existence of a family history of depression. We also know that people in employment are less prone to depression than people who are unemployed. A partial correlation analysis is carried out to clarify the relationship between family history of depression (FAMILYHIST) and susceptibility to DEPRESSION, controlling for ANXIETY (state – trait) pattern and employment (EMPLOY). The purpose of this analysis is to determine whether the family history–depression relationship can be construed as direct or indirect (i.e., mediated by anxiety (state – trait) pattern). A depression scale and state/trait anxiety scales are administered to 80 adults, and their status on the two binary variables (family history of depression and employment) is recorded.

Outcomes

All correlations among the four variables are significant except that between state – trait anxiety and employment. The bivariate correlation between family history and depression is $r = .31$, indicating that people with a family history of depression had higher depression scores. However, when state – trait anxiety and employment are controlled, the correlation drops to $r = .06$. The bivariate correlation between state – trait anxiety and depression is $r = -.45$, which tells us that people with higher scores on trait than on state anxiety have higher depression scores. In this case, the relationship remains strong ($r = -.41$) when family history and employment are controlled. We conclude that a higher trait than state anxiety score predicts a higher depression score regardless of family history of depression and employment status.

Alternative variables for use in SPSS
The full dataset, med.partial.sav, can be found on the book website

Variable	Psychology	Medicine
Outcome variable	CA Computer anxiety	DEPRESSION Score on a depression scale
Predictor variables	SEX Biological gender (male = 1, female = 2)	FAMILYHIST Family history of depression (no history = 1, history = 2)
	PSYGEN Psychological gender (masculinity – femininity)	ANXIETY Difference score on anxiety scales (state – trait anxiety)
	FACULTY Faculty membership (arts/ social science = 1, science = 2)	EMPLOY Employment status (unemployed = 1, employed = 2)

Semipartial (or part) correlations

Recall that in partial correlation analysis common variance is removed from both the IV and DV. It is possible, however, to remove the contribution of the antecedent or intermediate variable from only the IV or only the DV. When this is done, the correlation between the IV and DV, with the common variance of the other variable removed from just one of them, is called the *semipartial* (or *part*) correlation. It has been suggested (e.g., Diekhoff, 1992, p. 266) that a semipartial correlation may be the correlation of choice when it seems highly likely that the covariate you are interested in may influence only one of the two principal variables (IV or DV). An example might be a study looking at the relationship between age (the IV) and income (the DV), where we may want to take account of amount of education (a covariate), but this variable would not be expected to influence age. Therefore, according to the criterion expressed by Diekhoff, it may be reasonable to remove its effect only from the DV (income). However, we are not clear that this is necessarily the best course of action. Although amount of education cannot influence age, it is plausible that age will influence education. In other words, amount of education should be construed as an intermediate (mediating) variable rather than an antecedent variable. This does not seem to us a compelling reason for using a semipartial correlation. If it were, it would apply to all cases of intermediate covariates. Our view is that a partial correlation should be the default and, when the decision is to use a semipartial correlation, a clear justification should be provided.

In our first partial correlation analysis, neither of the covariates (psychological gender nor faculty) could influence biological gender, so should we have used a semipartial analysis? We do not think so, but perhaps it would be instructive to re-do that analysis using semipartial correlations. SPSS does not offer semipartial correlations in the **Correlate** procedure, but they can be requested in the **Regression** procedure. Incidentally, this is a good illustration of the interrelatedness of these analysis methods

(R^2 Change when a covariate is added is the square of the semipartial correlation). Furthermore, looking ahead to Chapter 7, it will become apparent that the flow diagrams in Figure 6.2 could be the start point for a path analysis.

Semipartial correlation: Requesting the analysis in SPSS

To get the semipartial correlation of SEX with CA, with PSYGEN and FACULTY controlled, choose **Analyze**, then **Regression**, then **Linear**. Select CA and move it into the **Dependent** box, then select SEX and move it into the **Independent(s)** box and click **Next** to obtain **Block 2 of 2**. Then select the IVs to be controlled (PSYGEN and FACULTY) and move them into the **Independent(s)** box. The dialog box will now look like SPSS Dialog Box 4.6 in the chapter on regression, except that different variables will be displayed and **Block 2 of 2** will be displayed instead of **Block 4 of 4**. Click the **Statistics** button at the bottom and select **Part and Partial Correlations** (the statistics dialog box can be seen in SPSS Dialog Box 4.2). Click **Continue** and **OK** to get the analysis.

Semipartial correlation analysis: Understanding the output

We have effectively done a hierarchical regression analysis with sex entered first, followed by the IVs to be controlled. The Coefficients output table (shown in SPSS Output 6.3) contains the partial and semipartial (part) correlations. You can see that the partial correlation between SEX and CA (.065) is as we found using the partial correlation procedure in SPSS (see SPSS Output 6.2), and the semipartial (part) correlation between these two variables is .055. So, in this case it makes very little difference whether we compute a partial or semipartial correlation.

Coefficients[a]

Model		Unstandardized Coefficients B	Unstandardized Coefficients Std. Error	Standardized Coefficients Beta	t	Sig.	Correlations Zero-order	Correlations Partial	Correlations Part
1	(Constant)	1.101	0.335		3.289	.002			
	sex	.541	0.188	.310	2.879	.005	.310	.310	.310
2	(Constant)	2.421	0.455		5.325	.000			
	sex	0.110	0.193	.063	0.567	.572	.310	.065	.055
	psygen	-0.330	0.085	-.415	-3.868	.000	-.452	-.406	-.373
	faculty	-0.538	0.195	-.276	-2.758	.007	-.307	-.302	-.266

a. Dependent Variable: ca

SPSS Output 6.3 Partial and semipartial (part) correlation between SEX and CA.

Reporting results: Partial correlation analysis

The following paragraphs illustrate how you might report the results of carrying out the two partial correlation analyses investigating the relationship between biological gender and CA and between psychological gender and CA, controlling for two covariates in each case.

We performed two partial correlation analyses on the variables, SEX, PSYGEN, FACULTY and CA, described in the Method section. The first investigated the relationship between SEX and CA, with PSYGEN and FACULTY controlled. The zero-order (bivariate) correlation between SEX and CA was significant: $r(df = 78) = .31$,

$p = .005$, two-tailed. This indicated that the female students (coded 2) had higher scores on CA than the male students (coded 1). When PSYGEN and FACULTY were controlled, the correlation was no longer significant: $r(df = 76) = .06, p = .57$, two-tailed. This suggested that the relationship between biological gender and CA was mediated by psychological gender and/or faculty.

The second analysis investigated the relationship between PSYGEN and CA, with SEX and FACULTY controlled. The zero-order correlation between PSYGEN and CA was significant: $r(df = 78) = -.45, p < .001$, two-tailed. Psychological gender was computed as 'masculinity' minus 'femininity' score, so high scores meant higher masculinity and the negative correlation means that students with higher masculinity scores showed less CA. When SEX and FACULTY were controlled, the relationship remained significant: $r(df = 76) = -.41, p < .001$, two-tailed. This suggested that the relationship between PSYGEN and CA was a direct one, not dependent on correlations with SEX and FACULTY. Students who reported a preponderance of stereotypically 'feminine' characteristics over 'masculine' characteristics (i.e., low scorers on PSYGEN) were more likely to have relatively high levels of CA, regardless of sex or faculty membership.

Mediation effects

We have seen that a variable may be said to function as a mediator when it can account for the relation between an IV (predictor) variable and a DV (outcome) variable. We have also seen that partial correlation can be used to test a mediation hypothesis: that the relationship between biological gender and computer anxiety is mediated by psychological gender, in our example.

Testing a mediation effect using regression

An alternative, conceptually direct and computationally straightforward regression approach to testing mediation hypotheses is growing in popularity. According to this approach, which was first spelled out in detail by Baron and Kenny (1986), neither the computation of partial correlations nor the application of hierarchical regression is involved. All that is required is the computation of three regression equations involving the variables shown in Figure 6.2(b):

(1) The IV is treated as the predictor variable and the DV as the outcome variable. This is necessary to establish that there is a significant relationship that could be mediated. The regression coefficient (IV → DV) is recorded.
(2) The IV is treated as the predictor variable and the presumed mediator (the intermediate variable) is treated as the outcome variable. This is necessary to establish that the effect of the IV could act on the DV via a relationship with the presumed mediator. The regression coefficient (IV → presumed mediator) is recorded.
(3) The IV and the presumed mediator are treated as predictor variables and the DV as the outcome variable. This is necessary to control for the direct effect of the IV. Two regression coefficients (IV → DV and presumed mediator → DV) are recorded.

If the presumed mediator is a complete mediator of the relationship between the IV and the DV, the effect of IV → DV when we control for the mediator (regression coefficient for IV → DV in regression 3) should be zero (or at least non-significant). If, however, it is only a partial mediator of the relationship, the effect (regression coefficient for IV → DV in regression 3) should only be reduced from the effect when the mediator effect is not controlled (regression coefficient for IV → DV in regression 1). The amount of mediation can be obtained by subtracting the IV → DV regression coefficient in regression 3 from that in regression 1, but we also need a way of interpreting the size of the difference.

Testing the significance of a mediation effect

A procedure for testing the significance of a mediation effect is provided in the Sobel test, which results in a Z statistic that can be interpreted in relation to the normal distribution in the usual way. Several versions of this test have been proposed. The one we describe is the simplest and for most purposes is an acceptable approximation. You will need the values of:

a = unstandardized regression coefficient for the relationship:

IV → presumed mediator (regression 2)

s_a = standard error of a

b = unstandardized regression coefficient for the relationship:

presumed mediator → DV when the IV is also a predictor of the DV (regression 3)

s_b = standard error of b

These values are entered into the equation: $Z = \dfrac{a * b}{\sqrt{b^2 * s_a^2 + a^2 * s_b^2}}$.

Mediation: Requesting the analysis in SPSS (the psychology partial correlation example continued)

The three regression analyses are carried out as in Chapter 4 by choosing **Analyze**, then **Regression**, then **Linear** to get Dialog Box 4.1. For the first regression, move CA into the **Dependent** box and SEX into the **Independent(s)** box and click **OK**. The second regression is carried out in the same way except that the proposed mediator variable, PSYGEN, is moved into the **Dependent** box in place of CA. For the third regression, put CA in the **Dependent** box and put both SEX and PSYGEN in the **Independent(s)** box.

Mediation analysis: Understanding the output

The required unstandardized coefficients and their standard errors are shown in the Coefficients output tables (SPSS Output 6.4). It can be seen from the first and third tables that the regression coefficient for SEX → CA reduces from 0.541 to 0.249 when PSYGEN is added to the regression, suggesting that PSYGEN may be exerting a partial mediating effect. The relevant values needed for the Sobel test for mediation are: SEX → PSYGEN unstandardized coefficient (a) = −0.938, standard error (s_a) = 0.224 (2nd table);

Coefficients[a]

Model		Unstandardized Coefficients		Standardized Coefficients	t	Sig.
		B	Std. Error	Beta		
1	(Constant)	1.101	0.335		3.289	.002
	sex	0.541	0.188	.310	2.879	.005

a. Dependent Variable: ca

Coefficients[a]

Model		Unstandardized Coefficients		Standardized Coefficients	t	Sig.
		B	Std. Error	Beta		
1	(Constant)	1.409	0.399		3.528	.001
	sex	-0.938	0.224	-.428	-4.187	.000

a. Dependent Variable: psygen

Coefficients[a]

Model		Unstandardized Coefficients		Standardized Coefficients	t	Sig.
		B	Std. Error	Beta		
1	(Constant)	1.539	0.337		4.570	.000
	sex	0.249	0.194	.143	1.281	.204
	psygen	-0.311	0.089	-.391	-3.509	.001

a. Dependent Variable: ca

SPSS Output 6.4 Regression coefficients for a mediation analysis.

and PSYGEN → CA, with SEX controlled: unstandardized coefficient (b) = −0.311, standard error (s_b) = 0.089 (3rd table).

Application of the Sobel approximate formula to these unstandardized coefficient and standard error values yields the statistic Z = 2.68, p = .008. So, according to this mediation analysis, it is confirmed that PSYGEN significantly mediates the relationship between SEX and CA. This confirms our earlier partial correlation analysis of the same data. Note, however, that the partial correlation analysis did not allow us to test the *difference* between the two correlations of SEX and CA with and without controlling for PSYGEN. The Sobel test in the mediation analysis described here has provided us with a way to check whether the reduction when PSYGEN is controlled is significant. The mediation analysis has used unstandardized regression coefficients rather than correlation coefficients to measure the effect of the IV on the DV, and Baron and Kenny (1986) suggest that this is always preferable. We endorse that conclusion. Nonetheless, it is necessary to keep an eye on the possibility of substantial *multicollinearity* when using the regression approach, and we consider this in the next section.

Example Box 6.2

A continuation of the alternative medical example for partial correlation applied to mediation effects

The full analysis for this example can be found at www.psypress.com/multivariate-analysis/medical-examples (click on Chapter 6).

The variables depression, family history of depression (measured as a binary variable) and anxiety (state – trait) pattern, are again used, this time to illustrate an analysis designed to test that the relationship between family history and depression is mediated by state – trait anxiety. Three regression equations are computed – (1) FAMILYHIST → DEPRESSION, (2) FAMILYHIST → ANXIETY, (3) FAMILY-HIST & ANXIETY → DEPRESSION – and regression coefficients and standard error values are entered into the Sobel formula to test for a significant mediation effect of ANXIETY on the relationship between FAMILYHIST and DEPRESSION.

Outcomes

The reduction in the FAMILYHIST → DEPRESSION coefficient when ANXIETY is controlled is 0.29, which suggests a partial mediating effect. The Sobel test gave a value of $Z = 2.68$, confirming that anxiety significantly mediates the relationship between FAMILYHIST and DEPRESSION.

Alternative variables for use in SPSS
The full dataset, med.partial.sav, can be found on the book website

Variable	Psychology	Medicine
Outcome variable	CA Computer anxiety	DEPRESSION Score on a depression scale
Predictor variables	SEX Biological gender (binary)	FAMILYHIST Family history of depression (binary)
	PSYGEN Psychological gender (masculinity – femininity)	ANXIETY Difference score on anxiety scales (state – trait anxiety)

Mediation analysis: Multicollinearity and power

Multicollinearity refers to the existence of a strong correlation between the IV and the mediator. Of course, if there is mediation a correlation necessarily exists, but if it is very high it will explain virtually all of the variance in the mediator, leaving minimal unique variance in the mediator to explain variance in the IV. When substantial multicollinearity is present, the power of tests of the regression coefficients is compromised. So, with a strong mediation effect, a larger sample size is needed to achieve power equivalent to that available with a smaller sample when we have a weak mediator. In our case, the correlation between SEX and PSYGEN was moderate ($r = -.43$), so multicollinearity was not a serious problem.

Mediation analysis: Measurement error

Another problem that arises in mediation analysis is when the assumption that the measurement of the mediator is free of error is not realistic. In such circumstances, the estimates of the regression coefficients are likely to be biased: typically overestimation of the IV → DV coefficient and underestimation of the mediator → DV coefficient. The best way to circumvent this problem is to use multiple indicators of the mediator, treated as a *latent* variable: that is, one that cannot be measured directly. This is the approach taken in confirmatory factor analysis and, by extension, in structural equation modelling. These approaches will be discussed in Chapter 8.

Reporting results: Mediation analysis

The following is an example of how you might report the results of carrying out the analysis to test the mediating effect of psychological gender on the relationship between biological gender and computer anxiety.

Moderate correlations between the variables suggested that a mediation hypothesis might be entertained and that multicollinearity would not be a problem. We performed three regression analyses: one in which SEX (the IV) was treated as the predictor variable and CA (the DV) as the outcome variable; another in which SEX was treated as the predictor variable and PSYGEN (the presumed mediator) was treated as the outcome variable; and a third in which SEX and PSYGEN were both treated as predictor variables with CA as the outcome variable. The amount of mediation was obtained by subtracting the regression coefficient (SEX → CA) in the third regression (i.e., with PSYGEN controlled) from the regression coefficient (SEX → CA, again) in the first regression (with PSYGEN not controlled). The reduction in the SEX → CA coefficient when PSYGEN was controlled was $0.541 - 0.249 = .292$, which suggests a partial mediating effect. The mediation effect was tested by application of the Sobel approximate formula (*give a reference here*) to the unstandardized coefficient and standard error values for SEX → PSYGEN (2nd regression) and PSYGEN → CA (3rd regression). This yielded a value of $Z = 2.68$, $p = .008$, so it was confirmed that PSYGEN significantly mediates the relationship between SEX and CA.

Moderating effects

Moderation as an interaction effect

The terms mediation and moderation have frequently been used interchangeably, but since the appearance of Baron and Kenny's (1986) article the distinction between them has been widely recognized. Briefly, we have seen that a mediating variable is one on which an IV has an effect and in turn exerts an influence on a DV. Thus, the influence of the IV on the DV is transmitted indirectly via the intermediate mediating variable. Moderating variables, on the other hand, are variables for which the effect of an IV upon a DV differs at different levels of the moderator. In the context of ANOVA, this is easily recognized as an interaction effect, where a test of the interaction term is, in effect, a test of the existence of a moderation effect. The factorial ANOVA provides a special case of a moderating effect in that, assuming there are two factors, both of the IVs (a focal IV and a moderator) are categorical variables.

Moderation: Continuous IV and categorical moderator

When one or both of the focal IV and the assumed moderator variable are continuous variables, however, the hypothesized interaction cannot be tested using ANOVA. If the moderator is a categorical variable (we will assume the simplest case of a dichotomy) and the IV is a continuous variable, a correlational analysis is possible, in which the difference is tested between correlations of the IV with the DV at each level of the moderator. As in the case of testing for a mediating effect, however, a regression analysis is preferable. In this case, the difference between two unstandardized regression coefficients would be tested.

Moderation: Continuous moderator and categorical or continuous IV

If the moderator is a continuous variable and the IV is a dichotomy, or both of these variables are continuous, and the effect of the moderator is assumed to be linear, a hierarchical regression approach to testing the interaction is possible. This regression approach has been gaining in popularity, particularly in relation to testing moderating effects within social psychological models. Sani's (2005) examination of a model of schism in groups provides a good recent example.

A psychological moderation hypothesis requiring a hierarchical regression

We will continue to use our computer anxiety example. We will look at the proposed causal relationship between psychological gender (PSYGEN) and computer anxiety (CA). For those variables, we will use the same data as in Table 6.1, but we will add fabricated data for another continuous variable: total hours of computer experience (COMPEXP), which we hypothesize will exert a moderating effect on the relationship between PSYGEN and CA. The first few cases for PSYGEN, CA and COMPEXP are shown in Table 6.2 (the full dataset can be found as psy.moderation.sav on the book website). Specifically, we suggest that the negative influence of psychological gender (masculine characteristics minus feminine characteristics) on computer anxiety will be stronger the less computer experience a person has had. So, we have three continuous variables – a predictor variable, an outcome variable and a hypothesized moderator variable – and our goal is to test the interaction between the IV (PSYGEN) and the proposed moderator (COMPEXP).

Table 6.2 The first few rows of data on computer anxiety, psychological gender and computer experience for 80 students. The data for the first two variables were real, but the data for the computer experience variable were fabricated (the full dataset can be found as psy.moderation.sav on the website)

CA	PSYGEN	COMPEXP
2.06	−0.15	351
3.65	−1.38	290
2.06	−0.35	333
1.24	−0.50	324
2.29	−0.85	343
1.24	−0.55	319

Moderation: The application of the regression approach

The interaction can be tested by creating an interaction term (PSYGEN * COMPEXP) and entering it after entry of PSYGEN and COMPEXP. Then, if addition of the new PSYGEN * COMPEXP variable results in a significant increase in R^2, it can be claimed that a moderating effect of COMPEXP on the relationship between PSYGEN and COMPEXP has been confirmed. Of course, generating a new variable by multiplying together two existing variables risks creating a multicollinearity problem, that is, either PSYGEN or COMPEXP, or both, will be highly correlated with PSYGEN * COMPEXP, which will seriously affect the estimation of the regression coefficients for the main effects. In addition, any effect of PSYGEN or COMPEXP will be tested at a value of zero for the other variable. For example, the effect of PSYGEN on CA would be tested for the rather extreme circumstance in which participants had no computer experience whatever.

Moderation using regression: Centring and standardizing

These two problems can be avoided by converting PSYGEN and COMPEXP to Z scores that have a mean of zero and a standard deviation of 1. To obtain a set of data with the same spread but with zero mean we need to subtract the mean from each of our values. This process is called centring. If the resulting data are divided by the standard deviation to obtain (raw score – mean)/*sd*, these values have a mean of zero and a standard deviation of 1. This process is called standardizing. The result is that the effect of the transformed variable, ZPSYGEN on the CA, for example, would be tested in relation to participants with an average level of computer experience, which seems considerably more reasonable. This procedure has the additional advantage of reducing the problem of multicollinearity by reducing the size of any high correlation of the IV or the moderator variable with the new interaction variable. The two standardized variables are then multiplied together to create the interaction variable.

Moderation: Requesting the analysis in SPSS

Open the file psy.moderation.sav in SPSS and create the two new Z score variables (the predictor and the moderator) by selecting **Analyze**, then **Descriptive Statistics**, then **Descriptives**. Move PSYGEN and COMPEXP into the **Variable(s)** box and click on **Save standardized values as variables** and then on **OK**. Check that the two new variables (automatically named as ZPSYGEN and ZCOMPEXP) have been added to the datasheet. Next, create an interaction term by selecting **Transform**, then **Compute**. Enter a name (e.g., PSYCOMP) in the **Target Variable** box and ZPSYGEN * ZCOMPEXP in the **Numeric Expression** box, and click **OK** and check that the interaction variable (PSYCOMP) has been added to the datasheet.

Now we are ready for the moderator analysis. Select **Analyze**, then **Regression**, then **Linear** to get a dialog box like SPSS Dialog Box 4.1. Move CA into the **Dependent** box and PSYGEN and COMPEXP into the **Independent(s)** box. Then click on **Next**, just as when doing a hierarchical regression described in Chapter 4. When **Block 2 of 2** appears, enter PSYCOMP in the **Independent Variable(s)** box and click the **Statistics** button. Select **R Squared Change**, then click **Continue** and **OK**.

Moderation analysis: Understanding the output

We focus on the Model Summary table shown in SPSS Output 6.5. Under Change Statistics, we see that R^2 Change is .045 when the interaction variable is added (model 2) to the predictor and moderator variables. This change is significant: $F(1,76) = 4.65, p = .034$. The significant interaction tells us that our presumed moderator (COMPEXP) does indeed moderate the effects of the predictor (PSYGEN) on the outcome variable (CA).

Model Summary

Model	R	R Square	Adjusted R Square	Std. Error of the Estimate	Change Statistics R Square Change	F Change	df1	df2	Sig. F Change
1	.461[a]	.213	.192	.70488	.213	10.396	2	77	.000
2	.508[b]	.258	.229	.68875	.045	4.649	1	76	.034

a. Predictors: (Constant), compexp, psygen

b. Predictors: (Constant), compexp, psygen, psycomp

SPSS Output 6.5 R Square Change when an interaction variable (PSYCOMP) is added to the model.

Example Box 6.3

A continuation of the alternative medical example for partial correlation applied to a test of a moderation hypothesis requiring a hierarchical regression

The full analysis for this example can be found at www.psypress.com/multivariate-analysis/medical-examples (click on Chapter 6).

The variables DEPRESSION and ANXIETY (state – trait) pattern are again used. In addition, another variable is introduced. The 80 adults have been keeping an anxiety diary for 2 years and the new variable we are going to introduce is the number of days during that period when no feelings of anxiety are recorded. The data are used on this occasion to illustrate an analysis designed to test that the relationship between ANXIETY (state – trait) pattern and DEPRESSION is moderated by the number of anxiety-free days. This involves testing the interaction between the predictor variable (ANXIETY) and the proposed moderator (ANXFREEDAYS) with respect to the outcome variable (DEPRESSION). To achieve this, it is necessary to create an interaction term (ANXIETY * ANXFREEDAYS), and to convert the predictor and moderator variables to Z scores (ZANXIETY and ZANXFREEDAYS).

Outcomes

The value of R^2 Change when the interaction variable is added to the predictor and moderator variables is significant. This tells us that our presumed moderator (number of anxiety-free days) does indeed moderate the effects of the predictor (ANXIETY) on the outcome variable (DEPRESSION). The negative influence of the anxiety (state – trait) pattern on the depression score is stronger the fewer anxiety-free days a person has.

Alternative variables for use in SPSS
The full dataset, med.moderation.sav, can be found on the book website

Variable	Psychology	Medicine
Outcome variable	CA Computer anxiety	DEPRESSION Score on a depression scale
Predictor variables	PSYGEN Psychological gender (masculinity – femininity) COMPEXP Computer experience (hours) PSYCOMP Constructed interaction term (PSYGEN * COMPEXP) ZPSYGEN Z score of PSYGEN ZCOMPEXP Z score of COMPEXP	ANXIETY Difference score on anxiety scales (state – trait anxiety) ANXFREEDAYS Anxiety-free days ANXDAYS Constructed interaction term (ANXIETY * ANXFREEDAYS) ZANXIETY Z score of ANXIETY ZANXFREEDAYS Z score of ANXFREEDAYS

Graphical clarification of the moderation effect

In order to see whether the significant moderator effect is in the predicted direction (the greater the computing experience, the weaker the negative effect of psychological gender on computer anxiety) we can look at the cases with the highest and lowest amounts of computer experience. A boxplot of COMPEXP shows that the upper quartile is at about 370, and the lower is at about 270. We can use **data**, then **select cases** and then click **If condition is satisfied** and the **If** button to select those cases with COMPEXP > 370. With this selection in place, plot CA against PSYGEN and also find the correlation between CA and PSYGEN. The results are shown in SPSS Output 6.6 overleaf. You can see that we have 21 cases here, which is about a quarter of the full set of 80. These are the ones with the highest COMPEXP scores and, for them, the correlation between CA and PSYGEN is $-.21$ ($p = .37$), and the graph shows that the relationship between CA and PSYGEN is very weak.

Now go back to **Select cases**, but this time select those with COMPEXP < 270 and repeat the graph and correlation. We get SPSS Output 6.7 (shown on p. 157), where you can see that we have 19 cases (again about a quarter of the full set) but this time those with the lowest COMPEXP. The graph shows a much stronger relationship and the correlation is $-.58$ ($p = .01$).

These brief investigations confirm our expectation that the effect of PSYGEN on CA weakens with more computer experience. The Sani paper to which we referred earlier illustrates a different approach to investigating the interaction from that adopted here.

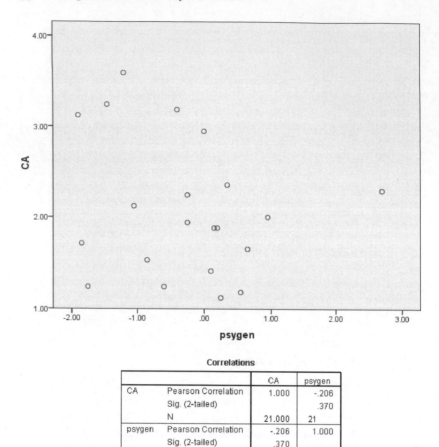

Correlations		CA	psygen
CA	Pearson Correlation	1.000	-.206
	Sig. (2-tailed)		.370
	N	21.000	21
psygen	Pearson Correlation	-.206	1.000
	Sig. (2-tailed)	.370	
	N	21	21.000

SPSS Output 6.6 Plot and correlation for the cases with COMPEXP > 370.

Reporting results: Moderation analysis

The following is an example of how you might report the results of carrying out the analysis to test the moderating effect of computer experience on the relationship between psychological gender and computer anxiety:

Psychological gender (the IV) and computer experience (the presumed moderator) were centred by converting them to Z scores with means of zero, and an interaction variable (PSYCOMP) was created by multiplying the two Z scores together. The IV (PSYGEN) and the presumed moderator (COMPEXP) were entered into a hierarchical regression as a group, followed by the entry of the interaction variable (PSYCOMP). The value of R^2 Change when the interaction variable was added to the predictor and moderator variables was .045 and that change was significant: $F(1,76) = 4.65$, $p = .034$. The significant interaction tells us that our presumed moderator (COM-PEXP) did indeed moderate the effects of the predictor (PSYGEN) on the outcome variable (CA). The nature of the moderation effect was as predicted, that is, the negative influence of psychological gender (masculine characteristics minus

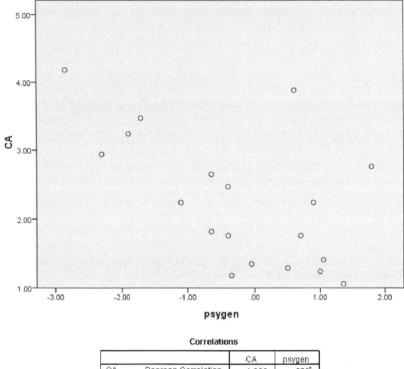

Correlations

		CA	psygen
CA	Pearson Correlation	1.000	-.575*
	Sig. (2-tailed)		.010
	N	19.000	19
psygen	Pearson Correlation	-.575*	1.000
	Sig. (2-tailed)	.010	
	N	19	19.000

*. Correlation is significant at the 0.05 level (2-tailed).

SPSS Output 6.7 Plot and correlation for the cases with COMPEXP < 2/0.

feminine characteristics) on computer anxiety was stronger the less computer experience a person had. This moderation effect can be seen clearly in Figure A (*the plots from SPSS Outputs 6.6 and 6.7*) showing the relationship between CA and PSYGEN for the cases with the highest and lowest COMPEXP scores.

Complex path models

The approaches to mediation and moderation analysis that we have taken generalize to more complex designs with more than two IVs. For example, multiple IVs may be mediated in their effects by one or more variables. Further, a variable may have both mediator and moderator status within a path model. Also, there can be mediated moderation and moderated mediation. We will not be dealing with these complexities but we note that, in general, as path models become more complex, researchers tend to find it necessary to turn to approaches that are designed to deal with multiple variables and multiple relationships concurrently. These are the approaches taken in confirmatory factor analysis and path analysis, and in structural equation modelling, which combines the two. We will consider these approaches in Chapters 7 and 8. Once again, we commend Sani's (2005) article as an excellent example of dealing with a complex model.

References

Baron, R. M., & Kenny, D. A. (1986). The moderator–mediator variable distinction in social psychological research: Conceptual, strategic and statistical considerations. *Journal of Personality and Social Psychology, 51*, 1173–1182.

Diekhoff, G. (1992). *Statistics for the social and behavioural sciences: Univariate, bivariate, multivariate*. Dubuque, IA: Wm. C. Brown.

Sani, F. (2005). When subgroups secede: Extending and refining the social psychological model of schism in groups. *Personality and Social Psychology Bulletin, 31*, 1074–1086.

Todman, J., & Day, K. (2006). Computer anxiety: The role of psychological gender. *Computers in Human Behavior, 22*, 856–869.

7   Path analysis

Introduction

Path analysis is an extension of multiple regression. It focuses on the pattern of relationships among a set of variables rather than just on which IVs predict a DV and how strongly. It is used to test the fit of causal models against correlation matrices for the variables in the models. Right away, we need to be very clear that we are not talking about inferring causal relationships between variables. *Causal modelling,* as the term is applied to path analysis, refers to *assumptions* made by researchers in developing their models. They propose that certain causal relationships exist among a set of variables and they represent these in a path diagram. They then use the techniques of path analysis to test some propositions about the model represented in the path diagram. If the propositions are supported, it is tempting to infer that the causal assumptions are correct. Emphatically, this is not the case; all of the usual cautions about not inferring causation from correlational data apply.

So, what is the point of path analysis? Well, at its best, it may indicate the relative importance of various paths in the *output path diagram* – the result of the path analysis – which may tell us which of several causal hypotheses is better supported by the data. Often, interest lies in whether *direct* or *indirect* effects of variables on other variables are more plausible. We discussed the analysis of specific indirect (mediation) effects in Chapter 6. Path analysis is a more general technique for investigating direct and indirect relationships among a number of variables that are usually specified in, often quite complex, *input path diagrams.*

Path analysis is essentially a technique to be used for confirmatory purposes, to determine which of two or more a priori theoretical models conforms best to the data. It may be that a model will be modified as a result of inspecting the results of a confirmatory path analysis, but the modified model then has the status of a new hypothesis that needs to be tested with fresh data. If path analysis is used in an exploratory fashion, models will usually be generated but, again, these should be given the status of hypotheses rather than discoveries. It is also the case that the more models are tested, the more likely are Type I errors to occur (i.e., confirmation by chance).

Path diagrams and terminology

Input path diagrams

Path analysis begins with one or more input path diagrams, which specify proposed causal relationships among a set of variables. There are conventions for displaying relationships in these flow diagrams, though they do vary a bit. Usually variable names are located within rectangular boxes and relationships are indicated with arrows between the boxes. Correlations between variables are shown with double-headed curved arrows and a proposed causal relationship is shown with a straight arrow from the presumed causal variable (on the left) to the variable on which it is proposed to have an effect (to its right). Figure 7.1 shows three possible input path diagrams of proposed relationships among the three variables: relaxed early experience with computers (RELAX), computer anxiety (CA) and time spent using computers (USE). Figure 7.1(a) suggests that RELAX and CA are correlated, but says nothing about the direction of influence. It also suggests that both RELAX and CA have *direct* causal effects on USE. The signs on the arrows indicate the predicted directions of the correlation and causal effects. Figure 7.1(b) suggests that RELAX has direct effects on CA and USE, and that CA also has a direct effect on USE. As well as its direct effect on USE, RELAX also has an *indirect* effect on USE via its effect on CA (partial mediation). Figure 7.1(c) suggests that RELAX has a direct effect on CA, which, in turn, has a direct effect on USE (complete mediation). You may recognize Figures 7.1(b) and 7.1(c) as representing the same issue as was illustrated in Figure 6.2 in the chapter on partial correlation, mediation and moderation. Indeed, partial correlation or the regression approach to mediation described in that chapter can tell us whether or not the relationship between

(a) Correlation and direct effects on DV

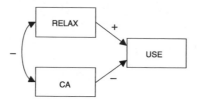

(b) Direct effects and indirect (mediated) effect on DV

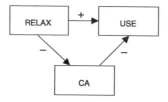

(c) Indirect (mediated) effect on DV

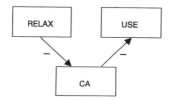

Figure 7.1 Three possible input path diagrams of proposed relationships among three variables.

the IV (RELAX) and the DV (USE) is mediated by CA. We do not need path analysis for that, but path analysis comes into its own when more complex path diagrams are proposed, and it also considerably simplifies the business of evaluating goodness of fit.

Model identification

Path models are evaluated by estimating the parameters (indicated by arrows): the curved arrows are correlations and the straight arrows are *path coefficients* (*standardized regression coefficients* or *beta weights*) obtained from regression analyses. Path models are described as *just-identified, under-identified* or *over-identified*. A model is just-identified when the number of *data points* is equal to the number of parameters to be estimated. The number of data points in this case is the number of variances and co-variances, and is given by $k(k + 1)/2$, where k equals the number of observed variables. The number of parameters to be estimated is a constant plus the number of beta values, correlations and residuals specified in the model. When a model is just-identified, the estimated parameters will perfectly reproduce the covariance matrix, and chi square (goodness of fit) and its *df*s will be zero. The model is unable to test any hypothesis and is therefore without interest. If a model has more parameters to be estimated than the number of data points, it is *under-identified* and a unique solution cannot be obtained, so under-identified models are also uninteresting. If a model contains fewer parameters to be estimated than there are data points, it is over-identified and its fit with the data, which may be better or worse than competing models, may be worth investigating.

Ideally, path analysis is a confirmatory procedure. Competing, theoretically interesting models are specified and the fit of each to the data is evaluated. The one with the best fit is generally retained, though a model with fewer parameters (a more parsimonious model), possibly a subset of those in a competing model, may be preferred if its fit is only a little worse than the model with more parameters.

The variables in a path analysis

In path analysis, a variable may be an IV in one regression and a DV in another; later we will explain and illustrate the various regression analyses that together make up a path analysis. In the meantime, you should be aware that another classification of variables is made in relation to path analysis. Those variables that have no one-way arrows pointing at them can only be IVs and they are sometimes referred to as *exogenous* variables. All the rest, which have at least one one-way arrow pointing at them, are capable of functioning as DVs and are referred to as *endogenous* variables. Nothing is predicted perfectly, and all endogenous variables have residuals pointing to them in the final input model. These are usually indicated by r1, r2, r3, etc. (or sometimes, e1, etc., where 'e' stands for 'error'), one for each endogenous variable. Exogenous variables are not assumed to have any prior effects, so do not have residuals pointing at them. Thus, in Figure 7.1(b), for example, there are two endogenous variables, making five model parameters to be estimated. Counting the constant, that amounts to six parameters. As there are also six data points (3 * 4/2), the model is just-identified, chi-square degrees of freedom will be zero (*df* = data points – model parameters – 1) and the model cannot be tested. The same is true for Figure 7.1(a). In that case, the curved arrow implies a correlation and an error to be estimated, so there are again six parameters. In Figure 7.1(c), on the other hand, there are again six data points but there are only four model parameters to be estimated. So, $df = 6 - 4 - 1 = 1$. The model is over-identified and its fit can be tested. Its fit can also be compared with that for the just-identified model.

Assumptions for path analysis

Some assumptions need to be made for path analysis. First, the variables are measured without error – in practice, that means that values of each variable are either obtained with a single measurement or, if several measurements (indicators) of a variable are combined, the reliability with which the variable is measured is not considered in the path model. At the end of the next chapter (on factor analysis), we briefly consider how *structural equation modelling* combines confirmatory factor analysis with path analysis to handle measurement error. Second, the model must be *recursive*, that is, all straight arrows flow the same way (usually from left to right), so that feedback loops and reciprocal effects are not allowed. Third, residual (unmeasured) variables are uncorrelated with any other variables in the model besides the one they point to.

Conducting a path analysis using regression

Path analysis proceeds by means of a series of regression analyses, beginning with the furthest right variable as the DV and all variables to its left that point at it as IVs. If there is more than one variable at the extreme right of the diagram, each is treated as the DV in turn. Then the next furthest right variable(s) is treated in turn as the DV and all variables to its left that point to it as IVs. The series of regression analyses (working backwards toward the left) continues until the only remaining IV(s) is the exogenous variable(s) at the extreme left.

Sample size

We will illustrate a path analysis using a small, fabricated sample of 20 cases that can easily be copied into an SPSS datasheet. This is far too small a sample for a real path analysis, but it will do for an illustration. When deciding on the number of cases needed for a real path analysis, bear in mind that we are using regression models, so the rule of thumb from regression analysis may give a good idea of a sensible number of cases. In a real example later in this chapter we have five variables, one of them being the principal DV. Applying the rule of thumb provided in Chapter 4 suggests that we would need $104 + 4 = 108$ (for testing an individual IV), or $50 + 8 * 4 = 82$ (for testing the overall regression), where $4 =$ number of IVs in each case. If we choose the bigger value, it seems that around 110 cases would be sufficient. In fact there are 211, which is more than adequate for a study with five variables. It should be emphasized that although the rule of thumb is often adequate, a formal power calculation should be undertaken if the conclusions from the experiment rely on statistical significance.

A simple psychology example of an input path model

Data for the 20 cases in our first demonstration are shown in Table 7.1, where it can be seen that the variables are those used in the computer anxiety example above, with the addition of another variable: experience of being in control when using computers (CONTROL). Scores for RELAX and CONTROL each ranged from 4 to 12, those for CA ranged from 20 to 90 and those for USE ranged from 2 to 6.

Table 7.1 Fabricated data for a path analysis (psy.path1.sav)

Case	CA	RELAX	CONTROL	USE
1	48	8	8	4
2	87	4	4	4
3	52	9	8	3
4	37	11	4	4
5	39	8	6	4
6	46	6	10	6
7	54	8	5	5
8	36	7	12	5
9	37	8	8	6
10	58	9	4	3
11	65	6	8	3
12	77	7	4	2
13	51	10	6	3
14	20	12	9	5
15	59	6	8	4
16	63	6	8	4
17	55	7	6	5
18	42	10	6	5
19	63	7	8	4
20	68	8	6	3

An input path diagram representing a proposed causal model involving the four variables in Table 7.1 is shown in Figure 7.2. The causal model in Figure 7.2 proposes that relaxed early experiences with computers result in lower computer anxiety (a negative effect: high on RELAX → low on CA). It is also proposed that high computer anxiety results in less USE of computers in the future and in less experience of feeling in CONTROL when using computers (both negative effects). Finally, it is proposed that more experience of feeling in CONTROL results in more USE of computers in the future (a positive effect). There are 10 data points and 7 parameters to be estimated, so the model is under-identified, with $10 - 7 - 1 = 2$ *df*s.

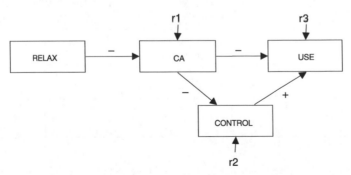

Figure 7.2 Input path diagram representing a proposed causal model.

Path analysis: Requesting the regression analyses in SPSS

So, we need to conduct a series of regression analyses. These can be specified as follows:

> USE is the DV, regressed on CA and CONTROL as IVs
> CONTROL is the DV, regressed on CA as the sole IV
> CA is the DV, regressed on RELAX as the sole IV

First, enter the data for the four variables into an SPSS datasheet (20 cases in four columns). For the first regression, select **Analyze** from the menu bar, then **Regression**, then **Linear**, to get a dialog box like SPSS Dialog Box 4.1 shown in the chapter on regression. Move USE into the **Dependent** box and CA and CONTROL into the **Independent(s)** box. Check that **Enter**, the default **Method**, is selected. Click the **Statistics** button and select **Descriptives** in order to get the correlations. Click **Continue** and **OK** to get the analysis.

Path analysis: Understanding the output

The relevant output is in the Correlations, Model Summary and Coefficients tables, shown in SPSS Output 7.1. The first table in the output (not reproduced here) gives descriptive statistics such as the means and standard deviations. Next comes the Correlations table, and we see that the correlations that our model specified as causal effects are all statistically significant. This is encouraging. The next table (not reproduced here) is Variables Entered/Removed, and this just tells us that CA and CONTROL were entered and that USE was the DV. Next is the Model Summary, in which we

Correlations

		use	ca	control
Pearson Correlation	use	1.000	-.567	.457
	ca	-.567	1.000	-.448
	control	.457	-.448	1.000
Sig. (1-tailed)	use	.	.005	.022
	ca	.005	.	.024
	control	.022	.024	.
N	use	20	20	20
	ca	20	20	20
	control	20	20	20

Model Summary

Model	R	R Square	Adjusted R Square	Std. Error of the Estimate
1	.611[a]	.373	.300	.896

a. Predictors: (Constant), control, ca

Coefficients[a]

Model		Unstandardized Coefficients		Standardized Coefficients	t	Sig.
		B	Std. Error	Beta		
1	(Constant)	4.881	1.298		3.761	.002
	ca	-0.031	0.015	-.454	-2.114	.050
	control	0.125	0.106	.253	1.180	.254

a. Dependent Variable: use

SPSS Output 7.1 Output from the first regression analysis for path analysis of the model in Figure 7.2.

see that $R^2 = .37$. Then comes an ANOVA table (not reproduced here) that just confirms that the regression equation is significant. Finally, we have the Coefficients table, in which we see that the standardized beta coefficients are −.45 for CA → USE, which is just significant ($p = .05$), and .25 for CONTROL → USE, which is not significant ($p = .25$).

The remaining two regression analyses required by the path model are carried out in the same way, using regression dialog boxes. CONTROL is entered as the DV and CA as the sole IV for the second regression, and CA is entered as the DV and RELAX as the sole IV for the third regression. We will not reproduce the output tables again, but the relevant information from them is as follows: the correlations specified in the model are both significant (CA → CONTROL = −.45, $p < .05$; RELAX → CA = −.70, $p < .0001$), the IV in each regression was entered and the ANOVAs confirmed that both were significant. The R^2 value for the regression with CONTROL as the DV is .20 and that for the regression with CA as the DV is .49. The standardized beta coefficients are −.45 for CA → CONTROL and −.70 for RELAX → CA (both significant, $p < .05$). The partial regression coefficients are displayed in our *output path diagram* in Figure 7.3, where we also display the r1, r2 and r3 values of R^2 (proportion of variance accounted for). Sometimes, instead of the R^2 values, the values entered in an output path diagram are $\sqrt{1 - R^2}$ (the *residuals*) or $1 - R^2$ (proportion of variance not accounted for).

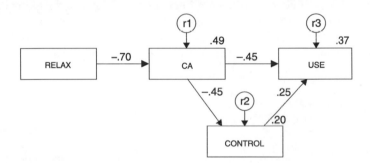

Figure 7.3 Output path diagram for data in Table 7.1.

Example Box 7.1

An alternative simple medical example of an input path model

The full analysis for this example can be found at www.psypress.com/multivariate-analysis/medical-examples (click on Chapter 7).

As part of a larger study of variables implicated in susceptibility to suicidal tendencies, a path model linking family history of mental health problems (FAMILYHIST), positive mental health (POSMENTAL) and susceptibility to depression following adverse life events (SUSCEPTIBILITY) with suicidal thoughts (THOUGHTS) is tested using a series of regression analyses in SPSS. Twenty adults between the ages of 25 and 45 are recruited and they complete self-report inventories designed to yield scores on the four variables. The regression analyses are specified as follows:

> THOUGHTS is the DV, regressed on POSMENTAL and SUSCEPTIBILITY as IVs
> SUSCEPTIBILITY is the DV, regressed on POSMENTAL as the sole IV
> POSMENTAL is the DV, regressed on FAMILYHIST as the sole IV

A causal model proposes that a family history of mental problems decreases the likelihood of positive mental health (a negative effect: high on FAMILYHIST → low on POSMENTAL). It is also proposed that good mental health (POSMENTAL) results in fewer and less serious suicidal thoughts (THOUGHTS) and lower SUSCEPTIBILITY to depression following adverse life events (both negative effects). Finally, it is proposed that high SUSCEPTIBILITY to depression following adverse life events results in more suicidal THOUGHTS (a positive effect).

Outcomes

Standardized beta coefficients are generated for all paths and R^2 values for all endogenous variables (i.e., those with arrows pointing at them). The beta values and the residuals ($\sqrt{1 - R^2}$) are as shown in Figure 7.3 (with the medical variables substituted for the psychology variables). The path from SUSCEPTIBILITY to THOUGHTS is not significant and the goodness of fit indicator, chi square, is highly significant, suggesting that the fit of the model to the data is not good. Given that we already know that there is a strong link between depression and suicidal thoughts, we conclude that the validity of our self-report measures, especially SUSCEPTIBILITY, is suspect.

Alternative variables for use in SPSS
The full dataset, med.path1.sav, can be found on the book website

Variable	Psychology	Medicine
Principal DV	USE Time using computers	THOUGHTS Suicidal thoughts
Exogenous variable (can only be an IV)	RELAX Relaxed early experience	FAMILYHIST Family history of mental health problems
Endogenous variables (can act as a DV)	CA Computer anxiety CONTROL Experience of feeling in control	POSMENTAL Positive mental health SUSCEPTIBILITY Susceptibility to depression following adverse life events

Goodness of fit

We need some further information to tell us how well the data fit our proposed models. We used a simple example to illustrate the idea of the fit of a model at the end of

Chapter 4 on regression. The last section of that chapter, on non-linear relationships, showed how we could fit a linear regression to some data from astronomy. The linear regression was highly significant, but a graph showed clearly that fitting a straight line was not appropriate for these data. Another way to say this is that the linear regression model is a very poor fit for these data. Because in this example we were using only one IV and one DV, we could easily check our model in simple graphical ways, but for more complex models with more than two variables we have to use numerical methods to decide whether a model is a good fit for the data. A range of methods is available under the general heading of *goodness of fit statistics*. A problem with using SPSS regression to do the analysis, as we did here, is that no estimate of fit is provided. We note that one beta value, for the path from CONTROL to USE, was not significant (beta = .25, p = .25, from SPSS Output 7.1), which is not encouraging. However, we will delay discussion of goodness of fit indicators until we analyse some real data using AMOS, a relatively new program marketed by SPSS that has impressed us with its excellent graphic interface and ease of use. Then, we will be able to discuss the goodness of fit indices computed by the program. In the meantime, we just note that the value of chi square (obtained from AMOS), which should be non-significant if the model is a good fit, is highly significant: χ^2 = 22.24, with 2 *dfs*, given by number of data points (10) minus number of parameters estimated (7) minus the constant (1).

For the moment, we just note that, as our model turned out to be a bad fit, we might choose to modify it by adding additional variables, by adding more paths between the existing variables or rethinking the directions of influences within our model. For example, a case might be made for expecting experience of CONTROL to cause changes in CA, rather than the reverse. Of course, it would have been better if we had generated some alternative models at the outset, so that we could compare their fit with our preferred model now. Incidentally, chi square tends to reach significance rather readily as sample size increases, so it is not generally the best indicator of fit when the sample size is high. It could still be useful though, even if it were significant for all of the proposed models, because it would tell us something if its value was much smaller for one model than for another. If we make changes to our model at this stage, we really need new data to test the new models, though it would still be alright to explore new models with our existing data in order to get an idea of whether it would be worth collecting new data to carry out valid tests.

Direct and indirect effects

Before leaving this example, which we analysed with regression analyses in order to reveal the logic that underlies the computations in dedicated packages, we note that sometimes researchers want to know the overall impact of one variable on another: the total of direct and indirect effects. For example, we might want to know the overall effect of CA on USE. To answer that question we need to take the direct effect of CA (−.45) and add to it the indirect effect via CONTROL. Indirect effects are obtained by multiplying the effects along each indirect path. In this example, there is only one indirect path from CA to USE and the coefficients along that path are −.45 and .25, so the indirect effect of CA on USE is −.45 × .25 = −.113. So the total effect of CA on USE is (−.45) + (−.113) = −.56.

Using a dedicated package (AMOS) to do path analysis

As with the next chapter on factor analysis, we make an exception here to our general procedure of confining ourselves to using SPSS to illustrate the data analyses. We do that because there are packages available that are far easier to use than SPSS for all but the most simple path models. In particular, these packages allow us to specify the model by constructing an input path diagram like Figure 7.2, which is the natural way to do it, and they give the results in the form of an output path model like Figure 7.3, as well as in various tables. They also provide a wide range of goodness of fit indicators. Another advantage of using a dedicated package is that, unlike in SPSS, indirect routes do not have to be calculated by hand. We do not intend to attempt to provide a general coverage of the AMOS package. Rather, we will give you detailed instructions for replicating a real path analysis. This will, we hope, get you started in a 'hands on' fashion, and prepare you for consulting manuals or texts to find out more about how to use the packages for your own purposes. A reference to a guide to using AMOS is given in the 'Further reading' at the end of the book.

A real dataset and a social psychological path model to be tested

Questionnaire data on five variables were obtained from 211 priests and deacons who were opposed to the ordination of women to the priesthood within the Church of England (Sani & Todman, 2002). One variable, schismatic intentions (SCHISM), was the principal DV. The remaining variables were the extent to which the ordination of women was perceived as changing a core aspect of the C of E (CHANGE), the perception that ordination subverted the identity of the C of E (SUBVERT), the extent to which the C of E is perceived as entitative, that is, as an entity (ENTITATI), and the perceived ability of opponents of ordination to voice their dissent (VOICE). It was proposed that CHANGE would affect SUBVERT, which would in turn affect VOICE and ENTITATI, that VOICE would affect ENTITATI and SCHISM and that ENTITATI would also affect SCHISM. All of the effects, with the exception of CHANGE → SUBVERT and VOICE → ENTITATI were predicted to be negative. Three plausible alternative models were also generated, but they will not be described here.

Using AMOS to test the model: Getting the data file

We will begin with the data in five columns in an SPSS datasheet. The first few cases can be seen in Table 7.2 and the full data file, psy.path2.sav, is available on the book website.

Table 7.2 First few cases of schism data (the full dataset can be found as psy.path2.sav on the website) (adapted from Sani & Todman, 2002)

Case	CHANGE	SUBVERT	VOICE	ENTITATI	SCHISM
1	12	19	15	7	1
2	12	25	22	10	2
3	12	26	24	6	3
4	14	29	14	4	2
5	10	22	13	9	2
6	12	26	15	missing	2

Note the presence of missing data that will need to be dealt with. To begin the path analysis, open AMOS Graphics (you have the option of using AMOS basic, which is an equation-based format, but we think most people will like the graphics version best). The screen will look as in AMOS Screen 7.1. First you need to identify the SPSS datafile to use, so go to **File** on the menu bar, then **Data Files**. Click the **File Name** button and browse to find the file you want (psy.path2.sav). Click **OK** to close the dialog box.

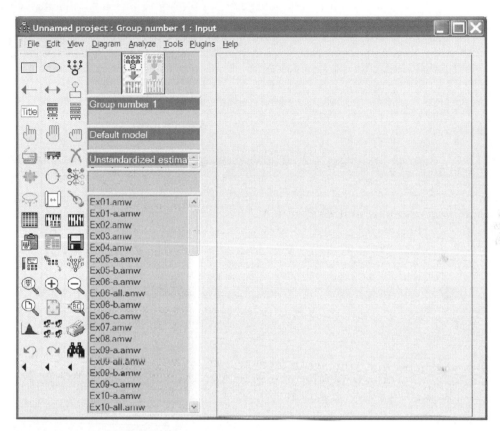

AMOS Screen 7.1 The AMOS graphic screen at the start.

Using AMOS to test the model: Constructing the input path diagram

You can begin drawing your input path diagram immediately. Go to the **Rectangle** icon at the top left of the icon box and click on it. It will then be highlighted to show that it is active. All of the icons toggle on and off, so you could deselect the rectangle icon by clicking on it again. While the rectangle icon is active, move to the diagram space on the right of the screen. When you click and hold down the mouse button, you can drag the mouse to draw a rectangle. We have five variables, so you need to draw five rectangles. The easiest way is to use the **Copy** icon (5th down in the left column). While it is active, click on the rectangle you have drawn and drag to where you want a copy. Repeat this until you have the five variable boxes positioned as you want them. You can change their size and shape at any time by activating the icon with arrows pointing in four directions (6th down in the left column) and you can move objects at any time by activating the **Truck** icon (5th down in the centre column). You can also delete any object by activating the **Cross-out** icon (5th down in the right column). You add arrows to the diagram by activating the appropriate **Arrow** icon, which is a single arrow in our case (2nd down in the left column). Click where you want the arrow to start and drag it to where you want it to point. You need to realize that all of the icon locations we refer to are as shown in AMOS Screen 7.1. Your columns may be arranged differently depending on the width that is set for the icon display.

Next, you can give the rectangles variable names (they must match the names used in your SPSS data file). Right click on a rectangle and select **Object Properties** from the menu that opens, then select the **Text** tab and type the name. When you have entered text in the dialog box, just close the box – there is no **Continue** or **OK** button. Next, activate the **Add a unique variable to an existing variable** icon (2nd down in the right column). This will enable you to attach R^2 value boxes to the four endogenous variables by clicking on the variables. Recall that we mentioned earlier that the values entered in an output path diagram may be R^2, $1 - R^2$ or $\sqrt{1 - R^2}$; AMOS shows R^2. You can then name these variables. We will call them r1, r2, r3 and r4, remembering that each of these labels stands for an R^2 value. You should end up with an input path diagram looking something like that shown in AMOS Screen 7.2. This would be a good time to save your work so far: use **File** and **Save As** from the menu bar in the usual way. The name you choose appears in the lowest box to the right of the tools.

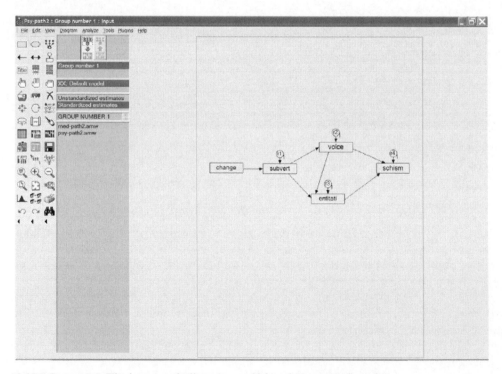

AMOS Screen 7.2 The input path diagram specifying the proposed model.

Using AMOS to test the model: Requesting output

Now select **Standardized estimates** to the right of the icon columns. Next, click on **View** in the menu bar at the top left, then **Analysis Properties** and the **Estimation** tab. Leave the defaults on and put a tick in **Estimate means and intercepts**. This deals with missing data (recall that we do have data missing in our file, see Table 7.2). Now click on the **Output** tab and put ticks against **Standardized estimates** and **Squared multiple correlations**.

Now you need to locate the **Calculate estimates** icon. It has thick and thin vertical stripes and is 8th down in the right-hand column in the icon box. Click on it and you should see a chi-square value appear in the box below **Standardized estimates**. The analysis has been done and you can look at the output path diagram, with beta coefficients and R^2 values entered, by clicking on the large icon at the top left of the screen with the red arrow pointing upwards. If you click on the magnifying glass icon with the plus sign on it, your output diagram will be enlarged. Should that result in the diagram becoming too big for the screen, click on the large icon at the top left of the screen with the down arrow to return to your input path diagram, and use the **resizing** and/or the **truck** icon to make the diagram fit. You can then click again on the up arrow icon to recover your output path diagram. The screen should now look something like that shown in AMOS Screen 7.3.

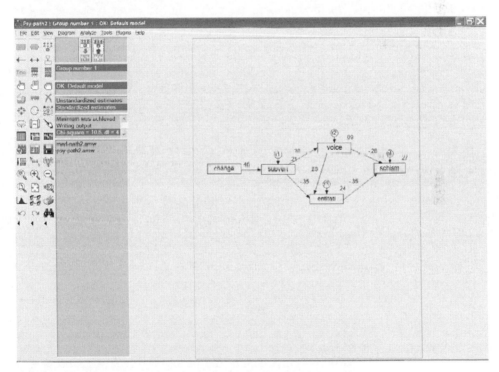

AMOS Screen 7.3 The output path diagram for the schism data in psy.path2.sav.

Using AMOS to test the model: Understanding the output

If it is unclear to you which values in the output diagram are beta coefficients and which are R^2 values, move the mouse pointer over an arrow and it, and its beta coefficient, will show up red. Likewise, if you move the arrow over a variable box it, and its associated R^2 (labelled r1, etc.) value, will show up red.

We see (on the left of AMOS Screen 7.3) that chi square for goodness of fit is 10.5 with 4 *df*s. This was the first statistic to be developed to give information about how well the data fit a proposed model. Our value in this case is significant at $p < .05$ (the probability $p = .033$ is given in the **Text Output**, which we will come to next). Just before we do, we may note that although the fit of the model to the covariance matrix is not 'good' (i.e., chi square just reaches significance), this is not a serious setback because, as noted in the section on interpreting the SPSS output, chi square very readily reaches significance with large sample sizes even when all other indices indicate a good fit, and in this case chi square is only just significant and its value is only slightly more than double the *df*s.

Using AMOS to test the model: Goodness of fit indices

Turning to those other indices, we can look at their values by clicking on the **View text output** icon, which is supposed to represent columns of text (9th down in the centre column). The goodness of fit indices come near the end of the file (select **Model Fit** from the list on the left). The beginning of the goodness of fit summary of models is shown in AMOS Screen 7.4.

For each index, goodness of fit is given for the model being tested (the **Default model**), the **Saturated model** (the just-identified model) and the **Independence model** (all correlations among variables are zero). The fit of the default model will lie somewhere between the extremes represented by the other two models. Evaluation of a model hinges on its position between the extremes relative to competing models. In other words, a comparative interpretation is called for. The first index we refer to is CMIN, which is actually the likelihood ratio chi square. We have already noted that its value of 10.5 with $df = 4$ is not inconsistent with a reasonably fitting model. Other indices have been developed to reduce the dependence on sample size. The next block of indices include two such indices, NFI (normed fit index) and CFI (comparative fit index), which are among those most frequently reported. The NFI is an example of a so-called *descriptive fit index* and indicates the proportion of improvement of the overall fit of the model relative to the independence model. The CFI is also a descriptive fit index and is interpreted in the same way as the NFI, but may be less affected by sample size. For these indices, values close to 1 are generally considered to indicate a good fit, so our values for NFI (.95) and CFI (.96) suggest that our model is quite a good fit.

Quite a few more batches of related indices follow. Of these, another that is frequently referred to, the RMSEA (root mean square error of approximation) index, is one of a number of measures that evaluate the extent to which a model fails to fit the data per degree of freedom, and tends to favour more complex models. It is considered to indicate a bad fit if it is greater than .1. It is not on the first screen of fit indices shown in AMOS Screen 7.4, but scroll down and see that the value we get is .09, with lower and upper bounds for the confidence interval of .02 to .16.

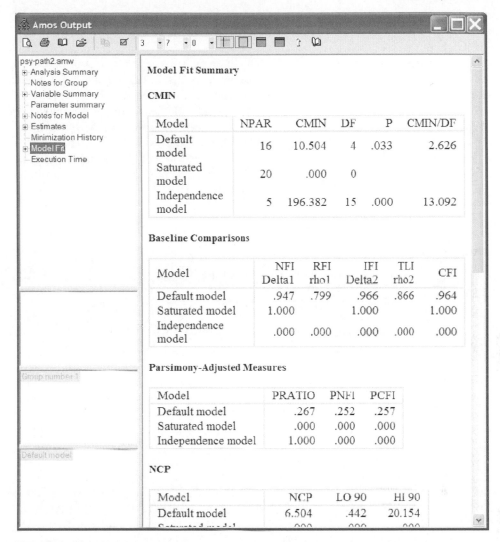

AMOS Screen 7.4 Goodness of fit indices for the schism (data in psy.path2.sav) model.

This suggests that the fit is not very good. There are detailed discussions of all of the indices in the guide to AMOS text (Arbuckle & Wothke, 2003) and in Marcoulides and Hershberger (1997), both of which we reference in 'Further reading' at the end of the book.

Before leaving the indices though, there is an index called AIC (Akaike's information criterion) that is a modification of the standard goodness of fit χ^2 statistic that includes a penalty for complexity. This index does not tell us anything about the fit of a particular model, but it is extremely useful for making comparisons among two or more models, including non-nested models (a model is nested under another when it is identical except that one or more paths have been removed). Generally, the model with the lowest AIC value is considered to have the best fit. If it is computed for several models estimated from the same dataset, the model with the lowest AIC value is considered the best fit. We tested three alternative, theoretically plausible models and they all yielded higher AIC values (the lowest was 48.85) than the value obtained for our proposed model (42.50).

There are many competing goodness of fit indices to choose from and, as no one index is considered clearly preferable in all respects, it is usual to consider a number. If the indices all lead to the same conclusion, you can be reasonably confident in selecting three or four, representing different types, in a report of the results of a path analysis. If the conclusions diverge, it is likely that there is a problem of some kind with the model. One final caution is that the relatively good performance of our model with respect to the goodness of fit criteria does not guarantee the plausibility of the model. In fact, it is possible for a model to fit well yet still be incorrectly specified, but discussion of how this may arise is beyond the scope of this book.

Example Box 7.2

An alternative medical example of a path model to be tested

The full analysis for this example can be found at www.psypress.com/multivariate-analysis/medical-examples (click on Chapter 7).

For this example we use the same (real) social psychological data but we have fabricated a medical context for it, so the results for this example do not derive from real medical research. Data on five variables were obtained from 211 patients with chronic fatigue syndrome (CFS) in an attempt to identify direct and indirect influences contributing to a reduction in occupational, educational and social ACTIVITY. This is the principal DV, measured on a scale of 1–5. The remaining variables are as follows: MONTHS since the onset of the illness; MANAGE, the extent to which the illness is managed by diet, graded exercise, education, etc.; FUNCTION, loss of function based on a checklist of physical and cognitive functions; PAIN, a rating of amount and severity of myalgia (muscle pain) experienced. It is proposed that MONTHS since onset will affect MANAGE, which in turn will affect PAIN and FUNCTION, that PAIN will affect FUNCTION and ACTIVITY and that FUNCTION will also affect ACTIVITY. All of the effects, with the exception of MONTHS → MANAGE and PAIN → FUNCTION, are predicted to be negative. The path model is tested using the AMOS package.

Outcomes

Standardized beta coefficients are generated for all paths and R^2 values for all endogenous variables (i.e., those with arrows pointing at them). The output includes a path diagram showing the computed values and a table showing values on a range of goodness of fit indices. These values are interpreted by comparison with equivalent values on several alternative plausible models. For these data, the proposed model appears to have a reasonable fit with the covariance matrix and its fit is superior to any of the plausible alternative models that were tested. We conclude that the proposed model has merit and further research aimed at refining it is justified.

Alternative variables for use in SPSS
The full dataset, med.path2.sav, can be found on the book website

Variable	Psychology	Medicine
Principal DV	SCHISM Intention to leave C of E	ACTIVITY Reduction in activity with CFS
Exogenous variable (can only be an IV)	CHANGE C of E identity change	MONTHS Months since onset of CFS
Endogenous variables (can act as a DV)	SUBVERT Extent of subversion of identity of C of E	MANAGE Extent to which illness is managed
	VOICE Ability to voice dissent	PAIN Amount of pain experienced
	ENTITATI Perception of C of E as an entity	FUNCTION Loss of physical and cognitive functions

Reporting results

It is usual to include a description of what has been done, together with an output path diagram for the proposed model and, preferably, diagrams for competing models that have been tested. As indicated above, it is usual to provide several indices of goodness of fit, and there may also be a summary of direct and indirect effects. A report of the path analysis might go something like this:

The AMOS graphics program was used to construct an input path diagram representing the causal model linking the variables CHANGE, SUBVERT, VOICE, ENTITATI and SCHISM, as described in the Method section. Data were entered for 211 cases (again, as described in the Method section) and standardized beta coefficients were generated for all paths and R^2 values for all endogenous variables. The output path diagram showing the computed values is in Figure A (*this would be a copy of the diagram in AMOS Screen 7.3*). The goodness of fit given by chi square was $\chi^2 = 10.5$, $df = 4$, $p = .033$. Because the chi square value increases rapidly with sample size, the obtained value does not necessarily indicate a bad fit. Indeed, some other goodness of fit indices suggested that the model fit was good. Values greater than .95 for NFI and CFI are considered indicative of a good fit (*give reference*). The obtained values were .996 and .998, respectively. A value less than .10 for RMSEA is considered a reasonable fit (*give reference*) and the obtained value was .09 (but with a CI of .02 to .16). The fits of three competing models shown in Figure B (*we have not reproduced these*) were also tested and were found to be inferior to the proposed model on all indices (*give details*). The AIC index is particularly useful for comparing models that are evaluated using the same data, the model with the lowest value being considered the best fit (*give reference*). The AIC value for the proposed model was 42.50 and values for the other three models were (*give values*). So, the proposed model appears to have a reasonable fit with the covariance matrix and its fit is superior to any of the theoretically plausible alternatives that were considered.

Reference

Sani, F., & Todman, J. (2002). Should we stay or should we go? A social psychological model of schisms in groups. *Personality and Social Psychology Bulletin*, *28*(12), 1647–1655.

8 Factor analysis

Introduction

Exploratory factor analysis (EFA)

Factor analysis was first considered by early twentieth century psychologists who were attempting to understand, define and measure intelligence. If we have a large set of measurements on each of our cases, the idea of factor analysis is to explain these measurements in terms of a smaller number of unobservable factors. So, for instance, a set of 20 or so scores on various tasks may be explainable in terms of two unobservable abilities (*latent factors*): 'verbal intelligence' and 'spatial intelligence'. If this were so, we would expect that there would be large correlations among the scores on those tasks that depend on verbal intelligence and also large correlations among the scores on those tasks that depend on spatial intelligence, but much smaller correlations between scores on tasks from the different groups. If this idea is correct, then we would have a good approximation to the original data if we had the scores for each case just on the two factors, and instead of dealing with a problem with 20 variables we would retain most of the information while dealing with only two. So, *exploratory factor analysis* (EFA) may help in two ways: by giving some insight into the structure of our dataset and also by reducing its dimensionality.

Confirmatory factor analysis (CFA)

There is, however, another approach to factor analysis. This is known as *confirmatory factor analysis* (CFA). This was the original approach developed by Spearman early in the previous century, in his endeavour to confirm his so-called two-factor theory of intelligence. We say 'so-called' because he really only specified one underlying factor: general intelligence (*g*). The second 'factor' was actually a large number of factors specific to each particular test in a battery of tests used to measure intelligence, each specific factor being unique to a single test. He proposed a criterion for testing his model (referred to as *tetrad equalities*, which we will not describe here) that, if met, would imply a correlation matrix from which only one factor could be extracted.

Q Method

In contrast to the above methods, which look for correlations among the variables across the subjects, the Q method looks for correlations among the subjects across the variables. It is usually used to assess subjects' viewpoints. We do not consider this method here.

Measurement models and structural models

Despite this initial emphasis on CFA, much of the subsequent development of factor analysis tended to be along EFA lines. CFA began to reappear with the development of a maximum likelihood chi-square goodness of fit test of the difference between an original correlation matrix and a matrix reproduced from a factor analysis solution. It became possible to hypothesize a theoretical factor structure and to test it against a structure produced by factor analysis. This led to the development of *structural equation modelling* programs, such as LISREL (Linear Structural Relations) and EQS (Structural Equations Program), which could be used to test models involving influences among latent variables (factors) and measured variables. Structural equation modelling has two components: a *measurement model* that relates measured variables to factors and a *structural model* that concerns hypothesized relationships among the constructs. This chapter will be concerned with the measurement model (i.e., CFA) after we have dealt with EFA. We deal with EFA first because it can be carried out within SPSS, whereas CFA requires a dedicated program for the analysis. Although LISREL and EQS are well established, we have chosen to demonstrate CFA with AMOS, which was introduced in the previous chapter on path analysis.

One version of the structural model is path analysis, discussed in the last chapter. At the end of this chapter we give a brief introduction to full structural equation modelling, for which we will again use AMOS as our demonstration tool. Full structural equation modelling involves a combination of CFA and structural modelling (of which path analysis is an example), so this chapter and the previous one are very closely related.

Exploratory factor analysis (EFA)

If you have measurements on a number of variables that are all thought to be related to a construct (a latent variable that cannot be directly measured), you may want to know whether responses to the variables can be grouped together to provide a better indicator of the construct than any of the variables considered singly. On the other hand, you may like to know whether there are subgroups of the variables that provide good indicators of different aspects, or components, of the broad concept.

As noted earlier, EFA can be thought of as a data reduction technique. The question we ask is whether we can use factors (latent variables) to represent the measured variables, and how many of them are needed to avoid losing too much information.

An intuitive explication: From correlation matrix to factor matrix

We will use some very simple fabricated data to try to convey the essence of what factor analysis does. We begin with a *correlation matrix* (the correlations among a set of variables). One such matrix, representing the correlations among scores of a sample of students on tests for a range of academic subjects, is shown in Table 8.1(a). From this a *factor matrix*, shown in Table 8.1(b), is obtained (we explain how below). This shows the correlations of each test with each of two factors that have been extracted. These correlations are usually referred to as *loadings* of the tests on the factors. Note that all

Table 8.1 Examples of (a) a correlation matrix, (b) an unrotated factor matrix and (c) a rotated factor matrix

(a) Correlation matrix

	English	French	History	Physics	Chemistry
English	1.00				
French	.63	1.00			
History	.65	.45	1.00		
Physics	.31	.27	.10	1.00	
Chemistry	.20	.18	.05	.55	1.00

(b) Unrotated factor matrix

	Factor 1	Factor 2
English	.90	−.27
French	.66	−.13
History	.61	−.35
Physics	.52	.62
Chemistry	.39	.56

(c) Rotated factor matrix

	Factor 1	Factor 2
English	.92	.20
French	.64	.21
History	.71	−.01
Physics	.16	.79
Chemistry	.07	.68

of the tests have positive loadings on the first factor and a mix of positive and negative loadings on the second factor. The first factor can be thought of as a general factor; the loadings on it indicate the extent to which all of the tests are measuring aspects of the same underlying (latent) construct, maybe academic ability in this case.

An intuitive explication: Rotating the factor matrix

Next, we have the option of *rotating* the factor matrix. This procedure is best explained using a graphical representation of the tests and factors. We will do this later, but for the moment we want to focus on the result of performing a rotation. A *rotated factor matrix* is shown in Table 8.1(c). For the rotated version of the factors, we see that the first three tests have high loadings on factor 1 and low loadings on factor 2. Similarly, the last two tests have high loadings on factor 2 and low loadings on factor 1. We might be inclined to interpret factor 1 as the latent construct, 'language (or humanities) ability', because that is what the tests that load on the factor seem to have in common, and we might think it reasonable to label factor 2 as 'science ability'.

A factor matrix such as that in Table 8.1(b) is obtained using an *iterative process*. First, some simple rule is used to generate a first attempt at a factor matrix, and this matrix is then used to reconstruct the correlation matrix (remember that the factor matrix is supposed to contain an abbreviated summary of the information in the correlation matrix). The original and reconstructed correlation matrices are then compared and changes are made to the factor matrix to reduce the discrepancy between the two correlation matrices. The modified factor matrix is again used to reconstruct the correlation matrix, the original and newly reconstructed correlation matrices are compared and the factor matrix is further modified to reduce the discrepancy. Iterations of this procedure are continued until the discrepancy cannot be reduced any further.

An intuitive explication: Reconstructing the correlation matrix

As an example of using a factor matrix to reconstruct the correlation matrix from which it was derived, consider the loadings of English and French on the first and second factors in Table 8.1(b). If the loadings of English and French on factor 1 are multiplied together (.90 × .66 = .59) and the same is done for the loadings of English and French on factor 2 (−.27 × −.13 = .04), and the two products are added together (.59 + .04 = .63), we end up with the original correlation between English and French (.63). All of the other correlations can be reconstructed in the same way. In this artificial example, the correlation matrix was constructed to fit perfectly a model comprising two independent (*orthogonal*) factors, so it is possible to get a perfect reconstruction of the correlation matrix from loadings on the two factors. With real data this would not be obtainable, as some information is always lost in the move from correlation matrix to factor matrix. This is why an iterative procedure is needed to move, by successively improving approximations, to the best reconstruction that is possible.

An intuitive explication: Theoretical interpretation of a rotated solution

At this point, we can note that there is an infinite number of mathematically equivalent factor matrix solutions that would produce an equally good reconstruction of the correlation matrix. The solution in Table 8.1(b) is simply the one that assigns as much of the variance as possible to factor 1. The rotated solution in Table 8.1(c) is produced by one of an infinite number of possible rotations of the factor axes. In this case, it is the solution that preserves orthogonality (independence) between the factors and comes as close as possible to producing a factor matrix in which each test has a high loading on one factor only. This is referred to as *rotation to simple structure*.

The idea is that if a small number of factors underlie the scores on the measured variables, then you would expect to find that some of the variables are measuring aspects of one of the factors, other variables are measuring aspects of another factor, and so on. In this case the data would have a simpler structure than that suggested by the number of measured variables. In our example we have five measured variables, but just two factors are sufficient to explain all the correlations in their correlation matrix. If a structure like this can be found in a complex dataset, then it immediately becomes more understandable. This is the motivation for looking for a simple structure, but of course we may not find it. Our example has been constructed to have a simple structure so that you can see how it works in a simple case. The factors in Table 8.1(c) are often referred to as group factors, because they emphasize the group structure of the tests and their correlations (a humanities group and a science group). You might like to carry out for the rotated factor solution the same reconstruction of the English/French correlation that we demonstrated for the unrotated factor matrix. You will find that the sum of the products of the English and French loadings again comes to .63, as would be the case for any of the other possible factor solutions. The reason for our interest in the two particular solutions in Tables 8.1(b) and 8.1(c) is their theoretical interpretability.

An intuitive explication: Factor scores and factor means

Although the factors cannot be measured directly, *factor scores* can be estimated as weighted combinations of the variable loadings on each factor. These factor scores are sometimes used in subsequent analyses. An alternative to factor scores is to use *factor means*, which are calculated using the mean of scores on variables that have high loadings (above some criterion such as .5) on a factor. *Factor scores* have the merit of using all of the available information to provide values for scores on the factors, but they include a good deal of information that is attributable to chance. Factor means have the merit of only using the variables that contribute substantially to a factor.

A graphical representation of initial and rotated factor solutions

As we indicated earlier, the concept of factor rotation may be clarified by means of a graphical representation (Figure 8.1 overleaf). We can represent the tests as points in two-dimensional space by using their unrotated loadings on the two factors as coordinates with respect to two axes at right angles (the factor axes). The tests are represented in this way in Figure 8.1(a). Note that factor 1 goes through the 'centre of gravity' of the tests, which all have positive loadings on the factor, and there are positive and negative loadings on factor 2. In the figure, we show how the loadings for two of the tests (History and Chemistry) relate to the factor axes.

In Figure 8.1(b), we show the points representing the tests in the same positions but their coordinates are now those for the rotated solution. In other words, the factor axes have moved (rotated) so that they are closer to the two clusters of variables. The statistical effect of the rotation is generally to increase the high loadings and reduce the low ones. The factors are still at right angles, therefore orthogonal. It is possible, however, to allow the factor axes to be at an oblique angle (less than 90°), therefore non-orthogonal, as in Figure 8.1(c). This *oblique rotation* has the merit of letting the factor axes pass through the middle of each cluster of tests, but at the cost of the factors themselves being correlated.

EFA: The Wechsler Adult Intelligent Scale (WAIS) data

We will use data relating to the construct of intelligence for our example of EFA. Specifically, we will use data from the administration of the Wechsler Adult Intelligence Scale (WAIS) to a sample of psychology students. The WAIS is supposed to provide a measure of verbal intelligence based on six subtests, a measure of non-verbal intelligence (or performance) based on five subtests and a measure of global intelligence based on all eleven subtests. The first six subtests (information, digit span, vocabulary, arithmetic, comprehension and similarities) comprise the *verbal intelligence* scale. The last five subtests (picture completion, picture arrangement, block design, object assembly and digit symbol) make up the *non-verbal intelligence* (or *performance*) scale. In this case we have a good idea of what the relationships among the variables (subtests) ought to be like, but that does not stop us from doing an exploratory analysis and seeing what emerges. We will use CFA to analyse the same data later.

(a) Unrotated factor solution

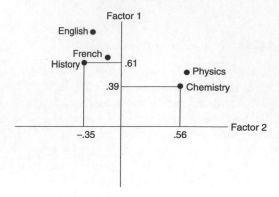

(b) Rotated orthogonal factor solution

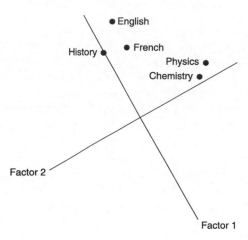

(c) Oblique rotated factor solution

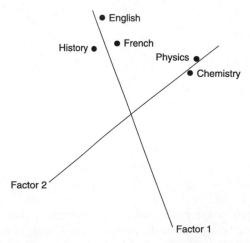

Figure 8.1 Unrotated, rotated orthogonal and oblique rotated factor solutions to the academic test data.

EFA: Missing values

Factor analysis is a large sample technique, and Tabachnick and Fidell (2007, p. 613) again give a rule of thumb: 'it is comforting to have at least 300 cases for a factor analysis'. Because the dataset will be large, it is almost certain that the problem of missing values will have to be addressed. The factor analysis **Options** dialog box allows you three choices for dealing with any missing values. The default is to exclude any cases with missing values (exclude cases listwise). The next option is to calculate each correlation using all data available for the two variables in that correlation (exclude cases pairwise). Finally, a missing observation can be replaced with the mean of the available observations on that variable (replace with mean). These choices were discussed briefly in the section on 'Missing data' in Chapter 3. We just remind you here that while the second option does make use of all available data, internal constraints on the correlation matrix may be breached if the correlations are not all calculated on the same set of cases. As always, it is worth investing a lot of effort to reduce missing data to an absolute minimum. Our example dataset for this chapter is rather small (only 128 cases) but at least there are no missing observations.

The first few cases of the data are shown in Table 8.2. The full dataset of 128 cases (psy.factor.sav) is available on the book website.

Table 8.2 The first few cases of the WAIS subtest scores of a sample of 128 psychology students (the full dataset can be found as psy.factor.sav on the website)

INFORM	DIGSPAN	VOCAB	ARITH	COMPREH	SIMIL	PICCOMP	PICARRAN	BLOCK	OBJASSEM	DIGSYM
20	16	52	10	24	23	19	20	23	29	67
24	16	52	7	27	16	16	15	31	33	59
19	21	57	18	22	23	16	19	42	40	61
24	21	62	12	31	25	17	17	36	36	77
29	18	62	14	26	27	15	20	33	29	88
18	19	51	15	29	23	19	20	50	37	54
19	27	61	12	19	24	17	11	38	21	72

EFA: Requesting the factor analysis in SPSS

Enter the data into SPSS in 11 columns as in Table 8.2. Select **Analyze**, then **Data Reduction**, then **Factor**. Use the arrow to move all 11 subtests into the **Variables** box. Ignore the **Selection Variable** box, which you could use if you wanted to analyse a subset of cases. The main dialog box for factor analysis then looks like that in SPSS Dialog Box 8.1.

If you click on **Descriptives**, you will see that **Initial solution** in the **Statistics** group has a tick against it. This will give you initial eigenvalues, communalities (we will explain what these are shortly) and the percentage of variance explained by each factor. You might like to look at the eigenvalues and proportions of variance, so leave the tick on. You could also request **Univariate descriptives**, but we do not need them so we will not bother. In the **Correlation Matrix** group are a number of diagnostic statistics. We will just select **KMO** and **Bartlett's test of sphericity** as examples. The KMO (Kaiser-Meyer-Olkin) index is a measure of sampling adequacy and the sphericity

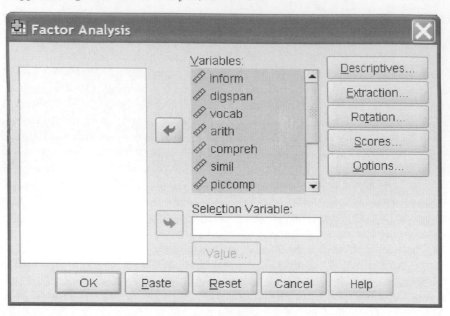

SPSS Dialog Box 8.1 The main dialog box for factor analysis.

statistic tests whether the correlations among variables are too low for the factor model to be appropriate. The other diagnostics are clearly explained in Tabachnick and Fidell (2007) (see 'Reference' at the end of the chapter and 'Further reading' at the end of the book). The entries in this dialog box are straightforward so it is not reproduced here.

If you click on **Extraction** (see SPSS Dialog Box 8.2), you will see that the default for extracting factors is the **Principal components** method. Strictly speaking, the principal components method is not factor analysis, in that it uses all of the variance, including error variance, whereas factor analysis excludes the error variance by obtaining *estimates* of *communalities* of the variables (a communality is the proportion of variance accounted for by a factor in a factor analysis). However, principal components is the method most commonly used in the analysis of psychological data, and we will use it here. Also, as it is commonly referred to as a method of factor analysis in the psychology literature, we will follow that practice. So, we will accept the default, **Principal components**, as our method of factor extraction. In the **Analyze** group, **Correlation matrix** has been selected and that is what we will use. The program will automatically generate a correlation matrix from the data. In the **Display** group, you will see that **Unrotated factor solution** is ticked. Add a tick against **Scree plot**. In the **Extract** group, the number '1' has been entered against **Eigenvalues over**. In principal components analysis, it is possible to extract as many factors as there are variables. That would not, however, involve any reduction of the data, and it is normal to set some criterion for the number of factors that are extracted. The sum of the squared loadings of the variables on a factor is known as the *eigenvalue* (or latent root) of the factor. Dividing the eigenvalue by the number of variables gives the proportion of variance explained by the factor. The higher the eigenvalue, the higher the proportion of variance explained by the factor, so it is possible to set a criterion eigenvalue for the acceptance of a factor

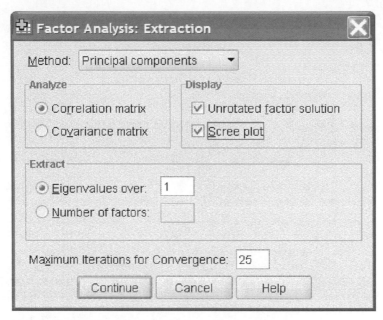

SPSS Dialog Box 8.2 Extracting factors from a correlation matrix.

as being important enough to consider. By convention, the usual criterion value is 1. The value of **Eigenvalue over** can be changed to allow more or fewer factors to be extracted, or you can decide on the number of factors you want to be extracted by clicking on the **Number of factors** button and entering the desired number in the box. At the bottom of the dialog box, the **Maximum Number of Iterations** is set at 25. This simply means that the analysis will stop after 25 iterations of the procedure to generate successive approximations to the best possible factor solution. This number can be increased, but we will leave it as it is. So the box now looks as in SPSS Dialog Box 8.2. Click **Continue**.

Next, click **Rotation** to get SPSS Dialog Box 8.3. You will see that the default **Method** is **None**. We want a rotated solution as well as an unrotated one and the most usual method for an orthogonal rotation is **Varimax**. Click that button. If we had wanted an oblique solution, we probably would have clicked **Direct Oblimin** and retained the default value of **Delta** = zero. In the **Display** group, **Rotated solution** has been ticked, which is what we want. If you love complex graphics, you can tick **Loading plot(s)** to see a three-dimensional plot of the rotated factor loadings, but we will not do that. At the bottom, the **Maximum Iterations for Convergence** on the best obtainable rotated solution is set at 25. We will accept that value. The box now appears as shown. Click **Continue** again.

If we wanted to make use of factor scores, we could click on **Scores** and **Save as variables**. This would result in a new column for each factor being produced in the datasheet. We do not wish to save the factor scores so we do not reproduce the dialog box here.

Click on **Options**. If you have any missing data, refer to our discussion at the start of the preceding section (Missing values) and make the best choice you can for dealing with the problem. In our example dataset we do not have any missing data, so we ignore

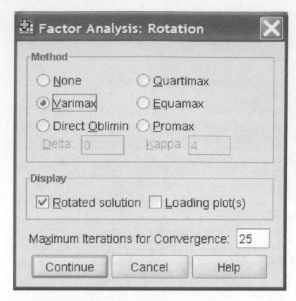

SPSS Dialog Box 8.3 Rotating the factors.

the **Missing Values** box. In the **Coefficient Display Format** box, you can, if you wish, put ticks against **Sorted by size** and/or **Suppress absolute values less than**. The former will result in variables that load on the same factor being located together in successive rows of the rotated factor matrix, and the latter will eliminate loadings below some threshold from both of the factor matrices. The default for the threshold value is **.1**, but if you wanted to suppress low loadings in the output you would probably choose a value closer to .5 to get an uncluttered view of the factor structure. Of course you can choose a value in between (.3 is often used): it is a trade-off between losing some information and ease of interpretation of the results. The higher the value chosen, the fewer results are displayed, making the results easier to interpret, but you run the risk of missing something interesting just below the threshold. We will not select either of these options on this occasion and we do not reproduce the dialog box here. Click on **Continue** to close any secondary dialog box that is open, then click on **OK** in the main dialog box to run the analysis.

EFA: Understanding the diagnostic output

The first table in the output (see SPSS Output 8.1) contains the diagnostics we requested. For the KMO index of sampling adequacy, values above .6 are required for good factor analysis. Our value of .69 is satisfactory. We need a significant value for Bartlett's test of sphericity and we have that. However, it is notoriously sensitive to sample size and is likely to be significant even when correlations are substantial. Consequently, this test is only recommended (e.g., by Tabachnick and Fidell – see 'Further reading') when there are fewer than about five cases per variable. We have about 11 cases per variable, so it is of no help to us here.

KMO and Bartlett's Test

Kaiser-Meyer-Olkin Measure of Sampling Adequacy.		.687
Bartlett's Test of Sphericity	Approx. Chi-Square	330.640
	df	55.000
	Sig.	.000

Total Variance Explained

Component	Initial Eigenvalues			Extraction Sums of Squared Loadings			Rotation Sums of Squared Loadings		
	Total	% of Variance	Cumulative %	Total	% of Variance	Cumulative %	Total	% of Variance	Cumulative %
1	3.379	30.720	30.720	3.379	30.720	30.720	2.388	21.705	21.705
2	1.483	13.480	44.200	1.483	13.480	44.200	2.135	19.406	41.111
3	1.251	11.369	55.569	1.251	11.369	55.569	1.590	14.458	55.569
4	0.980	8.913	64.482						
5	0.769	6.989	71.471						
6	0.733	6.664	78.136						
7	0.640	5.822	83.957						
8	0.622	5.656	89.614						
9	0.528	4.803	94.417						
10	0.352	3.199	97.616						
11	0.262	2.384	100.000						

Extraction Method: Principal Component Analysis.

Scree Plot

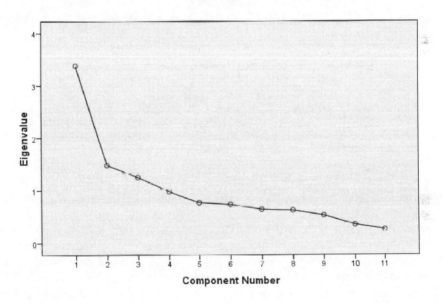

SPSS Output 8.1 Selected parts of the factor analysis output. (*Continued overleaf*)

EFA: Understanding the initial factor solution

The next table gives communalities (since this is principal components analysis, the *actual* proportion of variance accounted for by the factors), which you can ignore, so we do not reproduce that table here. Next comes the table with initial eigenvalues and proportions of variance explained by each factor. You will see that only the first three factors have eigenvalues greater than 1. As '1' was our criterion for retention of a factor,

Component Matrix[a]

	Component		
	1	2	3
inform	.605	-.247	-.219
digspan	.320	-.471	.559
vocab	.700	-.300	-.279
arith	.584	-.199	.564
compreh	.610	-.059	-.479
simil	.469	-.435	-.231
piccomp	.670	.132	-.106
picarran	.484	.350	.333
block	.638	.287	.285
objassem	.587	.461	-.059
digsym	.232	.665	-.074

Extraction Method: Principal Component Analysis.

a. 3 components extracted.

Rotated Component Matrix[a]

	Component		
	1	2	3
inform	.659	.124	.160
digspan	.110	-.085	.785
vocab	.783	.127	.170
arith	.185	.286	.763
compreh	.731	.230	-.135
simil	.646	-.107	.185
piccomp	.486	.480	.102
picarran	.016	.620	.289
block	.180	.652	.336
objassem	.264	.699	-.041
digsym	-.066	.649	-.277

Extraction Method: Principal Component Analysis.
Rotation Method: Varimax with Kaiser Normalization.

a. Rotation converged in 5 iterations.

SPSS Output 8.1 (Continued)

this tells us that only the first three factors to be extracted are in the factor solution. Looking at the proportions of variance, we see that the bulk of the variance attributable to the retained factors was explained by the first (general) factor (30.7% out of 55.6%) in the initial solution, whereas the variance was more evenly distributed in the rotated solution (21.7%, 19.4% and 14.5%, respectively). This is always the case. Next comes the scree plot. What we are looking for here is an indication of how many factors should be retained. The eigenvalue criterion tells us that three factors should be retained, but the criterion of 'greater than one' is somewhat arbitrary, and the scree plot might suggest a different number. A sudden change in the slope is often a useful guide. In our plot, this discontinuity seems to occur at two factors rather than three, and we might therefore consider whether a two-factor solution might be preferable. In the end, though, we should generally make the decision on the basis of how many factors are theoretically interpretable. There is little point in retaining factors that do not make sense.

The next table presents the loadings of variables on the factors (or *components*, because we used the principal components method of extraction) for the initial (unrotated) solution. We just note that all of the variables have positive loadings on the first (general) factor, which suggests that an intelligence score based on all 11 subtests might be reasonable. On the other hand, some of the loadings are quite modest, so we should not anticipate that the measure of general intelligence would be highly reliable.

EFA: Understanding the rotated factor solution

Next comes the rotated factor (or component) matrix. We see that the effect of the rotation is, as usual, to increase the size of high loadings and reduce the size of low loadings. The first two factors seem readily interpretable as verbal intelligence, with high loadings of information, vocabulary, comprehension and similarities. There is also a relatively high loading (.49) of picture completion on the first factor, which was not anticipated. The second factor seems to be quite clearly identifiable as non-verbal intelligence (or performance), with high loadings of picture arrangement, block design, object assembly and digit symbol. Picture completion, which is supposed to belong with this group of subtests, also has a moderately high loading (.48) on this factor. The fact that this test has very similar high loadings on two factors is an indication of a lack of *factor purity*. A solution is said to have factor purity when each test loads highly on just one factor, so that the factors are clearly defined by the groupings of tests that load on them. The situation is further complicated by the emergence of a third factor. This has high loadings on two subtests: digit span and arithmetic. Both of these tests involve working with numbers, so perhaps the third factor represents something like numerical ability, which might be distinct from both verbal intelligence and performance. Remember that, even though we had some expectations about the factor solution, we are engaged in exploratory factor analysis so our findings (and their interpretations) have the status of hypotheses, not model confirmation.

Before we leave our discussion of the rotated factor solution, we show in SPSS Output 8.2 a version of the rotated factor matrix that was obtained when the **Options** button in the main dialog box was clicked and ticks were put against **Sorted by size** and **Suppress absolute values less than** in the **Coefficient Display Format** box, and the default value of minimum size was changed from .1 to .5. You can see that these options make it easier to see the structure of the solution.

Rotated Component Matrix[a]

	Component		
	1	2	3
vocab	.783		
compreh	.731		
inform	.659		
simil	.646		
piccomp			
objassem		.699	
block		.652	
digsym		.649	
picarran		.620	
digspan			.785
arith			.763

Extraction Method: Principal Component Analysis.
Rotation Method: Varimax with Kaiser Normalization.

a. Rotation converged in 5 iterations.

SPSS Output 8.2 Rotated factor matrix, sorted and with loadings below .5 suppressed.

Example Box 8.1

EFA: An alternative medical example for the WAIS data set

The full analysis for this example can be found at www.psypress.com/ multivariate-analysis/medical-examples (click on Chapter 8).

For this example we use the same (real) WAIS data but we have fabricated a medical context for it, so the results for this example do not derive from real medical research. It is proposed to offer all adults between the ages of 40 and 75 years a free medical check-up accompanied by advice about maintaining good health. A Positive Health Inventory (PHI) is being developed in order to monitor the effectiveness of the free check-up program. The PHI comprises 11 subtests, 6 of which are biomedical indicators (e.g., blood counts) of healthy function. We may suppose that the subtests concern healthy function of lungs, muscular system, liver, skeletal system, kidneys and heart. The remaining five subtests are functional measures of health. We may suppose that these are scores on a step test, a stamina test, a stretch test, a blow test and a urine flow test. We have a good idea of what the relationship among variables should be like in a healthy population, but it is acceptable to do an exploratory factor analysis to see what emerges. A principal components analysis with varimax rotation is carried out, followed by reliability checks on the factor scales.

Outcomes

With an eigenvalue criterion set at 1 three factors emerge, accounting for 56.6% of the variance, though a scree plot suggests that a two-factor solution accounting for 41.1% of the variance could be considered. The first (general) factor in the unrotated solution accounts for 30.7% of the variance. In the rotated solution, the three factors account for 21.7%, 19.4% and 14.5% of the variance, respectively. As all of the variables have positive loadings on the first (general) factor, a positive health index based on all 11 subscales might be reasonable. On the other hand, some of the loadings are quite low, so a global measure of positive health may not have high reliability. In the rotated solution, the first two factors are readily interpretable as biomedical health and performance health subscales, though there is a relatively high loading of the step test on the biomedical factor as well as on the performance factor. The third factor, with high loadings of the muscular and skeletal biomedical indicators, may represent something like muscular/skeletal health, and be distinct from both of the first two factors. The relatively high loadings of the stamina and stretch tests on the third factor seem consistent with this interpretation. The reliability of the full scale is $\alpha = .64$, though this increases to .74 if the urine flow test is removed. The reliability of the biomedical subscale is $\alpha = .69$ and the reliability of the performance subscale is $\alpha = .44$ (.54 with removal of the urine flow test). The relatively low reliabilities for the full scale and the subscales suggest that the most useful feature of the PHI may be the clinical identification of patterns of subtest scores.

Alternative variables for use in SPSS
The full dataset, med.factor.sav, can be found on the book website

Subtest variable	Psychology	Medicine
Subscale 1	Verbal tests	Biomedical indicators
Test 1	INFORM (information)	LUNG (lung function)
Test 2	DIGSPAN (digit span)	MUSCLE (muscular system)
Test 3	VOCAB (vocabulary)	LIVER (liver function)
Test 4	ARITH (arithmetic)	SKELETON (skeletal system)
Test 5	COMPREH (comprehension)	KIDNEYS (kidney function)
Test 6	SIMIL (similarities)	HEART (heart function)
Subscale 2	Performance (non-verbal) tests	Medical performance tests
Test 1	PICCOMP (picture completion)	STEP (step test)
Test 2	PICARRAN (picture arrangement)	STAMINA (stamina test)
Test 3	BLOCK (block design)	STRETCH (stretch test)
Test 4	OBJASSEM (object assembly)	BLOW (blow test)
Test 5	DIGSYM (digit symbol)	URINE (urine flow test)

The reliability of factor scales: Internal consistency of scales

Many real correlation matrices may have no clear factor solution. When a factor solution is obtained, we need to consider how confident we can be about using it to measure factors. As far as the meaning of the factors is concerned, it is a matter of subjective theoretical judgement, about which there may be considerable disagreement. We can, however, resolve the statistical question of the *reliability* of factors. Even though we cannot be certain of the meaning of a factor, it is worth knowing whether a scale defined by factor loadings really is measuring a unitary construct. The usual index of the *internal consistency* of a scale (all of the items or tests that load on the factor are tapping into the same construct) is Cronbach's *coefficient alpha*. This may be thought of as the average of all of the possible split-half reliabilities of the items or tests that are taken to be indicators of the construct. Values of alpha range from zero to 1 and generally values over .8 are required for the claim to be made that a scale has high internal consistency.

Requesting a reliability analysis in SPSS

According to our factor analysis, there are several scales that we might be interested in. First, there is the presumed general intelligence scale, the first factor in the unrotated solution. We will begin with the assumption that all of the subtests contribute to this scale, though we may entertain some doubts about the contributions of the digit symbol test (loading = .23) and the digit span test (loading = .32). To obtain Cronbach's alpha for this scale, click on **Analyze**, then **Scale**, then **Reliability Analysis**. Use the arrow to move all of the subtests into the **Items** box. You will see that **Alpha** is the default in the **Model** box and that is what we want. You can ignore **Scale label** unless you want to give a name to the scale. This dialog box is straightforward and is not shown here.

Click on **Statistics** and put a tick against **Scale if item deleted**. There are a lot of other options in this dialog box, but we do not need any others and we have not shown it here. Click **Continue** and **OK** for the analysis.

Understanding the reliability analysis for the full scale

The first thing in the output is a Case Processing Summary table, which we do not reproduce here. This is followed by the Reliability Statistics table (see SPSS Output 8.3), which tells us that alpha = .64, based on all 11 subtests. This value is a bit low and we wonder whether removal of one or more subtests might improve the internal consistency of those remaining. The final table, Item-Total Statistics (see SPSS Output 8.3), is able to help us with that question. Looking in the final column of the table, we see that if the digit symbol test were deleted the value of alpha would increase to .74. If you remove DIGSYM from the variables in the **Items** box of main dialog box and re-run the analysis, you will find that the new alpha is indeed .74. If you also look at the new Item-Total Statistics box (which we do not reproduce here), you will discover that there are no further improvements to be made by removal of any other variables, so alpha = .74 is the best we are going to get for the general intelligence scale.

Reliability Statistics

Cronbach's Alpha	N of Items
.642	11

Item-Total Statistics

	Scale Mean if Item Deleted	Scale Variance if Item Deleted	Corrected Item-Total Correlation	Cronbach's Alpha if Item Deleted
inform	306.50	789.055	.427	.602
digspan	307.64	861.193	.159	.641
vocab	271.77	685.189	.452	.582
arith	313.59	834.243	.423	.615
compreh	300.82	803.755	.454	.604
simil	303.28	837.054	.257	.628
piccomp	310.29	832.412	.543	.610
picarran	310.59	850.338	.380	.622
block	287.65	675.316	.444	.584
objassem	292.92	784.718	.499	.595
digsym	259.55	673.320	.130	.743

SPSS Output 8.3 Main output from reliability analysis.

Understanding the reliability analyses for the group scales

You can repeat the reliability analysis for the verbal and performance groupings of tests (they are shown clearly in SPSS Output 8.2). We will just summarize the results here. For the four tests comprising the verbal scale, alpha = .69 and the reliability would not be improved by removal of any of the tests. For the four tests comprising the performance scale, alpha = .44, which can be increased to .54 by removal of the digit symbol subtest. These values do not give us confidence in the internal consistency of the scales. However, perhaps the rather modest alpha values for all three scales might have been expected given that the set of subtests was supposed to be doing two different things:

providing a general measure of intelligence and measures of two (probably related) components of intelligence. High reliability of the general scale would mean that the components were not being well separated. Conversely, high reliabilities for the component scales would mean that the general measure might be less satisfactory.

An alternative index of reliability: Coefficient theta

There is another index of reliability (internal consistency) of the scale based on the first (general) factor to be extracted. This is coefficient theta, which is closely related to coefficient alpha. This index takes advantage of the fact that the first factor to be extracted accounts for the largest proportion of the variance. It is not provided in SPSS, but it is easily calculated using the formula:

$$\theta = \left(\frac{n}{n-1}\right)\left(1 - \frac{1}{\lambda}\right)$$

where n = number of items in the scale and λ = the first (largest) eigenvalue. The largest eigenvalue for our unrotated solution was 3.38 (see SPSS Output 8.1). For our general intelligence scale, that gives a reliability of $\theta = (11/10)(1 - 1/3.38) = 0.77$, which is approaching respectability.

Confirmatory factor analysis (CFA)

As we indicated at the beginning of the chapter, CFA comprises the measurement modelling component of the broad approach known as structural equation modelling. Path analysis, which represents one approach to the other component, structural modelling, was covered in the last chapter.

CFA: The input diagram for the psychology (WAIS) example

We begin by specifying the measurement model (or models) that we wish to test. The specification is normally in the form of an *input diagram*. In the diagram, hypothesized factors (latent variables) are usually represented by circles or ovals and the measured indicators of the factors are shown as rectangles. We will use the same WAIS data that we used in our EFA and we will propose a two-factor model with the factors verbal intelligence (VERBAL) and performance (PERFORM). There are six indicators of verbal intelligence (the subtests INFORM, COMPREH, ARITH, SIMIL, VOCAB and DIGSPAN) and five indicators of performance (the subtests PICCOMP, PICARRAN, BLOCK, OBJASSEM and DIGSYM). The hypothesized model is shown in Figure 8.2, where c1, c2, . . ., c11 indicate regression coefficients (beta values) for influences of factors on measured indicators. Since the variables are only partly explained by the factors, each variable must have a *residual* (the unexplained part). This is $\sqrt{1 - R^2}$, where R is just the beta value (the correlation between the factor and the variable). AMOS displays R^2 rather than the residual. We denote these R^2 values by r1, r2, etc. The covariance between factors we denote by 'cor'. The straight arrows from factors to measured variables indicate that the factor constructs predict the measured variables. The arrows pointing at the measured variables indicate that 'error' also has an influence on them. The curved two-headed

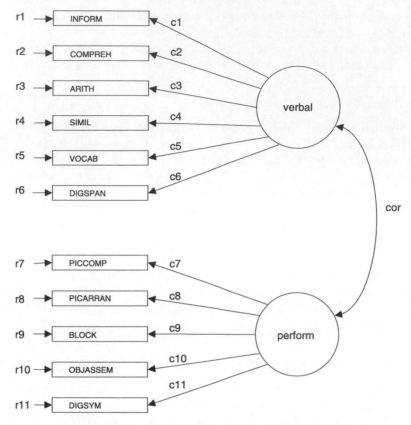

Figure 8.2 Diagram representing a measurement model for the WAIS data.

arrow indicates a hypothesized relationship between the two factors, with no implied direction of effect.

There are two main hypotheses to be considered. We can ask whether a two-factor model with rotation to simple structure (each variable loads on only one of the two factors) fits the data or whether there is a significant covariance between the two factors.

Model identification

At this point, it is sensible to check the identification status of our model. Just as in path analysis, a model is just-identified when the number of data points is equal to the number of parameters to be estimated. The number of data points is the number of variances and covariances, and is given by $k(k + 1)/2$, where k equals the number of observed variables. The number of parameters to be estimated is the number of beta values, correlations and residuals specified in the model. You should refer to the discussion of just-identified, under-identified and over-identified models in the section on 'Model identification' in Chapter 7. In our case, the number of data points is $11(11 + 1)/2 = 66$, and the model requires 23 parameters to be estimated (11 beta values, 1 covariance and 11 residuals). So, our model is over-identified and there will be $66 - 23 = 43$ *df*s when its fit is tested.

Using AMOS to do the CFA: Constructing the input diagram

To begin the confirmatory factor analysis, open AMOS Graphics. The screen will look as in AMOS Screen 7.1 shown in the previous chapter on path analysis. First you need to identify the SPSS datafile to use, so go to **File** on the menu bar, then **Data Files**. Click the **File Name** button and browse to find the file you want (psy.factor.sav). Click **OK** to close the dialog box.

You can begin drawing your input path diagram immediately. We have 11 variables, so you will need to draw 11 rectangles. Draw these using the **Rectangle** and **Copy** icons as described for path analysis.

Next, click on the **Oval** icon (top of the middle column) and draw two ovals to represent the factors. Then add arrows to the diagram by activating the appropriate **Arrow** icon: a single straight arrow for the influences of the factors on the variables (2nd down in the left column) and a two-headed curved arrow for the covariance between the two factors (2nd down in the middle column). The covariance arrow is drawn as a two-headed curved arrow between the two variables that are presumed to be correlated. In each case, click where you want the arrow to start and drag it to where you want it to point. Next, you can give the rectangles variable names (they must match the names used in your SPSS data file) and the ovals factor names. Right click on a rectangle or oval and select **Object Properties** as described in path analysis. Next, activate the **Add a unique variable to an existing variable** icon (2nd down in the right column) and attach R^2 value boxes to the 11 measured variables by clicking on the rectangles. Recall that AMOS enters R^2 into the output path diagram instead of residuals $\sqrt{1 - R^2}$. To position them to the left of the variables, click on each variable seven times. The reason for clicking seven times is to position the unique (residual) variable directly to the left of each variable, which will result in a less cluttered diagram. If you just clicked once, the residual would be located above the variable and that would make the diagram quite confusing because the residual would be competing for space with the arrows from the factors. Each click after the first rotates the variable 45° in a clockwise direction, so it ends up to the left of the variable where there is plenty of space. You can then name these variables. We will call them r1, r2, r3, etc., remembering that each of these labels stands for an R^2 value.

Using AMOS to do the CFA: Constraining parameters

There is one more thing to add to the input diagram. If you tried to run the analysis with the diagram as it is, and then clicked on the **View text** icon (9th down in the middle column) and selected **Notes for Models** from the menu that appears, you would get a message telling you that: 'the model is probably unidentified. In order to achieve identifiability, it will probably be necessary to impose 2 additional constraints.' The theoretical rationale underlying the application of constraints to models is complex and beyond the scope of this book. This issue is discussed in the books listed under 'Further reading' for this chapter at the end of the book. We will just tell you that one reason why constraints are needed is to set a measurement scale (a unit of measurement) for each latent variable, which is of course unknown because it is not directly measured. It is often the case in CFA that additional constraints on one of the regression coefficients (beta values) from each factor to one of its measured variables are required. This is achieved by assigning the value of 1 to the regression coefficient of one of the six arrows from the verbal factor and similarly to one of the five arrows from the performance factor. It should be noted that a *constrained* parameter is not the same as a *fixed* parameter, and the standardized parameter estimates in the output model are not affected by the scaling constraints. The constraints are necessary, though, in order to solve the identification problem. To introduce the constraints that we have described, select one arrow from the verbal factor and right click on it and then on **Object Properties** (a normal left click) in the menu that appears. Click on the **Parameters** tab and enter '1' in the **Regression weight** box and close the dialog box. Repeat this for one of the arrows from the performance factor. You should end up with an input path diagram looking something like that shown in AMOS Screen 8.1. This would be a good time to save your work so far: use **File** and **Save As** from the menu bar in the usual way. The name you choose appears in the lowest box to the right of the tools.

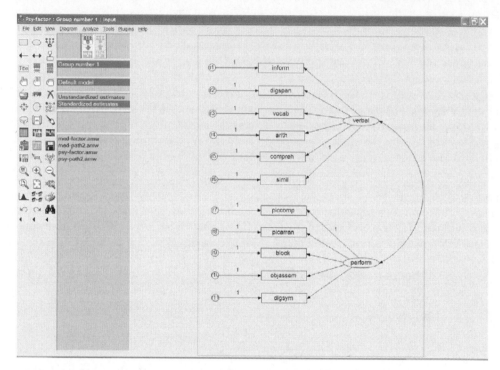

AMOS Screen 8.1 The input path diagram specifying an intelligence model for the WAIS data.

Using AMOS to do the CFA: Requesting output

Now select **Standardized estimates** to the right of the icon columns. Next, click on **View** in the menu bar at the top left, then **Analysis Properties** and the **Output** tab, and put ticks against **Standardized estimates, Squared multiple correlations, Residual moments** and **Modification indices**.

Click the **Calculate estimates** icon (or else use **Analyze** from the menu bar and then **Calculate estimates**). You should see a chi square value appear in the box below **Standardized estimates**. The analysis has been done and you can look at the output path diagram, with beta coefficients and R^2 values entered, by clicking on the large icon at the top left of the screen with the large red arrow pointing upwards. The screen should now look something like that shown in AMOS Screen 8.2.

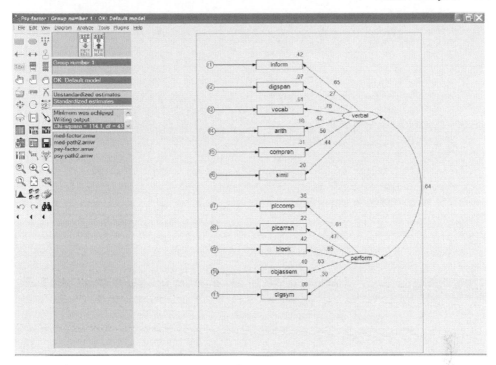

AMOS Screen 8.2 The output path diagram for the WAIS intelligence data.

CFA: Understanding the AMOS output

Remember that if it is unclear to you which values in the output diagram are beta coefficients and which are R^2 values, move the mouse pointer over an arrow and it, and its beta coefficient, will show up red. Likewise, if you move the arrow over a variable box it, and its associated R^2 (labelled r1, etc.) value, will show up red.

We see (on the left of AMOS Screen 8.2) that chi square for goodness of fit is 114.1 with 43 *df*s, which is significant at $p < .001$ (the probability $p = .000$, meaning $p < .001$, is given in the **Text Output**, which we will come to next). Just before we do, we may note that although the chi square fit of the model to the covariance matrix is poor, this may not guarantee that the model is without merit, because chi square very readily reaches significance with large sample sizes even when all other indices indicate a good fit. A very rough guide to the interpretation of the significant chi square is that if the value of chi square is more than double the *df*s it should be taken seriously. In our case, chi square is 114 with 43 *df*s, so the omens are not good.

It is still worth looking at some of the other indices. To see their values, click on the **View Text output** icon (9th down in the centre column). The goodness of fit indices come near the end of the file (select **Model Fit** from the list on the left). The beginning of the goodness of fit summary of models is shown in AMOS Screen 8.3.

For each index, goodness of fit is given for the model being tested (the **Default model**), the **Saturated model** (the just-identified model) and the **Independence model** (all correlations among variables are zero). The fit of the default model will lie somewhere between the extremes represented by the other two models. Evaluation of a model hinges

AMOS Screen 8.3 Goodness of fit indices for the intelligence model.

on its position between the extremes relative to competing models. In other words, a comparative interpretation is called for. First look at the CMIN (the likelihood ratio chi square). We have already noted that its value of 114.1 with $df = 43$ probably indicates a poorly fitting model. The NFI and CFI in the next but one block of indices are probably the most frequently reported. For these indices, values close to 1 are generally considered to indicate a good fit, so our values for NFI (.67) and CFI (.75) look distinctly discouraging. Other batches of indices follow. RMSEA is not on the first screen of fit indices shown in AMOS Screen 8.3, but scroll down and see that the value we get is .11. This index is considered to indicate a bad fit if it is greater than .1, which confirms that our model is unsatisfactory. There is a detailed discussion of the various indices in the AMOS guide (Arbuckle & Wothke, 2003) listed in 'Further reading' at the end of the book.

Example Box 8.2

CFA: The input diagram for the alternative medical (PHI) example

The full analysis for this example can be found at www.psypress.com/multivariate-analysis/medical-examples (click on Chapter 8).

A confirmatory factor analysis (CFA) is carried out using the AMOS package. Once again we use the same (real) WAIS data but we continue with our fabricated medical context, so as with the EFA example, these results are not from a real medical research project. The specification of the model to be tested is as shown in Figure 8.2, except that the six Positive Health Inventory (PHI) biomedical tests (LUNG, MUSCLE, LIVER, SKELETON, KIDNEYS, HEART) are substituted for the six WAIS verbal tests (INFORM, COMPREH, ARITH, SIMIL, VOCAB, DIGSPAN), and the five medical performance tests (STEP, STAMINA, STRETCH, BLOW, URINE) are substituted for the five WAIS performance tests (PICCOMP, PICARRAN, BLOCK, OBJASSEM, DIGSPAN). Also, the PHI subscale label, BIOMED, is substituted for the WAIS sub-scale label, VERBAL (the subscale label, PERFORM, happens to be the same for both examples). One hypothesis that may be considered is that a two-factor model with rotation to simple structure fits the data, and another is that there is a significant covariance between the two factors.

Outcomes

The output diagram containing the beta coefficients and R^2 values is as shown in AMOS Screen 8.2, except that the PHI labels replace the WAIS labels. The chi square for goodness of fit is 114.1, which is highly significant and therefore not encouraging. Other goodness of fit indices confirm that the hypothesis that the model fits the data is not supported. The second hypothesis, that the biomedical and medical performance factors are correlated, is clearly supported ($r = .64$). If a single factor model is proposed, the fit is even less satisfactory, as is the fit for a model proposing no correlation between the two factors. Attempts at post hoc modifications are reported.

Addition of a path from the BIOMED factor to the URINE flow performance test, for which there is a high modification index (MI), does not improve the fit of the model much. However, progressive removal of variables with high residual values until there are only three variables remaining that are predicted by the BIOMED factor (LUNG, LIVER, KIDNEYS) and three predicted by the PERFORM factor (STEP, STAMINA, BLOW) results in a much improved fit (e.g., chi square is reduced to 14.8, which is not significant with 8 dfs), and other indices are in the moderately good fit range. It seems possible that these six variables best define the two PHI factors, and we might consider using them instead of the full 11-variable scale. However, the modified model has not been subjected to CFA and it really has the status of an untested hypothesis and needs to be tested in a CFA with new data.

Alternative variables for use in SPSS
The full dataset, med factor.sav, can be found on the book website

Factors and variables	Psychology	Medicine
Factor 1	VERBAL (verbal tests)	BIOMED (biomedical tests)
Test 1	INFORM (information)	LUNG (lung function)
Test 2	DIGSPAN (digit span)	MUSCLE (muscular system)
Test 3	VOCAB (vocabulary)	LIVER (liver function)
Test 4	ARITH (arithmetic)	SKELETON (skeletal system)
Test 5	COMPREH (comprehension)	KIDNEYS (kidney function)
Test 6	SIMIL (similarities)	HEART (heart function)

Factor 2	PERFORM (non-verbal performance tests)	PERFORM (medical performance tests)
Test 1	PICCOMP (picture completion)	STEP (step test)
Test 2	PICARRAN (picture arrangement)	STAMINA (stamina test)
Test 3	BLOCK (block design)	STRETCH (stretch test)
Test 4	OBJASSEM (object assembly)	BLOW (blow test)
Test 5	DIGSYM (digit symbol)	URINE (urine flow test)

From CFA to EFA: Post hoc modifications to the model

So, the first hypothesis, that the model fits the data, is not supported. The second hypothesis, that the verbal and performance factors are correlated, is clearly supported ($r = .64$; see AMOS Screen 8.2). If variations of the model had been proposed a priori, we would now proceed to test the fit of these models. It is generally desirable to consider alternative, theoretically plausible models at the outset, because structural equation modelling, of which CFA is a part, is best conceived as a comparative procedure. We might well have proposed an alternative model with just one factor, intelligence, influencing all 11 measured variables. If we had, we would have found the fit even less satisfactory (chi square = 137.51 with 44 *df*s; CFI = .68; NFI = .60; RMSEA = .13). On the other hand we might have proposed a model with no correlation between the verbal and performance factors. Not surprisingly, since we know that they are in fact correlated, that model fares even worse (chi square = 143.25 with 44 *df*s; CFI = .66; NFI = .58; RMSEA = .13). We will say a bit more about making direct comparisons between model fits a little later.

At this point, we have come to the end of our strictly confirmatory procedure, but it remains possible, having seen the outcome, to consider some post hoc modifications and to perform factor analyses on them using the same techniques but recognizing that this is exploratory rather than confirmatory in nature: we would be generating hypotheses rather than testing them. For example, we might look at the output and at some diagnostics and, on the basis of what we see, we might try out some variants of our model. Two useful diagnostics that can be requested are *standardized residuals* and *modification indices*. A particularly high standardized residual for the covariance between two variables tells us that the relationship between those variables is not well accounted for by the model. A high value of the modification index (MI) for a relationship between a factor and a variable, where that relationship does not feature in the model, may suggest that inclusion of this arrow in the model might be expected to improve the fit of the model, as indicated by a high value for the *parameter change* statistic.

Requesting the modification indices

Recall that we obtained the modification diagnostics at the outset. If we had not done it then, we could request them by opening the **Analysis Properties** dialog box (either via **View/Set** on the top menu bar or via the icon, which is 8th down in the middle column). Then we would click on **Output** and put ticks against **Residual moments** and **Modification indices** and re-run the analysis. To see the residuals, click on the **View text** icon and, in the output menu that appears, click on the **+** sign to the left of **Estimates**, then on the **+** beside **Matrices** and, finally, on **Standardized Residual Covariances**. To see the modification output, just click on **Modification Indices**.

Using the indices to progressively modify the model

AMOS Text Output 8.1 shows the modification indices (and predicted parameter changes) and the standardized regression covariances for our model (the column of variable names is omitted from the left of the standardized regression covariance matrix to allow it to fit across the page). We note that there is a large modification index (MI = 5.24, giving a parameter change of −4.53) for the regression path predicting DIGSYM from the verbal factor (top row of MI table), and a large residual between ARITH and DIGSPAN (3.13) in the residuals table. The large MI suggests that an improved model might result if we added a path from the verbal factor to DIGSYM, and the large residual suggests that we might get an improved model if we removed DIGSPAN and/or ARITH from the model. In fact, addition of an arrow between the verbal factor and DIGSYM had a quite minor effect on the goodness of fit indicators. For example, chi square reduced from 114.1 to 107.8 and changes in the other indices were small. Removal of both of the variables ARITH and DIGSPAN was more promising. Chi square reduced to 47.8 and CFI (.90), NFI (.81) and RMSEA (.08) all moved substantially in the right directions. Encouraged by this, we continued progressively to remove variables with high residual values until we had just six variables remaining, three (INFORM, VOCAB and COMPREH) predicted by the verbal factor and three (PICCOMP, PICARRAN and OBJASSEM) predicted by the performance factor. This resulted in a reduction of chi square to 14.8 with 8 *dfs*, an increase in CFI to .95 and NFI to .90, with RMSEA at .08. These values are all in

Modification Indices (Group number 1 – Default model)
Covariances: (Group number 1 – Default model)

			M.I.	Par Change
r11	↔	verbal	5.242	−4.534
r7	↔	verbal	5.203	0.784
r6	↔	r9	10.962	−7.349
r5	↔	r6	4.795	2.444
r4	↔	perform	7.124	1.039
r4	↔	r9	14.650	6.153
r3	↔	r4	7.146	−3.673
r2	↔	r4	13.842	3.606
r1	↔	r3	4.845	3.897

Standardized Residual Covariances (Group number 1 – Default model)

digsym	objassem	block	picarran	piccomp	simil	compreh	arith	vocab	digspan	inform
0.000										
1.041	0.000									
−0.542	0.527	0.000								
0.837	0.637	−0.510	0.000							
0.388	−0.907	−0.117	−0.062	0.000						
−1.409	0.199	−2.311	−0.615	0.843	0.000					
0.258	1.046	0.054	−0.573	1.607	1.465	0.000				
−0.642	−0.147	3.143	1.891	1.013	1.089	−0.667	0.000			
−1.843	−0.722	−0.243	−0.385	0.938	−0.221	0.063	−1.170	0.000		
−1.599	−1.083	−0.007	0.441	0.128	1.001	−1.351	3.129	0.092	0.000	
−1.076	−0.925	0.229	−0.752	0.468	−0.830	−0.744	0.016	0.734	−0.776	0.000

AMOS Text Output 8.1 Modification indices for covariances and standardized residual covariances for the original intelligence model.

the moderately good fit range and the reduced model seems to 'make sense'. If you wanted measures of verbal and performance components of intelligence, you may do better using just the six variables in this final model; these are the variables that seem to best define the underlying factors. Since, however, this modified model has not been subjected to CFA, it is really only an untested hypothesis, and still needs to be the subject of a CFA with new data.

Comparisons among models

Finally, recall the AIC (Akaike's information criterion), which is useful for making comparisons among two or more models. Generally, the model with the lowest AIC value is considered to have the best fit. The value of AIC for our original model was 160.07 and the value for the final modified model was 40.8. If we follow the post hoc (exploratory) strategy that led to our final modified model, however, we will likely capitalize on chance, and it will be necessary to cross-validate the modified model with a new sample before we can have much confidence in it.

Structural equation modelling

In the previous chapter we looked at how to do a path analysis using AMOS, and in this one we have shown how to do a confirmatory factor analysis. In fact, structural equation modelling is a combination of confirmatory factor analysis (the measurement model) and, for example, path analysis (the structural model). For the sake of simplicity in the path analysis, we presented our schism data as though each variable had been measured in a single operation and as if the variable was synonymous with that operation. Recall that an assumption required for path analysis is that variables are measured without error. This is not really realistic. In fact most of our variables were really *latent variables* measured with multiple indicators (none synonymous with the variable in question). We have seen in this chapter that it is possible to deal with the issue of reliability of measurement indirectly, by computing reliability coefficients (coefficient alpha) for the indicators of variables. These reliabilities can then be incorporated into the path model. Alternatively, we can use structural equation modelling, representing our variables as factors (i.e., as latent variables rather than measured variables), as in confirmatory factor analysis.

Structural equation modelling: The 'Schism' data from Chapter 7

We now reconsider our schism data from the path analysis and see how to use the concepts of factor analysis to take the structural equation modelling approach. Recall that we represent the factors as ovals or circles to distinguish them from measured variables (indicators of a factor), which are represented as variables (squares) that are predicted by the factors (i.e., arrows lead from a factor to its measured indicators). As with measured (endogenous) variables in path analysis, with at least one arrow pointing at them, the indicators have residuals (measurement error) pointing at them. We actually measured our latent variables with between two and six indicators each, but to avoid having a very cluttered input diagram as in our example, we imagine that there were just two indicators (measured variables) per latent variable.

Structural equation modelling: Constructing the input diagram

To draw the diagram, we begin as with our path analysis, except that we draw ovals instead of rectangles. We can make better use of the space available by having the flow go from top to bottom instead of from left to right on the screen, so we do that. Next, we activate the **Draw latent variables and indicators** icon (top of the right column) and click twice inside each latent variable ellipse, once for each of the two indicator variables. Then activate the **Draw unique variables** icon (one down on the right) and, inside each of the endogenous latent variables (all except CHANGE), click 5 times. The reason for clicking five times is to position the unique (residual) variable below the latent variable. Recall that if you just clicked once, the residual would be located above the latent variable and that would make the diagram quite confusing because the residual would be competing for space with the indicators. Each click after the first rotates the variable 45° in a clockwise direction, so it ends up below the latent variable where there is plenty of space. Finally, all of the variables and latent variables must be given names. The procedure is the same as already used in both CFA and path analysis. Apart from the 10 measured (indicator) variables, which must be given the same names as they have been given in the SPSS data file, they may be given any convenient names. The names we used for the indicator variables were c1, c2, s1, s2, v1, v2, e1, e2, sc1 and sc2, the letters standing for the latent variable with which each was associated. The input diagram should look something like that in AMOS Screen 8.4.

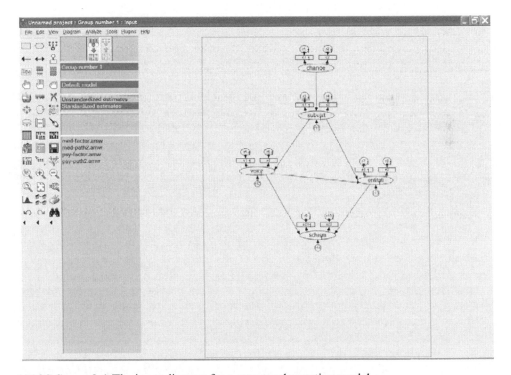

AMOS Screen 8.4 The input diagram for a structural equation model.

Structural equation modelling: The output and final comments

The procedure for running the analysis would be the same as that described for the path analysis. The output diagram would be similar, with all of the estimated parameter values added, and the interpretation of the goodness of fit criteria would be as for the path analysis results, so we do not reproduce either an output diagram or any of the text output for the structural equation analysis that would be carried out on this model. We have gone almost as far as we intend to go in introducing you to structural equation modelling. If you plan to use this technique, you will certainly need to read more advanced texts, but before concluding we will again, very briefly, draw your attention to a feature of the input diagram that you will need to learn more about. If you look carefully, you will see that there are a number of 1s associated with particular paths. These represent constraints that it is necessary to impose on the estimation of parameters to ensure that the model is *identified*. AMOS has done this automatically, so this model can be used to analyse 10 columns of data, two indicators for each of five variables, as it stands. However, it is sometimes necessary, as in our CFA, for the researcher to impose additional constraints, and deciding what parameters to constrain is far from straightforward. AMOS offers help with this and the issue is discussed in the two books listed in 'Further reading' at the end of the book.

The caveats concerning causation that we mentioned in connection with path analysis apply equally to structural equation modelling, but it is still a very powerful technique. The mathematics underlying it are not easy, but it is certainly true that packages such as AMOS make it possible to do the analyses with considerably less mathematical understanding than used to be the case.

Reporting results

It is usual to include a description of what has been done, together with an output diagram for the proposed measurement model and, preferably, diagrams for competing models that have been tested. In addition, several goodness of fit indices are normally provided. A report of the CFA might go something like this:

> The AMOS graphics program was used to construct an input path diagram representing the measurement model linking the hypothesized intelligence factors (latent variables) Verbal and Performance with the WAIS subtests (the indicator variables) that it was proposed they would predict. As described in the Method section, the subtests predicted by the Verbal factor were INFORM, DIGSPAN, VOCAB, ARITH, COMPREH and SIMIL, and those predicted by the Performance factor were PICCOMP, PICARRAN, BLOCK, OBJASSEM and DIGSPAN. The model also included a covariance between the two factors. Data were entered for 211 cases (again, as described in the Method section) and standardized beta coefficients were generated for all regressions of indicator variables on factors that were included in the model and the covariance between the factors was obtained. R^2 values for all 11 subtest variables were also generated. The output path diagram showing the computed values is in Figure A *(this would be a copy of the diagram in AMOS Screen 8.1)*. The goodness of fit given by chi square was $\chi^2 = 114.1$ ($df = 43$, $p < .001$). With a sample of this size, a significant value for chi square does not necessarily lead to rejection of the model, but our value is more than double the dfs, which suggests that the fit is likely

to be poor. Other goodness of fit indices confirmed this conclusion. Values greater than .95 for NFI and CFI are considered indicative of a good fit (*give reference*). The obtained values were .67 and .75, respectively. A value of less than .10 for RMSEA is considered a reasonable fit (*give reference*) and the value obtained was .11.

Alternative a priori models did not fare any better than the proposed model, but post hoc successive removal of poorly fitting variables, based on inspection of standardized residual and modification index tables, resulted in the modified model shown in Figure B (*we have not reproduced this*). This model includes three variables predicted by each factor. The fit indices suggest a good fit (chi square = 14.82, $df = 8$, $p = .06$; NFI = .90; CFI = .95; RMSEA = .08). This modified model appears to make sense. It remains a hypothesis, however, until such time as it is tested in a confirmatory factor analysis with new data.

Reference

Tabachnick, B. G., & Fidell, L. S. (2007). *Using multivariate statistics* (5th ed.). Boston, MA: Allyn & Bacon.

9 Discriminant analysis and logistic regression

Discriminant analysis

Introduction

Discriminant analysis was developed for two distinct purposes, *classification* and *separation*. Classification is concerned with locating things within known categories (or groups) on the basis of their values on a number of variables, with the least possible errors of classification. Separation is concerned with finding dimensions along which groups differ from one another and the extent to which they can be reliably discriminated. This amounts to discovering and interpreting combinations of variables that separate groups in various ways. We shall be using discriminant analysis for classification, and separation will be discussed only briefly. We can use discriminant analysis for classification when we have a categorical variable representing the groups into which we want to classify our cases and a set of measurements on each case that will be used to make the classification. The technique can be used to classify cases into one of several groups on the basis of two or more measurements. The groups must already be defined. If what you are trying to do is decide *whether* a set of cases falls into subgroups or not, then discriminant analysis is not the tool for the job: you need cluster analysis, the subject of Chapter 10.

The following are examples of problems for which discriminant analysis might be appropriate:

(1) Suppose that we want to classify convicted criminals into those who are likely and those who are unlikely to offend again within 5 years; that is our categorical variable, for which the values will be known if our sample comprises criminals who were released 5 years ago. The set of measurements that we hope may be used to classify them might be, for example, number of previous convictions, age and time spent in a rehabilitation programme.

(2) If we wanted to distinguish between accident survivors who developed serious, mild or no traumatic stress symptoms (our categorical variable with three possible values), we might use measurements of extent of social network, time spent in counselling, job satisfaction and scores on a test measuring resilience to try to classify them.

So, to get started we need a set of cases where we already know the group membership as well as the measurements on some variables for each case. This dataset is called the *training set.* We use it to work out a classification rule, then we can apply the rule to classify new cases just using the measurements. The grouping variable should be a categorical variable and the levels should be given numerical codes. To see how the method works, we start with a simple example that would not have any practical use, and then we move on to a more realistic case of the kind that is useful in practice.

If we are classifying into only two groups, then logistic regression can be a better option than discriminant analysis because it allows us to use categorical variables (factors) as well as measurements to make the classification. We discuss this method later in the chapter.

A simple example and an intuitive explication

Almost all people can be unequivocally classified as male or female. The two sexes form our groups, only two in this simple case, and we code males and females as 1 and 2. It is very easy to obtain for each person their height and weight. Table 9.1 lists the first few and last few rows of data on sex, height (cm) and weight (kg) for 35 people (the full dataset is on the book website as discriminant.sav).

Table 9.1 The first few and last few rows of data on sex, height and weight of 35 adults (the full dataset can be found as discriminant.sav on the website)

Sex	Height	Weight
1	184	67
1	179	55
1	180	50
1	166	63
⋮		⋮
2	180	62
2	176	67
2	170	66
2	170	67

If we plot the weights and heights on a scatterplot, with males and females showing as different symbols, we see that in general, because most men are taller and heavier than most women, the male symbols are towards the top right and the female symbols towards the bottom left. Figure 9.1 shows the plot.

In this example, we say that the grouping variable is sex (with two groups, male and female) and the independent or classification variables are weight and height. If we tried to use the height and weight measurements to classify the cases as male or female we could rule a straight line across the graph, sloping from top-left to bottom-right, and assign cases above and to the right of the line as males and cases below and to the left as females. By placing the line carefully we could get most of the cases correctly assigned. Try it yourself with a ruler. You should be able to place it so that only two triangles fall above and to the right of it and only four stars are below and to the left, so only 6 out of 35 cases would be misclassified. Discriminant analysis tells you exactly where the line should go to maximize the separation between the groups and thereby minimize misclassifications.

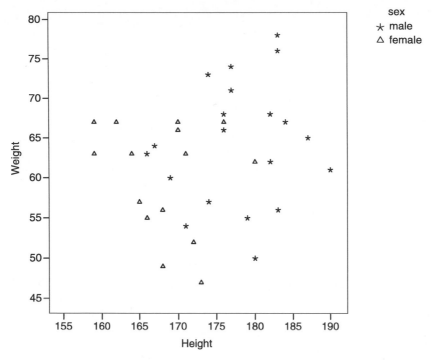

Figure 9.1 Heights and weights of males and females.

Discriminant functions

In practice, the position of the line defines a *discriminant* (or classification) *function* (or rule). A discriminant function is like a regression equation in which each predictor (equivalent to a classification variable) is weighted by a coefficient and there is a constant. The discriminant (or classification) function consists, then, of a set of coefficients for each classification group. Fortunately, you do not need to know about the mathematics used to obtain the coefficients; you just need to know what to do with them.

The general form of each discriminant function equation, where *a* is a coefficient, is:

Discriminant function = a_1 * height + a_2 * weight + constant

For each case, the measurements are multiplied by the coefficients and added to give a score for each group, and the case is assigned to the group with the highest score. In effect, the discriminant function line is at the boundary between the two groups and the decision to be made is which side of the boundary each case falls. If you have more than two measurements per case, or more than two classification groups, it would not be easy to just draw the lines by eye, but the underlying mathematics is the same; the discrimination function is calculated in the same way.

For the height and weight data the classification rule is shown in Table 9.2. Take the first case in Table 9.1: height 184 cm and weight 67 kg. The score for sex 1 (male) is

4.488 * 184 + 1.117 * 67 − 435.945 = 464.686

Table 9.2 Classification function (rule) for sexes based on height and weight

Classification variables	Sex (grouping variable)	
	1 (male)	2 (female)
Height	4.488	4.241
Weight	1.117	1.041
Constant	−435.945	−388.785

and the score for sex 2 (female) is

$$4.241 * 184 + 1.041 * 67 - 388.785 = 461.306$$

so, because the male score is higher, this case would be (correctly) assigned to sex 1 (male). How about a person 180 cm tall who weighs 62 kg? Their male score will be

$$4.488 * 180 + 1.117 * 62 - 435.945 = 441.149$$

and their female score will be

$$4.241 * 180 + 1.041 * 62 - 388.785 = 439.137$$

so this person will also be assigned to sex 1 (male). This is actually the fourth from last case in our training set, and was one of those incorrectly assigned by the rule. If you know your own height and weight in cm and kg, work out whether the classification rule assigns you to the correct sex.

Of course you may well ask, why bother to classify people as male or female using height and weight measurements when you can perfectly well classify them just by looking at them, usually getting a lot fewer than 6 misclassified out of 35. The sort of situation where this method is useful is one where you cannot identify the correct group membership until some later date, or else by using some expensive or intrusive test, but you do have some easily obtained measurements that would enable you to classify most cases correctly immediately, perhaps in time to take some decision about appropriate training or help for them. We now consider an example of this type. We have fabricated a set of data that will demonstrate the main features of classification using discriminant analysis.

A psychology example of a discriminant analysis problem

Many children in their first year at school make little or no progress in learning to read even though they appear to be of at least average intelligence. Various types of intervention and remedial work are usually tried on an ad hoc basis depending on the experience and preferences of the teacher. For most children, some method is eventually found that enables them to progress. For a few, nothing works and they leave primary school still functionally illiterate, which is a terrible handicap for the rest of school and life. We might reduce the stress and save time and money if we had a way to assign children who do not progress in reading to the type of intervention most likely to help them right away, rather than using trial and error. We have some research that may help us with this. All of the children from one school who failed to progress in reading in their first year took three tests, which it was hoped might be used in future as diagnostic. Then each child was assigned at random to one of two types of intervention. If the child was progressing after 6 weeks, they continued with their assigned intervention method for 6 more weeks, when progress was assessed. Any child failing to progress after 6 weeks on the assigned intervention was switched to the other intervention, and their progress was assessed after 12 weeks on the new intervention. The children were classified at the end according to whether they progressed on intervention 1 (group 1), intervention 2 (group 2) or still failed to progress on either intervention (group 3). See Figure 9.2 for a schematic illustration of the classification process.

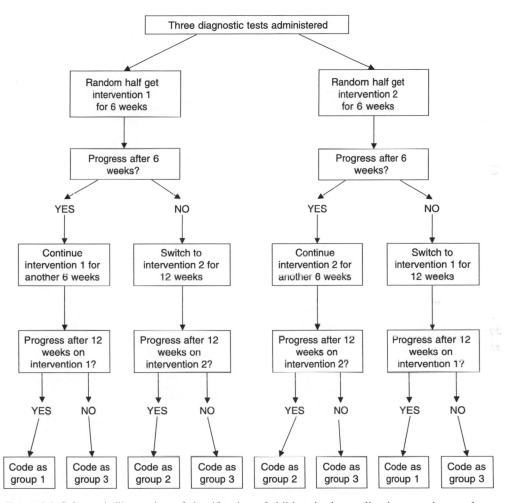

Figure 9.2 Schematic illustration of classification of children in the reading intervention study.

Some (fabricated) data

The data on the initial test results and their final classification appear in Table 9.3 (psy.discriminant.sav on the book website). Also in Table 9.3 is an extra column of data

Table 9.3 Test results and group membership of 54 children
(psy.discriminant.sav)

Group	Test 1	Test 2	Test 3	Later
1	8	11	7	6
1	4	8	7	5
1	4	9	6	4
1	7	10	9	5
1	6	10	7	7
1	7	9	8	6
1	6	10	6	6
1	5	9	6	3
1	8	8	6	6
1	8	10	7	7
1	7	11	8	6
1	6	8	4	6
1	4	10	5	6
1	5	8	7	4
1	5	10	7	7
1	7	9	6	6
1	8	10	7	6
1	7	11	7	9
1	8	8	7	7
1	6	10	7	5
1	7	10	8	6
1	5	11	7	6
1	8	10	8	7
1	5	7	8	2
1	7	8	9	7
1	6	9	7	7
2	7	8	4	6
2	8	8	6	5
2	6	6	4	2
2	8	6	4	5
2	7	9	5	4
2	8	7	7	6
2	9	9	6	6
2	9	7	5	5
2	10	8	6	5
2	7	7	4	4
2	7	7	7	4
2	9	8	6	6
2	7	7	5	5
2	8	7	6	4
2	9	8	6	4
2	8	8	7	6
2	8	8	6	7
2	6	6	5	6
3	7	6	5	4
3	4	5	6	5
3	3	5	5	3
3	4	5	7	4
3	5	6	5	4
3	6	6	6	3
3	4	5	5	4
3	5	4	6	2
3	5	6	8	4
3	7	6	7	3

called LATER. This is for use near the end of the treatment of discriminant analysis and will be ignored until then. There are 26, 18 and 10 children, respectively, in the three outcome groups. As a minimum, we need more cases in the smallest group than there are classification variables. Initially we have three classification variables (the tests) and 10 cases in the smallest group, so we can proceed. Even when we use our extra variable LATER, we shall still have enough cases.

Plots of pairs of the test results do show some separation of the three groups, though no pair of test scores gives a separation as good as in our initial example with weights and heights. Figure 9.3 shows the plot of the first two tests, with the three groups displayed as different symbols. Note that there are fewer symbols than there are cases because quite a lot of the cases (including cases in different groups) have identical values on the two tests. For example, there are two cases from GROUP1 and three cases from GROUP2 at the point where TEST1 = 8 and TEST2 = 8.

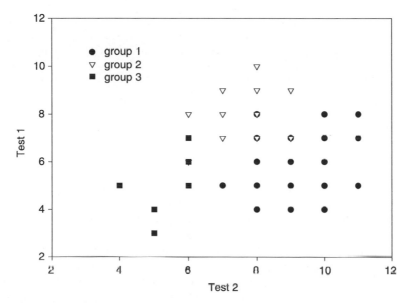

Figure 9.3 Results for tests 1 and 2 for the three groups of children.

Perhaps, using all three tests, the discriminant analysis can divide up the space of test results in a way that assigns most cases correctly to their final group. We now tackle this in SPSS.

Requesting a discriminant analysis in SPSS

To do discriminant analysis in SPSS you need to enter the data for the training set just as in Table 9.1, with the correct group membership as one variable and the measurements to be used for classification as the other variables. From the menu bar we select **Analyze**, then **Classify**, then **Discriminant**. In SPSS Dialog Box 9.1, use the arrow to enter the **Grouping Variable** (GROUP in our case). Then click the **Define Range** button so that we can say how many groups there are. A small dialog box opens: enter 1 as **Minimum** and 3 as **Maximum** since we have three groups coded as 1, 2 and 3. Click

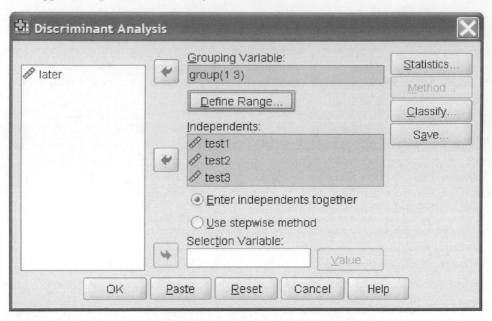

SPSS Dialog Box 9.1 Starting a discriminant analysis of reading data.

Continue to return to the main dialog box. Then use the arrow to put the three tests into the **Independents** box and we have the discriminant analysis dialog box as shown.

The default options only provide the information needed to use discriminant analysis for separation, and to get what we need for classification we need to click the **Statistics** button. In the dialog box that opens up (not reproduced here), click **Fisher's** in the **Function Coefficients** group, since this is what we need for discrimination. It may also be useful to see the **Means** of the test scores for each group, so click that box in the **Descriptives** group. This is all we need for now, so click **Continue** to return to SPSS Dialog Box 9.1.

Near the bottom of SPSS Dialog Box 9.1 you see radio buttons for the options **Enter independents together** and **Use stepwise method**. The default, **Enter independents together**, will immediately try the classification using all the variables in the **Independents** list. An alternative approach, especially useful if you have a long list of variables only some of which are likely to be useful for classification, is to use a *stepwise* method and we consider this option later. For now, we accept the default, **Enter independents together**.

Now, if we click the **Classify** button we get SPSS Dialog Box 9.2. The default choice for **Prior Probabilities** is **All groups equal**. This means that, if we had no classification variables, a randomly chosen case would be equally likely to belong to any of the groups. But if our groups were of unequal sizes, in the absence of any information on classification variables, the probability of a randomly chosen case belonging to a particular group would be proportional to the size of that group. Our groups are not all the same size so we choose **Compute from group sizes**. This will slightly improve our probability of successful classification. From the **Display** group we click **Summary table**. The summary table will give the results of classifying into groups 1–3 using the three tests. We accept the defaults for the other choices and click **Continue** to return to SPSS Dialog Box 9.1.

Now, if we click the **Save** button, and then click the **Predicted group membership** box,

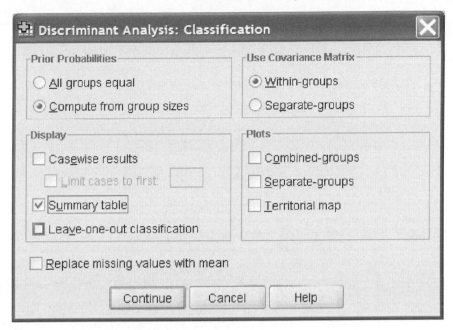

SPSS Dialog Box 9.2 Classification dialog box.

SPSS will add a column to our data window, with the group assigned to each case by the discriminant functions. This makes it easy to identify the particular cases that are misclassified. Click **Continue** and **OK** to get the discriminant analysis.

Understanding the output and calculating the discriminant functions

There is a lot of information in the output window, much of it concerned with using discriminant analysis for separation, which does not interest us at the moment. The first table in the output just shows whether any cases were omitted because of missing data. We had no missing data, so all our cases were included in the analysis. Then there is a table showing the mean scores on the three tests for the members of each of our groups. This may be of interest if we are trying to understand the differences among the groups more clearly. However, these tables have not been reproduced here.

Now if we go right to the end of the output, the last two tables are shown in SPSS Output 9.1. Look at the last table first. This is the summary table we requested in SPSS Dialog Box 9.2. It shows the results of classifying the children into our three groups using the data on the tests. Of the actual GROUP1 members, 22 were correctly classified into GROUP1, 3 were put into GROUP2 and 1 into GROUP3. All of the GROUP2 members were correctly classified. All but one of the GROUP3 members were also correctly classified, with just one being put in GROUP2. Overall, just over 90% were correctly classified using the data on the three tests. This would be good news for teachers, who would be able to offer the most effective intervention to 40 (22 + 18) of 54 children just on the basis of three diagnostic tests. They could also identify most of those who need some new approach because neither of the interventions used in this experiment was helpful. Of course, a few children (5 of 54) would be misclassified, and in their cases the usual trial and error approach would usually work eventually.

Classification Function Coefficients

	group		
	1	2	3
test1	0.583	2.615	0.888
test2	8.266	5.805	4.201
test3	4.304	2.701	4.072
(Constant)	-56.335	-40.374	-27.464

Fisher's linear discriminant functions

Classification Results[a]

		group	Predicted Group Membership			
			1	2	3	Total
Original	Count	1	22	3	1	26
		2	0	18	0	18
		3	0	1	9	10
	%	1	84.6	11.5	3.8	100.0
		2	0.0	100.0	0.0	100.0
		3	0.0	10.0	90.0	100.0

a. 90.7% of original grouped cases correctly classified.

SPSS Output 9.1 Part of the output from a discriminant analysis of reading data.

But how would they actually do the classification for a new set of children for whom they only have the test results? Look at the first table in SPSS Output 9.1. The columns give the coefficients for three discriminant functions, one for each group. For a new child with test results of 6 on TEST1, 10 on TEST2 and 8 on TEST3, we calculate each discriminant function and assign the child to the group with the highest value, as follows:

Function for group 1: $0.583 * 6 + 8.266 * 10 + 4.304 * 8 - 56.335 = 64.255$
Function for group 2: $2.615 * 6 + 5.805 * 10 + 2.701 * 8 - 40.374 = 54.974$
Function for group 3: $0.888 * 6 + 4.201 * 10 + 4.072 * 8 - 27.464 = 52.450$

So this pupil is assigned to GROUP1: intervention 1 is most likely to help. These calculations are quite laborious but SPSS will do them for us, and we consider this next.

Classifying new cases using SPSS

All you need to classify new cases is the first of the tables in SPSS Output 9.1, a calculator, the test results for the new cases and a lot of patience. Alternatively, you can get SPSS to do the calculations using the **Selection Variable** box in SPSS Dialog Box 9.1 as follows. Add the test results for the 10 new cases shown in Table 9.4 to the bottom of the SPSS data window. The GROUP variable will be missing for these cases.

We also need a new variable that can be used to select the 54 cases in the training set for the discriminant analysis, then SPSS will use the discriminant functions to assign the new cases to their predicted groups. We could call the new variable CHOOSE and give it the value 1 for the cases in the training set and 2 for the new cases. In SPSS Dialog Box 9.1, select the CHOOSE variable and move it into the **Selection Variable** box at the bottom using the arrow. Then press the **Value** button and insert 1. The dialog box now has CHOOSE = 1 in the **Selection Variable** box at the bottom.

Remember to use the **Save** button to get the predicted group membership for all cases, including the new ones. The predicted group membership is in a new column in

Table 9.4 Test results for new cases
(psy.discriminant.newcases.sav)

Test 1	Test 2	Test 3
7	10	8
4	8	9
7	7	5
7	8	7
6	9	5
5	6	8
6	10	6
5	5	7
4	6	5
6	8	7

the datasheet, and, if you look at the data window you will see an extra added column that shows the new cases assigned to groups 1, 1, 2, 1, 1, 3, 1, 3, 3 and 1, respectively.

Estimating the probability of misclassifying new cases

When we did our discriminant analysis on the 54 cases from the original experiment, the classification using the three test results was correct in 90.7% of the cases. When we apply the results to new cases we are unlikely to achieve quite such a high proportion of correct assignments because the original data, and any future data, will contain some random variation as well as the relationships among the test scores and the group membership. When we perform the discriminant analysis on any set of data, the results will be best for that dataset, including its random components. The next set of data will have different random elements and classification will have a slightly increased probability of being wrong. There are several ways to deal with this, all of which are used in practice.

First, you can just go ahead and apply the discriminant functions to new data, then, when actual group membership is eventually ascertained, you can find what proportion of classifications your discriminant functions got right. This is a great method if it is available to you. However, it can be a problem if ascertaining actual group membership for your new cases is difficult or expensive, and not just a matter of waiting until later results are available. This could apply in our example, because those assigned to GROUP3 will not be exposed to either intervention, but will be the subject of new experimental work to try to find some new way to help them. So we shall not find out (perhaps until much later if continued lack of progress results in everything being tried) whether any of those assigned by the discriminant functions to GROUP 3 would in fact have progressed on one of the interventions.

Another approach is available if you have a large body of data to start with. In this case you could randomly assign each case to one of two datasets. You would then use one of them as the training set to derive the discriminant functions, and the other one as the *cross-validation set* to calculate misclassification probabilities. The snag about this method is that you get better estimates of your discriminant functions by using a bigger dataset to calculate them, so it seems wasteful to use only half of the available data for this task just so that you can get a better estimate of the proportion of misclassifications. However, if you want to do this, SPSS makes it easy. All you need to do is make a new variable (you could call it xval for cross-validation) and give this new variable the value 1 for the cases you want in the training set and value 2 for all the others. You would make the assignment to training set and validation set at random. Then you would use the **Selection Variable** box, just as we did for classifying new cases, only this time you would be classifying the members of the cross-validation set (coded 2). You would end by clicking **Save** and then **Predicted group membership** in order easily to see how many were misclassified both in the training set and in the validation set.

The last approach is called *leave-one-out* classification in SPSS, though some packages use the term *cross-validation*. Here the full dataset is used to calculate the discriminant functions, then each case is classified using the discriminant functions calculated from all cases other than the one being classified. The probability of misclassification is then calculated from these results. To get this done, we tick the **Leave-one-out** classification box in SPSS Dialog Box 9.2. SPSS Output 9.2 shows the results for our example. From this we would expect to get 87% (see footnote to output table) of new cases correctly classified using the three tests. The snag about this approach is that there is some evidence that it still gives somewhat optimistic estimates of misclassification rates.

Classification Results[b,c]

		group	Predicted Group Membership 1	2	3	Total
Original	Count	1	22	3	1	26
		2	0	18	0	18
		3	0	1	9	10
	%	1	84.6	11.5	3.8	100.0
		2	0.0	100.0	0.0	100.0
		3	0.0	10.0	90.0	100.0
Cross-validated[a]	Count	1	22	3	1	26
		2	1	16	1	18
		3	0	1	9	10
	%	1	84.6	11.5	3.8	100.0
		2	5.6	88.9	5.6	100.0
		3	0.0	10.0	90.0	100.0

a. Cross-validation is done only for those cases in the analysis. In cross-validation, each case is classified by the functions derived from all cases other than that case.

b. 90.7% of original grouped cases correctly classified.

c. 87.0% of cross-validated grouped cases correctly classified.

SPSS Output 9.2 Leave-one-out classification for the reading data.

Example Box 9.1

An alternative medical example of a discriminant analysis problem

The full analysis for this example can be found at www.psypress.com/multivariate-analysis/medical-examples (click on Chapter 9).

For people with primary traumatic brain injury (TBI), we can discriminate among those who make a good recovery such that they are back to work at 6 months (group = 1), those who make a reasonable recovery with many functions restored but are not able to return to work at 6 months (group = 2), and those who are very dependent or dead at 6 months (group = 3). A study is carried out to see how well it is possible to predict, shortly after the injury has been sustained, who will be in which group at 6 months. The study is carried out on 54 people with primary TBI who have been scored (3–15) on the revised Glasgow coma scale. Data are obtained on the following variables: (1) an EEG-derived score (EEG), (2) the coma score (COMA) and (3) a pupil reactivity to light score (PUPIL). In addition, data derived from a scan are called LATER to remind us that it is not used in the initial analysis. Following the initial discriminant analysis, a bivariate variable (CHOOSE) is used to distinguish between cases in the training set and new cases, and it is suggested that another bivariate variable (XVAL) might be used to facilitate a cross-validation.

Outcomes

Considering the results for the first three variables, of the actual GROUP1 members, 22 are correctly classified into GROUP1, 3 are put in GROUP2 and 1 is put in GROUP3. All of GROUP2 and all but one of GROUP3 are also correctly classified. Overall, just over 90% are correctly classified. A *leave-one-out* classification shows that we would expect to classify 87% of new cases correctly using the data for the three variables. With stepwise entry of the three classification variables, it is confirmed that they all contribute significantly to successful classification. When LATER, which is correlated with EEG, COMA and PUPIL, is included in a stepwise analysis it does not get entered into the model and the number of misclassifications actually increases. From this, we learn that it is usually worth using the stepwise method, especially if one or more variables may be redundant.

Alternative variables for use in SPSS
The full dataset, med.discriminant.sav (or med.discriminant.newcases.sav with the addition of new cases), can be found on the book website

Variable	Psychology	Medicine
Classification variable	GROUP Outcome groups 1, 2 and 3	GROUP Outcome groups 1, 2 and 3
Independent variables	TEST1 TEST2 TEST3 LATER Another measure	EEG EEG-derived score COMA Glasgow coma score PUPIL Pupil reactivity LATER Scan data
Additional variables	CHOOSE Training vs. new cases XVAL Training vs. validation set	CHOOSE Training vs. new cases XVAL Training vs. validation set

Assumptions used in classification by discriminant analysis

The classification method we have been using in this chapter has the optimal property that it minimizes the total probability of misclassification, but only if one assumption is satisfied. That assumption is that the *covariance matrices* of the independent (classification) variables are the same for all groups. This requires the IVs to be measured on an interval scale, so dichotomous variables are not possible. However, even if that assumption is not satisfied, you may still achieve a useful classification, and you can estimate the misclassification probabilities for new cases using one of the methods described in the previous section.

You can check the assumption of equal covariance matrices using Box's *M* test for equality of covariance matrices. Click the **Statistics** button and then click **Box's M test** in the **Descriptives** group. The result appears at the start of the discriminant analysis, just after the table of group means. For our example the test statistic is shown in SPSS Output 9.3. We see that the result is not significant ($p > .05$) so we do not reject the hypothesis that the three covariance matrices are equal.

Test Results

Box's M		8.918
F	Approx.	0.664
	df1	12.000
	df2	3936.777
	Sig.	.787

Tests null hypothesis of equal population covariance matrices.

SPSS Output 9.3 Box's test of equality of covariance matrices.

Other parts of the output

After the first few tables showing whether cases have been omitted and displaying group means and the Box test for equality of covariance matrices, if requested, the discriminant analysis begins with a summary of the *canonical discriminant functions*. This information is not of direct importance for our purpose of classification, but the following paragraph gives a brief account of the tables, though we have not reproduced them here.

The idea behind the canonical discriminant functions is to find a set of linear combinations of the IVs that will separate the groups as well as possible, while being fewer in number than the IVs. In other words, is it possible to achieve good separation of the groups using fewer dimensions than the number of IVs? The first canonical discriminant function is the linear combination of IVs that separates the groups as much as possible, the second is the linear combination that achieves the best separation in a direction orthogonal to the first, and so on. Often, you can find a set of linear combinations of IVs that is fewer than the total number of IVs, which will achieve good separation of the groups. The Wilks' lambda table shows whether the canonical discriminant functions achieve significant separation (look at the 'Sig.' column), but the only relevance of this for our purpose of classification is that you are unlikely to achieve a useful classification unless there is significant separation. But we discussed above more direct ways to find out whether your classification is likely to be useful for new cases. The *eigenvalue* table shows the proportion of the within-groups variance that is accounted for by each canonical discriminant function (each eigenvalue divided by the total of eigenvalues gives the proportion of variance accounted for by that canonical discriminant function). The coefficients for the canonical discriminant functions are given in another table, and also the correlation of each IV with each canonical discriminant function.

Using a stepwise method

Since there are correlations among our three tests (look ahead to Table 9.5) we may wonder whether they all do contribute significantly to the classification into our three groups. We can check this by using the stepwise method instead of entering all our independent (classification) variables together. Look again at SPSS Dialog Box 9.1. This time we will click the radio button **Use stepwise method**. This is rather like doing a stepwise regression, and is especially useful in similar circumstances, namely when we have rather a long list of possible classification variables and it is unlikely that all will make a useful contribution to a set of discriminant functions. We would like to find the best subset, or else something close to that. By taking a stepwise approach we ask SPSS to choose first the single variable that gives the best classification into our groups. Then it checks to see that it does achieve a significant classification (i.e., it does better than just assigning the cases to the groups in the correct proportions but otherwise at random). Then it looks at the remaining variables and adds the one that gives the biggest improvement. It checks the two variables now in the discriminant functions and makes sure each makes a significant contribution in the presence of the other. At each step we see whether another variable can be added that will make a significant improvement, and whether any previous ones can be removed. The process stops when no more variables can be added or removed at the level of significance we are using. To choose the method by which variables will be added and removed, we click the **Method** button in SPSS Dialog Box 9.1 to obtain SPSS Dialog Box 9.3.

The default method uses **Wilks' lambda**, a *likelihood ratio* method. It has the advantage that it does not depend on the scale parameters of the variables and we will use it. The *F* values offered as defaults for entering and removing variables are the 5% and 10% levels for *F* with 1 and infinite degrees of freedom. If we have a fairly large dataset

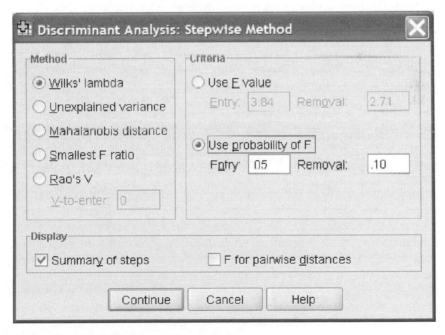

SPSS Dialog Box 9.3 Using the stepwise method.

this will approximate using the *F* probability values 5% and 10% for entry and removal. As probabilities of 5% and 10% would be typical, we may as well use the default probabilities and we click the radio button **Use probability of F**. Click **Continue**.

If we apply this process to our example data, all three test scores are entered into the discriminant functions and they remain there, so the extra information in test 3 does contribute significantly to successful classification. The table of stepwise results appears at the beginning of the analysis and is shown in SPSS Output 9.4.

Variables Entered/Removed[a,b,c,d]

		Wilks' Lambda				Exact F			
Step	Entered	Statistic	df1	df2	df3	Statistic	df1	df2	Sig.
1	test2	.293	1	2	51.000	61.503	2	51.000	.000
2	test1	.168	2	2	51.000	36.075	4	100.000	.000
3	test3	.129	3	2	51.000	29.182	6	98.000	.000

At each step, the variable that minimizes the overall Wilks' Lambda is entered.

a. Maximum number of steps is 6.

b. Maximum significance of F to enter is .05.

c. Minimum significance of F to remove is .10.

d. F level, tolerance, or VIN insufficient for further computation.

SPSS Output 9.4 Stepwise discrimination using tests 1, 2 and 3: Variables entered/removed.

Now at last we use the final column of data from Table 9.3, the one called LATER, to remind us to ignore it until now. This column actually shows the result of another measurement taken on the children, but you can see from the table of correlations in Table 9.5 that it is correlated with all of tests 1, 2 and 3.

Table 9.5 Correlations among tests 1, 2 and 3 and 'later'

	Test 1	Test 2	Test 3
Test 2	0.259		
Test 3	0.045	0.415	
Later	0.356	0.647	0.278

Perhaps including it as an extra IV will not improve the classification. In fact if we add it to the list of IVs and use the **Stepwise** method, the results are exactly as before: the extra variable LATER never gets added to the discriminant functions. If we include it and use the **Enter independents together** method, we get the summary table shown in SPSS Output 9.5.

We can see that we actually achieve *less* successful classification than we did with just the three tests, all of which contributed useful information. The inclusion of redundant variables can reduce the proportion of correctly classified cases. It is therefore worth using the stepwise method, especially if you suspect that some of your variables may be redundant.

Reporting results: Discriminant analysis

As an example of reporting the results of classification using discriminant analysis we will take the full set of data from Table 9.3: the grouping variable GROUP; the three tests;

Classification Results^a

		group	Predicted Group Membership			Total
			1	2	3	
Original	Count	1	22	3	1	26
		2	0	17	1	18
		3	0	1	9	10
	%	1	84.6	11.5	3.8	100.0
		2	0.0	94.4	5.6	100.0
		3	0.0	10.0	90.0	100.0

a. 88.9% of original grouped cases correctly classified.

SPSS Output 9.5 Classification including an extra (redundant) variable.

and the extra IV LATER, which turned out to be redundant. We could report as follows the results of classification with the IVs added in a stepwise process, and using *leave-one-out* as our method of estimating future probabilities of correct assignment.

> The three groups into which we wish to classify our 54 cases are coded 1, 2 and 3. Our IVs (TEST1, TEST2, TEST3 and LATER) are all measurements as described in the Method section. We used SPSS to classify the cases, using the stepwise method to add the IVs. The maximum significance of *F* for entry was .05, and the minimum for removal was .10. At each step, the variable that minimized the overall Wilks' lambda was entered. By these criteria, LATER was not included in the classification (the three tests were entered in the order TEST2, TEST1, TEST3, and none was removed).
>
> The three sets of coefficients for Fisher's discriminant functions are given in Table A (*this is the first table in our SPSS Output 9.1*). The numbers and percentages correctly and incorrectly classified are shown in Table B (*this is our SPSS Output 9.2*). Using the leave-one-out procedure for cross-validation, the overall probability of correct classification of future cases was estimated as 87%. This can be seen below Table B.

Note that Tables A and B are SPSS output tables, which, if the report were to be submitted for publication in a journal, would probably need to be modified to meet the table formatting requirements of the particular journal.

Logistic regression: An alternative approach to classification into two groups

Introduction

The idea behind *logistic regression*, as for linear regression, is that a DV may be predicted from a combination of IVs. In the case of logistic regression, however, the DV is a categorical variable, most usually a binary variable, such as membership/non-membership of a group. This gives rise to the other main difference from linear regression, that is, rather than calculating the predicted value of the DV we calculate the predicted probability of a case falling within a category. The probability of a category can be expressed in terms of the *odds* of a category, which is simply the ratio of the number of times the category occurs to the number of times it does not occur. For example, if the odds of people passing a test are 2 to 1 (i.e., 2/1 = 2), the probability of people passing is given by odds/(1 + odds) = 2/(1 + 2) = 0.67, which is the answer we get if we calculate the probability in the usual way (e.g., if there were a total of 30 people and 20 passed the test, the probability of someone passing would be 20/30 = 0.67).

It makes intuitive sense that a given change in a predictor variable will have most impact on the odds of a category (e.g., passing or failing) occurring near the middle of its range; a small change may easily tip the DV one way or the other. The effect of a given change in the predictor variable will be much less at either end of its range. To see this, think about students taking an exam. For those who do very little or no work at all, the odds of failure will be similarly high. Likewise, those who do a great deal of work will have low odds of failure. There will be diminishing returns for doing even more work as they cannot reduce the already low odds of failure by much. But in the middle of the range, among those who do a moderate amount of work, doing just a bit more may noticeably reduce the odds of failure since every bit of work adds to skills already in place. This variable strength of relationship between predictor variables and a categorical DV can be represented as an S-shaped curve, as in Figure 9.4. This curve can be expressed as a function known as the log of the odds, or *log(odds)* or *logit*.

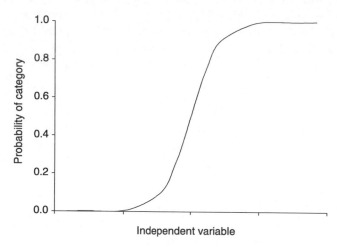

Figure 9.4 A logistic regression curve.

Although the probability of a category is not a linear function of the IVs (we referred to a single IV in the preceding discussion for the sake of simplicity), it can be assumed that the log(odds) is a linear function of the IVs. This is because an asymmetry between high and low odds – for a very likely event, the odds can be huge (e.g., 200/1 = 200), but for an unlikely event the odds must lie between zero and 1 (e.g., 1/200 = 0.005) – is removed by rescaling odds as log(odds). You do not need to be concerned if this is unfamiliar territory but, for the sake of completeness, we can tell you that the log in question is the *natural logarithm* (i.e., log to the base e).

So, the approach in logistic regression is to assume that the logarithm of the odds – the log(odds) – of being in the group coded with the higher number is a linear function of the IVs, which may be measurements (covariates) or categorical variables (factors) as in analysis of covariance. Let us say that the probability of being in GROUP1 is p_1 and of being in GROUP2 is p_2, so the odds of a case being in GROUP2 are p_2/p_1. Now we treat

$\log(p_2/p_1)$ as the DV in a model that is just like the one for analysis of covariance. Just as in ANCOVA, the model gives a predicted value for the DV in terms of the covariates and factors. This predicted value for a case will be multiples of the factor and covariate levels for the case, together with a constant. To use this predicted value as a way to classify cases into GROUP1 or GROUP2, we put a case into GROUP2 if the predicted odds value is greater than evens (i.e., the probability estimate for GROUP2 is greater than .5).

Comparison with discriminant analysis

To see how the results compare with discriminant analysis, we applied this method to the data in Table 9.1: the heights and weights of 20 men and 15 women. We found that the same six cases were misclassified as were misclassified by the discriminant analysis. So, in a case where either method could be used, the results were similar.

An example with psychology data

Now we will consider a variant of the reading example where discriminant analysis would not be able to make use of all the available data because we introduce an extra IV, which is a factor called SUPPORT.

Suppose that we now want to classify all the children in our previous example according to whether or not they progress on the first of our interventions. We will call this new classification variable INITIAL, and code the groups as 1 (did progress on intervention 1) and 2 (did not progress on intervention 1). We still have tests 1 and 2, but instead of test 3 we record whether the child has help and SUPPORT with reading at home from a parent or guardian. The first few and last few rows of the amended data appear in Table 9.6 (the full dataset is on the book website as psy.logistic.sav).

Table 9.6 The first few and last few rows of amended reading data on 54 children (the full dataset can be found as psy.logistic.sav on the website)

Initial	Test 1	Test 2	Support
1	8	11	Yes
1	4	8	Yes
1	4	9	No
1	7	10	Yes
⋮	⋮	⋮	⋮
2	4	5	No
2	5	4	No
2	5	6	Yes
2	7	6	No

Now we see how to set up a logistic regression in SPSS.

Logistic regression: Requesting the analysis in SPSS

With the data arranged in the SPSS data window as in Table 9.6, we proceed as follows. We choose **Analyze** from the menu bar, then **Regression**, then **Binary Logistic**, and get

SPSS Dialog Box 9.4. The grouping variable is the **Dependent** (INITIAL in our example). Only two levels are possible so we do not have to enter a range as we did in discriminant analysis. The IVs TEST1, TEST2 and SUPPORT are the **Covariates**. If any categorical variables are coded numerically, we would need to press the **Categorical** button to get a dialog box that allows us to say which these variables are. In our case, since we have used the words 'yes' and 'no' as levels of SUPPORT, SPSS recognizes this as a categorical variable. If we were to press the **Categorical** button, we would find that SPSS has already entered SUPPORT for us. The default **Method** enters all the variables from the **Covariates** list in the model. There are stepwise options that we will consider later. Press the **Save** button to keep the predicted group membership in an extra column of the datasheet, just as we did in discriminant analysis. In the **Save** dialog box, click **Group membership** in the **Predicted Values** group. Click **Continue** and **OK** to get our logistic regression.

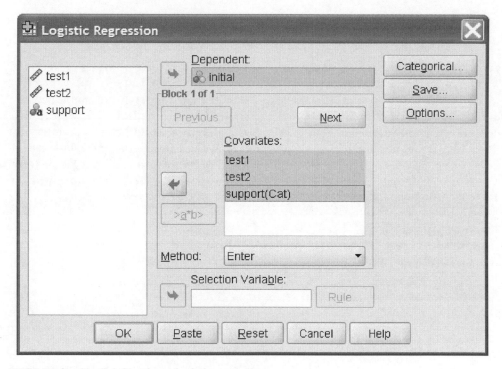

SPSS Dialog Box 9.4 Starting a logistic regression.

Logistic regression: Understanding the output

The first table in the output, called Case Processing Summary but not reproduced here, shows that all our 54 cases were included in the analysis and none were missing. The next two tables (also not reproduced here) show the codings given within the logistic regression to the DV and our categorical IV, SUPPORT. The DV is always given the codings 0 and 1 within the logistic regression, so our codings of 1 and 2 become 0 and 1, respectively, for the analysis. SUPPORT was given codes 0 for 'yes' and 1 for 'no' (you can change this by clicking the **Categorical** button and changing the **Reference Category** from **Last** to **First**).

Next comes a heading 'Block 0: Beginning Block'. This section is not very interesting because here SPSS starts by assigning all cases to the largest group. We do not reproduce this here. The next section is headed 'Block 1: Method = Enter'. This means that all our covariates are added, since we did not specify a stepwise method. The first two tables in this section show the overall significance of the model and we consider this later. Then we have a summary of the classification, as shown in SPSS Output 9.6. Here we see that we got just over 94% correctly assigned, and underneath the table we are told that the cut value is .5; in other words, if the probability of belonging to the group with INITIAL coded as 2 is greater than .5, then the case is classified as belonging to this group.

Classification Table[a]

			Predicted		
			initial		
Observed			1	2	Percentage Correct
Step 1	initial	1	25	1	96.2
		2	2	26	92.9
	Overall Percentage				94.4

a. The cut value is .500

Variables in the Equation

		B	S.E.	Wald	df	Sig.	Exp(B)
Step 1	test1	1.236	0.629	3.857	1	.050	3.441
	test2	-2.691	0.971	7.674	1	.006	0.068
	support(1)	3.109	1.589	3.831	1	.050	22.402
	Constant	11.471	6.492	3.122	1	.077	95901.429

SPSS Output 9.6 Classification results using logistic regression.

The second table in SPSS Output 9.6 gives the parameter values in the B column. These can be used to classify new cases. The mathematics is a bit off-putting and we will not show how it is done by hand, since you can also use the **Selection Variable** box in SPSS Dialog Box 9.4 to get SPSS to do this for you, as explained in the next section.

If we look in the data window we find that a new column called PGR_1 has been added. This gives the group membership code that was assigned by the logistic regression. If you do this yourself and look down the new column you will see that case 9 is incorrectly assigned to group 2, and cases 31 and 42 are incorrectly assigned to group 1. These are the three misclassified cases shown in SPSS Output 9.6.

Example Box 9.2

Logistic regression: An alternative example with medical data

The full analysis for this example can be found at www.psypress.com/multivariate-analysis/medical-examples (click on Chapter 9).

A study is carried out to find out how well people with traumatic brain injury (TBI) can be classified, shortly after the injury is sustained, either as having made a sufficiently good recovery to be back at work at 6 months (WORK = 1) or as not having recovered sufficiently to be back at work at 6 months (WORK = 2). The study is carried out on 54 people with TBI who have Glasgow coma scores below 12. Data are obtained on the following covariates: (1) an EEG-derived score (EEG), (2) the coma score (COMA) and bivariate (yes/no) pupil reactivity (REACT), the first two being the same variables that were used in the preceding discriminant analysis. The data are analysed using logistic regression. First, all covariates are entered together and then they are re-entered stepwise. As with discriminant analysis, a bivariate variable (CHOOSE) is used to distinguish between cases in the training set and new cases, and another bivariate variable (XVAL) is used to select cases for a training set and a validation set to carry out a cross-validation.

Outcomes

With all covariates entered together, only three cases are misclassified and all of the covariates are significant, though EEG and REACT are only marginally so. However, when we omit either of these from the model it does make a significant difference, and when we enter the covariates stepwise all three are entered. The overall fit of the model is good ($-2\log(\text{likelihood}) = 15.53$), though case 9 is not well fitted, with a Z residual of -4.34. The cross-validation shows only two of the 27 training cases and one of the 27 validation cases to be misclassified. However, when the roles of training and validation sets are reversed all of the training set are correctly classified, but there are four misclassifications in the validation set. In light of this, and with 94% correctly classified when all 54 cases are used as the training set, we expect to be able to achieve at least 85% correct classifications for new cases, that being the lowest result for the cross-validations carried out (i.e., 23/27 * 100). This suggests that we have a useful practical tool.

Alternative variables for use in SPSS
The full dataset, med.logistic.sav, can be found on the book website. The dataset med.logistic.predict.sav has new cases and the CHOOSE variable added. Med.logistic.crossvalidation.sav has the original 54 cases and the additional variable XVAL for crossvalidation.

Variable	Psychology	Medicine
Classification variable	INITIAL Outcome groups 1 and 2	WORK Outcome groups 1 and 2
Independent variables	TEST 1 TEST 2 SUPPORT	EEG EEG-derived score COMA Glasgow coma score REACT Pupil reactivity
Additional variables	CHOOSE Training vs. new cases XVAL Training vs. validation set	CHOOSE Training vs. new cases XVAL Training vs. validation set

Logistic regression: *Assigning new cases to* INITIAL = *1 or 2*

For new cases, you can if you wish calculate the probabilities of belonging to INITIAL = 2 using the parameters from SPSS Output 9.6 and a calculator. However, as indicated above, we can persuade SPSS to do this job for us. We enter the 10 new cases in Table 9.7 at the bottom of the datasheet. These new cases are the same ones we used to try out our discriminant functions, but with TEST3 replaced by the SUPPORT variable. The variable INITIAL will be missing in the datasheet for the new cases.

Table 9.7 New cases to be classified by logistic regression (psy.logistic.newcases.sav)

Test 1	Test 2	Support
7	10	Yes
4	8	Yes
7	7	No
7	8	Yes
6	9	No
5	6	Yes
6	10	No
5	5	Yes
4	6	No
6	8	Yes

Now we also need a variable to allow us to select the original cases that formed our training set to be included in the logistic regression, and then to use the parameters from the regression to assign all cases, including the new ones, to the two groups. We can call the selecting variable CHOOSE, and give it the value 1 for the 54 training set cases and 2 for the 10 new cases. The complete dataset with the original and new cases, and the CHOOSE variable added in a new column, can be found as psy.logistic.predict.sav on the book website. Then in SPSS Dialog Box 9.4, we put the variable CHOOSE in the **Selection Variable** box with the arrow. Click the **Rule** button and put **equals 1** in the box and click **Continue**. The dialog box now has CHOOSE = 1 in the **Selection Variable** box at the bottom.

We remember to **Save** the predicted group membership as before. When we press **OK** we get the usual output, with the additional information that 54 of 64 cases were selected for the analysis. The parameters and classification tables appear as before, but in the data window the new column called PGR_1 assigns all of the cases, including the 10 new ones, to one of the two groups. In fact they are assigned to groups 1, 1, 2, 1, 1, 2, 1, 2, 2 and 1, respectively.

Logistic regression: *Estimating misclassification probabilities for new cases*

SPSS does not offer a cross-validation option for logistic regression, so the only way to get a realistic estimate of misclassification probabilities on new cases is either to await final correct assignment on a new dataset, if that will eventually be available, or else divide the training set at random into two, using half to calculate the parameters, then using these parameters to assign the other half to get the misclassification rate.

Random assignment to the two halves is best, but to make it easy for you to reproduce our results we used alternate cases, starting with the first, from our dataset in Table 9.6 as a training set to perform a logistic regression. The other 27 cases will be our validation set. Remove the 10 new cases if you still have them at the bottom of the dataset. Then we can use a variable called, for example, xval, and set it as 1 or 2 in alternate rows, and use the selection procedure described in the previous section. The modified dataset with the original 54 cases and xval added as an extra column is available as psy.logistic.crossvalidation.sav on the book website.

When we did this cross-validation, 2 of the 27 cases in the training set were misclassified (we have not shown the output here). The parameter estimates corresponding to the B column in SPSS Output 9.6 were 0.497, −2.322, −3.672 and 17.184, which are different from those in SPSS Output 9.6 because only the 27 cases with xval = 1 were used to calculate the regression. SPSS used these to calculate the predicted group membership for the remaining cases. This time we saved the probabilities as well, and these are shown in Table 9.8, along with the predicted and actual group membership for the 27 cases with xval = 2 (the validation set).

Table 9.8 Probabilities of belonging to INITIAL = 2 for validation set

Probability	Predicted group	Actual group
.04426	1	1
.00198	1	1
.01980	1	1
.22721	1	1
.00325	1	1
.11130	1	1
.07077	1	1
.44291	1	1
.00019	1	1
.00120	1	1
.00007	1	1
.43713	1	1
.01213	1	1
.93022	2	2
.99928	2	2
.77546	2	2
.99555	2	2
.98805	2	2
.95638	2	2
.99270	2	2
.25299	1	2
.99805	2	2
.99948	2	2
.99948	2	2
.99805	2	2
.99997	2	2
.99882	2	2

For these 27 cases we find we have only one misclassification, or 96% correctly classified. This is one less misclassified than we got from the 27 cases we used as the training set, so we could be quite optimistic that in future we should be able to get about the same proportion correctly classified. However, if we reverse the roles of our training and validation sets, by setting xval = 2 in the **Selection Variable** box, we get all cases correct in the training set but four misclassified (15%) in the validation set. This should be a warning not to exaggerate our claims for our results. We may prefer to use the parameters calculated from the full training set of 54 in classifying new cases in future, and in that case we expect to get at least 23/27 * 100 = 85% classified correctly (our worst result from the cross-validation exercises described in this paragraph).

Logistic regression: More about the model parameters and their significance

Return to SPSS Output 9.6 and look again at the parameters in the B column of the second table. At the right of the table there is a column labelled 'Sig.' that tells you whether each parameter is significant in the model: if the probability in this column is less than .05, you would reject at the 5% level the hypothesis that the parameter is zero. The probabilities for our three parameters are .050 for TEST1, .006 for TEST2 and .050 for SUPPORT, so TEST2 makes a significant contribution to predicting the probability of belonging to INITIAL = 2, and TEST1 and SUPPORT are right on the borderline of significance. We could try removing each of these, one at a time, to see the effect on our correct classification rate.

If we remove SUPPORT (use the arrow to remove it from the **Covariates** box in SPSS Dialog Box 9.4), we get four instead of three misclassifications in the summary table, similar to that shown in SPSS Output 9.6. The 'Sig.' column in the table of variables now gives .009 and .001 for TEST1 and TEST2, as shown in SPSS Output 9.7. If we remove TEST1 and put SUPPORT back in, we get five misclassified and the 'Sig.' column for TEST2 and SUPPORT reads .004 and .010 (we do not show the output this time). There is a difficult decision to make here, since we can always get better estimates if we have fewer parameters for any given size of dataset. On the other hand, excluding either of the variables at the borderline of significance increases the number of misclassifications in the training set. But if we remember that the 5% significance level is a boundary imposed on a continuum that runs from 'extremely unlikely to be a chance effect' through to 'very likely to be a chance effect' we may decide that on balance it is better to include both TEST1 and SUPPORT as predictors with TEST2. We consider this further when we look at stepwise procedures.

Variables in the Equation

		B	S.E.	Wald	df	Sig.	Exp(B)
Step 1	test1	1.442	0.555	6.745	1	.009	4.227
	test2	-2.565	0.751	11.679	1	.001	0.077
	Constant	10.512	4.011	6.869	1	.009	36754.312

SPSS Output 9.7 Significance of TEST1 and TEST2 when these are the only IVs in the logistic regression.

Look at the signs of the parameters in the second column in SPSS Output 9.6 or 9.7, labelled 'B'. TEST1 has a positive sign for B, so an increase in the TEST1 score increases the odds of being in group 2 (INITIAL = 2). TEST2 is negative, so an increase in the TEST2 score reduces the odds of belonging to the group INITIAL = 2. If you look at the data in Table 9.6 you see that the TEST2 scores for INITIAL = 1 are generally higher than they are for INITIAL = 2.

Logistic regression: Checking the fit of the model

The overall fit of the model can be checked by looking for the *–2 Log(likelihood)* in the Model Summary table, which appears at the beginning of the output, and is shown in SPSS Output 9.8. If the model fits well, then –2Log(likelihood) is approximately χ^2 with degrees of freedom equal to the number of cases minus the number of estimated parameters, including the constant. This is $54 - 4 = 50$ when we include TEST1, TEST2 and SUPPORT in our model. If the value does not exceed that for significance at the 5% level, we would not reject at the 5% level the hypothesis that the model is a good fit. Our value of 15.533 is way below the value of 67.5, which is the critical value for the 5% significance level with 50 degrees of freedom, so we conclude that our model fits well.

Model Summary

Step	-2 Log likelihood	Cox & Snell R Square	Nagelkerke R Square
1	15.533ᵃ	.666	.889

a. Estimation terminated at iteration number 8 because parameter estimates changed by less than .001.

Casewise Listᵇ

		Observed			Temporary Variable	
Case	Selected Statusᵃ	initial	Predicted	Predicted Group	Resid	ZResid
9	S	1**	.950	2	-.950	-4.343

a. S = Selected, U = Unselected cases, and ** = Misclassified cases.

b. Cases with studentized residuals greater than 2.000 are listed.

SPSS Output 9.8 Fit of the model and cases that are not fitted well.

Another way to check the fit is to click the **Options** button and request **Casewise listing of residuals** (accept the default of **Outliers outside 2 sd**). Then if any cases are not well fitted by the model, you get a table listing them like the second one in SPSS Output 9.8. Here we see that our case 9, belonging to INITIAL = 1, is more typical of INITIAL = 2 and is not well fitted by the model. It has a very large residual, $Z = –4.343$. Sometimes examining a case that is an outlier like this one will help us to understand our problem better. But one outlier in 54 cases when the model fit is good overall is probably not enough to make us lose confidence in our ability to classify new cases. Of course, we should always monitor the performance of a classification tool that is being used in a practical situation.

Logistic regression: Using a stepwise method

In the previous section we saw that all the IVs in our logistic regression had parameters that were significantly different from zero or were on the borderline, so all make a significant contribution in estimating the probability of belonging to INITIAL = 2. Just as in discriminant analysis, we can choose to enter the variables by a stepwise method. Clicking the arrow to the right of the **Method** box in SPSS Dialog Box 9.4 produces a list of alternative stepwise methods. The first three are *forward* selection methods: start with no variables and add them one at a time if they pass a criterion. The last three are *backward* elimination methods: start with all the variables and remove them one at a time if they fail a criterion. We prefer forward selection, since parameter estimates are more reliable if we have fewer parameters. The different selection criteria will usually give similar results, so we just take the first one and re-do the regression. We find that all our variables are added in three steps, which supports our argument for retaining all three variables in the above section entitled 'More about the model parameters and their significance'. SPSS does not offer a procedure for combining forward selection and backward elimination as it does for discriminant analysis, but you can see from the table shown in SPSS Output 9.9 that it does provide the significance of the change if you do remove any of the entered variables. At every step, removing any of the entered variables would be a significant change. We should keep them in.

Model if Term Removed[a]

Variable		Model Log Likelihood	Change in -2 Log Likelihood	df	Sig. of the Change
Step 1	test2	-37.401	41.043	1	.000
Step 2	test2	-30.837	39.484	1	.000
	support	-18.574	14.959	1	.000
Step 3	test1	-11.749	7.964	1	.005
	test2	-31.111	46.688	1	.000
	support	-11.775	8.017	1	.005

a. Based on conditional parameter estimates

SPSS Output 9.9 The significance of removing variables from a logistic regression.

Logistic regression: Interaction terms

Logistic regression allows *interaction terms* to be included in just the same way as does covariance analysis. However, the main effects for any variables in interaction terms must always be included. Adding them one at a time yourself, and using the **Enter** method rather than a stepwise procedure, is the best way to ensure that this is done. We consider this next. First put INITIAL in the **Dependent** box and put the three IVs TEST1, TEST2 and SUPPORT in the **Covariates** box as before. To add the TEST1 * TEST2 interaction term to the model, we select these two variables, which are still in the box at the left, and the **>a * b>** button becomes available. Click it and the interaction term TEST1 * TEST2 appears in the **Covariates** box, as shown in SPSS Dialog Box 9.5 overleaf.

Click **OK** and we get the parameter estimates shown in SPSS Output 9.10. Now none of our variables is significant. We did still get only three misclassified, but the case that was not very well fitted by the model is still not well fitted. The model summary (not reproduced here) shows that -2Log(likelihood) is 15.274. With just the main effects it was 15.533. The difference is only 0.259. This is approximately χ^2 with 1 degree of freedom (the number of degrees of freedom is the number of extra parameters in the more complex model), so is certainly not significant. We do better without the TEST1 * TEST2 interaction.

Similar results are obtained if we add either of the other second-order interactions. We cannot add the third-order interaction since none of the second-order ones is significant.

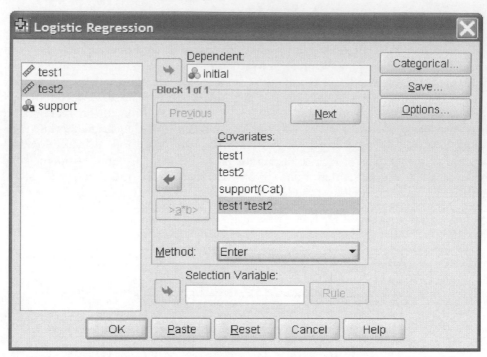

SPSS Dialog Box 9.5 Adding an interaction term to a logistic regression.

Variables in the Equation

		B	S.E.	Wald	df	Sig.	Exp(B)
Step 1	test1	-1.271	5.268	0.058	1	.809	0.280
	test2	-4.787	4.741	1.020	1	.313	0.008
	support(1)	2.973	1.568	3.594	1	.058	19.544
	test1 by test2	0.328	0.691	0.224	1	.636	1.388
	Constant	27.355	35.403	0.597	1	.440	7.588E11

SPSS Output 9.10 The effect of adding an interaction term.

Reporting results: Logistic regression

The main items to go into a report of results are the proportion of correct classifications achieved, the result of any cross-validation checks and the fit of the model. For our example we could present these results as follows:

> We used logistic regression to classify our 54 cases into two groups coded as INITIAL = 1 and 2, with covariates TEST1, TEST2 and SUPPORT as described in the Method section. SUPPORT was entered into the model as a categorical variable with values yes and no. Only three cases (6%) were misclassified. All covariates were significant, though TEST1 and SUPPORT were only marginally so. However, omitting either of these from the model did make a significant difference, and when we used a stepwise forward selection method to enter covariates, all three were entered. The parameter values and significance levels are shown in Table A (*this is the second table in our SPSS Output 9.6*).

The overall fit of the model as judged by the value of 15.533 for -2Log(likelihood) on 50 *df*s is good. However one case, case 9, was not well fitted and had a Z residual of -4.343.

We divided our dataset into two halves for a cross-validation exercise to estimate the probability of correct classification on new cases. Of the 27 cases used as the training set 2 were misclassified, but only 1 of the 27 validation cases was misclassified. However, when we reversed the roles of training and validation set, we found all of the training set correctly classified but four misclassifications in the validation set. In the light of this, and with 94% correctly classified when all 54 cases were used as the training set, we expect that we shall achieve correct classification in at least 85% of new cases, making this a useful practical tool.

As for the reporting of discriminant analysis, the format of Table A (SPSS Output 9.6) may need to be modified if the report is to be submitted to a journal.

10 Cluster analysis

Introduction

Cluster analysis is an exploratory tool that may help you to understand the story your data have to tell, but many choices and decisions influence the results, few of the many questions have clear correct answers and you should regard any conclusions you reach as tentative until they are confirmed by other methods.

The idea of cluster analysis is to group together cases that are *close together* in some sense, based on their values on variables you recorded for them, and see if they fall into natural subgroups or clusters that may help you to understand them better, or to explore possibilities for helping or treating subgroups more effectively. Typically, the question addressed in cluster analysis is whether *cases* (often, though not necessarily, participants) can be grouped. It is also possible to look for groupings of *variables*, based on how close together they are in terms of cases having similar values on them, though, typically, this question is addressed in factor analysis. However, as we discussed in Chapter 8, we do occasionally use factor analysis to look for clusters of cases, and also if you have recorded at least five or six variables for each case you can use cluster analysis to look for clusters of variables. We consider this use of cluster analysis near the end of this chapter.

Clustering methods all begin with a matrix of *distances* (or *similarities*) between each pair of cases. You have seen examples of a *distance matrix* in road atlases, where there is a triangular display giving the distances between pairs of cities, as illustrated with just a small number of cities in Table 10.1.

Notice that such matrices are *symmetric*, because the distance from Manchester to London is the same as the distance from London to Manchester, so usually only half of the matrix is printed, either the upper triangle as here or else the equivalent lower triangle. The distance between any case (or city here) and itself is, of course, zero. A common example of a *similarity matrix* is a correlation matrix (which is also

Table 10.1 A distance matrix for some British cities (in miles)

	Birmingham	*Manchester*	*Bristol*	*Edinburgh*	*Inverness*
London	110	184	116	373	529
Birmingham		80	88	288	444
Manchester			159	211	367
Bristol				365	521
Edinburgh					156

symmetric). Similarity matrices are the inverse of distance matrices. Any two cases that are close in terms of their similarity will necessarily be at a small conceptual distance from one another. Distances can always be converted into similarities, and vice versa.

First, we explore this idea of distance (or similarity) between cases. Then we consider some of the methods for using distance between cases to form clusters. We shall use some of the data we used for discriminant analysis to show that the interpretation of results is often not simple. Because there are so many different ways to calculate distances or similarities *between cases*, and also so many ways to calculate distances *between clusters*, the introductory parts of this chapter are rather long, but it does mean that once we start setting up a cluster analysis in SPSS we do not need such lengthy explanations of some of the choices to be made.

Calculating distance between cases

One of the fundamental problems with distance measures is deciding which variables to include. Unfortunately we usually do not know which may be relevant to assigning our cases to clusters since we do not know what distinguishes the clusters, or even if there are any. The problem is most acute when we have a great many variables recorded for each case, though this is more common in biology than in psychology or medicine. If many variables are included and most turn out to be irrelevant, then differences between cases can be swamped by similarities on the many irrelevant variables. So if you find yourself with a problem where many variables have been recorded, you should not assume that including all of them is necessarily the best approach. The only general advice we can offer on the choice of variables is that they should be relevant to the task in hand. What is your reason for looking for clusters among your cases? If you are hoping to improve what you can offer in the way of treatment, help or support, then include just the variables that you believe are relevant to the problem or the way in which the treatment or support works. If you are hoping to gain more understanding of the cases, then include just the variables that define these cases for you in the context of your study.

Now we go on to consider ways to define distance between cases for different kinds of data.

Distance measures for interval or ratio scale variables

A familiar example of a similarity matrix for a set of cases is the correlation matrix, and a distance matrix can always be obtained from a matrix of similarities, though the process is not always simple. But you can easily see that if a pair of cases has a high similarity (close to 1 in the correlation matrix), then the distance between them should be close to zero, and conversely if the cases are very dissimilar (e.g., with a correlation close to 0), then the distance between them should be large. The details of the transformation are handled by SPSS.

If your cases are described by variables on at least interval scales, you can imagine them as points in a space where the variables are the axes, like the people who are points on the graph in Figure 10.1. These are 52 students who have taken aptitude tests for maths and communication skills. Each of them appears as a point on the graph according to their scores on the two aptitude tests, called MATH and LANG.

Here you can see that some individuals are close together and others are far apart. The eye of faith may even discern some tendency of the points to form a cluster

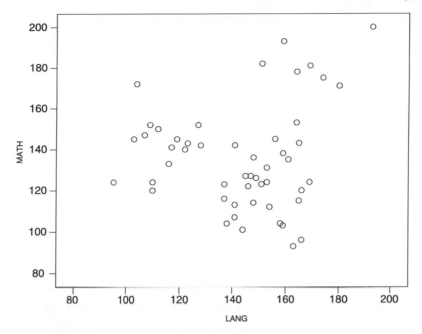

Figure 10.1 Cases shown as points in MATH and LANG space.

towards the left and a slightly larger cluster towards the right, with perhaps a small cluster up towards the top right. Perhaps many people who are strong on communication skills are not so gifted in mathematical skills, while many who are gifted in maths may not have such good communication skills, and a few fortunate people are very gifted in both. The idea that people could perhaps be grouped in this way fits in with some of our preconceptions. Actually we should point out that we fabricated this dataset to demonstrate some features of cluster analysis, and you do not need to believe that abilities actually follow this pattern.

Clustering methods all begin with a matrix of distances (or similarities) between each pair of cases. The first question is how we should calculate these distances. You could of course measure or calculate the distance between each pair of cases on the graph in Figure 10.1. This would be the *Euclidean distance*, which is the usual one we use: the length of a straight line drawn between the two points. To calculate the Euclidean distance between cases 1 and 2 (they are listed in Table 10.4 if you want to look ahead), with MATH 143 and 133 and LANG 123 and 116, we apply Pythagoras' theorem to the points on the graph and get

$$d_{12} = \sqrt{(143 - 133)^2 + (123 - 116)^2} = 12.21$$

Euclidean distance is the one usually used when we have data on interval scales, but other options are available. One alternative is the city block, or *Manhattan distance*. To get this distance, instead of taking the straight line between the two cases we move only horizontally and vertically, like walking around Manhattan where buildings are built in rectangular blocks and you cannot just make a beeline through the buildings. For cases 1 and 2 the Manhattan distance is

$$d_{12} = \text{abs}(143 - 133) + \text{abs}(123 - 116) = 17$$

Here, abs, stands for absolute value, or ignore the sign of the difference. One advantage of using the Manhattan distance is that outlying observations receive less weight, or influence the final result less. Euclidean distance and Manhattan distance are illustrated in Figure 10.2.

A

C = Euclidean distance ($C = \sqrt{A^2 + B^2}$)

B

$A + B$ = Manhattan distance

Figure 10.2 Distance measures for use with interval data.

In Figure 10.3 (from the SPSS help file) you can see the full list of options for use with interval data. The length of this list is an indication of the uncertainty about what is best. We shall use Euclidean distance for our example.

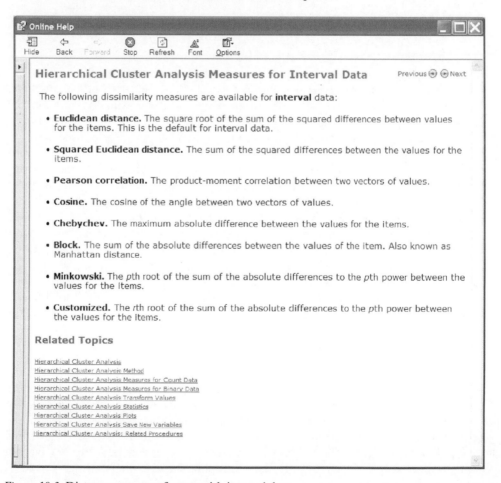

Figure 10.3 Distance measures for use with interval data.

A further problem in many investigations is that the variables are recorded in several different units, all of them arbitrary. We shall look again later at the data on heights and weights that we used to demonstrate discriminant analysis. They were recorded in centimetres and kilograms, but we might have used metres instead of centimetres, or grams instead of kilograms, or we could have used imperial units of inches (or feet) and pounds (or stones). Any change we make will change the distance matrix. Worse, our choice of centimetres or metres for height will change the contribution that height makes to the distances. Likewise we can change the contribution of weight by switching from kilograms to grams. These considerations suggest that if measurements are on different scales they should all be standardized in some way. SPSS offers several options, but for interval measurements Z scores are probably the best.

Distance measures for binary variables

If our variables are binary then we have an even wider choice of possible distance or similarity measures. The sort of problem where this arises is most commonly one where a list of characteristics is recorded as present or absent for each case. Two cases that have identical lists of presences and absences have zero distance between them. But in less extreme instances, should the 'distance' between two cases make use of all concordant presences and absences or only concordant presences? If there are many characteristics, most of which are absent in any particular case, using concordant absences may give undue weight to the many characteristics possessed by neither. Table 10.2 shows a presence/absence table for two cases. There are a characteristics possessed by both and d possessed by neither, while $b + c$ are possessed by just one of the two cases.

Table 10.2 Numbers of presences and absences for two cases

		Case 1	
		Present	*Absent*
Case 2	Present	a	b
	Absent	c	d

With binary data, the most commonly used measures are similarity measures. Should we base the similarity measure for the cases in Table 10.2 on $a/(a + b + c)$ or $(a + d)/(a + b + c + d)$? The first of these two is called the Jaccard similarity and the second is the simple matching coefficient. SPSS offers these measures and 25 others to choose from, including an analogue of Euclidean distance. Many pages in many books have debated this issue. The best choice of distance measure will depend on the particular problem, and it is unlikely to be an easy decision. Probably, you will do best to use one of the measures referred to above, and, only if there seems to be a problem with interpretation of the analysis, start finding out about the properties of alternative measures.

Distance measures for categorical data

If binary data offer us too many plausible measures for the distance between two cases, categorical data perhaps offer us too few. One approach is to use each level of a categorical variable, except the last, as a binary variable. For instance, if we have a variable EMPLOYMENT that defines employment status with four levels (full time, part time, student, other), then we need three binary variables (FULLTIME, PARTTIME, STUDENT), each with two levels, yes and no (the 'other' level will be 'no' for all three). If we do this, we are back to the plethora of choices offered for binary variables.

If our 'cases' are populations, for example groups of students taking different courses at a university, then for any categorical variable two 'cases' can be represented by a frequency table just as you would use for a χ^2 test of association. For example, for each group of students we may have recorded the frequencies in each of the categories of a variable such as PAID EMPLOYMENT (works at weekends, works on weekdays, works weekdays and weekends, does not work in term-time). For a pair of courses such as medicine and economics we might have a table such as the one shown in Table 10.3.

Table 10.3 Table for χ^2 test of association for two courses

Paid employment	Medicine	Economics
Works at weekends	17	23
Works on weekdays	6	14
Works weekdays and weekends	4	7
Does not work in term-time	3	6

A distance measure can be based on the χ^2 value for the usual test of association. This is so because a large χ^2 arises when the 'distance' between courses is great (i.e., they differ significantly from one another). A similar table can be obtained for each pair of courses, so we can obtain a distance matrix for the courses. If there are other categorical variables, these distance measures can be summed to give a total distance between each pair.

Using the distance matrix to form clusters

Once you have a matrix giving the distance between each pair of cases, you have to decide on a method for linking cases together in clusters and then linking clusters to form bigger clusters. There are two basic approaches: *hierarchical* and *non-hierarchical* clustering. Non-hierarchical, or *K*-means clustering, can be used if you know how many clusters to expect and if your variables are interval. The method attempts to form *K* relatively homogeneous clusters based on the variables, and it assumes you have chosen the correct number of clusters and included all relevant variables. For the rest of this chapter we consider hierarchical clustering, which permits a more exploratory approach.

Hierarchical clustering

The results of a hierarchical clustering are often displayed using a *dendrogram* or tree diagram. SPSS Output 10.1 shows the one obtained for the data on the graph in Figure 10.1. (SPSS always scales the distances from 0 to 25.) We show how to get one of

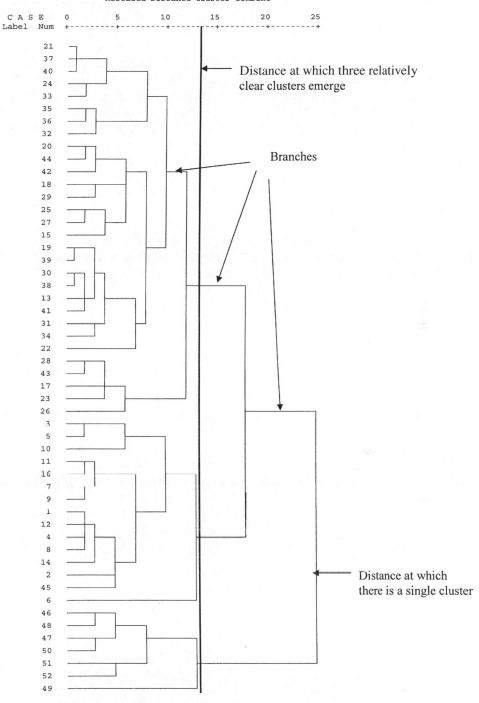

SPSS Output 10.1 Dendrogram for clusters based on MATH and LANG scores.

these later, but for now just look at the structure: cases are down the left side, and the most similar ones are joined with vertical bars. These pairs or triples, such as cases 21, 37 and 40 at the top or 51 and 52 near the bottom, are the beginnings of clusters. To the right, at greater distances, pairs and single cases join to form bigger clusters. These bigger ones join together yet further to the right, until if you place a ruler down the page at a distance a little to the left of 15 just three horizontal lines (or branches) will cross it. By this distance, all cases have been assigned to one of just three clusters. Even further to the right these coalesce into two and then one cluster. Look at the three clusters that form a little more than halfway across. The branches (horizontal lines) that join these clusters together further to the right are quite long, indicating that the clusters are separated by relatively long distances; looking at the dendrogram you could perhaps think that there are three natural clusters there. Following the branches left across the diagram, you see that the biggest cluster, at the top, has 30 cases. The small cluster at the bottom has 7 cases and the one in the middle has 15. Later we consider some ways to decide whether there is a natural place to put a line down the dendrogram and decide how many clusters there are.

The dendrogram illustrates very well how the clustering process works and why it is called hierarchical: there is a hierarchy of clusters as you move across the diagram left to right from the smallest to the greatest distance. Now we consider the methods used to decide which cases should be linked into clusters and when.

Agglomerative techniques

In *agglomerative* techniques, which are used by SPSS, each case starts as a separate cluster and those pairs of cases with the shortest distance between them are linked to form clusters. The distance between a cluster and a case or another cluster may be calculated as the *shortest* distance between any pair of cases with one in each cluster (single linkage or nearest neighbour), the *longest* distance between any pair of cases with one in each cluster (complete linkage or furthest neighbour) or some kind of *average* distance between pairs with one in each cluster (average linkages). Nearest neighbour and furthest neighbour are illustrated in Figure 10.4.

Among the different averaging methods used are between-group (maximize the average distance between members of different groups), within-group (minimize the average distance between members of the same groups), centroid, median and mean. The

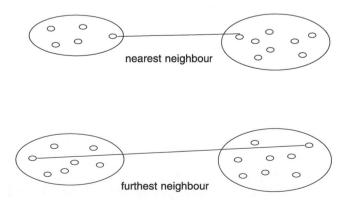

Figure 10.4 Two distance measures between clusters.

centroid method takes the distance between clusters to be the distance between their centroids (centres of gravity), and similarly for the median and mean. *Ward's linkage* attempts to minimize the within-cluster sums of squares. The appropriate distance measure to use with Ward's, centroid and median linkages is the squared Euclidean distance.

Clusters are amalgamated to form bigger clusters at increasing distances between them, until finally all cases are in one cluster. The method of calculating distances between clusters influences the kind of clusters that are obtained. Single linkage tends to produce long straggly clusters where the most distant pair of cases within a cluster may be much further away from each other than either is from neighbouring members of other clusters. Ward's linkage tends to produce clusters with similar numbers of members.

We used the Euclidean distance measure with between-group and within-group linkage on the data graphed in Figure 10.1 and got exactly the same results at the level with three clusters. Using Ward's linkage and the squared Euclidean distance we got the same again. However, with single linkage and the Euclidean distance at the level of three clusters, all but seven cases were in one big cluster, six of the seven (cases 46–48 and 50–52) made another cluster and one case (49) was the sole member of cluster 3. The dendrogram is shown in SPSS Output 10.2 overleaf, with the cases in clusters 2 and 3 in bold italics. Most people use one of the average linkages because such long straggly clusters seldom help us with understanding our data. Should you want to see how dendrograms are constructed, there are some very simple and clear examples provided in Everitt et al. (2001).

Instead of starting with each case being a separate cluster, some algorithms start with all cases in one big cluster and keep splitting clusters until all cases are separate. This reverse technique is known as a *divisive* hierarchical method. We will use agglomerative techniques because that is what SPSS offers.

Some examples and (fabricated) data

In this chapter we use three sets of data, two of which were used previously in illustrations of discriminant analysis. We begin by considering the set of three test scores on children who were poor readers that we used in discriminant analysis. We already know quite a bit about this dataset from the discriminant analysis. However, this time we shall ignore the grouping data based on how they progressed with different interventions. Instead we focus on the question of whether, based on the three test results, we can identify subgroups among the poor readers. If we can, then by looking at such subgroups separately we may gain a better understanding of the problems experienced by the children. The data were shown in Table 9.3 and appear on the book website as psy.discriminant.sav. Figure 9.3 showed a plot of two of the variables.

A second set of data that we already know quite a bit about is the height and weight data that we used in our earlier discriminant analysis. We use this dataset to consider what happens when we do cluster analysis on data where we know there are subgroups. This dataset is sufficiently general to make a parallel medical example unnecessary. The first and last few rows of data were shown in Table 9.1 and the full dataset is discriminant.sav on the book website. They are graphed in Figure 9.1.

Finally, we look at a set of data with three measures, two of which are aptitude scores on language and mathematics (LANG and MATH) that were graphed in Figure 10.1. The

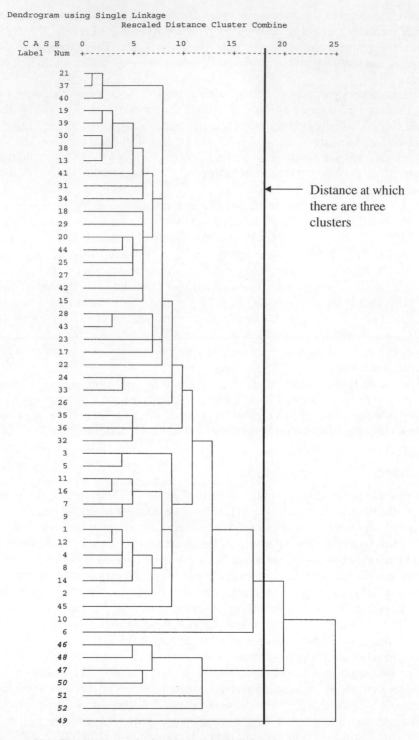

SPSS Output 10.2 Dendrogram obtained using single linkage.

Table 10.4 The first few rows of aptitude and manual dexterity data on 52 students (full set is cluster.sav on the website)

Test		
MATH	LANG	MANUAL
143	123	123
133	116	104
124	110	110
145	119	112
120	110	123

third measure is a score on a test of manual dexterity (MANUAL). As this example is likely to be readily accessible to readers with a medical background as well as those with a psychology background, we do not provide a parallel medical example in this case. The first few rows of data are shown in Table 10.4 (the full set can be found as cluster-.sav on the book website). We have already considered a graph of the first two variables (Figure 10.1) and a dendrogram from a clustering based on the same two variables (SPSS Output 10.1). With three variables, graphs like Figure 10.1 can give us only a partial picture of the data, but a cluster analysis using all three variables may help us to decide whether there are natural subgroups in our dataset.

The poor readers example: Requesting a cluster analysis in SPSS

To start a cluster analysis in SPSS we go to **Analyze** on the menu bar, then **Classify**, then **Hierarchical Cluster**, . . . and we get SPSS Dialog Box 10.1. We begin with our poor

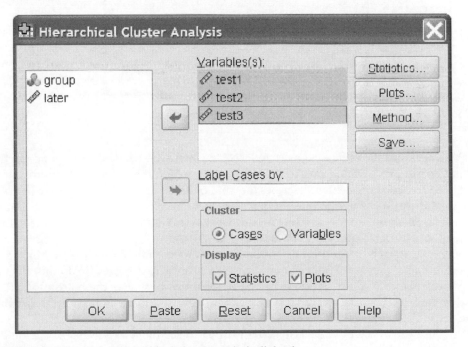

SPSS Dialog Box 10.1 Hierarchical cluster analysis dialog box.

readers data and enter all three test variables into the **Variable(s)** box using the arrow. Make sure the radio button for **Cases** is selected under **Cluster** (click it if not), since we are hoping to form clusters from our cases (not our variables).

Click the **Plots** button and then the **Dendrogram** box. The **Plots** dialog box also offers an *icicle plot*, which is another way to illustrate the step by step amalgamation of cases into clusters, but to start with click the **None** radio button to suppress this (see George & Mallery, 2009, for an example of an icicle plot). Click **Continue** to get back to SPSS Dialog Box 10.1.

The **Statistics** button allows you to decide what to display in the Output Viewer. We can accept the defaults here. If you press the **Save** button you get the dialog box in SPSS Dialog Box 10.2, and we have selected a single solution at the level of three clusters to be saved in the data window. We could instead have chosen to save cluster membership at a range of levels, perhaps from two to four clusters, by clicking the bottom radio button. This could be useful if you have little idea whether there are clusters in your data, or if there are, how many. Click **Continue** to get back to SPSS Dialog Box 10.1.

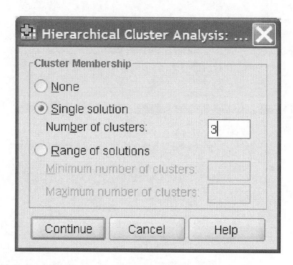

SPSS Dialog Box 10.2 Saving cluster membership in the data window.

We have saved the difficult choices to last. Now press the **Method** button and get the dialog box in SPSS Dialog Box 10.3. First look at the radio buttons for **Measure**. Here you need to click the one that describes the kind of data you have. Our data are interval scales, and the arrow by the **Interval** box gives a choice of distance measures available. As discussed above, we will choose **Euclidean distance**. We will not transform the values since all our variables are scores on similar scales.

When we try the method on height and weight data, which are measured on quite different scales, then we should standardize our variables to Z scores. To do this, use the arrow to replace **None** by **Z scores** in the **Standardize** box near the bottom of SPSS Dialog Box 10.3. Since we are clustering cases, leave the radio button at **By variable** (the default).

Now use the arrow by the **Cluster Method** box to see the list of available agglomeration methods. You may want to try several of these when you have a new problem and

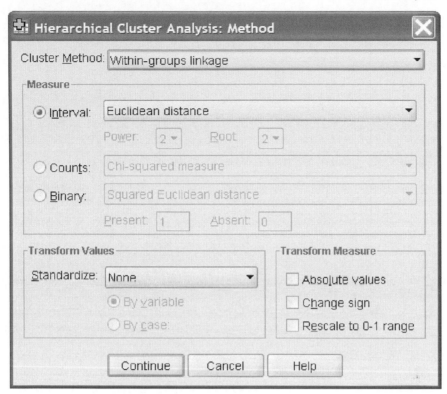

SPSS Dialog Box 10.3 Choosing the distance measure and agglomeration method.

know little about your data. The first two on the list are averaging methods, putting together cases or clusters in the way that minimizes the average within-group distance or maximizes the average between-group distance. Either of these averaging methods may be useful, as may one of the other averaging methods (median or centroid) or Ward's method. Here we have chosen **Within-groups linkage** as our clustering method.

Click **Continue** and **OK** to get the cluster analysis.

The poor readers example: Understanding the output

First in the output is a table showing whether any cases have been omitted because of missing data. All ours have been included and we do not reproduce this table. Then comes the Agglomeration Schedule, shown in SPSS Output 10.3. Here you can see (in the Cluster Combined columns) that the first two cases to be joined in a cluster are 28 and 43. This cluster will now be known as number 28 (i.e., its lowest numbered case). Over to the right in the Next Stage column we see that this new cluster will be joined to something else at stage 4. Look down to stage 4 in the left-hand column and see that cluster 28 (cases 28 and 43) now joins case 9. This is now a three-case cluster and will be referred to as cluster 9. The Next Stage column tells us that the next join is at stage 7, where we see that case 40 joins the cluster. The Next Stage column tells us that the next join is at stage 15, where we see that cluster 19 joins. In the Stage Cluster First Appears (Cluster 2) column, you can see that cluster 19 first appeared at stage 9. Look back to

Agglomeration Schedule

Stage	Cluster Combined		Coefficients	Stage Cluster First Appears		Next Stage
	Cluster 1	Cluster 2		Cluster 1	Cluster 2	
1	28	43	0.000	0	0	4
2	19	42	0.000	0	0	9
3	38	41	0.000	0	0	8
4	9	28	0.000	0	1	7
5	5	20	0.000	0	0	10
6	10	17	0.000	0	0	11
7	9	40	0.500	4	0	15
8	33	38	0.667	0	3	12
9	19	32	0.667	2	0	15
10	5	26	0.667	5	0	13
11	10	23	0.667	6	0	14
12	33	35	0.902	8	0	36
13	5	15	0.902	10	0	28
14	1	10	0.902	0	11	34
15	9	19	0.908	7	9	32
16	37	54	1.000	0	0	47
17	24	53	1.000	0	0	44
18	47	51	1.000	0	0	42
19	44	50	1.000	0	0	29
20	46	48	1.000	0	0	37
21	39	45	1.000	0	0	38
22	27	36	1.000	0	0	30
23	16	31	1.000	0	0	41
24	4	21	1.000	0	0	31
25	11	18	1.000	0	0	34
26	2	14	1.000	0	0	44
27	3	8	1.000	0	0	39
28	5	7	1.024	13	0	33
29	44	49	1.138	19	0	35
30	12	27	1.138	0	22	43
31	4	6	1.138	24	0	40
32	9	34	1.172	15	0	36
33	5	22	1.203	28	0	45
34	1	11	1.218	14	25	40
35	29	44	1.305	0	29	48
36	9	33	1.372	32	12	41
37	46	52	1.382	20	0	42
38	30	39	1.382	0	21	43
39	3	13	1.382	27	0	45
40	1	4	1.478	34	31	46
41	9	16	1.598	36	23	47
42	46	47	1.598	37	18	52
43	12	30	1.619	30	38	48
44	2	24	1.639	26	17	49
45	3	5	1.702	39	33	49
46	1	25	1.729	40	0	51
47	9	37	1.785	41	16	50
48	12	29	1.856	43	35	50
49	2	3	2.323	44	45	51
50	9	12	2.439	47	48	52
51	1	2	2.724	46	49	53
52	9	46	3.039	50	42	53
53	1	9	3.565	51	52	0

SPSS Output 10.3 Agglomeration of cases and clusters.

stage 9, and in the Cluster Combined columns you see clusters 19 and 32 joining to make the new cluster 19. You can tell that cluster 32 must just be case 32 because in the Stage Cluster First Appears (Cluster 2) column we have a zero, so the second cluster in the join (32) must be just a single case. In the Stage Cluster First Appears (Cluster 1) column we see that cluster 19 was started at stage 2, and looking back to stage 2 we see cluster 19 being formed from cases 19 and 42. So when clusters 9 and 19 join at stage 15, we have a seven-case cluster with members 28, 43, 9, 40, 19, 42 and 32. In this way the history of all the clusters can be followed.

Now look at the dendrogram, which appears next. When looking at it in the SPSS output window, you may have to click on it, then pull down the bottom of the frame to get the whole diagram into view. It is shown in SPSS Output 10.4. At the top of the dendrogram we see cases 28, 43 and 9 joining, then being joined by case 40. Cases 19 and 42 join just below and are joined by case 32. These two clusters then join to form a seven-case cluster. At the bottom of the diagram you can see cases 3 and 8 forming a cluster that is joined by case 13. Of course, in this example we do have some extra knowledge: we have test data on poor readers whom we previously put

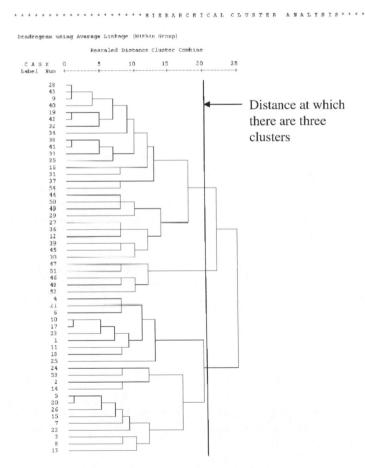

SPSS Output 10.4 Dendrogram for 54 poor readers.

into three groups according to their response to two interventions. So we may be specially interested to see whether we can see three clusters in our data. In the dendrogram we have added a vertical line at a distance just above 20, where it crosses just three branches.

We can easily compare cluster membership with our original group membership since we saved cluster membership at the level of three clusters and we now have an extra column in the datasheet recording this. Use **Analyze, Descriptive statistics** and **Crosstabs** to get SPSS Output 10.5. Here we see that there is quite good correspondence between our new clusters and the original groups. However, four of the group 1s and four of the group 3s are clustered with the group 2s, and one of the group 3s is clustered with the group 1s. Careful study of unexpected results may reveal useful details previously unnoticed, especially in an area where much remains unknown.

group * Average Linkage (Within Group)   Crosstabulation

Count

		Average Linkage (Within Group)			
		1	2	3	Total
group	1	22	4	0	26
	2	0	18	0	18
	3	1	4	5	10
	Total	23	26	5	54

SPSS Output 10.5 Comparing cluster membership with group membership.

Example Box 10.1

Clustering cases: An alternative medical example

The full analysis for this example can be found at www.psypress.com/multivariate-analysis/medical-examples (click on Chapter 10).

We already know from our discriminant analysis that there are three groups in the traumatic brain injury (TBI) data (GROUP 1: back at work at 6 months; GROUP 2: reasonable recovery but not back at work at 6 months; GROUP 3: dependent or dead at 6 months). As the scales for the three IVs (EEG, COMA and PUPIL) all happen to be similar, we do not need to standardize the scores for this dataset. Apart from that, a cluster analysis is carried out in the same way as for the height and weight example, with cluster membership for three clusters being saved and the tabulated results being obtained as shown in SPSS Output 10.7.

Outcomes

A rather surprising feature of the clustering result is that the second cluster contains four cases from each of groups 1 and 3 as well as 18 from group 2. This suggests that it may be worth looking more closely at these eight cases from groups 1 and 3. Such consideration of surprising results can sometimes shed new light on problems where, as with TBI, there are many unknowns.

Alternative variables for use in SPSS
The full dataset, med.discriminant.sav, can be found on the book website

Variable	Psychology	Medicine
Classification variable	GROUP Outcome groups 1, 2 and 3	GROUP Outcome groups 1, 2 and 3
Independent variables	TEST1 TEST2 TEST3	EEG EEG-derived score COMA Glasgow coma score PUPIL Pupil reactivity

The poor readers example: Comparing distance measures and linkage methods

We repeated our analysis of the poor readers data using the three tests and the between-group linkage method. At the level of three clusters, membership was just as shown above for within-group linkage, except that three of the group 1s were clustered with the group 3s, and also the group 3 case that was formerly clustered with the group 1s is now with the group 3s.

To use the centroid or Ward's method we need to use the squared Euclidean distance. We tried this and found that centroid linkage reproduced our three clusters from within-group linkage except for moving the group 3 and one of the group 1 cases from cluster 1 to cluster 3. Ward linkage (with squared Euclidean distance) produced exactly the same result as between-groups linkage (with Euclidean distance).

Using Manhattan (block) as the distance measure and within-group linkage we found five group 1s and five groups 3s clustered with the group 2s. This result is very similar to that obtained with Euclidean distance and shown in SPSS Output 10.5. The similarity of the results obtained using several methods gives us some comfort that when the data are structured in clusters, as ours are here, the choice of distance measure and linkage method may not affect our results very much. Experimenting with these changes can help you to see whether your results seem fairly robust or are very dependent on the choices you make for the distance measure and linkage method.

Selection of cases

In addition to the problems of choosing variables on which to base distance measures, choosing distance measures and deciding which clustering method to use, there is the usual problem of deciding how many cases are needed and selecting a suitable sample. Unlike factor analysis, it is the cases that are usually grouped on the basis of some variables that identify characteristics of the cases, and we do not necessarily need a large number of cases to identify clusters. If the data do have some structure and there are subsets to be found, then the choice of cases and even the number of them may not be important as long as all subsets are represented.

In order to see the effect of reducing the number of cases selected, we made an extra variable called SELECT and added it to the data on the three test scores. We gave alternate cases the values of 1 and 2, starting with 1, on SELECT. Then we tried using **Data** and **Select cases** to select just those with SELECT = 1, and applied the hierarchical cluster analysis just to this half of the dataset (using Euclidean distance and within-group linkage). At the level of three clusters, all but one of the cases in this half of the dataset fell into the same clusters as they did when the full dataset was used. The same was true when we repeated the analysis with SELECT = 2. It is easy for you to try this experiment for yourself. You could of course do the same sort of thing with a real dataset, and perhaps have added confidence in any clusters you identify if you can still find them using just part of the dataset.

Using discriminant analysis to confirm findings

One way to investigate possible clusters further is to see whether a discriminant analysis can classify the cases successfully into the clusters. To try this, all you need to do is save the cluster membership in the data window for the number of clusters you think is appropriate, then use the cluster membership as the grouping variable in a discriminant analysis. We did this for our poor readers data: we saved cluster membership for three clusters, then used this as the grouping variable for a discriminant analysis. We used a stepwise method to add the variables TEST1, TEST2 and TEST3. All three variables were entered and all cases were correctly classified into their clusters.

So, looking at the dendrogram in SPSS Output 10.4, we might think that our cases fall into three clusters and that discriminant analysis can classify all of them correctly using our variables. However, we may discern subclusters in the larger clusters so that four or five clusters, or perhaps some different number, may also be possible. We considered the possibility that discriminant analysis would classify the cases into four clusters.

Still looking at the dendrogram in SPSS Output 10.4, you find that by placing a vertical ruler carefully you can find a position where it crosses four branches. At this distance level, the 23 cases that form cluster 1 at the bottom of the dendrogram form two clusters. How would discriminant analysis perform on these four clusters? To try it, all you need do is save the cluster membership in the data window for four clusters and use this as the grouping variable for a discriminant analysis. We did this, again using a stepwise method to enter the variables TEST1, TEST2 and TEST3. All but one case was correctly classified. So, discriminant analysis can classify the cases into four clusters quite successfully, though not quite as well as into three.

Results for other datasets

The heights and weights example

It is useful to see what happens when we try to form clusters in a dataset where we know there are certainly subgroups. The data on heights and weights of 35 men and women is a simple example. We know there are two groups (men and women) and we have data on just two measurements. We also know, from the graph in Figure 9.1 of the previous chapter, that the points do not really form distinct clusters. However, this is clearly a case where standardizing to Z scores for the heights and weights would be sensible.

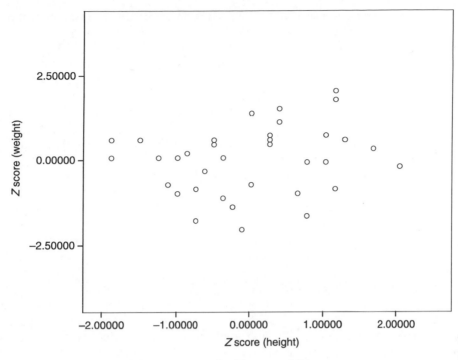

Figure 10.5 Heights and weights as Z scores for 20 men and 15 women.

Figure 10.5 shows the graph when we do this, and we can see that the general pattern of points is little changed. This time men and women are not distinguished, since we are asking whether there are clusters in the data.

We used the standardized heights and weights as our clustering variables by selecting **Z scores** from the drop-down list in the **Standardize** box in SPSS Dialog Box 10.3 and ensuring that the **By variable** radio button was selected. We used the **Save** button in the main dialog box to save the cluster membership for the single solution of two clusters (SPSS Dialog Box 10.2, but with two instead of three clusters specified) and then returned to the data window and tabulated the results by selecting **Analyse, Descriptive Statistics** and **Crosstabs**. Put SEX and the saved variable (AVERAGE LINKAGE) in the row and column boxes. You can see the output in SPSS Output 10.6. Cluster 1 is nearly all males (just two females), but eight of the males are in cluster 2 with most of the females. The two clusters derived from the (standardized) height and weight measurements do not correspond very closely with the two groups that we know make up the data. This is a useful reminder that cluster analysis looks for clusters of observations in the space

sex * Average Linkage (Within Group)   Crosstabulation

Count

		Average Linkage (Within Group)		
		1	2	Total
sex	male	12	8	20
	female	2	13	15
	Total	14	21	35

SPSS Output 10.6 Cluster membership for males and females.

defined by the variables we use. If there are distinct groups in the dataset they will only be identified by a cluster analysis if the variables we use reflect these groups. In this case, we find that height and weight do not adequately reflect membership of the male and female groups. We need to keep in mind that it is usual for us not to know whether the variables we are using are those that will separate any clusters that there may be.

The aptitude example

In our discussion of distance measures we showed part of an aptitude dataset for 52 students (Figure 10.1). For these students we have scores on VERBAL, MATH and MANUAL aptitude tests. The first few rows appear in Table 10.4 and the full dataset is on the book website (cluster.sav). We already suggested that study of Figure 10.1 may lead an optimist to discern three clusters here. We did perform a cluster analysis and found, at the level of three clusters, a cluster of seven cases (those on the top right of Figure 10.1) and two other clusters of 15 and 30 cases. If we save cluster membership at the level of three clusters, we find that a discriminant analysis can successfully separate the clusters obtained.

On the dendrogram, it appeared that we could reasonably consider four clusters, so we tried saving cluster membership at that level (using Euclidean distance and within-group linkage). Then we used the saved cluster membership as the grouping variable for a discriminant analysis and used the stepwise method to enter VERBAL, MATH and MANUAL. The summary table is shown in SPSS Output 10.7, where you can see that classification was quite successful.

Classification Results[a]

		Average Linkage (Within Group)	Predicted Group Membership				
			1	2	3	4	Total
Original	Count	1	15	0	0	0	15
		2	0	20	1	0	21
		3	0	2	7	0	9
		4	0	0	0	7	7
	%	1	100.0	0.0	0.0	0.0	100.0
		2	0.0	95.2	4.8	0.0	100.0
		3	0.0	22.2	77.8	0.0	100.0
		4	0.0	0.0	0.0	100.0	100.0

a. 94.2% of original grouped cases correctly classified.

SPSS Output 10.7 Discrimination into four clusters using the variables MATH and LANG.

Deciding how many clusters there are

There is no simple way to decide how many clusters there are. You can put a ruler on the dendrogram at any chosen distance and the number of branches that cross it is the number of clusters at that distance (using your chosen distance measure and linkage method). The greater the distance, the fewer the clusters, but is there a natural place to stop? Usually, you are not interested in solutions with a great many clusters, since you are looking for ways to understand your data and this generally needs some simplification. If you are trying to consider a great many clusters you may as well consider individual cases. Probably you are hoping to see some evidence of clustering into between two and five or six groups. Is there a distance on the dendrogram where the process of branches and twigs (the lines linking cases or clusters of cases) joining seems to slow down, so that there are longer lengths of branch between joins? This can be an indication that you have reached a level where the clusters formed so far do have some separation between them.

Trying the process again using a different linkage method can also be helpful. If you get similar results with the number of clusters you suspect may be the right one, then this increases your confidence that there really are clusters in your data and that you have found them. With our height and weight data we tried using within-group linkage with Euclidean distance and centroid linkage with the squared Euclidean distance (standardizing to Z scores in both cases). We found the same cases in the same clusters at the level of two clusters. This would tend to confirm our belief in the reality of these clusters. But, recall that we already know that the graph does not suggest the existence of clusters at all using these variables, and that the clusters found in the cluster analysis do not correspond closely with the known groups of males and females, so our belief would be mistaken. We include this result as a cautionary tale!

Clustering variables and some (fabricated) binary data

So far we have only looked at clustering cases. We have also only looked at dealing with interval data. So, while we have a brief look at clustering variables, we also use a different kind of data, namely binary data. Once again we have fabricated it to bring out an important point. Difficulties with reading are often associated with various behaviour problems, some of which may contribute to the reading problems and some of which may be caused by the inability to progress with reading. Table 10.5 gives the first few rows of presence (coded 1) and absence (coded 0) data on eight problems for 50 children at the end of the first year of school (the full dataset can be found as psy.cluster.variables.sav on the book website). These problems, which we have abbreviated as PROB1 to PROB8, are listed below:

PROB1	daily tantrums
PROB2	cannot take turns for teacher's attention
PROB3	poor coordination
PROB4	short attention span
PROB5	cannot share equipment
PROB6	poor concentration
PROB7	shows off to classmates when asked to work without teacher
PROB8	little or no progress with reading

Table 10.5 The first few rows of presence/absence of eight problems in 50 children (full set is psy.cluster.variables.sav on the website)

PROB1	PROB2	PROB3	PROB4	PROB5	PROB6	PROB7	PROB8
0	0	0	1	0	0	0	1
0	0	0	1	0	1	1	0
0	0	0	0	0	1	0	1
0	0	0	1	0	1	0	0
0	0	0	1	0	0	1	1

Binary variables: Requesting the cluster analysis

Looking at the table of presences and absences certainly does not convey much impression of how the variables may be related, if they are. To see whether cluster analysis throws any light on this, we once again used **Analyze**, then **Classify**, then **Hierarchical Cluster**, . . . to get SPSS Dialog Box 10.1. We entered all of the variables, PROB1 to PROB8, into the **Variables** box and this time we clicked the radio button for **Cluster Variables**. We then clicked the **Plot** button and again asked for a **Dendrogram** and omitted the icicle diagram. For the Cluster **Method**, we chose **Within-groups linkage** (SPSS Dialog Box 10.3) and clicked the **Binary** radio button in the **Measure** group. We used the drop-down list to choose a similarity measure (which will be converted to a distance measure). There is a long list, as mentioned in the discussion of distance measures in the introduction.

Distance measures: Simple matching coefficient

We began by choosing the **Simple matching coefficient**. SPSS Output 10.8(a) shows the resulting dendrogram. This suggests that problems 1 and 8 may be linked, and also 3, 5 and (less closely) 2. Problems 4 and 6 also make a pair, but not grouped as closely as 1 with 8, or 3, 5 and 2. Problem 7 joins the 3, 5, 2 cluster but only just before it is joined by the loose 4 and 6 pair. Looking at the list of problems, these clusters do seem quite plausible. Perhaps the tantrums (PROB1) are related to loss of self-esteem if the child sees itself as failing at the all-important reading skill (PROB8). Short attention span (PROB4) and poor concentration (PROB6) do seem likely to be linked. Inability to share attention (PROB2) or equipment (PROB5) may be a sign of immaturity, and poor coordination (PROB3) could also indicate this.

Distance measures: The Jaccard coefficient

But what happens if we use a different similarity/distance measure? SPSS Output 10.8(b) shows the dendrogram obtained using the Jaccard coefficient. Apart from the cluster of problems 1 and 8, this looks very different from SPSS Output 10.8(a). The choice of distance measure for binary data is particularly difficult and, as here, can have a marked effect on the results. In this case, many people would suggest that the simple matching coefficient is more appropriate than the Jaccard, because none of the problems is rare. Problem 1 occurs in 12 out of 50 cases, and all others are more common than that. Because this technique is exploratory, if your results help you to understand your data you do not need to be too concerned if you do not have clear justification for your choice of distance measure or linkage method. But of course if results that help your understanding are not robust to changes in the choices you make, you must be careful not to claim too much for them and only use them as a guide to further work.

Clustering method: Comparing within-group and between-group linkage

Here we have one more dendrogram to consider. In SPSS Output 10.8(c) we see the result of using the simple matching coefficient with between-group linkage. This time the result is similar to SPSS Output 10.8(a), but problem 7 joins the cluster with 4 and 6 instead of 3, 5 and 2.

(a) Dendrogram for variable clusters using simple matching coefficient

```
* * * * * * * * * * * * * * * * * * * H I E R A R C H I C A L   C L U S T E R   A N A L Y S I S * * * * * * * * * * * * * * * * * * * * *

Dendrogram using Average Linkage (Within Group)

                    Rescaled Distance Cluster Combine

   C A S E     0         5        10        15        20        25
   Label   Num +---------+---------+---------+---------+---------+

   PROB1     1
   PROB8     8
   PROB4     4
   PROB6     6
   PROB3     3
   PROB5     5
   PROB2     2
   PROB7     7
```

(b) Dendrogram for variable clusters using Jaccard coefficient

```
* * * * * * * * * * * * * * * * * * * H I E R A R C H I C A L   C L U S T E R   A N A L Y S I S * * * * * * * * * * * * * * * * * * * * *

Dendrogram using Average Linkage (Within Group)

                    Rescaled Distance Cluster Combine

   C A S E     0         5        10        15        20        25
   Label   Num +---------+---------+---------+---------+---------+

   PROB1     1
   PROB8     8
   PROB6     6
   PROB4     4
   PROB2     2
   PROB3     3
   PROB7     7
   PROB5     5
```

(c) Dendrogram for variable clusters using simple matching coefficient with between-group linkage

```
* * * * * * * * * * * * * * * * * * * H I E R A R C H I C A L   C L U S T E R   A N A L Y S I S * * * * * * * * * * * * * * * * * * * * *

Dendrogram using Average Linkage (Between Groups)

                    Rescaled Distance Cluster Combine

   C A S E     0         5        10        15        20        25
   Label   Num +---------+---------+---------+---------+---------+

   PROB1     1
   PROB8     8
   PROB3     3
   PROB5     5
   PROB2     2
   PROB4     4
   PROB6     6
   PROB7     7
```

SPSS Output 10.8 Dendrograms for variable clusters using different distance measures and clustering methods.

It is of course possible to cluster the cases here as well as the variables, and consideration of each cluster of children may suggest helpful interventions or better ways to understand the problems. If so, then the technique has been useful, whether or not you can fully justify your choice of distance measure or linkage method.

Example Box 10.2

Clustering variables: An alternative medical example with (fabricated) binary data

The full analysis for this example can be found at www.psypress.com/multivariate-analysis/medical-examples (click on Chapter 10).

There is a range of symptoms associated with traumatic brain injury (TBI). Various combinations of symptoms may be present in different victims, and it may be that an exploration of what combinations (or clusters) of symptoms tend to occur together would be revealing. From a long list of possible symptoms, we have selected just eight for the purpose of this example analysis:

SYMPT1   fatigue
SYMPT2   feelings of helplessness
SYMPT3   disorientation
SYMPT4   confrontational attitude
SYMPT5   blurred vision
SYMPT6   explosive temper
SYMPT7   depression
SYMPT8   irritability

The file med.cluster.variables.sav on the web has data on the presence (coded 1) and absence (coded 0) of eight symptoms (in reality, there would be many more) for 50 patients who have recently suffered mild to moderate TBI. Three cluster analyses are carried out on these data: (1) the average (within-group) linkage method is used with the simple matching coefficient as the distance measure, (2) the same method is used with the Jaccard coefficient as the distance measure and (3) the average (between-group) linkage method is used with the simple matching coefficient as the distance measure, as in the first analysis.

Outcomes

In the first analysis, symptoms 1 and 8 are linked, which makes intuitive sense: a physical state of fatigue may lead to the emotional state of irritability. Also symptoms 3, 5 and 2 are linked and it does seem plausible that the physical state of blurred vision may be associated with cognitive disorientation and, eventually, feelings of helplessness. Symptom 7, depression, joins the 3, 5, 2 cluster just before it is joined by the 4 and 6 pair of symptoms (confrontational attitude and explosive temper). Apart from the cluster comprising symptom 1 and symptom 8, the results using the Jaccard coefficient look very different. Probably, in a situation like this in which none of the symptoms is rare, the average linkage method would generally be considered more appropriate. The average (between-group) linkage method yields very similar results to the within-group linkage method, which increases confidence in the stability of the clusters. It is interesting that links are found across physical, cognitive, emotional and behavioural categories of symptoms, and this is something that might be worth pursuing in future research.

Alternative variables for use in SPSS
The full dataset, med.cluster.variables.sav, can be found on the book website

Variable	Psychology	Medicine
Binary variables	PROB1 Daily tantrums PROB2 Can't take turns for attention PROB3 Poor coordination PROB4 Short attention span PROB5 Cannot share equipment PROB6 Poor concentration PROB7 Shows off to classmates PROB8 Little or no reading progress	SYMPT1 Fatigue (physical) SYMPT2 Depression (emotional) SYMPT3 Disorientation (cognitive) SYMPT4 Confrontational (behavioural) SYMPT5 Blurred vision (physical) SYMPT6 Explosive temper (behav.) SYMPT7 Feelings of helplessness (emot.) SYMPT8 Irritability (emot.)

Reporting results

As we have already said, if you are reporting results from a study using an exploratory technique like this you can really only describe what you did and how it helped your understanding of the data, perhaps suggesting a different way of looking at it, which in turn suggests some further work. In this spirit we offer the following paragraphs suggesting how you might report the attempt to cluster variables in the last section.

Our data on the presence or absence of eight problems in 50 children who have not progressed well in their first year at school have been described above. In an attempt to gain more understanding of the problems and how they may be related, we performed a cluster analysis on the variables. For the distance measure we chose the simple matching coefficient. None of the problems was rare in our dataset (problem 1, the least common, was present in 12 of 50 cases), so the simple matching coefficient was a reasonable choice. Using an average linkage method (within-group linkage), we found the dendrogram shown in Figure A (*this is our SPSS Output 10.8(a)*). The variables most closely linked were problems 1 and 8: daily tantrums and lack of progress in reading.

Problems 3, 5 and 2 also formed a cluster, though 2 was not as close as 3 and 5. This cluster links the inability to share attention or resources with poor coordination. Perhaps all these are indications of immaturity. At a greater distance, this cluster was joined by problem 7 (showing off as soon as they do not have the teacher's attention), which is perhaps a further indication of immaturity.

Poor concentration and short attention span (4 and 6) are clearly related, and here they were grouped together, though not as closely as we might have expected.

Using the between-group linkage method the results were similar, though this time problem 7 was loosely linked to the pair of 4 and 6.

These results suggest to us that perhaps tantrums may be related to loss of self-esteem when a child feels it is failing at an important skill. Perhaps efforts to improve the self-esteem of children experiencing some failure may help them to avoid behaviour that further compromises their progress. We propose to investigate this in a further study. Our results also suggest that some children may just need longer to achieve the maturity needed for some of the behaviour expected in school, and if their inability to share attention and resources can be sympathetically treated they may be helped just to grow out of this. Also, we could try to teach the skills of sharing explicitly, perhaps helping children towards greater maturity by focussing on the specific skills required of them. Again, a follow-up study on these children will investigate this.

References

Everitt, B. S., Landau, S., & Leese, M. (2001). *Cluster analysis* (4th ed.). London: Hodder & Arnold.

George, D., & Mallery, P. (2009). *SPSS for Windows step by step: A simple guide and reference* (16.0 update). Boston, MA: Pearson Education.

11 Multidimensional scaling

Introduction and intuitive explication

A road atlas example

Most people are familiar with the distance matrix in a road atlas. It gives the distance in miles or kilometres between the main towns in the atlas. Since the distance between A and B is the same as the distance between B and A, usually just the lower or upper triangle of the symmetric matrix is shown, like the small one in Table 11.1. Of course, a matrix like this is produced from a map, but the question tackled by multi-dimensional scaling (MDS) is: Can we reconstruct the map if we only have the distance matrix?

Table 11.1 Lower triangle of a distance (in miles) matrix for eight British cities (mds1.sav)

	Wick	*Glasgow*	*York*	*Oxford*	*Cardiff*	*Exeter*	*Bristol*	*London*
Wick	0							
Glasgow	277	0						
York	477	212	0					
Oxford	633	370	184	0				
Cardiff	662	397	243	107	0			
Exeter	716	451	298	154	113	0		
Bristol	643	380	226	74	44	84	0	
London	675	410	211	56	153	200	120	0

The answer is that we can, approximately at least. Of course, the road distances are not the shortest straight line distances between the towns; roads are not straight and they have to divert from the shortest route in order to cross rivers, or go round mountains or inlets from the sea. If our distance matrix gave the straight line distances between the towns then the reconstructed map would correspond to the original, but with a real distance matrix like we have here the reconstructed map will not be exactly right, and the bigger the road diversions from the straight line distances, the bigger will be the discrepancy between the original and the reconstructed map. So a country like Norway, with many natural barriers round which roads must go, will have a less satisfactory reconstructed map than a country like Belgium, with few natural barriers. For the towns in Table 11.1, we expect some distortion of the map because the Bristol Channel blocks the shortest route between Exeter and several

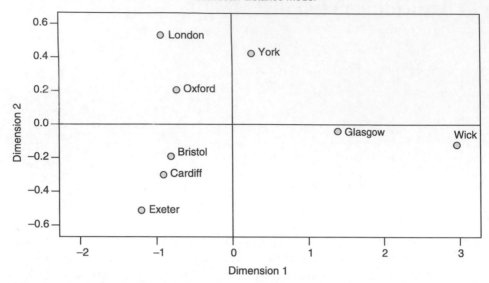

Figure 11.1 Map produced from distance matrix in Table 11.1.

places to the north. Also, the wide exit from the Moray Firth in the east coast of Scotland blocks the shortest route between Wick and places to the south-east. In fact Figure 11.1 shows the reconstructed map, which at first glance does not look promising.

However, if we remember that having north at the top and west at the left of the map is just a convention, we see that this map is not so far from the original. Just rotate it anticlockwise through a quarter turn, then turn it over and you have something not very different from the positions of these towns on a normal map of Britain.

So, we can do this, but you may well ask why anyone should want to. In fact it is a useful technique for producing a visual display of distances between items, and the distances can be conceptual instead of geographical. In the previous chapter we applied cluster analysis to distance or similarity matrices to see if we could identify subgroups of cases (or variables) in our dataset. Now we are considering a visual display that will show relationships among cases or variables as a two-dimensional map. This can be a useful aid to understanding data where we have no reason to expect clusters or subsets. As we shall see, it can also help us to see whether relationships change after some intervention or event, or just after the lapse of time.

Multidimensional scaling and cluster analysis compared

Like cluster analysis, MDS is basically a descriptive technique that may be useful at an exploratory stage of research into some problem. It is also like cluster analysis in that it examines the distances between (or proximities of) a set of entities to reveal their structure. Indeed, the distinction between cluster analysis and MDS is not clear-cut. Both can be used to obtain structural descriptions of the same set of data. However, they differ in the aspect of structure that they focus on. Whereas cluster analysis focuses on the identification of groupings (or categories) of entities (cases or variables), MDS focuses on the identification of continuous dimensions along which the entities are perceived to vary, although groupings may still be referred to within the dimensional structure where this aids interpretation of the data.

MDS Stage 1: Obtaining proximity (or distance) data

There are three stages to MDS. First, distance (or proximity) data for all pairings of entities (either physical or conceptual) are generated. The distance data may be obtained *directly*, as when someone is asked to rate the similarity (e.g., in attractiveness or relatedness) between each pair of entities, or *indirectly*, as when the entities are rated on a number of variables and the correlation, or some measure of difference (i.e., distance), between each pair of entities is obtained. One such measure of distance would be the squared Euclidean distance, defined as the sum of the squared differences between a pair of entities on all of the rated variables: $\Sigma_i (x_{1i} - x_{2i})^2$. Of course the distance measures do not have to be subjective ratings. They could just as well be objective observations, such as number of interactions between pairs of children as a measure of their 'closeness'. Typically, indirect measures have been used in cluster analysis and direct measures in MDS. Although there is no necessity for this distinction, users of MDS tend to claim that direct measures are to be preferred because they tap into the dimensions that raters use spontaneously to interpret their world.

MDS Stage 2: Scaling in spatial dimensions

Second, the distances are used to create scales in some (usually small) number of spatial dimensions on which the entities of interest can be located. You do not need to know the details of the scaling computation but it may help to have an idea of the general approach. Suppose we have proximities for the three possible pairings of entities A, B and C and that these proximities are AB = 4, BC = 2 and AC = 5. We can start by representing A as a point in an empty space. Then we can represent B as a point 4 units (let us make the units centimetres) in any direction away from A. Next, we know that C must be 2 cm from B, so it must lie somewhere on the circle with radius – 2 cm with its centre at B (see Figure 11.2). We find a location on the circle whose distance from A is 5 cm and label that point C. In this example, two dimensions were needed to represent

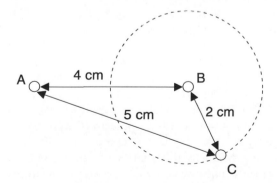

Figure 11.2 A simple example of multidimensional scaling of distances between three entities.

the distances on a spatial map. Had the distance between A and C been 6 cm instead of 5 cm, then one dimension would have sufficed: A, B and C could all have been accommodated on a single straight line. Returning to our two-dimensional example, perhaps, within acceptable limits of error, all remaining distances involving AD, BD, . . ., JK, etc., could be accommodated within two dimensions. If not, we would need to add a third dimension, and we could add yet more dimensions as necessary. The mathematics work just as well with, say, six dimensions as with two, though the attraction of MDS is its capability of representing a lot of relational information in a very accessible two-dimensional spatial map. Generally, the more dimensions that are needed, the less useful will be the structural summary for understanding the data.

MDS Stage 3: Interpretation and an example from social psychology

The final, third, stage in MDS is interpretation of the dimensional structure obtained. This is best discussed in the context of realistic examples. Here we show you some results from a published example.

Table 11.2 Distance matrix for church organizations according to opponents of women's ordination, obtained before the first ordinations took place (mds2.sav)

	MOW	PWO	WAOW	CofCon	FiF	Bishops	RCC	Orth	CofE
MOW	0.000								
POW	1.800	0.000							
WAOW	4.600	4.533	0.000						
CofCon	4.444	4.556	2.111	0.000					
FiF	4.591	4.511	2.000	1.935	0.000				
Bishops	2.822	2.978	4.200	4.156	4.200	0.000			
RCC	4.533	4.422	3.455	2.932	3.000	4.311	0.000		
Orth	4.717	4.622	3.022	3.250	3.089	4.391	2.911	0.000	
CofE	3.556	3.467	3.622	3.711	3.756	3.364	3.696	3.870	0.000

An example of a distance matrix from social psychology is shown in Table 11.2. This was obtained as part of a study of Identity and Schism, which used the contentious issue of the ordination of women as priests in the Church of England in 1994 (Sani & Reicher, 1999). The entities (or items) in the matrix are nine church organizations, including several pressure groups promoting or opposing the ordination of women. Before the first ordinations took place, a sample of opponents to the ordination of women were each asked to rate all pairings among the nine organizations on a scale of 1 (very similar) to 5 (very different). The ratings of the sample members were averaged to form the distance matrix in Table 11.2. The organizations are MOW (Movement for the Ordination of Women), PWO (Priests for Women's Ordination), WAOW (Women against the Ordination of Women), CofCon (Cost of Conscience, an anti group), FiF (Forward in Faith, an anti group), Bishops (the House of Bishops of the Church of England), RCC (the Roman Catholic Church), Orth (the Orthodox Church) and CofE (the Church of England).

The result of applying MDS to this matrix of conceptual distances is shown in Figure 11.3. The three organizations opposed to women's ordination are very close together, as you might expect. However, it is interesting to see that the Church of

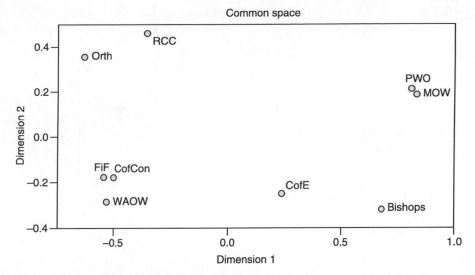

Figure 11.3 Map of church organizations as seen by opponents of women's ordination, produced from distance matrix in Table 11.2.

England and its leadership, the bishops, are quite far apart, and the bishops are closer than is the Church of England as a whole to the two organizations promoting women's ordination. The Orthodox and Catholic churches are as far as they can be from the bishops.

Using a sample of supporters of women's ordination, another distance matrix (Table 11.3) was obtained in exactly the same way as Table 11.2. The map produced from it is shown in Figure 11.4, and it is interesting to see the difference from the perception of the opponents. Here the Church of England and its leadership, the bishops, are close together, and quite close to the organizations supporting women's ordination. The opponents' organizations are seen as closer to the Catholic and Orthodox churches than to their own.

Table 11.3 Distance matrix for church organizations according to supporters of women's ordination, obtained before the first ordinations took place (mds3.sav)

	MOW	*PWO*	*WAOW*	*CofCon*	*FiF*	*Bishops*	*RCC*	*Orth*	*CofE*
MOW	0.000								
POW	2.091	0.000							
WAOW	4.647	4.579	0.000						
CofCon	4.504	4.598	2.288	0.000					
FiF	4.432	4.423	2.267	2.221	0.000				
Bishops	3.220	3.402	4.295	4.231	4.015	0.000			
RCC	4.244	4.176	3.649	3.248	3.473	3.931	0.000		
Orth	4.466	4.279	3.612	3.519	3.595	4.108	3.450	0.000	
CofE	3.115	3.092	4.100	4.124	3.977	2.354	3.692	3.886	0.000

These two figures show how a visual representation of conceptual distances can be very revealing. The two samples of supporters and opponents of women's ordination perceive quite differently the relationships of their church and its bishops to other

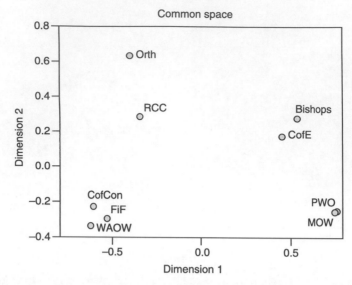

Figure 11.4 Map of church organizations as seen by supporters of women's ordination, produced from distance matrix in Table 11.3.

churches and the various pressure groups. Such a visual display can be very helpful in understanding complex data.

Interpreting the dimensions on the maps is not important: it is the relative positions on the maps that we hope will aid understanding. Nevertheless, sometimes an interpretation of the dimensions can be made, and if so it may further assist our understanding of the data. Sani and Reicher (1999) interpreted dimension 1 on both maps, shown here as *ideology*, with conservatism on the left and emancipation/liberalism on the right. In Figure 11.3, dimension 2 can be seen as reflecting *involvement* in the issue of women's ordination, with the Orthodox and Roman Catholic churches not involved at all. In Figure 11.4, dimension 2 might reflect *organization*, with the churches and bishops at the top and pressure groups at the bottom.

Multidimensional scaling: A psychology example and (fabricated) data

Here we use the number of interactions between pairs of people to derive a measure of distance between them. Fourteen secondary school students studying social science agreed to participate in an experimental evaluation of a course unit on citizenship and diversity. The students all got on quite well in the classroom context and were accustomed to working individually and in self-selected pairs on loosely supervised classroom projects where the teacher acted as a consultant. They agreed that the classroom could be videoed during three sessions of such work so that, in the words of the experimenter, 'their methods of working together could be studied'. In fact the interactions between all pairs of students were counted. If more than two were discussing or working together then all pairs of students in the group were counted as interacting. The numbers of interactions are shown in Table 11.4(a). The students studied the new course unit soon after, and in it they worked intensively on the costs and benefits to a community of cultural differences and on the differences and similarities in approaches

Table 11.4 Numbers of interactions between pairs of students

(a) In the first three project sessions (mds.similaritya.sav)

	Adam	Ana	Chila	Colin	Dee	Dom	Ewan	Holly	Jim	Krish	Laura	Mira	Pete	Sanjiv
Adam														
Ana	5													
Chila	4	10												
Colin	7	7	7											
Dee	4	7	8	6										
Dom	6	7	6	6	4									
Ewan	8	7	6	9	5	8								
Holly	3	7	8	6	9	4	5							
Jim	9	5	4	8	4	5	7	4						
Krish	7	6	5	6	3	8	8	3	6					
Laura	3	7	8	6	9	4	5	9	4	3				
Mira	3	8	9	5	7	5	5	7	3	4	7			
Pete	8	6	6	9	5	7	8	4	8	7	5	5		
Sanjiv	6	6	5	6	4	10	8	3	5	9	3	5	7	

(b) In the three project sessions after the citizenship course (mds.similarityb.sav)

	Adam	Ana	Chila	Colin	Dee	Dom	Ewan	Holly	Jim	Krish	Laura	Mira	Pete	Sanjiv
Adam														
Ana	7													
Chila	6	9												
Colin	9	7	6											
Dee	5	8	9	5										
Dom	9	8	7	9	6									
Ewan	7	9	8	7	7	8								
Holly	4	7	8	4	8	5	7							
Jim	4	6	8	4	9	5	6	8						
Krish	5	8	8	5	8	6	8	9	7					
Laura	8	9	8	8	7	9	8	6	6	7				
Mira	7	9	9	6	8	7	9	8	7	8	8			
Pete	6	9	9	7	9	7	8	7	7	7	8	8		
Sanjiv	9	8	7	9	6	10	8	6	5	6	9	7	7	

to problems shown by the boys and the girls. Then the next three sessions of working on classroom projects were videoed as before, and the interactions counted once again. These counts are shown in Table 11.4(b).

Obtaining a distance measure

The counts of interactions provide a measure of proximity between each pair of students, and we can use these measures directly or we can convert them into distances. We prefer to use the counts to derive a distance measure, since MDS is based on the idea of producing a visual display of the distances between pairs of items. However, SPSS does enable you to use proximities directly, as we see in the next section.

The highest number of interactions between any pair is 10, so if you subtract all the proximities in Table 11.4 from some number greater than 10, for instance from 12, then those who spoke to each other least often will have the highest scores and we shall have a measure of distance. The distance of each person from him/herself must be taken as zero, by analogy with distances in space. Table 11.5 shows the result for the first set of

Table 11.5 'Distances' between pairs of students in the first three project sessions (mds.distancea.sav)

	Adam	Ana	Chila	Colin	Dee	Dom	Ewan	Holly	Jim	Krish	Laura	Mira	Pete	Sanjiv
Adam	0													
Ana	7	0												
Chila	8	2	0											
Colin	5	5	5	0										
Dee	8	5	4	6	0									
Dom	6	5	6	6	8	0								
Ewan	4	5	6	3	7	4	0							
Holly	9	5	4	6	3	8	7	0						
Jim	3	7	8	4	8	7	5	8	0					
Krish	5	6	7	6	9	4	4	9	6	0				
Laura	9	5	4	6	3	8	7	3	8	9	0			
Mira	9	4	3	7	5	7	7	5	9	8	5	0		
Pete	4	6	6	3	7	5	4	8	4	5	7	7	0	
Sanjiv	6	6	7	6	8	2	4	9	7	3	9	7	5	0

project sessions. (For the later set of project sessions the results can be found as mds.similarityb.sav on the book website.)

We can use either Table 11.4(a) or Table 11.5 as the basis of on MDS and the results will be equivalent.

Entering the data in SPSS

As in cluster analysis, we can get SPSS to calculate a distance matrix from a data matrix of cases and variables, and the same considerations apply to the choice of distance measure. Alternatively we can enter a distance matrix as a lower or upper triangle like the one in Table 11.1. We note, in passing, that SPSS offers MDS of non-metric (ordinal) data as well as scaling of metric data (distances or proximities on an interval scale), though we will not be looking at any ordinal examples.

First enter the data in Table 11.5 into the SPSS datasheet, with the students' names as the variable NAMES and the upper triangle missing (note that the names do not appear as the first column as they do in Table 11.5). We can apply scaling to variables or cases, but the default is variables and if we apply it to cases then they appear as case 1, case 2, etc. on the map, whereas variables are named. As this is the only difference in the results, we will let our students be variables.

Requesting the analysis in SPSS

Once the data are entered, choose **Analyze**, then **Scale**, then **Multidimensional Scaling (PROXSCAL)** to get SPSS Dialog Box 11.1.

Our data are distances (SPSS includes distances under the term 'proximities'), we have one matrix and our distances are entered as a lower triangle across the columns, so accept the defaults and click **Define**. This gives us SPSS Dialog Box 11.2, where we enter all the students' names in the **Proximities** box using the arrow.

First click the **Model** button to get SPSS Dialog Box 11.3. We can accept most of the defaults here. Ours is a **Lower triangular matrix**, and our 'proximities' are distances or **Dissimilarities**. Usually a distance matrix will be square symmetric, because the distance

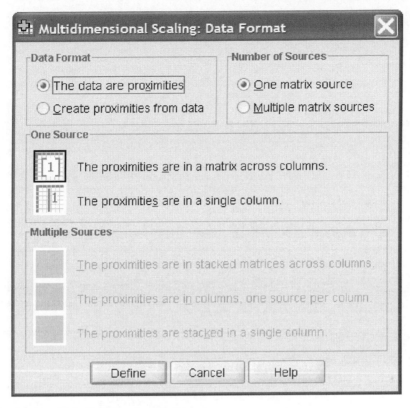

SPSS Dialog Box 11.1 Defining the data layout.

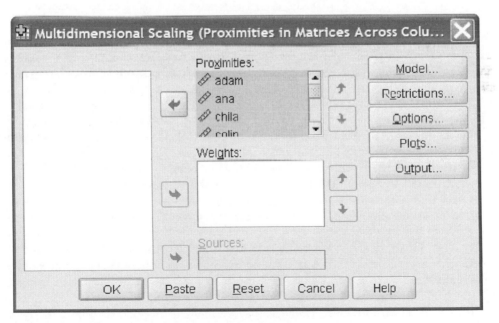

SPSS Dialog Box 11.2 Starting a multidimensional scaling.

SPSS Dialog Box 11.3 Defining the model.

from A to B is the same as that from B to A. However, if instead of counting interactions between our students we had asked each student to rate each of the others on a scale from 1 (we are very friendly) to 5 (we do not like each other), then we would have two measures of distance for each pair, one contributed by each member of the pair, and these two measures need not be the same. In a case like this it is necessary to enter the complete matrix, not just the upper or lower triangle, and to select **Full matrix** for the **Shape**.

For the moment, we are only interested in two dimensions, so leave both **Minimum** and **Maximum** at **2**. However, it would be more realistic perhaps to describe our data as **Interval** rather than ratio, since we subtracted numbers of interactions from an arbitrary number greater than the maximum number. Even if we had used numbers of transactions directly as a similarity measure, however, there would still have been the same arbitrariness in deciding a number for each person with themselves. Click **Continue** to return to the main dialog box.

We need not consider the **Restrictions** button, since we only consider problems with no restrictions, the default. (It is possible to impose values for some coordinates in the final map but we do not consider these problems.) We can also ignore the **Options** button, which allows us to choose different ways of starting the process of trying to form the two-dimensional map from the distances and also to choose different criteria to end the process. The defaults will be fine for us, and for most purposes.

Clicking the **Plots** button gives us SPSS Dialog Box 11.4, and if we opt for **Transformed proximities vs distances** as well as **Common space** we get an additional idea of the goodness of fit. It is the **Common space** plot that is the map constructed from the matrix of distances. Note that the first plot (greyed out here) is called **Stress**. This becomes available if the **Maximum** is greater than the **Minimum** dimensions in SPSS Dialog Box 11.3, and we shall need this later. Click **Continue** to return to SPSS Dialog Box 11.2.

SPSS Dialog Box 11.4 Selecting plots.

The last button, **Output**, allows us to save the coordinates of the points on the map to a file (these are the **Common space coordinates**). Further details of the fitting process can also be obtained but the defaults are enough for most problems. If we provided data on a set of variables and asked for SPSS to create the distance matrix then it may be useful to click **Distances** in the **Display** group, but we do not need this as we submitted a matrix of distances. Click **OK** to get the results, which we consider in the next section. First we briefly describe how to proceed if you start with variables recorded for each case instead of with a distance or similarity matrix.

If instead of a distance or similarity matrix we have a set of variables recorded on each case, we can ask SPSS to create a distance matrix by selecting **Create proximities from data** in SPSS Dialog Box 11.1, then clicking **Define**. SPSS Dialog Box 11.5 appears (here we have used some non-proximity data from one of our cluster analyses as our example).

Enter the variables into the **Variables** box using the arrow, and click the **Measure** button. SPSS Dialog Box 11.6, which then appears, is similar to SPSS Dialog Box 10.3, which we considered in the chapter on cluster analysis, and we must make the same kind of choice as we did there.

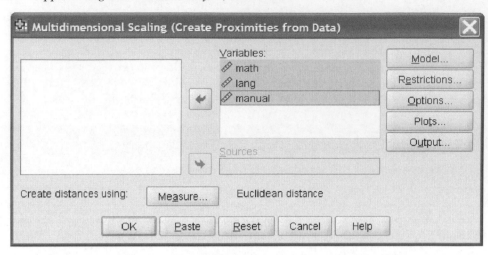

SPSS Dialog Box 11.5 Creating a distance matrix from data on variables.

SPSS Dialog Box 11.6 Choosing a distance measure and deciding how the distance matrix should be created.

We must choose a distance measure appropriate for our data and decide whether standardization is necessary. Standardization should be used unless all variables are on the same scale. In this example, all three variables are on similar scales so we need not standardize. We also have to choose between applying MDS to variables (the default) or cases. In our example here we have 52 cases (rows of the data matrix) and three variables (columns), so we need to calculate the distance matrix **Between cases**. Remember that if you apply MDS to variables they are labelled on the map, whereas cases are only numbered, so we may often prefer to call the items of interest (whatever they are) variables and arrange them as columns in the datasheet. But with 52 cases, as we have here, numbering them on the map is more realistic than trying to use names, which will unduly clutter the map. Click **Continue** and proceed as we did when we already had a distance matrix.

Understanding the output tables

First in the output is a summary of the data (not shown here), which tells us how many objects were mapped (14 students in our example) and how many distances were submitted (14 * 13/2 = 91 in our example).

A table showing how well the data are fitted by a two-dimensional map follows, which is the first table in SPSS Output 11.1. For a good fit, we want to see low measures of stress (less than .15) and values close to 1 for Dispersion Accounted For (DAF)

Stress and Fit Measures

Normalized Raw Stress	.00491
Stress-I	.07006[a]
Stress-II	.16614[a]
S-Stress	.00881[b]
Dispersion Accounted For (D.A.F.)	.99509
Tucker's Coefficient of Congruence	.99754

PROXSCAL minimizes Normalized Raw Stress.

a. Optimal scaling factor = 1.005.

b. Optimal scaling factor = .990.

Final Coordinates

	Dimension	
	1	2
adam	-.722	.412
ana	.291	-.233
chila	.479	-.190
colin	-.125	.304
dee	.720	.212
dom	-.409	-.503
ewan	-.362	-.027
holly	.823	.275
jim	-.516	.643
krish	-.721	-.316
laura	.826	.152
mira	.649	-.463
pete	-.392	.238
sanjiv	-.540	-.504

SPSS Output 11.1 Measures of goodness of fit and coordinates in two dimensions.

and Tucker's Coefficient of Congruence. The coordinates of the students in the two-dimensional map follow; see the second table in SPSS Output 11.1.

Understanding the graphical output

The coordinates may be useful but by far the most important part of the output is the plot shown in SPSS Output 11.2. It is this visual display that we hope will give us some insight into our data. In fact what this map shows is all the girls on the right and the boys on the left. There are six students from ethnic minorities and they are the ones at the bottom. So although this group of students get on quite well in the classroom and work together without friction, the boys and girls each interact mostly with their own sex, and within each sex there is some separation of the ethnic groups. Dom, Sanjiv and Krish, the ethnic minority boys, are closer to some of the indigenous boys than to any of the girls. The indigenous girls, Holly, Dee and Laura, form a close group that may be difficult for any of the others to approach.

Object Points

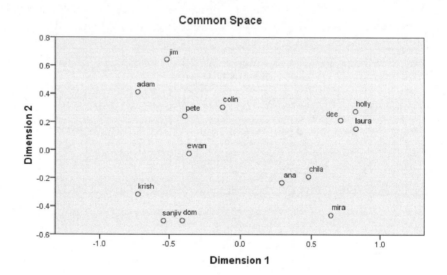

SPSS Output 11.2 Two-dimensional map of the students from the distance matrix in Table 11.5.

The final piece of output, shown in SPSS Output 11.3, is a plot of the distances from the matrix against the distances from the map. This would be a straight line if the fit were perfect. In the road map example, this would correspond to all distances between towns being the shortest straight line distances rather than actual road distances. Even if the fit is good, it can be useful to look at this plot in case one or two points are somewhat further than the rest from the line, which would indicate that one of the items mapped was fitted less well than the rest.

To illustrate the value of looking at the plot, we show in SPSS Output 11.4 a plot we obtained after we altered one of the distances in Table 11.5. We changed the distance

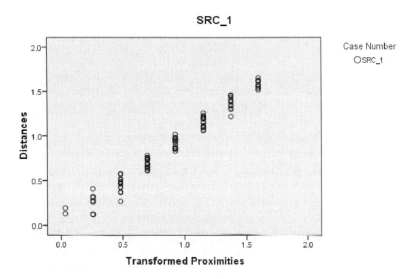

SPSS Output 11.3 Plot of actual and fitted distances.

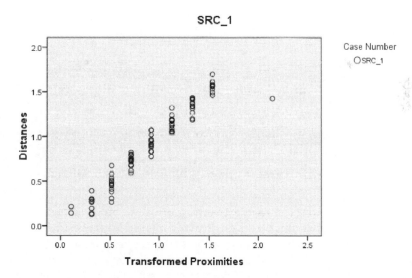

SPSS Output 11.4 Plot of actual and fitted distances when one distance in the matrix is altered.

between Adam and Ana from 7 to 12. The DAF value was still high at almost .99, but the stress values are all higher and the point at the top right of the plot suggests that the lack of fit is confined to one of the distances.

Example Box 11.1

An alternative medical example of MDS

The full analysis for this example can be found at www.psypress.com/multivariate-analysis/medical-examples (click on Chapter 11).

There are 14 people with multiple sclerosis (MS) who regularly attend an occupational therapy group. We know that there are numerous possible combinations of MS symptoms and some of the patients have been complaining that there is a tendency for occupational therapy staff to treat some of them inappropriately as rather distinct groups with similar needs on the basis of a few obvious symptoms. A pilot study is carried out to explore the extent to which this complaint appears justified, and to see how far staff perceptions of similarities are modified when they are given an opportunity to study the responses of the MS patients to a checklist of MS symptoms. Prior to the checklist intervention, mean staff ratings of similarities between MS pairs are obtained on a scale from 1 to 10. A multidimensional scaling (MDS) analysis seeking two dimensions is carried out on a distance measure derived from the proximity data. Following the checklist intervention, similarities among pairs of MS patients are rated again and the MDS analysis is repeated.

Outcomes

The MDS map is as shown in SPSS Output 11.2. Dimension 1 may be interpreted as the presence of obvious physical symptoms, such as poor coordination and balance, involuntary movements, visual disturbance and numbness, and dimension 2 as severity of symptoms. The tight group at the upper right of the map comprises people with obvious and severe physical symptoms. Towards the lower left is a group with few physical symptoms and whose symptoms are less severe. People towards the upper left have severe symptoms but not generally of an obvious physical kind (e.g., loss of sensation, facial pain, constipation, memory problems). Finally, at the lower right there is a group with obvious physical symptoms that are not yet severe. The MDS map after the intervention is as in SPSS Output 11.5. People with different degrees of obvious physical symptoms and different degrees of severity of symptoms are now spread throughout the map. It appears that staff now use a wider range of symptoms when judging similarities and, presumably, needs in common among the MS patients. Concerning the interpretation of the dimensions in the second map, when asked about the ordering along dimension 1, the MS patients suggest that those towards the left tend to be more vociferous than their peers, and, for dimension 2, that those at the bottom tend to be among the most enthusiastic participators in therapeutic activities.

Understanding the post-course output

If we convert the interaction counts in Table 11.4(b) to distances, just as we obtained Table 11.5 from Table 11.4(a), we can produce a new map of the students after the course on citizenship and diversity. This is shown in SPSS Output 11.5. Again the stress and DAF values suggest a good fit.

Here we see a more homogeneous mix of students on the map, with girls and boys, and ethnic minority and indigenous students, all spread throughout the map. As we said in the Introduction, interpreting the map dimensions is not a priority but, nevertheless, if it can be done it may be useful. On the first map of the students (SPSS Output 11.2), we could interpret dimension 1 as sex, with the girls on the right and boys on the left. Dimension 2 could be interpreted as ethnicity, with the minorities at the bottom.

Object Points

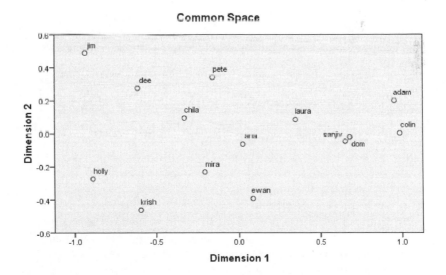

SPSS Output 11.5 Two-dimensional map of the students after the citizenship and diversity course.

The second map, in SPSS Output 11.5, offers no such obvious interpretation of the two dimensions. If we list the students in their order along dimension 1 we get Jim, Holly, Dee, Krish, Chila, Mira, Pete, Ana, Ewan, Laura, Sanjiv, Dom, Colin, Adam. At this point, we will imagine that we asked the students whether this meant anything to them, and we will invent some responses that they might have given, in order to illustrate the kind of interpretation that might arise. Suppose the students said they thought the dimension 1 order corresponded roughly to their interest in environmental issues, with Jim, Holly and Dee all being committed greenies. Suppose also that the project they were working on for the second set of videos did deal with some environmental problems, then their suggestion would seem plausible. When asked about the order on dimension 2 they might have said it did not correspond to anything that was clear to them, but they thought those at the low end (Krish, Mira, Holly and Ewan) were more sociable and extravert than those near the high end (Pete and Jim), so perhaps it could be interpreted as a sociability dimension.

Asked for their comments on the usefulness of the maps in evaluating the citizenship and diversity course, we can suppose that the students might have said that if they had seen the first map, even before the course, it would have shown them how narrow their perceptions were and they would have begun to be more open with each other even without the course. But they might also say that they had enjoyed the course and were pleased that the second map showed that, for whatever reason, they were now interacting as a more inclusive group.

The scree diagram: Considering more than two dimensions

If we have a sufficiently large set of items it is possible to make a check on whether our two-dimensional map is appropriate by graphing the stress against the number of dimensions for a range of dimensions, say 1–4. This graph is called a *scree diagram*, and we hope to observe a sharp change in gradient at the most appropriate number of dimensions for our data. For a map derived from the road distances between cities we would expect that two dimensions would give the best representation. However, if we had the distances between some places in the Himalayas, where enormous changes in height occur over fairly short distances, we might expect that three dimensions would be needed to give an adequate representation.

The scree diagram: Number of cases needed

When we collect data of the sort described in the Introduction and for our experiment, there is no guarantee that a visual representation in two dimensions will display the inter-item distances without distortion. But with sufficient items in our distance matrix we can do a check with a scree diagram. The number of coordinates required to map (for instance) 14 students in two dimensions is $2 * 14 = 28$. In three dimensions we need $3 * 14 = 42$, and for four we need $4 * 14 = 56$. Our distance matrix for 14 students gives us $14 * 13/2 = 91$ distances, which is not a lot to use in estimating 56 coordinates. If we only had six students ($6 * 5/2 = 15$ distances), we would be unable to estimate $4 * 6 = 24$ coordinates for a four-dimensional representation or, indeed, $3 * 6 = 18$ coordinates for a three-dimensional representation. This is why you can only check the scree diagram if you have a large enough set of items: at least nine ($9 * 8/2 = 36$ distances), preferably more, for four dimensions (with $4 * 9 = 36$ coordinates).

We obtained a scree plot for the students' second distance matrix. In SPSS Dialog Box 11.3, replace the values for **Minimum** with **1** and for **Maximum** with **4**. In SPSS Dialog Box 11.4 we can now click the **Stress** plot.

The scree diagram: Understanding the output

Map plots are produced for representations in four, three and one dimension as well as in two dimensions. The plots in four and three dimensions are hard to read; probably this visual approach will only be useful if two dimensions (as in SPSS Output 11.5) suffice. The one-dimensional plot arranges the items in a line, which is also unlikely to be revealing. We therefore do not reproduce the map plots for one, three and four dimensions.

SPSS Output 11.6 was produced as a result of clicking **Stress** in SPSS Dialog Box 11.4. We see from the graph, known as a scree diagram, that stress increases as the number of dimensions is reduced, showing that the fit becomes progressively less good. The biggest increase is from two to one dimension. The sharp change in the slope at dimension 2 shows that a visual representation in two dimensions is the best for this distance matrix.

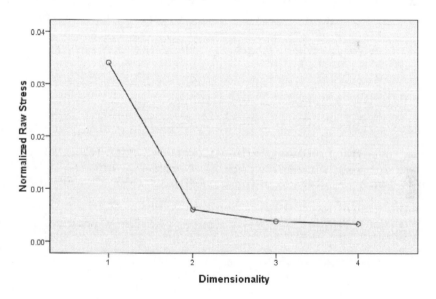

Scree Plot

SPSS Output 11.6 Stress for solutions in one to four dimensions.

Multidimensional scaling and seriation

Seriation: An archaeological example

Multidimensional scaling can be used to pick out one-dimensional structure in a dataset. The most common example is seriation, where we want to ascertain the chronological ordering of the data. Note that although MDS can be used to order the data in time, the direction of time must be determined independently. Even when the data are one-dimensional, they need not lie on the axis of the first dimension but can sometimes lie on a curve. If our two-dimensional plot of the data shows the items lying along a curve in the plane, then their order along the curve may correspond to their order along a dimension, time for example, that has not been recorded or is unknown. This idea has been used in archaeology, one of the early application areas for MDS. In an early archaeological application, a distance matrix for a set of tombs was obtained by recording the presence/absence of several pottery types for each tomb, then distances were obtained using one of the methods described in Chapter 10. On the MDS map obtained from this distance matrix, the tombs formed a shallow curve and their order along this curve was taken to be their temporal order.

Seriation: A psychology example

Could this idea have an application in psychology? Consider this: We are interested in the possible existence of a personality dimension, control freakery perhaps. If there is such a dimension, then people at one extreme will need to control their lives, their loved ones and their environment, while people at the other extreme will be relaxed and able to go with the flow, and there will be a continuum along which everyone could be placed. We devise a list of yes/no questions that we think may be relevant to various aspects of a need to control (Do you plan what time to leave the party? Would you rather be a passenger than a driver? Do you let your partner have the remote? . . .) and we ask some student volunteers to answer them. Psychology students may be too smart for this one, so we might try the maths class. From the answers, we calculate the simple matching coefficient for each pair of students (this is discussed in Chapter 10). We could use 1 – the matching coefficient – as a distance measure. Table 11.6 shows the (fabricated) results of an experiment like this.

Table 11.6 'Distances' between pairs of students calculated from 'control' questions (mds.distancec.sav)

Case	1	2	3	4	5	6	7	8	9	10	11	12
1	0.00											
2	0.13	0.00										
3	0.41	0.49	0.00									
4	0.22	0.10	0.57	0.00								
5	0.36	0.46	0.17	0.57	0.00							
6	0.44	0.53	0.08	0.54	0.13	0.00						
7	0.36	0.29	0.78	0.20	0.74	0.81	0.00					
8	0.04	0.18	0.39	0.26	0.32	0.41	0.40	0.00				
9	0.52	0.57	0.15	0.65	0.32	0.20	0.86	0.52	0.00			
10	0.43	0.49	0.02	0.58	0.19	0.10	0.80	0.40	0.12	0.00		
11	0.29	0.18	0.67	0.09	0.64	0.70	0.12	0.33	0.74	0.67	0.00	
12	0.22	0.33	0.32	0.43	0.19	0.32	0.57	0.17	0.47	0.35	0.50	0.00

Seriation: Understanding output from the psychology example

The resulting map is shown in SPSS Output 11.7. The stress values and DAF suggest that a two-dimensional map is a good fit. The cases are arranged along a curve. If we

Object Points

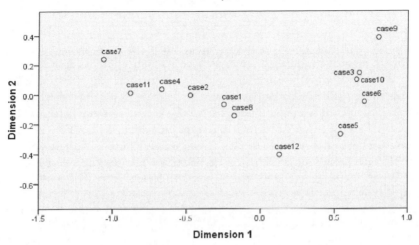

SPSS Output 11.7 Map of cases from the distance matrix in Table 10.7.

list them in order (case 7, case 11, case 4, . . ., case 9) we can then consider whether it would be reasonable to see them as arranged along a continuum according to their need for control. We may also consider whether the two dimensions of the map reflect different aspects of a need for control (control of others and the environment, and control of self, perhaps). If we think the ordering of the cases along the curve does correspond to the participants' need for control, then the questions we used to form the distance matrix would enable us to begin the process of developing a questionnaire and a scale to measure this personality dimension.

Example Box 11.2

Seriation: Continuing the alternative medical example of MDS

The full analysis for this example can be found at www.psypress.com/ multivariate-analysis/medical-examples (click on Chapter 11).

The MS patients are asked yes/no questions about how they see their lives in the future (e.g., Do you expect to take holidays abroad? Will you make the major decisions about your living environment? Are better treatments on the way?). The curve in SPSS Output 11.7 might represent a continuum according to their optimism and the two dimensions could be optimism about the course of their illness and optimism about their ability to cope. The data for this extension are given on the book website as mds.distancec.sav.

Reporting results

The main thing in a report of a multidimensional scaling is the visual representation, the map, and a description of how it assisted understanding. However, stress and DAF values for the two-dimensional solution should be given, and if possible a scree diagram. Here we report on the student data.

We performed a multidimensional scaling on the first distance matrix obtained from the counts of student interactions described in the Method section. For the solution in two dimensions the normalized raw stress was less than .005 and other stress measures were also small. The Dispersion Accounted For (DAF) exceeded .99, so a two-dimensional map is a good fit. The map is shown in Figure A (*this is our SPSS Output 11.2*). The six girls are all at the right and the eight boys are all at the left. Among the boys, there is some separation between the five indigenous boys and the three ethnic minority boys, Sanjiv, Dom and Krish, who appear towards the bottom. The three indigenous girls, Holly, Dee and Laura, form a close group towards the upper right, while the three ethnic minority girls are lower down and further apart. Sanjiv, Dom and Krish are closer to some of the indigenous boys (Ewan and Pete) than they are to any of the girls. This picture suggests that although the students get on quite well in the classroom and work together without friction, they mostly confine their interactions to others within their ethnic and sex group.

This contrasts with the results from the second distance matrix, obtained after the course in citizenship and diversity as described in the Method. This time the normalized raw stress was .005 and the DAF exceeded .99, again indicating a good fit. The map is shown in Figure B (*this is our SPSS Output 11.5*). This time we see a more homogeneous mix of the students, with both sexes and all ethnic groups spread throughout.

To check that a two-dimensional representation was best for these data, we plotted a scree graph of stress against number of dimensions for each of the two analyses. Figure C (*this is our SPSS Output 11.6*) shows the one for the second distance matrix (the other was similar). The sharp change in slope at two dimensions is quite clear, and shows that two dimensions is correct for these data.

Interpreting the map dimensions is not a priority, but if it can be done it may be useful. On the first map of the students (Figure A), we could interpret dimension 1 as sex, with the girls on the right and boys on the left. Dimension 2 could be interpreted as ethnicity, with the minorities at the bottom. The second map (Figure B) offers no such obvious interpretation of the two dimensions. If we list the students in their order along dimension 1 we get Jim, Holly, Dee, Krish, Chila, Mira, Pete, Ana, Ewan, Laura, Sanjiv, Dom, Colin, Adam. The students suggested that this roughly corresponded to their interest in environmental issues, and as they were working on some environmental problems during the second set of videos this made sense. They had no clear idea of what dimension 2 could be, but said that those at the low end (Krish, Mira, Holly and Ewan) were more sociable and extravert than those near the high end (Pete and Jim), so perhaps it was a sociability dimension.

Asked for their comments on the usefulness of the maps in evaluating the citizenship and diversity course, the students said that if they had seen the first map, even before the course, it would have shown them how narrow their perceptions were and they would have begun to be more open with each other, even without the course. But they had enjoyed the course and were pleased that the second map showed that, for whatever reason, they were now interacting as a more homogeneous group.

Reference

Sani, F., & Reicher, S. (1999). Identity, argument and schism: Two longitudinal studies of the split in the Church of England over the ordination of women to the priesthood. *Group Processes and Intergroup Relations*, 2(3), 279–300.

12 Loglinear models

Introduction and intuitive explication

Two-way contingency tables

Loglinear models are often useful in dealing with multivariate discrete data. Two-way contingency tables to deal with bivariate discrete data are familiar to all students who deal with quantitative data, and Pearson's χ^2 test of association in such tables is the oldest statistical test. There are only two null hypotheses that can be tested for a two-way table: (1) that the row and column variables are independent, and (2) that the row (or column) proportions are equal. Which of these two is tested depends on whether the data were obtained as a single sample with cases classified on both variables, or as a sample from each level of one of the variables, with cases classified on the other variable. For example, we could obtain a single sample of 60 adults and classify them as male or female and as high or low on salary. Alternatively, we could obtain a sample of 30 males and 30 females (though there is no need for the samples to be of equal size) and classify cases in each sample as high or low on salary. But the contingency table is the same in both cases and the test statistic is calculated in exactly the same way. As the same process can be used to test either hypothesis, the distinction is not that important.

Multidimensional contingency tables

If we move from two variables to three, we have several possible null hypotheses that may be of interest. For instance, we may test the hypothesis that all three variables are independent (the most common hypothesis), that two of them are independent at each level of the third (*conditional independence*) or that one of them is independent of the other two. There are still other possibilities. In more than three dimensions the possibilities are even more numerous. All such hypotheses can be tested using the same method as the Pearson χ^2 test for a two-way table: expected values for all the cells are calculated from the marginal totals, according to the hypothesis of interest, and then the χ^2 statistic is calculated from the observed and expected frequencies for all the cells. Thus, to test the conditional independence hypothesis referred to above, expected values for cells relating to the first two variables and the first level of the third variable would be based only on the marginal totals at the first level of the third variable, and similarly for cells relating to the first two variables and subsequent levels of the third variable. The degrees of freedom can be calculated as:

No. of cells – 1 – No. of probabilities estimated from the table according to the hypothesis

In our conditional independence example, if there were two levels of each of the first and third variables and three levels of the second variable, the degrees of freedom would be $12 - 1 - 6 = 5$. There are six probabilities that have to be estimated because at each of the two levels of the third variable there is a 3×2 table, and if the two variables in this table are independent we must estimate three probabilities, one for the two-level variable and two for the three-level variable.

So we can use familiar methods for dealing with multidimensional contingency tables, but the process can become rather unwieldy even with only three variables. A different approach, attempting to find a suitable model to describe the data, can give a clearer insight, and this is where we use loglinear models.

The multiplicative law of probability

The name loglinear arises as follows. In the simple two-way contingency table, the hypothesis of interest states that the row and column variables are independent. This is equivalent to saying that the probability for cell *ij* (the *i*th row and *j*th column) is the *product* of the *i*th row and *j*th column probabilities. Our experience is that many medical and psychology students are not wholly comfortable with basic concepts of probability, so it might be worth pausing to try to relate the multiplicative law of probability, to which we have just alluded, to something that will be familiar to most of our readers. Recall that, in order to compute χ^2 for a two-way contingency table you need first to obtain expected (expected under the null hypothesis, that is) frequencies for each cell. Recall also that the expected frequency for a cell is obtained as:

Row total * Column total/Grand total

This is simply the application of the multiplicative law to obtain the probability for cell *ij* (Row prob * Col prob = (Row total/Grand total) * (Col total/Grand total)), which is then multiplied by the grand total because the expected frequency in the cell is just the probability applied to the number of cases available. Thus:

Expected frequency = (Row total/Grand total) * (Col total/Grand total) * Grand total

which, with cancellation of 'grand total' in the numerator with one of its occurrences in the denominator, reduces to our original formula for the expected frequency in a cell. We hope that helped!

An additive model: The log of the probability

So, given that the probability for cell *ij* is the *product* of the *i*th row and *j*th column probabilities, the log of the probability for cell *ij* is the *sum* of the logs of the row and column probabilities. Do not worry if you have forgotten (or never knew) how logarithms work. All you need to know is that if two numbers are to be multiplied together you can look up the log values of the two numbers and add these to one another and then look up the antilog of the sum. So:

3.6481 * 0.0056 = antilog(log 3.6481 + log 0.0056)

which is a much easier calculation to perform by hand (less so now that we have electronic calculators, which is why you may know less about logarithms than us oldies). In our case, we are not adopting logarithms to make calculations easier, but to enable us to build an *additive* model rather than a *multiplicative* model. We want to do this because there is a greater conceptual simplicity about additive (linear) models of the kind we use in ANOVA.

Hypotheses for tables with more than two dimensions also have a multiplicative form, so if we are looking for linear models similar to those used in ANOVA it is natural to use the logs of the probabilities (or expected values).

Requirements for loglinear models

Because loglinear models resemble the models used in ANOVA, we often refer to the variables as factors and describe relationships among them in terms of interactions.

It is standard to use models that are *hierarchical* (like logistic models), which means that if any interaction term is included in the model, all the lower order terms associated with it must be included. So if an interaction term between two variables is included, the main effects for both must also be included. If an interaction between three variables is included, all the pairwise interactions and all the main effects for those three variables must be included as well.

Any constraints on the marginal totals also impose requirements to include particular terms in the model. For a three-dimensional table the sampling scheme is usually one of the following:

(i)   A single sample of fixed size is taken and cases are classified on three variables.
(ii) One of the variables is used for stratification and a fixed size sample is taken at each level of this variable. Cases are classified on the other two variables. Models must contain the main effect for the stratifying variable.
(iii) Two variables are used for stratification and a fixed size sample is taken at each combination of levels for these two variables. Cases are classified on the other variable (which may be called the response variable). If this method is used, models must contain the interaction term for the two stratifying variables. The hierarchy requirement means that the main effects of both of these variables must also be included.

With more than three variables, combinations of levels of variables after the first two are sometimes regarded as levels of a third (compound) variable. For example, if SMOKER (yes or no) and SEX (male or female) are variables 3 and 4, we could define a new variable, perhaps called SEXANDSMOKING, with four levels corresponding to male smokers, female smokers, male non-smokers and female non-smokers. In this way we could treat our four-variable problem as a three-variable one.

Main effects in ANOVA and loglinear analysis

Although we have said that loglinear analysis is similar to ANOVA in some respects, there are also some important differences and these can be a source of confusion if they are not appreciated. The most important distinction is that ANOVA models cell means (which have an error component), whereas loglinear analysis models cell frequencies (which have a single score in each cell and, therefore, no error term in the model). Why does this matter? Well, basically, in an ANOVA, if we find a significant main effect of an IV (let us say sex), this tells us that the mean scores of participants on the DV (let us say reading comprehension level) differ between males and females sufficiently for it to be unlikely (given the variance within these levels) that this was a chance effect. This would be true regardless of whether the number of participants was equal for males and females.

Now consider what a significant main effect would tell us in a loglinear analysis (where the DV is now a categorical variable: e.g., high, medium, low reading comprehension) if the number of participants differed for males and females. To make it concrete, let us assume that we have 30 males and 50 females. In the loglinear model we will probably find a significant main effect of sex even if sex has no effect on reading comprehension! The reason is that we are trying to model *cell frequencies*, not *means*, on reading comprehension. We want to explain why there are higher frequencies in some cells than others, not to ask whether males have different scores on reading comprehension. Cells dealing with females will generally have higher frequencies than those dealing with males simply because there are more of them in our total sample. In a similar way, if there were an equal number of males and females there would be no main effect of sex even if they differed greatly in their reading comprehension. In *asymmetric* loglinear models (when there is one variable that is conceived of as the DV, analogous to the DV in an ANOVA), the main effects of the IVs, and their interactions with one another, may just reflect our sample sizes. They still need to be included in the model, but they are often of no interest. It is the *interaction* of these IVs with the DV that we are interested in. For example, we might ask whether frequencies of high, medium and low reading comprehension differ between male and female cells.

A psychology example of loglinear analysis

Size of dataset required

Loglinear models can be applied to any number of variables or factors in a way that resembles analysis of variance but, just as in ANOVA, if there are more than three or four factors it may be hard to see the wood for the trees. In addition, the more cells you have in your model, the more data you need. Recall that even in a simple two-way contingency table, if any of the cells have expected numbers less than 5 then the χ^2 test may not be a good enough approximation. Even a large dataset is not a guarantee that all expected numbers are at least 5 (if some categories are sparse), but a small dataset almost guarantees that some expected values will be too small. In a loglinear model you may have some cells with small expected values but you still need a dataset of adequate size, taking account of the number of cells. As a minimum, you need at least five times as many observations as cells in your model.

Some (fabricated) data

Even for three factors each at only two levels, a loglinear model can make clear the relationships among the factors, whereas looking at the relationships between pairs

Table 12.1 Frequencies for three factors each at two levels

Layer 1: Index finger longer				Layer 2: Third finger longer			
	Male 1	Female 2	Totals		Male 1	Female 2	Totals
Maths ability 1	5	9	14	Maths ability 1	29	10	39
2	17	54	71	2	49	27	76
Totals	22	63	85	Totals	78	37	115

of factors can be quite misleading. We will illustrate the problem with the data in Table 12.1, and then show how to elucidate the data using the loglinear facility in SPSS. Notice that we have eight cells (2 * 2 * 2) and 200 cases, with a ratio of cases to cells of 25. Our three variables are sex (M = 1, F = 2), mathematical ability (good = 1, not so good = 2) and relative lengths of the index and third fingers of the right hand (index longer = 1, third longer = 2). We are giving numerical codes to our factor levels from the start since this is necessary when using the SPSS loglinear facility.

The relative length of fingers seems quite unlikely to have anything to do with mathematical ability or indeed anything else of interest, so ignore it for the moment and add up the two layers of Table 12.1 to get Table 12.2.

Table 12.2 Two-way table showing mathematical ability by sex

	Male 1	Female 2	Totals
Maths ability 1	34	19	53
2	66	81	147
Totals	100	100	200

Conditional independence within the data

Here we see that we have 100 each of males and females, and the χ^2 test of association gives $\chi^2 = 5.78$ on one degree of freedom, so $p < .05$. We would reject the null hypothesis of no association between mathematical ability and sex. However, if we apply the same test to each of the two layers shown in Table 12.1 we get $\chi^2 = 0.845$ and 1.154, neither of which is significant at the 5% level. So what are we to believe? Among those with a longer index finger there is no association between mathematical ability and sex, and among those with a longer third finger there is no association between mathematical ability and sex. However, if we ignore finger length, which surely cannot have anything to do with anything of interest, we find an association between mathematical ability and sex that is significant at the 5% level.

The problem is that the factor over which we have summed – relative finger length – is associated with each of the other two factors. In fact what we have here is an example of *conditional independence*: sex and mathematical ability are independent within each level of finger length.

The nature of a loglinear model

We need a method that allows us to look at all the factors and their interactions. The idea of a loglinear model is to express the logarithm of each expected cell frequency as the sum of an overall mean of the main effects of the factors and the interaction terms, just as we express an observation in ANOVA. The terms in the model, main effects and interactions, will all be logs of expected values of cells or marginal totals.

We have already shown you our first set of illustrative data. We have taken a random sample of 100 male and 100 female students entering a university for the first time and asked them to show us their right hands, laid palm down on the desk. After we assign them to one of the finger length categories, we assess their mathematical ability by the rather rough method of determining from their entry qualifications whether or not they have a mathematical qualification higher than GCSE level. If they have they are coded 1, otherwise 2.

Facts underlying our fabricated data

We fabricated these data to illustrate the point, but they are in fact based on some surprising truths that make the relationships among our three factors impossible to understand by looking at two-way tables as we did first. Here are the facts on which we based this set of data.

The majority of men (about 80%) have a longer third than first finger, while for the majority of women the opposite is true. Among women working in the male strongholds of maths and physics, the proportion with a longer third than first finger is higher than in the general population of women. Among those men working in areas that need very good communication skills (a strength more common among women), the proportion of men with a longer first than third finger is higher than in the general population of men. It has been conjectured that there are differences in typical brain organization that mean good communication skills are more common in women than men and good spatial or mathematical skills (the two are related) are more common among men than women. Amazingly, these differences in brain organization are thought to begin at a stage in foetal development when finger lengths are also being established.

So, in our dataset, relative finger length and sex are associated and relative finger length and mathematical ability are associated. These associations are concealed when we collapse the table over finger length to get Table 12.2, and so the χ^2 test based on the collapsed table is misleading.

A loglinear model: Entering the data in SPSS

We have already warned you that factor levels must be given numerical codes if you want to do a loglinear analysis in SPSS, so do not code the males and females as M and F or the mathematical ability as Yes and No. Once you have the data represented with suitable codes, there are two ways to present it to SPSS. If you already have the cell frequencies, you can enter these in the SPSS data window as in Table 12.3, which we have set out for the data in Table 12.1.

The first three columns show all eight combinations of factor levels, and the column of frequencies gives the cell frequency for each combination of factor levels. To use

Table 12.3 Presenting a frequency table to SPSS
(psy.loglinear.sav)

SEX	INDEX	MATHS	FREQS
1	1	1	5
1	1	2	17
1	2	1	29
1	2	2	49
2	1	1	9
2	1	2	54
2	2	1	10
2	2	2	27

these frequencies we select **Data** from the menu bar, then **Weight Cases**. A small dialog box opens; click the radio button **Weight cases by**, then enter FREQS into the **Frequency Variable** box using the arrow. When you save the data file, the weighting will be saved with it, so you only need to do this the first time you use the frequency table.

If instead of the layout in Table 12.3 you have each case listed with the levels of each factor for the case, you can enter the data in the usual way, with each case making one row and each factor or variable making one column. SPSS will calculate the cell frequencies when the analysis is requested.

A loglinear model: Requesting the analysis in SPSS

Whichever way the data were entered, select **Analyze** from the menu bar, then **Loglinear**, then **General**, and SPSS Dialog Box 12.1 appears. Enter the factors using the arrow, and click the radio button to select **Multinomial**. The other boxes are left empty as we only have factors in this problem.

The multinomial model is the one to choose if we took one or more random samples and classified the cases according to one or more variables or factors. This is usually how data are obtained. We took two samples, one each of men and women. We could have used exactly the same methods if we had taken one sample and classified the cases as male or female as well as on the other two variables, but the sampling method used does affect which terms have to be included in any model.

Click the **Model** button to get SPSS Dialog Box 12.2 and define the model. The *saturated* model includes all main effects and all interactions. This is equivalent to estimating a separate probability for every cell. Usually we are interested in a model with fewer terms than this, and then we must click the **Custom** radio button. You can add terms one at a time or in groups using the arrow and the drop-down menu below it. For instance we can select **Main effects** on the menu, select all three factors and click the arrow to enter all main effects. Then select **All 2-way** from the menu, select all the factors again and click the arrow to get all two-factor interactions entered. In Dialog Box 12.2 you can see all the terms of the saturated model entered. We could just have used the **Saturated** radio button, but we shall want a series of **Custom** models later and it is convenient to start with the list of terms as we have them here.

The model corresponding to complete independence of the three factors is that with only the main effects. However, we are usually interested in models that fall somewhere between complete independence and the saturated model.

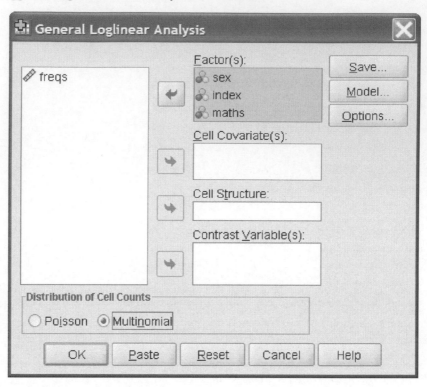

SPSS Dialog Box 12.1 Starting a loglinear analysis.

Click **Continue** and then the **Options** button from Dialog Box 12.1. We can accept all the defaults here except that we want the **Estimates** of the effects, so click that box in the **Display** group. Now click **Continue** and **OK** to get the analysis.

The loglinear analysis: Understanding the output for the saturated model

The output for the saturated model begins with a warning: All residuals are zero so no charts will be created. This is because we have estimated separate probabilities for every cell in the table, so the model is a perfect fit with no residuals.

Next a data information table (not shown here) tells us that 8 cases are accepted but 200 weighted cases are used in the analysis (this is because we entered our data as frequencies), 8 cells are defined and no cases are rejected because of missing data. Then there is a list of the variables (factors) and the number of levels for each. Three more tables follow, which are not shown here as none of them is very interesting for the saturated model. The convergence information table shows that 5 iterations out of a possible 20 were sufficient: the saturated model is a perfect fit so the process of fitting is not difficult. The goodness of fit tests show that the fit is perfect: both goodness of fit statistics are zero. The table of cell counts and residuals again just repeats the information that the saturated model is a perfect fit: all cell frequencies fitted by the model are just the actual cell frequencies, so all residuals are zero.

Next comes a list of the parameters, shown as SPSS Output 12.1. At the bottom of the list is a note saying that all those parameters with a superscript b are set to zero

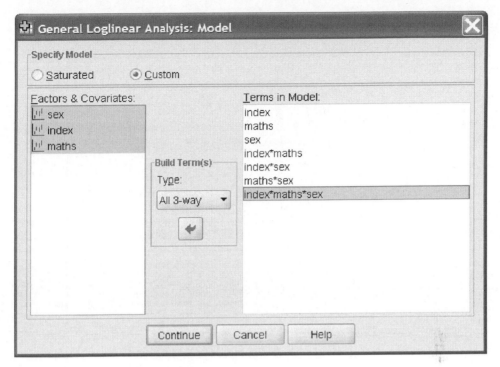

SPSS Dialog Box 12.2 Defining the model.

because they are redundant. This is because, as in ANOVA, all effects are measured from an overall mean, so when the probability is known for one of only two levels, the value for the other level is known as well. We show how to calculate expected cell values from the parameter estimates later. Other notes at the bottom of the table remind us that we used the multinomial model and all main effects and interactions are included. Each of the main effects and interactions has one non-zero term (estimate) in the model (because each of the three factors has just two levels), and for each of these terms a Z value, a confidence interval and a significance level are given in the table.

We see that the Z values (column 4) for the third-order interaction term and the terms for INDEX * MATHS and SEX * MATHS are all less than 2 in absolute value, which suggests that the corresponding model terms may not be needed (1.96 is the 5% critical value for Z). We could try omitting all these three terms from the model, but we will use a more systematic approach and begin by omitting just the three-factor interaction. The final two tables in the output window (not shown here) give the correlations and also covariances of the estimates.

Selecting a reduced model

Removing the three-factor interaction

If we return to SPSS Dialog Box 12.2 we can remove the three-factor interaction from the model using the arrow. We repeat the analysis and look through the output until we find the goodness of fit statistics (shown in SPSS Output 12.2(a)). The less familiar one,

Parameter Estimates[c,d]

Parameter	Estimate	Std. Error	Z	Sig.	95% Confidence Interval Lower Bound	95% Confidence Interval Upper Bound
Constant	3.314[a]					
[index = 1]	0.684	0.234	2.924	.003	0.226	1.142
[index = 2]	0[b]	.	.	.	.	.
[maths = 1]	-0.963	0.363	-2.654	.008	-1.674	-0.252
[maths = 2]	0[b]	.	.	.	.	.
[sex = 1]	0.588	0.238	2.471	.013	0.122	1.054
[sex = 2]	0[b]	.	.	.	.	.
[index = 1] * [maths = 1]	-0.784	0.505	-1.552	.121	-1.774	0.206
[index = 1] * [maths = 2]	0[b]	.	.	.	.	.
[index = 2] * [maths = 1]	0[b]	.	.	.	.	.
[index = 2] * [maths = 2]	0[b]	.	.	.	.	.
[sex = 1] * [index = 1]	-1.724	0.363	-4.744	.000	-2.436	-1.012
[sex = 1] * [index = 2]	0[b]	.	.	.	.	.
[sex = 2] * [index = 1]	0[b]	.	.	.	.	.
[sex = 2] * [index = 2]	0[b]	.	.	.	.	.
[sex = 1] * [maths = 1]	0.445	0.431	1.033	.302	-0.399	1.290
[sex = 1] * [maths = 2]	0[b]	.	.	.	.	.
[sex = 2] * [maths = 1]	0[b]	.	.	.	.	.
[sex = 2] * [maths = 2]	0[b]	.	.	.	.	.
[sex = 1] * [index = 1] * [maths = 1]	0.144	0.740	0.195	.846	-1.307	1.595
[sex = 1] * [index = 1] * [maths = 2]	0[b]	.	.	.	.	.
[sex = 1] * [index = 2] * [maths = 1]	0[b]	.	.	.	.	.
[sex = 1] * [index = 2] * [maths = 2]	0[b]	.	.	.	.	.
[sex = 2] * [index = 1] * [maths = 1]	0[b]	.	.	.	.	.
[sex = 2] * [index = 1] * [maths = 2]	0[b]	.	.	.	.	.
[sex = 2] * [index = 2] * [maths = 1]	0[b]	.	.	.	.	.
[sex = 2] * [index = 2] * [maths = 2]	0[b]	.	.	.	.	.

a. Constants are not parameters under the multinomial assumption. Therefore, their standard errors are not calculated.

b. This parameter is set to zero because it is redundant.

c. Model: Multinomial

d. Design: Constant + index + maths + sex + index * maths + sex * index + sex * maths + sex * index * maths

SPSS Output 12.1 Estimates of the parameters (terms in the model).

(a) Goodness of fit of model with all two-factor interaction terms

Goodness-of-Fit Tests[a,b]

	Value	df	Sig.
Likelihood Ratio	0.017	1	.897
Pearson Chi-Square	0.017	1	.896

a. Model: Multinomial

b. Design: Constant + index + maths + sex + index * maths + sex * index + sex * maths

(b) Goodness of fit of model with INDEX * MATHS and SEX * INDEX

Goodness-of-Fit Tests[a,b]

	Value	df	Sig.
Likelihood Ratio	1.979	2	.372
Pearson Chi-Square	1.999	2	.368

a. Model: Multinomial

b. Design: Constant + index + maths + sex + index * maths + sex * index

SPSS Output 12.2 Goodness of fit of two models.

based on the likelihood ratio, is sometimes called the Goodman statistic and it has the advantage that it can be partitioned in a way that enables us to test hypotheses about terms in a hierarchical set of models. Like the Pearson statistic, it has an approximate χ^2 distribution if the model is a good fit. In practice there is usually little difference between the two values. In our example, using either of these χ^2 tests, we would not reject the hypothesis that the model is a good fit.

Removing a two-factor interaction

Now we would like to see if the model can be further simplified by removing one or more of the two-factor interactions. Looking at the new list of parameter estimates (not shown here), we find that the two-factor interaction with the smallest Z value is that for MATHS * SEX, so we try removing this one first. (In SPSS Output 12.1, the MATHS * SEX interaction is also the two-factor interaction with the smallest Z value.)

So, omitting MATHS * SEX, using the arrow in SPSS Dialog Box 12.2, we search down the output for the Goodness of fit Statistics and find SPSS Output 12.2(b). Again we would not reject the null hypothesis that the fit is good. The Z values for all remaining terms exceed 2.

The conditional independence model

This is the model for the conditional independence of MATHS and SEX within each level of INDEX. If we try further reductions by removing either of the other two-factor interactions we find that the goodness of fit statistics cause us to reject the models as poorly fitting, so we settle for the model with all main effects and the interactions MATHS * INDEX and SEX * INDEX. In this model both SEX and MATHS are each associated with INDEX.

We now have two models that both fit well. We are usually interested in finding a model with fewer terms than the saturated one, but which still fits well. In fact, we usually only want to use a more complex model if including the extra term(s) provides a significant improvement in the fit. Equivalently, we only want terms in the model if they differ significantly from zero. We now show how to test hypotheses about terms in a nested set of hierarchical models where a simpler model contains a subset of the terms from a complex model with which it is being compared.

Testing the hypothesis that the three-factor interaction effect is zero

The saturated model contains all main effects and interactions. The reduced model with all two-factor interactions is nested within it since it contains a subset of these parameters. To test the hypothesis that the three-factor interaction is zero, find the difference between the χ^2 statistic for the likelihood ratio for the reduced model with all two-factor interactions and that for the saturated model. For the saturated model, the goodness of fit statistics are zero (since the fit is perfect) and there are no degrees of freedom for them. So the difference between χ^2 statistics is $0.017 - 0 = 0.017$ (SPSS Output 12.2(a)). This is approximately χ^2, with degrees of freedom equal to the difference between the degrees of freedom for the χ^2 in the two models ($1 - 0 = 1$). Since our value is much less than the critical value of 3.84 for a test at the 5% level, we do not reject the null hypothesis that the three-factor interaction is zero.

Testing the hypothesis that the MATHS by SEX interaction effect is zero

The model without the MATHS * SEX interaction is nested within that with all two-factor interactions, since it contains a subset of the parameters in the model with all two-factor interactions. To test the hypothesis that the MATHS * SEX interaction is zero, find the difference between the χ^2 statistic for the likelihood ratio for the model without this term (SPSS Output 12.2(b)) and the model with all two-factor interactions (SPSS Output 12.2(a)). This is $1.979 - 0.017 = 1.962$, and is approximately χ^2, with degrees of freedom equal to the difference between the degrees of freedom for the χ^2 in the two models ($2 - 1 = 1$). Since our value is much less than the critical value of 3.84 for a test at the 5% level, we do not reject the null hypothesis that the MATHS * SEX interaction is zero.

Testing several interactions together

It is possible to test a hypothesis that several parameters are zero. For instance, we could test the hypothesis that the three-factor interaction and the MATHS * SEX interaction are both zero. To do this, use the χ^2 statistic for the likelihood ratio for the model without these two terms (SPSS Output 12.2(b)) and for the saturated model (which is zero). This gives us $1.979 - 0 = 1.979$ on $2 - 0 = 2$ degrees of freedom, so we do not reject the hypothesis. We could have gone to our selected model in one step instead of two.

Example Box 12.1

An alternative example with medical data

The full analysis for this example can be found at www.psypress.com/multivariate-analysis/medical-examples (click on Chapter 12).

People with a particular variant of the FTO gene (the abbreviation derives from an observation of fused toes and other abnormalities in mice following a deletion in a homologous area) have increased risk of being obese (30% increase with one copy; 70% increase with two copies). There is also a causal relationship between obesity and type II diabetes. One hundred adults with and 100 without the FTO variant are recruited and the presence or absence of type II diabetes is recorded, together with the presence or absence of obesity, based on a body mass index (BMI) cutoff of 30. The data in Table 12.1 may be taken to represent these variables as follows: layers 1 and 2 respectively may be substituted by not obese and obese; sex 1 and 2 by variant FTO present and not present; maths ability 1 and 2 by diabetes and no diabetes. The frequency data in Table 12.3 are entered, from left to right, as FTO, OBESITY, DIABETES and FREQS, and a loglinear analysis is carried out.

Outcomes

We can fit a loglinear model with three main effects (OBESITY, DIABETES, FTO) and the two-factor interactions between OBESITY and FTO and between OBESITY and DIABETES. Using the Goodman statistic for goodness of fit, based on the likelihood ratio, the goodness of fit is 1.979, which is not significant, allowing us to conclude that the model is a good fit. The three-factor interaction and that between DIABETES and FTO are shown to not differ significantly from zero. The fact that the DIABETES * fto interaction is not included in the model tells us that these two variables are conditionally independent within levels of OBESITY. This means that among those with obesity there is no association between diabetes and presence of the FTO variant, and among those without obesity there is also no association between diabetes and presence of the FTO variant. There are, however, significant associations between obesity and the FTO variant, and between obesity and diabetes.

Alternative variables for use in SPSS
The full dataset, med.loglinear.sav, can be found on the book website

Variable	Psychology	Medicine
Binary variables	SEX Male = 1, female = 2 INDEX Index finger longer = 1 Index finger shorter = 2 MATHS High ability = 1 Lower ability = 2	DIABETES Diabetes = 1, no diabetes = 2 OBESITY Not obese = 1, obese = 2 FTO FTO variant present = 1 FTO variant not present = 2
Frequency count variable	FREQS Frequencies within categories	FREQS Frequencies within categories

Automating model selection

Requesting a backward elimination loglinear analysis

You can get SPSS to automate the process of working down from the saturated model to a reduced model that fits well. Use the menu commands **Analyze, Loglinear** and **Model Selection** to get SPSS Dialog Box 12.3 (overleaf). After using the arrow to enter the factors we must define the range for each. Selecting each factor in turn, click the **Define Range** button and fill in the **Minimum** and **Maximum** values (1 and 2 for each of ours) for that factor in the small dialog box that opens.

Make sure the radio button **Use backward elimination** is selected for **Model Building**.

Backward elimination analysis: Understanding the model evaluation output

The process of selection will start from the saturated model, then try removing the three-factor interaction. The goodness of fit will be checked, then the hypothesis that the third-order interaction is zero will be tested. If the fit is good and the hypothesis not rejected, the two-factor interaction that contributes least to the goodness of fit will be removed. The fit will again be checked and the hypothesis that the interaction is

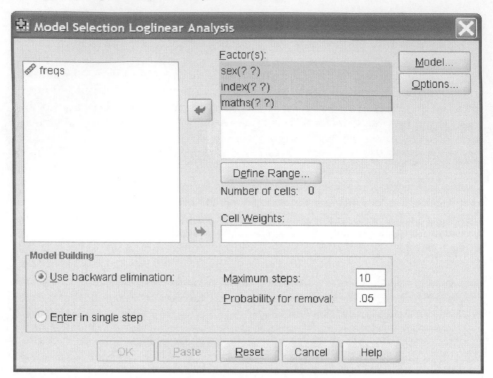

SPSS Dialog Box 12.3 Getting SPSS to do the model selection.

zero will be tested. The process continues until no more terms can be removed from the model without significantly worsening the fit. The process is exactly the same as the one we went through in the previous two sections, and the result is the same. The history is shown in a table, the first in SPSS Output 12.3. The *generating class* just means the set of highest order interactions in the model: because models are hierarchical, the presence of any interaction implies the presence of all related lower order interactions and main effects. The changes in goodness of fit statistics are also shown for each model as the interaction effects are removed one at a time. For instance, if you look at the row of the table for Step 1, Deleted Effect 2, you see the change in χ^2 of 1.962 that we derived in the previous section. For the original saturated model and for the final one we have a small table like the second one shown in SPSS Output 12.3, which is for the final model, the same one that we arrived at using **Analyze, Loglinear** and **General Loglinear**.

There is also a table of expected values for the final model and we discuss this in the next section.

Backward elimination analysis: The expected values table

Observed and expected values are given in the Cell Counts and Residuals table shown in SPSS Output 12.4(a). Here we use the version obtained from **Analyze, Loglinear** and **General Loglinear**, where we asked for adjusted and deviance residuals. You can see that SEX is used for the layers: this is because it was entered first in the list of factors

Step Summary

Step[a]		Effects	Chi-Square[c]	df	Sig.	Number of Iterations
0	Generating Class[b]	sex*index*ma ths	0.000	0	.	
	Deleted Effect 1	sex*index*ma ths	0.017	1	.896	4
1	Generating Class[b]	sex*index, sex*maths, index*maths	0.017	1	.896	
	Deleted Effect 1	sex*index	31.694	1	.000	2
	2	sex*maths	1.962	1	.161	2
	3	index*maths	4.052	1	.044	2
2	Generating Class[b]	sex*index, index*maths	1.979	2	.372	
	Deleted Effect 1	sex*index	35.569	1	.000	2
	2	index*maths	7.927	1	.005	2
3	Generating Class[b]	sex*index, index*maths	1.979	2	.372	

a. At each step, the effect with the largest significance level for the Likelihood Ratio Change is deleted, provided the significance level is larger than .050.

b. Statistics are displayed for the best model at each step after step 0.

c. For 'Deleted Effect', this is the change in the Chi-Square after the effect is deleted from the model.

Convergence Information[a]

Generating Class	sex*index, index*maths
Number of Iterations	.000
Max. Difference between Observed and Fitted Marginals	.000
Convergence Criterion	.250

a. Statistics for the final model after Backward Elimination.

SPSS Output 12.3 Backward elimination history and model summary for the final model in an automated loglinear model fitting.

(SPSS Dialog Box 12.1). You can control the layout of the table of expected values by altering the order in which factors are entered. Enter INDEX first if you want it to form the layers like in Table 12.1.

Backward elimination analysis: Parameter estimates

The table of estimates for the terms in the model with MATHS and SEX conditionally independent is shown in SPSS Output 12.4(b) overleaf. These parameter estimates are analogous to the sizes of effects in ANOVA. Their relationship to the expected frequencies is hard to comprehend if you do not have a mathematical background and it will be okay to skip over the rest of this section and rejoin us at 'Residuals and their plots'. For those readers who are strong on mathematics or are masochists, however, we include an attempt to show how expected frequencies are obtained from the parameter estimates.

Obtaining expected frequencies from parameter estimates

To see how the expected values relate to the parameter values, look first in SPSS Output 12.4(a) at the cell where all factors are at level 2 (third finger longer, females, not so good at maths). The expected count for this cell is given as 24.452. From the list of parameter values for the model (see footnote d to SPSS Output 12.4(b) for the model summary) we see that for this cell (all terms that include a factor at level 2) all parameter values in SPSS Output 12.4(b) are zero (because they are redundant, indicated by the superscript b). That leaves the overall mean (the constant), which has

(a) Observed and expected values for well-fitting model

Cell Counts and Residuals[a,b]

sex	index	maths	Observed Count	Observed %	Expected Count	Expected %	Residual	Standardized Residual	Adjusted Residual	Deviance
male	index longer	high ability	5	2.5%	3.624	1.8%	1.376	.730	0.919	1.794
		low ability	17	8.5%	18.376	9.2%	-1.376	-.337	-0.919	-1.627
	third longer	high ability	29	14.5%	26.452	13.2%	2.548	.532	1.074	2.309
		low ability	49	24.5%	51.548	25.8%	-2.548	-.412	-1.074	-2.229
female	index longer	high ability	9	4.5%	10.376	5.2%	-1.376	-.439	-0.919	-1.601
		low ability	54	27.0%	52.624	26.3%	1.376	.221	0.919	1.670
	third longer	high ability	10	5.0%	12.548	6.3%	-2.548	-.743	-1.074	-2.131
		low ability	27	13.5%	24.452	12.2%	2.548	.550	1.074	2.314

a. Model: Multinomial

b. Design: Constant + index + maths + sex + index * maths + sex * index

(b) Parameter list and estimates for well-fitting model

Parameter Estimates[c,d]

Parameter	Estimate	Std. Error	Z	Sig.	95% Confidence Interval Lower Bound	95% Confidence Interval Upper Bound
Constant	3.197[a]					
[index = 1]	0.766	0.223	3.439	.001	0.330	1.203
[index = 2]	0[b]	.	.	.	.	.
[maths = 1]	-0.667	0.197	-3.387	.001	-1.053	-0.281
[maths = 2]	0[b]	.	.	.	.	.
[sex = 1]	0.746	0.200	3.736	.000	0.355	1.137
[sex = 2]	0[b]	.	.	.	.	.
[index = 1] * [maths = 1]	-0.956	0.353	-2.713	.007	-1.647	-0.265
[index = 1] * [maths = 2]	0[b]	.	.	.	.	.
[index = 2] * [maths = 1]	0[b]	.	.	.	.	.
[index = 2] * [maths = 2]	0[b]	.	.	.	.	.
[sex = 1] * [index = 1]	-1.798	0.318	-5.652	.000	-2.421	-1.174
[sex = 1] * [index = 2]	0[b]	.	.	.	.	.
[sex = 2] * [index = 1]	0[b]	.	.	.	.	.
[sex = 2] * [index = 2]	0[b]	.	.	.	.	.

a. Constants are not parameters under the multinomial assumption. Therefore, their standard errors are not calculated.

b. This parameter is set to zero because it is redundant.

c. Model: Multinomial

d. Design: Constant + index + maths + sex + index * maths + sex * index

SPSS Output 12.4 Observed and expected values, and parameter list and estimates, for well-fitting model.

the value 3.197, so the expected value for this cell is the natural log of the constant, that is, $\exp(3.197) = 24.5$. If you want to check this on your calculator, look for a button labelled 'ln' and above it will probably be e^x in a colour indicating that it is a *second function* on the calculator. Select the second function mode and then ln and enter the value (on some calculators the sequence will be different: e.g., enter the value, select mode (sometimes labelled 'inverse'), then select ln).

If INDEX = 1 and SEX and MATHS are both 2, only the main effect for INDEX and the constant (the non-redundant parameters) are needed, so the expected value is $\exp(3.197 + 0.766) = 52.6$, as indicated in row 4 within Table 12.4. The other expected values and the parameter combinations needed are also shown in Table 12.4.

Table 12.4 Parameter combinations to give expected values

SEX	INDEX	MATHS	Exp of these terms are computed	Expected frequency
1	1	1	$3.197 + 0.746 + 0.766 - 0.667 - 0.956 - 1.798$	3.6
1	1	2	$3.197 + 0.746 + 0.766 - 1.798$	18.4
1	2	1	$3.197 + 0.746 - 0.667$	26.5
1	2	2	$3.197 + 0.746$	51.6
2	1	1	$3.197 + 0.766 - 0.667 - 0.956$	10.4
2	1	2	$3.197 + 0.766$	52.6
2	2	1	$3.197 - 0.667$	12.6
2	2	2	3.197	24.5

Residuals and their plots

The residuals are the differences between the observed and expected cell frequencies. Adjusted residuals and deviance residuals are both derived from the raw residuals because they each have the useful property that, for a well-fitting model, they will be approximately normal provided the sample size is not too small. So, plotting either of these against the expected values should give a shapeless cloud of points if the model fits well. Patterns in the residuals may give a clue about how a model does not fit. In a well-fitting model, none of the residuals should be much larger than the rest (in absolute value). Any residual with an absolute value larger than about 3 (roughly corresponding to the 1% value for a standard normal distribution) suggests that the model does not provide an adequate fit for that point.

The Q–Q (quantile–quantile) plot, not shown here, will be approximately a straight line if the residuals are standard normal random variables, which should be the case for a well-fitting model.

Raw, adjusted and deviance residuals are displayed (and can be saved if required, using the **Save** button in SPSS Dialog Box 12.1). The deviance residuals are calculated from the contribution that each cell makes to the Likelihood Ratio goodness of fit statistic. This makes them particularly useful if you are trying to find the cell(s) where the fit is bad. If you want the deviance residuals rather than the adjusted residuals plotted, click the box in the **Options** dialog box.

Residuals and their plots for the conditional independence model

The residuals can be seen in SPSS Output 12.4(a) (none had an absolute value above 2.55), and we show in SPSS Output 12.5 one of the plots provided to assist in identifying any lack of fit. Only three of the small graphs are needed as the other three are just mirror images. The observed and expected counts form a nearly straight line: the expected values are all close to the observed values. The plot of the residuals against expected counts shows no pattern or exceptional values. The plot of residuals against observed counts is similar since observed and expected values are close for this model.

Multinomial Model

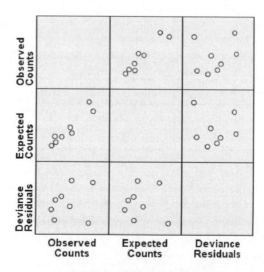

SPSS Output 12.5 Graphical diagnostics for well-fitting model.

Residuals and their plots for an alternative (badly fitting) model

For comparison, we show the same graphs for the model with only one two-factor interaction, INDEX * SEX, in SPSS Output 12.6. This model did not fit well according to

Multinomial Model

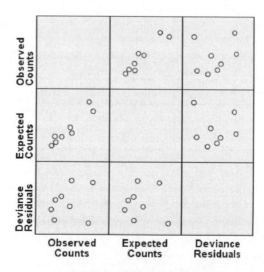

SPSS Output 12.6 Graphical diagnostics for poorly fitting model.

the goodness of fit statistics (χ^2 for the likelihood ratio was 9.906 on three degrees of freedom). Here we see that the observed and expected points form a less good approximation to a straight line, as we expect since this model was not a good fit. The residuals against expected counts do not, in this case, show a pattern that is helpful in identifying the problem, but we can at least see that we do not have just one or two large residuals, which would indicate that the fit was much worse for one or two cells than for the rest. In fact, using the parameter estimates from the saturated model (SPSS Output 12.1) we can easily see how to improve it: just try adding the term that has the largest Z value that is not already in the model (i.e., MATHS * INDEX).

Collapsing a table

If a variable in a three-dimensional table is at least conditionally independent of one of the other two variables at each level of the third, then we can collapse the table over that variable and it will not affect the interaction between the other two variables. In our example, MATHS and SEX are conditionally independent at each level of INDEX, so we could collapse over either MATHS or SEX and see the interaction between the other two. Collapsing over MATHS gives us Table 12.5(a), and collapsing over SEX gives Table 12.5(b).

Table 12.5 Collapsing a table
(a) Collapsing Table 12.1 over MATHS

	Male 1	Female 2	Totals
INDEX 1	22	63	85
2	78	37	115
Totals	100	100	200

(b) Collapsing Table 12.1 over SEX

	Math 1	Math 2	Totals
INDEX 1	14	71	85
2	39	76	115
Totals	53	147	200

Both of these tables show significant association between the row and column variables (the χ^2 values are 34.39 and 5.95 on one degree of freedom). This is why our attempt to collapse the table over INDEX when we first described the experiment was misleading: the table can be collapsed over either of the other two variables (which are conditionally independent within levels of INDEX) but not over INDEX, which is associated with both of the other variables.

There is another situation where a table can be collapsed. If a two-way table has independent row and column variables and if there are more than two categories for the row or the column, categories can be combined and the row and column variables will still be independent.

Measures of association and size of effects

The odds ratio for 2 × 2 tables

In a 2 * 2 table with frequencies *a* and *b* in the first row and *c* and *d* in the second, the odds of the levels of the row variable are *a/c* and *b/d* for the two levels of the column variable. The ratio of these odds, $(a/c)/(b/d) = ad/bc$, will be close to 1 in the case of independence, and the stronger the association between row and column variables, the further from 1 this ratio will be. If we rearranged the category order in the rows or columns, the odds ratio would be inverted (e.g., 0.6 would become 1/0.6 = 1.67). It is just as valid to look at either version. For Tables 12.5(a) and 12.5(b), both with significant association between row and column variables, the values of *ad/bc* are 0.17 and 0.38. The association between SEX and INDEX (0.17) is stronger than between MATHS and INDEX (0.38). For the two tables in Table 12.1, neither of which shows a significant association between row and column variables, the values are 1.76 and 1.60 (their reciprocals are 0.57 and 0.62, which are closer to 1 than 0.17 and 0.38). This odds ratio for a 2 * 2 table is one of several possible measures of association. The odds ratio cannot be applied to tables with more than two categories in rows or columns. Other measures, which can be applied to a two-way table with more than two categories in one or both variables, are based on the χ^2 statistic for the table.

For tables in more than two dimensions, measures of association can only be calculated for pairs of variables within levels of the third variable, or combinations of levels of the third and any other variables (i.e., compound variables). Only if the table turns out to be collapsible down to two dimensions can a single measure of association tell us all we want to know.

Using parameter estimates and odds ratios to indicate the size of an effect

The odds ratio suggests how we can use the parameter estimates to indicate the size of an effect. We will look at the odds of being good at maths for each sex within level 2 of INDEX, which is the level with a zero parameter in SPSS Output 12.4(b). For a person who is SEX 1 (male) or SEX 2 (female) and INDEX 2 (third finger longer), the odds of being MATHS 1 (good) against MATHS 2 (not so good) can be obtained from the ratios of expected values (26.45/51.55 = 0.51 for males or 12.55/24.45 = 0.51 for females; see SPSS Output 12.4(a)). This value can also be obtained from the main effect for MATHS level 1, which is −0.667 (see SPSS Output 12.4(b)). The odds ratio we want from this main effect is exp(−0.667) = 0.51. The odds ratio of being good at maths is the same for the two sexes within a level of INDEX because of the conditional independence of MATHS and SEX within levels of INDEX. To get this odds ratio from the list of parameter estimates in SPSS Output 12.4(b) we only need the main effect of MATHS because we used level 2 of INDEX, which has a zero parameter estimate, and we are finding the odds ratio within each sex.

At the other level of INDEX, the odds will again be the same for both sexes, the value being 0.20 this time. We can get this from the ratios of expected values in SPSS Output 12.4(a) (i.e., 3.62/18.38 and 10.38/52.62), as we did for level 2 of INDEX. Alternatively, we can use the main effect for MATHS and the interaction for MATHS and INDEX from SPSS Output 12.4(b). We need the main effect for MATHS since that is the factor for which we are calculating an odds ratio. We need the interaction term for MATHS and

INDEX for level 1 of INDEX (the non-zero level) because it is the strength of the interaction that the odds ratio measures. We are doing an odds ratio for each sex so we need no term for SEX. So the odds ratio for being good at maths within level 2 of INDEX is exp(−0.667−0.956) = 0.20 for either sex, as we got from the ratios of expected values.

INDEX interacts with both MATHS and SEX, so the odds of being INDEX 1 are not the same for both sexes at a given level of MATHS. For MATHS 2 (parameter zero) and SEX 2 (parameter zero) for instance, the odds of being INDEX 1 are 52.624/24.452 = 2.15 from the ratio of expected values in SPSS Output 12.4(a). Alternatively, we can get it from the main effect for INDEX found in SPSS Output 12.4(b): exp(0.766) = 2.15. For MATHS 2 and SEX 1 we need the main effect of INDEX (which is the one we want the odds for) and the interaction of INDEX and SEX, exp(0.766 − 1.798) = 0.36, which is the same as we get from the ratio of expected values, 18.376/51.548 = 0.36. These ratios reflect the fact that many more females than males are INDEX 1.

In the previous paragraph we considered those less good at maths (MATHS 2). Even if we look at those who are good at maths (MATHS 1) we still find many more females than males at INDEX 1, and this is reflected in the odds ratios of INDEX 1 for the two sexes. So we can now take MATHS 1 and SEX 2 and find the odds ratio of INDEX 1 from the expected values: 10.376/12.548 = 0.83. Using the parameter estimates from SPSS Output 12.4(b) we need the main effect for INDEX, since we are finding its odds ratio, and the interaction for INDEX and MATHS to find it at MATHS 1, exp(0.766 − 0.956) = 0.83, which is the same as we got from the expected values. For SEX 1 the odds are 3.624/26.452 = 0.14 or exp(0.766 − 0.956 − 1.798) = 0.14. This time we needed the interactions for INDEX and MATHS and for INDEX and SEX, since we want the odds of INDEX 1 at the non-zero parameter levels of both MATHS and SEX. Once again the odds ratio for INDEX 1 is much higher for females than males, even though we considered only those good at maths.

A general solution for using parameter estimates to calculate odds

If you compare the results in the previous two paragraphs with Table 12.4 you can see that reference to this table enables any required odds to be calculated. Just identify the two relevant rows, and use the exp of the terms that are only in one of the rows. For instance, to get the odds of being INDEX 1 for MATHS 1 and SEX 2 we would need rows 5 and 7 (where MATHS is 1, SEX is 2 and INDEX is 1 in row 5, and MATHS is 1, SEX is 2 and INDEX is 2 in row 7) to give us the odds for INDEX 1. The terms 0.766 and −0.956 are in row 5 (INDEX 1) but not row 7, so we need exp(0.766 − 0.956) = 0.83, as in the previous paragraph.

We recognize that the computation of effect sizes that we have demonstrated in this section is far from straightforward. We have included more computational detail than we have in general throughout the book because we think that, in this case, the effort of trying to follow the detailed examples offers the best hope of arriving at an intuitive understanding of what is going on in broad terms. If it is too much for you, however, do not despair. Many researchers have conducted and published loglinear analyses without understanding the relationship between odds ratios, parameter estimates and effect size. If you do succeed in grasping the essentials of this relationship, you will probably be ahead of the pack. These considerations remind us that relationships among three variables are not simple unless all three are independent.

As we noted at the beginning of this section, if the odds ratio *ad/bc* in the 2 * 2 table is equal to 1, or equivalently if the log(odds) is zero, then the rows and columns are independent, so testing the hypothesis of independence is equivalent to testing that the odds ratio is 1 or the log(odds) is zero. However, looking at the odds for one value of a factor, as we have done in this section, is one way to gain more insight into the magnitude of the interactions or the scale of the departures from independence.

Variables with more than two categories

Another example for loglinear analysis

We now briefly show an example where one of three variables in a contingency table has three categories (the others have just two). This example will also illustrate a case where one variable is independent of the other two. The data relate to the voting behaviour of old and young people, and are shown in Table 12.6. The age groups are coded 1 (old, over 50) and 2 (young, under 25). There are three parties coded 1–3 (actually two parties and a catch-all 'other' category). Those who voted at the last election are coded 1 and those who did not are coded 2. The data are set out as in the SPSS datasheet, with the frequencies in column 4 used to weight the data.

Table 12.6 Voting behaviour of old and young people (loglinear.sav)

AGE	PARTY	VOTE	FREQS
1	1	1	15
1	1	2	6
1	2	1	18
1	2	2	8
1	3	1	9
1	3	2	4
2	1	1	6
2	1	2	13
2	2	1	7
2	2	2	18
2	3	1	5
2	3	2	11

We do not provide a medical alternative for this example, as the context will be readily meaningful to readers with different academic backgrounds.

Requesting loglinear analysis

If we use the **Model selection** method (SPSS Dialog Box 12.3) we soon find that the best model has just one two-factor interaction, as shown in SPSS Output 12.7. Here the generating class must list the main effect, PARTY, since that does not appear in any interaction in the model. If we want to see parameter estimates and residual plots we can easily get these by using **General Loglinear** and using a **Custom** model (see SPSS

Convergence Information[a]

Generating Class	age*vote, party
Number of Iterations	.000
Max. Difference between Observed and Fitted Marginals	.000
Convergence Criterion	.250

a. Statistics for the final model after Backward Elimination.

Parameter Estimates[c,d]

					95% Confidence Interval	
Parameter	Estimate	Std. Error	Z	Sig.	Lower Bound	Upper Bound
Constant	2.317[a]					
[age = 1]	-0.847	0.282	-3.008	.003	-1.399	-0.295
[age = 2]	0[b]	.	.	.	.	.
[party = 1]	0.322	0.244	1.319	.187	-0.156	0.800
[party = 2]	0.565	0.233	2.427	.015	0.109	1.020
[party = 3]	0[b]	.	.	.	.	.
[vote = 1]	-0.847	0.282	-3.008	.003	-1.399	-0.295
[vote = 2]	0[b]	.	.	.	.	.
[age = 1] * [vote = 1]	1.695	0.398	4.254	.000	0.914	2.475
[age = 1] * [vote = 2]	0[b]	.	.	.	.	.
[age = 2] * [vote = 1]	0[b]	.	.	.	.	.
[age = 2] * [vote = 2]	0[b]	.	.	.	.	.

a. Constants are not parameters under the multinomial assumption. Therefore, their standard errors are not calculated.

b. This parameter is set to zero because it is redundant.

c. Model: Multinomial

d. Design: Constant + age + party + vote + age * vote

SPSS Output 12.7 The best model for the voting data has just one interaction term.

Dialog Box 12.2) with all main effects and just one two-factor interaction, AGE * VOTE. We also show the parameter estimates from this analysis in SPSS Output 12.7 (a reminder of the model we used appears in footnote d). The main difference from previous results is that there are two non-zero terms for PARTY, because it has three levels. Since the interaction term is between the two variables with only two levels, there is only one non-zero term for the interaction.

Loglinear analysis: Understanding the output

In SPSS Output 12.8 overleaf we show the residual plots for the model using only the main effects. This model does not fit well: we have not shown the Goodness of Fit Tests here (look for the box like those shown in SPSS Output 12.2) but we find that the likelihood ratio statistic is 20.292 on seven degrees of freedom, significant at the 1% level. We show this just to illustrate how a residual plot for a badly fitting model may give a clue to where the problem lies.

The plot of observed by expected values shows the points falling on two well separated straight lines, and this usually means that an important effect has been omitted. The plot of residuals against expected values also shows two clearly separated groups, indicating that there is an important term missing from the model. To find which term this might be, we should look at the saturated model and consider those with Z values of 2 or above that have not been included.

Multinomial Model

Analysis weighted by freq

SPSS Output 12.8 Residual plots for model with main effects only.

Reporting results

The main items to include when reporting results are the final model with either the expected values or parameter estimates, the goodness of fit statistic and the χ^2 value for the test of the hypothesis that all omitted interactions are zero. It may then be useful to describe what the resulting model means: for instance conditional independence means that the IVs that are conditionally independent are independent within levels of the other variable. For our example of the 2 * 2 * 2 table we suggest the following:

For the frequency data described in the Method section we were able to fit a loglinear model with the three main effects and the two-factor interactions between INDEX and SEX and between INDEX and MATHS. The Goodman statistic for goodness of fit, based on the likelihood ratio, was 1.979. If the model is a good fit, this is approximately χ^2 on two degrees of freedom (8 cells $-$ 1 $-$ 5 estimated parameters). Our value is well below the critical 5% value of 5.991 and we conclude that the model fits well.

To test the null hypothesis that the three-factor interaction and the two-factor interaction between MATHS and SEX are both zero, we compare the Goodman statistics for the model without these terms and for the saturated model. For the saturated model the Goodman statistic is zero, as are the degrees of freedom, so the test statistic for the hypothesis is again 1.979, which is χ^2 with $2 - 0 = 2$ degrees of freedom under the null hypothesis.

Table A shows the observed and expected frequencies, which are in good agreement.

Table A Observed and expected frequencies

SEX	INDEX	MATHS	Obs freq	Exp freq
1	1	1	5	3.62
1	1	2	17	18.38
1	2	1	29	26.45
1	2	2	49	51.55
2	1	1	9	10.38
2	1	2	54	52.62
2	2	1	10	12.55
2	2	2	27	24.45

Because the MATHS * SEX interaction is not included in the model, we know that these two variables are conditionally independent within levels of INDEX. This means that among those with a longer index finger there is no association between sex and mathematical ability, and among those with a longer third finger there is also no association between sex and mathematical ability. However there are significant associations between INDEX and SEX (more females have a longer index finger) and between INDEX and MATHS (more of those with a longer third finger are good at maths).

13 Poisson regression

Introduction

In many areas of psychology and medical research, the investigator is interested in the number of times a fairly rare event occurs within some defined time interval. The event of interest might be the number of epileptic seizures a person has during a known period of time or the number of occurrences of a particular adverse event reported by a participant during a clinical trial. Examples from other fields include the number of accidents at a particular road junction in a year and the number of spam e-mails received in a day.

It is often the case that events such as these occur independently: in other words, the chance of a new event occurring in the next short time interval is not affected by whether or not an event has recently occurred. If this assumption holds and the events occur at random, then it can be shown that the number of events in a given time period follows a Poisson distribution. This provides a formula to calculate the probability of a given number of events depending on the mean. If the mean is small (less than 10), then the Poisson distribution is positively skewed so that smaller numbers of events have a relatively large probability. For larger means, the Poisson distribution can be approximated by a normal distribution.

The kind of independence assumed by the Poisson distribution is extremely common in nature. If you watch people arriving to join a queue for instance, you will observe that the chance of a new arrival in the next minute does not depend on whether someone arrived in the minute just past. The chance that a radioactive object will emit a gamma ray in the next 5 seconds does not depend on whether it emitted one in the last 5 seconds. A similar independence can be observed in space as well as time: the chance of finding a misprint on the next page of this book does not depend on whether there was a misprint on the previous page. The Poisson distribution is frequently used to model counts in equal-sized grid squares, including the number of plants of a given species within a quadrant. It was even observed in flying bomb hits on London in World War II: a grid of kilometre squares placed over a map of the city showed that the chance of a hit in one square did not depend on whether neighbouring squares experienced a hit.

However, although extremely common, this kind of independence is not universal: events that tend to be periodic do not show it, and neither do events that tend to occur in groups. Some migraine sufferers tend to be afflicted at the weekend, so for them the chance of getting a migraine tomorrow will depend on how many days since the last one. At the airport passport check queue, people do not arrive at random but in bunches as aircraft arrive. A person who makes an error and becomes flustered may then make several more errors, so the errors are not independent in the sense described above. By counting the events that occur in consecutive time intervals it is easy to check whether or not they follow a Poisson distribution. We do not show the process here, but details can be found in the Further reading, at the end of the book.

In this chapter, we shall be assuming that counts of events do occur at random and independently. Usually we shall be interested in whether the number of events in the specified time is influenced by a factor such as treatment or experimental condition, and also whether covariates such as age and gender have any effect. To begin with we consider a study where the observation period is the same for all participants. Later we can relax this requirement.

It turns out that we can approach this problem using a combination of the ideas in the chapters on ANCOVA and loglinear models. Like logistic regression and loglinear models, Poisson regression is an example of a Generalized Linear Model, which is an extension of the General Linear Model that includes ANOVA, MANOVA, ANCOVA and regression. As in loglinear models where we considered an additive model for the log of the *cell probabilities*, here we consider the log of the *number of events* occurring in the specified time, or its *rate* if the time periods for our observations differ. (The logs in this chapter are all natural logs, sometimes denoted ln or $\log_e$.) As before, our model may contain a linear combination of continuous covariates and dummy variables that represent levels of factors.

A psychology experiment and (fabricated) data with equal observation periods

We begin by considering the first case above, that is, where the time intervals for all observations are equal. Later, we relax this assumption. Consider an investigation into how to reduce the number of violent incidents (those that required the intervention of staff) involving prisoners convicted of violent offences. Eligible prisoners (those who had been at the prison for at least 1 year and still have at least 1 year left before they can be released) were randomly allocated to one of three TREATMENTS: cognitive behaviour therapy (CBT, treatment 1), group therapy aimed at anger control (treatment 2) and rigorous exercise (treatment 3). Details were also taken of two potentially confounding variables: ESTEEM, which is their score on Rosenberg's Self-Esteem Scale (ranging from 0 to 30, with scores below 15 indicating low self-esteem); and ABUSE, which is a Yes/No variable indicating whether the participant was abused as a child. The DV is the number of violent incidents requiring the intervention of staff, where the participant is the antagonist (EVENTS), during the year following the end of the treatment. For the remainder of the chapter these are referred to as violent incidents. Data were collected for all participants for the whole year. Table 13.1 shows the first four cases within each treatment group.

A first look at the data

Before starting our Poisson regression analysis we might begin by looking at the mean numbers of events for the three TREATMENT groups: 2.95, 6.07 and 9.36, respectively. You can easily obtain these using **Analyze**, then **Compare means** and then **Means**. Put EVENTS in the **Dependent List** box and TREATMENT in the **Independent List** box, as shown in SPSS Dialog Box 13.1, and click **OK**.

Table 13.1 The first four cases from each treatment group in the prison trial (the full dataset can be found as psy.poissonregression.equaltimes.sav on the website)

ESTEEM	ABUSE[1]	TREATMENT[2]	EVENTS
13	0	1	6
15	0	1	5
16	0	1	4
15	0	1	4
16	0	2	9
19	0	2	8
23	0	2	7
13	0	2	9
12	0	3	16
22	0	3	11
11	1	3	14
13	0	3	12

1 0 = No, 1 = Yes.
2 1 = cognitive behaviour therapy, 2 = group therapy, 3 = exercise.

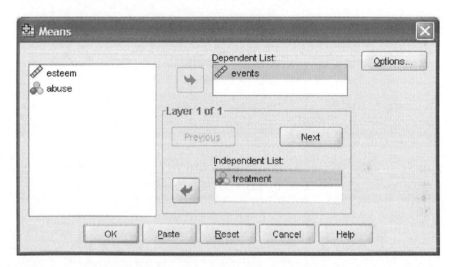

SPSS Dialog Box 13.1 Obtaining the mean number of events for each treatment group.

It is also interesting to consider the contingency table showing the numbers of events by treatment group. This can be obtained using **Analyze**, then **Descriptive Statistics** and then **Crosstabs** to obtain SPSS Dialog Box 13.2. Put EVENTS in the **Row(s)** box and TREATMENT in the **Column(s)** box. Click **OK** to get SPSS Output 13.1.

The contingency table and means suggest that there are differences among the three treatments. CBT (treatment 1) has the lowest mean and six is the highest number of events for any participant in that group. Rigorous exercise (treatment 3) has the highest mean and 16 is the highest number of events for any participant in that group.

Now we will fit a Poisson regression with EVENTS as the DV, TREATMENT and ABUSE as

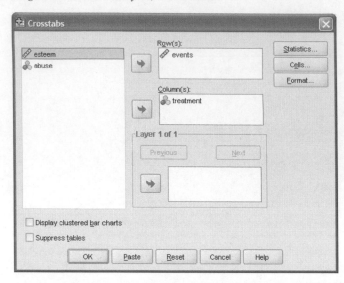

SPSS Dialog Box 13.2 Producing a contingency table of the number of events for each treatment group.

events * treatment Crosstabulation

Count

		treatment			
		1	2	3	Total
events	1	3	0	0	3
	2	3	1	0	4
	3	9	3	0	12
	4	3	3	0	6
	5	1	5	0	6
	6	1	3	2	6
	7	0	8	4	12
	8	0	3	4	7
	9	0	4	5	9
	10	0	0	3	3
	11	0	0	3	3
	12	0	0	2	2
	14	0	0	1	1
	16	0	0	1	1
Total		20	30	25	75

SPSS Output 13.1 The number of events (violent incidents requiring staff intervention) for three treatment arms. Treatment 1 = cognitive behaviour therapy, treatment 2 = group therapy, treatment 3 = exercise.

factors and ESTEEM as a covariate. Because TREATMENT is a categorical variable with three levels, we will need two dummy variables to define it. The process is as described in the section, 'Creating dummy variables' in Chapter 4, illustrated in Table 4.2. The first of the dummy variables will take the value 1 for cases in treatment group 1 (CBT) and zero otherwise, and the second will take the value 1 for cases in treatment group 2 (group therapy) and zero otherwise. So the two dummy variables will have values (1, 0) for treatment group 1, (0, 1) for treatment group 2 and (0, 0) for treatment group 3. This arrangement, with treatment group 3 being (0, 0), is the SPSS default and is referred to as making the last category the reference category.

Since ABUSE is a categorical variable with only two categories, we can just code No as zero and Yes as 1, making just one dummy variable. ESTEEM is a numerical variable and can be treated as a covariate in the usual way.

The Poisson regression model uses a linear combination of factors and covariates, just like ANCOVA, but instead of using this to predict the DV as ANCOVA does, it is used to predict the log of the DV. This is analogous to the loglinear model where we used a linear combination of factors to predict the log of the cell probabilities in a contingency table. In the loglinear case we used the logs so that the *multiplicative* law of probability could be modelled by a *sum* of the effects of factors and their interactions. In the Poisson regression case, if the count of events has a Poisson rather than a normal distribution it can be shown that we can predict the log of the count rather than the count itself, using a sum of the effects of factors and covariates. We will see later how this affects how we obtain predicted values from parameter estimates.

Requesting a Poisson regression with equal times in SPSS

With the data arranged as in Table 13.1 we can proceed to our Poisson regression model using TREATMENT, ABUSE and ESTEEM as our predictor variables. Choose **Analyze**, then **Generalized Linear Models**, then **Generalized Linear Models**. Click the **Type of Model** tab if it is not already selected, so that you see SPSS Dialog Box 13.3 (overleaf). Our DV, EVENTS, is a count, so look at the **Counts** section, second down on the left. Click the **Poisson loglinear** radio button since we shall be using a linear model for the log of the number of events, as explained at the end of the Introduction.

We now work our through the other tabs. Select the **Response** tab and put EVENTS in the **Dependent Variable** box.

Select the **Predictors** tab and put TREATMENT and ABUSE in the **Factors** box and ESTEEM in the **Covariates** box.

Select the **Model** tab and make sure that **Main effects** appears in the **Build Terms** box (use the drop-down list if it does not). Use the arrow to put ABUSE, ESTEEM and TREATMENT in the **Model** box, so your dialog box now looks like SPSS Dialog Box 13.4 on page 319. (The order in which you put the predictor variables in the model box only affects the *order* in which parameter values are listed in the output, not their values.) We do not consider possible interactions among our factors and covariates in this introductory account of Poisson regression.

Select the **Save** tab and tick **Standardized deviance residuals**. You may also want to save the values predicted by the model. If you tick **Predicted value of linear predictor** from the list, you will get the predicted value of the log of the EVENTS count for each case. If you tick **Predicted value of mean of response**, you will get the predicted count. SPSS displays this to the nearest whole number as a default, but you can change this. Click on **Variable view** in the dataset and then on the cell in the decimals column and the **Mean Predicted** row. Use the up arrow to select the required number of decimal places. Click **OK** to get the analysis.

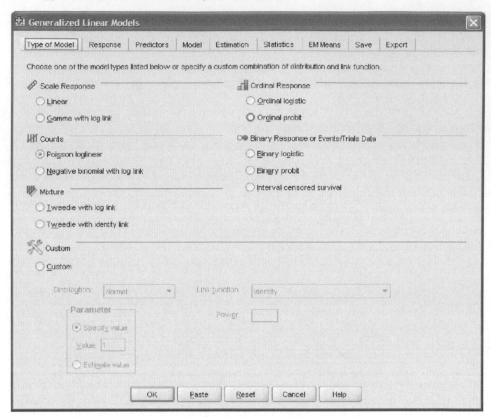

SPSS Dialog Box 13.3 The main dialog box for Poisson regression.

Understanding the output: Checking the fit of the Poisson regression model with equal times

The first four tables in the output show us the model we have chosen, the number of cases excluded because of missing data (none in our example), the numbers at each level of TREATMENT (20, 30 and 25 in our example) and ABUSE (52 and 23) and what continuous variables have been used. This last table lists variables that are not factors (i.e., are not categorical variables) and we see here our covariate ESTEEM and our DV EVENTS. If you are of a critical turn of mind you may notice that these variables are discrete, not continuous. They are numerical variables on a ratio scale, but 'continuous' is not a correct description. However, just take it that variables listed here are not categorical.

Next come the goodness of fit tests, shown in SPSS Output 13.2. The deviance and Pearson residuals are used to assess whether the model assumptions have been violated. Each should approximately equal its degrees of freedom and so Value/df (value divided by degrees of freedom) should be close to 1. You can see that we have 0.560 and 0.549 in the Value/df column, both of which are less than 1. This means that our values are probably more bunched up around the mean than would be expected in a Poisson distribution, but not seriously so. This is a case where we have mild *underdispersion*. A more serious departure from the Poisson assumption is *overdispersion*, which would result in our values being less tightly clustered around the mean. This gives values

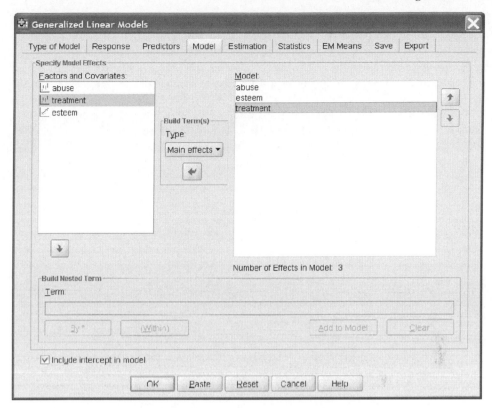

SPSS Dialog Box 13.4 Specifying our Poisson regression model.

exceeding 1 in the Value/df column. Here we can be satisfied that there is no evidence that the Poisson regression model is a poor fit.

An additional check on the model fit uses the standardized deviance residuals. They should approximately follow a standard normal distribution. Since we saved them

Goodness of Fit[b]

	Value	df	Value/df
Deviance	39.214	70	0.560
Scaled Deviance	39.214	70	
Pearson Chi-Square	38.441	70	0.549
Scaled Pearson Chi-Square	38.441	70	
Log Likelihood[a]	-153.371		
Akaike's Information Criterion (AIC)	316.742		
Finite Sample Corrected AIC (AICC)	317.611		
Bayesian Information Criterion (BIC)	328.329		
Consistent AIC (CAIC)	333.329		

Dependent Variable: events
Model: (Intercept), abuse, esteem, treatment

a. The full log likelihood function is displayed and used in computing information criteria.

b. Information criteria are in small-is-better form.

SPSS Output 13.2 Goodness of fit tests for the Poisson regression with equal times.

(using the **Save** tab in SPSS Dialog Box 13.3), they now occupy a new column in the datasheet and we can obtain a histogram. Select **Graph** from the menu bar, then **Chart builder**. Drag the icon showing a simple histogram into the chart area, and drag **Standardized deviance residual** from the variable list into the *X*-axis box. In the **Element Properties** dialog box to the right of the **Chart builder** dialog box, tick **Display normal curve** and click **Apply**. Then click **OK** in the **Chart builder** dialog box to get SPSS Output 13.3. This shows that the standardized deviance residuals are approximately normally distributed and that all values are between −2 and +2.

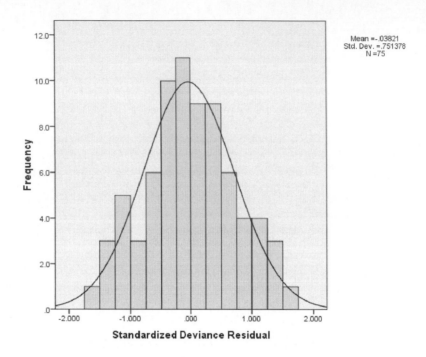

SPSS Output 13.3 Histogram of standardized deviance residuals for the Poisson regression with equal times.

These two checks give us some confidence that the Poisson regression model assumptions are not being violated.

Understanding the output: Testing hypotheses for the Poisson regression model with equal times

We shall ignore the next two tables since we can get all we want from the table of parameter estimates, shown as SPSS Output 13.4. Look first at the two rows of the table for ABUSE. This is a dummy variable coded zero for No (no childhood abuse) and 1 for Yes. The default for SPSS is to use the last category as reference, so the parameter value for ABUSE = 1 is zero (look in the B column). The parameter value for ABUSE = 0 is −0.004. Because it is negative, the effect of ABUSE = 0 is to reduce the expected count of EVENTS compared with the reference category, ABUSE = 1 (assuming TREATMENT and ESTEEM are fixed). However, as the B value is very close to zero this effect is very small.

Parameter Estimates

Parameter	B	Std. Error	95% Wald Confidence Interval		Hypothesis Test		
			Lower	Upper	Wald Chi-Square	df	Sig.
(Intercept)	2.753	0.2084	2.345	3.162	174.559	1	.000
[abuse=0]	-0.004	0.1032	-0.206	0.198	0.002	1	.967
[abuse=1]	0ᵃ	.	.	.	.	.	.
esteem	-0.034	0.0139	-0.061	-0.007	5.958	1	.015
[treatment=1]	-1.153	0.1457	-1.439	-0.868	62.637	1	.000
[treatment=2]	-0.457	0.0994	-0.652	-0.263	21.178	1	.000
[treatment=3]	0ᵃ	.	.	.	.	.	.
(Scale)	1ᵇ						

Dependent Variable: events
Model: (Intercept), abuse, esteem, treatment

a. Set to zero because this parameter is redundant.

b. Fixed at the displayed value.

SPSS Output 13.4 Parameter estimates for the Poisson regression with equal times.

Now look at the Sig. column on the right: the *p* value for ABUSE is close to 1 (.967) so it is almost certain that this small effect is only random variation. We certainly cannot reject the null hypothesis that ABUSE has no effect on EVENTS, consistent with its very low value of B. We conclude that being abused as a child does not affect the count of violent EVENTS significantly.

The *p* value for ESTEEM is .015 and hence this covariate is significant. The negative value of B for ESTEEM shows that the predicted value of the DV decreases as ESTEEM increases.

Because TREATMENT is a categorical variable with three levels, and once again the last category is used as the reference, we have two parameter estimates and corresponding *p* values, for TREATMENT = 1 (CBT) and TREATMENT = 2 (group therapy). Both parameter values (the B column) are negative, so both CBT and group therapy have lower predicted EVENTS counts than rigorous exercise (assuming ABUSE and ESTEEM are fixed). The *p* value for TREATMENT = 1 is less than .001, so we can certainly reject the null hypothesis that, compared with rigorous exercise, CBT has no effect on EVENTS. The *p* value for TREATMENT = 2 is also less than .001, so we can certainly also reject the null hypothesis that, compared with rigorous exercise, group therapy has no effect on EVENTS. Notice that, so far, we have no way to see whether CBT and group therapy differ significantly from each other; all we know is that each differs significantly from rigorous exercise, after allowing for ABUSE and ESTEEM.

Example Box 13.1

An alternative medical example with equal observation times

The full analysis for this example can be found at www.psypress.com/multivariate-analysis/medical-examples (click on Chapter 13).

A study aimed at reducing the number of epileptic seizures is carried out on participants who had been diagnosed with epilepsy for at least 1 year. Participants are randomly allocated to one of three treatments: high drug dose (treatment 1), low drug dose (treatment 2) and placebo (treatment 3). Scores are recorded on a measure of self-esteem, ESTEEM (0–30), and ALCOHOL, a Yes/No variable indicating whether the participant drinks more than the recommended upper limit of alcohol. The DV is the number of epileptic seizures (EVENTS) during the year following the end of the treatment. Data are collected for all participants for the whole year.

Outcomes

A Poisson regression analysis shows that high self-esteem is associated with a reduced number of epileptic seizures, whereas consumption of alcohol above or below the recommended limit has very little effect on the number of seizures. Both high and low drug doses have lower predicted EVENTS counts than the placebo after account is taken of the two covariates (ESTEEM and ALCOHOL). However, the high drug dose is associated with fewer seizure events than the low drug dose.

Alternative variables for use in SPSS
The full dataset, med.poissonregression.equaltimes.sav, can be found on the book website

Variable	Psychology	Medicine
IV	TREATMENT Treatment 1 = CBT Treatment 2 = group therapy Treatment 3 = rigorous exercise	TREATMENT Treatment 1 = high drug dose Treatment 2 = low drug dose Treatment 3 = placebo
DV	EVENTS = violent incident count	EVENTS = epileptic seizure count
Covariates	ESTEEM ABUSE (binary variable: abused/not abused))	ESTEEM ALCOHOL (above/not above recommended limit)

Obtaining expected EVENTS *counts from the parameter values*

We told you how to save predicted values of the EVENTS count and its log at the end of the section 'Requesting a Poisson regression with equal times in SPSS'. However, you may find it helps your understanding of the Poisson regression model if you work out some of the expected values yourself from the parameter values. Just be aware that the table in SPSS Output 13.4 gives parameter values correct to three decimal places, but more precise values are used by SPSS in its own calculation of expected values. Hence in the calculations shown below, and in any you do yourself, you may find small discrepancies in the last decimal place.

To see how to obtain expected values of EVENTS using the parameter values, first consider a case with ABUSE = 1 and TREATMENT = 3. Because these are the reference categories for the two factors, the parameter values for TREATMENT and ABUSE for this case are both zero. You can see such a case in the penultimate row of Table 13.1. This participant had an esteem score of 11, was abused as a child, was in treatment group 3 and had an events count of 14. In SPSS Output 13.4 you see that the intercept is 2.753 and the B value for ESTEEM is −0.034. So, with zeros for ABUSE and TREATMENT, and 11 for ESTEEM, our predictor for this case is

$$2.753 - 0.004 * (0) + 0 * (1) - 0.034 * 11 - 1.153 * (0) - 0.457 * (0) + 0 * (1) = 2.379$$

If this were ordinary regression, this would be the predicted value of the DV. However, in Poisson regression this predictor is for the *log* of EVENTS, so to get the predicted value of EVENTS we need exp(2.379) = 10.8, or 11 to the nearest whole number. Remember though that you can display more accurate values in the dataset file by specifying the number of decimal places using variable view. To get this from your calculator, look for e^x or the inverse of ln (the natural log). You may have to use the Shift or Inverse key. The observed value of EVENTS for this individual was 14.

Now consider a case with ABUSE = 0 and TREATMENT = 3. You can find such a case in the last row of Table 13.1. The ESTEEM score is 13 and the EVENTS count is 12. This time the B value for ABUSE is −0.004 and that for TREATMENT is still zero. Our predictor of log(EVENTS) will be

$$2.753 - 0.034 * 13 - 0.004 = 2.307$$

and the predicted value for EVENTS is exp(2.307) = 10.0, which is again slightly below the observed value of 12.

Now consider a case with ABUSE = 0 and TREATMENT = 1. You can find such a case in the first row of Table 13.1. The ESTEEM score is 13 and the EVENTS count is 6. This time the B value for ABUSE is −0.004 and for TREATMENT is −1.153. Our predictor of log events will be

$$2.753 - 0.034 * 13 - 0.004 - 1.153 = 1.154$$

and the predicted value for EVENTS is exp(1.154) = 3.17, or 3 to the nearest whole number, compared with the observed value of 6. To find the predicted value for a person in treatment group 2, replace −1.153 by −0.457 and insert the correct value of esteem where we have 13 here.

Changing the reference category from last to first

If we want to test the null hypothesis that there is no difference between the effects of treatments 1 and 2 on EVENTS, we can do it by changing the reference category from the last to the first, so that treatments 2 and 3 will each be compared to treatment 1. Note that all factors will have the reference category changed to the first, so ABUSE = 1 will be compared to ABUSE = 0 instead of the other way round, but because ABUSE has only two categories this will just reverse the sign of the parameter.

Before you re-run the analysis you need to delete the columns containing the predicted values of the event count, the predicted value of the linear predictor and the standardized deviance residuals, if you created them. Select **Data View** within the dataset, click on **MeanPredicted**, ensuring that the column of data is highlighted, and then press the **Delete** key. Repeat for **StdDeviance Residual** and **XBPredicted**.

When you click the **Predictors** tab in SPSS Dialog Box 13.3, you see an **Options** button at the bottom of the **Factors** box. Click this after putting ABUSE and TREATMENT in the box. Click the radio button for **Descending**, as shown in SPSS Dialog Box 13.5. Repeat the analysis, and this time you see the table of parameters shown in SPSS Output 13.5.

As expected, you can see that in the B column we now have 0.004 for ABUSE = 0

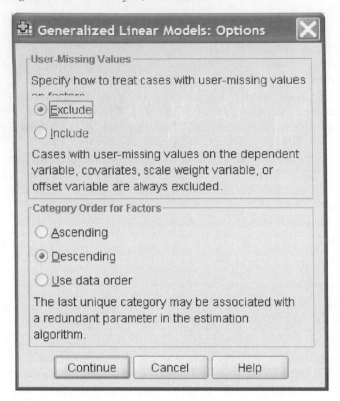

SPSS Dialog Box 13.5 Changing the reference category for factors from last to first.

Parameter Estimates

Parameter	B	Std. Error	95% Wald Confidence Interval		Hypothesis Test		
			Lower	Upper	Wald Chi-Square	df	Sig.
(Intercept)	1.596	0.2552	1.096	2.096	39.102	1	.000
[abuse=1]	0.004	0.1032	-0.198	0.206	0.002	1	.967
[abuse=0]	0ᵃ	.	.	.	.	.	.
esteem	-0.034	0.0139	-0.061	-0.007	5.958	1	.015
[treatment=3]	1.153	0.1457	0.868	1.439	62.637	1	.000
[treatment=2]	0.696	0.1504	0.401	0.991	21.404	1	.000
[treatment=1]	0ᵃ	.	.	.	.	.	.
(Scale)	1ᵇ						

Dependent Variable: events
Model: (Intercept), abuse, esteem, treatment

a. Set to zero because this parameter is redundant.

b. Fixed at the displayed value.

SPSS Output 13.5 Parameter estimates with the reference category for factors changed from last to first.

instead of −0.004 for ABUSE = 1. The *p* value remains unchanged. The parameter for ESTEEM is also unchanged. The B value for TREATMENT = 3 (compared to TREATMENT = 1) is 1.153. Previously we had −1.153 for TREATMENT = 1 compared to TREATMENT = 3. But the comparison of interest is TREATMENT = 2 compared to TREATMENT = 1. Here we have B = 0.696 and a *p* value of less than .001. The B value is positive so, compared with TREATMENT = 1, TREATMENT = 2 increases the expected value of EVENTS (assuming that ABUSE and ESTEEM are fixed). As the p value is so low we can certainly reject the null hypothesis that there is no difference between treatments 1 and 2. It appears that group therapy increases the number of EVENTS significantly, compared with CBT.

Poisson models with unequal observation periods

So far we have assumed that each case is observed over the same period of 1 year. We now extend the approach to consider cases where observations in the dataset may be taken over different time intervals. This would occur in the previous example if the number of violent incidents were counted until the individual left the prison rather than over a fixed period of 1 year.

Since we are recording individuals over different time intervals we would expect the count of the events to depend on the time interval even if the rate remains constant. Consider a prisoner who was observed to have four violent incidents in the year of the study. If the experiment had been designed to follow the participants for 6 months we would expect to have observed two such events if the Poisson rate were constant for the year. Similarly, if we had observed the prisoner for 2 years we would expect to observe eight such incidents, again assuming that the Poisson rate did not change over time.

A similar situation arises in many clinical trials. Consider a trial to determine if an adverse event depends on the length of exposure to a drug. Participants may be followed for varying lengths of times, noting their number of adverse events and duration of exposure to the drug. It is common to combine participants and report the adverse event rate for each person-year. A similar approach of reporting the rate to a common unit is taken when the number of events is recorded over space rather than time. For example, a forester may wish to use many forests in their Poisson model and determine if the density of trees above a given height depends on a number of factors, such as time since logging, species composition, etc. The forests are unlikely to have a common area and so the rate of trees above the given height may be reported per hectare.

We now adapt our example using prisoners and violent incidents to model the average number of events over the reporting period (violent incidents per year). We then estimate the expected count over the period by taking into account the reporting period. For example, if we have observed an individual for 3 years and their predicted Poisson rate was 7 violent incidents per year, then we would predict that they would have had a total of 21 violent incidents during the 3 years they had been observed.

A psychology experiment and (fabricated) data with unequal observation periods

After reviewing the results of the experiment above where each participant was observed for 1 year, the research team wondered if the relative success of treatment 1 (CBT) was because participants in that group were less aggressive before the experiment began. Since records of violent incidents are retained throughout a prisoner's stay, the team decided to count the number of violent offences for each participant in the study from the time they arrived at the prison until the start of the intervention. The team would then test for differences among the treatment groups, allowing for ESTEEM and ABUSE, for the period preceding the original study. If the TREATMENT group effect is non-significant, then the research team will have more confidence that their results were due to their intervention.

Since the participants in the experiment have been in the prison for different lengths of time, we need to modify the Poisson model. Instead of modelling the event count over a fixed interval of time we model the average number of events per year over the observed time. For each participant we shall need the number of violent incidents from when the participant arrived at the prison until the start of the experiment (which we call pretreatment events, PRE_TRT_EVENTS), and also the number of years that the participant has been at the prison before the experiment (YEARS). We shall also need the natural log of years, which, for a reason that will become apparent later, is called OFFSET. Table 13.2 shows the first four cases from each treatment group. You can see that the first four columns are the same as Table 13.1, but we now have three extra columns containing the new variables. Our analysis will not include EVENTS this time, since we are now focussing on the period before the start of the experiment. YEARS will appear only through its log OFFSET.

Table 13.2 The first four cases from each treatment group in the extended prison trial (the full dataset can be found as psy.poissonregression.unequaltimes.sav on the website)

ESTEEM	ABUSE [1]	TREATMENT [2]	EVENTS	YEARS	OFFSET [3]	PRE_TRT_EVENTS
13	0	1	6	1.95	0.667829	15
15	0	1	5	3.36	1.211941	24
16	0	1	4	3.30	1.193922	28
15	0	1	4	4.14	1.420696	27
16	0	2	9	3.07	1.121678	28
19	0	2	8	5.18	1.644805	28
23	0	2	7	4.44	1.490654	18
13	0	2	9	2.34	0.850151	30
12	0	3	16	3.47	1.244155	34
22	0	3	11	3.16	1.150572	28
11	1	3	14	4.77	1.562346	35
13	0	3	12	2.04	0.71295	21

1 0 = no, 1 = yes.
2 1 = cognitive behaviour therapy, 2 = group therapy, 3 = exercise.
3 Log (YEARS).

A first look at the unequal times data

Since participants have been in the prison for varying times, it would not be particularly useful to compare the mean number of violent incidents to the start of the experiment for each treatment group. Instead, we find the mean number of pretreatment events *per year* for each treatment group. To obtain this, we first calculate the number of events per year for each case by dividing the number of pretreatment events (PRE_TRT_EVENTS) by the time the participant has been in the prison before the experiment (YEARS). From the menu bar select **Transform** and then **Compute Variable**. (You can see an example of the dialog box in the chapter on MANOVA, SPSS Dialog Box 3.2.) In the **Target Variable** box, type a name for the new variable (we called it PRE_TRT_EVENTS_PER_YEAR). Use the arrow to put PRE_TRT_EVENTS in the **Numeric Expression** box, then click on the / for divide, then use the arrow again to put in YEARS. The numeric expression should now read PRE_TRT_EVENTS/YEARS. Click **OK** and check that the datasheet now contains your new variable PRE_TRT_EVENTS_PER_YEAR.

Now we want a table giving the mean of PRE_TRT_EVENTS_PER_YEAR for each treatment group. You can obtain this by using **Analyze**, then **Compare means** and then **Means**, as we did above (see SPSS Dialog Box 13.1). Put PRE_TRT_EVENTS_PER_YEAR in the **Dependent List** box and TREATMENT in the **Independent List** box and click **OK**.

The result is shown in SPSS Output 13.6. We can see that the mean annual number of violent incidents for each participant in the period before the experiment is approximately equal for each treatment group at around eight incidents per year. So the *rate* at which violent incidents were occurring before the experiment began was similar for all the treatment groups. Now we will do a Poisson regression analysis, taking account of ESTEEM and ABUSE, which we have ignored in this first look at the data.

Report

pre_trt_events_per_year

Treatment	Mean	N	Std. Deviation
1	7.6624	20	1.17110
2	8.0759	30	2.33067
3	8.4821	25	2.35803
Total	8.1010	75	2.09418

SPSS Output 13.6 Mean annual number of pretreatment events by treatment group.

Requesting a Poisson regression with unequal times in SPSS

In this analysis we attempt to predict the rate of our PRE_TRT_EVENTS. Our DV is PRE_TRT_EVENTS, and as before we use ABUSE and ESTEEM as predictors. Also, because we want to know whether the treatment groups for the 1-year experiment differed in their levels of violence before the experiment started, we include TREATMENT to see whether there are significant differences in PRE_TRT_EVENTS among treatment groups. It remains to consider YEARS. Since the observation periods for PRE_TRT_EVENTS are not all the same, we have to allow for time during which PRE_TRT_EVENTS was counted for each participant. We do this by adding the log of YEARS to the linear combination of predictor variables, and this extra term is called the *offset* (hence our name for it in Table 13.2). If you are old enough to have used log tables before the arrival of calculators you can see how this works by remembering that to multiply two numbers you add their logs. If the linear combination of the predictor variables gives the log of the event count per year, then adding the log of the number of years will give the total event count over that number of years. It is called the offset because it shifts the prediction up or down according to whether the observation period was long or short.

Notice that other time units might be appropriate in other problems, and you can even use the same idea when counting in space rather than time. In the forestry example briefly mentioned above, you might count trees above 40 metres tall in several patches of forest, and the area of each patch of forest would take the place of years of observation. The offset would be log(area). In this case you would most likely use hectares as the unit of area.

Now we fit the model. Choose **Analyze**, then **Generalized Linear Models**, then **Generalized Linear Models**. Click the **Type of Model** tab if it is not already selected, so that you see SPSS Dialog Box 13.3 again. Our DV, PRE_TRT_EVENTS, is a count as before, so look at the **Counts** section and again click the **Poisson loglinear** radio button.

Select the **Response** tab and put PRE_TRT_EVENTS in the **Dependent Variable** box.

Select the **Predictors** tab and put TREATMENT and ABUSE in the **Factors** box, ESTEEM in the **Covariates** box and OFFSET in the **Offset** box, as in SPSS Dialog Box 13.6. Select the **Model** tab and specify TREATMENT, ABUSE and ESTEEM as main effects, exactly as in SPSS Dialog Box 13.4. Select the **Save** tab and check **Standardized deviance residuals**. Click **OK**.

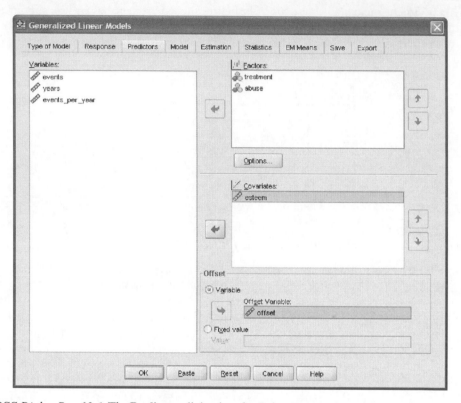

SPSS Dialog Box 13.6 The **Predictors** dialog box for Poisson regression with unequal times.

Understanding the output: Checking the fit of the Poisson regression model with unequal times

As with the first experiment, we consider goodness of fit in two ways. These help to determine whether there have been gross violations of the assumptions made by our model. Note that these results are identical whether we use the ascending or descending order of factor categories. First consider SPSS Output 13.7, the goodness of fit table that appears near the beginning of the output.

As in the equal times model, the deviance and Pearson residuals are used to assess whether the model assumptions have been violated. Each should approximately equal its degrees of freedom and so Value/df (value divided by degrees of freedom) should be close to 1. We see that our values are 1.005 and 1.013, both of which are very close to 1.

Goodness of Fit[b]

	Value	df	Value/df
Deviance	70.361	70	1.005
Scaled Deviance	70.361	70	
Pearson Chi-Square	70.888	70	1.013
Scaled Pearson Chi-Square	70.888	70	
Log Likelihood[a]	-222.601		
Akaike's Information Criterion (AIC)	455.201		
Finite Sample Corrected AIC (AICC)	456.071		
Bayesian Information Criterion (BIC)	466.789		
Consistent AIC (CAIC)	471.789		

Dependent Variable: pre_trt_events
Model: (Intercept), treatment, abuse, esteem, offset = offset

a. The full log likelihood function is displayed and used in computing information criteria.

b. Information criteria are in small-is-better form.

SPSS Output 13.7 Goodness of fit tests for the Poisson regression with unequal time intervals.

SPSS Output 13.8 shows the histogram of the standardized deviance residuals, which we saved as we did for the equal times model (and we obtained the histogram in the same way as SPSS Output 13.3). As before, you can see that we have an approximately

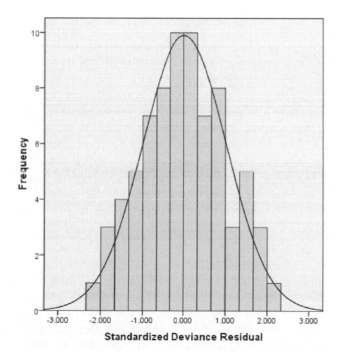

SPSS Output 13.8 Histogram of standardized deviance residuals for the unequal time interval experiment.

standard normal distribution. Note that two values fall just outside the interval −2 to +2. However, this is not particularly worrying as −2 to +2 is the 95% confidence interval for the standard normal distribution. Hence we might expect a small number of the 75 observations to fall outside the range −2 to +2. Both of our checks suggest that we have a well-fitting model for the unequal times data.

Understanding the output: Testing hypotheses for the Poisson regression model with unequal times

As before, we can find most of what we need in the table of parameter estimates, shown in SPSS Output 13.9. First consider the *p* values (from the Sig. column) for the two covariates. The *p* values for ABUSE and ESTEEM are .246 and .000 (i.e., < .001), respectively. Consistent with the results of the experiment, ABUSE is found to be non-significant while ESTEEM is very highly significant.

After allowing for these covariates, the two TREATMENTS are found to be non-significant (with *p* values of .105 and .150). This shows that neither treatment 1 nor treatment 2 has a PRE_TRT_EVENTS rate that is significantly different from the PRE_TRT_EVENTS rate for treatment 3. However, it is still possible that there is a difference between treatments 1 and 2. We cannot use the results in SPSS Output 13.9 to ascertain whether this is the case because treatment 3 is the reference category. The values of B for treatments 1 and 2 are very similar (−0.095 and −0.078) and their 95% confidence intervals have a large overlap. However, to be sure that treatment groups 1 and 2 do not have a significantly different rate of PRE_TRT_EVENTS we change the reference category to treatment 1.

Parameter Estimates

Parameter	B	Std. Error	95% Wald Confidence Interval		Hypothesis Test		
			Lower	Upper	Wald Chi-Square	df	Sig.
(Intercept)	2.634	0.1029	2.432	2.836	655.168	1	.000
[abuse=0]	0.060	0.0514	−0.041	0.160	1.345	1	.246
[abuse=1]	0ᵃ		.	.	.	.	.
esteem	−0.037	0.0070	−0.050	−0.023	27.604	1	.000
[treatment=1]	−0.095	0.0585	−0.209	0.020	2.622	1	.105
[treatment=2]	−0.078	0.0540	−0.184	0.028	2.077	1	.150
[treatment=3]	0ᵃ		.	.	.	.	.
(Scale)	1ᵇ						

Dependent Variable: pre_trt_events
Model: (Intercept), abuse, esteem, treatment, offset = offset

a. Set to zero because this parameter is redundant.

b. Fixed at the displayed value.

SPSS Output 13.9 Poisson regression model for unequal times, including TREATMENT, ABUSE, ESTEEM and OFFSET.

First, delete the columns containing the predicted value of the linear predictor and the predicted event counts if you have saved them. We have already seen how to change the reference category: when you click the **Predictors** tab in SPSS Dialog Box 13.3, you see an **Options** button at the bottom of the **Factors** box. Click this after putting ABUSE and TREATMENT in the box. Click the radio button for **Descending**, as shown in SPSS Dialog Box 13.5. Repeat the analysis, and this time you see the table of parameters shown in SPSS Output 13.10.

Parameter Estimates

Parameter	B	Std. Error	95% Wald Confidence Interval		Hypothesis Test		
			Lower	Upper	Wald Chi-Square	df	Sig.
(Intercept)	2.599	0.1188	2.366	2.832	478.958	1	.000
[abuse=1]	-0.060	0.0514	-0.160	0.041	1.345	1	.246
[abuse=0]	0ᵃ	.	.	.	.	.	.
esteem	-0.037	0.0070	-0.050	-0.023	27.604	1	.000
[treatment=3]	0.095	0.0585	-0.020	0.209	2.622	1	.105
[treatment=2]	0.017	0.0561	-0.093	0.127	0.090	1	.764
[treatment=1]	0ᵃ	.	.	.	.	.	.
(Scale)	1ᵇ						

Dependent Variable: pre_trt_events
Model: (Intercept), abuse, esteem, treatment, offset = offset

a. Set to zero because this parameter is redundant.

b. Fixed at the displayed value.

SPSS Output 13.10 Poisson regression model including TREATMENT, ABUSE, ESTEEM and OFFSET. Reference category levels are the lowest.

Comparing this model with the version that used the highest category as the reference, we note that the estimate associated with ESTEEM is unchanged. The estimate for ABUSE is −0.060 rather than +0.060 as we are measuring the difference from 1 to 0 (Yes to No) rather than 0 to 1 (No to Yes). Similarly the parameter estimate for treatment 3 compared to treatment 1 is just the negative of treatment 1 compared to treatment 3. Note that the *p* values for both ABUSE and ESTEEM are unchanged. The *p* value associated with treatment 3 is the same as we found for treatment 1 in the earlier model, as both are comparing treatments 1 and 3.

However we can now see the *p* value we wanted: that for treatment 2 compared with treatment 1. It is .764, which is certainly not significant. We have now shown that the annual rate of violent incidents before the treatment did not vary significantly between the CBT/group therapy/rigorous exercise treatment arms after allowing for ESTEEM and ABUSE. Hence, the research team have more confidence that the differences found in the number of violent incidents in the year after the experiment were related to their intervention and not to a difference in the average number of violent incidents prior to the experiment.

This was our purpose in fitting this Poisson regression model with unequal times, but we will explore it a bit more to enhance your grasp of the unequal times model.

Example Box 13.2

An alternative medical example with unequal observation times

The full analysis for this example can be found at www.psypress.com/multivariate-analysis/medical-examples (click on Chapter 13).

The previous epilepsy study is re-examined, this time taking into account the number of seizures for each participant from the time they were referred to the treatment unit until the start of the intervention. The number of pretreatment events (PRE_TRT_EVENTS) and the number of years the participant has been at the treatment unit before the experiment (YEARS) are recorded. A variable (OFFSET) is obtained that is just the natural log of YEARS.

Outcomes

The mean annual number of seizures per participant in the period preceding the experiment is found to be similar for all treatment groups and does not differ significantly after allowing for ESTEEM and ALCOHOL. The possibility that the original treatment effects could have been due to treatment groups being more or less prone to seizures before the experiment commenced is therefore ruled out.

Alternative variables for use in SPSS
The full dataset, med.poissonregression.unequaltimes.sav, can be found on the book website

Variable	Psychology	Medicine
IV	TREATMENT Treatment 1 = CBT Treatment 2 = group therapy Treatment 3 = rigorous exercise	TREATMENT Treatment 1 = high drug dose Treatment 2 = low drug dose Treatment 3 = placebo
DV	PRE_TRT_EVENTS = pre-intervention violent incident count	PRE_TRT_EVENTS = pre-intervention seizure count
Covariates	ESTEEM ABUSE (binary variable: abused/not abused)	ESTEEM ALCOHOL (above/not above recommended limit)
Offset	OFFSET (log(YEARS))	OFFSET (log(YEARS))

Obtaining expected PRE_TRT_EVENTS rates and totals from the parameter values

As before, we can use the **Save** button to get the predicted value of the linear predictor added to the datasheet. This time the **Predicted value of mean of response** will be the predicted value of the total of PRE_TRT_EVENTS, the predicted number over the time the case was observed. We now show how to use the parameter values in SPSS Output 13.9 to obtain these. You can achieve the same results with the values in SPSS Output 13.10, as we will demonstrate for one case. Note that, as in the case of equal times, your calculations may differ slightly from the predicted values calculated by SPSS, with more decimal places than are shown in the output.

First consider a case with ABUSE = 1 and TREATMENT = 3. There is such a case in the last but one row of Table 13.2. This participant has an esteem score of 11. Since ABUSE = 1 and TREATMENT = 3 are the reference categories for SPSS Output 13.9, we have zeros for these variables. Look in the B column to see that the constant is 2.634 and the parameter for ESTEEM is −0.037. So, for this case, the log of predicted *rate* of PRE_TRT_EVENTS is

2.634 − 0.037 * 11 = 2.227

For the predicted rate of PRE_TRT_EVENTS per year, use your calculator to find exp(2.227) = 9.272 (look for e^x or the inverse of ln). This is the predicted rate of PRE_TRT_EVENTS per year.

Multiply by 4.77 years to get the predicted total, which is 44.22, or 44 to the nearest whole number. Alternatively, to get the log of the predicted total count over the 4.77 YEARS this case was observed, we need to add the log of 4.77 YEARS, the OFFSET (1.562), to give us 3.789. For the predicted count of events of the 4.77 years, find exp(3.789) = 44.21. Once again we have 44 predicted PRE_TRT_EVENTS to the nearest whole number (the observed number was 35).

If ABUSE = 0 but TREATMENT = 3, we need to add the parameter 0.060 from the B column of SPSS Output 13.9. The case on the bottom row of Table 13.2 is an example, and this person has an ESTEEM score of 13, so the log of the predicted rate of PRE_TRT_EVENTS per year is

2.634 + 0.060 − 0.037 * 13 = 2.213

This gives a predicted rate of exp(2.213) = 9.143. Multiply by the time this case was observed, 2.04 years, to get the predicted total PRE_TRT_EVENTS, which is 18.65, or 19 to the nearest whole number. The observed value was 21.

If the TREATMENT category is not 3 then we need to add the appropriate parameter from the B column of SPSS Output 13.9. If we take the first case from the TREATMENT = 2 group in Table 13.2 (this person has ABUSE equal to 0 and an ESTEEM score of 16), we get the log of the predicted rate of PRE_TRT_EVENTS per year as

2.634 + 0.060 − 0.078 − 0.037 * 16 = 2.024

Find exp(2.024) = 7.569 to get the predicted rate per year. Multiply this by the years observed, 3.07, to get the predicted total of PRE_TRT_EVENTS, which is 23.24, or 23 to the nearest whole number. The observed count was 28.

To use the values in SPSS Output 13.10 to obtain the same result for the TREATMENT = 2 case we just considered, notice that this time the constant is 2.599 and the parameter for ABUSE = 0 is zero because we used the first instead of the last categories as the reference. The parameter for TREATMENT = 2 is 0.017 and the parameter for ESTEEM remains the same at −0.037. So the predicted log of the rate of PRE_TRT_EVENTS per year is

2.599 + 0.017 − 0.037 * 16 = 2.024

This is the same as the result from SPSS Output 13.9.

A common way to summarize the parameter values for publication is to give an equation for the log of the predicted rate, listing all the parameters as below (we are using SPSS Output 13.9, so the reference categories are the last ones, the default):

log (annual pretreatment violent incident rate) =
2.634 − 0.095 (TREATMENT = 1) − 0.078 (TREATMENT = 2) + 0.060 (ABUSE = 0) − 0.037 (ESTEEM)

where TREATMENT = 1, TREATMENT = 2 and ABUSE = 0 are indicator variables. This is interpreted to mean that, if TREATMENT = 1, the parameter −0.095 is included, but otherwise it is not. If TREATMENT = 2, the parameter −0.078 is included, but otherwise it is not. If TREATMENT = 3, neither of these parameters is included. Likewise, the parameter 0.06 is included if ABUSE = 0, but not if ABUSE = 1. The ESTEEM score will be multiplied by −0.037 for all cases.

Reporting results

When reporting Poisson regression models, you should indicate whether you have used data with a fixed time interval or not. If the time intervals are not all equal then you need to indicate the standard unit used.

You may wish to report the model in full, as with other regression models, or just state which variables in the model were significant. For significant variables you should also indicate whether the variable increases or decreases the Poisson rate.

For example, for the experiment with unequal time intervals you might want to report as follows:

> An experiment was undertaken to reduce the number of violent incidents within a prison. Prisoners convicted with violent offences who had been in the prison for at least 1 year and who had at least 1 year before they could be released were randomly allocated to one of three treatment groups: CBT (treatment 1), group therapy (treatment 2) and exercise (treatment 3). The number of violent offences (PRE_TRT_EVENTS) and the time since arriving in the prison (YEARS) before the experiment were determined.
>
> As a check that the treatment groups did not differ in the amount of violence exhibited before the start of the experiment, a Poisson regression model was fitted to determine if the average number of violent offences per year committed by participants differed significantly among the three treatment groups. The Poisson regression model contained an offset because the duration the prisoners had been in the prison before the experiment differed. The model also contained two potentially confounding effects: ESTEEM (Rosenberg's Self-Esteem Scale, where higher scores are related to greater esteem); and ABUSE, a 1/0 variable indicating whether the participant was abused as a child (0 = not abused).
>
> The fitted model was:
>
> log (annual pretreatment violent incident rate) =
> 2.634 − 0.095 (TREATMENT = 1) − 0.078 (TREATMENT = 2) + 0.060 (ABUSE = 0) − 0.037 (ESTEEM)
>
> where TREATMENT = 1, TREATMENT = 2 and ABUSE = 0 are indicator variables. The p value for ABUSE was not significant ($p = .246$), indicating that being abused as a child was not related to the average annual rate of violent incidents. The p value for ESTEEM was very highly significant ($p < .001$). The negative regression coefficient in the model is consistent with an increasing self-esteem decreasing the mean annual violent incident rate.
>
> After allowing for these two covariates, treatment groups 1 and 2 were not significantly different ($p = .105$ and $p = .150$, respectively) from treatment group 3.

The *p* value for comparing treatment groups 1 and 2 was .764. This shows that the annual rate of violent offences did not differ significantly among the three treatment groups in the period before the experiment began.

Standard diagnostic checks did not show any severe departure from the model assumptions.

14 Survival analysis

Introduction

Survival analysis is a technique for investigating the effect of treatments or covariates on the first time to reach some important event. You could think of it as an extension to covariance analysis when the DV is time taken to reach the event, but where not all cases are observed for long enough for the event to occur. These cases, to which the event has not occurred by the end of the study, are said to be *censored* observations. For historical reasons the event of interest is usually referred to as *failure*. So in an industrial context (where this method has been extensively used) we might want to know whether particular materials or methods of manufacture affect the useful life of a component: its time to failure. In the context of a serious illness we might want to know whether a change in treatment regime might affect the length of time in remission. Here, failure would be the end of remission. But, equally, with a less serious illness we may be interested in the time taken to recovery, and then failure is actually a misnomer for the event of interest, which would be recovery. In psychology we could use the method to investigate treatments for behavioural difficulties, and our demonstration example for this chapter will be methods to help people to give up smoking. Here the failure event is relapse: a return to smoking.

You can probably already see from these examples that a key feature of any investigation of this type will be the cases that do not fail by the end of the study. If they are successful in giving up, the smokers will not reach the failure event (relapse) at all, and certainly not by the end of a study, which may last for just a few months or perhaps a year. Likewise a successful new treatment may mean a considerable extension in the lives of the seriously ill patients, and many will be still alive or in remission long after the end of the study. These are the censored cases, and it was finding a way to deal with them that made survival analysis possible. SPSS uses the more neutral term *event* instead of failure, and we shall do this also in what follows.

First we introduce some terminology. At any time, the *hazard* is the probability of the event occurring, given that it has not occurred so far. The *survival function* gives the fraction of the study sample for which the event has not occurred at each observation time. Figure 14.1 shows a typical survival function: this one is for a group of smokers who were trying to give up. The event of interest is relapse – a return to smoking – and for each observation time (horizontal axis) we have the proportion still off cigarettes (vertical axis). These participants were only observed for 20 weeks, and you can see that at the end of the trial about 40% of them were still not smoking. At week 10 about two-thirds of them were not smoking.

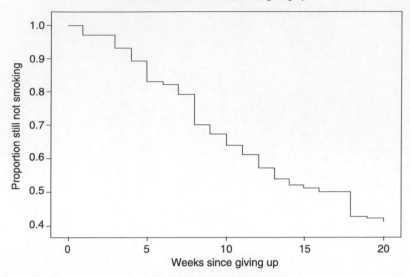

Figure 14.1 Survival function for 20-week smoking cessation trial.

The survival function is easier to understand but the hazard function turns out to be easier to work with. Each can be derived from the other (in fact the cumulative hazard function is minus the natural log of the survival function). As time moves on, the proportion of survivors (those still not smoking) falls, as we see in Figure 14.1, and correspondingly the hazard (the potential to fail) rises. Figure 14.2 shows the cumulative hazard function that corresponds to the survival function shown in Figure 14.1. You can see how, as the weeks go by, the proportion that have not smoked falls while the accumulated hazard rises.

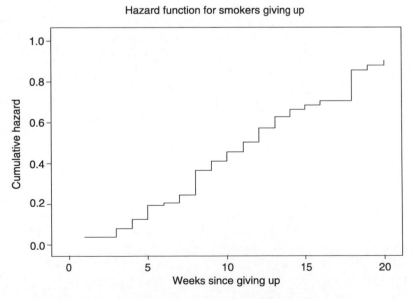

Figure 14.2 Cumulative hazard function for 20-week smoking cessation trial.

The *baseline hazard rate* depends on time but ignores any treatment effects and covariates. Treatments or other covariates may affect the hazard rate, making the event less likely or more likely. In our smoking example, nicotine patches or hypnosis may reduce the hazard rate, while a high daily average number of cigarettes smoked prior to giving up may increase the hazard rate. In a medical example, a new treatment may decrease the hazard rate, but having a more severe form of the illness may increase it.

Kaplan-Meier survival analysis allows us to compare treatment groups but ignores any other covariates. You could think of this as analogous to a one-way ANOVA. We will show you how to obtain the survival plots from a Kaplan Meier survival analysis, but our main discussion is around the approach developed by David Cox, known as *Cox regression* or *proportional hazard modelling*. You could think of this as analogous to a covariance analysis (ANCOVA), where the effect of being in different treatment groups is modified by covariates.

We assume that the effect of a treatment or covariate on the hazard rate remains the same throughout the time of the study. If, for instance, type of employment is a covariate that affects the hazard rate, we are assuming that this effect does not increase or decrease during the study period.

To continue this example, suppose we have two cases in different types of employment, so that each will have a hazard rate that depends on the employment type as well as on time. At any particular time, the ratio of hazard rates for this pair of cases depends only on their employment types. Assuming their employment types stay the same throughout the study, their two hazard rates will have the same ratio at all times. So the two cases have a *hazard ratio* determined by their covariate values, and this ratio will not change during the time of the study. This applies to any two cases from the study. This is the *proportional hazard assumption*. Later we will show you a way to check whether it is reasonable.

Cox's method can be extended to include covariates whose effect varies over time, but we shall not consider this here. SPSS offers a good tutorial showing how to use this extension. To find it, type **Cox Regression** in the **Help Topics** index, double click **Cox Regression** when it shows in the index, then **Cox Regression Analysis** in the list of **Topics found**. Double click **Show me** to get the tutorial. The second example in the tutorial uses a time-dependent covariate.

A psychology example: An experiment with fabricated data

Surveys show that the majority of smokers want to give up, and many say they have tried and failed. Some make multiple attempts, sometimes lasting for weeks but still relapsing eventually. Since the health risks of smoking have become so well documented, a number of methods have been developed to help smokers who want to quit. In the past, the only way to give up was 'cold turkey': just stop, and endure the pain of the withdrawal symptoms. This has always worked for some people, though perhaps only for those with exceptional qualities of endurance and determination. Nicotine replacement therapy is aimed at enabling people to give up smoking and all the behaviours associated with it, before tackling the nicotine addiction. Skin patches supply the nicotine in gradually reducing amounts over several months, so the physiological symptoms of withdrawal are more manageable and are only tackled after the patient is used to not having a cigarette in their hand. A more radical approach is hypnotherapy. Here the smoker receives one or more sessions with a hypnotist specializing in work with smokers. The smoker is usually then able to go 'cold turkey', but some combine hypnotherapy with nicotine patches. We have fabricated data for a supposed trial of methods of giving up smoking. The three methods (TREATMENT) are nicotine patches (treatment 1), hypnotherapy without patches (treatment 2) and cold turkey (treatment 3). Our data do show the sort of results you might expect, in that there are relapses (observed failures) for all methods, as well as plenty of censored observations (people who are still not smoking at the end of the study). However, if you are a smoker, bear in mind that our main concern is to provide a good illustration of the main features of the technique, so do not use our made-up example as a guide when choosing your own approach to giving up!

We are assuming we have 100 mature student volunteers, most of them in their twenties. Most have made at least one attempt at cold turkey and failed, and are now willing to try anything. Due to practical considerations, we have assigned them at random: 50 to nicotine patches, 30 to hypnosis and 20 to cold turkey. In the month before the start of the study all participants recorded all cigarette purchases, and from this they have calculated their average daily consumption (NUMBER). They have also recorded the number of years since they began smoking (YEARS). The covariates NUMBER and YEARS will be ignored when we obtain the Kaplan-Meier plots, but we will include them in the Cox regression analysis.

The number of weeks to relapse is recorded as TTF (time to failure). This is the study week in which relapse occurred, if it did. Those still not smoking at the end of the 20-week study have a TTF of 20, but are the censored ones, and are coded 1 on the variable RELAPSE. Those with a recorded time to relapse are coded zero on RELAPSE. Note that one participant relapsed in the last week of the study, so has a TTF of 20 but a RELAPSE code of zero. Table 14.1 shows the first four cases for each treatment group, and the full dataset can be found on the book website as psy.survival.sav.

Table 14.1 The first four cases from each treatment group in the smoking cessation trial (the full dataset can be found as psy.survival.sav on the website)

YEARS	NUMBER	TTF	RELAPSE[1]	TREATMENT[2]
11	28	8	0	1
9	38	8	0	1
13	29	20	1	1
13	28	16	0	1
12	30	14	0	2
12	31	5	0	2
12	24	20	1	2
12	29	11	0	2
6	33	4	0	3
10	29	1	0	3
11	30	13	0	3
9	37	4	0	3

[1] 0 = relapse occurred, 1 = censored (no relapse).
[2] 1 = nicotine patches, 2 = hypnosis, 3 = cold turkey.

So, do our data suggest that one of the strategies for giving up smoking is more effective? We would expect that if one is better, then participants using it would have longer times to relapse and more censored observations (still not smoking when the study ends) than those using the others. In fact treatment 2 (hypnosis) has 14 out of 30 censored cases while treatment 1 (patches) has 26 out of 50: both are close to a half. Only one of those on cold turkey is censored, the other 19 all having relapsed. The uncensored observations have a mean TTF of 10.6 weeks for patches, 11.4 for hypnosis and 6.5 for cold turkey.

You can easily obtain these means by using **Analyze**, **Compare Means**, **Means**. In the dialog box put TTF in the **Dependent List** box and TREATMENT in the **Independent List** box. Click **Next** so that **Layer 2 of 2** replaces **Layer 1 of 1**, and put RELAPSE in the **Independent list** box, as in SPSS Dialog Box 14.1. Click **OK** to get the table of means. Note that when RELAPSE = 1 (censored cases) the mean is 20 for all treatments, because this is the TTF recorded for censored cases.

SPSS Dialog Box 14.1 Obtaining treatment group means for uncensored and censored observations.

These preliminary results suggest that there may not be a lot of difference between patches and hypnosis but that either may be more effective than cold turkey. But can survival analysis give us more detail and a test of significance?

Requesting a Kaplan-Meier survival plot in SPSS

First arrange the datasheet as in Table 14.1. An essential requirement is the variable indicating whether or not the observation is censored. In our example this variable is RELAPSE, and we have used zero for the cases in which relapse is observed to have occurred, and 1 for censored cases. Any coding is possible since SPSS will ask us to state it. The variable giving times to the event must contain a value for censored cases, since if we leave the time blank SPSS will omit those cases from the whole analysis. So these censored cases have the time for which they were observed recorded, which is always 20 weeks in our example. But you could have a study where people entered at different times and so were observed for different periods up to the end, and then the censored cases would not all have the same time recorded. We have three treatment categories. Our other two covariates are quantitative.

With the datasheet set up, we can get the Kaplan-Meier analysis and plots as follows. Choose **Analyze** from the menu bar, then **Survival** and **Kaplan-Meier** to get SPSS Dialog Box 14.2. Use the arrow to put TREATMENT in the **Factor** box and TTF in the **Time** box (this is the variable for the time to the event). In the **Status** box goes the variable to indicate whether the observation was censored, so use the arrow to put RELAPSE in here. There will be a question mark in the brackets following RELAPSE and the **Define Event** button will now be available.

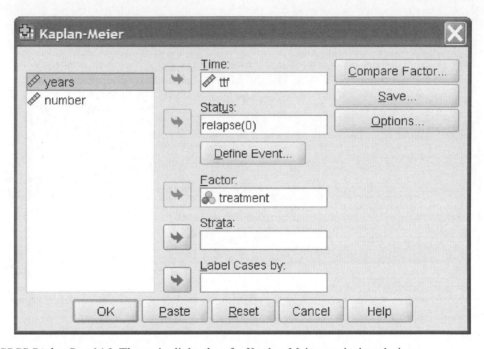

SPSS Dialog Box 14.2 The main dialog box for Kaplan-Meier survival analysis.

We have to define our code so click **Define Event** to get SPSS Dialog Box 14.3. We have a single value, zero, to indicate that the event (RELAPSE) occurred, so type a zero in the box (in our code, 1 indicates censorship, which is when we do not observe the event). Click **Continue** to return to the main dialog box.

Now click the **Options** button to get SPSS Dialog Box 14.4. All we want from this analysis is the survival plot, so in the **Plots** group tick **Survival** and untick all the statistics boxes. Click **Continue** and **OK**.

Understanding the Kaplan-Meier plot output

We only requested a plot from this analysis, but the output begins with a table showing the number and percentage of censored observations in each treatment group, as shown in SPSS Output 14.1. We see that just over half of the observations from treatment 1 (patches) were censored, so just over half of these people were still not smoking when

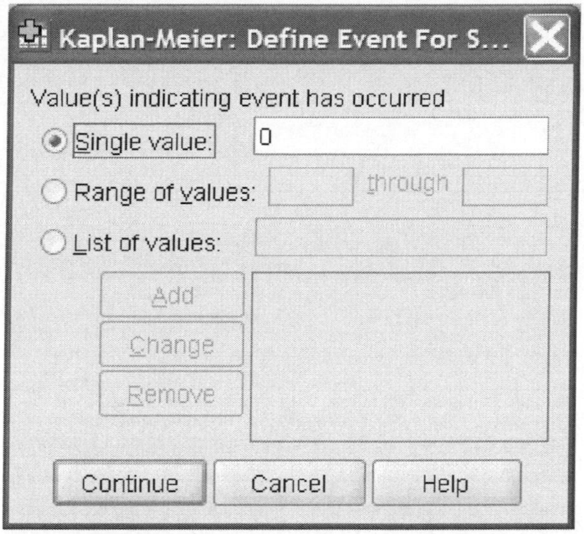

Kaplan-Meier: Define Event For S...

Value(s) indicating event has occurred

◉ Single value: `0`

○ Range of values: ☐ through ☐

○ List of values: ☐

Add

Change

Remove

Continue   Cancel   Help

SPSS Dialog Box 14.3 Coding for censored observations.

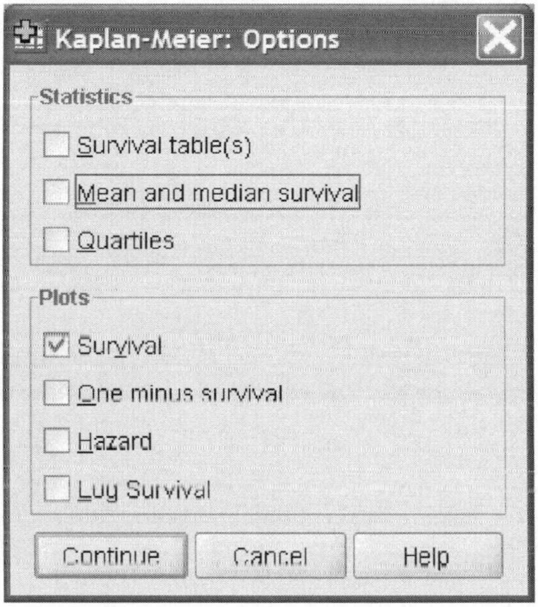

Kaplan-Meier: Options

Statistics

☐ Survival table(s)

☐ Mean and median survival

☐ Quartiles

Plots

☑ Survival

☐ One minus survival

☐ Hazard

☐ Log Survival

Continue   Cancel   Help

SPSS Dialog Box 14.4 Ordering a Kaplan-Meier survival plot.

the study ended. Just under half of the hypnosis group (treatment 2) were censored but only one of the cold turkey group was still not smoking at the end of the study.

The survival plot, also shown in SPSS Output 14.1 (overleaf), shows the proportion of each group still not smoking at the end of each week of the study. Two of the cold turkey group (10%) were already smoking again at the end of week 1, and you can see that .9 of that group (treatment 3) are survivors at the end of week 1. Then no one else from that group goes back to smoking until week 3, when one person succumbs (.05 of

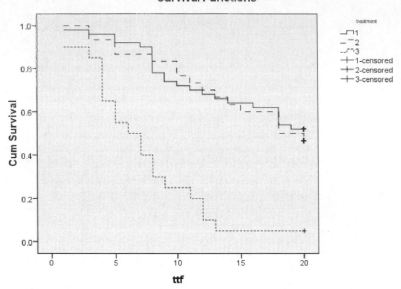

Case Processing Summary

treatment	Total N	N of Events	Censored N	Percent
1	50	24	26	52.0%
2	30	16	14	46.7%
3	20	19	1	5.0%
Overall	100	59	41	41.0%

SPSS Output 14.1 Numbers of censored observations and the survival plot from a Kaplan-Meier
survival analysis.

the group of 20). Four more of treatment group 3 (.2 of the group) start smoking again
by the end of week 4 and you can see the big step down in their survival function. For
the hypnosis group (treatment 2), no one starts smoking again until week 3, so the
survival function for that group stays at 1.0 until week 3: the whole group still survives
until then.

There are tests of significance for the differences among treatments, and they can be
requested by clicking the **Compare Factor** button. Three tests are offered, of which the
log rank test is most commonly used. However we do not discuss these here since
we want to allow for the possible effect of our covariates, YEARS and NUMBER, when
comparing treatments. To do this we need the Cox regression method.

Requesting a Cox regression analysis in SPSS

Now we do the Cox regression and take account of NUMBER and YEARS, which may
well influence the results: choose **Analyze** from the menu bar, then **Survival** and **Cox
Regression**, to get SPSS Dialog Box 14.5. Use the arrow to put TTF in the **Time** box
(this is the variable for the time to the event). In the **Status** box goes the variable to
indicate whether the observation was censored, so use the arrow to put RELAPSE in here.

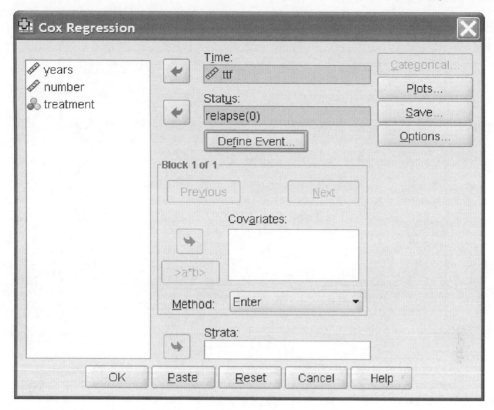

SPSS Dialog Box 14.5 The main dialog box for survival analysis.

There will be a question mark in the brackets following RELAPSE and the **Define Event** button will now be available, just as in the Kaplan-Meier analysis above.

Clicking **Define Event** produces a dialog box just like SPSS Dialog Box 14.3 and once again we have a single value, zero, to indicate that the event (RELAPSE) occurred, so type a zero in the box as before. Click **Continue** to return to the main dialog box.

Cox regression includes treatment factors in the term 'covariates', so our covariates are YEARS since starting to smoke, NUMBER smoked per day and TREATMENT, and we are primarily interested in whether the treatments are equally effective or not. The other covariates are there because the difficulty of giving up may be affected by them. We could just put in all the covariates and see which have a significant effect, but as we did in multiple regression we can take a hierarchical approach. We shall enter YEARS and NUMBER as covariates in Block 1, and TREATMENT in Block 2, as we now explain.

First use the arrow to put YEARS and NUMBER in the **Covariates** box. Whenever we have more than one covariate in a block, we can use a stepwise method (see Chapter 4 on regression) by clicking the arrow next to the **Method** box. Here we have chosen to enter both of our covariates for Block 1 together, so we left **Method** at the default setting of **Enter**. Now click **Next** so that **Block 2 of 2** replaces **Block 1 of 1**. Now use the arrow again to put TREATMENT in the **Covariates** box. So now the effect of TREATMENT will be examined, having allowed for the effects of YEARS and NUMBER.

We still have to specify which covariates are categorical, so click **Categorical** and

Cox Regression: Plots

Plot Type
- ☑ Survival   ☐ Hazard   ☐ Log minus log
- ☐ One minus survival

Continue

Cancel

Help

Covariate Values Plotted at:

years(Mean)
number(Mean)

◄

Separate Lines for:

treatment(Cat)

Change Value
- ⦿ Mean   ◯ Value: [   ]

Change

SPSS Dialog Box 14.6 Specifying a plot.

in the dialog box that appears put TREATMENT in the **Categorical covariates** box and click **Continue**. We also want to specify a graph, so click the **Plots** button to get SPSS Dialog Box 14.6. Tick **Survival** and put TREATMENT in the **Separate Lines for** box. This will give us survival graphs showing our three treatment groups as separate lines.

Click **Continue** and when you return to the main dialog box click the **Save** button. In the dialog box that appears, select **Partial residuals** in the **Diagnostics** group and click **Continue** again.

Click the **Options** button. In the dialog box that appears select **CI for exp(B)**. (This box also allows you to alter the criteria for entering and removing variables when using a stepwise method, just as in regression.) Click **Continue** then **OK** to get the analysis.

Understanding the Cox regression output

The first table (which we have not shown) just gives a case processing summary, showing the number of cases, the number that were censored and how many with missing data (none of ours). The second table (SPSS Output 14.2) shows the coding used by SPSS for any categorical variables. We only have one, TREATMENT, and we used 1, 2 and 3 to denote patches, hypnosis and cold turkey. The SPSS default is to use the last category as the reference category and to assign a code of zero to it. The other categories are defined by dummy variables, just as in multiple regression. Because we have three categories, there are two dummy variables: the first takes the value 1 for treatment 1 and zero for treatments 2 and 3; the second takes the value 1 for treatment 2 and zero for treatments 1 and 3. Thus the three treatments are defined by the pairs of values $(1, 0)$, $(0, 1)$ and $(0, 0)$.

Because treatment 3 is the reference category, treatments 1 and 2 will each be compared with treatment 3 in the analysis. You can change this if you want and use the first instead of the last category as reference (we show you how in the next section).

Categorical Variable Codings [b]

		Frequency	(1)	(2)
treatment[a]	1	50	1	0
	2	30	0	1
	3	20	0	0

a. Indicator Parameter Coding

b. Category variable: treatment

SPSS Output 14.2 Dummy variables for categories defined by SPSS.

The analysis begins by ignoring all the covariates (Block 0), just as the Kaplan-Meier analysis does. You could think of the likelihood statistic that is given here as analogous to the total sum of squares in ANOVA or ANCOVA. Subsequently, as covariates are added, the reduction in this statistic is the basis for tests of significance for the covariates. We omit this table but the statistic from it is also shown (note a) below the first table in SPSS Output 14.3 (−2 Log likelihood = 502.587). SPSS Output 14.3 shows the results of entering our Block 1 variables, YEARS and NUMBER. Because we chose not to use a stepwise method of entering these two, we are reminded that they were both entered together (Method = Enter).

In the first table of SPSS Output 14.3, look at the column labelled Change From Previous Step. This gives a chi-square value of 37.804 on two degrees of freedom, which is a highly significant value. The 2 *df*s refer to the two covariates we added at this step, YEARS and NUMBER. The chi-square value is the reduction in the likelihood ratio statistic for this step. You get the Block 0 value (no covariates included) from note a or from the Block 0 table we have not shown (this is 502.587). The Block 1 value (464.783) is

Block 1: Method = Enter

Omnibus Tests of Model Coefficients [a,b]

-2 Log Likelihood	Overall (score)			Change From Previous Step			Change From Previous Block		
	Chi-square	df	Sig.	Chi-square	df	Sig.	Chi-square	df	Sig.
464.783	36.583	2	.000	37.804	2	.000	37.804	2	.000

a. Beginning Block Number 0, initial Log Likelihood function: -2 Log likelihood: 502.587

b. Beginning Block Number 1. Method = Enter

Variables in the Equation

	B	SE	Wald	df	Sig.	Exp(B)	95.0% CI for Exp(B)	
							Lower	Upper
years	0.039	0.071	0.298	1	.585	1.040	0.904	1.196
number	0.245	0.041	36.296	1	.000	1.277	1.179	1.383

Variables not in the Equation [a]

	Score	df	Sig.
treatment	31.185	2	.000
treatment(1)	11.359	1	.001
treatment(2)	0.018	1	.894

a. Residual Chi Square = 31.185 with 2 df Sig. = .000

SPSS Output 14.3 The effect of YEARS and NUMBER on the relapse hazard rate.

in the left column of this table, hence the chi-square Change From Previous Step is $502.587 - 464.783 = 37.804$. So we know that together our two covariates have a significant effect on the probability of relapse at any time (the hazard rate). The column on the right, Change From Previous Block, just gives the same information since we added both of our covariates at the same time.

The next table shows the significance levels separately for the two variables and we see that YEARS is not significant: the significance observed above is entirely due to NUMBER. (The test statistic used here, which is assumed to follow a normal distribution, is the Wald statistic, simply $(B/SE)^2$, the square of the parameter estimate divided by its standard deviation.) Look at the right-hand column of this table: if Exp(B), the hazard ratio, is > 1, as here, the hazard rate will increase (so expected time to the event, RELAPSE, will decrease) for increasing values of the covariate. The fact that the hazard ratio for YEARS is so close to 1 reflects its non-significance. For each unit increase in NUMBER the hazard rate will be multiplied by 1.277. As you would expect, the more our participants smoked before starting the study, the greater the chance they will start smoking again at any stage.

The last table in SPSS Output 14.3 tells us which covariates are omitted. Only TREATMENT is omitted at this stage, but because it is a categorical variable the two dummy variables that represent it are also listed in the table, together with the significance in each case. We consider this in SPSS Output 14.4, which shows the tables for Block 2 when we entered TREATMENT.

The first table in SPSS Output 14.4 again shows the chi-square statistic for the

Block 2: Method = Enter

Omnibus Tests of Model Coefficients[a,b]

-2 Log Likelihood	Overall (score)			Change From Previous Step			Change From Previous Block		
	Chi-square	df	Sig.	Chi-square	df	Sig.	Chi-square	df	Sig.
441.467	66.371	4	.000	23.316	2	.000	23.316	2	.000

a. Beginning Block Number 0, initial Log Likelihood function: -2 Log likelihood: 502.587
b. Beginning Block Number 2. Method = Enter

Variables in the Equation

	B	SE	Wald	df	Sig.	Exp(B)	95.0% CI for Exp(B)	
							Lower	Upper
years	0.057	0.072	0.622	1	0.430	1.059	0.919	1.220
number	0.264	0.045	34.738	1	0.000	1.302	1.193	1.422
treatment			26.209	2	0.000			
treatment(1)	-1.709	0.338	25.550	1	0.000	0.181	0.093	0.351
treatment(2)	-1.324	0.377	12.353	1	0.000	0.266	0.127	0.557

Covariate Means and Pattern Values

	Mean	Pattern		
		1	2	3
years	11.600	11.600	11.600	11.600
number	28.880	28.880	28.880	28.880
treatment(1)	0.500	1.000	0.000	0.000
treatment(2)	0.300	0.000	1.000	0.000

SPSS Output 14.4 The effect of TREATMENT on the relapse hazard rate after allowing for YEARS and NUMBER.

Change From Previous Step (23.316). There are 2 *df*s again even though we only added one covariate, because TREATMENT is categorical with three categories and hence two dummy variables are needed to define it. Once again we see that the change from the previous step is significant. The change from the previous block again repeats the same information since the two dummy variables were entered together.

Now look at the second table in SPSS Output 14.4. Here we see that, with all covariates included, YEARS still does not have a significant effect on the hazard rate. NUMBER does have a significant effect, with a hazard ratio of 1.302 (the 95% confidence interval for this value is shown as 1.193 to 1.422). TREATMENT is also significant, but more interesting than the overall significance of this covariate is whether either of the therapies gives a significant reduction of the hazard rate compared with cold turkey. In fact we see that both do. Patches (treatment 1) has a significant effect, with a hazard ratio of 0.181 (the 95% CI is 0.093 to 0.351), or about 18%, of that on cold turkey. Likewise hypnotherapy is significant and reduces the hazard rate to about 27% of that on cold turkey. We consider whether the difference between patches and hypnosis is significant later. For now, look at the last table in SPSS Output 14.4.

The first column gives the mean values for all the covariates. The mean time participants have smoked is 11.6 years, and they have smoked an average of 28.88 cigarettes per day before giving up. The first dummy variable for TREATMENT has a mean of 0.5 because 50 of our 100 participants received treatment 1, so the first dummy variable was coded 1 for them and zero for everyone else. The second dummy variable was coded 1 for the 30 participants on treatment 2 and zero for everyone else, so its mean value is 0.3. The three columns labelled Pattern 1, 2 and 3 repeat the means for YEARS and NUMBER, and give the dummy variable codings for the three treatments: (1, 0), (0, 1) and

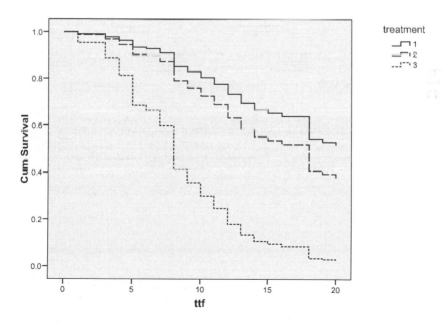

Survival Function for patterns 1 - 3

SPSS Output 14.5 Survival functions for each TREATMENT in the smoking cessation study.

(0, 0). These are patterns 1–3 in the title for the survival graph we requested, which is shown in SPSS Output 14.5.

These survival graphs for the three treatment groups are the expected values for the Cox regression model. Since they are also affected by the values of the covariates YEARS and NUMBER that we also have included, they are calculated using the mean values of YEARS and NUMBER. On the graphs you can see that the expected proportion of those who have not relapsed falls more rapidly for cold turkey than for either therapy, and is nearly zero by the end of the 20 weeks. This agrees well with our observation that only one participant was still not smoking. The two therapies each have expected proportions of around a half not relapsed by the end, which is close to what we observed by counting the censored observations at the start of our analysis.

SPSS also provides a single survival graph for all treatment categories together. Since the values of the other covariates affect this, it is also calculated for the mean values of YEARS and NUMBER, and is the one shown in the Introduction as Figure 14.1.

Before leaving this stage of the analysis we consider how we might check the proportional hazards assumption. We requested that partial residuals should be saved, and these will be added to the datasheet. The columns in the datasheet are labelled PR1_1, PR2_1, etc., but if you let the mouse rest over the column names, the more helpful 'Partial residual for years', 'Partial residual for number', etc., will be shown. Since only NUMBER of our quantitative covariates was significant, we will use it to illustrate our check. From the menu bar, choose **Graphs** and then **Chart builder**. Click **OK** when you

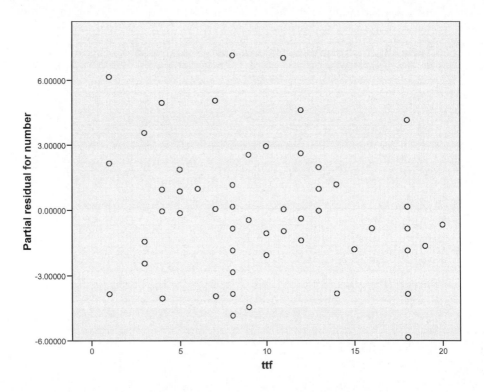

SPSS Output 14.6 A check on the proportional hazards assumption.

get the warning about defining your variables correctly. From the gallery, choose a simple scatterplot and drag and drop it into the graph area. Then drag TTF from the variable list into the X-axis space and PARTIAL RESIDUAL FOR NUMBER into the Y-axis space. Click **OK** and get the graph in SPSS Output 14.6.

If the effect of NUMBER on the hazard rate is constant over time, there should be no pattern in this graph of residuals. In fact it looks as if there is a slight downward trend from left to right. If you fit a simple linear regression (**Regression**, then **Linear**, TTF as **Independent** and PARTIAL RESIDUAL FOR NUMBER as **Dependent**) you find that the negative correlation you see in the graph is very small and does not approach significance. So our proportional hazards assumption seems reasonable here.

Example Box 14.1

An alternative example with medical data

The full analysis for this example can be found at www.psypress.com/multivariate-analysis/medical-examples (click on Chapter 14).

A Phase IIB clinical trial is conducted to assess the efficacy of a new anticholinergic agent in reducing chronic obstructive pulmonary disease (COPD) dyspnoea events in smokers. The trial has three TREATMENT arms: treatments 1 and 2 are low and high doses, respectively, of the drug, while treatment 3 is a placebo. A hundred patients diagnosed with COPD are followed for 20 weeks and the number of weeks until their first dyspnoea event (TTF) is recorded. Patients who have not experienced any dyspnoea events at 20 weeks (censored data) are coded 1 on the bivariate variable RELAPSE and those with a recorded time to relapse are coded zero on RELAPSE. Covariates included in the analysis are NUMBER (the average number of cigarettes smoked per day in the month before the screening date) and YEARS (the number of years the subject has smoked cigarettes before the trial). Survival analyses, using Kaplan-Meier and Cox regression procedures, are carried out.

Outcomes

In combination, the covariates NUMBER and YEARS have a significant effect on hazard rate (the probability of relapse at any time), but considered separately, only NUMBER is significant. The effect of TREATMENT is also significant; both low and high drug doses (treatments 1 and 2) are better than the placebo (treatment 3), but there is no significant difference between the drug doses. This suggests that the low drug dose should go forward to a full trial.

Alternative variables for use in SPSS
The full dataset, med.survival.sav, can be found on the book website

Variable	Psychology	Medicine
IV	TREATMENT Nicotine patches = 1 Hypnosis = 2 Cold turkey = 3	TREATMENT Low dose = 1 High dose = 2 Placebo = 3
DVs	TTF (time to failure) RELAPSE (binary: censored/not censored)	TTF (time to failure) RELAPSE (binary: censored/not censored)
Covariates	NUMBER (mean cigarettes smoked/day) YEARS (years smoked before trial)	NUMBER (mean cigarettes smoked/day) YEARS (years smoked before trial)

Changing the reference category

One way to find out whether the difference between patches and hypnosis is significant is to repeat the analysis above but using the first instead of the last of our treatment categories as the reference category. This will mean the effect of hypnosis and of cold turkey will be compared with patches. After clicking the **Categorical** button and putting TREATMENT in the **Categorical Covariates** box, click the **First** radio button at the bottom. You also have to click the **Change** button to make this happen. The dialog box now looks like SPSS Dialog Box 14.7.

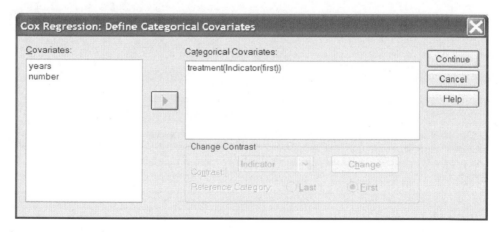

SPSS Dialog Box 14.7 Changing the reference category.

Now repeat the analysis exactly as before. The Categorical Variable Codings table (like the one in SPSS Output 14.1) now shows that the dummy variables code treatments 1, 2 and 3 as (0, 0), (1, 0) and (0, 1), respectively. The middle table in SPSS Output 14.4 is replaced by the one in SPSS Output 14.7. Here we see that, while the effects of YEARS and NUMBER are the same as before, only the second dummy TREATMENT variable has a significant effect. The first TREATMENT dummy compares treatment 2 (hypnosis) to the new reference category, treatment 1 (patches), and the significance of this ($p = .252$) is well above .05. However, the second dummy compares treatment 3 (cold turkey) to treatment 1 (patches), and here the effect is highly significant, just as we found when we made the comparison in reverse above. The hazard ratio, 5.521, is just the reciprocal of 0.181 (i.e., 1/0.181), as we would expect, because if the effect of treatment 1 compared to treatment 3 is to multiply the hazard rate by 0.181, as we found above, then the effect of treatment 3 compared to treatment 1 should be the inverse of the multiple. So, as we suspected when we looked at our data at the start, both patches and hypnosis reduce the hazard rate compared with cold turkey, and there is no significant difference between their effects.

Variables in the Equation

| | B | SE | Wald | df | Sig. | Exp(B) | 95.0% CI for Exp(B) | |
							Lower	Upper
years	0.057	0.072	0.622	1	.430	1.059	0.919	1.220
number	0.264	0.045	34.738	1	.000	1.302	1.193	1.422
treatment			26.209	2	.000			
treatment(1)	0.305	0.336	1.312	1	.252	1.469	0.781	2.839
treatment(2)	1.709	0.338	25.550	1	.000	5.521	2.847	10.710

SPSS Output 14.7 Comparing therapies by changing the reference category.

Using a stepwise method

Since one of our covariates turned out not to have a significant effect on the hazard rate, we may want to repeat our analysis omitting this variable (YEARS). However, had we used a stepwise method to enter the two variables in the first block, we could have saved ourselves this step. Here we repeat the first analysis, though keeping the first category of TREATMENT as reference, but this time when we put YEARS and NUMBER in the **Covariates** box (SPSS Dialog Box 14.4) we click the arrow by the **Method** box and choose **Forward LR** from the list. (LR stands for likelihood ratio.) SPSS Output 14.8 shows the tables from the Block 1 steps.

In the notes below the first table we see that at the first step NUMBER was added (note a). As before, the likelihood ratio with no covariates is also shown (note b). The chi-square value for the Change From Previous Step is 37.505 (37.804 when we added YEARS and NUMBER together; SPSS Output 14.3), with only 1 *df* since only one covariate was added at this step. The Change From Previous Block is just the same since this is the first step in this block.

In the second table we see that NUMBER does have a significant effect. The default settings will add a covariate if the significance level is less than .05. You can change the default probabilities for entry and removal in the stepwise procedure by clicking the **Options** button in the main dialog box. Next comes a table showing the significance levels for variables not currently included. Then we have a table showing the effect of removing NUMBER. As it is the only variable included at this step, it is not surprising that removing it will increase the chi-square value by exactly the amount that entering the variable reduced it. However, if we had just added a variable to several already there, then the entry of the new variable might possibly make redundant one that had been added at a previous step. So, as in regression, when a new variable is entered, all those currently included will be checked to see if they

Omnibus Tests of Model Coefficients [b,c]

Step	-2 Log Likelihood	Overall (score)			Change From Previous Step			Change From Previous Block		
		Chi-square	df	Sig.	Chi-square	df	Sig.	Chi-square	df	Sig.
1[a]	465.082	36.522	1	.000	37.505	1	.000	37.505	1	.000

a. Variable(s) Entered at Step Number 1: number

b. Beginning Block Number 0, initial Log Likelihood function: -2 Log likelihood: 502.587

c. Beginning Block Number 1. Method = Forward Stepwise (Likelihood Ratio)

Variables in the Equation

		B	SE	Wald	df	Sig.	Exp(B)	95.0% CI for Exp(B)	
								Lower	Upper
Step 1	number	0.238	0.039	38.267	1	.000	1.269	1.177	1.368

Variables not in the Equation [a]

		Score	df	Sig.
Step 1	years	0.298	1	.585
	treatment	30.488	2	.000
	treatment(1)	0.001	1	.974
	treatment(2)	29.244	1	.000

a. Residual Chi Square = 31.100 with 3 df Sig. = .000

Model if Term Removed

Term Removed	Loss Chi-square	df	Sig.
Step 1 number	37.505	1	.000

SPSS Output 14.8 Block 1 tables with a stepwise method.

could now be removed. The default setting for removal is a significance level that exceeds .10.

In Block 2, as before, we see TREATMENT added. The table giving the significance levels and Exp(B) values and confidence intervals for the final version, which includes just NUMBER and TREATMENT, is shown in SPSS Output 14.9. This is similar to the one we had in SPSS Output 14.7, when YEARS was included, and it confirms that there is not a significant difference ($p = .198$) between treatments 1 and 2 (patches and hypnosis). Each extra cigarette smoked per day increases the hazard rate by a factor of about 1.3, and cold turkey increases the hazard rate by a factor of about 5.4 compared with patches.

Variables in the Equation

	B	SE	Wald	df	Sig.	Exp(B)	95.0% CI for Exp(B)	
							Lower	Upper
number	0.257	0.043	34.950	1	.000	1.293	1.188	1.408
treatment			25.796	2	.000			
treatment(1)	0.429	0.333	1.659	1	.198	1.535	0.800	2.949
treatment(2)	1.693	0.337	25.243	1	.000	5.435	2.808	10.520

SPSS Output 14.9 The effects of number of cigarettes smoked per day and treatment group on the hazard, with patches (treatment 1) as the reference category.

Other ways to compare treatment effects

By using treatment 3 as a reference category, we were able to compare each of our two therapies with cold turkey. Or, using treatment 1 as a reference category, we could compare hypnosis with patches, and cold turkey with patches.

There is another approach to comparing treatment effects, which resembles the use of contrasts explained near the end of our description of one-way ANOVA in Chapter 2. In that section we showed how to conduct post hoc comparisons of the five levels (in order: COUNTING, RHYMING, ADJECTIVE, IMAGERY and INTENTIONAL) of the IV DEPTH on the DV RECALL. In particular, we compared the average of the last three levels with the average of the first two levels of the variable DEPTH. We considered the difference between the two averages:

$$-\frac{1}{2}\,\text{counting} - \frac{1}{2}\,\text{rhyming} + \frac{1}{3}\,\text{adjective} + \frac{1}{3}\,\text{imagery} + \frac{1}{3}\,\text{intentional}$$

The coefficients for the three categories must sum to zero and to avoid fractions we used small whole numbers in the same proportions (−3, −3, 2, 2, 2). Note that these numbers need to be in the same order as the factor levels.

Using this method, we can consider the difference between the two therapies (hypnosis − patches) and then the difference between cold turkey and the average of the two therapies:

$$\text{cold turkey} - \frac{1}{2}\,\text{patches} - \frac{1}{2}\,\text{hypnosis}$$

In survival analysis, SPSS offers a short list of contrasts to choose from, but we cannot make up our own, and the coefficients are chosen by SPSS. We will now show you how to use this facility.

Return to the main dialog box with TTF in the **Time** box and RELAPSE(0) in the **Status** box. Once again we will enter YEARS and NUMBER into Block 1 of **Covariates** and select the stepwise method **Forward LR**. Then TREATMENT is entered in Block 2 of **Covariates** as before. Now click the **Categorical** button to see SPSS Dialog Box 14.7 again. Move TREATMENT into the **Categorical Covariates** box as before, then click the arrow on the indicator button below **Change Contrast** to get the list of contrasts on offer. Select **Difference** from the list and click **Change**. Click **Continue** and **OK** to repeat the analysis.

This time the categorical variable codings table, giving the dummy variables to define the categories, is as shown in the first SPSS Output 14.10 table. The first dummy variable assigns values −1/2, 1/2 and 0 to treatments 1, 2 and 3, and the second dummy variable assigns values −1/3, −1/3 and 2/3. Once again the three treatments are defined by two dummy variables, this time with the following values: (−1/2, −1/3), (1−2, −1/3) and (0, 2/3). However the first dummy variable contrasts treatments 1 and 2, and the second contrasts treatment 3 with the average of the first two. SPSS has used fractions, but we only want to know whether the contrasts differ significantly from zero, so any multiple of (hypnosis − patches) will do, as will any multiple of (cold turkey $-\frac{1}{2}$ patches $-\frac{1}{2}$ hypnosis).

The results appear in the second table of SPSS Output 14.10, which corresponds to SPSS Output 14.9 from our previous analysis. You can see that the first dummy

Categorical Variable Codings [b]

		Frequency	(1)	(2)
treatment[a]	1	50	-.500	-.333
	2	30	.500	-.333
	3	20	0	.667

a. Difference Parameter Coding

b. Category variable: treatment

Variables in the Equation

	B	SE	Wald	df	Sig.	Exp(B)	95.0% CI for Exp(B)	
							Lower	Upper
number	0.257	0.043	34.950	1	.000	1.293	1.188	1.408
treatment			25.796	2	.000			
treatment(1)	0.429	0.333	1.659	1	.198	1.535	0.800	2.949
treatment(2)	1.478	0.312	22.487	1	.000	4.386	2.381	8.081

SPSS Output 14.10 Dummy variables defined for the difference contrast, and the tests of significance.

treatment variable does not approach significance ($p = .198$), so the difference between hypnosis and patches is not significant. The p value is the same as that in SPSS Output 14.9, where we made the same comparison using treatment 1 as the reference category and comparing each of treatments 2 and 3 to it. The second dummy variable for treatment does show a significant effect, but the Wald statistic is not the same as the one in SPSS Output 14.9 because this time cold turkey is compared with the average of patches and hypnosis instead of just with patches as the reference category. Likewise the hazard ratio also differs for the second dummy treatment variable.

There are several other available contrasts. To see a list of definitions, click the **Help** button in SPSS Dialog Box 14.7. When using any of these, check the table of Categorical Variable Codings to make sure it is what you want.

Incomplete records

In our smoking cessation example, all participants were successfully followed for 20 weeks to the end of the study: there were no dropouts. So, whenever an observation was censored, that participant had not returned to smoking by the end of the study. Of course, sometimes participants are lost to a study, especially if it is a long one. People move and do not report a change of address, they get bored with the repeat appointments, they go on holiday and then forget about our study. If the event of interest has not occurred up to the last time we see a participant, then we may still be able to use this as a censored observation, though the time to censoring will be shorter than for those who complete the study. However, if we are to do this we need to consider the same issue as that raised in our discussion of missing data in the chapter on MANOVA: Do missed observations occur at random or not?

If participants are lost to the study for reasons that are unrelated to the study, then there is no problem in using the censored observation arising in this way. But it is not difficult to think of situations where the probability of dropping out may be related to some aspect of our investigation. First we will imagine a scenario where participants who are lost to the study may be more likely than those with complete records to experience the event. In our example, it would be possible that some participants who return to smoking may be ashamed of not succeeding and so fail to check in with us once they start smoking again. If this happened, the last time we saw them they would still be succeeding in giving up, then the next week they relapse but we never see them again, so they would appear as censored observations with a record shorter than the study length. Meanwhile, those successful in giving up are only lost for the sort of random reason that affects everyone equally. As with other kinds of missing data, it may be possible to track down a sample of those with incomplete records to see whether there is any evidence that they differ in any systematic way from those who completed.

Also in the context of our example, we can imagine a situation where members of one treatment group may be more or less likely than the others to remain to the end of the study. Suppose that those on treatment 1 in our example were given a supply of patches for the next week at each of the weekly check-ins. This might provide a good incentive to members of this group to turn up every week till the end of the study, while those on cold turkey or hypnosis would only be checking in to enable us to complete our research. In a case like this, incomplete records giving rise to censored observations would be more likely in the two treatment groups where members did not receive anything at the check-ins. Here a little foresight and imagination might have warned us that we were not treating all the participants in an equitable way.

If all our participants complete the study with none dropping out, as in our worked example, the censoring process is said to be *uninformative*. This is also the case if you can be confident that the reasons for losing any dropouts are entirely random and unrelated to any aspect of the study. If there is any reason to suspect that participants lost to the study differ in any systematic way from those who remain to the end, then this must be explained when reporting the results.

Reporting results

When describing the study you need to state whether any of the censored observations are incomplete records. If you have any of these but believe that the reasons for incomplete records are entirely random, then give your reasons for your confidence in this. If you suspect otherwise, then explain how this may affect your findings. Include the numbers and proportions of censored observations and the mean times to the event of interest. If you are comparing treatment or other groups, then include these details for each group. If you have performed any checks on the adequacy of the proportional hazards model for your data, then include this information. For the smoking cessation trial we described, you might report the results as follows:

> As described in the Method section, we had three treatment groups with 50 participants using nicotine patches, 30 who underwent hypnosis and 20 who attempted to quit smoking with no support (cold turkey). All 100 participants were followed for 20 weeks: there were no dropouts. The numbers still not smoking at the end of the study (censored observations) were 26 (52.0%), 14 (46.7%) and 1 (5.0%), respectively. The mean times to relapse for the cases where relapse occurred by the end of the study were 10.58 for patches, 11.44 for hypnosis and 6.53 for cold turkey. These preliminary results suggest that while there may not be much difference between patches and hypnosis, both may improve a smoker's chance of giving up over cold turkey.

To test for significance we performed a Cox regression analysis where YEARS and NUMBER were entered as Block 1 covariates and TREATMENT was entered as the Block 2 covariate. Since TREATMENT is a categorical variable with three categories, we need two dummy variables and initially these were defined to make treatment 3 (cold turkey) the reference category. In Block 1, only NUMBER was significant. When TREATMENT was added in Block 2, the chi-square statistic for the change was 23.3 on 2 *df*s (because we have two dummy variables), with $p < .001$. So there are highly significant differences among our treatments. The hazard ratios in Table A (*this is the middle table from our SPSS Output 14.4*) show that for each extra cigarette smoked per day the hazard rate is multiplied by 1.302 and patches (treatment 1) reduces the hazard rate to 0.181 (or about 18%) of that on cold turkey. Likewise hypnotherapy reduces the hazard rate to about 27% of that on cold turkey.

We repeated the analysis with treatment 1 (patches) as the reference category and omitting YEARS, as this covariate was not significant. This analysis showed that there was no significant difference between treatments 1 and 2 (patches and hypnosis), with $p = .198$ (Table B, *which would be our SPSS Output 14.9*). Figure A (*this would be our SPSS Output 14.5*) shows the survival functions for the three treatment groups, allowing for the covariates YEARS and NUMBER. Residual plots gave no reason to suppose that the proportional hazard assumption used in Cox regression was inappropriate here.

15 Longitudinal data

Introduction

It is common for studies in the human sciences to record measures on each participant at intervals over the course of the investigation. The intervals at which measures are recorded may be regular, every week or month or year, or may be at intervals determined by the need for treatment or by convenience for the participants. Data from such studies are said to be *longitudinal*. They are repeated measures studies but we cannot randomize the order in which measurements are taken as we did in a within-subjects ANOVA. Time moves on and some of the measures will have some time dependence. However, including time as a regressor variable will violate the assumption of independent observations for a regression. Longitudinal data present some particular problems and in fact are the subject of a considerable literature. In this chapter we briefly discuss how some of the techniques in previous chapters may be helpful, and also indicate where you can learn more about this large subject.

Some benefits and some problems

There are many advantages of using a longitudinal study. If each person is able to try more than one treatment or condition then they can act as their own control, and since variation within a participant is typically less than that between participants we may achieve greater sensitivity or power. Also, for a fixed number of participants, we obtain more information if we can record measures on several occasions. But most important, if we want to find out about a process for individuals, then a record of their progress is essential. If we want to know about growth or decline or progress on a treatment or training program, then a record that follows each individual over a period of time will be much more informative than data on different individuals who are measured at different stages of the process.

However, there are difficulties particular to longitudinal studies. Missing data can be a bigger problem when we try to see each participant several times. They may get tired of turning up for the appointments and drop out. They may move and be too far away to come for appointments, or may forget to tell us their new address so we lose touch. They may become ill or go on holiday and miss appointments but then return. So we will have cases where the record stops before the end of the study and also records with points missing in the middle. As with all missing data (recall our discussion in the chapters on MANOVA and survival analysis) we need to know whether only random events cause missed observations, or whether something about the investigation causes some cases to have a higher probability of being lost to us.

Another problem is the correlations among observations from the same participant. These are likely to be higher for observations that are close in time than for those widely separated. The methods we use for analysis must take account of these correlations.

Especially if a study extends over several years, many things may change with time in ways that only hinder us. People age, health may improve or decline and events unrelated to our study may affect our measures: bereavements, divorce, the joys of love or birth may intervene when we were hoping to observe the uneventful progress of whatever process we were studying. The longer the study, the more the mere passage of time is likely to cause us extra difficulties of data collection or interpretation.

In addition to the effects of the passage of time on our participants we must remember that many things are correlated with time. The annals of statistical blunders and cautionary tales contain many examples of spurious correlations between variables, both of which happen to be increasing or decreasing with time, so we need to be careful not to fall into such errors with whatever variables interest us. We have cautioned our students by showing them the strong correlation between the length of the railways and the consumption of shoe leather over the years in which railways were being extended in Britain: the population was increasing and using more shoe leather at the same time as the railway network was being developed. For those old enough to remember the soap advert that showed a stork flying along with a baby suspended in a snow-white sheet from its beak, we could also give a tongue in cheek demonstration that the decline in the stork population in Europe was associated with a decline in the birth rate. But it was not the shortage of storks available for delivering babies, it was just that during the process of industrialization the stork habitat was destroyed so their population fell, and at the same time birth rates were falling for reasons probably associated with industrialization. These examples may be amusing, but we do need to be aware that if we observe variables increasing or decreasing together over time, it may mean nothing more than each reflecting some other process affected by the passage of time.

Still, even with the difficulties outlined above, longitudinal studies can be an attractive option and we outline below how some of the techniques explored in previous chapters may show the way forward.

ANCOVA

The experiment we described in the chapter on ANCOVA is an example of the simplest possible longitudinal study: each participant is measured on two occasions. In our experiment we wanted to compare two training methods with an untrained control group. We measured each participant, including those in the control group, before the start of the training. Then we measured them all after the training, again including those who received no training. This design is often called a pretest–posttest control group design, and it can be applied in any situation where we want to test the effect of some intervention. We may hope that training may improve scores, as in our example, or we may be trying to find an intervention that will improve quality of life for people with an untreatable illness, or we may be attempting to find a drug dose that will cause a reduction in blood pressure. Any investigation of this sort could be carried out using a pretest–posttest design and analysed as shown in Chapter 5. This is an excellent way to study a measure that may be influenced by some intervention, but it does not extend to studies where we want to observe a process developing over more than two occasions.

Within-subjects ANOVA

Our medical example (Example Box 2.3) was an example of the use of a within-subjects ANOVA to analyse a longitudinal design where each participant was recorded at three time points (at intervals of a year). You may recall that Mauchly's test of sphericity was not significant (SPSS Output 2.11). This test concerns the correlations among the observations, which are assumed to have a simple form for the ANOVA. The correlation between observations at any pair of time points is assumed to be the same, however close or far apart the time points are. It is also assumed that the variances remain constant at all time points. Mauchly's test checks that it is reasonable to assume this simple structure, and in our example the test is not significant. However, especially in a study extending over a long time and with more numerous observation occasions, we would expect that observations close together in time would be more alike than observations made at widely separated times. Also it is commonly observed that over time the variance of observations increases. Here we have fabricated new data for the example in Example Box 2.3, and this time it fails the Mauchly test. The data are shown in Table 15.1 and appear on the website as longitudinal.anova.sav.

Table 15.1 Data from a design with two within-subjects variables (longitudinal.anova.sav)

| Participant | Year of test | | | | | |
| | Year 1 | | Year 2 | | Year 3 | |
	Visual	Auditory	Visual	Auditory	Visual	Auditory
1	284	310	333	348	409	441
2	258	273	283	333	347	383
3	272	291	327	293	346	385
4	303	318	306	345	291	296
5	298	303	351	373	308	310
6	279	284	362	333	417	443
7	266	284	289	309	221	236
8	283	317	272	310	255	254
9	292	288	335	351	355	358
10	283	301	349	376	247	262

Mauchly's test is shown as SPSS Output 15.1. It is significant for YEAR ($p = .007$) and for the YEAR by MODE interaction ($p = .023$). In this case, since sphericity cannot be assumed, we must use one of the tests with degrees of freedom adjusted, as shown in SPSS Output 15.2. We see that neither YEAR nor MODE reaches significance when we cannot use the sphericity assumption. Had we been able to assume sphericity then the effect of YEAR would have been significant ($p = .046$). If you check the correlations and the variance of the observations for each year, you will see that we fabricated these data to have exactly the properties that cause failure of the Mauchly test: the variance increases with time, and correlations are higher between neighbouring observations than between those separated by 2 years.

Mauchly's Test of Sphericity^b

Measure:rt

Within Subjects Effect	Mauchly's W	Approx. Chi-Square	df	Sig.	Epsilon^a		
					Greenhouse-Geisser	Huynh-Feldt	Lower-bound
year	.293	9.809	2	.007	.586	.621	.500
mode	1.000	0.000	0		1.000	1.000	1.000
year * mode	.391	7.514	2	.023	.621	.672	.500

Tests the null hypothesis that the error covariance matrix of the orthonormalized transformed dependent variables is proportional to an identity matrix.

a. May be used to adjust the degrees of freedom for the averaged tests of significance. Corrected tests are displayed in the Tests of Within-Subjects Effects table.

b. Design: Intercept
Within Subjects Design: year + mode + year * mode

SPSS Output 15.1 Mauchly's test is significant.

Tests of Within-Subjects Effects

Measure:rt

Source		Type III Sum of Squares	df	Mean Square	F	Sig.
year	Sphericity Assumed	26913.433	2	13456.717	3.678	.046
	Greenhouse-Geisser	26913.433	1.172	22964.636	3.678	.078
	Huynh-Feldt	26913.433	1.242	21675.951	3.678	.075
	Lower-bound	26913.433	1.000	26913.433	3.678	.087
Error(year)	Sphericity Assumed	65848.900	18	3658.272		
	Greenhouse-Geisser	65848.900	10.548	6243.045		
	Huynh-Feldt	65848.900	11.175	5892.710		
	Lower-bound	65848.900	9.000	7316.544		
mode	Sphericity Assumed	5742.817	1	5742.817	36.734	.000
	Greenhouse-Geisser	5742.817	1.000	5742.817	36.734	.000
	Huynh-Feldt	5742.817	1.000	5742.817	36.734	.000
	Lower-bound	5742.817	1.000	5742.817	36.734	.000
Error(mode)	Sphericity Assumed	1407.017	9	156.335		
	Greenhouse-Geisser	1407.017	9.000	156.335		
	Huynh-Feldt	1407.017	9.000	156.335		
	Lower-bound	1407.017	9.000	156.335		
year * mode	Sphericity Assumed	441.233	2	220.617	1.115	.349
	Greenhouse-Geisser	441.233	1.243	354.995	1.115	.330
	Huynh-Feldt	441.233	1.344	328.179	1.115	.334
	Lower-bound	441.233	1.000	441.233	1.115	.318
Error(year*mode)	Sphericity Assumed	3560.433	18	197.802		
	Greenhouse-Geisser	3560.433	11.186	318.283		
	Huynh-Feldt	3560.433	12.100	294.241		
	Lower-bound	3560.433	9.000	395.604		

SPSS Output 15.2 If sphericity cannot be assumed YEAR does not show a significant effect.

Although the usefulness of within-subjects ANOVA for longitudinal studies is limited by the considerations discussed above, we see from our original medical example in Example Box 2.3 that it may enable us to analyse a series of observations taken over a fairly short time.

MANOVA

If we have two or more DVs measured on at least two occasions for each participant, then a within-subjects MANOVA may be what we need, as in our medical example for this method in Example Box 3.2. In that example we had measurements on choice reaction TIME from the within-subjects ANOVA, and also on STRENGTH of response for each participant in YEAR 1, YEAR 2 and YEAR 3. In the previous section we altered the choice reaction time data so that it would fail the Mauchly test, and called the altered variable RT instead of TIME. For the following demonstration we have added the data on STRENGTH to the RT data so that we have data for a within-subjects MANOVA that will fail the Mauchly test. The data are shown as Table 15.2.

Table 15.2 Data from a within-subjects experiment to compare effects of year of testing and stimulus mode on choice reaction time and strength of response in a decision task (longitudinal.manova.sav)

v1y1m1*	v1y1m2	v1y2m1	v1y2m2	v1y3m1	v1y3m2	v2y1m1	v2y1m2	v2y2m1	v2y2m2	v2y3m1	v2y3m2
284	310	333	348	414	456	17	25	23	25	26	24
258	273	283	333	352	398	21	20	18	18	15	17
272	291	327	293	351	400	20	19	23	23	18	23
303	318	306	345	296	311	20	19	12	21	25	21
298	303	351	373	313	325	20	20	20	20	17	19
279	284	362	333	422	458	23	20	20	20	20	18
266	284	289	309	226	251	20	21	19	19	19	17
283	317	272	310	260	271	21	21	20	17	21	20
292	288	335	351	360	373	20	17	23	21	16	22
283	301	349	376	252	275	18	23	23	19	19	20

v1 and v2 refer to the DVs RT and STRENGTH, y1, y2, y3 refer to the year of measurement, m1 and m2 refer to visual and auditory modes.

If we perform the within-subjects MANOVA as described in Chapter 3, we do indeed find that the Mauchly test is failed by the RT variable (SPSS Output 15.3).

Mauchly's Test of Sphericity[b]

Within Subjects Effect	Measure	Mauchly's W	Approx. Chi-Square	df	Sig.	Epsilon[a]		
						Greenhouse-Geisser	Huynh-Feldt	Lower-bound
year	rt	.293	9.809	2	.007	.586	.621	.500
	strength	.986	0.117	2	.943	.986	1.000	.500
mode	rt	1.000	0.000	0	.	1.000	1.000	1.000
	strength	1.000	0.000	0	.	1.000	1.000	1.000
year * mode	rt	.381	7.514	2	.023	.621	.672	.500
	strength	.971	0.238	2	.888	.972	1.000	.500

Tests the null hypothesis that the error covariance matrix of the orthonormalized transformed dependent variables is proportional to an identity matrix

a. May be used to adjust the degrees of freedom for the averaged tests of significance. Corrected tests are displayed in the Tests of Within-Subjects Effects table.

b. Design: Intercept
Within Subjects Design: year + mode + year * mode

SPSS Output 15.3 One of our two DVs fails the Mauchly test for sphericity.

However, we can still use the table of multivariate tests (SPSS Output 15.4, overleaf) to show that both YEAR and MODE have a significant effect on our pair of DVs. The interaction of YEAR and MODE is not significant.

However, when we come to look at the table of univariate tests, we find that when we consider RT and STRENGTH singly, year does not reach significance for either, since we cannot use the 'Sphericity Assumed' line for RT (SPSS Output 15.5 on page 365).

So, MANOVA makes less stringent assumptions than within-subjects ANOVA, and this may enable us to make some useful inferences about a short series of longitudinal data collected on two or more variables. Nevertheless, for those studies where the variance of observations shows a marked increase or correlations between pairs depend strongly on how far apart in time they were collected, we may be able to reach only rather general conclusions using this technique. It will usually not be very useful for studies with many observation points over an extended period of time.

Multivariate Tests[b]

Effect			Value	F	Hypothesis df	Error df	Sig.
Between Subjects	Intercept	Pillai's Trace	.996	1.062E3	2.000	8.000	.000
		Wilks' Lambda	.004	1.062E3	2.000	8.000	.000
		Hotelling's Trace	265.380	1.062E3	2.000	8.000	.000
		Roy's Largest Root	265.380	1.062E3	2.000	8.000	.000
Within Subjects	year	Pillai's Trace	.796	5.850[a]	4.000	6.000	.029
		Wilks' Lambda	.204	5.850[a]	4.000	6.000	.029
		Hotelling's Trace	3.900	5.850[a]	4.000	6.000	.029
		Roy's Largest Root	3.900	5.850[a]	4.000	6.000	.029
	mode	Pillai's Trace	.805	16.463[a]	2.000	8.000	.001
		Wilks' Lambda	.195	16.463[a]	2.000	8.000	.001
		Hotelling's Trace	4.116	16.463[a]	2.000	8.000	.001
		Roy's Largest Root	4.116	16.463[a]	2.000	8.000	.001
	year * mode	Pillai's Trace	.450	1.229[a]	4.000	6.000	.391
		Wilks' Lambda	.550	1.229[a]	4.000	6.000	.391
		Hotelling's Trace	0.819	1.229[a]	4.000	6.000	.391
		Roy's Largest Root	0.819	1.229[a]	4.000	6.000	.391

a. Exact statistic

b. Design: Intercept
Within Subjects Design: year + mode + year * mode

SPSS Output 15.4 YEAR and MODE have a significant effect on the pair of DVs.

Regression

Because the observations must be independent, if we have a series of observations made at different times on each participant it is not appropriate to use time as an IV and perform a regression analysis. Observations made on one participant are likely to be correlated, as are observations made at neighbouring times. However, the regression model that we discussed in Chapter 4 can be extended to include multiple observations made on each participant. These extended models are known as mixed-effect regression models (MRMs). They are beyond the scope of this book, though we will try to give you a flavour of what is involved at the end of this section. Also, a brief introduction showing an example of their use can be found in the SPSS Help file. Display **Linear Mixed Models** from the Help Index, and then click **Show me** to see an extended worked example. A more detailed treatment, including an extension to curvilinear models, can be found in the 'Further reading' at the end of the book. Note that SPSS does not support the extension to curvilinear models at present (version 16).

A disadvantage of ANOVA, MANOVA and ANCOVA for dealing with longitudinal data is that measurements must be taken at the same time points for all participants. It is often much easier to organize a longitudinal study that is free of this constraint, so that participants can be measured at various times during the course of the study, perhaps when they attend appointments that are for their treatment or other benefit. Regression methods do allow for measurement at various time points that need not be equally spaced nor the same for all participants. However, it is important to note that there is a difference between participants having individual schedules of measurement occasions and participants for whom regular measurements are planned but for whom some are missing. Missing data must always be considered in case they are missing for some reason associated with the study. If they are missing for reasons that appear to be random, then we can just ignore them and use the irregularly spaced observations that we have. But if we suspect that participants in some categories were more likely than

Univariate Tests

Source	Measure		Type III Sum of Squares	df	Mean Square	F	Sig.
year	rt	Sphericity Assumed	26913.433	2	13456.717	3.678	.046
		Greenhouse-Geisser	26913.433	1.172	22964.636	3.678	.078
		Huynh-Feldt	26913.433	1.242	21675.951	3.678	.075
		Lower-bound	26913.433	1.000	26913.433	3.678	.087
	strength	Sphericity Assumed	1.900	2	0.950	0.129	.880
		Greenhouse-Geisser	1.900	1.971	0.964	0.129	.877
		Huynh-Feldt	1.900	2.000	0.950	0.129	.880
		Lower-bound	1.900	1.000	1.900	0.129	.728
Error(year)	rt	Sphericity Assumed	65848.900	18	3658.272		
		Greenhouse-Geisser	65848.900	10.548	6243.045		
		Huynh-Feldt	65848.900	11.175	5892.710		
		Lower-bound	65848.900	9.000	7316.544		
	strength	Sphericity Assumed	132.767	18	7.376		
		Greenhouse-Geisser	132.767	17.743	7.483		
		Huynh-Feldt	132.767	18.000	7.376		
		Lower-bound	132.767	9.000	14.752		
mode	rt	Sphericity Assumed	5742.817	1	5742.817	36.734	.000
		Greenhouse-Geisser	5742.817	1.000	5742.817	36.734	.000
		Huynh-Feldt	5742.817	1.000	5742.817	36.734	.000
		Lower-bound	5742.817	1.000	5742.817	36.734	.000
	strength	Sphericity Assumed	2.400	1	2.400	0.970	.350
		Greenhouse-Geisser	2.400	1.000	2.400	0.970	.350
		Huynh-Feldt	2.400	1.000	2.400	0.970	.350
		Lower-bound	2.400	1.000	2.400	0.970	.350
Error(mode)	rt	Sphericity Assumed	1407.017	9	156.335		
		Greenhouse-Geisser	1407.017	9.000	156.335		
		Huynh-Feldt	1407.017	9.000	156.335		
		Lower-bound	1407.017	9.000	156.335		
	strength	Sphericity Assumed	22.267	9	2.474		
		Greenhouse-Geisser	22.267	9.000	2.474		
		Huynh-Feldt	22.267	9.000	2.474		
		Lower-bound	22.267	9.000	2.474		
year * mode	rt	Sphericity Assumed	441.233	2	220.617	1.115	.349
		Greenhouse-Geisser	441.233	1.243	364.006	1.115	.330
		Huynh-Feldt	441.233	1.344	328.179	1.115	.334
		Lower-bound	441.233	1.000	441.233	1.115	.319
	strength	Sphericity Assumed	0.300	2	0.150	0.020	.981
		Greenhouse-Geisser	0.300	1.943	0.154	0.020	.979
		Huynh-Feldt	0.300	2.000	0.150	0.020	.981
		Lower-bound	0.300	1.000	0.300	0.020	.891
Error(year*mode)	rt	Sphericity Assumed	3560.433	18	197.802		
		Greenhouse-Geisser	3560.433	11.186	318.283		
		Huynh-Feldt	3560.433	12.100	294.241		
		Lower-bound	3560.433	9.000	395.604		
	strength	Sphericity Assumed	137.033	18	7.613		
		Greenhouse-Geisser	137.033	17.488	7.836		
		Huynh-Feldt	137.033	18.000	7.613		
		Lower-bound	137.033	9.000	15.226		

SPSS Output 15.5 RT and STRENGTH fail to reach significance.

those in others to miss measurement occasions, then missing data could be a source of bias in the results. This is just the same issue as discussed above in the section 'Some benefits and some problems', in the section 'Incomplete records' in Chapter 14 and in the section 'Missing data' in Chapter 3. SPSS does not currently (version 16) support measurements made at irregular intervals or at different times for different participants.

Before leaving this large topic we will show you part of an analysis using an MRM. The (fabricated) data give the body mass index (BMI) for seven participants, each recorded at intervals of a month for 10 months. We also have the participants' ages at the start. All participants began with a BMI that was rather high and were trying to reduce it. Four of them were following a diet and exercise programme and the other three were following an exercise programme but eating as usual. The data are shown in Table 15.3.

Table 15.3 Data from a longitudinal study of BMI

Group	Age	BMI1	BMI2	BMI3	BMI4	BMI5	BMI6	BMI7	BMI8	BMI9	BMI10
1	32	27.0	27.1	26.8	26.7	26.5	26.5	26.4	26.4	25.9	25.7
1	39	25.6	25.3	25.8	27.3	26.5	25.9	26.6	25.8	26.2	26.0
1	34	30.0	28.4	28.3	28.9	26.1	28.4	27.6	26.8	27.6	27.8
1	40	26.5	27.6	26.9	23.4	25.1	24.8	23.9	24.6	24.6	24.3
2	31	27.4	27.6	28.6	28.2	27.8	27.1	28.8	26.7	27.2	28.5
2	35	27.5	28.9	30.2	27.7	26.5	28.0	25.7	28.8	27.2	25.5
2	37	27.7	27.6	27.1	26.7	26.8	28.5	26.0	26.9	25.6	26.7

First of all, ignore the fact that each participant has been recorded on 10 occasions, and just treat MONTH of measurement and AGE as covariates in a covariance analysis with GROUP as the only factor. It is necessary to organize the data so that we have 70 rows, each corresponding to a single BMI record. The variables (columns) will be participant ID (ignored for the moment), GROUP, AGE, BMI and MONTH. Arranged in this way, the data can be found on the book website as longitudinal.MRM.sav. Use **Analyze, General Linear Model** and **Univariate**, and put BMI in the **Dependent** box, GROUP in the **Factor** box and AGE and MONTH in the **Covariates** box. Use the **Model** button to specify a **Custom model** with just the main effects of GROUP, AGE and MONTH. In the **Options** dialog box, click **Parameter estimates**. Part of the output is shown as SPSS Output 15.6.

Parameter Estimates

Dependent Variable:BMI

Parameter	B	Std. Error	t	Sig.	95% Confidence Interval Lower Bound	95% Confidence Interval Upper Bound	Partial Eta Squared
Intercept	34.630	1.472	23.521	.000	31.690	37.570	.893
[group=1]	-0.654	0.267	-2.446	.017	-1.188	-0.120	.083
[group=2]	0ᵃ	.	.	.	.	.	.
age	-0.186	0.042	-4.430	.000	-0.269	-0.102	.229
month	-0.146	0.044	-3.320	.001	-0.234	-0.058	.143

a. This parameter is set to zero because it is redundant.

SPSS Output 15.6 Parameter estimates for a covariance analysis of the BMI data.

Here you can see that BMI falls with AGE and with MONTH (both B values are negative). Also being in GROUP 1 reduces BMI compared to GROUP 2. GROUP and both covariates have a significant effect. However, we have ignored an important fact: the data are repeat observations on just seven participants. We will now show how an MRM addresses this problem.

In Chapter 2 we briefly mentioned fixed and random factors but thereafter considered only fixed factors or fixed effects. In the BMI study, it may be reasonable to consider the participants in each group as a random sample from a population that could have been selected, and hence participants may be considered as a random effect. Analysis of a random effects model requires that we specify how the correlations among observations are correlated. In our example, do observations on a single participant have higher correlations than between participants? And are observations close in time more highly correlated than observations far apart? We shall not show you how to make these decisions, but only show the parameter estimates and goodness of fit statistics for two examples.

Using Analyze, Mixed Models and **Linear** produces SPSS Dialog Box 15.1. The variable identifying our participants (or subjects) is ID, and the variable that identifies the repeat occasions for measurements is MONTH. We have put these in the appropriate boxes. At the bottom is a long list of possible types of covariance (or correlation) structure for the observations. Here we have selected **Scaled Identity**, which effectively ignores the participant ID by choosing the simplest possible structure for the correlations among observations (it assumes that our observations are independent).

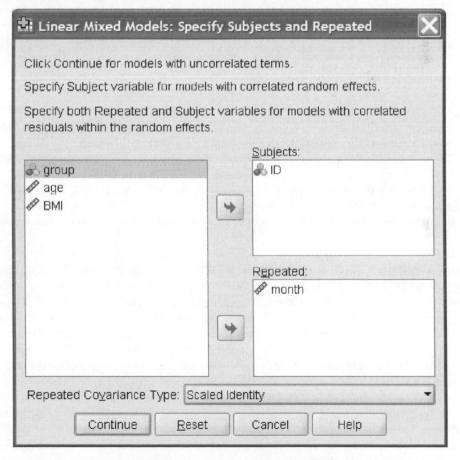

SPSS Dialog Box 15.1 An MRM that ignores the participant ID.

Click **Continue** to get SPSS Dialog Box 15.2, where we put BMI in the **Dependent Variable** box, GROUP in the **Factors** box and AGE and MONTH in the **Covariates** box. Click **Statistics**, and in the dialog box select **Parameter estimates**.

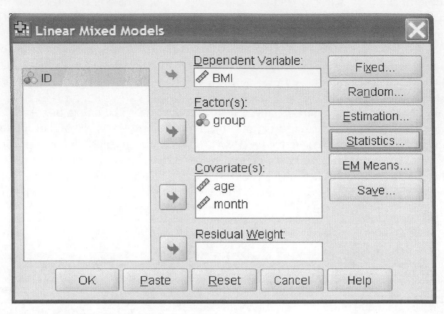

SPSS Dialog Box 15.2 Setting up an MRM.

Part of the output is shown in SPSS Output 15.7, and you can see that the parameter estimates in the third table are the same as those we obtained from an ANCOVA. Choosing the simplest correlation structure for our observations in an MRM analysis just reduces to our familiar ANCOVA. By assuming that our observations are independent we have effectively ignored the participant ID. The first table shows that there are five parameters in the model, one each for GROUP (two levels), AGE, MONTH, the intercept and the repeated effects. Note the value of the first of the 'Information Criteria' in the second table. We shall use this to compare the fit of this model, which has ignored important information, with a more complex model.

Now we repeat the analysis, but this time choosing **Compound Symmetry** (instead of **Scaled Identity**) for the covariance type. This structure also makes simplifying assumptions about the way our data are correlated, but it does allow for correlations among observations on the same participant. SPSS Output 15.8 shows part of the output.

This time, neither AGE nor GROUP shows a significant effect (there is still a significant effect of MONTH, with BMI reducing as time goes by). The first table shows that this time we have six parameters. To see whether this more complex model is a better fit to our data than the one ignoring participant ID, subtract the −2log(likelihood) statistic for the more complex model from that for the simpler model (214.375 − 201.314 = 13.061). Then subtract the degrees of freedom (6 − 5 = 1). The more complex model is a significantly better fit if the chi-square value (13.061) with these *df*s (1) is significant. Our value is well in excess of the critical value for a test at the 5% level (3.84), so we conclude that the more complex model is a better fit: we do need to take into account that our data are repeat observations on seven participants.

Model Dimension[a]

		Number of Levels	Covariance Structure	Number of Parameters	Subject Variables	Number of Subjects
Fixed Effects	Intercept	1		1		
	group	2		1		
	age	1		1		
	month	1		1		
Repeated Effects	month	10	Identity	1	ID	7
Total		15		5		

a. Dependent Variable: BMI.

Information Criteria[a]

-2 Restricted Log Likelihood	214.375
Akaike's Information Criterion (AIC)	216.375
Hurvich and Tsai's Criterion (AICC)	216.437
Bozdogan's Criterion (CAIC)	219.564
Schwarz's Bayesian Criterion (BIC)	218.564

The information criteria are displayed in smaller-is-better forms.

a. Dependent Variable: BMI.

Estimates of Fixed Effects[b]

Parameter	Estimate	Std. Error	df	t	Sig.	95% Confidence Interval	
						Lower Bound	Upper Bound
Intercept	34.629989	1.472331	66.000	23.521	.000	31.690385	37.569594
[group=1]	-0.653968	0.267374	66	-2.446	.017	-1.187798	-0.120139
[group=2]	0[a]	0					
age	-0.185756	0.041928	66.000	-4.430	.000	-0.269467	-0.102044
month	-0.145887	0.043937	66	-3.320	.001	-0.233610	-0.058165

a. This parameter is set to zero because it is redundant.

b. Dependent Variable: BMI.

SPSS Output 15.7 Part of the output for an MRM that ignores participant ID.

There is much more to learn about this large topic and how to make a sensible choice of covariance structure. However, we hope that this short exploration has given you some idea of how MRMs can be used to analyse longitudinal data.

Generalized estimating equations

The previous section shows how linear mixed models may be used to analyse longitudinal quantitative variables. In this section, we consider generalized estimating equations (GEE) used for analysing longitudinal qualitative variables.

As with linear mixed models, GEE are used when we expect the observations to be correlated. In this chapter we consider the case where the correlation may be found in longitudinal studies since observations are taken on the same subject over time. Other examples include observing subjects that are clustered (e.g., all the students within a particular class, patients within the same clinician practice or siblings). Unlike linear mixed models, however, our observations are counts, binary (yes/no responses) or interval censored data – the time to an event measured periodically (e.g., oncology patients in a clinical trial who are checked at regular intervals for the growth of a tumour).

For example, consider an experiment in which adults diagnosed with mild anxiety are allocated at random to one of three treatments. Treatment 1 is a monthly counselling

Model Dimension[a]

		Number of Levels	Covariance Structure	Number of Parameters	Subject Variables	Number of Subjects
Fixed Effects	Intercept	1		1		
	group	2		1		
	age	1		1		
	month	1		1		
Repeated Effects	month	10	Compound Symmetry	2	ID	7
Total		15		6		

a. Dependent Variable: BMI.

Information Criteria[a]

-2 Restricted Log Likelihood	201.314
Akaike's Information Criterion (AIC)	205.314
Hurvich and Tsai's Criterion (AICC)	205.504
Bozdogan's Criterion (CAIC)	211.693
Schwarz's Bayesian Criterion (BIC)	209.693

The information criteria are displayed in smaller-is-better forms.

a. Dependent Variable: BMI.

Estimates of Fixed Effects[b]

Parameter	Estimate	Std. Error	df	t	Sig.	95% Confidence Interval	
						Lower Bound	Upper Bound
Intercept	34.629989	3.322431	4.031	10.423	.000	25.433345	43.826633
[group=1]	-0.653968	0.610466	4.000	-1.071	.344	-2.348894	1.040957
[group=2]	0[a]	0					
age	-0.185756	0.095729	4.000	-1.940	.124	-0.451541	0.080030
month	-0.145887	0.037493	62.000	-3.891	.000	-0.220835	-0.070940

a. This parameter is set to zero because it is redundant.

b. Dependent Variable: BMI.

SPSS Output 15.8 A better fitting MRM for the BMI data.

session, treatment 2 is the provision of written and online information about reducing stress and treatment 3 is access to a telephone help line. The subject's gender and the scaled score on an SF 36 health/mood questionnaire are also noted. The response variable is the subject's answer to the question 'Have you had trouble sleeping in the last week?' (1 = yes, 0 = no).

If we had one observation on each subject (e.g., 6 months after the start of the intervention) then we could use the logistic regression techniques of Chapter 9 to determine if the proportion of yes/no responses depended on treatment after allowing for the covariates of gender and the SF 36 score. However if we continue the experiment we could ask the same question after 1 year and 18 months, thus having three responses for each subject. We can use GEE to analyse the set of three responses for each subject as they are likely to be correlated.

In the medical research context, a clinical trial for subjects with high blood pressure might allocate subjects to one of three treatments (placebo, low drug dose and high drug dose), with the subject's blood sodium level and their gender as covariates. The response variable is whether the blood pressure is at a clinically high level (yes/no). We could use logistic regression if we were to take a single reading but GEE if a number of readings are taken on the same individual over time.

Consider Table 15.4, which shows the (fabricated) data for the first two subjects in each treatment group for the anxiety experiment outlined above.

Table 15.4 The first two subjects in each treatment group from a repeated measures experiment to compare effects of treatment, gender and sf_36 score on response to a yes/no question. (The full dataset can be found as psy.gee.sav on the website)

Subject	Gender[1]	Treatment[2]	Visit	sf_36	Response[3]
1	1	1	1	87	1
1	1	1	2	89	0
1	1	1	3	67	0
2	1	1	1	68	0
2	1	1	2	83	0
2	1	1	3	77	1
11	2	2	1	79	1
11	2	2	2	72	1
11	2	2	3	81	1
12	2	2	1	66	1
12	2	2	2	62	1
12	2	2	3	67	1
21	1	3	1	54	1
21	1	3	2	59	1
21	1	3	3	61	1
22	1	3	1	82	1
22	1	3	2	84	1
22	1	3	3	89	1

Notes:
[1] 1 = male, 2 = female.
[2] 1 = counselling, 2 = access to written information, 3 = telephone help line.
[3] 0 = no, 1 = yes.

The format for GEE is similar to that of linear mixed models. Before we can do the analysis we have to make an assumption about how the observations on a participant are correlated. This assumption must be made with care, and should reflect the design of the experiment and our background knowledge as well as possible. SPSS provides five structures for correlations among repeat observations on a participant and, using the selected assumption, will estimate the correlations. The most restrictive assumption is that the observations on a participant are *independent*, so that the correlations between responses on visits 1 and 2, visits 1 and 3 and visits 2 and 3 are all zero.

A slightly less restrictive assumption is that the correlations between any pair of observations on a participant are the same. So the correlation between visits 1 and 2 will be the same as that between visits 2 and 3 and also the same as between visits 1 and 3. Thus, responses on adjacent observations are no more highly correlated than observations more widely separated in time. This correlation, between any pair of observations, is assumed to be the same for all participants. SPSS calls this correlation structure *exchangeable*. For the data in psy.gee.sav, each correlation is estimated to be .493.

Slightly less restrictive than *exchangeable* is *M exchangeable*. This assumes that the correlations between visits the same time apart have the same correlation. So in our example visits 1 and 2 and visits 2 and 3 are assumed to have the same correlation, whilst visits 1 and 3 have a different correlation. M can be chosen by the user, and observations greater than M apart are assumed to be uncorrelated. If M is set at 1, then any pair of adjacent observations will have the same correlation (.515 for the data in psy.gee.sav), but observations further apart, for instance visits 1 and 3 in our example, will have zero correlation. If M is set at 2, then in our example visits 1 and 2 will have the same correlation as visits 2 and 3 (.518) but visits 1 and 3 will have a different correlation (.512). If we had more observations, say a fourth visit, then visits 1 and 4 would have zero correlation.

Usually, observations further apart in time will have lower correlations than observations close in time, and AR(1) assumes a particular form for this reduction. (AR(1) is a term used in time series analysis, standing for autoregressive with order 1.) In the context of GEE we assume that the correlation between successive visits reduces geometrically, so that the correlation between visits 1 and 3 is the square of that between visits 1 and 2 (or 2 and 3). For the data in psy.gee.sav, using the AR(1) assumption, SPSS estimates the correlation for visits 1 and 2 or visits 2 and 3 as .513. For visits 1 and 3 the correlation is .263, or .513.

The least restrictive assumption is that the correlations among observations on a participant are *unstructured*. If this assumption is chosen, SPSS will estimate correlations for every pair of observations. It is still assumed that the correlations between pairs of observations are the same for all participants. Using this assumption with the psy.gee.sav data, SPSS estimates the correlation for visits 1 and 2 as .651, for visits 2 and 3 as .443 and between visits 1 and 3 as .505.

The M-dependent and AR(1) structures are likely to be appropriate only when the visits are equally spaced.

We now consider how to fit a GEE in SPSS, interpret the output produced and choose between two models. We first fit the model for response using gender and treatment as factors and SF_36 as a continuous covariate, assuming an unstructured correlation matrix.

Using Analyze, Generalized Linear Models and **Generalized Estimating Equations** produces SPSS Dialog Box 15.3. The subject variable is SUBJECT and the within-subjects variable that identifies the repeat occasions for measurements is VISIT. The working correlation matrix is chosen to be unstructured.

Click on the **Type of Model** tab and select binary logistic. Click on the **Response** tab and select response as the dependent variable. Click on the **Predictors** tab. We put GENDER and TREATMENT in the **factors** box and SF_36 in the **Covariates** box. Click on the **Model** tab and enter GENDER, TREATMENT and SF_36 as main effects. Select **Statistics** and **Working Correlation**. Click on **OK**.

The SPSS output is similar to that for other techniques and includes tables (not displayed here) showing the analysis performed and summaries of the categorical and continuous variables in the model. Since we ticked **Working Correlation**, we also find the estimated correlation matrix for the repeat observations. If you look at this you can check the values for the correlations between visits 1 and 2, visits 2 and 3 and visits 1 and 3, which we quoted when describing the unstructured correlation assumption. Here we begin by considering the parameter estimates, shown in SPSS Output 15.9 on page 374.

As with linear models fitted in earlier chapters, categorical variables have one fewer dummy variable than the number of levels. So, we need one variable to specify the gender effect but two to represent the three treatment groups. The default used by SPSS is to use the highest level of the response variable as the reference level. This means

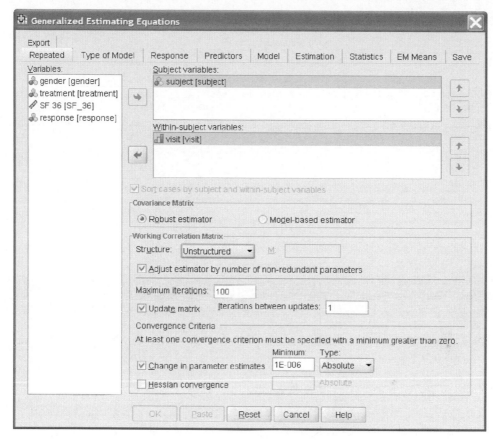

SPSS Dialog Box 15.3 A GEE using the unstructured correlation matrix.

that the model is using 'yes' (response = 1) as the reference level in our example. We could have changed this by clicking on reference level in the response tab. We did not do this, so positive model parameters mean a higher proportion of 'no' responses to the question 'Have you had trouble sleeping in the last week?'.

The value of the parameter estimates (B) in SPSS Output 15.9(a) can be seen for gender = 1 (males), although the associated significance level of .154 shows no significant difference in the proportion of yes/no responses between males and females. Similarly with a p value of .106, the SF 36 covariate does not have a significant effect on RESPONSE.

The significance values (.034 and .838, respectively) comparing treatments 1 and 2 with treatment 3 show that the response variable is significantly different for treatment 1 (counselling sessions) but not treatment 2 (written material) compared with a telephone help line. The positive value of B for treatment 1 shows that the proportion of 'no' responses to the sleeping question is reduced for the counselling group compared with the telephone help line.

The parameter estimates for the model assuming independence is given as SPSS Output 15.9(b). These show very little difference from the model using the unstructured correlation matrix.

(a) Parameter estimates for GEE with the Unstructured correlation matrix

Parameter Estimates

Parameter	B	Std. Error	95% Wald Confidence Interval		Hypothesis Test		
			Lower	Upper	Wald Chi-Square	df	Sig.
(Intercept)	2.257	1.5819	-0.843	5.357	2.036	1	.154
[gender=1]	0.540	0.5674	-0.572	1.653	0.907	1	.341
[gender=2]	0ᵃ						
[treatment=1]	1.366	0.6454	0.101	2.631	4.479	1	.034
[treatment=2]	0.136	0.6647	-1.167	1.438	0.042	1	.838
[treatment=3]	0ᵃ						
SF_36	-0.039	0.0244	-0.087	0.008	2.607	1	.106
(Scale)	1						

Dependent Variable: response
Model: (Intercept), gender, treatment, SF_36
a. Set to zero because this parameter is redundant.

(b) Parameter estimates for GEE with the Independent correlation matrix

Parameter Estimates

Parameter	B	Std. Error	95% Wald Confidence Interval		Hypothesis Test		
			Lower	Upper	Wald Chi-Square	df	Sig.
(Intercept)	1.977	1.5638	-1.088	5.042	1.598	1	.206
[gender=1]	0.547	0.5695	-0.569	1.663	0.923	1	.337
[gender=2]	0ᵃ						
[treatment=1]	1.442	0.6481	0.172	2.712	4.952	1	.026
[treatment=2]	0.094	0.6656	-1.210	1.399	0.020	1	.887
[treatment=3]	0ᵃ						
SF_36	-0.035	0.0245	-0.083	0.013	2.084	1	.149
(Scale)	1						

Dependent Variable: response
Model: (Intercept), gender, treatment, SF_36
a. Set to zero because this parameter is redundant.

SPSS Output 15.9 Parameter estimates for GEE with two different correlation assumptions.

To compare the models using the unstructured and independent correlation matrices we use the quasi-likelihood under independence model criterion (QIC). The model with the lower value is the better fitting model. SPSS Output 15.10(a) gives this output for our experiment using the assumption of an unstructured correlation matrix, and SPSS output 15.10(b) gives the value assuming independence. The model with the unstructured correlation matrix has a slightly lower value of QIC so it may be a better (but more complicated) model to fit these data.

Once we decide on a correlation structure using the QIC criterion, the QICC (the final C stands for corrected, which penalizes models with redundant variables) can be used to compare models with different variables. If we repeat our analysis using the unstructured correlation matrix but omitting the non-significant variables of GENDER and SF_36, we find that the value of QICC is 202.032. This is much lower than the 231.721 for the model with the same correlation matrix that contains the non-significant covariates GENDER and SF_36, although it should be noted that there is no consensus on deciding when a reduction in the QICC is 'large enough'.

Hence, our chosen model is to include only TREATMENT and use the unstructured correlation matrix. We conclude from the experiment that the within-subjects data are

(a) Goodness of Fit Measures for the model assuming the Unstructured correlation matrix.

Goodness of Fit[b]

	Value
Quasi Likelihood under Independence Model Criterion (QIC)[a]	240.473
Corrected Quasi Likelihood under Independence Model Criterion (QICC)[a]	231.721

Dependent Variable: response
Model: (Intercept), gender, treatment, SF_36

a. Computed using the full log quasi-likelihood function.

b. Information criteria are in small-is-better form.

(b) Goodness of Fit Measures for the model assuming the Independent correlation matrix.

Goodness of Fit[b]

	Value
Quasi Likelihood under Independence Model Criterion (QIC)[a]	240.905
Corrected Quasi Likelihood under Independence Model Criterion (QICC)[a]	231.998

Dependent Variable: response
Model: (Intercept), gender, treatment, SF_36

a. Computed using the full log quasi-likelihood function.

b. Information criteria are in small-is-better form.

SPSS Output 15.10 Goodness of fit measures for the model assuming two different structures for the correlations among observations on a participant.

correlated between visits and that counselling reduced the proportion of 'no' responses to the question 'Have you had trouble sleeping in the last week?' compared to a telephone help line. The provision of written information on stress-reducing techniques was as effective as a telephone help line and the proportion of 'no' responses was not related to gender or to the standardized scores on the SF 36 form.

Poisson regression and survival analysis

Although we observe each participant over a period of time that may be quite long, to do a Poisson regression we just record the number of times the event of interest occurs during the observation period. This count is the single observed DV for each participant, and studies such as this are not usually regarded as longitudinal.

Like Poisson regression, survival analysis involves observing our participants over a period of time but, once again, what we record is a single DV, the time to failure or the time to censoring. Of course each observation also carries a marker to indicate whether or not it was censored. But we do not have a series of observations taken at successive times, and survival studies are not generally regarded as longitudinal.

Time series

A well developed set of methods known as time series analysis may be useful if you have a long series of data, perhaps from a monitoring program. These methods were developed for use in economics and are most effective when you have hundreds of observations. They are especially useful for dealing with *seasonality*. This term was first used to denote the kind of changes in economic data associated with the seasons: unemployment usually rises in winter because some jobs are only available in summer (especially in tourism and construction). Many measures show this kind of seasonal effect: ice cream sales rise in summer and fall in winter; consumer spending goes up before Christmas. Often interest focuses on whether there is some underlying trend, up or down, that seasonal variation obscures.

However, seasonality can be used to denote any periodic feature of the data: animal temperatures go up and down on a daily cycle; productivity in the workplace is subject to a weekly cycle; distress caused by a depressive illness may peak every morning. There are hundreds of examples of this sort of cyclic variation. Time series analysis can be used to expose underlying features of the data once the seasonality is allowed for. Upward or downward trends are obvious features that may be of interest, but slow, irregular cycles may also become visible once seasonal effects are removed.

SPSS will perform time series analyses, and you can find out a bit about it by looking for **Time Series Modeler** in the Help file and again clicking **Show me**. However, time series is a very large subject area, and if you think this may be useful to you we recommend that you do some serious reading. The classic introduction by Christopher Chatfield (2003) is still a good place to start.

Reference

Chatfield, C. (2003). *The analysis of time series: An introduction* (6th ed.). Boca Raton, FL: Chapman & Hall/CRC Press.

Appendix
SPSS and SAS syntax

Introduction

If you are using version 16 of SPSS, you may have noticed that when you undertake analyses there are a few lines of text before the output is produced. This text – syntax – is a list of instructions that tells SPSS the analysis you wish to perform. It includes details of the technique used (e.g., one-way ANOVA), the DV, the IVs and any options you have chosen. Earlier versions of SPSS did not produce syntax as part of the output. However, users of earlier versions of SPSS can create syntax easily and use it as explained below. If you want to turn off the syntax output in version 16, go to **Edit**, then **Options** and the **Viewer** tab. Untick **Display commands in the log** at the bottom left.

Users of SAS will be aware of the SAS equivalent of SPSS syntax. This is the SAS program made up of PROC statements that contain the code to instruct SAS which analyses and options to use, just as with SPSS.

In this appendix we:

- outline the advantages of using SPSS syntax files;
- explain how to create and use SPSS syntax files;
- provide the SPSS and SAS syntax for a selection of the analyses within the book.

First though we give an example of SPSS and SAS syntax to show their main structure.

An example of SPSS and SAS syntax

Recall that in Chapter 2 we performed a one-way ANOVA with the DV RECALL, using DEPTH as the factor. We requested SPSS to produce descriptive statistics and perform a test for homogeneity of variance. We also requested a plot of the means and used the default method of dealing with missing values. We begin by examining the structure of the SPSS syntax before considering SAS code, which performs much the same task. Do not worry, you will not have to learn the syntax for any SPSS analysis you perform as it is produced automatically in the SPSS output file or through the **Paste** button (in SPSS), which we will meet later.

The SPSS syntax for this one-way ANOVA analysis with the DV RECALL and DEPTH as the factor is given below. Note that the syntax produced by SPSS is in upper case and variable names are in lower case.

```
ONEWAY recall BY depth
    /STATISTICS DESCRIPTIVES HOMOGENEITY
    /PLOT MEANS
    /MISSING ANALYSIS.
```

The first line of SPSS syntax shows which analysis is to be undertaken. Here, ONE-WAY in the first line specifies that we are performing a one-way ANOVA. In ONEWAY, this is always followed by the DV, then the *keyword* 'BY' and then the IV. A keyword has a special meaning in SPSS syntax and you cannot, for example, name a variable 'BY'. This is because SPSS would not be able to distinguish a variable 'BY' and the 'BY' that separates the DV and IV in the ONEWAY command. Note that since not all techniques use a response variable and a factor, other SPSS syntax commands do not have the DV and IV on the first line. The exact structure of SPSS syntax varies with the analysis undertaken but most follow the pattern of specifying which analysis is to be undertaken, followed by specifying any variables used. Options are shown after the '/' on the following lines. The end of the syntax is shown by a full stop.

In this example we requested descriptive statistics to be calculated and the test for homogeneity to be performed. These are shown after the '/' on the second line. The remaining lines, also starting with '/', give the other options we chose.

Although the syntax above is given on four lines (as produced in the output file), we could have written it as

```
ONEWAY recall BY depth /STATISTICS DESCRIPTIVES HOMOGENEITY
    /PLOT MEANS /MISSING ANALYSIS.
```

We need to remember though to retain the '/' and ensure that the full stop is given at the end.

The SAS syntax to perform one-way ANOVA, obtain descriptive statistics and perform Levene's test is given below. Here, and in the syntax given at the end of this appendix, SAS syntax is given in upper case and variables in lower case. The syntax used assumes that the user has SAS version 9 available. This allows more flexibility with variable names than earlier versions. For example, only eight characters are allowed for a variable in SAS version 8, so users of this version will have to change the variable 'treatment' to 'treatmen' (or similar).

Note that the first line of the SAS syntax shows that a General Linear Model is to be fitted. This procedure can be used for balanced and unbalanced designs and for more complicated models such as two-way ANOVA. For balanced designs (such as this experiment) PROC ANOVA can be used instead of PROC GLM, as it is computationally more efficient.

```
PROC GLM;
    CLASS depth;
    MODEL recall = depth;
    MEANS depth / HOVTEST = LEVENE;
RUN;
```

The CLASS statement in the second line specifies which variables in the model are qualitative: DEPTH in this example. For one-way ANOVA, the MODEL statement in the third line is always of the form, 'Model DV = IV;'. The MEANS statement in the next line requests summary statistics for the DV (RECALL) for each level of the IV (DEPTH) and Levene's test for homogeneity.

Unlike SPSS, SAS requires a semi-colon rather than a solidus (/) to separate the various logical parts of the syntax and options. The end of the command is signified by the 'RUN;' line rather than a full stop as in SPSS. As in SPSS, the commands do not need to be on one line. The syntax below works just as well.

PROC GLM; CLASS depth; MODEL recall = depth; MEANS depth / HOVTEST = LEVENE; RUN;

Although there are differences in style and detail, there are common features about SPSS and SAS syntax for equivalent analyses. You can see that each starts by specifying which technique is to be undertaken. Then the variables to be used are identified, followed by which options we require. In this example SAS has a CLASS statement that shows that DEPTH is a categorical variable. SPSS does not need this to be specified because it knows that the variable after BY in the first line must be categorical. In later examples where there might be some ambiguity we find that SPSS also requires us to specify which variables in the model are categorical, and this is given in the syntax.

At this point, you might be wondering why SPSS shows the syntax and how we can make use of this feature. After all, we did not need to know anything about syntax to perform the analyses shown in the book. A similar situation arises in SAS when drop-down menus available through SOLUTIONS > ANALYSIS > ANALYST can be used to perform many analyses.

In the next section we outline some advantages of using syntax before showing how we obtain syntax commands.

Uses of SPSS and SAS syntax

SPSS has a variety of associated files. We have already met SPSS data files with a .sav extension (e.g., psy.anova.oneway.sav) that hold our data. In addition, as soon as you perform an analysis in SPSS, an output file with extension .spv (in version 16, but .spo in earlier versions) is created where the results are displayed and stored. You can, of course, choose a name for an output file by selecting **File** and then **Save**.

A third type of SPSS-associated file is a syntax file, with extension .sps. A syntax file contains the instructions to perform your analyses. A simple example would be to open up a dataset and run a one-way ANOVA. The syntax file to do this for the example above is:

```
GET
  FILE='C:\data files\psy.anova.oneway.sav'.
  DATASET NAME DataSet4 WINDOW=FRONT.

ONEWAY recall BY depth
  /STATISTICS DESCRIPTIVES HOMOGENEITY
  /PLOT MEANS/MISSING ANALYSIS.
```

The GET FILE command opens the file psy.anova.oneway.sav, which is stored in the folder 'data files' on the c drive. The command starting with ONEWAY is the same as we investigated above. We will learn how to create these commands in the next section.

One advantage of using syntax files is now clear: you have a permanent record of which data you analysed and the analyses you performed. This allows you to quickly locate and open the data used and reproduce exactly the analyses you undertook.

Another immediate advantage is that syntax files can be shared with others, who can use them to verify your analyses or point out where you might have gone wrong. This is particularly important for medical researchers, who provide their data and analyses to regulatory authorities such as the FDA or EMEA.

Thirdly, if you have many similar analyses to perform you can copy, paste and edit the commands within a syntax file. For example, imagine that you wished to test whether RECALL depended on GENDER. We would then amend the copied syntax to:

> ONEWAY recall BY gender
> /STATISTICS DESCRIPTIVES HOMOGENEITY
> /PLOT MEANS
> /MISSING ANALYSIS.

We could then run this analysis without having to select the variables and options again through drop-down menus.

Finally, it should be noted that some SPSS commands are only available by using syntax. These include adding value labels and (as mentioned in Chapter 3) the Roy-Bargmann step-down procedure.

In the next section we learn how to create an SPSS syntax file.

How to create an SPSS syntax file

If you are using a version of SPSS earlier than 16, you need to skip the section below and go on to the next.

SPSS 16: Using the menus

There are two ways to create the syntax for a particular analysis for users of SPSS version 16. In the first method we perform the desired analysis as usual and so create an output file. We then copy and paste the syntax into a syntax file that we create. In the second method, which also works for earlier versions of SPSS, we create the syntax from the drop-down menus using the **Paste** button. This method automatically opens a syntax file and adds to it whenever you select the paste button.

We assume that you have created a folder called 'data files' on the c drive and stored the file psy.anova.oneway.sav within it. We now create a syntax file from the output file.

Open the dataset psy.anova.oneway.sav and use the drop-down menus to perform the one-way ANOVA shown above. This opens up an output file that starts with the information shown in SPSS Output A.1.

Click on the syntax shown at the top so that the contents of the syntax, starting from GET and including the full stop after ANALYSIS, are enclosed in a box with an arrow on the left. Copy this text using any of the methods you are familiar with (click on **Edit** and then select **Copy**, or right click on the mouse and select **Copy**, or use Control and C).

```
GET
  FILE='C:\data files\psy.anova.oneway.sav'.
DATASET NAME DataSet1 WINDOW=FRONT.
ONEWAY recall BY depth
  /STATISTICS DESCRIPTIVES HOMOGENEITY
  /PLOT MEANS
  /MISSING ANALYSIS.
```

Oneway

```
[DataSet1] C:\data files\psy.anova.oneway.sav
```

Descriptives

recall

	N	Mean	Std. Deviation	Std. Error	95% Confidence Interval for Mean		Minimum	Maximum
					Lower Bound	Upper Bound		
counting	10	7.00	1.826	0.577	5.69	8.31	4	10
rhyming	10	6.90	2.132	0.674	5.38	8.42	3	11

SPSS Output A.1 Syntax and start of ANOVA output.

Select **File** on the menu bar, then **New**, then **Syntax**, which opens a new syntax file. Paste the syntax you have just placed on the clipboard by using **Edit** and then **Paste**, or right click on the mouse and select **Paste**, or Control and V. You now see SPSS Output A.2.

*Syntax1 - SPSS Syntax Editor
File Edit View Data Transform Analyze Graphs Utilities Run Add-ons Window Help
Active: DataSet1

```
GET
  FILE='C:\data files\psy.anova.oneway.sav'.
DATASET NAME DataSet1 WINDOW=FRONT.
ONEWAY recall BY depth
  /STATISTICS DESCRIPTIVES HOMOGENEITY
  /PLOT MEANS
  /MISSING ANALYSIS.
```

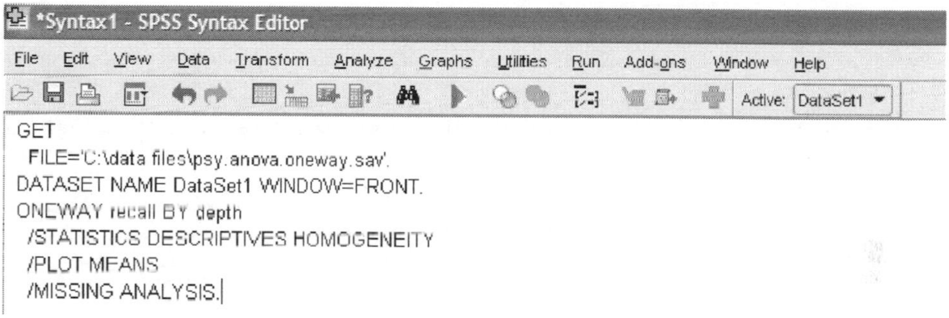

SPSS Output A.2 Syntax file contents.

Select **File** on the menu bar and then **Save** (or use Control and S). Browse to find the folder 'data files' and name the syntax file method1. Exit SPSS.

In the next section, we learn how to open the syntax file and run the commands from it. However, we next create an identical syntax file using the second method – the **Paste** button.

Previous versions: Using Paste

This method of creating syntax files works for SPSS 16 as well as previous versions, though the method above may be preferred if available. We begin by obtaining the syntax for opening the dataset. From the menu bar choose **File**, then **Open**, then **Data**. Use the drop-down list for **Look in** to get the folder 'data files'. Scroll to find psy.anova.oneway.sav and select it (click only once) so that it appears in the **File name** box, as shown in SPSS Dialog Box A.1. Now, instead of clicking **Open**, click the **Paste** button by the **File name** box.

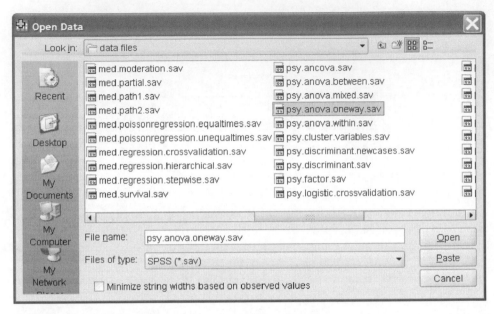

SPSS Dialog Box A.1 Pasting the syntax to identify a data file.

This creates a new syntax file and pastes in the syntax associated with opening the file psy.anova.oneway.sav. However, because you did not click on **Open** the file has not been opened. To open the dataset select **Run** on the syntax file menu bar, then **All**. This executes the commands you have just created using the **Paste** button and so opens the dataset.

Use the menus in the usual way to request the one-way ANOVA, choosing the appropriate options. However, when you are ready to perform the analysis, instead of clicking on **OK** in SPSS Dialog Box A.2, click on **Paste**. This causes the one-way ANOVA syntax to be pasted to the bottom of the syntax file you created when you opened the dataset. Check that the syntax file is the same as shown in SPSS Output A.2. Check the output window and notice that the analysis has not yet been performed.

We have now used two methods to create a syntax file and they produce identical results. We now learn how to edit an SPSS syntax file to enable us to perform similar analyses more quickly.

How to edit an SPSS syntax file

As an example of working with syntax files, imagine that you wish to produce the same output but without the plots of the means.

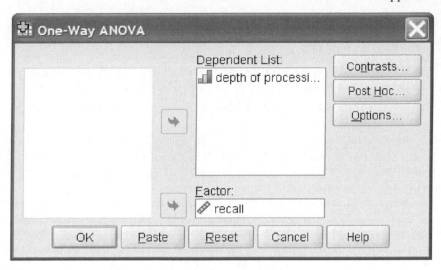

SPSS Dialog Box A.2 Pasting the syntax for one-way ANOVA.

Select the text in the syntax file, starting with ONEWAY until (and including) the full stop after ANALYSIS. Copy and paste this text underneath the existing syntax and then delete the line containing /PLOT MEANS (because we do not wish to plot the means). Close up the gap that this creates and check that you have the syntax shown in SPSS Output A.3.

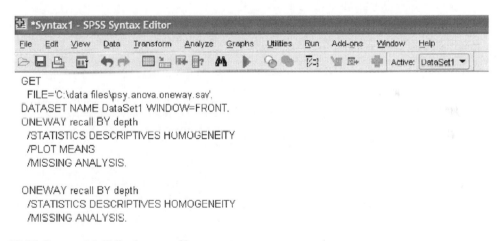

SPSS Output A.3 Edited syntax file contents.

Exit SPSS, saving the current syntax file as method2 in the 'data sets' folder.

Copying, pasting and editing SPSS syntax is a very efficient way of performing large analyses within SPSS. We can copy the 'Get File' syntax section to open a different file, we can replace the IV or DV by different variables for a new analysis or we can add or delete options or plots.

In the next section, we learn how to perform analyses using syntax files.

How to perform analyses using an SPSS syntax file

Recall that we created a syntax file called method2, which we stored in the 'data sets' folder. We now open this file and run the syntax stored in it.

Open SPSS and select **File**, then **Open** and then **Syntax** from the menu bar. Use the drop-down list to get the 'data sets' folder in the **Look in** box. Open the syntax file method2. We first open the dataset psy.anova.oneway.sav and perform the one-way ANOVA with the mean plots.

Select the syntax starting with 'Get' up to and including the full stop after the first ANALYSIS. This text should be highlighted. Now on the menu bar select **Run** and then **Selection**. Check that the dataset has opened and that the output window contains the one-way ANOVA with mean plots.

We now produce the one-way ANOVA without the mean plots. To do so, we wish to run only the second ANOVA syntax. Ensure that the cursor in the syntax file is in the blank line between the first ANALYSIS and ONEWAY. Select **Run** and then **To end**. Check in the output window that the one-way ANOVA has been performed without the mean plots.

Note that if we wished to perform both one-way ANOVAs we could have opened the Method2 syntax file and used **Run** and then **All**, or we could have highlighted all the syntax and used **Run** and then **Selection**.

Although you can perform SPSS analyses without using syntax files, becoming practised with their use has a number of advantages. You can use syntax files if you wish to keep a record of which datasets you have used and which analyses you have performed. You can copy or e-mail the files to colleagues so that they can check, reproduce or amend your analyses. Finally, using the editing functions, you can quickly create syntax files to perform similar analyses quickly.

In the next section, we give examples of SPSS syntax and SAS code for a selection of the analyses covered in this book. Note that SPSS and SAS often have different options available and so sometimes the syntax are not exactly matched. For some analyses in SPSS no direct SAS code is possible and this is left blank.

SPSS and SAS syntax for selected analyses

Chapter 2: One-way ANOVA (SPSS Dialog Box 2.2)

DV: RECALL
IV: DEPTH

SPSS data set: psy.anova.oneway.sav	SAS data set psy_anova_oneway stored in a library called 'datafold'
SPSS Syntax	SAS Syntax

ONEWAY recall BY depth 　/STATISTICS DESCRIPTIVES HOMOGENEITY 　/PLOT MEANS 　/MISSING ANALYSIS.	PROC GLM DATA = datafold.psy_anova_oneway; CLASS depth; MODEL recall = depth; MEANS depth / HOVTEST = LEVENE; RUN;

Chapter 2: One-way ANOVA with Tukey's post hoc analysis (SPSS Output 2.3)

DV: RECALL
IV: DEPTH

SPSS data set: psy.anova.oneway.sav

SAS data set psy_anova_oneway stored in a library called 'datafold'

SPSS Syntax

SAS Syntax

ONEWAY recall BY depth
  /STATISTICS DESCRIPTIVES
HOMOGENEITY
  /MISSING ANALYSIS
  /POSTHOC=TUKEY ALPHA(0.05).

PROC GLM DATA = datafold.psy_anova_oneway;
CLASS depth;
MODEL recall = depth;
MEANS depth / HOVTEST = LEVENE TUKEY
ALPHA=0.05;
RUN;

Chapter 2: Factorial between-subjects design (SPSS Outputs 2.6–2.9)

DV: SCORE
IV: TRAINING, TRIALS

SPSS data set: psy.anova.between.sav

SAS data set psy_anova_between stored in a library called 'datafold'

SPSS Syntax

SAS Syntax

UNIANOVA score BY training trials
  /METHOD=SSTYPE(3)
  /INTERCEPT=INCLUDE
  /PLOT=PROFILE(trials * training)
  /PRINT=ETASQ HOMOGENEITY
OPOWER
  /PLOT=RESIDUALS
  /CRITERIA=ALPHA(.05)
  /DESIGN=training trials training * trials.

PROC GLM DATA =
datafold.psy_anova_between;
CLASS training trials;
MODEL score = training trials training * trials;
RUN;

Chapter 2: Factorial within-subjects design (SPSS Outputs 2.10–2.12)

DV: TIME
IV: ANGLE, MODE

SPSS data set: psy.anova.within.sav

SAS data set psy_anova_within stored in a library called 'datafold'

SPSS Syntax

SAS Syntax

GLM a1m1 a1m2 a2m1 a2m2 a3m1 a3m2
  /WSFACTOR=angle 3 Polynomial mode 2
  Polynomial
  /MEASURE=time
  /METHOD=SSTYPE(3)
  /PLOT=PROFILE(angle * mode)
  /PRINT=ETASQ OPOWER
  /CRITERIA=ALPHA(.05)
  /WSDESIGN=angle mode angle * mode.

Chapter 3: Between-subjects MANOVA (SPSS Output 3.5)

DV: CORRECT, DELAY
IV: METHOD SESSIONS

SPSS data set: psy.manova.between.sav

SAS data set psy_manova_between stored in a library called 'datafold'

SPSS Syntax

SAS Syntax

GLM correct delay BY method sessions
　/METHOD=SSTYPE(3)
　/INTERCEPT=INCLUDE
　/PRINT=HOMOGENEITY
　/PLOT=SPREADLEVEL RESIDUALS
　/CRITERIA=ALPHA(.05)
　/DESIGN= method sessions method * sessions

PROC GLM DATA =
datafold.psy_manova_between;
CLASS method sessions;
MODEL time delay = method sessions
method * sessions;
MANOVA H=_ALL_;
RUN;

Chapter 4: Multiple regression (SPSS Outputs 4.1–4.5)

DV: SUCCESS
IV: APT1 APT2 EXTRAVER

SPSS data set: psy.regression.stepwise.sav

SAS data set psy_regression_stepwise stored in a library called 'datafold'

SPSS Syntax

SAS Syntax

REGRESSION
　/MISSING LISTWISE
　/STATISTICS COEFF OUTS R
　ANOVA COLLIN TOL
　/CRITERIA=PIN(.05) POUT(.10)
　/NOORIGIN
　/DEPENDENT success
　/METHOD=ENTER apt1 apt2 extraver
　/SCATTERPLOT=(*ZRESID, *ZPRED)
　/RESIDUALS NORM(ZRESID)
　/CASEWISE PLOT(ZRESID)
　OUTLIERS(2).

PROC REG DATA =
datafold.psy_regression_stepwise;
MODEL success = apt1 apt2 extraver;
RUN;

Note: For stepwise regression replace /METHOD=ENTER by /METHOD= STEPWISE in SPSS. For SAS replace the model statement by MODEL success = apt1 apt2 extraver/SELECTION = STEPWISE;.

Chapter 4: Hierarchical multiple regression (SPSS Output 4.11)

DV: SUCCESS
IV: EXTRAVER CONTROL then APT1 APT2 then ITDEGREE OTHERIT then TRAINING

SPSS data set: psy.regression.hierarchical.sav

SPSS Syntax　　　　　　　　　　　　　　　　　　SAS Syntax

REGRESSION
　/MISSING LISTWISE
　/STATISTICS COEFF OUTS R ANOVA
　/CRITERIA=PIN(.05) POUT(.10)
　/NOORIGIN
　/DEPENDENT success2
　/METHOD=ENTER extraver control
　/METHOD=ENTER apt1 apt2

/METHOD=ENTER itdegree otherit
/METHOD=ENTER training.

Chapter 5: Analysis of covariance (SPSS Output 5.1)

DV: POSTTEST1
IV: PRETEST1, TRAINING

SPSS data set: psy.ancova.sav

SAS data set psy_ancova stored in a library called 'datafold'

SPSS Syntax

SAS Syntax

UNIANOVA posttest1 BY training WITH pretest1
  /METHOD=SSTYPE(1)
  /INTERCEPT=INCLUDE
  /PRINT=ETASQ OPOWER
  /CRITERIA=ALPHA(.05)
  /DESIGN=training pretest1
  pretest1 * training.

PROC GLM DATA =
datafold.psy_ancova;
CLASS training;
MODEL posttest1 = pretest1 training
pretest1 * training;
RUN;

Note: For SPSS Output 5.2 remove pretest1 * training.
Note: For SPSS Output 5.3 remove pretest1 * training and training.

Chapter 5: Analysis of covariance with contrasts (SPSS Output 5.6)

DV: POSTTEST2
IV: PRETEST2, TRAINING

SPSS data set: psy.ancova.sav

SAS data set psy_ancova stored in a library called 'datafold'

SPSS Syntax

SAS Syntax

UNIANOVA posttest2 BY training WITH pretest2
  /CONTRAST(training)=Simple(1)
  /METHOD=SSTYPE(1)
  /INTERCEPT=INCLUDE
  /PRINT=ETASQ OPOWER
  /CRITERIA=ALPHA(.05)
  /DESIGN=training pretest2.

PROC GLM DATA = datafold.psy_ancova;
CLASS training;
MODEL posttest2 = pretest2 training;
ESTIMATE 'Level 2 vs. Level 1' training −1 0 1;
ESTIMATE 'Level 3 vs. Level 1' training −1 1 0;
RUN;

Chapter 6: Partial correlation (SPSS Output 6.1)

DV: SEX CA
IV: PSYGEN FACULTY

SPSS data set: psy.partial.sav

SAS data set psy_partial stored in a library called 'datafold'

SPSS Syntax

SAS Syntax

PARTIAL CORR
  /VARIABLES=sex ca BY psygen faculty
  /SIGNIFICANCE=TWOTAIL
  /MISSING=LISTWISE.

PROC CORR
DATA=datafold.psy_partial;
VAR sex ca ;
PARTIAL psygen faculty;
RUN;

Chapter 8: Factor analysis (SPSS Output 8.1)

IV: INFORM DIGSPAN VOCAB ARITH COMPREH SIMIL PICCOMP PICARRAN BLOCK OBJASSEM DIGSYM

SPSS data set: psy.factor.sav

SAS data set psy_factor stored in a library called 'datafold'

SPSS Syntax

SAS Syntax

FACTOR
  /VARIABLES inform digspan vocab arith
compreh simil piccomp picarran block
objassem digsym
  /MISSING LISTWISE
  /ANALYSIS inform digspan vocab arith
compreh simil piccomp picarran block
objassem digsym
  /PRINT INITIAL KMO EXTRACTION
ROTATION
  /PLOT EIGEN
  /CRITERIA MINEIGEN(1) ITERATE(25)
  /EXTRACTION PC
  /CRITERIA ITERATE(25)
  /ROTATION VARIMAX
  /METHOD=CORRELATION.

PROC FACTOR
DATA=datafold.psy_factor CORR EV
SCREE METHOD=PRIN
ROTATE=VARIMAX;
VAR inform–digsym;
RUN;

Chapter 8: Reliability analysis (SPSS Output 8.2)

IV: INFORM DIGSPAN VOCAB ARITH COMPREH SIMIL PICCOMP PICARRAN BLOCK OBJASSEM DIGSYM

SPSS data set: psy.factor.sav

SAS data set psy_factor stored in a library called 'datafold'

SPSS Syntax

SAS Syntax

RELIABILITY
  /VARIABLES=inform digspan vocab arith compreh
simil piccomp picarran block objassem digsym
  /SCALE('ALL VARIABLES') ALL
  /MODEL=ALPHA
  /SUMMARY=TOTAL.

PROC CORR
DATA=datafold.psy_factor ALPHA;
VAR inform–digsym;
RUN;

Chapter 9: Discriminant analysis (SPSS Output 9.1)

DV: GROUP
IV: TEST1 TEST2 TEST3

SPSS data set: psy.discriminant.sav

SAS data set psy_discriminant stored in a library called 'datafold'

SPSS Syntax

SAS Syntax

DISCRIMINANT
  /GROUPS=GROUP(1 3)
  /VARIABLES=TEST1 TEST2 TEST3
  /ANALYSIS ALL
  /SAVE=CLASS
  /PRIORS SIZE
  /STATISTICS=MEAN STDDEV COEFF TABLE
  /CLASSIFY=NONMISSING POOLED.

PROC DISCRIM DATA =
datafold.psy_discriminant;
CLASS group;
PRIORS PROPORTIONAL;
VAR test1 test2 test3 ;
RUN;

Note: For stepwise discriminant analysis
- SPSS: add /METHOD=WILKS /FIN = 3.84/ FOUT = 2.71 after CLASS to the SPSS syntax
- SAS: replace DISCRIM by STEPDISC and remove the PRIORS PROPORTIONAL line.

Chapter 9: Logistic regression (SPSS Output 9.6)

DV: INITIAL
IV: TEST1 TEST2 SUPPORT

SPSS data set: psy.logistic.sav

SAS data set psy_logistic stored in a library called 'datafold'

SPSS Syntax

SAS Syntax

```
LOGISTIC REGRESSION VARIABLES
initial
    /METHOD=ENTER test1 test2 support
    /CONTRAST (support)=Indicator
    /SAVE=PGROUP
    /CRITERIA=PIN(.05) POUT(.10)ITERATE(20)
CUT(.5).
```

```
PROC LOGISTIC DATA =
datafold.psy_logistic DESCENDING ;
CLASS support /REF = LAST;
MODEL initial (event='2') = test1 test2
support;
RUN;
```

Note: For stepwise logistic regression analysis (SPSS Output 9.9)
- SPSS: replace ENTER by FSTEP(COND)
- SAS: add / SELECTION = STEPWISE between support and the semi-colon.

Note: To add an interaction term (SPSS Output 9.10) add test1 * test2 after support on the METHOD line in SPSS (MODEL line in SAS).

Chapter 10: Cluster analysis of variables (SPSS Output 10.8)

IV: PROB1 – PROB8

SPSS data set: psy.cluster.variables.sav

SAS data set psy_cluster_variables stored in a library called 'datafold'

SPSS Syntax

SAS Syntax

```
PROXIMITIES prob1 prob2 prob3 prob4 prob5 prob6
prob7 prob8
    /MATRIX OUT('C:\Temp\spssclus.tmp')
    /VIEW=VARIABLE
    /MEASURE=SM(1,0)
    /PRINT NONE
    /STANDARDIZE=NONE.
CLUSTER
    /MATRIX IN('C:\Temp\spssclus.tmp')
    /METHOD WAVERAGE
    /PRINT SCHEDULE
    /PLOT DENDROGRAM.
ERASE FILE='C:\Temp\spssclus.tmp'.
```

```
PROC VARCLUS DATA =
datafold.psy_cluster_variables;
VAR prob1 – prob8;
PROC TREE;
```

Note: For SSPS Output 10.8(b) (Jaccard Coefficient) replace /MEASURE=SM(1,0) by / MEASURE=JACCARD(1,0).

Note: For SSPS Output 10.8(c) (simple matching with between groups) replace /METHOD WAVERAGE by /METHOD BAVERAGE.

Chapter 11: Multidimensional scaling (SPSS Outputs 11.1–11.5)

IV: ADAM – SANJIV

SPSS data set: mds.distancea.sav

SAS data set mds_distancea stored in a library called 'datafold'

SPSS Syntax

SAS Syntax

PROXSCAL VARIABLES=adam ana chila colin dee
dom ewan holly jim krish laura mira pete sanjiv
　/SHAPE=LOWER
　/INITIAL=SIMPLEX
　/TRANSFORMATION=INTERVAL
　/PROXIMITIES=DISSIMILARITIES
　/ACCELERATION=NONE
　/CRITERIA=DIMENSIONS(2,2) MAXITER(100)
DIFFSTRESS(.0001) MINSTRESS(.0001)
　/PRINT=COMMON STRESS
　/PLOT=COMMON RESIDUALS(ALL).

ALSCAL
　VARIABLES=adam ana chila colin dee dom ewan
holly jim krish laura mira pete sanjiv
　/SHAPE=SYMMETRIC
　/LEVEL=INTERVAL
　/CONDITION=MATRIX
　/MODEL=EUCLID
　/CRITERIA=CONVERGE(0.001)
STRESSMIN(0.005) ITER(30) CUTOFF(0)
DIMENS(2,2)
　/PLOT=DEFAULT ALL
　/PRINT=DATA HEADER.

PROC MDS DATA =
datafold.mds_distancea
PFINAL
OUT = test OCONFIG OCOEF
CONDITION = MATRIX;
RUN;
%PLOTIT (DATA = test,
DATATYPE = MDS);
RUN;

Note: The SPSS syntax using PROXSCAL is only available through the categories module. The SAS syntax
produces output similar to ALSCAL but the orientation of subjects is different.

Chapter 12: Loglinear models (SPSS Outputs 12.1, 12.2, 12.4(b) and 12.5)

IV: INDEX, SEX, MATHS

SPSS data set: psy.loglinear.sav

SAS data set psy_loglinear stored in a
library called 'datafold'

SPSS Syntax

SAS Syntax

GENLOG sex index maths
　/MODEL=MULTINOMIAL
　/PRINT=FREQ RESID ADJRESID ZRESID
DEV ESTIM CORR COV
　/PLOT=RESID(ADJRESID)
NORMPROB(ADJRESID)
　/CRITERIA=CIN(95) ITERATE(20)
CONVERGE(0.001) DELTA(.5)
　/DESIGN sex index maths index * maths index * sex
maths * sex index * maths * sex.

PROC CATMOD DATA =
datafold.psy_loglinear;
WEIGHT freqs
MODEL sex * index * maths =
RESPONSE /ML NOGLS;
LOGLIN sex|index|maths @3;
RUN;

Note: For SPSS Output 12.2(a)
• SPSS: remove index * maths * sex from the /DESIGN line
• SAS: replace @3 by @2 in the LOGLIN line.
For SPSS Output 12.2(b)
• SPSS: remove index * maths * sex and maths * sex from the /DESIGN line
• SAS: replace sex|index|maths @3 by sex index maths index * maths index * sex in the LOGLIN line.

Chapter 12: Loglinear models (SPSS Outputs 12.3 and 12.4a)

IV: INDEX, SEX, MATHS

SPSS data set: psy.loglinear.sav

SAS data set psy_loglinear stored in a
library called 'datafold'

SPSS Syntax

SAS Syntax

```
HILOGLINEAR sex(1 2) index(1 2) maths(1 2)
   /METHOD=BACKWARD
   /CRITERIA MAXSTEPS(10) P(.05)
ITERATION(20) DELTA(.5)
   /PRINT=FREQ RESID
   /DESIGN.
```

Chapter 13: Poisson regression (SPSS Dialog Box 13.1)

DV: EVENTS
IV: TREATMENT

SPSS data set:
psy.poissonregression.equaltimes. sav

SAS data set
psy_poissonregression_equaltimes stored in a
library called 'datafold'

SPSS Syntax

SAS Syntax

```
MEANS TABLES=events BY treatment
   /CELLS MEAN COUNT STDDEV.
```

```
PROC MEANS DATA =
datafold.psy_poissonregression_ equaltimes
mean std;
VAR events;
CLASS treatment;
RUN;
```

Chapter 13: Poisson regression (SPSS Output 13.1)

DV: EVENTS
IV: TREATMENT

SPSS data set:
psy.poissonregression.equaltimes. sav

SAS data set
psy_poissonregression_equaltimes stored
in a library called 'datafold'

SPSS Syntax

SAS Syntax

```
CROSSTABS
   /TABLES=events BY treatment
   /FORMAT=AVALUE TABLES
   /CELLS=COUNT
   /COUNT ROUND CELL.
```

```
PROC FREQ DATA =
datafold.psy_poissonregression_
equaltimes;
TABLES events * treatment/NOCOL
NOROW NOPERCENT;
RUN;
```

Chapter 13: Poisson regression (SPSS Outputs 13.2 and 13.4)

DV: EVENTS
IV: TREATMENT, ABUSE, ESTEEM

SPSS data set: psy.poissonregression.equaltimes.sav

SAS data set
psy_poissonregression_equaltimes
stored in a library called 'datafold'

SPSS Syntax

```
* Generalized Linear Models.
GENLIN events BY abuse treatment
(ORDER=ASCENDING) WITH esteem
   /MODEL abuse treatment esteem
INTERCEPT=YES
   DISTRIBUTION=POISSON LINK=LOG
   /CRITERIA METHOD=FISHER(1) SCALE=1
COVB=MODEL MAXITERATIONS=100
MAXSTEPHALVING=5
   PCONVERGE=1E-006(ABSOLUTE)
SINGULAR=1E-012 ANALYSISTYPE=3(WALD)
CILEVEL=95 CITYPE=WALD
   LIKELIHOOD=FULL
   /MISSING CLASSMISSING=EXCLUDE
   /PRINT CPS DESCRIPTIVES MODELINFO FIT
SUMMARY SOLUTION
   /SAVE MEANPRED(MeanPredicted)
XBPRED(XBPredicted)
DEVIANCERESID(DevianceResidual).
```

SAS Syntax

```
PROC GENMOD DATA= datafold.
psy_poissonregression_equaltimes;
Class abuse treatment;
MODEL events = abuse treatment
esteem
/ DIST = POISSON LINK = LOG;
RUN;
```

Note: For SPSS Output 13.5 change (ORDER=ASCENDING) to (ORDER=DESCENDING).

Chapter 13: Poisson regression (SPSS Output 13.3)

IV: DEVIANCERESIDUAL

SPSS data set:
psy.poissonregression.equaltimes.sav

SAS data set
psy_poissonregression_equaltimes stored in a library called 'datafold'

SPSS Syntax

```
GRAPH
   /HISTOGRAM(NORMAL)=-
DevianceResidual.
```

SAS Syntax

```
PROC UNIVARIATE DATA=datafold.
psy_poissonregression_equaltimes;
VAR DevianceResidual;
HISTOGRAM DevianceResidual
/NORMAL(COLOR=red FILL);
RUN;
```

Note: The SAS syntax assumes that you have created the variable DevianceResidual using SPSS and converted the data file to SAS by using **File** > **Save as** and choosing type SAS V7+ Windows long extension (* .sas7bdat).

Chapter 13: Poisson regression (SPSS Outputs 13.7 and 13.9)

DV: PRE_TRT_EVENTS
IV: ABUSE, TREATMENT, ESTEEM, OFFSET

SPSS data set:
psy.poissonregression.unequaltimes.sav

SAS data set
psy_poissonregression_unequaltimes stored in a library called 'datafold'

SPSS Syntax

```
* Generalized Linear Models.
GENLIN pre_trt_events BY abuse treatment
(ORDER=ASCENDING) WITH esteem
   /MODEL abuse treatment esteem
INTERCEPT=YES OFFSET=offset
   DISTRIBUTION=POISSON
```

SAS Syntax

```
PROC GENMOD DATA=datafold.
psy_poissonregression_unequaltimes;
   CLASS abuse treatment;
   MODEL pre_trt_events = abuse
treatment esteem
/ DIST = POISSON
```

```
    /CRITERIA METHOD=FISHER(1) SCALE=1       LINK = LOG
COVB=MODEL MAXITERATIONS=100                 OFFSET = offset;
MAXSTEPHALVING=5                             RUN;
    PCONVERGE=1E-006(ABSOLUTE)
SINGULAR=1E-012
ANALYSISTYPE=3(WALD) CILEVEL=95
CITYPE=WALD
    LIKELIHOOD=FULL
    /MISSING CLASSMISSING=EXCLUDE
    /PRINT CPS DESCRIPTIVES MODELINFO
FIT SUMMARY SOLUTION
    /SAVE MEANPRED(MeanPredicted)
XBPRED(XBPredicted)
DEVIANCERESID(DevianceResidual).
```

Note: For SPSS Output 13.10
- SPSS: change (ORDER=ASCENDING) to (ORDER=DESCENDING)
- SAS: use PROC FORMAT to put categories in correct order then add ORDER = FORMATTED at the end of the proc GENMOD line.

Chapter 14: Survival analysis (SPSS Output 14.1)

DV: TTF
IV: TREATMENT, RELAPSE

SPSS data set: psy.survival.sav   SAS data set psy_survival stored in a library called 'datafold'

SPSS Syntax   SAS Syntax

```
KM ttf BY treatment                    PROC LIFETEST DATA=datafold. psy_survival PLOTS = (S);
    /STATUS=relapse(0)                 STRATA treatment;
    /PRINT NONE                        TIME ttf * relapse(1);
    /PLOT SURVIVAL.                    RUN;
```

Chapter 14: Survival analysis (SPSS Outputs 14.2–14.5)

DV: TTF
IV: TREATMENT, RELAPSE, YEARS, NUMBER

SPSS data set: psy.survival.sav   SAS data set psy_survival stored in a
                                       library called 'datafold'

SPSS Syntax   SAS Syntax

```
COXREG ttf                             PROC TPHREG DATA =
    /STATUS=relapse(0)                 datafold.psy_survival;
    /PATTERN BY treatment              CLASS treatment;
    /CONTRAST (treatment)=Indicator    MODEL ttf * relapse(1)= treatment
    /METHOD=ENTER years number         relapse years number;
    /METHOD=ENTER treatment            RUN;
    /PLOT SURVIVAL
    /SAVE=PRESID
    /PRINT=CI(95)
    /CRITERIA=PIN(.05) POUT(.10) ITERATE(20).
```

Note: For SPSS Output 14.7 change /CONTRAST (treatment)=Indicator to /CONTRAST (treatment)=Indicator(1).
Note: For SPSS Outputs 14.8 and 14.9 also change /METHOD=ENTER years number to /METHOD= FSTEP(COND) years number.
Note: For SPSS Output 14.10 change /CONTRAST (treatment)=Indicator to /CONTRAST (treatment)=Difference.

Chapter 14: Survival analysis (SPSS Output 14.6)

SPSS data set: psy.survival.sav

SAS data set psy_survival stored in a library called 'datafold'

SPSS Syntax

SAS Syntax

GRAPH
   /SCATTERPLOT(BIVAR)=ttf WITH PR2_1
   /MISSING=LISTWISE.

PROC GPLOT DATA =
Datafold.psy_survival;
PLOT pr2_1 * ttf;
RUN;

Note: The SAS syntax assumes that you have created the variable PR2_1 using SPSS and converted the data file to SAS by using **File > Save** as and choosing type SAS V7+ Windows long extension (* .sas7bdat).

Chapter 15: Longitudinal analysis (SPSS Output 15.6)

DV: BMI
IV: AGE MONTH GROUP

SPSS data set: longitudinal.MRM.sav

SAS data set longitudinal_mrm stored in a library called 'datafold'

SPSS Syntax

SAS Syntax

UNIANOVA BMI BY group WITH age month
   /METHOD=SSTYPE(3)
   /INTERCEPT=INCLUDE
   /PRINT=PARAMETER
   /CRITERIA=ALPHA(.05)
   /DESIGN=group age month.

PROC GENMOD DATA = datafold.
longitudinal_mrm;
CLASS group;
MODEL bmi = group age month;
RUN;

Chapter 15: Longitudinal analysis (SPSS Outputs 15.7 and 15.8)

DV: BMI
IV: AGE MONTH GROUP

SPSS data set: longitudinal.MRM.sav

SAS data set longitudinal_MRM stored in a library called 'datafold'

SPSS Syntax

SAS Syntax

MIXED BMI BY group WITH age month
   /CRITERIA=CIN(95) MXITER(100)
MXSTEP(5) SCORING(1)
SINGULAR(0.000000000001) HCONVERGE(0,
   ABSOLUTE) LCONVERGE(0, ABSOLUTE)
PCONVERGE(0.000001, ABSOLUTE)
   /FIXED=group age month | SSTYPE(3)
   /METHOD=REML
   /PRINT=SOLUTION
   /REPEATED=month | SUBJECT(ID)
COVTYPE(ID).

PROC MIXED DATA = datafold.
longitudinal_MRM;
CLASS group;
MODEL BMI = group age month;
REPEATED / SUBJECT = id;
RUN;

Note: For SPSS Output 15.8
• SPSS: replace COVTYPE(ID) by COVTYPE(CS) in the line /REPEATED=month | SUBJECT(ID) COVTYPE(ID)
• SAS: add TYPE=CS after Subject = ID.

Chapter 15: Longitudinal analysis (SPSS Output 15.9)

DV: RESPONSE
IV: GENDER TREATMENT SF_36

SPSS data set: psy.gee.sav

SAS data set psy_GEE stored in a
library called 'datafold'

SPSS Syntax

SAS Syntax

* Generalized Estimating Equations.
GENLIN response (REFERENCE=LAST) BY
gender treatment (ORDER=ASCENDING) WITH
SF_36
  /MODEL gender treatment SF_36
INTERCEPT=YES
  DISTRIBUTION=BINOMIAL LINK=LOGIT
  /CRITERIA METHOD=FISHER(1) SCALE=1
MAXITERATIONS=100 MAXSTEPHALVING=5
PCONVERGE=1E-006(ABSOLUTE)
  SINGULAR=1E-012
ANALYSISTYPE=3(WALD) CILEVEL=95
LIKELIHOOD=FULL
  /REPEATED SUBJECT=subject
WITHINSUBJECT=visit SORT=YES
CORRTYPE=UNSTRUCTURED
ADJUSTCORR=YES
  COVB=ROBUST MAXITERATIONS=100
PCONVERGE=1e-006(ABSOLUTE)
UPDATECORR=1
  /MISSING CLASSMISSING=EXCLUDE
  /PRINT CPS DESCRIPTIVES MODELINFO
FIT SUMMARY SOLUTION.

PROC GENMOD DATA =
datafold.psy_GEE;
CLASS gender treatment subject;
MODEL response = gender treatment
SF_36 / dist = bin;
REPEATED SUBJECT = subject
/TYPE = UN;
RUN;

Note: For SPSS output 15.9(b)
- SPSS: replace CORRTYPE=UNSTRUCTURED by CORRTYPE=INDEPENDENT in the line starting with /REPEATED
- SAS: replace TYPE=UN by TYPE = IND.

Further reading

Chapters for which books in the list are relevant are indicated with a cross in the table overleaf.

Allison, P. D. (1999). *Multiple regression: A primer*. Thousand Oaks, CA: Pine Forge Press.

Arbuckle, J. L., & Wothke, W. (2003). *AMOS 5.0 user's guide*. Chicago, IL: SPSS Inc.

Borg, I., & Groenen, P. (2005). *Modern multidimensional scaling: Theory and applications* (2nd ed.). New York: Springer-Verlag.

Bray, J. H., & Maxwell, S. E. (1985). *Multivariate analysis of variance*. Thousand Oaks, CA: Sage Publications.

Byrne, B. M. (2001). *Structural equation modeling with AMOS: Basic concepts, applications, and programming*. Mahwah, NJ: Lawrence Erlbaum Associates.

Chatfield, C. (2003) *The analysis of time series: An introduction* (6th ed.). Boca Raton, FL: Chapman & Hall/CRC Press.

Clark-Carter, D. (2009). *Quantitative psychological research: A student's handbook* (3rd ed.). Hove, UK: Psychology Press.

Cox, T. F., & Cox, M. A. A. (2002). *Multidimensional scaling* (2nd ed.). London: Chapman & Hall.

Cramer, D. (2003). *Advanced quantitative data analysis*. Maidenhead, UK: Open University Press.

Der, G., & Everitt, B. S. (2006). *Statistical analysis of medical data using SAS*. Boca Raton, FL: Chapman & Hall.

Diekhoff, G. (1992). *Statistics for the social and behavioural sciences: Univariate, bivariate, multivariate*. Dubuque, IA: Wm. C. Brown.

Diggle, P., Heagerty, P., Liang, K-Y., & Zeger S. (2002). *Analysis of longitudinal data*. Oxford: Oxford University Press.

Dunbar, G. (1998). *Data analysis for psychology*. London: Arnold.

Everitt, B. (1992). *The analysis of contingency tables* (2nd ed.). London: Chapman & Hall/CRC.

Everitt, B. S., Landau, S., & Leese, M. (2001). *Cluster analysis* (4th ed.). London: Hodder & Arnold.

Field, A. (2005). *Discovering statistics using SPSS* (2nd ed.). London: Sage Publications.

George, D., & Mallery, P. (2009). *SPSS for Windows step by step: A simple guide and reference* (16.0 update). Boston, MA: Pearson Education.

Heiser, W. J., & Busing, F. M. T. A. (2004). Multidimensional scaling and unfolding of symmetric and asymmetric proximity relations. In D. Kaplan (ed.), *Handbook of quantitative methodology for the social sciences* (pp. 25–48). Thousand Oaks, CA: Sage Publications.

Howell, C. H. (2007). *Statistical methods for psychology* (6th ed.). Pacific Grove, CA: Duxbury.

Kinnear, P. R., & Gray, C. D. (2006). *SPSS for Windows made simple* (Release 14). Hove, UK: Psychology Press.

Machin, D., Campbell, M. J., & Walters, S. J. (2007). *Medical statistics: A textbook for the health sciences* (4th ed.). Chichester, UK: Wiley.

Book author(s)	Chapter number															
	1	2	3	4	5	6	7	8	9	10	11	12	13	14	15	A
Allison				X												
Arbuckle & Wothke							X	X								
Borg & Groenen											X					
Bray & Maxwell		X														
Byrne							X	X								
Chatfield															X	
Clark-Carter	X	X														
Cox & Cox											X					
Cramer		X		X		X	X	X	X			X				
Der & Everitt													X	X		X
Diekhoff	X	X	X	X			X		X	X	X					
Diggle et al.															X	
Dunbar				X								X				
Everitt												X				
Everitt et al.										X						
Field	X		X		X		X					X				
George & Mallery	X	X	X	X	X	X	X		X	X		X				

Book author(s)	Chapter number															
	1	2	3	4	5	6	7	8	9	10	11	12	13	14	15	A
Heiser & Busing											X					
Howell	X	X		X	X	X						X				
Kinnear & Gray	X	X		X			X					X				
Machin et al.														X		
Marascuilo & Levin			X	X			X		X			X				
Marcoulides & Hershberger		X					X	X	X							
Miles & Shevlin				X	X		X	X								
Sani & Todman	X															
Siegel & Castellan	X															
Stokes et al.												X	X			
Tabachnick & Fidell		X	X	X	X	X	X	X	X			X				
Tacq		X	X	X	X		X	X	X							
Winer et al.		X			X											
Woolson & Clarke														X		

Chapter: 1, Overview; 2, ANOVA; 3, MANOVA; 4, Regression; 5, ANCOVA; 6, Partial correlation, mediation and moderation; 7, Path analysis; 8, Factor analysis; 9, Discriminant analysis; 10, Cluster analysis; 11, Multidimensional scaling; 12, Loglinear models; 13, Poisson regression; 14, Survival analysis; 15, Longitudinal data; A, Appendix.

Marascuilo, L. A., & Levin, J. R. (1983). *Multivariate statistics in the social sciences: A researcher's guide.* Monterey, CA: Brooks/Cole.

Marcoulides, G. A., & Hershberger, S. L. (1997). *Multivariate statistical methods: A first course.* Mahwah, NJ: Lawence Erlbaum Associates.

Miles, J., & Shevlin, M. (2001). *Applying regression and correlation: A guide for students and researchers.* London: Sage Publications.

Sani, F., & Todman, J. (2006). *Experimental design and statistics for psychology: A first course.* Oxford: Blackwell Publishing.

Siegel, S., & Castellan, N. J., Jr. (1988). *Nonparametric statistics for the behavioural sciences* (2nd ed.). New York: McGraw-Hill.

Stokes, M. E., Davies, C. S., & Koch, G. G. (2000). *Categorical data analysis using the SAS system* (2nd ed.). Cary, NC: SAS Press.

Tabachnick, B. G., & Fidell, L. S. (2007). *Using multivariate statistics* (5th ed.). Boston, MA: Allyn & Bacon.

Tacq, J. (1997). *Multivariate analysis techniques in social science research.* London: Sage Publications.

Winer, B. J., Brown, D. R., & Michels, K. M. (1991). *Statistical principles in experimental design* (3rd ed.). London: McGraw-Hill.

Woolson, R. F., & Clarke, W. R. (2002). *Statistical methods for the analysis of biomedical data* (2nd ed.). Chichester, UK: Wiley.

Glossary

Agglomerative technique A method of cluster analysis where we start with each case as a separate cluster and put them together into clusters, and combine clusters, according to a similarity criterion. Divisive techniques start with all cases in a single cluster that is gradually split up.

Agreement measures (*see also* Similarity and distance) If several binary variables are recorded for each case, which for definiteness we could call presence/absence, then two cases agree on a variable if both record a presence or both record an absence. An agreement measure for the two cases is a count of joint presences and joint absences as a proportion of the number of variables, or some similar ratio based on joint presences only.

Analysis of covariance (ANCOVA) A method of analysing experimental data where there are both discrete and continuous IVs. The effects of one or more continuous variables are statistically controlled so that the effects of interest can be more clearly seen.

Analysis of variance (ANOVA) A method for comparing the means of three or more experimental conditions that are defined by the values of the IV(s). If there is only one IV, the analysis is called a one-way ANOVA.

Autocorrelation Neighbouring observations taken sequentially in time or space may be correlated, and this is called autocorrelation.

Backward elimination Stepwise methods that begin with all variables and remove them one by one if they fail a criterion.

Balanced design An ANOVA design with equal numbers of observations for all combinations of factor levels.

Beta weights Standardized regression coefficients.

Ceiling effect There are insufficient questions (or other opportunities for scoring) to allow those with potentially the highest scores to be discriminated from those with more modest scores.

Censoring Survival data give the times to an event (such as component failure times or patient recovery times). Not all cases are observed for long enough for the event to occur and the observation times for these cases are said to be censored.

City block or Manhattan distance A distance measure that does not use the shortest distance between points but (for two variables) sums the east–west and north–south distances, as if you had to walk along the streets in Manhattan to get from A to B. The idea easily extends to more variables.

Classification Attempts to predict group membership from measurements on a set of variables (**discriminant analysis**) or to identify subgroups in a dataset (**cluster analysis**).

Cluster analysis (*see also* **Classification**)   Looks for subgroups of cases in a dataset based on their similarity on recorded variables. It can also be used to look for subgroups of variables.

Communality   The proportion of variance accounted for by a factor in a factor analysis.

Confidence interval   A 95% confidence interval is the range of values that would not be rejected by a test of the null hypothesis at the 5% level.

Contingency table   A frequency table for discrete data where the possible values of the variables define the rows and columns (and layers, if more than two variables).

Contrast   A test of the difference on the DV between levels of an IV. A common example is the difference between an experimental and a control condition. More complex contrasts are possible: for instance, you could compare the average of all the experimental conditions with the control condition.

Counterbalancing   When we use a repeated measures design, so each participant experiences every experimental condition, any effects of the order in which the conditions are applied must be controlled. The order may be systematically balanced (e.g., AB, BA) or, if there are more than two or three conditions, partially balanced (e.g., Latin squares) or randomized independently for every participant. This process is called counterbalancing.

Covariance matrix   A matrix is just a rectangular array. If we have more than two variables, each pair has a covariance, and the covariance matrix just displays these in a systematic way.

Covariate   A variable that may influence our DV but we cannot control experimentally is called a covariate. Usually, especially in the context of ANCOVA, it is a continuous variable.

Cox regression   A method for analysing survival data, also known as the proportional hazard model.

Cross-validation   If we use a set of data (called the training set) to calculate a regression equation or discriminant function, when we use it to predict for a new dataset results will not be as good as those achieved on the training set. Various methods of cross-validation are used to estimate the probability of correct prediction for new data.

Degrees of freedom   Degrees of freedom are usually used as the denominator in calculating an average where there is some constraint on the values in the numerator. For instance, to estimate a variance we first obtain the sample mean, $\bar{x}$, then subtract this from each observation and square the results. But the sum of the differences between the observations and $\bar{x}$ is zero, which is a constraint. So to estimate the variance, instead of dividing the sum of squares by n, the number of squares, we divide by the degrees of freedom, $n - 1$.

Dendrogram   A diagram for displaying the process of clustering cases (or variables).

Diagnostics   Tools for checking on the assumptions made in an analysis.

Discriminant analysis (*see also* **Classification**)   A method of predicting group membership from measurements on other variables.

Effect   The difference made to the DV by a change in the IV. Estimating the statistical significance and the size of an effect is usually the task of ANOVA.

Endogenous variable   A variable that can function as a DV at some stage in a path analysis.

Euclidean distance   The shortest distance between points.

Exogenous variable   A variable that can only be an IV in a path analysis.

Expected value   In the simplest case an expected value is just a probability multiplied by the number of trials. But it is also used to define the value of a DV predicted by a regression, ANOVA or other model.

Exploratory methods   Methods of displaying or summarizing data to expose important features when we do not know enough to set up or test hypotheses.

Factor   In ANOVA the IVs are usually referred to as factors. The values they take are referred to as factor levels.

Factor analysis   Attempts to identify a small number of underlying variables or factors that cannot be measured directly but that explain the observed correlations among measured variables.

Factor loading   In a factor analysis, each measured variable is expressed as a sum of multiples of the factors. The numbers multiplying the factors in this sum are the factor loadings for the variable. A loading may be thought of as the correlation of a variable with a factor.

Factor score   Although the factors in factor analysis cannot be measured directly, factor scores can be estimated as weighted combinations of the variable loadings on each factor.

Factorial design   Describes an ANOVA, usually giving the number of levels for each factor, so a 2 * 3 factorial design has two factors, the first with two levels and the second with three. The design also usually specifies whether each factor is between or within subjects (independent groups or repeated measures).

Family of tests (*see also* **Multiple testing**)   A set of related tests on some data: for example, tests of differences between all pairs of means within a factor. The probability of making at least one Type I error in the family of tests is greater than the error rate per individual comparison (e.g., .05) and there are procedures for controlling the familywise error rate (e.g., making it equal to .05).

Floor effect   The measurement scale does not allow us to discriminate those with potentially the lowest scores from those whose scores could be a little higher. This can occur if the task is too difficult, so few participants can score anything at all.

Forward selection   In a stepwise analysis, forward selection starts with just one variable, the one that is the best single predictor. Variables are then added one at a time if they pass a criterion.

General Linear Model   A class of models including ANOVA, ANCOVA, MANOVA and regression (simple and multiple).

Generalized Linear Model   An extension of the General Linear Model that includes (among others) logistic regression, Poisson regression and loglinear models.

Generating class   In a hierarchical model where the main effects must be included if an interaction between them is included, the generating class is the list of main effects and interactions that tells us all the terms that are in the model. For instance, if we have factors A, B and C, and the generating class is given as B and A * C, we know that the model must include main effects A and C as well as B and the interaction A * C, because including the A * C interaction implies we must have the main effects A and C.

Goodness of fit   Various statistics, known collectively as measures of goodness of fit or goodness of fit statistics, are used to determine how well a model fits the data.

Hazard (in survival analysis)   The chance of an event occurring in the next short time interval given that it has not happened already.

Hierarchical methods   Cluster analysis methods where once a case has entered a cluster it remains in that cluster throughout. Methods considered in this book are all hierarchical.

Homogeneity of variance   The DV has the same variance for all experimental groups (this is assumed for ANOVA and ANCOVA). When applied to regression, it means that the variance of the DV is constant over the range of values of the IVs.

Independence   Observations or variables are independent if the value on one of them does not affect the probabilities for values on the other. A simple example of independent observations is two coin tosses. A head at the first toss does not affect the probability of a head at the second.

Interaction   Two factors in an ANOVA interact if the effect of one differs at different levels of the other (plots will show non-parallel lines). For instance, if we have factors MODALITY (visual and aural levels) and DELAY (short and long levels), we would have an interaction if the effect of long versus short delay on recall (the DV) were greater (or less) with visual than with aural presentation.

Intercept   The value at which a straight line graph intersects the vertical (DV) axis, so it is the constant a in the equation $y = a + bx$. With more than one IV it is the constant in the linear equation that predicts the DV.

Iterations, iterative process   Many calculations have to proceed by a process of successive approximation, starting with a guess or even a randomly chosen value. A process of refinement is repeated (iterated) until further iterations make little change. Some processes fail to converge, so they never reach a point where further iterations make little change. In case the process you are about to embark on is one of these, there is always some upper limit to the number of iterations that will be performed. The software may allow you to alter the upper limit.

Jaccard coefficient   A similarity measure for binary variables that counts joint presences but not joint absences.

Kaplan-Meier plot   A survival data plot showing survival times for treatment groups but ignoring covariates.

Latent variable   A variable that is not directly measured but is assessed indirectly by measurements on several other (indicator) variables.

Leave-one-out   A method for predicting the probability of successful discrimination on new data that calculates the discriminant function based on all observations in the training set except the first and uses it to classify the omitted observation (it may get the predicted group right or wrong). This is repeated for every observation to get the proportion of correct predictions. This is the estimated probability of correct predictions for new data.

Likelihood   The likelihood of a hypothesis or parameter value, given our data, is proportional to the probability of our data with that hypothesis or parameter value. Usually the likelihood is used as part of a likelihood ratio, which gives the ratio of the likelihood of a specific parameter value to the maximum likelihood for the other possible parameter values.

Linear function or linear combinations of variables   Each variable is multiplied by a number and these products are added together. Usually the multipliers are estimated as part of a statistical analysis.

Linkage methods   Methods of determining the distance between clusters (in cluster analysis). Several kinds of average may be used, or else single linkage (nearest neighbour), which uses the distance between closest members of a pair of clusters.

Logistic regression (*see also* Regression) In logistic regression we aim to predict the probability that a case falls into one of two categories from the values of the IV(s) The model assumes that a small change in an IV has the most effect on this probability in the middle of its range, and that small changes in the IV near the top or bottom of its range will have a smaller effect on the probability. It can be adapted for discriminant analysis if there are only two target groups.

Logit or log(odds) With two possible outcomes of a random process (such as getting a six or not when you roll a die) the odds of the outcome with probability p are $p/(1 - p)$. The logit or log(odds) is $\log(p/(1 - p))$

Loglinear analysis A method for analysing contingency tables that has analogies with ANOVA.

Longitudinal data Repeat observations taken, on each case, over time at fixed or variable intervals.

Main effect If we have more than one factor in an ANOVA, the main effect of a factor is the effect of that factor averaged over all the other factors.

Marginal distribution In a simple two-way table, the marginal totals appear in the bottom row and right-hand column (the margins). More generally, if we sum the frequencies in a contingency table over all the variables except one, we have the marginal totals for that one variable. Divide the marginal totals by the grand total to get estimates of the marginal probabilities that make up the marginal distribution for that variable.

Matrix A matrix is a rectangular array of numbers, usually used in statistics to display the correlations or variances and covariances among a set of variables, or the distances or similarities between pairs of variables.

Maximum likelihood The likelihood of a parameter value or hypothesis is a measure of its support by the data. The hypothesis or parameter that has the best support from the data maximizes the likelihood.

Measure of association If the variables in a contingency table are not independent we need some way to measure the strength of the association. Various measures have been suggested, some based on the value of the χ^2 statistic.

Mediating effects An indirect effect of an IV on a DV via its effect on a variable intermediate between the IV and DV in a hypothesized causal chain. For example, high levels of care from parents might lead to feelings of competence that in turn might lead to subsequent confident parenting.

Meta-analysis A statistical procedure for combining, testing and describing the results from different studies investigating the same broad hypothesis, with a view to establishing the degree of consistency of an effect or the overall effect size.

Misclassification When a discriminant function predicts the wrong group for a case, the case is said to be misclassified. Estimating the misclassification probabilities for new cases is one of the problems for discriminant analysis.

Missing observations If observations that are required by an experimental design are not obtained, perhaps because a participant is ill or drops out, then we have missing observations. Analysis may be considerably more difficult if there are missing observations.

Mixed regression models (MRMs) May be used for longitudinal data. Various methods can be used to model the correlations among observations made on the same case.

Model   The model is an equation that predicts or accounts for the observed values of the DV in terms of the values of the IV(s) and some random variation. A linear model predicts the DV as a sum of multiples of the IVs plus a constant and some random variation.

Moderating effects   If a correlation between two variables is affected by the level of a third variable, this third variable is said to have a moderating effect on the correlation between the other two.

Multicollinearity   If there are high correlations among IVs in a regression then estimates of the coefficients are unreliable and we say we have a multicollinearity problem.

Multidimensional scaling   A method for displaying the distances (which may be conceptual rather than geometrical) between pairs of cases (or variables) as a map, usually in two dimensions.

Multiple correlation coefficient   The correlation between the observed and predicted values of the DV in a regression analysis.

Multiple testing (*see also* **Family of tests**)   When a number of related tests are carried out on the same data and alpha is set at, say, .05, the probability of finding one or more significant results will be greater than .05. For example, if 20 correlation tests are carried out and the null hypothesis is true in each case, the probability of at least one significant finding will be .64. A correction for multiple testing can be applied.

Multivariate analysis of variance (MANOVA)   ANOVA with more than one DV.

Non-metric methods   In multidimensional scaling non-metric methods may be used if distances can only be ordered rather than given values.

Null hypothesis   In hypothesis testing, the null hypothesis is the one we test. It is so named because it often takes a form such as 'there is no difference between . . .' or 'there is no association between . . .'.

Odds   If only two outcomes of an experiment are being considered (for instance, that the horse may win or not), the odds of an outcome is the ratio of the probability of that outcome to the probability of the other. The odds of the horse winning is the ratio of the probability of a win to the probability of not winning.

Offset   The extra term needed in a Poisson regression when unequal observation times are used.

Order effects   If a participant is measured under more than one experimental condition there may be some effect such as practice, boredom or tiredness that affects measurements after the first one, and may in fact increase with successive measurements if there are more than two. These would be order effects.

Orthogonal   At right angles, indicating independence (e.g., of factors in factor analysis).

Outlier   An observation with a value far away from all the rest, which may have a disproportionate influence on statistics calculated for the set of observations.

Overdispersion   A departure from the Poisson distribution resulting in increased variance.

Paired comparisons   In an ANOVA, if the difference in the DV is tested for every pair of values taken by an IV, we call these paired comparisons.

Parameter   A numerical value that has to be estimated for a model (e.g., the slope of a regression line).

Parametric assumptions   The assumptions that the DV is (at least approximately) normally distributed and has a variance that is the same for all values of the IV(s) in the study.

Partial correlation The correlation between two variables with the influence of another variable controlled. Variance in the third variable that is common to each of the main variables is removed.

Path analysis An extension of multiple regression that focuses on the pattern of relationships among a set of variables rather than just on which IVs predict a DV and how strongly.

Path coefficient A standardized regression coefficient obtained from a path analysis.

Path diagram A representation of a proposed causal model in path analysis.

Planned comparisons (*see also* **Post hoc tests**) Comparisons or contrasts that are planned when the experiment is designed.

Poisson distribution If events occur at random and the chance of an event occurring in the next short time interval does not depend on whether one just occurred, the frequencies of counts in fixed time intervals follow a Poisson distribution.

Poisson regression A method of modelling counts of random events where the rate at which the events occur may be influenced by treatment conditions or covariates.

Polynomial A straight line such as $y = 3 + 7x$ is a polynomial of the first degree. A quadratic such as $y = 2 - 6x + 5x^2$ is a polynomial of the second degree. You can have a polynomial of any degree, and the degree is the highest power of x. Some powers can be missing, for example $y = 2 - 3x + 5x^4$ is a polynomial of the fourth degree.

Population The set of all items of interest for an investigation. It can be a population of people, animals, businesses, countries or anything else of interest.

Post hoc tests (*see also* **Planned comparisons**) Tests that are done after viewing the data, or multiple tests that are not based on specific planned comparisons.

Power The probability of rejecting a false null hypothesis, or the chance of detecting an effect that exists.

Pretest–posttest design Each participant is measured both before and after some experimental condition is applied.

Probability plot A method for checking whether data are likely to be from a normal distribution.

Proportional hazard model Also known as the Cox regression model in survival analysis.

Random assignment Each participant is assigned at random to one of the experimental conditions, using random numbers.

Random sample A sample where every member of the population has an equal chance of being included in the sample. A random number generator is used to select ID numbers if the population is listed and numbered.

Rate The number of events that occurred, divided by the observation time during which they were counted.

Reduced model (*see also* **Saturated model**) A model with fewer parameters than observations.

Regression A method for predicting the value of a DV from values of the IVs. Usually we mean linear regression, where the DV is predicted by a linear combination of the IVs.

Regression coefficients The numbers that are multiplied by the variables to get the predicted value in a regression.

Reliability analysis   A method for assessing consistency of measurements (e.g., in factor analysis, the consistency of the contributions of variables to a factor).

Repeated measures design   A design in ANOVA where each participant experiences each level of a factor.

Replicate   In ANOVA, observations with the same combination of factor levels are called replicates.

Residuals   The difference between an observed value of the DV and the value predicted by a model.

Retrospective or observed power   Power that is calculated after an experiment has been completed, based on the results of that experiment. It is the power that would result if the values of the population means and variances were as found in this experiment.

Robustness   A test or method is robust if it is not very sensitive to deviations from the underlying assumptions.

Saturated model (*see also* **Reduced model**)   A model in which the number of estimated parameters is the same as the number of observations. It is usually of interest only as a starting point for, or comparison with, reduced models with fewer parameters.

Scree diagram   A graph of the stress against the number of dimensions in multidimensional scaling – also a graph showing the diminishing contributions of factors in factor analysis.

Seasonality (in time series data)   Any regular cyclic effect, such as diurnal temperature variation or weekly productivity cycles.

Semi-partial or part correlation   The correlation between two variables with the influence of another variable controlled. Variance in the third variable that is common to just one of the main variables is removed.

Similarity and distance (*see also* **Agreement measures**)   Similarities are measures of how alike pairs of cases are, based on the variables recorded for them. Distances are measures of how different pairs of cases are. Similarities can be converted into distances, and vice versa. Similarities and distances between pairs of variables can also be calculated based on the number of cases where scores on the pair of variables agree.

Simple matching coefficient   A similarity measure for binary variables that counts joint absences as well as joint presences.

Simultaneous confidence intervals/regions   The probabilities associated with hypothesis tests and confidence intervals are calculated on the assumption that you are doing one test or confidence interval. If you want several tests or confidence intervals, for instance for the difference between each experimental condition and the control, the probabilities have to be adjusted.

Standardization   To standardize a variable, subtract from each observation the mean of the whole set and divide the result by the standard deviation of the whole set.

Stress   A measure of the distortion of between-pair distances in a map produced by multidimensional scaling.

Structural equation models   Combines confirmatory factor analysis with path analysis to deal with measurement error.

Survival analysis   A method of analysing times to an event when some observations are censored.

Time series   Observations taken sequentially at regular time intervals, usually over a period resulting in hundreds of observations.

Trace of a matrix   The sum of the terms down the diagonal of a square matrix.

Training set (*see also* **Validation set**)   The set of data used to calculate a regression equation or discriminant function.

Transformation of data   Using a function of the observations, such as the log, the square root or the reciprocal, in place of the original measurements.

Type I error   Rejecting a null hypothesis that is true.

Type II error   Failing to reject a null hypothesis that is false.

Unbalanced design   An ANOVA design that does not have equal numbers of observations at all combinations of factor levels.

Underdispersion   A departure from the Poisson distribution resulting in decreased variance.

Validation set (*see also* **Training set**)   The set of data used to estimate misclassification probabilities for a discriminant function or the error in prediction from a regression equation.

Abbreviations

AIC	Akaike's information criterion (comparative goodness of fit index)
AMOS	Analysis of Moment Structures (structural equation modelling program)
ANCOVA	analysis of covariance
ANOVA	analysis of variance
CFA	confirmatory factor analysis
CFI	comparative fit index (goodness of fit index)
CMIN	likelihood ratio chi square (goodness of fit index)
DAF	dispersion accounted for (fit of data to a dimensional map)
df	degrees of freedom
DV	dependent variable
EFA	exploratory factor analysis
EMEA	European Medicines Agency
EQS	Structural Equations Program (structural equation modelling program)
FDA	Food and Drug Administration
GEE	generalized estimating equations
GLM	General Linear Model
IV	independent variable
KMO	Kaiser-Meyer-Olkin (measure of sampling adequacy)
LISREL	Linear Structural Relations (structural equation modelling program)
MANOVA	multivariate analysis of variance
MRM	mixed regression model
MS	mean square (variance)
NFI	normed fit index (goodness of fit index)
RMSEA	root mean square error of approximation (goodness of fit index)
SAS	Statistical Analysis Software
sd	standard deviation
SEM	structural equation modelling
SPSS	Statistical Package for the Social Sciences
SS	sum of squares
WAIS	Wechsler Adult Intelligence Scale

Author index

Subject index